CENSORSHIP

CENSORSHIP

Volume I
Abelard, Peter – *Front, The*

Consulting Editors

Lawrence Amey
Dalhousie University

Timothy L. Hall
University of Mississippi Law School

Carl Jensen
Project Censored
Sonoma State University

Charles May
California State University,
Long Beach

Richard L. Wilson
University of Tennessee at Chattanooga

Project Editor
R. Kent Rasmussen

Salem Press, Inc.
Pasadena, California   Englewood Cliffs, New Jersey

Editor in Chief: Dawn P. Dawson
Managing Editor: Christina Moose *Project Editor:* R. Kent Rasmussen
Research Supervisor: Jeffry Jensen *Production Editor:* Janet Long
Acquisitions Editor: Mark Rehn *Layout:* James Hutson
Photograph Editor: K. L. A. Hyatt *Proofreading Supervisor:* Yasmine A. Cordoba
Research Assistant: Irene McDermott

Frontispiece: courtesy of National Archives

Library of Congress Cataloging-in-Publication Data
Censorship / consulting editors: Lawrence Amey, Timothy L. Hall, Carl Jensen, Charles May, and Richard L. Wilson; project editor, R. Kent Rasmussen
    p.   cm. — (Ready reference)
Includes bibliographical references and index.
    ISBN 0-89356-444-3 (set : alk. paper). — ISBN 0-89356-445-1 (vol. 1 : alk. paper).
    1. Censorship—United States—Encyclopedias. 2. Censorship—Encyclopedias. I. Amey, L. J., 1940-
II. Rasmussen, R. Kent.   III. Series.
Z658.U5C38   1997
363.3'1—dc21   97-14245
                                                                                                                    CIP

First Printing

PRINTED IN THE UNITED STATES OF AMERICA

Publisher's Note

As the twenty-first century approaches, censorship issues command daily public attention. The same might have been said at virtually any time in the past. At midcentury, for example, battles over obscenity in books and films were being fought in the courts with such frequency that the moral fabric of American society appeared to be under assault. Around this same time another fear arose: that the American government and its institutions were being subverted by unwelcome foreign ideologies. The very freedoms on which the nation had been built seemed to be threatened. To some, the solution to these problems lay in an evident paradox: Preservation of America's precious freedoms could best be achieved by restricting their exercise.

By the 1990's much had changed. The frankness with which literature, films, and even television were treating subjects such as sexual behavior would have been unimaginable a half century earlier. Likewise, unpopular political and social ideas were being expressed with unprecedented openness. However, while specific issues had changed, the impulse to censor unwelcome expression had not. Scarcely a day passed without a censorship issue making front-page news: calls for recording companies to label their rap music products with content warnings; legislative bodies debating whether government should dictate the content of children's television programming; national governments trying to block public access to the information superhighway of the Internet; Christian Fundamentalists campaigning to control school curricula; cigarette manufacturers charging that prosmoking viewpoints are being censored; and national leaders calling for public resistance to liquor advertising on television.

Each generation of the twentieth century has seen the world reinvent itself. Dramatic scientific and technological advances have helped to accelerate change at rates that would previously have been unimaginable. Colonial empires have come and gone, powerful political and economic ideologies have risen and fallen—along with the nation-states built on them—and the map of the world has been periodically redrawn. Even religious dogmas that once seemed immutable have evolved. Meanwhile, literary, musical, and artistic styles have developed at accelerating rates, and entirely new forms of expression have grown out of new technologies in film, broadcasting, and computers. Through all these changes, however, one force seems destined never to disappear: censorship—the deliberate efforts of governments, churches, groups, and individual persons to prevent others from freely expressing themselves. As each generation has tried to express new ideas and new art forms, opponents—often from earlier generations—have arisen to censor them. Specific issues have changed, along with the technology used to communicate new ideas, but the impulse to censor has been constant.

Censorship has taken many forms and has had many definitions. According to its classical definition, it occurs only when a government acts deliberately to limit expression. Indeed, governments have historically been among the most powerful censors in the world. Authoritarian governments have always been rigid censors, outlawing any and all expression that in any way threatens their power, prestige, or security. However, it has not been only authoritarian governments that have acted as censors. Under both democratic and authoritarian governments, censorship has taken many forms: from control over the licensing of publications, operas, films, and other forms of expression, to intimidation, imprisonment, and even death for transgressors. Nor have governments always limited their censorship efforts to politically objectionable expression. In many societies they have accepted the role of protectors of public morals and defenders of religious orthodoxy. The U.S. government has stood apart by being steadfast in not trying to censor religious heretics or blasphemers; however, it has played a leading role in defining obscenity and punishing its purveyors.

Organized religion has also long been a powerful censoring force in most societies. Indeed, since the rise of Christianity churches have waged a ceaseless, and often violent, war to stamp out heresy. As heresy usually consists of dissent from a certain religious dogma, the true believers of one faith may be the heretics of another. The Puritans of colonial New England, for example, came to America to escape religious persecution from the Church of England. After establishing their own governments in the New World, they did not hesitate to use their freedom to persecute dissenters in their own midst. The legacies of intolerance left by such groups have contributed greatly to the censoring forces of later generations.

* * *

The three volumes of *Censorship* contain 997 alphabetically arranged essays, including 333 on persons; 203 on general issues; 173 on books, films, and other works; 92 on organizations and government bodies; 66 on laws; 60 on events; 42 on places; and 28 on court cases. Each article begins with easily accessible ready-reference information. Articles on people, for example, give their names, full dates and places of birth and death, brief identifications, and concise statements of their significance with regard to censorship issues. Articles on other subjects begin with similarly concise information. Articles vary in length from several hundred to several thousand words, with each article emphasizing censorship issues. All articles are followed by lists of cross-references to other essays on closely related subjects and the subjects they mention. Additional references can be found in three indexes in the third volume. Brief annotated bibliographies appear at the ends of articles more than a thousand words in length, and a comprehensive bibliography on censorship can be found at the end of the third volume. More than 275 articles are illustrated with photographs, drawings, or maps. Many of these illustrations contain graphic examples of censorship.

The front of each volume of *Censorship* contains an alphabetical listing of all topics; the back lists topics by subject category. The third volume contains appendices providing details on important court decisions, a guide to censorship resources, a general glossary, and a bibliography. It also contains three indexes: an index of court cases, an index of film and book titles, and a comprehensive index.

As the extensive bibliographical notes in this reference set attest, there is an immense literature on censorship. It thus might be fairly asked what this work contributes to the field. Aside from meeting an ongoing need for up-to-date information on a subject changing as rapidly as modern technology, *Censorship* offers unique perspective. The approach taken throughout is one of open-minded inquiry. The 353 scholars who contributed to the set were not given a rigid definition with which to pinpoint exactly where "censorship" has or has not occurred. Instead, they were invited to explore the concept in all its dimensions, leaving it to readers to draw their own conclusions. The premise of this work is that any effort, originating from any source, to eliminate free expression of any manner may constitute a form of censorship. From this perspective, the set has an exceptionally broad sweep. In addition to covering such obvious censorship targets as public speaking, the news media, literature, music, and the arts, the set considers such matters as gang-related graffiti, school prayer, voting rights of minority groups, dress codes, and much more.

One of the novel approaches that this set takes is to examine every dimension of censorship: its targets and victims; its perpetrators and defenders; its rationale; and its subject matter. For example, the issue of what constitutes obscenity runs throughout this entire work. Censors of obscenity have included government agencies, churches, pressure groups, and private crusaders—who are covered under entries on persons, groups, laws, court decisions, and other topics. Targets of obscenity censorship have been even more numerous: writers, poets, artists, filmmakers, and even musicians. Far too many works have been attacked for their alleged obscenity to make it possible to discuss each of them. Instead, *Censorship* offers entries on a representative selection of important and intriguing examples of censored works. It also has entries on hundreds of creative people who have been attacked, as well as the content of their work. Readers will thus find essays on such subjects as pornography, nudity, prostitution, offensive language, and sex.

* * *

We are grateful to the many scholars who have contributed their time, talent, and expertise to make this set possible. A list of their names appears in the front of this volume. We are also indebted to our distinguished panel of consulting editors: Lawrence Amey of the School of Library Studies at Dalhousie University in Nova Scotia; Timothy L. Hall of the University of Mississippi Law School; Carl Jensen, founder-director of Project Censored at Sonoma State University in California; Charles May, of the Department of English at California State University, Long Beach; and Richard L. Wilson of the Department of Political Science at the University of Tennessee at Chattanooga.

Consulting Editors

Lawrence Amey
Dalhousie University
School of Library Studies

Timothy L. Hall
University of Mississippi Law School

Carl Jensen
Project Censored
Sonoma State University

Charles May
California State University, Long Beach
Department of English

Richard L. Wilson
University of Tennessee at Chattanooga
Department of Political Science

Contributors

Richard Adler
University of Michigan, Dearborn

Amy Allison
Los Angeles, California

William Allison
Bowling Green State University

Emily Alward
Greenwood Public Library

Lawrence Amey
Dalhousie University

Carolyn Anderson
University of Massachusetts at Amherst

Gerald S. Argetsinger
Rochester Institute of Technology

Robin Armstrong
Western Maryland College

Lessie Bass Artis
East Carolina University School of
Social Work

Mary Welek Atwell
Radford University

Bryan Aubrey
Fairfield, Iowa

H. C. Aubrey
Oregon City, Oregon

Charles Avinger
Washtenaw Community College

James A. Baer
Northern Virginia Community College

Matthew C. Bagger
Columbia University

Charles F. Bahmueller
Center for Civic Education

Barbara Bair
Duke University

Von Bakanic
College of Charleston

Ann Stewart Balakier
University of South Dakota

Carl L. Bankston III
University of Southwestern Louisiana

Paul Bateman
Southwestern University School of Law

Jeffrey A. Bell
Southeastern Louisiana University

Raymond A. Belliotti
State University College at Fredonia

Frances K. Bender
University of Tennessee at Chattanooga

Richard A. Bennett
Southern College of Technology

Milton Berman
University of Rochester

Arnold Blumberg
Towson State University

Kevin Bochynski
Salem State College

Pegge Bochynski
Beverly, Massachusetts

Christine M. Boeckl
University of Nebraska at Kearney

Steve D. Boilard
Western Kentucky University

Michael W. Bowers
University of Nevada, Las Vegas

Suzanne Riffle Boyce
Mexico, Missouri

Gerald Boyer
Maryville University, St. Louis

John H. Boyer
West Virginia University

Anthony D. Branch
Golden Gate University

John A. Britton
Francis Marion University

Wesley Britton
Grayson County Commuinity College

Jeffrey Brody
California State University, Fullerton

Daniel A. Brown
California State University, Fullerton

Thomas W. Buchanan
Ancilla Domini College

Fred Buchstein
Dix & Eaton, Inc.

Douglas S. Campbell
Lock Haven University

Edmund J. Campion
University of Tennessee, Knoxville

Thomas Cappuccio
Northern Michigan University

Andrea D. Cardwell
University of Tennessee at Chattanooga

Brian J. Carroll
California Baptist College

Christine R. Catron
St. Mary's University

John W. Cavanaugh
University of South Carolina

Donald E. Cellini
Adrian College

Jim D. Clark
Richland College

Thomas Clarkin
University of Texas at Austin

Martin Cloonan
University of York

Ross F. Collins
North Dakota State University

Helen O'Hara Connell
Barry University

Vanessa Moody Coombs
Hampton University

Michael Coronel
University of Northern Colorado

Patricia Coronel
Colorado State University

Jonathan L. Crane
University of North Carolina at Charlotte

Stephen Cresswell
West Virginia Wesleyan College

Norma Crews
Neosho, Missouri

Judith A. Cunningham
Eastern Kentucky University

Jeff Cupp
Cullman, Alabama

E. M. Dadlez
University of Central Oklahoma

Douglass K. Daniel
Kansas State University

Eddith A. Dashiell
Ohio University

Juliet Dee
University of Delaware

James E. Devlin
State University College at Oneonta

M. Casey Diana
University of Illinois

Gerard Donnelly
University of Mississippi

Davison M. Douglas
College of William and Mary Law School

Bruce E. Drushel
Miami University (Ohio)

Joyce Duncan
East Tennessee State University

Jennifer Eastman
Clark University

June Edwards
State University College at Oneonta

Susan Ellis-Lopez
Heritage College

Thomas L. Erskine
Salisbury State University

R. Ferrell Ervin
Southeast Missouri State University

Bette Novit Evans
Creighton University

Daniel C. Falkowski
Canisius College

David John Farmer
Virginia Commonwealth University

Randall Fegley
Pennsylvania State University

Mario D. Fenyo
Bowie State University

John P. Ferré
University of Louisville

Michael Shaw Findlay
California State University, Chico

Alan M. Fisher
California State University, Dominguez Hills

Shane Fitzpatrick
Centenary College

George J. Flynn
State University of New York at Plattsburgh

Rory Flynn
Hilo, Hawaii

Michael J. Fontenot
Southern University at Baton Rouge

Ella Forbes
Temple University

Paul A. Frisch
Washington and Jefferson College

Michael J. Garcia
Arapahoe Community College

Janet E. Gardner
University of Massachusetts, Dartmouth

Phyllis B. Gerstenfeld
California State University, Stanislaus

K. Fred Gillum
Colby College

Phillip Goggans
Seattle Pacific University

Marc Goldstein
Troy, New York

Robert Justin Goldstein
Oakland University, Rochester, New York

Nancy M. Gordon
Amherst, Massachusetts

Cecil E. Greek
University of South Florida

William Howard Green
University of Missouri, Columbia

Thomas Clifton Greenholtz
University of Tennessee at Chattanooga

Gwendolyn Griffith
Willamette University College of Law

Johnpeter Horst Grill
Mississippi State University

Scot M. Guenter
San Jose State University

Christopher E. Guthrie
Tarleton State University

Katheleen R. Guzman
University of Oklahoma College of Law

Nancy N. Haanstad
Weber State University

Lawrence W. Haapanen
Lewis-Clark State College

Robert A. Hackett
Simon Fraser University

Cathy Moran Hajo
New York University

Irwin Halfond
McKendree College

Timothy L. Hall
University of Mississippi Law School

Susan E. Hamilton
Honomu, Hawaii

Roger D. Haney
Murray State University

Gillian Greenhill Hannum
Manhattanville College

Paul Hansom
Los Angeles, California

Craig L. Hanson
Muskingum College

Roger D. Hardaway
Northwestern Oklahoma State University

Fred R. van Hartesveldt
Fort Valley State College

Fred Hartmeister
Texas Tech University

Fran J. Hassencahl
Old Dominion University

A. Waller Hastings
Northern State University

Pamela Hayes-Bohanan
McAllen Memorial Library

John Victor Heilker
University of Tennessee at Chattanooga

Mark C. Herman
Edison Community College

Steven R. Hewitt
University of Saskatchewan

David G. Hicks
Pollack & Hicks, P.C.

Stephen R. C. Hicks
Rockford College

Mark L. Higgins
Wayne State College

Kay Hively
Neosho, Missouri

Russell Hively
Neosho, Missouri

Teresa Holder
Bradley University

Hal L. Holladay
Middlebury, Connecticut

Kenneth M. Holland
University of Memphis

Fred Hoover
University of Texas at Arlington

Hilary Horan
University of Ottawa

Charles C. Howard
Tarleton State University

William L. Howard
Chicago State University

Peter Hőyng
University of Tennessee, Knoxville

Patricia J. Huhn
Trinidad State Junior College

Sue Hum
University of Massachusetts, Dartmouth

E. D. Huntley
Appalachian State University

Marian L. Huttenstein
Radford University

K. L. A. Hyatt
Pasadena, California

John Jacob
Northwestern University

Linda R. James
University of Wisconsin, Madison

Duncan R. Jamieson
Ashland University

Dave Jenkinson
University of Manitoba

Albert C. Jensen
Central Florida Community College

Carl Jensen
Sonoma State University

Dwight Jensen
Marshall University

Jeffry Jensen
Altadena, California

K. Sue Jewell
Ohio State University

Bruce E. Johansen
University of Nebraska at Omaha

Carolyn Johnson
Idaho State University

Harlan R. Johnson
Northern Arizona University

Dennis L. Kalob
New England College

Mathew J. Kanjirathinkal
East Texas State University

Max Kashefi
Eastern Illinois University

Richard Keenan
University of Maryland, Eastern Shore

Richard Keenan
Wayne State College

Nancy D. Kersell
Northern Kentucky University

Niaz Ahmed Khan
University of West Alabama

Howard M. Kleiman
Miami University (Ohio)

Bill Knight
Western Illinois University

Joseph M. Knippenberg
Oglethorpe University

Grove Koger
Boise Public Library

Barbara G. Kramer
Santa Fe Community College

Frederic Krome
Northern Kentucky University

Camille R. La Bossiere
University of Ottawa

Ralph L. Langenheim, Jr.
University of Illinois at Urbana

LaRae Larkin
Weber State University

Eugene Larson
Pierce College

Ritchie R. Latimore
Kent State University-Geauga Campus

Abraham D. Lavender
Florida International University

Barbara Leckie
Carleton University

Joseph Edward Lee
Winthrop University

David LeMaster
Centenary College of Louisiana

Dana Lesley-Draper
University of Tennessee at Chattanooga

Gregory A. Levitt
University of New Orleans

Leon Lewis
Appalachian State University

Thomas T. Lewis
Mount Senario College

Matthew J. Lindstrom
Northern Arizona University

Anne Lineberry
Dallas, Texas

Jeremy Harris Lipschultz
University of Nebraska at Omaha

Edward J. Lordan
Villanova University

Bill Loving
University of Oklahoma

Denise Low-Weso
Haskell Indian Nations University

Marnie K. Lucas
Flagstaff, Arizina

David C. Lukowitz
Hamline University

Joe E. Lunceford
Georgetown College

Wei Luo
Southern Illinois University

Robert McClenaghan
Pasadena, California

Glen McClish
Southwestern University

Mark McCulloh
Davidson College

Andrew Macdonald
Loyola University

Gina Macdonald
Loyola University

Robert W. McGee
Seton Hall University

Edgar V. McKnight, Jr.
John A. Logan College

Matthew D. McNary
Ohio University School of Film

Diane L. McNulty
Grand Prairie, Texas

Eduardo Magãlhaes III
Simpson College

Paul D. Mageli
Kenmore, New York

Scott Magnuson-Martinson
Normandale Community College

Patrick Malcolmson
St. Thomas University

Nancy Farm Mannikko
L'Anse, Michigan

Chogollah Maroufi
*California State University,
Los Angeles*

Charles E. Marske
St. Louis University

Eric Martin
Boston, Masschuessetts

Pamela Jane Martin
Saint Francis College

Dena Mattausch-Hicks
Rockford, Illinois

James T. Mattingly
Western Oregon State College

Bruce E. May
University of South Dakota

Charles May
California State University, Long Beach

Steve J. Mazurana
University of Northern Colorado

Michael E. Meagher
University of Missouri, Rolla

James S. Measell
Wayne State University

Joseph A. Melusky
Saint Francis College

Myra Mendible
University of South Florida, Ft. Myers

Rebecca Ellen Merlick
University of Texas at Arlington

Diane P. Michelfelder
California Polytechnic State University

Vasa D. Mihailovich
*University of North Carolina at Chapel
Hill*

Sharon Mikkelson
El Centro College

Randy E. Miller
University of South Florida

Daniel L. Mitchell
Silver City, New Mexico

William V. Moore
College of Charleston

Mario Morelli
Western Illinois University

Brian K. Morley
Frazier Park, California

Thomas J. Mortillaro
Nicholls State University

Turhon A. Murad
California State University, Chico

Francois N. Muyumba
Indiana State University

Kimberly R. Myers
*University of North Carolina at Chapel
Hill*

Linda G. Nation
University of Tennessee at Chattanooga

Byron Nelson
West Virginia University

Kristen Dollase Nevious
University of South Dakota

Joseph L. Nogee
University of Houston

Martin F. Norden
University of Massachusetts at Amherst

Robert H. O'Connor
North Dakota State University

Oladele A. Ogunseitan
University of California, Irvine

Gary A. Olson
San Bernardino Valley College

James F. O'Neil
Edison Community College

David E. Paas
Hillsdale College

Diane M. Pacetti
Bradley University

Maria A. Pacino
Pacific University

Lisa Paddock
Brooklyn, New York

Catherine Pagani
University of Alabama

Tim Palmer
Genesee Community College

William A. Paquette
Tidewater Commuity College

Richard A. Parker
Northern Arizona University

Constance A. Pedoto
Miles College

William A. Pelz
DePaul University

William E. Pemberton
University of Wisconsin, LaCrosse

John B. Peoples
University of Tennessee at Chattanooga

Marilyn Elizabeth Perry
Prospect Heights, Illinois

Nis Petersen
Jersey City State College

James Petrik
Ohio University

Peter Phillips
Sonoma State University

Erika E. Pilver
Westfield State College

Julio Cesar Pino
Kent State University

Nancy A. Piotrowski
University of California, Berkeley

Gregory G. Pitts
Arkansas State University

George R. Plitnik
Frostburg State University

Oliver B. Pollak
University of Nebraska at Omaha

Arthur Pontynen
University of Wisconsin, Oshkosh

Luke A. Powers
Tennessee State University

Verbie Lovorn Prevost
University of Tennessee at Chattanooga

Cliff Prewencki
Schenectady, New York

Edna B. Quinn
Salisbury State University

Gregory P. Rabb
Jamestown Community College

Brandon Raulston
University of Tennessee at Chattanooga

Paul L. Redditt
Georgetown College

Gerald L. Rettie
Sacramento, California

Robert D. Richards
Pennsylvania State University

Betty Richardson
*Southern Illinois University,
Edwardsville*

Thomas J. Roach
Purdue University Calumet

Claire J. Robinson
Fairfield, Iowa

Stephen F. Rohde
Los Angeles, California

Carl Rollyson
Bernard M. Baruch College

Peggy Waltzer Rosefeldt
New Orleans, Louisiana

Joseph R. Rudolph, Jr.
Towson State University

Vicki A. Sanders
Paine College

Udo Sautter
University of Windsor

Richard Sax
Madonna University

Jean Owens Schaefer
University of Wyoming

Helmut J. Schmeller
Fort Hays State University

Mareleyn Schneider
Yeshiva University

Robert O. Schneider
Pembroke State University

John Richard Schrock
Emporia State University

Elizabeth L. Scully
University of Texas at Arlington

Rose Secrest
Signal Mountain, Tennessee

Pamela K. Shaffer
Fort Hays State University

Fan A. Shen
Rochester Community College

Amy L. Shields
Mexico, Missouri

R. Baird Shuman
*University of Illinois at
    Urbana-Champaign*

Jerold L. Simmons
University of Nebraska at Omaha

Roger Smith
Portland, Oregon

Ted J. Smith III
Virginia Commonwealth University

David R. Sobel
Provosty, Sadler & deLaunay

Joseph L. Spradley
Wheaton College

Barbara C. Stanley
Johnson City, Tennessee

Glenn Ellen Starr
Appalachian State University

Michael R. Steele
Pacific University

David L. Sterling
University of Cincinnati

Roger J. Stilling
Appalachian State University

Geralyn Strecker
Ball State University

Leslie Stricker
Dayton, Ohio

Taylor Stults
Muskingum College

Susan A. Stussy
Madonna University

Douglas J. Swanson
Oklahoma Baptist University

James Tackach
Roger Williams University

Robert D. Talbott
University of Northern Iowa

Paul E. Tanner, Jr.
Annapolis, Maryland

G. Thomas Taylor
University of Maine

Susan M. Taylor
Indiana University at South Bend

Emily Teipe
Fullerton College

Tommy G. Thomason
Texas Christian University

Leslie V. Tischauser
Oak Park, Illinois

Brian G. Tobin
Lassen College

Paul B. Trescott
Southern Illinois University

Robert D. Ubriaco Jr.
Crestwood, Missouri

Siva Vaidhyanathan
University of Texas

Tamara M. Valentine
*University of South
    Carolina-Spartanburg*

Elizabeth Van Schaack
Yale Law School

Qun Wang
*California State University, Monterey
    Bay*

A. J. L. Waskey
Dalton College

John C. Watkins Jr.
University of Alabama, Tuscaloosa

Robert P. Watson
University of Hawaii at Hilo

Samuel E. Watson III
Midwestern State University

Ronald J. Weber
University of Texas at El Paso

David S. Webster
Oklahoma State University, Stillwater

Marcia J. Weiss
Point Park College

Marsha M. West
University of Texas at Arlington

Donald M. Whaley
Salisbury State University

Winifred Whelan
St. Bonaventure University

Richard Whitworth
Ball State University

Steve Wiegenstein
Culver-Stockton College

Lee Williams
Authors Guild

John F. Wilson
University of Hawaii at Manoa

Raymond Wilson
Fort Hays State University

Richard L. Wilson
University of Tennessee at Chattanooga

Sharon K. Wilson
Fort Hays State University

Thomas Aaron Wyrick
University of Tennessee at Chattanooga

Philip R. Zampini
Westfield State College

Barry J. Zaslow
Miami University (Ohio)

Noah R. Zerbe
Northern Arizona University

Loretta Ellen Zimmerman
University of Portland

CONTENTS

ALPHABETICAL LIST OF ENTRIES

Volume I

Volume II

Volume III

CENSORSHIP

A

Abelard, Peter

BORN: c. 1079, Le Pallet, near Nantes, Brittany

DIED: April 21, 1142, near Chalon-sur-Saône, Burgundy

IDENTIFICATION: French philosopher, theologian, and educator

SIGNIFICANCE: Later famous for his love affair with Heloise, Abelard was hounded during his lifetime because of his theology

The most important teacher at the new University of Paris, Abelard was notorious for publicly ridiculing rivals, and he easily made enemies who were anxious to seek revenge. His dialectical method of questioning nearly everything was the pretext used by his theological enemies to obtain the first condemnation of his work at the Provincial Council of Rheims, held at Soissons in 1121. At that council Abelard was not even given the right to respond. For a time he was confined to a monastic community at St. Medard. The only contemporary theologians whose criticisms of Abelard's theology have survived were insignificant figures, however, far removed from the site of Abelard's condemnations.

After his condemnation Abelard returned to Paris and became abbot of St. Denis. There he ridiculed the belief that the Dionysius the Areopagite—Saint Denis himself—had had anything to do with Paris, or the abbey named after him, causing his fellow monks to turn on him. Because France's king was patron and protector of the abbey, Abelard's remarks were also considered an offense against the Crown. Abelard fled to the Champagne region to escape arrest. The monks of Saint-Gildas-de-Rhuys in Breton invited him to be their abbot, but his abrasive personality again won him enemies and the monks evidently tried to kill him.

Abelard was back in Paris by 1135, again teaching theology and ethics; however, opposition against him never ceased. In fact, it grew more serious when theologians at the prestigious School of St. Victor, in company with William of Saint-Thierry, convinced Saint Bernard of Clairvaux to confront Abelard. Bernard helped to convince the Provincial Council at Sens to level charges against Abelard in 1140. Abelard appeared at the council, appealed his case to Rome, and left the session. As was pointed out at the time, "He was neither judged nor heard." Pope Innocent II, Bernard's friend and former student, upheld the accusation, but Abelard wanted to appeal his case in person. Because of his ill health, friends made sure that he did not rush off to Rome. Peter the Venerable, the abbot of Cluny, then reconciled Abelard and Bernard. (It was not until the eighteenth century that Bernard was denounced as an intolerant bigot and Abelard was regarded as an anticlerical free thinker.) Abelard died at a Cluniac abbey, without reaching Rome to make his personal appeal.

Abelard is most famous for his tragic love affair with a young woman named Heloise; however, this affair had no bearing on the trouble that he had over his writings and teachings. Modern collections of Abelard's correspondence with Heloise have been attacked by censors, and the U.S. Customs Service confiscated English editions several times before 1930.

See also *Areopagitica*; Bacon, Roger; Christianity; Customs laws, U.S.; Lateran Council, Fourth; Paris, Council of; Religion; Thomas à Kempis.

Abolitionist movement

DATE: 1780's-1860's

PLACE: United States

SIGNIFICANCE: In many parts of the United States opponents of slavery were rigorously censored

In 1619 the first Africans to land in North America were sold into indentured servitude in Virginia. From this beginning the institution of slavery gradually evolved. As it spread throughout Britain's American colonies, opponents to the institution began speaking out. In the 1770's Quakers and others began protesting the system that allowed Christians to hold other human beings in involuntary servitude; those calling for the abolition of slavery became known as abolitionists. The revolutionary ideologies of Thomas Paine and John Locke, emphasizing natural rights, added a philosophical base to abolitionism. At first slaveholders engaged in discussions about the legitimacy of slavery, but found they could not resolve the issues of social control and economics if slavery were ended.

After the independent United States arose from the American Revolution, most of the Northern states abolished slavery. However, invention of the cotton gin in the 1790's and the rapidly increasing world demand for cotton fabrics gave Southern slavery a new lease on life and caused white Southerners to view the institution as a necessary evil early in the nineteenth century. The antislavery movement matured, however, and grew more resolute as the concept of slavery, especially in a free country, lost credibility.

During the 1820's a growing radical segment of U.S. citizens called for slavery's immediate abolition. This rising antislavery tide caused a corresponding increase in participation in a proslavery movement, which resulted in Southern society's arguing that slavery was a positive good for American society. Those supporting slavery resorted to legal, extralegal, and illegal approaches to blunt the efforts of the abolitionists. Meanwhile, the slavery issue was a part of a larger discussion on the right of free speech and the rights to liberty of all Americans, especially those opposed to slavery.

Two of the numerous parts of the antislavery movement have a special bearing on questions of censorship. The first part is abolitionist literature, the second petitions sent to the U.S. Congress and congressional reaction to such petitions.

Censorship of Literature. The printed word provided one of the easiest ways for abolitionists to spread news of their activities, and there were several antislavery newspapers. At least two of them attracted enough attention to result in dire consequences. A Southern planter and slaveholder named James G. Birney sold his slaves during the early 1830's. After attempting to conduct antislavery work in Alabama and Kentucky, he moved to Cincinnati, Ohio. There he established an antislavery paper, the *Philanthropist*, early in 1836. His paper was short-lived, however. In July a mob that included Cincinnati's mayor, a bank president, and a former senator, destroyed Birney's paper. Afterward Birney tried to establish another antislavery paper in Danville, Kentucky. He was stopped from doing so on the grounds that it would create an unsafe environment. In a letter to fellow abolitionist Gerrit Smith, Birney concluded that an inextricable link existed between liberty and slavery. Denial of the opportunity to oppose slavery limited the freedom of whites.

The year after the *Philanthropist*'s destruction, an Alton, Illinois, mob that included the town's leading citizens, murdered Elijah Lovejoy, who edited an antislavery newspaper. William Elery Channing called a protest meeting to be held in Boston. Although many people opposed the rally, for fear of the reaction it might cause, more than five thousand defenders of free speech and abolitionism turned out on December 8, 1837. They heard Wendell Phillips declare that Lovejoy's murder was censorship that threatened the constitutionally guaranteed freedoms of speech and the press. Phillips charged that a mob had lynched Lovejoy merely for expressing his views on slavery. To Phillips, such actions undermined the nation's founding principles.

Lovejoy's martyrdom caused others to rise in defense of free speech and to speak out against this heinous form of censorship. Journalist Horace Greeley expressed his outrage that people could suggest Lovejoy was at fault. In a similar vein, Ralph Waldo Emerson praised Lovejoy in a speech on heroism.

The Gag Rule. Antislavery activists began petition drives to force Congress to abolish slavery in the District of Columbia and to restrict its spread into the territories. The first nationwide petition drive began in 1828. By 1836 petitions were arriving in sufficient numbers to disrupt the work of Congress. While there were enough Southern senators to vote to prevent petitions from being read on the floor, supporters of slavery enjoyed no such balance in the House of Representatives. Therefore, the House instituted a Gag Rule ordering petitions relating to slavery to be immediately tabled without being read. Despite opposition from congressmen Joshua Giddings of Ohio, William Slade of Vermont, and former president John Quincy Adams of Massachusetts, the rule was reinstated in 1837 and made permanent in 1842. The antiabolition forces succeeded in having Representative Giddings censured, whereupon he resigned his seat and returned to Ohio to be re-elected. Revocation of the Gag Rule in 1844 vindicated the free-speech congressmen.

John C. Calhoun. A major supporter of slavery, Senator Calhoun of South Carolina argued vehemently for the need to control actions that might undermine the institution. In fact, he demanded that the Northern states support slavery as vigorously as the Southern states were doing—even if they had to restrict First Amendment freedoms as the slaveholding states had already done. Calhoun defended the actions of a mob that had burned allegedly abolitionist literature by the American Anti-Slavery Society that had been found at the Charleston, South Carolina, post office. As a result, Amos Kendall, President Andrew Jackson's postmaster general, refused to order Southern postmasters to deliver abolitionist literature. Jackson supported Kendall, going so far as to ask—without success—for a law prohibiting the circulation of incendiary literature in the South. Calhoun called for a similar law.

While most censorship of abolitionist literature occurred in the Southern states, the Reverend Leonard Bacon issued the Connecticut Gag Law, which denied abolitionists the opportunity to use Congregational churches for their meetings. This law was adopted in other Northern states, thus limiting the places where abolitionists could hold their meetings.

Several Southern states passed laws censoring abolitionists following the incident in Charleston. Maryland made it a "high offense" to write or circulate literature that might cause discontent among slaves, with penalties of up to twenty years in prison. South Carolina made it a crime to subscribe to antislavery literature, while Arkansas specified prison terms for anyone speaking against slavery. The legislatures of Alabama, North and South Carolina, and Georgia called upon Northern states to outlaw the publication of abolitionist literature. Abolitionists used these and similar actions to gain support for their position, arguing that such attacks undermined basic democratic principles. Abolitionists kept reminding Americans that slavery was only one part of the general issue of freedom and liberty for all Americans. —*Duncan R. Jamieson*

See also African Americans; Civil Rights movement; Civil War, U.S.; Death; Douglass, Frederick; Gag order; Locke, John; Lovejoy, Elijah Parish; Paine, Thomas; Postal regulations; *Uncle Tom's Cabin*; Walker, David.

BIBLIOGRAPHY

Herbert Aptheker, *Abolitionism: A Revolutionary Movement* (Boston: Twayne, 1989), views abolitionism as a revolution, not a reform movement. Gilbert Hobbs Barnes, *The Antislavery Impulse, 1830-1844* (New York: Harcourt, Brace and World, 1964), is a classic study of the antislavery movement. Martin Duberman, *The Antislavery Vanguard* (Princeton, N.J.: Princeton University Press, 1965), is a collection of essays showing domestic and foreign perspectives of abolitionism. Alma Lutz, *Crusade for Freedom: Women of the Antislavery Movement* (Boston: Beacon Press, 1968), focuses on women and the abolitionist crusade. Russell B. Nye, *William Lloyd Garrison and the Humanitarian Reformers* (Boston: Little, Brown, 1955), is a biography of the most famous abolitionist. Alice Felt Tyler, *Freedom's Ferment* (New York: Harper and Row, 1962), is a classic study of nineteenth century reform.

Abortion gag rule

ENACTED: 1991
PLACE: United States (national)
SIGNIFICANCE: This amendment to Title X of the Public Health Service Act forbade discussion of abortion by federally funded agencies

In 1970 the U.S. Congress enacted Title X of the Public Health Service Act, authorizing the secretary of Health and Human Services to make grants to and enter into contracts with public or nonprofit private entities to assist voluntary family planning projects. The law provided that no funds could be used in programs advocating abortion as a method of family planning. In 1988 new regulations were issued, prohibiting Title X projects from providing counseling or referral or in any way "encouraging, promoting, or advocating" the use of abortion as a method of family planning. The new regulations also required projects to be organized so that they would be "physically and financially" separate from prohibited abortion activities.

These regulations were challenged in a case brought before the U.S. Supreme Court by Title X grantees and doctors, on the grounds that the law violated First Amendment free speech rights by "impermissibly imposing viewpoint-discriminatory conditions on government subsidies." In a 5-4 decision in *Rust v. Sullivan* the Court ruled that the Title X prohibition was constitutional. The Court ruled that the government was not discriminating on the basis of viewpoint because in choosing to fund one activity to the exclusion of another it was not attempting to suppress a dangerous idea. Four justices dissented, declaring that the majority's decision upheld a clear government restriction on the expression of dangerous ideas.

The question of whether Title X's "gag rule" constituted a form of censorship has become a matter of opinion, both on the Supreme Court and in society at large. However, the Court's majority ruling never went into effect. Health care providers led by Planned Parenthood of America mounted procedural challenges to the decision that delayed its implementation through 1992. The day after Bill Clinton was inaugurated as president of the United States in March, 1993, he signed an executive order nullifying the controversial Title X regulations.

See also Birth control education; Comstock Act of 1873; First Amendment; Gag order; Moral Majority.

Abridgment

DEFINITION: Abridgment is the condensing of a work by omitting either single words or entire passages, without changing its meaning; bowdlerization is the modification of a work's meaning by omission or revision of selected passages, often those considered vulgar

SIGNIFICANCE: Both methods are used by editors to alter the contents of literary works

Both abridgment and bowdlerization are usually carried out by editors, often after the death of an author; they are distinct processes which are often confused. Abridgment, in itself, is not a form of censorship. Many authors consent to the publication of shortened versions of their work in formats such as *Reader's Digest Condensed Books*. Theoretically, these abridged novels are merely shorter versions of longer works, with some descriptive and digressive passages not central to the narrative line having been weeded out, but with the larger meaning or messages of the work having been preserved.

The distinction between abridgment and bowdlerization blurs, however, with the example of texts prepared for use in schools and for juvenile audiences. The plays of William Shakespeare, probably the most abridged and bowdlerized works in existence, are often shortened for use in high schools. More often than not, it is the passages regarded as vulgar and lascivious that are omitted, those passages having been judged extraneous to the meaning of the play by the editor. Such abridgment can lead to the distortion of a work's meaning by excessive or selective cutting.

The term bowdlerization comes from the practices of the nineteenth century British editor Thomas Bowdler, who prepared sanitized versions of the Bible and of Shakespeare's plays for the genteel British family audience. His practices went far beyond simple abridgment, however; Bowdler actually attempted to "improve" on Shakespeare, for example, by rewriting passages and altering plots, such as his revision of the tragedy *King Lear*, for which he provided a happy ending.

One of the least known, though equally notorious, examples of bowdlerization in the United States concerns the publication in 1916 of what was purported to be one of Mark Twain's last works, a book given the title *The Mysterious Stranger*. The book was in fact a fraud concocted by Mark Twain's biographer and literary executor, Alfred Bigelow Paine, and the publisher Frederick A. Duneka. Two authentic Mark Twain manuscripts were patched together and heavily rewritten by Paine and Duneka to produce the appearance of a single complete work entitled *The Mysterious Stranger*. Paine and Duneka subsequently marketed the bowdlerized text as a Christmas book for children. For almost fifty years the reading public spuriously believed that *The Mysterious Stranger* was an authentic, complete work of Mark Twain's final years; it was not until 1963 that Twain scholar John S. Tuckey discovered the fraud.

See also Book publishing; Books, children's; Bowdler, Thomas; *Diary of Anne Frank, The*; Education; Shakespeare, William; *Tess of the D'Urbervilles*; Textbooks; Twain, Mark.

Academy Awards ceremonies

TYPE OF WORK: Annual stage production and television broadcast

FIRST STAGED: 1927

SUBJECT MATTER: Annual awards ceremony in which the Academy of Motion Picture Arts and Sciences recognizes achievement in filmmaking by awarding Oscars

SIGNIFICANCE: The high visibility of this ceremony has made it an increasingly attractive public platform on which participants have expressed their political and social views

Established in 1927 and first broadcast on television in 1953, the annual Academy Awards presentation ceremonies is one of the most watched television programs in the world. The gold statuettes awarded in this event—picturing a knight plunging a two-edged sword into a reel of film and popularly known as "Oscars"—are perhaps the most widely recognized trophies in the world. Because of this visibility, the awards ceremonies themselves have prompted many of the ceremony's participants to use this forum to express strongly held political and social sentiments.

In 1973, for example, Marlon Brando won the Academy's Best Actor award for his performance in *The Godfather*, but he

The earliest, and most publicized, attempt to use the Academy Awards presentation ceremonies as a platform for protest occurred in 1973 when actor Marlon Brando sent Marie Cruz ("Sacheen Littlefeather") to the ceremonies to read a statement on American Indians in his behalf. (AP/Wide World Photos)

declined to attend the awards ceremony. Instead, upon announcement of his award, a woman dressed in Native American clothes who called herself Sacheen Littlefeather (Marie Cruz) read a prepared statement from Brando in which he refused the award on account of "the condition of the American Indian." In 1975 Burt Schneider and Peter Davis were recognized for their anti-Vietnam war documentary *Hearts of Mind*. When Schneider included in his acceptance speech a wire from a Viet Cong leader, many viewers called the network to protest and Frank Sinatra—one of the program's emcees—disavowed the political remarks on behalf of the Academy and apologized for their assertion. In 1978 Vanessa Redgrave created a furor in accepting the best-actress Oscar for her performance in *Julia* when she spoke disparagingly of "Zionist hoodlums"—an allusion to her support of the Palestine Liberation Organization.

Because acceptance speeches of Oscar winners are delivered spontaneously, the producers of the annual Academy Awards ceremonies have had little control over their content. However, even award presenters whose remarks have been prepared in advance have sometimes interjected political asides. Producers have typically responded by essentially blacklisting such presenters from future ceremonies. In 1993 for example, Susan Sarandon and Tim Robbins appeared together as award presenters and appealed for better treatment of HIV-positive Haitian immigrants. That same year Richard Gere served as a presenter and made a statement about Tibetan human rights. None of these actors was invited to present awards in 1994.

Political controversies of other forms have also occasionally adorned the Oscar ceremony. In 1996 Iran announced that it was withdrawing its own entry for the Academy Award for best foreign-language film—the 1995 Cannes Film Festival winner *The White Balloon*—to protest moves in the U.S. Congress to fund covert action against its government. Occasionally protesters have gathered outside the location of the Academy Awards ceremony to demonstrate against particular films. In 1979 police arrested thirteen members of a group called Vietnam Veterans Against the War after they protested *The Deer Hunter*, a film about the Vietnam War that won five awards that year, including best picture and best director.

See also Film censorship; Motion Picture Association of America; Symbolic speech.

Accuracy in Media (AIM)

Founded: 1969

Type of organization: Conservative media-watchdog body dedicated to condemning inaccuracies and bias in media news

Significance: This organization's aggressive efforts to expose allegedly liberal bias in the news media have frequently led to calls for censorship

During the late 1960's, Reed Irvine, a bureaucrat in the Federal Reserve Board, decided to escalate his own personal war against liberal bias of American news organizations. Tired of writing letters to newspapers and television operations, Irvine wanted to form an organization that would point out what he considered to be liberal distortions of the news. His new organization, Accuracy in Media, began monitoring newspapers and television news, and it publicized examples of media bias and misdeeds in its own newsletter, weekly newspaper columns, regular radio commentaries, and a weekly television program—*The Other Side of the Story*—broadcast through satellite and cable television channels.

The organization has motivated letter-writing campaigns directed toward advertisers who sponsored television programs considered to have a liberal bias. AIM representatives have also attended shareholder meetings of large media corporations to critique their news services and to introduce resolutions urging what the organization considers a fairer hearing for conservative points of view. Charged with encouraging media self-censorship, AIM has countered that because the media are effectively censoring conservative ideas it is simply providing a necessary counterbalance to the left-leaning press.

See also Advertising as the target of censorship; Eagle Forum; FAIR; Morality in Media; News broadcasting; News media censorship; Pressure groups.

Action for Children's Television (ACT)

FOUNDED: 1968

TYPE OF ORGANIZATION: American media advocacy group

SIGNIFICANCE: ACT has worked to improve television programming for children by making it noncommercial

Made up of individual members and participating organizations, ACT is primarily concerned with the lack of responsible children's programming. Since it was founded, ACT has petitioned both the Federal Communications Commission and the Federal Trade Commission to require a reasonable amount of high-quality programming for children each week. It has commissioned studies on the effects of television on children and has conducted symposiums to disseminate their findings. Members of ACT have also testified before congressional committees investigating programming practices of television stations. Each year the group honors outstanding producers of children's television with achievement awards.

See also Federal Communications Commission; Foundation to Improve Television; Television, children's.

Adultery

DEFINITION: Consensual sexual relationships between married persons and persons other than their marriage partners

SIGNIFICANCE: Adultery is among the most commonly censored topics

Marriage is a social institution that enhances the stability of society. Adultery is forbidden by most religions, and depictions of adultery, especially those in which the adulterers do not suffer as a consequence of their actions, have long been controversial. Those opposed to censorship of adultery themes and depictions point out that although adultery may be bad, it is common, and that artistic representations of adult life that pretend that adultery does not exist do not make it go away.

The censorship of adultery serves as a barometer for changing definitions of public morality. While representations of sexuality have always been subject to censorship at particular historical moments, the representation of adultery, in particular, has been a focus for censors since the nineteenth century. Depicting adultery involves a representation of sexuality but also, because it contravenes the marriage vow, a challenge to public morality and the institution of the family.

Depictions of adultery, when censored, are typically cited as belonging to the category of obscene libel (as opposed to seditious libel or blasphemous libel). It is striking that three of the most notorious censorship trials in the West—the trial of Gustave Flaubert's *Madame Bovary* (1857) in France, the trial of *Ulysses* (1922) in the United States, and the trials of *Lady Chatterley's Lover* (1928) in the United States and England—involve novels that address adultery as a central theme.

The history of censorship indicates that subversive political and religious writings received the most prominent attention from censoring authorities, but with the rise of the bourgeois family, the stability of the marriage tie became increasingly important (much more important than it had been to, for example, the nobility, except regarding the legitimacy of the firstborn male). The stability of the family was linked to national stability, and any representation that challenged the integrity of the family was interpreted as a national threat. In terms of censorship, adultery became a potent focus of attention for three main reasons. First, on a political level, adultery posed a challenge to the family which could be translated as a challenge to the nation. Second, on a religious level, adultery contravened biblical tenets. Third, on the immediate level of the family and gender, a wife's adultery threatened the father, and thus the institution of patriarchy, by throwing into question a child's paternity. A wife's adultery also disturbed established ideas of womanhood. The censorship of adultery almost always involved a woman's, as opposed to a man's, adulterous actions. The three novels referred to above, for example, each involve a woman who is unfaithful to her husband. There are many examples in literature and drama of men who are unfaithful to their wives, yet these works are rarely the target of censorship. Adultery, then, brings together a political threat and a religious threat.

Adultery in the Novel. In 1857 Gustave Flaubert's novel *Madame Bovary* became the controversial subject of a censorship trial for its alleged "outrage to public morality and religion." The prosecution isolated the novel's representation of adultery as one of the key offenses. After a lengthy debate, the novel was acquitted. Upon completion of *Ulysses*, James Joyce recalled the trial of Flaubert's novel and when his novel, too, was subject to a censorship trial, he hoped for equally sensational results. A trial in 1922 found the novel obscene, but after being banned for eleven years in the United States, the novel was pronounced legal (that is, not obscene) in 1933. While *Ulysses* also focuses on adultery, the trial took more issue with Joyce's use of explicit language and his frank description of sexual scenes.

D. H. Lawrence's *Lady Chatterley's Lover* also addresses adultery, and it was banned in England and the United States after its limited-edition publication in Italy in 1928. The novel was not acquitted until 1959 in the United States and 1960 in England. Adultery was a focus of discussions at the trial. In the case of *Lady Chatterley's Lover*, however, the novel was easily acquitted, perhaps indicating the relative relaxation of strictures against literature and the change in public morality that had occurred by the late 1950's. It is likely, too, that the social antagonism to *Lady Chatterley's Lover* was, at least in part, related to the class difference between Lady Chatterley and her lover. These trials, in fact, suggest that adultery alone was not enough to attract the attention of the censor. In the first case adultery and religion is the problem, in the second, adultery and explicit language, and in the third, adultery and class difference.

Adultery in Drama. In Western Europe and North America drama has often been subject to a form of prior restraint. A powerful system of prior restraint was developed in Great Britain, for example. In 1737 the Lord Chamberlain was given authority over theatrical productions under the Stage Licensing Act. For the most part, this prior censorship was political in motivation, but in 1843 a new Stage Licensing Act was passed which introduced a focus on public morals—"the Preservation of good Manners, Decorum, or the public Peace"—and opened a space for the censorship of adultery in drama. This act and others like it not only prevented the production of certain plays but also worked to inhibit playwrights, who knew that if they took the trouble to write on certain controversial topics, they were likely to be censored. In Great Britain the Stage Licensing Act was not completely changed until 1968, and in many other European countries similar regulatory boards also continued into the late twentieth century.

In summary, adultery was perceived to be an offense to public morality and its censorship was advocated on these grounds. Public morality intersects with, but is not the same as, maintaining political stability and religious faith as a motivation for censoring questionable works. —*Barbara Leckie*

See also Family; Flaubert, Gustave; *Lady Chatterley's Lover*; Licensing Act of 1662; Licensing Act of 1737; Morality; Obscenity: legal definitions; Prior restraint; Sex in the arts; *Ulysses*.

BIBLIOGRAPHY

There is only one study that is devoted solely to adultery and censorship: Dominick LaCapra's *"Madame Bovary" on Trial* (Ithaca, N.Y.: Cornell University Press, 1982); it is, however, limited to Flaubert's novel. In *Girls Lean Back Everywhere: The Law of Obscenity and the Assault on Genius* (New York: Random House, 1992), however, Edward de Grazia offers a comprehensive overview of censorship in the United States and, to a lesser extent, England, that often touches on the relationship between adultery and censorship. Samuel Hynes and Peter Keating offer good overviews of censorship in England in *The Edwardian Turn of Mind* (Princeton, N.J.: Princeton University Press, 1968) and *The Haunted Study: A Social History of the English Novel, 1875-1914* (London: Secker and Warburg, 1989). Finally, several works discuss the representation of adultery in the novel without, for the most part, addressing the issue of censorship. These include Judith Armstrong's *The Novel of Adultery* (New York: Barnes & Noble Books, 1976) and Tony Tanner's *Adultery in the Novel: Contract and Transgression* (Baltimore: The Johns Hopkins University Press, 1979).

Adventures of Huckleberry Finn

TYPE OF WORK: Book

PUBLISHED: 1884

AUTHOR: Mark Twain (Samuel L. Clemens; 1835-1910)

SUBJECT MATTER: Through a series of comic and tragic misadventures, a white youth comes to terms with complex questions of morality, society, and humanity while drifting down the Mississippi River with a runaway slave

SIGNIFICANCE: Because of its heavy use of racially sensitive terms and descriptions, this novel has been regularly among the most criticized and censored books considered for high school curricula

The story of a poor and uneducated boy from eastern Missouri, *Adventures of Huckleberry Finn* is narrated by Huck himself. He relates his adventures as he travels down the Mississippi River on a raft with a runaway slave named Jim. The book satirizes antebellum Southern society and the constraints of civilization, which both Huck and Jim are attempting to escape. Mark Twain's use of dialects is one of the most original

and influential aspects of the novel, and in many ways sets it apart as a masterwork of American literature. However, his use of dialect has also sparked controversy.

Almost immediately upon publication, the rough language Huck uses evoked calls for excluding the book from libraries. As the *Boston Transcript* reported in March, 1885, that the Concord, Massachusetts, public library committee "decided to exclude Mark Twain's latest book from the library. One member of the committee says that, while he does not wish to call it immoral, he thinks it contains but little humor, and that of a very coarse type. He regards it as the veriest trash." Mark Twain responded that the calls for censorship would only help sell more copies.

Since the novel's publication, it has been removed from libraries or schools in Denver (in 1902), New York City (1957), Winnetka, Illinois (1976), San Jose, California (1995), and many other places. As late as the mid-1990's efforts to remove it from classroom use failed in Plano, Texas, and Tempe, Arizona. The civil liberties group People for the American Way estimated that *Adventures of Huckleberry Finn* was the third most-challenged book in America in 1996.

The most common reason for the controversy is the frequency with which Huck uses the racial epithet "nigger" to describe Jim. Although Huck clearly evolves over the course of the story in his appreciation of Jim as a friend, father figure, and human being (he even opts to risk damnation for helping Jim seek freedom), many critics have pointed out that Huck often portrays Jim as a shallow character with minstrel-like comic simplicity.

Late twentieth century debates have moved from the question of whether the book should be taught to how and at what level it should be taught. Scholars have shown that Mark Twain himself held sophisticated and enlightened views on race, slavery, and post-reconstruction treatment of African Americans. Many scholars and teachers have advocated adding historical context to the learning process, so that students are better prepared to decode the language and grapple with the deeper moral and historical issues the book raises.

See also Abolitionist movement; Banned Books Week; Books, young adult; Libraries, school; National Association for the Advancement of Colored People; Newspapers, African American; People for the American Way; Race; Twain, Mark.

Advertisers as advocates of censorship

DEFINITION: Business concerns and other bodies that use their clout to influence the editorial or artistic content of the media in which they advertise

SIGNIFICANCE: Advertisers have had considerable influence in censoring the content of the broadcast and print media because of their unwillingness to associate their own names, messages, and images with images, ideas, or persons of which they may disapprove

Advertisers wield considerable power over the content of publications and programs that serve as vehicles for conveying information to the public regarding their own goods and services. In many cases advertisers provide all the revenue for the media in which advertise. The two basic categories of advertis-

THE "DIRTY DOZEN" TELEVISION ADVERTISERS

A prime motive for advertisers to act as media censors is the pressure that they themselves receive from the public. For example, in 1996 the conservative American Family Association (AFA) published a list of "12 top sponsors of prime-time filth" on network television. After monitoring programs in May, 1996, the AFA used its own rating system to score companies on the basis of the offensive sexual content, profanity, and violence in the programs that they sponsored. The AFA also published the addresses and phone numbers of the offending sponsors and encouraged its readers to contact them to register their displeasure. The AFA's "dirty dozen":

Rank		Score
1	Sony Corp.	28.07
2	Upjohn Company	24.07
3	Schering-Plough Corp.	22.55
4	Hyundai Motor America	22.19
5	Merrill Lynch & Co.	20.63
6	Pfizer Inc.	19.81
7	MCI Communications	19.53
8	Toyota Motor Sales	19.39
9	Echo Star Comm. Corp.	19.08
10	American Honda Motor	19.02
11	Slimfast Foods Company	18.58
12	Warner-Lambert Co.	17.76

Source: AFA Journal. September, 1996.

ers are national and local. National advertisers are mostly major corporations that are seeking to inform the public of a particular brand of product or service that they provide. By contrast, local advertisers are generally interested in persuading members of their own communities to purchase products or services from their local businesses. The ability of national advertisers—because of their greater resources—to impose censorship is substantially greater than that of local advertisers.

Targeted Markets. One reason that advertisers attempt to control the content of the media in which they advertise is their desire to convey their messages to predesignated markets that they wish not to offend. In amassing information on the make-up, or profile, of their targeted markets, advertisers believe that the content and style of their messages must make an overall favorable appeal, or they will be ineffective. Advertisers further assume that the information in the medium carrying their advertising must be compatible with what they perceive to be the interests and values of their markets. Advertisers therefore prefer to use the media whose content and style conform to their own judgments about interests, values, likes, and dislikes of their predesignated markets.

The media that advertisers select are also aware of the characteristics of their own audiences or readers, as well as the markets which their advertisers target. Advertisers consider numerous social, economic, and political factors in designing their advertising and in selecting the media in which to advertise their products and services. These include race, ethnicity, gender, age, social class, occupation, income, education, religion, political affiliations, and regional characteristics.

Mainstream advertisers are generally interested in targeting a single primary market for their goods and services. In the United States members of predesignated markets are typically young, white, and middle-class people. Therefore, advertisers will frequently seek to impose control over the content and style of media that handle their advertising to conform to the interests and lifestyle of this particular market. When conflicts arise regarding the style and content of advertisement, as well as in the overall media, advertisers tend to exercise censorship in the interest of accommodating their targeted market.

Censoring Through Imagery. Aside from controlling the content of publications and programs, advertisers also influence images that are purveyed by the media which carry their messages. Although information must be geared toward the interests, values, and culture of an advertiser's targeted market, so must the images that media use to inform the designated market of the advertiser's product or service. Visual images are an integral part of most advertising campaigns. Even when a nonvisual medium is used such as radio, advertisers present advertising sounds—such as rushing water or high-performance automobile engines—that invoke visual images in the minds of the listening audience.

Advertisers have used many means to control images used by the broadcast and print media in order to appeal to their young, white, middle-class target markets. These means have included omission of certain kinds of images, use of stereotypes, and the purveying of nonrepresentative images. Despite challenges from marginal groups, particularly African Americans, advertisers have tended to exclude them from mainstream advertisements.

Both national and local advertisers have generally been unwilling to sponsor or have their advertisements appear in television programs whose casts are predominately African American. In still other cases, when African American-oriented publications have signed major advertisers, the advertisers have often refused to modify their advertisements to include African American models. It is not uncommon to see white models portrayed in African American-oriented publications. Whether advertisers provide a rationale for such policies, such as cost-efficiency or time constraints, such decisions tend to influence the editorial content of publications.

Advertisers also control the visual content of advertisements by using stereotypical imagery. Gross caricatures of African Americans to advertise products such as soap, baking powder, and cooking oil were common during the nineteenth century. Advertisers continued this practice in the twentieth century by using stereotyped African American images on food products such as Aunt Jemima pancake mix—whose product logos have depicted a stereotypical African American domestic worker. Similarly, Uncle Ben's Rice has long used pictures of an older African American man. These and other stereotypical images that appear in advertising have been challenged because they suggest that African Americans are best suited for certain occupational roles. There has also been a tendency among advertisers to portray women of all races in stereotypical roles performing domestic tasks and providing support for their husbands and children.

Censoring Advertisers. Despite the considerable power that advertisers exercise over the media, they have also been subject to censorship themselves. There have been constant efforts to place bans on advertising by citizen groups, government policymakers, and other businesses. Such efforts have typically tried to prevent the advertising of certain products, notably tobacco products, alcohol, condoms, artificial sweeteners, firearms, and certain films and books. Advertisers have responded to such attacks by maintaining that efforts to ban advertising may lead to a controlled economy, the demise of the First Amendment, and ultimately a dictatorship.

Other Countries. Throughout Europe greater control has been imposed upon advertisers than in the United States. In Great Britain, for example, radio and television services were originally established as public service systems—in contrast to the commercially oriented broadcasting systems in the United States. Concern over the danger of exploiting the public contributed to greater control over advertisers in Britain and throughout Europe. It is generally held that advertisers have considerably more freedom to advertise in the United States than in Britain.   —*K. Sue Jewell*

See also Accuracy in Media; Advertising as the target of censorship; British Broadcasting Standards Council; Campaign for Press and Broadcasting Freedom; Federal Communications Commission; Jackson, Michael; National Coalition Against Censorship; News media censorship.

BIBLIOGRAPHY

For broad surveys of advertising, see S. Watson Dunn et al., *Advertising: Its Role in Modern Marketing* (Chicago: Dryden Press, 1990); Maurice I. Mandell, *Advertising* (3d ed. Englewood Cliffs, N.J.: Prentice-Hall, 1980); James S. Norris, *Advertising* (2d ed. Reston, Va.: Reston Publishing Company, 1980); and Gillian Dyer, *Advertising as Communication* (London: Methuen, 1982). *American Voices* (New York: Philip Morris, 1987), published by a tobacco company, contains the winners of an essay contest that address how free speech is threatened by advertising bans.

Advertising as the target of censorship

DEFINITION: Censorship of commercial messages
SIGNIFICANCE: Commercial speech is sometimes protected by the First Amendment, but not as broadly as other forms of speech

Radio and television commercials, billboard messages, print advertisements, and other forms of commercial announcements are often unprotected from government regulation. In the United States, constitutional debate focuses on the extent to which the First Amendment protects commercial speech. In Great Britain, with no written constitution, political and commercial speech is more strictly controlled than in the United States, although Britain is much freer in permitting advertise-

ments for products and services such as contraceptives and abortion facilities, areas of commercial speech that have resulted in extensive constitutional debate in the United States. In Canada, the Canadian Charter (1982) constitutionally protects speech broadly described as "thought, belief, opinion and expression" restricting commercial speech only in the interests of protecting consumer groups such as children.

Historically, commercial speech in the United States has not been thought worthy of First Amendment protections. The eighteenth century, however, was a period of dynamic commercialism in the United States; had the authors of the Bill of Rights intended to exclude commercial speech from First Amendment protection, they could easily have so indicated. Even commercial messages protected by the First Amendment may still suffer censorship when newspapers, television stations, and other forms of the media refuse to run an announcement because of pressure from consumer groups or because of the media's own professional codes of conduct.

Commercial Speech and First Amendment Protection. Not until 1942, in *Valentine v. Chrestensen*, did the U.S. Supreme Court decide whether commercial speech should be protected from government regulation. In the Valentine case, the Court upheld a New York statute forbidding the distribution of handbills containing a commercial message, reasoning that commercial advertising was unprotected speech. Although that decision's cursory opinion was criticized for not clearly delineating between commercial speech and political speech, this decision stood for thirty years. By the 1970's several Supreme Court decisions recognized limited First Amendment protections to commercial messages containing information deemed of such high public interest that its regulation would deprive the public of useful information. For example, in *Bigelow v. Virginia* (1975) the Court held that a newspaper in Virginia, where abortions were illegal, that ran an advertisement containing information about the availability of abortions in New York, where they were legal, fell within First Amendment protections. Within a year of that decision, the Court afforded limited First Amendment protection to advertisements containing information that would otherwise be withheld under a state's code banning advertising by such professional groups as pharmacists and lawyers.

In *Virginia State Board of Pharmacy v. Virginia Citizens Consumer Council* (1976), the Court extended limited First Amendment protection to commercial messages when the content not only proposed a commercial transaction but also included information about prescription drugs of great interest to consumers. This trend continued so that members of highly regulated professions, such as lawyers, were allowed to advertise their services because of consumer interest in the message. The trend also extended to product labeling, with the Supreme Court deciding in *Rubin v. Coors Brewing Co.* (1985) that beer companies could indicate the alcohol content of their beverages despite Washington's paternalistic view that consumers needed to be protected from information that might lead to competition founded on alcohol strength, rather than beer taste. However, just how much First Amendment protection is afforded commercial speech was still unclear by the late

1980's. In *Posadas de Puerto Rico Associates v. Tourism Company of Puerto Rico* (1986), the Court upheld a ban on advertising of legal casino gambling, thus departing from its trend to offer commercial speech at least some protection from government regulation.

Commercial Speech and Political Speech. Court decisions denying free speech protections to commercial speech received intense criticism. Often it was impossible to differentiate between unprotected commercial speech and protected political speech, especially when the advertised product or service was associated with lifestyle preferences that rose to the level of protected political speech. For example, while the Supreme Court held that a drug company's pamphlet mailed to consumers containing information about condoms was unprotected commercial speech, a Federal Trade Commission judge held that an editorial advertisement by the R. J. Reynolds tobacco company that disputed scientific evidence about the hazards of smoking should be protected. While this decision was later reversed, it illustrated the difficulty courts had in distinguishing between the two forms of speech. Indeed, some commercial speech is political speech when the message carries social and political implications.

Bans on Radio and Television Tobacco Advertising. After 1971, the Public Health Cigarette Smoking Act banned cigarette advertising on television in the United States. In 1964 then Surgeon General Luther L. Terry announced a connection between smoking tobacco and mortality. The ban, intended to decrease cigarette smoking, extended only to the publicly owned airways; cigarette advertisements continued to appear in newspapers, in magazines, and on billboards. One side effect was that revenue from cigarette advertisements increased significantly for magazines and billboard companies. Some magazines dropped cigarette advertising as a matter of public policy, but many magazines resumed running the advertisements because of the substantial revenue cigarette advertisements represented. Cigarette advertisements appearing in print and billboards are still heavily regulated, especially where those messages might be seen by minors. However, how a cigarette advertisement would differ if a minor rather than an adult might see it is unclear. The tobacco industry has generally managed this problem by using messages that indicate that smoking should be an adult choice. Nevertheless, newspaper groups such as Knight-Ridder pressed its newspapers to drop the Joe Camel character from advertisements for Camel cigarettes since young children recognized that figure as easily as they recognized their comic book heroes. In the 1990's, the Food and Drug Administration proposed banning billboards close to schools or playgrounds, and it proposed banning brand-name sponsorship of sporting or entertainment events.

Advertisements for Alcohol. Although cigarette commercials are no longer on television, federal rules do not forbid commercials for beer and wine. However, television networks themselves have refused to air advertisements that connect alcohol consumption with social status, personal achievement, or as a stress reliever. In addition, the commercials are not allowed to portray someone actually drinking the beverage.

Some states and cities have enacted much stricter controls over the way alcohol is advertised. The state of Mississippi's regulations effectively ban liquor advertising on billboards, in print, and on the airways. Some cities enacted bans on alcohol advertisements. In the 1990's, the city of Baltimore banned billboard advertising for alcoholic drinks. This ban was intensely criticized by advertising groups because of the ban's First Amendment ramifications and because of the city's paternalistic efforts to protect its citizens from the evils of alcohol.

Federal and State Regulations. With its inception in 1914, the Federal Trade Commission (FTC) became responsible for protecting consumers from deceptive advertising. Under its advertising substantiation program, the FTC investigates advertisements that do not reasonably substantiate their claims and so pose a potential risk to consumers. While deceptive advertising is not itself entitled to First Amendment protections (and is illegal), some forms of advertising that contain incomplete or scientifically controversial information may be banned by the FTC. The ban may then result in a void of information such that interested consumers remain unaware of competing views regarding the value of a medicine, diet, or other form of useful consumer information. The landmark case on this issue, *In re Pfizer, Inc.* (1972), involved a suntan product whose makers claimed it stopped sunburn pain, a claim made without benefit of scientific studies. However, over time, the FCC relaxed its policies, so long as any misrepresentation would not mislead its intended audience. While the FTC relaxed its advertisement compliance policies, state regulations, the advertisement industry itself in self-regulation, and private lawsuits took up the slack in regulating the speech of advertisers.

Industry Self-Regulation. Some censorship has been self-imposed by the advertising industry itself through associations such as the National Association of Broadcasters, which sets the code for approximately 35 percent of radio stations and for about 60 percent of television stations. Compliance is voluntary. Each major network also has its own advertising guidelines and standards. The association has banned advertisements for such products as toilet paper and contraceptives. Since 1969 these standards have relaxed so that products such as genital deodorants, hemorrhoid treatments, and tampons are no longer considered taboo by the industry. However, by the 1990's, commercials for condoms were slowly making inroads into television, though usually with the public service message of disease prevention. Groups such as Planned Parenthood and others proposed far wider broadcasting of these advertisements.

Boycotts from Consumer Groups. Various consumer groups have censored advertisements that otherwise fell outside government or industry regulation. For example, clothing companies that target young consumers have often offended groups such as child welfare advocates, religious organizations, the American Family Association, and Stop the Starvation Imagery Campaign. In 1995 groups such as these promoted boycotts of Calvin Klein clothing when its advertisements appeared on television, in newspapers, and on billboards and posters. The advertisements featured adolescent

A news bulletin announcing a government investigation of Calvin Klein's alleged "kiddie porn" advertising campaign lights up the zipper sign adjacent to one of the offending advertisements in New York City's Times Square. (AP/Wide World Photos)

males and females modeling underwear. Critics charged that since the advertisements were "kiddie porn," a boycott was not censorship. Because of the adverse reaction, the clothing company dropped the advertising campaign. In 1992 the Benetton clothing company experienced similar negative response when its advertisements featured controversial subjects such as a nun kissing a priest or floating condoms. Benetton featured controversial images reflecting the 1990's such as the AIDS crisis, environmental problems, and political violence. Negative reaction to these commercial messages resulted in several magazines refusing to run the advertisements. However, in both the Calvin Klein and Benetton campaigns, the publicity gained from the apparent censorship boosted interest in the advertisements.

Stereotyping in Commercial Messages. Advertisers have not escaped the wrath of various groups who have seen negative stereotypes depicted in commercials. Beer commercials, for example, have often been criticized for depicting women as merely sex objects. One beer company used a "Swedish Bikini Team" of women in bikinis to promote its beer. This commercial was viewed by some as debasing women and as fostering sexual harassment. A television commercial for an automobile company was forced to change its depiction of a Charlie Chan character, who spoke broken English, to one who spoke standard English. Advertisers typically respond

that to force changes in their commercials is censorship and that their commercial messages are targeted to particular segments of the population who respond favorably to their messages. —*Paul Bateman*

See also Action for Children's Television; Commercial speech; Fairness doctrine; Federal Communications Commission; First Amendment; Mill, John Stuart; *New York Times Co. v. Sullivan*; Prior restraint.

BIBLIOGRAPHY

Daniel Morgan Rohrer, *Mass Media, Freedom of Speech, and Advertising: A Study in Communication Law* (Dubuque, Iowa: Kendall-Hunt, 1979), contains an extensive collection of essays and the text of the major censorship and advertising cases. Edwin P. Rome and William H. Roberts, *Corporate and Commercial Free Speech: First Amendment Protection of Expression in Business* (Westport, Conn.: Quorum Books, 1985), thoroughly analyzes legal developments in commercial speech censorship. It also contains an extensive index of censorship and advertising cases. For opposing views on the extent to which First Amendment protections should be afforded to newspapers, see Tom Goldstein, *A Two-Faced Press?* (New York: Priority Press, 1986), and Michael G. Gartner, *Advertising and the First Amendment: A Twentieth Century Fund Paper* (New York: Priority Press, 1989). Richard T. Kaplar, *Advertising Rights, the Neglected Freedom: Toward a New*

Doctrine of Commercial Speech (Washington, D.C.: Media Institute, 1991), argues for extending full First Amendment protection to commercial speech.

Advocacy

DEFINITION: Active support of a cause

SIGNIFICANCE: Since the U.S. Supreme Court's decision in *Brandenburg v. Ohio* (1969), advocacy of causes thought to be subversive has been treated as speech protected by the First Amendment

Until 1969, lawmakers at the state and federal level, supported by the courts, acted on the assumption that advocacy of radical political change by illegal means so threatened the American political system that such advocacy was not protected expression. Suppression of advocacy is motivated by a desire to preserve the nation's security. Following the assassination of President William McKinley by the anarchist Leon Czolgosz in 1901, two-thirds of the states, over a twenty-year period, made it a crime to advocate the violent overthrow of the government. Congress, in the 1918 amendments to the Espionage Act of 1917, banned expression advocating interference with the war effort. The Supreme Court consistently upheld the thousands of convictions that were obtained by state and federal prosecutors in cases in which advocacy was considered a threat to the nation's security. In *Schenck v. United States* (1919), the justices sustained the conviction of Charles Schenck, general secretary of the Socialist Party, for conspiring to obstruct military recruitment and to cause insubordination in the armed forces. He had mailed leaflets to young men arguing that the draft was unconstitutional.

After World War II, many members of Congress and the state legislatures became increasingly concerned about the threat that Soviet communism posed to the survival of American democracy. The Communist Party of the United States and groups considered fronts for the Soviets became objects of concern. The Department of Justice initiated prosecutions of Communist Party officials residing in the United States under the Smith Act of 1940 that prohibited advocating, teaching, or organizing to advocate or to teach the use of force to overthrow the government. In *Dennis v. United States* (1951) the U.S. Supreme Court upheld the convictions of twelve leaders of the Communist Party for conspiring to advocate and to organize to advocate the violent overthrow of the government. Subsequent to the Supreme Court's decision, the federal government obtained an additional ninety-six convictions of Communist Party officials.

As the Soviet threat waned, the Supreme Court began to extend the umbrella of the First Amendment to verbal support of communism. In *Yates v. United States* (1957), the Court narrowed the meaning of advocacy to verbal backing of the act of overthrowing the government. The Court said the Smith Act does not proscribe speech which merely calls on the audience to believe something. To be punished, the speaker must urge the listeners to do something, now or in the future. To obtain a conviction against a party leader, the prosecutor would have to prove active participation in a conspiracy to overthrow the government.

In *Brandenburg v. Ohio* (1969) the Court found unconstitutional Ohio's Criminal Syndicalism Act, which penalized persons advocating or teaching the duty of violence as a means of accomplishing industrial or political reform. The opinion made clear that mere advocacy of a set of ideas, no matter how subversive they might seem, was protected speech, thus effectively overturning precedent. Under the First Amendment, only incitement to imminent lawless action can be punished.

See also Communist Party of the U.S.A.; Criminal syndicalism laws; Espionage Act of 1917; National security; *Schenck v. United States*; Smith Act.

African Americans

DEFINITION: Americans of African descent

SIGNIFICANCE: African Americans have systematically had their freedom of expression limited through laws and institutional practices

Freedom of speech was denied African Americans upon their arrival to the colonies and later the United States. Slave codes, which were strictly enforced as a means of social control, prohibited slaves from having any form of freedom of speech. Slave owners deprived African Americans freedom of speech because of fear that free communication among slaves would threaten the institution of slavery. Therefore, slave owners established policies and practices that prevented slaves, individually and collectively, from expressing themselves except under specific preestablished conditions.

While there were myriad constraints that limited free expression among slaves, many restrictions were more universally applied. For example, slaves were denied the right to converse in their African languages. Slave owners also prohibited slaves from using drums, which were considered a telegraph system. In addition, slaves were not permitted to meet without a white person being present. Further, slave owners denied slaves the right to be educated, which limited their ability to learn and use standard English. Moreover, severe penalties were imposed on any individual who was found to be educating slaves, especially teaching them to read. The formulation and implementation of such policies, practices, and laws that restricted the communication of slaves with others were intended to foster control of the slaves. That is, the propertied class believed that it would be able to maintain the profitable system of slavery if it could prevent slaves from fleeing the plantation and planning revolts. Among the preventive measures that slave owners took was the prohibition of communication, except under the supervision of the slave owner or his designees.

In addition, the ability of slaves to use standard English as a method of communication presented a major threat to the institution of slavery by enabling slaves to inform critics and individuals involved in the abolitionist movement with information regarding the inhumane treatment that characterized the institution of slavery in the United States. While slave owners developed rigid policies to prevent and control communication between slaves, their methods of enforcement were designed to ensure that these policies and laws were strictly followed. When slaves violated the slave codes and rules that governed plantations that prohibited communication, the common practice was whipping. Generally, whippings were administered by an overseer hired by the slave owner. State laws as well as the Constitution protected the right of the slave owner to control the behavior of slaves, as they were considered chattel or property of slave owners. Accordingly, the slave owner's use of any means to retain his property, including censorship, was supported by the legal system.

Reconstruction. The censoring of African Americans continued after emancipation. Black Codes were enacted throughout the United States to prevent African Americans from becoming integrated into the American social, economic, and political system. These efforts became universally accepted and protected by the Constitution in the legislation that enforced what was called separate but equal treatment of African Americans in most institutions throughout the United States. In effect, African Americans were limited regarding their access to quality education, medical care, housing, employment, legal protection, and the use of public transportation and facilities. Depriving African Americans of the benefits of these important services and access to these institutions was an effective method of preventing African Americans from expressing their needs, interests, and desires. Equally important, this form of censorship precluded African Americans from correcting the distortions and omissions regarding their history that were reflected in U.S. history, science, literature, and the natural sciences. They were also prevented from expressing their views and concerns that would have enabled them to contribute to the shaping of the direction of the country and that would have strengthened their own community. Other legal actions that Southerners enacted were vagrancy laws that also restricted the ability of African Americans, particularly African American men, to acquire the freedom necessary to communicate freely. These laws required African American men to have a full-time job or business, during a period when jobs for African American men were virtually nonexistent. Newly freed African American men found themselves forced to work as sharecroppers or tenant farmers, in a system of servitude for farmers. This system was similar to the institution of slavery that had recently been abolished.

Basically African Americans were forced to work and live on the land in exchange for a substandard rented shelter, food, clothing, seed, and borrowed farm animals. They were kept in abject poverty because they were compelled to borrow, but were not permitted to generate sufficient money from the sale of their crops to rise out of poverty. This subsistence living made African Americans totally dependent upon Southern farmers for survival. African American men who were without a job or business were jailed and released to the farmer who paid their bail. When this occurred they became indentured servants, providing free labor to Southern farmers. Therefore, white Southerners were able to continue to control the behavior of African American men, women, and children.

Southern whites exerted control over African American expression by dissuading African Americans from voting and expressing their interest in various activities that would have enhanced their social and economic position. Throughout much of the United States after the Civil War, African Americans could not register to vote, obtain library cards, or use media for their purposes.

The Black Media. The mainstream media have not been vehicles through which African Americans views, opinions, and interests have been expressed. Consequently, African Americans have founded their own journals, newspapers, and publishing companies to transmit their ideas, points of view, and information. *Freedom's Journal*, founded in 1863, was the first African American publication. Two publications that have provided the African American community with critical news and information for fifty years are *Jet* and *Ebony*, a weekly and monthly magazine respectively, both founded by John H. Johnson in 1945. In addition to numerous publications, African Americans have sought freedom of expression through black-owned and -oriented radio stations and television programs. The Black Entertainment Network is an African American-oriented network that offers news, sports, and entertainment.

The Twentieth Century. There are myriad ways in which constraints have been placed on African Americans relative to the freedom of expression. The electronic media have excluded African American voices from radio, television, and film. During the 1920's, when African Americans were portrayed in movies and on radio, it was usually the case that they were portrayed by white actors and that the roles reinforced stereotypes. These actors spoke in Southern dialect and engaged in dialogue that contained broken English. For example, the *Amos 'n' Andy* radio program of the 1940's employed white actors whose speech perpetuated stereotypes of African American men as ignorant, lazy, and untrustworthy. In addition, African American women remained speechless in radio.

Historically, American films that have included African American casts have restricted their roles. Films have generally portrayed African Americans using stereotypical imagery. Until the 1970's speaking films that represented African Americans at all generally portrayed them as slaves and domestic servants. In the 1970's, in the wake of the Civil Rights movement, the U.S. film industry began to market movies with African American casts. However, the actors were compelled to portray characters that continued to conform to racial stereotypes and to perpetuate the themes of the African American male as hypersexed, a criminal, or a shady detective. The African American writer, actor, and producer Robert Townsend, in his *Hollywood Shuffle* (1987), satirizes the Hollywood film industry's systematic efforts to distort and silence the actual voices of African Americans. He depicts the behind-the-scenes activities of white directors who insist that African American actors speak and use mannerisms, gestures, and behaviors that are consistent with stereotypical beliefs. A comical scene in the film shows a television commercial for a black acting school, run by whites, that teaches students the completely unrealistic and stereotypical black English of the film and television industry and that shows how to perform such roles as slaves, butlers, street hoods, and dope addicts.

Another common practice on the part of the U.S. film industry is the refusal of major filmmakers to finance movies that

Among the objections that many African Americans had to the Amos 'n' Andy *radio program was that its black characters were portrayed by white actors Freeman F. Gosden and Charles J. Correll, photographed here in blackface.* (AP/ Wide World Photos)

accurately portray the positive qualities of African American culture.

The print media is also a vehicle thorough which African Americans have not had the opportunity to freely express their views. News reports of African American events and community concerns have not historically been presented in mainstream newspapers in the United States. Aside from the established pattern of omitting African American's voices, another factor that contributes to the failure of U.S. newspapers to provide a medium for African Americans to express their views is the mainstream newspapers' underrepresentation of African American journalists, editors, and executives.

Education. Throughout the educational system in the United States, textbooks covering a variety of subjects have historically prevented African Americans an opportunity to express their perspectives, values, beliefs, and experiences. To a large extent, when multicultural curricula have been adopted the experiences of African Americans in the United States are generally presented by white Americans rather than African Americans.

There are many practices within the United States that result in the censorship of African Americans as individuals and as a cultural group. While these practices vary depending on the societal institution in which these restrictions occur, the mass media are responsible for the most pervasive and comprehen-

sive efforts to constrain the free expression of African Americans. For the most part, the mass media have either submerged the voices of African Americans through omission or distorted the expressions of African Americans through stereotypical imagery. Nevertheless, African Americans have continued to challenge the mass media and various institutional policies and practices that limit the free expression of African Americans. —*K. Sue Jewell*

See also *Amos 'n' Andy*; *Birth of a Nation, The*; Civil Rights movement; Film censorship; Garvey, Marcus; King, Martin Luther, Jr.; Malcolm X; National Association for the Advancement of Colored People; Newspapers; Newspapers, African American; Race; Simpson, O. J., case.

BIBLIOGRAPHY

John Hope Franklin and Alfred A. Moss, Jr., *From Slavery to Freedom: A History of Negro Americans* (6th ed. New York: Alfred A. Knopf, 1988) examines the harsh social and economic conditions and the deprivation of rights and liberties that African Americans have experienced in the United States. Bell Hooks, *Outlaw Culture: Resisting Representations* (New York: Routledge, 1994), describes how white supremacy, capitalism, and patriarchy distort and omit images and information based on race, ethnicity, and gender. Peter McLaren, *Critical Pedagogy and Predatory Culture* (New York: Routledge, 1995), examines how those in power have constructed structures of domination that are eroding American culture and education. He proposes methods of educating contemporary youth. Ella Shohat and Robert Stam, *Unthinking Eurocentrism: Multiculturalism and the Media* (New York: Routledge, 1994), explores the diverse approaches employed by the mass media to prevent African Americans and other people of color from being accurately represented.

Agnew, Spiro T.

BORN: November 9, 1918, Baltimore, Maryland
DIED: September 17, 1996, Berlin, Maryland
IDENTIFICATION: Governor of Maryland (1967-1969) and vice president of the United States (1969-1973)
SIGNIFICANCE: As vice president during most of Richard M. Nixon's presidency, Agnew attacked intellectuals and students for their political beliefs and condemned the U.S. press for its criticism of American military policy

A self-professed spokesperson for the great "silent majority" of the American population, Agnew was critical of students and intellectuals who criticized U.S. participation in the Vietnam War as well as the reporters and editors who reported on the antiwar movement of the late 1960's. As early as October, 1969, he spoke out against "a minority of pushy youngsters and middle-aged malcontents" who were critical of the U.S. military. He broadened his criticism in Des Moines, Iowa, on November 13, 1969, when he claimed to identify a "small band of 'self-appointed analysts,' who raise doubts in a million minds about the veracity of a public official or the wisdom of a government policy."

Agnew claimed that the administration's critics were part of an "Eastern establishment" largely confined to Washington, D.C., and New York City. He suggested that television net-

During President Richard M. Nixon's first term, Vice President Spiro T. Agnew played a classic "hatchet man" role by stridently denouncing administration critics as dangerous radicals. (AP/Wide World Photos)

works were not entitled to the same First Amendment protection as newspapers because they held a "virtual monopoly" on a whole outlet of communication. The networks claimed that Agnew was proposing suppression and harassment. Frank Stanton, president of the Columbia Broadcasting System, charged that the statements had "ominous" implications for a medium that must have a federal license to operate, and that Agnew's charges would send a chilling message throughout the mass media. Agnew was forced to resign in disgrace from the vice presidency when it was revealed that he had avoided paying income taxes; he was later found to have taken bribes while governor of Maryland.

See also Chilling effect; Federal Communications Commission; Music; Nixon, Richard M.; Presidency, U.S.; Television; Television networks; Vietnam War; Watergate scandal.

Airline safety news

DEFINITION: News media coverage of airline safety violations

SIGNIFICANCE: News media, dependent on their advertisers for economic survival, may have avoided affecting advertisers negatively

Consumer groups have criticized the Federal Aviation Administration (FAA) for its inability to maintain high safety stand-

ards. In their book *The Truth About Airline Safety* (1994), Ralph Nader and Wesley Smith discuss the impact that deregulation has had on the safety of air travel. They have argued that the industry is crumbling financially while equipment of major airlines is aging and inspections or repairs are being ignored to save money.

In 1994 accidents by scheduled U.S. major airlines resulted in 239 deaths, compared with one fatality in 1993. National Transportation Safety Board (NTSB) chairman James Hall indicated that if a new system had been adopted as planned, a TWA jet and a small plane might not have collided on a runway in St. Louis in November, 1994, killing two people. In another TWA accident which killed all 68 people on board near Roselawn, Indiana, the probable cause was ice on the wings. The problems related to icing had been documented in several earlier crashes. Based on the initial investigation, the NTSB recommended that the FAA ban certain planes from flying in known or predicted icing conditions. The FAA did not comply for another five weeks.

While the FAA tries to balance safety standards with containing costs, the press tries to balance corporate profits with freedom of speech. The degree to which consumers are adequately informed about airline safety issues may be affected by having a press system that is dependent on advertising dollars.

The crash of a PanAm jumbo jet at Lockerbie, Scotland, in 1988 attracted unprecedented news media coverage. (AP/Wide World Photos)

According to a study of newspaper editors in the January 16, 1993 issue of *Editor & Publisher*, more than 90 percent admitted they had been pressured by advertisers. According to the study, 93 percent of the editors indicated that advertisers had threatened to withdraw advertising from their newspapers because of news content. A majority of editors also believed that advertisers would follow through on their threats. Small-circulation papers were much more likely to be affected by advertiser pressures than large metropolitan dailies, and more than half of the responding editors reported pressure from within their newspapers to write, or position, news stories to please advertisers.

See also Advertisers as advocates of censorship; Automobile safety news; Pharmaceutical industry; Toxic waste news.

Akhmatova, Anna

BORN: June 23, 1889, Bol'shoy Fontan, near Odessa, Ukraine, Russian Empire

DIED: March 5, 1966, Domodedovo, Soviet Union

IDENTIFICATION: Russian poet

SIGNIFICANCE: Soviet condemnation of Akhmatova's poetry stopped her from writing for several decades, but her work was rediscovered after her death

Akhmatova's life and literary career illustrate the challenges that creative intellectuals faced under the restrictions imposed by the Soviet Union's communist regime. Her poetry is introspective and personal, with unfulfilled love and strained relationships common themes throughout her graceful composi-

Russian poet Anna Akhmatova. (Library of Congress)

tions. Her imagery contrasts hardship and disappointment with elements of tenderness and even optimism. She also occasionally addressed political themes. Her famous "Requiem" deals with the Stalinist purges of the 1930's.

After Akhmatova published her earliest work between 1912 and 1922, she endured a literary hiatus until the early 1940's, when she was allowed to publish *A Selection from Six Books*. In 1946, on the threshold of the Cold War, Soviet authorities branded Akhmatova's poetry as "bourgeois" and expelled her from the Union of Soviet Writers. What little writing she did over the last twenty years of her life conformed to Communist Party rules.

Under the more open atmosphere of Mikhail Gorbachev's regime during the 1980's, Akhmatova's writings were again published in the Soviet Union. Since the Soviet Union's collapse in 1991, appreciation of her poetry has seen a renaissance, and Akhmatova has won recognition as one of the significant Russian poets of the twentieth century.

See also Babel, Isaac Emmanuilovich; Bulgakov, Mikhail Afanasyevich; Communism; Gorbachev, Mikhail; Intellectual freedom; Poetry; Soviet Union; Stalin, Joseph; Voznesensky, Andrey Andreyevich; Zhdanov, Andrei.

Alabama

DESCRIPTION: Politically and religiously conservative and comparatively poor state in the Deep South of the United States

SIGNIFICANCE: At various times in the past Alabama's white government leaders have tried to preserve the racial status quo by silencing opposing voices

Although generally acknowledged as a state in which various forms of censorship have long flourished, Alabama produced Hugo L. Black, one of the U.S. Supreme Court's most ardent champions of the First Amendment. In 1940 Black voted with the Court's majority, in *Thornhill v. Alabama*, to strike down Alabama's own antipicketing law because it permitted arbitrary government interference in peaceful labor union demonstrations. This decision later served the Court well when it faced Civil Rights movement cases during the 1950's and 1960's, and was arguably the beginning of Black's reputation as a traitor to the South.

Alabama's public officials long used state libel law to silence opposition until 1964, when the U.S. Supreme Court's landmark *New York Times v. Sullivan* decision ruled that speech on public issues was protected by the U.S. Constitution. Before that decision, government officials could chill speech merely by forcing their critics to assume the heavy costs of libel defenses. For example, *The New York Times*, which was often under attack in the South for its extensive coverage of racial integration, not only faced a half-million-dollar judgment in the Sullivan case but had eleven other suits pending against it in Alabama courts as well. Harrison Salisbury, a *Times* correspondent in the South, could not safely return to Alabama for several years, and general media coverage throughout the South was inhibited.

In 1975 the Federal Communications Commission, citing the failure of the Alabama Educational Television Commission (AETC) to meet the programming needs of the state's black minority, denied the latter's request for a license renewal, forcing the AETC to address that issue before it could reapply. In contrast, in a case brought by Alabama residents seven years later, a federal court held that AETC's programming decision to cancel its scheduled broadcast of a film dramatizing the execution of a Saudi Arabian princess and her lover for adultery was an editorial decision, not censorship.

Communism also came under state scrutiny in the 1950's, when state law mandated that the political loyalty of the authors and publishers of all books in the state's libraries be certified; in the case of fictional works, the loyalty of major characters had to be certified. Since this law would have required verification of millions of loyalty oaths, it remained largely unenforced. Other laws passed during that period, which have remained in force, spelled out detailed rules for the selection of textbooks statewide. Local textbook committees have been allowed to select books only from lists recommended by the state textbook committee and adopted by the state's board of education at public meetings. Books by communist authors were specifically excluded, and school teachers using unapproved texts were subject to criminal proceedings.

The most prominent challenges to Alabama's textbook laws have arisen not from political issues, but from religious issues. During the 1980's conservative Christians attempted to force state schools to present Christian teachings by asking the courts to declare secular humanism a religion that would require a balancing textual viewpoint. An Alabama court ruling for the plaintiffs was reversed in federal courts. Other conservative Christian challenges during the 1980's included an incident in Mobile County in which school officials declared— and a state court agreed—that the U.S. Supreme Court had erred in applying the First Amendment to the state of Alabama and declaring public school prayer unconstitutional; a federal court reversed the decision.

See also Bumper stickers; Chilling effect; *New York Times Co. v. Sullivan*; Picketing; School prayer; Secular humanism; Textbooks.

Albania

DESCRIPTION: Balkan nation bounded by Greece, Macedonia, Yugoslavia, and the Adriatic Sea

SIGNIFICANCE: Albania has a long history of government censorship under a succession of authoritarian regimes

Albanian political opinion and cultural expression was systematically suppressed under Ottoman and Greek rule. In 1879 the Society of Albanian letters was organized, an alphabet adopted, and book and newspaper publication followed, mostly in foreign countries. In the autumn of 1885 the Porte authorized teaching Albanian, a reform largely frustrated in Muslim and Orthodox schools.

From its independence in 1912 Albania was in constant turmoil until 1925, when the government of Achmet Zogu, later King Zog, took control. Zog dissolved opposing political and cultural organizations and either imprisoned active opponents or drove them into exile. Press freedom was curtailed and private correspondence was censored. In 1939 Italy annexed Albania, which remained under Italian and, briefly, German, control until 1944.

From 1944 to 1961 Albania was ruled by the communist dictatorship of Enver Hoxha and his successor, Ramiz Alia. All publishing, broadcasting, schools, and cultural enterprises were in the hands of the state. Rigid censorship extending to private conversations was enforced by the secret police (*Sigurimi*). Citizens conversing with foreigners were subject to arrest and imprisonment.

In 1974 the communists began denouncing families possessing television antennae capable of receiving Italian or Yugoslavian broadcasts. Thousands of political opponents, dissidents and members of ethnic minorities died in concentration camps. Foreign travel was stringently restricted. Ordinary Albanians who had left the country were denied return. Works of authors falling from governmental acceptance were collected and destroyed, including works in technical journal articles. In 1967 religion was banned, almost all places of worship were closed, and clergy were imprisoned, executed, or "retrained." In spite of this, Ismail Kadare wrote and published novels of a quality making him a serious candidate for the Nobel Prize. By using metaphor and ironic flattery, Kadare avoided total suppression, but was heavily attacked for ignoring stylistic "Socialist Realism."

The dictatorship began to relax after Hoxha's death in 1985. In 1990 his successor, Ramiz Alia, ended the bans on religion and foreign travel and a new, democratic constitution was adopted. In March, 1991, Alia was forced to hold elections, which he won. By September, 1991, eight newspapers representing as many political parties appeared and the circulation of *Zeri i Popullit*, the Communist (later Socialist) Party paper, dropped by two thirds. Continuing protests and demonstrations forced another election in early 1992, resulting in a democratic regime under Sali Berisha.

Artistic style was no longer censored; by 1994 a gallery devoted to contemporary Tirana artists and writers opened. Official censorship, however, remained. The new constitution made those who "insult the high personalities of state" subject to imprisonment, and an October, 1994, referendum rejected a more liberal constitution. In 1994 the British Broadcasting Corporation lost access to a medium-wave transmitter, had FM service threatened, and had correspondents harassed by SHIK (or, secret police) agents for coverage of a corruption trial. Also, Aleksander Frangaj, the editor of *Koha Jone*, was tried, but acquitted, for publishing official secrets. One of his staff received an eighteen-month jail sentence and the judge was arrested. An appeals court gave Frangaj a five-month sentence. Frangaj fled to Greece. During late 1993 and 1994, twenty-two critics of the regime, former communist officials and Greek minority leaders, were imprisoned.

See also Communism; Greek junta; Italy; Police states; Socialist Realism.

Alberta Press Act Reference

DECIDED: 1938
PLACE: Canada (national)
SIGNIFICANCE: This decision by the Supreme Court of Can-

ada struck down a provincial bill restricting news reporting, thereby reaffirming freedom of the press in Canada

This court decision was a ruling on the constitutionality of a legislative bill introduced in the provincial government of Alberta by the Social Credit Party, led by Premier William Aberhardt. Unhappy at hostile newspaper coverage, Aberhardt's government introduced the Accurate News and Information Act, which many critics immediately denounced as an attempt to curtail freedom of the press. The bill required newspapers to publish government rebuttals to any articles to which it objected as unfair. Government responses were to be given the same prominence within the newspapers that the original articles received. The bill also required newspapers to disclose to the government the identities of the sources they used in their stories. Before the bill was passed into law, however, Alberta's lieutenant governor reserved the bill so that the Supreme Court of Canada could rule on its constitutionality. In the Alberta Press Act Reference, the court ruled the bill unconstitutional and struck it down.

See also Canada; Free speech; News media censorship; Newspapers.

Alcoholic beverages

DEFINITION: Fermented and distilled liquors containing ethanol, a behavior-altering drug when consumed

SIGNIFICANCE: Portrayals of alcohol in the media present conflicts between expression protected by the Constitution and the need to decrease the health problems associated with alcohol use

Alcohol use is a part of human culture. It provides relaxation and pleasure when consumed prudently, and even has medicinal uses. As a commodity, alcohol also provides numerous jobs, ranging from production and bottling, to promotion, transport, and sales. In essence, it composes a huge industry affecting many through the consumption of its products and the size of the workforce it employs.

Alcohol also brings costs to society. In 1980 a survey of Americans found 60 percent reporting alcohol to be one of the most harmful influences on family life. Car accidents, traffic fatalities, firearm injuries, decreased work performance, crime, violence, alcoholism, miscellaneous accidental deaths and injuries, and other mental and physical health problems all have been linked to problematic alcohol use. In 1985 in the United States alone, a conservative estimate of the public and private costs of alcohol-related problems was fourteen billion dollars.

Controlling Alcohol Consumption. Given such problems, it is no surprise that controls for alcohol use have been receiving increased attention. Stricter public drunkenness laws, harsher penalties for those driving while intoxicated, and new responsible server laws are some examples of legislative actions to punish overconsumption and control drinking. Public health prevention efforts also have focused on increasing drinking ages, establishing added "sin taxes" on alcoholic beverage purchases, and creating tighter restrictions on the proximity between schools and alcohol distribution outlets. Finally, business owners have contributed to control efforts by increasing alcohol- and drug-testing in the workplace.

Portrayals of Alcohol Consumption. Since the mid-1980's, there also has been a growing interest in regulating alcohol advertising and portrayals of alcohol in the media. Critics argue that such alcoholic beverage advertising targets younger individuals and thereby promotes underage drinking. Research suggesting relationships between exposure to alcohol-related advertising and later drinking in teenagers and young adults has reinforced such critiques. Knowledge about how individuals learn social behavior via observation has served to encourage consumers to exert more pressure on advertisers. Protests and boycotts by consumers against advertising using youthful performers, along with demands for the promotion of healthy role models on television and in other popular media have been common. Combined with campaigns to raise awareness about drinking problems, such as those sponsored by Mothers Against Drunk Driving in the 1980's, it is no surprise that a 1989 Roper poll showed 56 percent of adult Americans were in favor of alcohol advertisements' being banned. Similarly, a 1991 Roper poll showed that 33 percent of Americans thought that the alcohol industry should do more to address drunk driving. Such poll results demonstrate the public's perception that alcohol advertising should address the risks of alcohol consumption.

Concurrent to this shift in public opinion, alcohol advertisers began a different approach to marketing. Encouragement of moderate alcohol consumption, responsible drinking, designated driver programs, and the use of responsible servers all became the topics of advertising. No formal censorship was instated; rather, the alcohol industry responded to public concerns. Some critics argued, however, that these advertisements were not enough because they did not suggest abstinence as an option and thus were still promoting drinking. The efforts of U.S. vintners to initiate a campaign promoting their products following a 1991 broadcast on noted television news show *60 Minutes* on the benefits of red wine provide one example. In this case, despite a televised report indicating that moderate alcohol use might be related to beneficial health effects, advertisement promoting the curative or therapeutic effects of alcohol were forbidden by the Bureau of Alcohol, Tobacco, and Firearms (ATF). The vintners, some organized as a group called Wine First, as well as others, were confused by the ATF prohibition. Reports are that some felt they had been subject to censorship in that their rights to advertise were restricted. As of 1995, however, there was a lack of consensus among experts regarding the costs and benefits of moderate alcohol consumption on health. Thus, the issue of whether or not the ATF committed an act of unconstitutional censorship remained debatable, as the truth behind the advertising remains, to an extent, unknown.

Contrastingly, the Alcoholic Beverages Labeling Act passed by the U.S. Congress in 1988 required alcohol containers to carry warning labels. Based on evidence suggesting that such labels might promote reductions in drinking and that counter-advertising might be more effective and feasible than an outright advertising ban, warning labels entered the national spotlight as a suitable intervention. The labels indicate that alcohol may cause health problems and that pregnant women and those operating machinery or driving should be aware that drinking poses special risks. The effectiveness of such labels to decrease birth defects, drunk driving, or machine-related accidents, however, has not been certified. Further, there has been controversy over whether the labels do more to protect the public or the alcohol industry. In short, the presence of a warning label effectively releases the producer from many liabilities related to the effects of the product on the consumer. Some opponents of the labels might argue that the labels have harmed industry sales, others have suggested that the labels have provided protection against lawsuits.

Alcohol Industry Perspective. In 1976 the U.S. Supreme Court constitutionally protected truthful commercial speech or advertising. Critics argue that products with harmful effects should not be given the same protection as benign or healthful products. In contrast, alcohol industry officials feel that their products should not be singled out for exclusion, as nearly any product can be used to ill effects. The alcohol industry, officials argue, has a product that is legal to sell and so they should be permitted to advertise it. In addition, some feel that an outright ban on advertising would be harmful to consumers by depriving them of important information about such products and their appropriate use.

The Need for Balance. The destructive aspects of censorship must be kept in mind. At an extreme, efforts to control the portrayal of alcohol in the media can be puritanical. In 1990, for example, two California school districts banned an edition of *Little Red Riding Hood*; the book had an illustration showing a bottle of red wine in Red Riding Hood's basket. This caused the book to be deemed inappropriate for minors. It has been argued that such censorship is counterproductive: Frank and open discussion dispels the attractive aura of taboo that surrounds censored materials.

There are trade-offs between protecting the public good and the dangers of censorship. As these trade-offs come to be better understood, it is important that caution be exercised regarding censorship of alcohol in the media. Censorship against may create dangerous precedents.   —*Nancy A. Piotrowski*

See also Advertising as the target of censorship; Boycotts; Broadcast media; *44 Liquormart, Inc. v. Rhode Island*; Smoking.

BIBLIOGRAPHY

Nicholas Dorn and Nigel South, *Message in a Bottle: Theoretical Overview and Annotated Bibliography on the Mass Media and Alcohol* (Aldershot, Hants, England: Gower, 1983) is an overview of prevention and media campaigns on alcohol and drinking. Retold and illustrated by Trina Schart Hyman, *Little Red Riding Hood* (New York: Holiday House, 1983) is an example of a fairy tale banned for its portrayal of alcohol. Editor Richard T. Kaplar's *Bad Prescription for the First Amendment: FDA Censorship of Drug Advertising and Promotion* (Washington, D.C.: Media Institute, 1993) discusses the pros and cons of the Food and Drug Administration's control over drug advertising. Marcia J. Summers et al., *Our Chemical Culture* (Cambridge, Mass.: Schenkman, 1982) is written for high school students and describes drug use and abuse in society. Andrew Weil and Winifred Rosen's *From*

Chocolate to Morphine (Boston: Houghton Mifflin, 1993) discusses the use and history of mind-altering substances in society.

Alexandria library

DATE: 391 C.E.

PLACE: Alexandria, Egypt

SIGNIFICANCE: The destruction of the great Alexandria library by Christians has long stood as a spectacular example of cultural censorship

After Alexander the Great founded the port city of Alexandria in Egypt in the fourth century B.C.E., his successor, Ptolemy I, built a great library in the city. The Athenian exile Demetrius of Phaleron modeled the new library on a similar institution in Athens, Greece. A century later, part of the library's holdings were housed in the nearby Serapeum—the temple of Serapis, a god who combined elements of both Greek and Egyptian deities. It is believed that over the next two centuries, the library's holdings grew to many more than 500,000 volumes, with manuscripts from all over the known world.

Around 48 B.C.E. part of the library's holdings were said to have been destroyed, but evidence for this event is sparse. By the most popular accounts, most of the library was ruined during a Roman siege, when Julius Caesar razed part of the city in order to protect his troops' position. What actually happened, and how many of the library's books were lost, is not known. In any case, Alexandria's libraries afterward made the city the most important intellectual center in the Mediterranean world during the era of Roman rule. Meanwhile, the Serapeum expanded and absorbed Alexandria's main library. By the late fourth century C.E. the Serapeum was probably the greatest pagan shrine remaining in the developing Christian world.

In 391 Constantinople's Emperor Theodosius ordered the destruction of all major pagan centers of worship in his Christian empire. In the ensuing holocaust, the contents of Alexandria's ancient library were allegedly destroyed—in an act of extreme Christian intolerance. There are, however, reasons to doubt that this destruction actually occurred at that time. Some evidence indicates that the library may have been destroyed in 646, when Muslims conquered Egypt.

See also Athens, ancient; Book burning; Historiography; Islam; Religion.

Ali, Muhammad

BORN: January 17, 1942, Louisville, Kentucky

IDENTIFICATION: American boxer

SIGNIFICANCE: Stripped of his world heavyweight title and prosecuted as a draft evader, Muhammad Ali became a symbol for African Americans and those protesting the Vietnam War

Born Cassius Clay, Muhammad Ali changed his name in 1964 to reflect his conversion to the Nation of Islam. Done at the height of his boxing career, his conversion led him to assume the status of conscientious objector on the grounds that his religion prohibited his serving in the U.S. military during the Vietnam War. His action outraged many white Americans, who saw Ali's action as unpatriotic.

Ali had been very outspoken before his religious conversion, but his adoption of the Nation of Islam ideology was particularly controversial. He had been given a "1-Y" draft status, meaning that he had not passed the examination necessary for induction into the armed services. (Top athletes had sometimes been granted military deferments.) However, just four weeks after Ali announced his conversion, he was retested amid calls to reclassify his draft status from people who were offended by his conversion. Bowing to pressure, his draft board reclassified him as "1-A" and ordered him to report for induction. He refused on religious grounds. His appeal of the rejection of conscientious objector status was based on the fact that no African Americans were on the Selective Service boards that heard his case.

Convicted of violating the Selective Service Act in 1967, Ali was sentenced to five years in prison and fined ten thousand dollars. The same year, he was stripped of his heavyweight boxing championship title by the World Boxing Association and the New York Athletic Association and barred from boxing for four years. His passport was also revoked. In 1970 his conviction was overturned, based on a 1969 U.S. Supreme Court ruling which allowed conscientious objectors to base their claims on philosophical and moral, as well as religious, grounds. Muhammad Ali returned to the boxing ring and resumed his successful career.

See also African Americans; Draft resistance; Islam; Malcolm X; Sports news; Vietnam War.

Alice's Adventures in Wonderland

TYPE OF WORK: Book

PUBLISHED: 1865

AUTHOR: Lewis Carroll (Charles Lutwidge Dodgson; 1832-1898)

SUBJECT MATTER: Fantasy in which a young girl dreams about a world in which she changes sizes, encounters bizarre creatures, and is threatened with execution

SIGNIFICANCE: Although one of the most popular works of fantasy for children, this classic book and its dramatizations have been condemned as sadistic and perverse

Certain critics—including psychoanalyst Paul Schilder and author Katherine Anne Porter—have argued that *Alice's Adventures in Wonderland* should be kept away from children because it is riddled with material that causes anxiety. For example, Schilder has cited the book's frequent references to devouring small animals as evidence of the work's "preponderant oral sadistic trends."

The government of China banned the book in 1931, charging that its talking animals were offensive because their use of language placed them inappropriately on the same level with humans. In 1966, after the book was read over the radio in Britain, the British Broadcasting Corporation was inundated by phone calls from listeners outraged over the book's description of using hedgehogs as croquet balls.

The Disney Company released an animated film adaptation of *Alice in Wonderland* in 1951. Although this film was somewhat sanitized, it later merited a warning to parents in psychologist Harold Schecter's 1986 guide to children's video for its threats of violence and its scenes of baby oysters being eaten. Meanwhile, Disney withdrew the film from 16 mm rental distribution during the late 1960's, although it had won some fans on the college circuit. At that time the company's animated feature *Fantasia* (1940) was drawing fire because of its association with the drug culture, so Disney may have acted to protect its wholesome image.

See also Books, children's; British Broadcasting Corporation; China; Dahl, Roald; Disney films.

All Quiet on the Western Front

TYPE OF WORK: Book
PUBLISHED: 1929
AUTHOR: Erich Maria Remarque (1898-1970)
SUBJECT MATTER: Novel about the disillusionment of an idealistic young German soldier who experiences the grim realities of fighting in World War I
SIGNIFICANCE: This best-selling novel was censored in the United States because it contained scenes of sex and latrines; it was banned in Germany and Italy because of its antihero themes, and in Russia and other Eastern Bloc countries because of its alleged bourgeois intellectualism

The rapid popular success of Erich Maria Remarque's novel after it appeared in January, 1929, attracted special attention from the political parties vying for ascendancy in Germany's Weimar Republic. Reviews by Adolf Hitler's National Social-

The film All Quiet on the Western Front *(1930) raised objections in Great Britain, France, and the United States because of its powerful antiwar message and sympathetic treatment of German soldiers in World War I.* (Museum of Modern Art/Film Stills Archive)

ists ridiculed the novel as unauthentic, the work of an imaginative Jew intent on pulling down the ideal of heroism. German Marxists judged Remarque as ideologically noncommittal and insufficiently critical of the war it depicted. In Great Britain and Australia, criticism of *All Quiet on the Western Front* followed similar ideological lines.

In the United States Little, Brown published a version of *All Quiet on the Western Front* from which passages mentioning latrines and a scene of sexual encounter in a hospital were removed. This edition, which also softened the book's raw language, was a Book-of-the-Month Club choice in 1929. The first unexpurgated American edition of the novel did not appear until 1975.

In 1930 an American film company, Universal Pictures, adapted *All Quiet on the Western Front* to the screen; both the film and its director, Lewis Milestone, won Academy Awards. When the film opened in Berlin, Germany, Joseph Goebbels led a group of Hitler Youth in a violent demonstration. Afterward the Weimar government found reasons to banish the film from Germany on aesthetic grounds. Three years later, after Hitler took power, the National Socialist government banned the novel from the country as well.

In a silent film version that was adapted for French-speaking audiences, scenes depicting the killing of a French soldier and a gathering of German soldiers and French women were removed. When the film was rereleased in the United States in 1938, an anti-Nazi prologue was added.

See also Germany; Literature; *Red Badge of Courage, The*; World War I.

Amants, Les

TYPE OF WORK: Film
RELEASED: 1958
DIRECTOR: Louis Malle (1932-1995)
SUBJECT MATTER: A young French woman in an unhappy marriage finds other lovers and eventually leaves her husband
SIGNIFICANCE: After numerous attempts to censor this film because of its perceived obscenity, the U.S Supreme Court ruled the film not to be obscene and therefore a constitutionally protected form of expression

Adapted from the nineteenth century novel *Point de Lendemain* by Dominique Vivant and directed by Louis Malle, *Les Amants* is about an unhappy and neglected young wife who has affairs with a sophisticated Parisian and a young archeologist, for whom she eventually leaves her husband. The film met a cool reception in many U.S. cities, where many theaters that exhibited it were prosecuted for obscenity, or moved to edit the film themselves to avoid prosecution.

One obscenity case occurred in Ohio, where the manager of a Cleveland Heights theater was convicted in a county court for exhibiting an obscene film. Although Ohio's state supreme court affirmed this conviction, the case eventually reached the U.S. Supreme Court, in *Jacobellis v. State of Ohio* (1964). The Court ruled the film not to be obscene and therefore constitutionally protected from government censorship. Joining in this decision, Justice Potter Stewart noted the difficulty of defining

Bannings of Les Amants *in the United States led to many legal battles in courts.* (Museum of Modern Art/Film Stills Archive)

obscenity but observed, "I know it when I see it, and the motion picture involved in this case is not that."

See also Adultery; *Ecstasy*; Film censorship; Obscenity: legal definitions.

American Bar Association (ABA)

FOUNDED: 1878

TYPE OF ORGANIZATION: Voluntary national association of law students and lawyers admitted to practice and in good standing in any state

SIGNIFICANCE: The association has promoted improvement in the administration of justice and the uniformity of laws

Established largely through the efforts of the older Connecticut bar association, the ABA—with a membership approaching 400,000 in the 1990's—coordinates the activities of scores of state and local bar associations. A subsidiary, the American Bar Foundation, sponsors and funds legal research, education, and social studies. Through the operations of approximately twenty-five committees devoted to specific legal topics, the ABA has sought to promote professional standards among lawyers and to improve the administration of justice. The Section of Intellectual Property Law, for example, has worked for adoption of changes in federal laws governing patents, trademarks, and copyrights. It lobbied heavily for the adoption

in 1992 of a new fair use provision in the Copyright Act of 1976. A series of court decisions ruling against use of unpublished materials had created an atmosphere of self-censorship among publishers, making it increasingly difficult for reporters, historians, and biographers to get into print. Finally, the statute was amended to state that the fact that a work is unpublished does not mean that it cannot be used for such purposes as analysis and criticism.

See also Copyright law; Courtrooms; Courts and censorship law; Irish Republican Army; Privileged communication.

American Booksellers Association, Inc. v. Hudnut

COURT: U.S. Supreme Court

DECIDED: February 24, 1986

SIGNIFICANCE: In this case the Supreme Court summarily affirmed an appellate court's holding that an Indiana antipornography ordinance violated the First Amendment

The *Hudnut* decision involved an Indianapolis-Marion County ordinance that defined pornography not a causal factor that harmed women but as an injury per se. The ordinance defined pornography as "graphic sexually explicit subordination of women through pictures and/or words" that dehumanized women as sexual objects, presented them in sexually degrading situations, showed them being sexually penetrated by objects or animals, or depicted them in other physically degrading situations in contexts that make the conditions sexual. After heated debate over the problems of pornography and sex discrimination in American society, the Indianapolis City-County Council enacted an ordinance that restricted the availability of materials depicting the sexual subordination of women.

A district court held that the state's interest in eradicating sex discrimination was insufficiently compelling to outweigh the public interest in free speech. The court paid particular attention to obscenity as the category of speech most closely resembling pornography. Defenders of the ordinance contended that because pornography was a broader category than obscenity the court should recognize it as a new category of unprotected speech. They also argued that the ordinance regulated conduct and not speech, since—by their own definition—pornography was more than a mere expression of ideas. They saw it as unconstitutional sex-based discrimination.

Opponents of the ordinance contended that it failed to provide fair notice to residents of Indianapolis and those doing business there as to what it covered or exempted, and that it thereby violated the Fifth and Fourteenth amendments of the U.S. Constitution. They also claimed that the ordinance had a "chilling effect" on the exercise of free speech rights and that its provision for cease and desist orders constituted an illegal prior restraint by allowing the government to act as a censor.

The district court ruled that it could not permit every group claiming to have been victimized by unfair expression special legislative exceptions to the First Amendment. Finally, the court suggested that while sociological patterns might need alteration, defendants should remember that free speech, "rather than being the enemy, is a long-tested and worthy ally," that could be used to protect against tyranny.

See also Chilling effect; Courts and censorship law; First Amendment; *Miller v. California*; Obscenity: legal definitions; Pornography; Prior restraint; Unprotected speech; Women, violence against.

American Booksellers Foundation for Free Expression (ABFFE)

Founded: 1990

Type of organization: Advocacy branch of the American Booksellers Association

Significance: This organization has worked for full First Amendment protections of the arts, publishing, and Internet computer communications

The ABFFE was founded to serve as the free expression arm of the American Booksellers Association (ABA), a national organization founded in 1901 to serve bookstores and sellers. The foundation's mission was to ensure full First Amendment protections of people in the bookselling industry. The ABFFE has been active in all areas of First Amendment issues. In 1996 for example, it worked with similar groups to protest the Communications Decency Act of 1996, which proposed to regulate many forms of expression on the Internet.

Dedicated to the principle that booksellers and publishers cannot be held responsible for criminal acts, the ABFFE has stood ready to support individual book retailers who face censorship challenges because of what they sell. At the ABA conferences it has held panel discussions on free speech issues. ABFFE has also been a strong supporter of Banned Books Week and it has produced information supplies to aid bookstores in increasing awareness on the subject.

See also American Library Association; Banned Books Week; Internet; Moral Majority; Obscenity: sale and possession; Thurmond, Strom.

American Civil Liberties Union (ACLU)

Founded: January 20, 1920

Type of organization: Private, nonprofit rights advocacy group

Significance: Formed to defend and to protect the Bill of Rights, especially its free expression clauses, the ACLU has been involved with more Supreme Court cases than any nongovernmental organization

In 1917 Roger Nash Baldwin, a young New York social worker, founded the National Civil Liberties Bureau to defend the free expression rights of those who spoke out against U.S. participation in World War I. In 1920 the bureau renamed itself the American Civil Liberties Union (ACLU) and broadened its agenda to become a nationwide nonpartisan, nonprofit organization dedicated to defending the Bill of Rights of the U.S. Constitution. Since then the ACLU has built a nationwide network of chapters, with affiliates in every state. Many lawyers volunteer their time to provide legal counsel in ACLU cases. The organization has functioned in three primary ways: by litigating cases, by educating the public on civil liberties matters, and by advocating legislation. Its policy decisions have been made by a national board, with the advice of a national committee, and have been implemented by the national organization and its affiliates.

The ACLU has centers of activity in New York City and Washington, D.C. The former houses its national headquarters and public education activities—such as alerting the public to potential or actual civil liberties violations. Washington houses the ACLU's office for legislative activity, which lobbies the federal government. The organization advocates legislation requiring greater public disclosure of information on government activities and on preventing the passage of legislation that may violate the Constitution.

The Early Years. The ACLU initially restricted its activities to First Amendment issues. In 1924, however, it played a role in supporting the legal appeal of Nicola Sacco and Bartolomeo Vanzetti, Italian anarchists who had been convicted of a 1920 murder in Massachusetts. The ACLU attorneys were interested in Sacco and Vanzetti's case because it appeared that the men were actually being prosecuted for having expressed unpopular political views. Despite lengthy appeals, Sacco and Vanzetti were executed in 1927.

The following year the ACLU came to national prominence during the trial of John T. Scopes, a Tennessee high school teacher who had challenged a state law prohibiting the teaching of evolution. With William Jennings Bryan, a Christian

ACLU executive director Ramona Ripston (left) leads a team of attorneys presenting a suit brought by a student newspaper against California governor Pete Wilson for violating an open-meeting law by influencing University of California regents before they voted on an affirmative action resolution. (AP/Wide World Photos)

Fundamentalist and former presidential candidate as prosecutor, and Clarence Darrow, a famous Chicago criminal lawyer and agnostic, as defense counsel, the trial was a national sensation that dominated news reporting. Scopes was eventually convicted and fined one hundred dollars; his conviction was overturned on a technical matter. More importantly, the constitutionality of Tennessee's law was upheld by the state's supreme court. Seven decades later, the ACLU was still battling some of the same issues in cases in which religious Fundamentalists demanded that public schools teach "scientific creationism." Likewise, the guilt of Sacco and Vanzetti was still being debated.

Jehovah's Witnesses. The Jehovah's Witnesses are a Christian sect that believes in divine revelation and in actively proselytizing on street corners and on door-to-door missions. Because of its members' aggressive persistence, many people have found their missionary work offensive. Moreover, the sect's strong prohibition of all forms of idolatry has taught members to regard symbols such as national flags as idols and to refuse to salute them. The sect also advocates conscientious objection to military service. Beliefs such as these have caused the patriotism of Jehovah's Witnesses to be questioned in the United States.

During the late 1930's and early 1940's, the Jehovah's Witnesses were targets of both official and popular persecution. In the case of *Minersville School District v. Gobitis* (1940), the U.S. Supreme Court was asked to decide whether Jehovah's Witness children who refused to salute the flag on religious grounds should be expelled from school. The Court ruled against the Witnesses, holding that the state's interest in pro-

moting national unity by compelling school children to salute the flag outweighed the students' exercise of freedom of conscience. Three years later, the Court reversed itself, in *West Virginia State Board of Education v. Barnette*. Through these so-called flag salute cases, the ACLU supported the right of Jehovah's Witnesses to express themselves according to their consciences and religious beliefs.

Aside from various attacks on the Jehovah's Witnesses during these years, the ACLU reported a remarkable lack of repression during World War II—in contrast to what had happened during World War I.

The Red Scares. During the early 1950's the ACLU strongly resisted the efforts of Wisconsin senator Joseph McCarthy to "root out" the "communist conspiracy" that he claimed permeated the arts, the entertainment industry, the U.S. State Department, and the army. During this period McCarthy's Senate committee and the House Committee on Un-American Activities (HUAC) held hearings on communism. Eventually the anticommunist movement ran out of steam. Meanwhile, however, a special Senate committee chaired by Senator Arthur Watkins investigated possible censure of McCarthy. The ACLU heartily endorsed McCarthy's censure, but insisted that his own civil rights be protected by demanding that Watkins' committee grant him the right to confront and cross-examine witnesses against him. When McCarthy confronted his enemies, he participated, for the first time in his political career, in a Senate hearing that afforded due process.

Skokie Controversy. In 1976 members of the National Socialist (Nazi) Party of America wanted to march through the small Chicago suburb of Skokie, Illinois, the home to many

Jewish families, including survivors of concentration camps during the Jewish Holocaust. When local officials tried various tactics to prevent the march, attorneys for the ACLU supported the Nazis' right to express themselves by marching. Federal courts eventually struck down Skokie's attempts to block the march, but after achieving the publicity they had sought, the Nazis decided not to march there.

The ACLU's support of the Nazis in the Skokie case alienated many Americans; however, this incident did not represent a new policy for the organization. Since its inception, it had defended many groups such as the Nazis that were devoted to eliminating civil liberties. Nevertheless, negative public reaction to this case was unprecedented; a significant number of ACLU members resigned. The ACLU soon found itself facing serious fiscal problems, but its membership rolls eventually rebounded to surpass pre-Skokie levels.

Later Years. During the 1990's, the ACLU opposed campus speech codes aimed at mandating political correctness in colleges and universities around the nation. In 1991, for example, it assisted a student newspaper and several students in a successful court challenge to the University of Wisconsin's speech code that prohibited expression of demeaning comments about the race, sex, religion, sexual orientation, or physical disability of persons. Three years later the ACLU criticized the Federal Bureau of Investigation's arrest of a University of Michigan student charged with interstate transmission of a threat to injure, for having written and published on the Internet a sexually violent piece of fiction that used the name of a female student.

On May 26, 1994, President Bill Clinton signed into law the Freedom of Access to Clinic Entrances Act, which was designed to protect the patients and staff of abortion clinics from attacks, blockades, and acts of intimidation. The ACLU hailed this legislation as a congressional milestone in the protection of reproductive rights. A year later the ACLU provided legal consul for a student's unsuccessful Supreme Court challenge of the Veronia, Oregon, school district's policy of random drug testing for student athletes. The court ruled on June 26, 1995, that community efforts to deter drug usage among teens overrode the right to individual privacy.

Although the ACLU has been best known for resisting almost all forms of censorship in its defenses of free expression, it has also supported a broad range of civil liberties. For example, it opposed the interment of Japanese Americans during World War II, and it supported the right to abortions after the Supreme Court's 1973 *Roe v. Wade* decision. Consistently nonpartisan, the ACLU has represented groups on both the Left and the Right. Nevertheless, its philosophical position against censorship has continued to draw criticism from many Americans. —*Daniel C. Falkowski*

See also Campus speech codes; Constitution, U.S.; First Amendment; Frankfurter, Felix; Internet; Jehovah's Witnesses; Political correctness; Scopes trial; Skokie, Illinois, Nazi march; World War I.

BIBLIOGRAPHY

Charles Lam Markman's *The Noblest Cry: A History of the American Civil Liberties Union* (New York: St. Martin's Press, 1965) is a sympathetic history of the ACLU that attributes the organization's prestige to its "utter lack of partisanship and its concentration on matters of principle." William A. Donohue's *The Politics of the American Civil Liberties Union* (New Brunswick, N.J.: Transaction, 1985) is a critical analysis of twentieth century American liberalism and an attack on the ACLU. Donohue contends that the "ACLU is no more free from partisanship than the Republican and Democratic parties. Quite simply, the ACLU has politics, and that politics is liberalism." For accounts of the ACLU's involvement in the Skokie incident, see James L. Gibson, *Civil Liberties and Nazis: The Skokie Free Speech Controversy* (New York: Praeger, 1985); Aryeh Neier, *Defending My Enemy: American Nazis, the Skokie Case, and the Risks of Freedom* (New York: E. P. Dutton, 1979); or David Hamlin, *The Nazi/Skokie Conflict: A Civil Liberties Battle* (Boston: Beacon Press, 1980).

American Library Association (ALA)

FOUNDED: 1876

TYPE OF ORGANIZATION: The largest library association in the world, ALA has 57,000 members representing school, academic, state, and special libraries

SIGNIFICANCE: ALA is one the most active U.S. bodies opposing censorship of information, preserving free public access to library materials, and promoting librarians' right of intellectual freedom

Selecting and guarding books in libraries are two traditional tasks of librarians. Selecting and guarding books entails screening books and controlling access to them. At times, therefore, librarians consciously or unconsciously act as censors. In the past many librarians favored censorship. During its early years in the late nineteenth century even ALA itself listed books it approved for the public to read. Such attitudes and practices significantly changed in 1896, when the delegates to an ALA conference approved free access to shelves in public libraries. This decision contrasted sharply with sentiments shown at earlier conferences.

During World War I many American librarians believed that pro-German literature should be withdrawn from public libraries. As a result, the ALA's governing council appointed a committee to prepare a list warning of books whose misuse should be guarded against. However, this committee never produced the proposed list.

In 1929 ALA's executive board spoke out in opposition to a proposed federal tariff bill that would prohibit importing materials advocating or urging treason, insurrection, or forcible resistance to U.S. laws. The board also opposed tariffs on obscene books, papers, or the like. Its members argued that this law would create effective censorship over foreign literature and keep out material relating to revolutions in foreign countries. The board also argued that this law was a reflection upon the intelligence of the American people by implying that they were too stupid and untrustworthy to read about revolutions without immediately becoming traitors and revolutionaries themselves.

Before the 1930's many articles published in library literature tended to support censorship, while only a few supported intellectual freedom. This situation dramatically changed as ALA took a stronger position against censorship. In 1934 the association recorded its first protest against the banning of a specific publication. In 1939 John Steinbeck's new novel, *The Grapes of Wrath*, became the target of censorship pressures and was banned from libraries around the country. ALA responded by adopting the Library Bill of Rights to support librarians and library boards opposed to censorship of materials. Since then, the Library Bill of Rights has become the library profession's basic policy statement on protecting the rights of librarians and library users to intellectual freedom.

Intellectual Freedom Committee. During and after World War II, demands increased for strict control over the dissemination of propaganda and "subversive" publications. The challenge of censorship became an everyday problem encountered by the library profession during this era. In response to the continuing pressure on libraries regarding material thought to be subversive, ALA established a special committee on censorship. In late 1940 the ALA council appointed a new committee on intellectual freedom, empowering it to act for ALA in safeguarding the rights of library users. Establishment of this committee strengthened ALA's role in censorship disputes and helped many librarians change their attitudes toward intellectual freedom.

During the postwar years, especially between 1949 and 1954, the anti-intellectual freedom activities were greater than in the prewar period because of nationwide fears of communism. Censorship activities against libraries were on the increase throughout the country. Patriotic and religious organizations, such as the Sons of the American Revolution, attempted to force libraries to label dangerous materials to alert patrons. For example, labels were to be applied to publications advocating communism or issued by communist agencies. On July 13, 1951, the ALA council unanimously adopted a strong statement, recommended by the Intellectual Freedom Committee, condemning attempts to label library materials. The statement pointed out that labeling was a tool of censorship and a violation of the First Amendment to the Constitution.

In early 1953 the principle of freedom of information was severely tested in the library community once again when U.S. State Department libraries in foreign cities came under pressure from Senator Joseph McCarthy to remove books about communism or by communist authors. In response to this situation, in May, 1953, ALA with the American Book Publishers' Council adopted the Freedom to Read Statement attacking censorship and the attempts at suppression of reading materials. The statement expressed ALA's concern that citizens had been constantly threatened with censorship from the public and the private sectors. The statement also indicated that freedom to read was essential in any democracy. A further statement was adopted by ALA condemning U.S. interference with American libraries in other countries. From 1940 until 1967 most intellectual freedom activities were centered in the Intellectual Freedom Committee. The committee not only recommended policies to fight censorship but also directed a variety of educational efforts to promote intellectual freedom.

To relieve the Intellectual Freedom Committee's task of educating librarians and the general public on the importance of intellectual freedom and allow it to concentrate on developing policy, ALA established the Office for Intellectual Freedom (OIF) in 1967. It served as an ALA headquarters unit to conduct and coordinate intellectual freedom activities. The OIF has since served as the administrative arm of the Intellectual Freedom Committee and has borne responsibility for implementing official ALA policies on intellectual freedom. The specific goal of the OIF has been to educate librarians and the public about the importance of concepts embodied in the Library Bill of Rights.

Since its inception, the OIF has created and maintained a broad program of informational publications, projects, and supportive services. Its regular publications are the bimonthly *Newsletter on Intellectual Freedom* and the monthly *OIF Memorandum*. Special OIF publications prepared for librarians have included the *Banned Books Week Resource Kit, Censorship and Selection: Issues and Answers for Schools, Confidentiality in Libraries: An Intellectual Freedom Modular Education Program*, the *Intellectual Freedom Manual*, and miscellaneous bibliographies. In addition, the OIF has accepted speaking engagements, given interviews to news media on intellectual freedom, and maintained exhibits on banned books and non-mainstream publications. In a supportive role, the OIF advises and consults with librarians confronting potential or actual censorship.

The OIF has also coordinated the Intellectual Freedom Committee's relations with other agencies and organizations having similar concerns. It has worked closely with the Freedom to Read Foundation, an ALA sister organization dedicated to litigating court cases affecting the rights of libraries and librarians, allocating and disbursing grants to individuals and groups primarily for the purpose of aiding them in litigation, and providing funds for the direct participation in litigation dealing with freedom of speech and of the press.

In June, 1973, ALA set up the Intellectual Freedom Round Table (IFRT) as the association's membership activity program for intellectual freedom. The IFRT has provided a forum for discussions of activities, programs, and problems related to the intellectual freedom of libraries and librarians. It has served as a channel of communications on intellectual freedom matters, promoted opportunities for involvement by ALA members in defense of intellectual freedom, and promoted feelings of responsibility in implementation of ALA policies on intellectual freedom.

Goals for the Twenty-first Century. ALA has been generally successful in promoting and preserving the idea of intellectual freedom. It has set goals for the twenty-first century. ALA Goal 2000, an initiative endorsed by ALA's executive board in 1994, aims to ensure that the association is as closely associated with the public's right to a free and open information society—intellectual participation—as it is with the idea of intellectual freedom.

The key goal is to make the voices of ALA and libraries heard in the board rooms of government and corporations where information policies are being developed. These policies will determine who will have access to new information technology and at what price. ALA considers that it and the voice of the American people are outnumbered, outspent, and too often absent.

To implement ALA Goal 2000, ALA has called for expanding its Washington office and establishing an Office for Information Technology Policy to increase its ability to influence national information policy and support its members in addressing these issues at the local and state levels. Issues of immediate concern include renewal of the Library Services and Construction Act, funding for library programs under the Higher Education Act, and favorable telecommunications access rates for libraries. ALA Goal 2000 also has focused its energies and resources on positioning its association as a force for the public interest in the arena of electronic information.

—Wei Luo

See also Canadian Library Association Statement on Intellectual Freedom; Freedom to Read Foundation; Freedom to Read Week; *Grapes of Wrath, The*; Intellectual freedom; Libraries; Libraries, Canadian; Libraries, school; Library Bill of Rights; Privacy Protection Act of 1980.

BIBLIOGRAPHY

Intellectual Freedom Manual compiled by the Office for Intellectual Freedom of American Library Association (4th ed. Chicago: American Library Association, 1992). The first edition was published in 1974, and the manual has become an indispensable tool for librarians, library trustees, and others concerned with defending intellectual freedom for librarians and libraries. *Newsletter on Intellectual Freedom* (Chicago: Intellectual Freedom Committee of the American Library Association). Published six times per year since 1952, this is the official publication of the Intellectual Freedom Committee of ALA. Dennis Thomison's *A History of the American Library Association, 1876-1972* (Chicago: American Library Association, 1978) also discusses the history of ALA's early procensorship years and its anticensorship stance since the late 1930's.

American Psycho

TYPE OF WORK: Book
PUBLISHED: 1991
AUTHOR: Bret Easton Ellis (1964-   )
SUBJECT MATTER: Novel about a Wall Street investment banker who leads a double life as a sadistic serial killer
SIGNIFICANCE: This novel aroused controversy when its original publisher canceled plans to print it because of its graphic violence; another company published it, leading to widespread criticism, particularly from women's groups

The author of *Less Than Zero* (1985), Ellis completed his third novel, *American Psycho*, for the publishing house Simon and Schuster in 1989. Its story about a wealthy young businessman whose greed for money and material possessions is matched only by his taste for sadism and murder contains detailed descriptions of acts ranging from cannibalism to necrophilia, as well as extended scenes of sexual torture and mutilation. As the book was nearing publication in 1990, reports of its extraordinarily violent content began to surface in magazines such as *Time* and *Spy*, which printed excerpts from some of its most gruesome passages. As criticism of the novel grew, Si-

mon and Schuster canceled plans to publish the novel, despite having paid Ellis an advance of three hundred thousand dollars. The book was immediately purchased by Random House and published as a Vintage Contemporary paperback in 1991.

Feminist groups criticized the novel's depiction of violence against women, leading to a boycott of its publishers by the National Organization for Women. The furor surrounding the book's publication fueled public debate about corporate censorship and corporate responsibility, as well as the literary quality and moral implications of the book itself.

See also Book publishing; *Caligula*; Violence; Women, violence against.

American Society of Composers, Authors & Publishers (ASCAP)

FOUNDED: 1914
TYPE OF ORGANIZATION: One of three major performance rights organizations that collect performance payments from broadcasters and other sources
SIGNIFICANCE: Through its agreements with broadcasters in the 1920's and 1930's, this organization had a significant impact on the kind of music aired on radio

Founded in 1914, ASCAP was the first major American performance rights organization. Since then it has acted as a kind of intermediary between musicians, songwriters, and music publishers on one hand and broadcasters and others who play music on the other hand. It contracts with musicians and associated interests to collect fees from broadcasters and other entities that play music. In the early years of its existence, ASCAP had a virtual monopoly on the collection of such fees and used its economic power to affect the kind of music broadcast. First, it screened the musicians for which it would collect performance fees and refused to admit blues, country, and rock musicians. Second, through its agreements with broadcasters, ASCAP was able to limit music broadcast to that produced or performed by its members. Ultimately, ASCAP's monopoly was broken by Broadcast Music, Inc. (BMI), which has actively recruited the very kinds of musicians and musical interests that ASCAP itself has shunned. In so doing, BMI has created opportunities for more kinds of music to be aired.

See also Broadcast Music, Inc.; Music; Recording industry; Rock 'n' roll music.

Americans for Democratic Action (ADA)

FOUNDED: 1947
TYPE OF ORGANIZATION: Liberal American citizen group
SIGNIFICANCE: Dedicated to promoting liberalism in American public policy, ADA publishes appraisals of Congress and develops resolutions on issues such as civil rights, employees rights, and censorship

This Washington, D.C.-based political action organization was established in 1947 by leaders in politics, journalism, academia, and labor, including Eleanor Roosevelt, Hubert Humphrey, and Arthur Schlesinger, Jr. ADA was founded primarily to promote a liberal, anticommunist agenda. By the 1990's the nonpartisan organization was promoting liberalism and had become a central player in the fight against censorship. With sixty-five thousand members, ADA has continued to attract leading figures from the political Left. Past ADA presidents include former Democratic senator Paul Wellstone of Minnesota and Democratic representatives Patsy Mink of Hawaii and John Lewis of Georgia.

ADA is the nation's oldest liberal lobbying group and has been in the forefront of debate on important political issues since its inception. ADA achieves its goals of social and economic justice through several initiatives. One approach is political action, whereby ADA is involved in grassroots issue advocacy. A separate political action committee, ADA/PAC, supports progressive candidates for office and is committed to assisting women, minority, and nonincumbent candidates. ADA is also active in youth issues and its Youth for Democratic Action organization, made up of members under the age of thirty, builds chapters on college campuses, lobbies and works with political campaigns, and encourages community service. Another affiliated program, ADA's Education Fund, an independent, charitable organization, sponsors drug awareness conferences and voter registration drives for young individuals and promotes parental involvement in education. Perhaps ADA's most popular initiative is its publishing. A legislative update of key votes and issues is provided in *ADAction News & Notes*, published every week that Congress is in session. The ADA *Annual Voting Record* has been published since 1947 and has become a leading source of assessing legislators' voting and performance.

ADA is active in developing positions on important policy issues. Through its large research staff, conferences and seminars, and publications, ADA promotes its agenda of civil rights, health care reform, employee rights, full employment, fair immigration standards, reproductive rights, and a fair minimum wage. ADA is also committed to fighting censorship. ADA's policy resolution "Censorship in Education and the Arts," adopted in 1995, states: "Liberty of thought and conscience and the freedom to express the ideas to which they give rise are the foundations upon which the edifice of American democracy rests." ADA has fought attempts to censor the National Endowment for the Arts and the Corporation for Public Broadcasting by some members of Congress, such as North Carolina's Republican Senator Jesse Helms, who cite a supposed liberal bias and sexually offensive, antireligious content as justification for censorship. Another issue of concern to ADA is that of banning books from libraries and educational curricula, including award-winning classics. ADA has opposed right-wing groups such as Focus on the Family and the American Family Association that have been engaged in efforts to ban books that do not conform to their beliefs.

New challenges to free expression are emerging in cyberspace. ADA has opposed plans by Congress to limit free access to the Internet and interactive media. ADA continues to be a leader in the fight for First Amendment rights and a champion of free expression.

See also Advocacy; American Civil Liberties Union; Committee to Defend the First Amendment; First Amendment Congress; National Coalition Against Censorship; People for the American Way.

Amerika

TYPE OF WORK: Television miniseries
BROADCAST: February 15-22, 1987
WRITER AND DIRECTOR: Donald Wrye
SUBJECT MATTER: A fictional look at the lives of ordinary Americans ten years after the Soviet Union occupies the United States
SIGNIFICANCE: Airing during the last years of the Cold War, this production drew strong protests from the Soviet Union, the United Nations, and both the Left and the Right

This seven-part miniseries aired on the American Broadcasting Company (ABC) in the spring of 1987. The drama was set in 1997, ten years after a bloodless Soviet takeover of the United States.

The miniseries faced a barrage of potential censorship starting with the government of the Soviet Union in late 1985. The ABC News Desk in Moscow was implicitly threatened with denial of access if the production continued. When publicly revealed in the United States, this threat was condemned by daily newspapers as a violation of freedom of speech. Later, the Soviets reversed their position and eventually bargained with ABC for rights to air *Amerika* in their own country.

The United Nations was disturbed by the series' portrayal of its peacekeeping forces and the use of recognizable portions of U.N. symbols. In the fall of 1986 the United Nations sent a list of requests to the network, including free air time to promote their organization. ABC agreed to air disclaimers during the show but retained the use of the symbols.

Citizen groups aimed letter writing campaigns threatening boycotts at sponsors; shortly before *Amerika* aired, Chrysler Corporation withdrew about seven million dollars in advertisements. Conservatives denounced the miniseries because it portrayed Americans as apathetic and the Soviets as too sympathetic. Liberals protested the show as "red-scare paranoia." In response, some ABC affiliates allowed critics air time after the broadcast to offer opposing views.

See also Advertisers as advocates of censorship; Communism; *Last P.O.W.?: Bobby Garwood Story, The*; Pressure groups; Soviet Union.

Amos 'n' Andy

TYPE OF WORK: Radio and television series
BROADCAST: 1926-1951 (radio); 1951-1953 (television)
CREATORS: Freeman Gosden and Charles Correll
SUBJECT MATTER: Comedy about black life in Harlem
SIGNIFICANCE: After long popularity on radio, the first all-black television version raised objections from black advocacy groups

In 1928 white radio entertainers Freeman Gosden and Charles Correll created the black-dialect characters of Amos Jones and Andy Brown on Chicago's radio station WMAQ, based on their "Sam and Henry" series on Chicago's WGN (1925-1928). In 1929 the radio network of the National Broadcasting Company (NBC) launched the fifteen-minute situation comedy series built on racial stereotypes, exaggerated black dialect, urban poverty, and trickery, which was a near-daily broadcast until 1948, when the Columbia Broadcasting System (CBS) bought the rights to the show and turned it into a one-hour variety program. The show's popularity during the years of the Great Depression was reflected in the fact that Louisiana governor Huey P. Long was nicknamed "The King-fish" after a central character in the show, George "Kingfish" Stephens. At the show's peak, presidents Herbert Hoover and Franklin D. Roosevelt both listened to it, British author George Bernard Shaw praised it, and most American film theaters interrupted their programs in order to let their audiences hear each episode.

Using black actors from 1951 to 1953, CBS televised the series despite the objections of the National Association for the Advancement of Colored People (NAACP). Under this pressure CBS dropped the show's production in 1953; however, it aired reruns until 1966, when NAACP protests finally persuaded CBS to withdraw it altogether. In later years *Amos 'n' Andy* was both praised for its pioneering use of black actors and criticized for stereotyping African Americans. Both Gosden and Correll refused to comment on attacks against their creation.

See also African Americans; National Association for the Advancement of Colored People; Race; Radio; Television; Television networks.

Anaxagoras

Born: c. 500 B.C.E., Clazomenae, Anatolia (now Turkey)
Died: c. 428 B.C.E. Lampsacus (now Turkey)
Identification: Ancient Greek philosopher prosecuted for his impiety and atheism
Significance: A pre-Socratic philosopher credited with advancing scientific philosophy, Anaxagoras was prosecuted for his views

Information about Anaxagoras and his works is incomplete and contradictory. Only fragments of his book on natural history survive; most of these are quoted in the seventh century C.E. writings of Simplicius, who may have quoted them from another source. Others assert that Anaxagoras' book was lost as early as the third century B.C.E. In addition to these fragmentary texts, Aristotle and Plato describe Anaxagoras' concepts and philosophy. From these sources, several contrasting versions of Anaxagoras' works have been constructed. Despite inconsistencies, a general understanding of Anaxagoras' contributions to the philosophy of science does exist.

Anaxagoras' treatise on natural philosophy became a standard text in ancient Athens. In contrast to earlier Greek thinkers, he postulated an infinite number of fundamental elements in the universe, rather than one or a few elements. He also asserted that *nous*, or mind, created the cosmos. According to Anaxagoras, *nous* first formed all of the elements by a process of mixing and revolving. Thus all of "the dark" came together to form the night, all "the fluid" formed the ocean, and all other elements formed similarly. During a second stage flesh and other elements were brought together by *nous* to create living things. Because ethical concerns are not addressed in Anaxagoras' cosmology, it was later criticized by Aristotle and Plato. However, this omission and Anaxagoras' scientific inquiries—such as his discovery of the true cause of eclipses—make him the earliest known natural philosopher, or true scientist.

Around 480 B.C.E. Anaxagoras moved to Athens, where he probably remained for thirty years. While there he attracted a "school" and was accepted in the highest circles. Pericles was one of his students and openly acknowledged his indebtedness to Anaxagoras. Aristotle based part of his work on that of Anaxagoras, some of whose teachings were inserted into drama, either seriously or as subjects for lampoon. Around 433-430 B.C.E., Anaxagoras was prosecuted by Cleon for impiety and atheism. Anaxagoras' statement that the sun was an incandescent stone somewhat larger than the Peloponnese Peninsula was given as the reason for his prosecution; however, it is thought that the prosecution was actually an attack upon Pericles. Pericles was able to save Anaxagoras' life, but could not prevent his exile. Thereafter Anaxagoras resided at Lampsacus where he reestablished his school and continued his work until his death.

See also Aristotle; Athens, ancient; Bacon, Francis; Plato; Science; Socrates.

And God Created Woman

Type of work: Film
Released: 1956 (France); 1957 (United States)
Director: Roger Vadim (1928-   )
Subject matter: A young French woman rebels against the sexual conventions of her village
Significance: The sexual attitudes expressed in the film broke ground for future French films

Roger Vadim was only twenty-eight years old when he directed *And God Created Woman*. He had married the film's star, Brigitte Bardot, in 1952, and had contributed dialogue to a number of undistinguished films in which she appeared. Vadim had received financial backing for his directorial debut in 1955 with the help of the film's producer Raoul Lévy. The screenplay was written by Vadim and Lévy. Released in Paris on November 28, 1956, the film instantly became the center of controversy. French censors had to be convinced that the eroticism of *And God Created Woman* was not too blatant for French audiences. The controversy surrounding the film helped it to become an international success.

Shot on location in Saint-Tropez, *And God Created Woman* launched Bardot as an international sex symbol. While the plot of the film is flawed, it is undeniable that Bardot's bold and reckless sexuality makes the film remarkable. To ensure that the film could enter the United States, Vadim shot alternate versions of some of its most provocative scenes. *And God Created Woman* was a major success in English-speaking countries, especially the United States. Even though the film had no trouble being exhibited in a number of American locations, it ran into legal difficulties in Philadelphia, Pennsylvania. In 1958 Philadelphia's assistant district attorney stated that the film violated a state obscenity law. It was later determined by the state's supreme court that he had overstepped his jurisdiction. Eventually, the distributor of the film argued before the court of equity that *And God Created Woman* rightfully should be exhibited in Philadelphia because it already

The 1958 film And God Created Woman *catapulted French actress Brigitte Bardot to international stardom and helped launch new assaults on the bounds of acceptable sexuality on the screen.* (Museum of Modern Art/Film Stills Archive)

had been found legal by U.S. Customs authorities and that it had been shown in numerous other American locations.

See also *Amants, Les*; Customs laws, U.S.; Foreign Agents Registration Act of 1938; *Ronde, La.*

Andrews, V. C.

BORN: June 6, 1924(?), Portsmouth, Virginia
DIED: December 19, 1986, Virginia Beach, Virginia
IDENTIFICATION: Author of controversial books for young people
SIGNIFICANCE: After Andrews' death, a ghostwriter was hired to continue writing stories under Andrews' name and the legality and ethics of doing so were questioned

Andrews wrote several popular books during her lifetime that were controversial because of their plots about incest and graphic family violence. After she died in 1986, Anita Diamant, her agent, and the head of Simon and Schuster's mass-market division decided to hire a ghostwriter to continue her works. After an unsuccessful attempt by Diamant to write the books herself, professional novelist Andrew Neiderman was hired to carry out the task. Using computers to analyze Andrews' style, Neiderman created several successful new novels. No credit for his authorship was given until the fifth book, in which only an acknowledgment of a "carefully selected writer" to finish the collection was noted. Critics claimed that it was fraudulent to use Andrews' name on works she did not herself write. The legality of doing this was questioned when the Internal Revenue Service declared that marketing these books made the name "V.C. Andrews" itself a taxable asset worth more than one million dollars. Repre-

sentatives for both Andrews' estate and Simon and Schuster argued that the success of the posthumous novels could not have been foreseen, and sued for a tax refund of nearly one million dollars.

See also Books, young adult; Tax laws; Violence.

Anti-Defamation League (ADL)

FOUNDED: 1913
TYPE OF ORGANIZATION: Investigative and educational organization formed to combat discrimination against Jews and later to combat discrimination against all peoples
SIGNIFICANCE: Efforts of the ADL to suppress negative ethnic stereotyping have raised charges of censorship, even within the organization

B'nai B'rith International, the largest Jewish men's service organization in the world, was founded in New York City in 1843 to foster educational and philanthropic causes. Among the many affiliated organizations that it has created is the Anti-Defamation League, which began in 1913 to help strengthen cooperation among religious communities and to monitor anti-Jewish activities.

One of the problems that the ADL has addressed has been negative stereotyping of minorities—especially Jews—in the arts. In fact, the tendency in early twentieth century Vaudeville to depict Jews as comical or as greedy "Shylocks" was a major reason that the ADL was founded in 1913. Since then the ADL has consistently held that depictions of negative Jewish stereotypes do not merit protection as free speech and should be stopped. This policy has, however, always been controversial, even within the ADL, and civil libertarians have frequently complained that the organization's attitude smacks of censorship.

Dramatic depictions of stereotyped Jewish characters such as Fagin in Charles Dickens' *Oliver Twist* and Shylock in William Shakespeare's *The Merchant of Venice* have generated arguments over exactly what constitutes censorship. During the early twentieth century, *The Merchant of Venice* was required reading in many U.S. high schools, and three silent films were adapted from the play between 1908 and 1922 alone. Partly because of ADL pressure, many schools removed the play from their reading lists, substituting other Shakespearean plays. Anti-Semitism in Nazi Germany and the horrors of the ensuing Holocaust made it even more difficult in the United States to produce dramatic adaptations of any works containing anti-Jewish stereotypes. By 1962, however, these horrors had faded enough in the minds of the public for a major production of *The Merchant of Venice* to be staged in New York City. In consideration of the sophistication of modern audiences, and in recognition of the play's stature as a classic, the ADL was content merely to remind the play's producers of their social responsibility in staging it. In contrast, the ADL protested the American Broadcasting Company's airing of a television adaptation of the play to a mass audience in 1974. In a compromise of sorts, Sir Laurence Olivier—who played Shylock in the production—made an opening statement in the hope of neutralizing the play's anti-Semitic undertones.

The Anti-Defamation League has called for stiffer penalties against anti-Semitic graffiti, such as the swastika that Bud Almassy is removing from a Jewish cemetery in Saddle Brook, New Jersey, in 1995. (AP/Wide World Photos)

The sneaking criminal character Fagin in *Oliver Twist* has generated similar controversies. During the first decades of the twentieth century, seven films were adapted from the book. In 1947 a sound version was produced with Alec Guinness playing Fagin. ADL protests convinced the Production Code office of the Motion Picture Association of America to withhold its seal of approval from the film. The damage that this action did to the film's box-office success moved its producers to cut nine and a half minutes of footage from the film. These cuts satisfied the ADL and the MPAA gave the film its seal of approval.

See also Dickens, Charles; Film adaptation; Holocaust, Jewish; Judaism; Music; Pressure groups; Religious education; Shakespeare, William.

Arabian Nights, The

TYPE OF WORK: Book
FIRST COLLECTED: Fifteenth century
AUTHOR: Unknown
SUBJECT MATTER: Collection of Arabic and Persian folktales
SIGNIFICANCE: The diverse subject matter of these classic Middle Eastern stories has frequently been censored and

expurgated in Western attempts to remold them into harmless children's tales

The Arabian Nights' Entertainments (also known as *A Thousand and One Nights*) is a medieval collection of Middle Eastern folktales about heroic figures such as Aladdin, Ali Baba, and Sinbad whose luck and ingenuity carry them through perilous adventures. First collected in the fifteenth century, the stories found their way into Western culture in the early eighteenth century when they were translated into French. The first English edition followed a century later. Since then they have been retranslated and rewritten for both children and adults many times.

Translations have variously recast the stories as moral tales or expanded their exotic and erotic aspects. Sir Richard Francis Burton challenged Great Britain's Obscene Publication Act of 1857 and the obscenity definition laid down by *Bradlaugh v. The Queen* (1872) when he published his own unexpurgated translation of *The Arabian Nights* for private subscribers in London during the mid-1880's.

In May, 1927, an English translation made from the French version of J. C. Mardus by E. Powys Mathers was imported into the United States and seized as obscene by U.S. Customs in New York. Authorization of such action came from a section of the Tariff Act of 1842, which left discretion to the local customs officers, whose decisions were usually held upon appeal to the U.S. Customs Court. Customs rulings were also subject to review by the Treasury Department. Such seizures superseded state and local laws and usually meant a loss of access to the total U.S. market by the importer. These broad powers were challenged by the importer. The Department of the Treasury released the books on the grounds that unexpurgated versions had been imported previously and that new rules were in the process of being drafted.

See also *Bradlaugh v. The Queen*; Burton, Richard Francis; Customs laws, U.S.; Fairy tales; Obscene Publications Acts; Obscenity: sale and possession.

Archaeology

DEFINITION: Scientific study of human artifacts and structures whose interpretation can help to explain the past

SIGNIFICANCE: Archaeological discoveries and interpretations that contradict accepted versions of history have often been subject to censorship

Archaeological excavation yields objective artifacts; these materials are then subjectively interpreted. Interpretations are more often the target of censorship than the artifacts. For example, in thousands of backyards in Texas, one may find fossils of sea life. It is impossible to censor such abundant objective evidence. The interpretation that Texas was once the floor of a sea, however, argues against the biblical account of the creation of the world; such interpretation is often the target of censorship. Censorship in archaeology has appeared in at least two forms: religion and politics.

Religion and Archaeology. Much early archaeology from the 1700's was conducted by Europeans concerned with proving the accuracy of the Bible. A time line based on the creation of the earth related in Genesis was the early framework into which archaeological discoveries were forced. That the earth was created in six literal days was accepted as absolute by the Church as early as the early fourth century C.E. The Genesis chronology of humankind, dating human habitation from the time of Adam to Christ as about four thousand years, influenced scientific thought in Europe for several centuries. This chronology was generally accepted as late as the 1700's.

Additionally most early archaeologists, such as Thomas Blackwell and James Burnett, built their ideas about human development on the medieval notion that all of life was based on the plan of a higher being in which every creature was located in a hierarchical position, with men of Northwest European extraction (as Blackwell and Burnett happened to be) at the pinnacle. Artifacts such as stone tools were explained as thunderbolts and fairy arrows.

The European discovery in the 1500's of the Stone Age people of the Americas began the debate that the stone artifacts found in Europe were truly products of ancient people rather than natural productions. There were thinkers such as Isaac de la Peyrere and John Frere who maintained a greater age for the earth than what could be extrapolated from the Bible.

Evidence for the antiquity of the human race accumulated in spite of opposition, including acts of censorship, from the Church, which was concerned that Christian faith would be undermined if the literal interpretation of Genesis was found to be wrong. The biblical time line was firmly discredited in the late 1800's with the development of fluvial geology. The geological processes that formed stratigraphy, a key in archaeological excavation, were recognized by the late 1600's. This recognition culminated in Charles Lyell's works, including *The Principles of Geology* (1930-1933) and *The Antiquity of Man* (1863). Lyell wrote specifically to refute theories more accommodating to the biblical interpretation of the origin of the world. Charles Darwin's *On the Origin of the Species by Means of Natural Selection* (1859) was widely denounced from pulpits; work such as Lyell's also signalled, at mid-nineteenth century, a clear demarcation between religious and scientific interpretation of the origins of the world.

Lyell's work marked a juncture in archaeology. Some antiquarians continued to use the Bible as the focal point of archaeology, but more began looking objectively at the evidence. During the 1800's, the struggle between the two positions continued as Europeans discovered archaeological sites in Africa and the Americas. For example, the site of Great Zimbabwe in Zimbabwe, Africa, when discovered by Europeans in 1870, was determined to be of Semitic origin, probably built by the biblical Queen of Sheba. The prevailing European belief was that the native African population did not have the capability to build such a superbly crafted structure. In the Americas, great mounds were explored in the Midwest area of the United States. Archaeologists, in a stunning display of Old World chauvinism, credited these mounds, now known to be products of the early Indians of Ohio, to Hindus from India traveling to Mexico. John Lloyd Stephens worked against this biblical bias and maintained that the Mayan cities he discovered were products of local civilizations, not the results of builders from the Old World.

Politics and Archaeology. Old World-centered theories abounded during the 1800's and 1900's. Much archaeological theory of the time came from England. Grafton Elliot Smith proposed that all civilizations proceeded from Egypt. In 1939 Lord Raglan suggested a correction: that all civilizations originated in Sumeria. Other archaeologists worked against these Egypto- and Sumerocentric theories but many, scholar and layperson alike, found such simplistic theories acceptable and comfortable.

During the mid-1800's archaeological theory turned political. This was especially evident in Germany. Gustav Kossinna wrote of the superiority of the Germanic race and substantiated his claims by biased archaeological findings. His theories were the basis for the Nazi precept of Aryan superiority. Prior to the rise of Hitler, prehistoric archaeology had been largely ignored in Germany in favor of classical archaeology. Under Adolf Hitler, prehistoric archaeologists combed the area for "Germanic" artifacts, and wherever "Germanic" sites were found (for example, in Poland and Czechoslovakia) the land was declared to belong to Germany. All excavation was focused on supporting Germany's claim to territory, extending these claims as far into prehistory as possible. Revisionist

German history books of the time showed maps with Germany in the center of great waves of diffused Germanic culture carrying civilization to the rest of the continent. Excavation information that did not support German claims to territory and cultural superiority was suppressed.

Other areas of the world that have been affected by political censorship include China and Guatemala. During the Cultural Revolution in China archaeological sites were viewed as the remains of an antiquated lifestyle, and many were destroyed. In Guatemala, the government attempted to negate the importance of Mayan research with the intent of devaluing the history of the living Maya Indians, whom the government considered racially inferior.

Politics and religion continued to affect archaeology into the 1990's. In the political arena, Germany emerged again. As new museums were built and excavations proceeded, the question arose as to how to portray the Hitler era. Much concern was voiced over whether Nazi sites should be excavated, destroyed, or left buried, and over what the results of each of these actions would be.

Religion again became an issue in archaeology with the Native American Grave Protection and Repatriation Act, signed into effect in 1990. The religious position of many North American Indian groups affected the fate of past and current excavations, and artifacts from both, including human remains. Open archaeological sites such as the Dickson Mounds Museum were forced to close because of protests by American Indian groups against the open-burial exhibits. The Native American Grave Protection and Repatriation Act required human remains to be removed from museums and returned to their tribes of affiliation. Additionally, tribes such as the Hopi and Zuni sued for return of religious objects from museums to their area of origin. With this precedent burial items, which make up a good portion of archaeological artifacts, became reclaimable from museums. —*Susan Ellis-Lopez*

See also Archival laws; Bible; Cultural Revolution, Chinese; Darwin, Charles; Education; Evolution; Germany; Historiography; Maya books, destruction of; Native Americans; Science.

Bibliography

Bettina Arnold's "The Past as Propaganda," in *Archaeology* 45, no. 4 (July-August, 1992) discusses the use of archaeology as a political tool of the 1900's, focusing on Hitler's use of the discipline to justify racist designs. Glyn Daniel's *A Short History of Archaeology* (New York: Thames and Hudson, 1981) is an excellent summary of the evolution of archaeology from its earliest beginnings, the issues confronted, and the men and women who were instrumental in its development. Robert W. Ehrich's "Some Reflections on Archeological Interpretation" in *American Anthropologist* 53, no. 4 (October-December, 1950) is a thoughtful consideration of the goals of archaeology and the means by which those goals are achieved. Roderick J. McIntosh, Susan Keech McIntosh, and Tereba Togola's "People Without History," in *Archaeology* 42, no. 1 (January-February, 1989) focuses on the looting of cultural resources from Third World countries and on the problem of political agendas that deny a valid history to dominated societies.

Archival laws

Definition: Access regulations imposed by governments on stored records

Significance: By restricting outside access to their archives, governments have been able to conceal information about sensitive, controversial, and embarrassing matters

Government archives are historical records of various events, actions, and policies. Most local, state, and national governments maintain archives, though they vary widely. Other archives are maintained by universities, businesses, organizations, and private individuals.

Nearly all governments restrict access to their records in some way, by offering them to only a select group and by maintaining a certain period of time before a particular set of documents may be accessed. In some places, such as the Vatican, records are almost inaccessible to the general public; other nations, such as Sweden, are relatively open in matters not relating to national security.

History of Archives. The first known attempt to record human history in public records was made by the ancient Sumerians in approximately 3500 B.C.E. Laws were recorded on large clay tablets. Their preparation, however, was a laborious process. Archives improved significantly under the ancient Egyptians, who around three thousand years later began to maintain information on papyrus. Preserving data on such material was easier and more efficient, and assisted the Egyptians in everyday matters such as tax collection.

The archives of ancient Egypt, which required most matters to be written on papyrus before they became legal, were extensive. Papyrus disintegrated with the years, however, and although some of the archives contained reading rooms, a forerunner of the modern public library, many documents were available only to certain individuals. Historical events were recorded so as to exclude any criticism of the pharaohs. Alexander the Great kept extensive documents concerning the history of his empire, as did the kings of medieval Europe. The records of the kings in the middle ages were considered protected under the divine right of kings, and could not be accessed by anyone lacking permission of the monarch. Also, their accuracy has been disputed; the archivists were on the royal payroll and dared not record events that exposed the shortcomings of the king.

In some cases, documents were hidden so that there was no trace of mistakes made by a ruler. Such was the case of the notorious Secret Treaty of Dover. In 1670 Charles II, then king of England, made a pact with Louis XIV saying he would declare his allegiance to the Roman Catholic church and help destroy the Dutch Republic. Charles underestimated the strength of the Dutch, however, and was forced to agree on a peace agreement when he could no longer afford to continue the attack on Holland. Fearing discovery of his failed plans, he asked an influential member of his royal court, a baron named Thomas, to hide the only English copy of the treaty in his home.

Although most of these earlier archives were not available to the average citizen, low rates of literacy made them of little interest to the commoner. The French Revolution established

France's national archives, which gave citizens unprecedented access to public files. Following the French Revolution, much of Europe began to follow more open archival policies, for as literacy and democratic awareness increased, so did public interest in government documents.

In Soviet Russia and the rest of Eastern Europe, a large portion of archives were severely damaged in World War II. During communist rule of Eastern Europe, archives were seen as an official organ of the state. Joseph Stalin ordered various czarist documents destroyed, and the manuscripts of dissident writers and historians were burned. Much of the information contained in the archives under Stalin was falsified. Stalin tried to cover up documents showing that Adolf Hitler was dead, believing that he could convince the people of his nation that the West was hiding Hitler. After the fall of the Soviet Union, public records that had been secret became public; spouses discovered that their spouses were on the payroll of secret police; historians began writing histories that made use of accurate documents that had been secret.

Control of History. In many cases, regimes have attempted to control history by manipulating its archival files. Very often, if these records are later opened to the public, they can change the way historians interpret the past. Argentina had long kept its archives regarding the resettlement of Nazi war criminals into their nation tightly closed. Throughout the latter part of the twentieth century, Argentine leaders feared outcry both from the people of Argentina and the international community if the real numbers concerning the hiding of Nazis were released. Argentine President Carlos Saul Menem vowed to open the government's so-called Nazi files in 1991. It was not until strong protest in 1993 over its hesitancy to release the archives, however, that significant documents were made public. Historians, who had earlier thought that several dozen Nazi war criminals had immigrated to Argentina, discovered the number was at least one thousand. The archives also revealed that Martin Bormann, Hitler's deputy, was thought to have lived for some time in northern Argentina. Historians had previously believed that his body had been found in Berlin.

In some countries, archives relating to foreign trade are kept tightly controlled. In the case of South Africa, a 1985 law restricted the release of any information concerning the importation of oil to South Africa. Strong international outcry over its policies of apartheid, and the trade embargo that followed, forced South Africa to keep secret the names of its suppliers. Considered to be the largest underground trade ever, it greatly distorted the trade figures for other nations. Daily records of ships were no longer made public to protect nations willing to forgo the international sanctions and sell oil to South Africa. It was later revealed that the oil sold in secrecy to South Africa was as much as fifteen million tons per year. In 1989 the government prepared a report concerning the effects of the oil embargo, but it was never released to the public.

U.S. Archival Law. In the United States, a national system of archives took place later than in most of Europe. In 1934 the National Archives Act was passed, allowing for the preservation of key documents to serve the needs both of the govern-ment and the public. The Federal Property and Administrative Services Act of 1949 gave the National Archives an expanded role in the management and compilation of government records. This ultimately led to broadening the scope of files maintained, as well as increased efficiency of America's archival system. In 1966 the Freedom of Information Act (FOIA) was passed to provide greater public access to federal government records. Several types of documents (for example, trade and military secrets, and issues of personal privacy) were exempted, however, and the cooperation of federal agencies has been inconsistent. This is particularly true in that some presidents have been more receptive to legislative efforts to increase government records made public, though most have sought more restrictive information policies. Ronald Reagan, for example, often attempted to widen the various types of exemptions to the Freedom of Information Act as they applied to the executive branch. Presidents and other officials have not wanted information that would embarrass the government released.

Although the National Archives, located in Washington, D.C., is open to the public, researchers must agree to adhere to a strict set of regulations concerning the use of its material. Users must first secure a user identification card. The card is given only to persons more than sixteen years old, with a proper photo identification card, and who are engaging in a specific project that can be reasonably pursued at the National Archives. Anyone taking personal notes with them as they examine the documents are required to provide an explanation of why such notes are needed; any notes brought in are subject to limitations or controls by the National Archives staff. Also, any copies of a previously classified document that does not display the declassifying authority will not be allowed out of the National Archives, although this process can usually be done by a staff member. There are numerous other rules and regulations regarding the use of the National Archives. Most of them, however, are common-sense measures to preserve the documents maintained by the archives.

The Library of Congress also serves as an important archival deposit for Americans. Its vast collection includes 36 million manuscripts, including the personal papers of numerous early presidents. It also houses what it claims to be the most extensive film and television archive in the world, as well as various important maps, photographs, audio tapes, art prints and periodicals. In 1992 Librarian of Congress James Billington announced that the public would no longer be allowed to wander through the stacks of books that make up the majority of the library. It is now required that the book be requested by the patron and delivered by a staff member. The library claimed the move was necessary due to increased theft and damage to its holdings.

Controversies in U.S. Archival Law. The Supreme Court has made numerous rulings concerning public access to archives. In *Kissinger v. Reporters Committee for Freedom of the Press* (1980), various groups and individuals sought to claim that taped conversations of former secretary of state Henry Kissinger should be available immediately to journalists under the Freedom of Information Act. Kissinger had donated the tapes to the Library of Congress with the stipulation that they were not to be released for a set period of time. The court ruled that the tapes were not the records of an agency, which, under the provisions of the FOIA, would be subject to immediate release, but rather under the aegis of the office of the president, whose records are excluded from FOIA provisions.

In *Forsham v. Harris, Secretary of Health, Education, and Welfare* (1980), the Supreme Court ruled that data produced by a private organization, even if it is receiving federal funds, is not to be considered agency records under the FOIA. *Department of the Air Force v. Rose* (1976), was the case that forced the United States Air Force Academy to turn over files relating to the academy's Academic Honor Board to a group of law students writing a journal article. The information was not initially provided because the academy claimed it would violate the privacy rights of those involved. The Supreme Court denied this, saying it was sufficient privacy to simply omit the specific names of those involved.

Everyday issues in archival law have generated a number of controversies. The Internal Revenue Service (IRS) has long been criticized by scholars, taxpayers, and other officials for its policy of strict secrecy. In 1995, however, John W. Carlin, the archivist of the United States, issued a report saying that the IRS had failed to turn over important documents that were required by law to be turned over to the National Archives. The IRS claimed that privacy was the reason such documents could not be surrendered, since tax returns constitute confidential information. Carlin insisted that the records be given to him within ninety days, however, saying that he had requested information such as commissioners' files and its annual report, which contain no information about individual tax returns.

—Paul E. Tanner, Jr.

See also Archaeology; Canadian Access to Information Act; Classification of information; Freedom of Information Act; Historiography; Military censorship; Official Secrets Act (Canada); Official Secrets Act (U.K.); Sunshine laws.

BIBLIOGRAPHY

For an overview of the issues concerning restrictions on government archives, see Peter Hernon's *Public Access to Government Information* (Norwood, N.J.: Ablex Publishing Corporation, 1988), which provides information on various legislative and administrative efforts to control government archives. David Sadofsky's *Knowledge as Power: Political and Legal Control of Information* (New York: Praeger, 1990) includes a comprehensive discussion of how statutory regulations restrict access to government records and gives information concerning some of the recent United States Supreme Court decisions relating to freedom of information. *Managing Institutional Archives: Foundational Principles and Practices* (Westport, Conn.: Greenwood Press, 1992), by Richard J. Cox, discusses some of the legal issues involved in the management of private archives, including privacy and access. An excellent reference for comparative information on access to government records and data is Article 19's *Information Freedom and Censorship: World Report 1991* (Chicago: American Library Association, 1991). Another source for international information is the periodic *Freedom of Information: A Compilation* (New York: United Nations Department of Social Affairs, 1950-). For policies concerning the American National Archives, see the U.S. National Archives and Records Administration's *Basic Laws and Authorities of the National Archives and Records Administration* (Washington, D.C.: Government Printing Office, 1986).

Areopagitica

TYPE OF WORK: Essay
PUBLISHED: 1644
AUTHOR: John Milton (1608-1674)
SUBJECT MATTER: An impassioned argument against prior censorship or licensing of books
SIGNIFICANCE: Milton's arguments against prior censorship have gained classic status, and have stood for centuries as a milestone in the history of liberalism

Milton's *Areopagitica* is among the most eloquent protests against prior censorship ever written. Its context lies in the religious politics of seventeenth century England, where the religious cross-currents of the Reformation and the Counter-Reformation inflamed passions, as the French Revolution and Soviet communism did in later centuries.

England's Civil War. The English Civil War began in the summer of 1642 over constitutional and religious issues, pitting Parliament against royalist forces. Fears were rife of religious sectarianism and covert support for Roman Catholicism, especially after a deluge of sectarian books and pamphlets followed Parliament's early noncensorship policy. Parliament responded in 1642 by requiring every publication to bear the name of its printer; but on June 14, 1643, Parliament went even further by requiring approval and licensing of all publications before printing, instituting a regime of prior censorship.

Milton was an ideal writer to respond to Parliament's order. A brilliant student at St. Paul's School in London and at Cambridge University, Milton read Greek, Latin, and Hebrew and was steeped in the Bible and the Greek and Roman classics. Urged to reply to Parliament, Milton published *Areopagitica* without official approval, in November, 1644. His tract's title refers to a speech known as "Logos aeropagitikos" that the ancient Athenian Isocrates addressed to Athens' governing council. This council, drawn from ordinary citizens, had reduced the power of the Areopagus, a council of elders named for the Athenian hill on which it met. Milton's essay did not take Parliament to be the Areopagic council; rather, the Areopagus was the English people, whose powers had been diminished by the censorship order.

Milton's Arguments. Many of the arguments of Milton's essay became classics in the history of modern liberal thought, but they were not all liberal. For example, he did not champion freedom to publish all persuasions, especially Catholicism. Within limits, however, his arguments marked a giant stride on the road to freedom of expression. As demanded by the occasion, Milton cast his arguments in the context of the times. He repeatedly stressed that the practice of prior censorship had been started by the very same religious persuasion that his audience was so keen to condemn—Roman Catholicism—and had been carried even further by the hated Spanish Inquisition. To drive his point home, Milton surveyed the whole of ancient Greek, Roman, and biblical practices, using his immense erudition. He pointed out that although Greece and Rome had condemned libellous material, they had never embraced prior censorship. The Spartan lawgiver Lycurgus even invited residence by foreign poets who might soften the city's crude manners. In the late Roman Republic, Cato the Elder had tried to have Cynic philosophers banished, but the Senate would not permit it.

Only with the Roman church after the year 800 had books been prohibited. The policy had grown stricter in Spain and Italy in the fifteenth century and had been endorsed by the Council of Trent, the conference on Catholic doctrine which had ended in 1563. By then, Milton wrote, "No book, pamphlet, or paper" could be printed unless "approved and licensed under the hands of two or three glutton friars." To underline the evil of the policy, Milton alluded to his poignant 1638 meeting with Galileo Galilei in Florence, where the old man—broken by the Roman Inquisition for endorsing Copernicanism—was living under house arrest.

To Milton, books were not dead things, but they contained "a potency of life." Suppressing a good book is like killing a good person, he wrote, perhaps worse: "Who kills a man kills a reasonable creature, God's image; but he who destroys a good book, kills reason itself, kills the image of God." Suppressing books destroys stored reason and "slays an immortality rather than a life." Truths lost may never be replaced and whole nations suffer in consequence; Protestant England seemed poised for a "second tyranny over learning."

Milton's Second Argument. Milton also praised study as necessary for great spiritual creation, citing Moses, Daniel, and St. Paul as masters of learning. He argued that reading impious material was not dangerous, since "to the pure all things are pure." Bad books no more corrupt a good person than good books alone reform a bad person. The search for truth is among the highest human callings, and its practitioners should neither be discouraged and stultified nor insulted by censorship. Censors, indeed, will often be younger and less learned than the writers they judge.

More important was Milton's emphasis on the nature of moral action and the effect that censorship has on the moral life of the individual. The essence of the moral life is choice. God gave humanity reason and the ability to choose right action as opposed to making all human behavior instinctual, requiring no choice. But censorship seeks to remove moral choice because only the censor chooses. Milton repeatedly argued that censorship treats mature adults as children, unable to exercise reason and choice.

Milton's Third Argument. Milton's final argument was that Parliament's order was useless, since censorship must necessarily be imperfect. If people are to be kept from corruption, shielding them from books will not suffice alone. Their entire experience must be controlled. The moral life, by contrast, must be confronted with temptation and therefore choice:

"I cannot praise a fugitive and cloistered virtue," Milton wrote, "unexercised and unbreathed, that never sallies out and sees her adversary." Virtue that counts is virtue tested: life's trials purify those of good character.

Censorship damps down learning and blunts the ability to reason, slowly strangling truth. Truth benefits in its struggle with falsehood, as good benefits from confrontation with evil. Good and evil cannot be separated by mere mortals. Echoing Saint Augustine, Milton argued that truth and falsehood are inextricably intertwined. Error cannot be eliminated without also removing truth. Censorship implies adherence to orthodox tradition. Far from respecting the past, Milton viewed tradition as an obstacle to furthering truth, which he argued is revealed only gradually, not all at once. Parts of the truth are encompassed by tradition, but cannot be advanced unless writers are free to depart from the past. Truth, moreover, can be anesthetized by tradition into "conforming stupidity."

Areopagitica's Legacy. Read by generations in Western democracies as a signal event in the history of freedom, Milton's essay has been deeply influential. His arguments anticipated Baruch Spinoza's demands for free expression in *Tractatus Theologico-Politicus* (1670), and Immanuel Kant's admonition "dare to know" in "What Is Enlightenment?" (1784)—which also warned readers not to allow others to think for them, and which interpreted "enlightenment" as humanity's passage from childhood to maturity. Above all, Milton's essay influenced John Stuart Mill's *On Liberty* (1859), which consciously adopted various of its arguments, carrying them even further than the poet intended in pleading for freedom of action as well as of thought and expression.

Areopagitica was a significant event in the history of the modern West because it established the idea that censorship attacks elemental human liberties, especially the free use of one's mind. "Give me the liberty to know, to utter, and to argue freely, according to conscience, above all liberties," Milton wrote. His teaching advanced the notion that free inquiry—the search for truth—is an essential well-spring of humanity's spiritual life.

—*Charles F. Bahmueller*

See also Galileo Galilei; *Index Librorum Prohibitorum*; Intellectual freedom; Mill, John Stuart; Milton, John; Reformation, the.

BIBLIOGRAPHY

A helpful account of the *Areopagitica* that locates it in the context of both Milton's life and his era is Emile Saillens' biography *John Milton: Man, Poet, Polemist* (Oxford, England: Basil Blackwell, 1964). Junita J. Whitaker argues that the text develops the theme of censorship as "perverted wisdom and misdirected strength" in " 'The Wars of Truth': Wisdom and Strength in *Areopagitica,*" in James D. Simmonds, ed., *Milton Studies*, vol. 9 (Pittsburgh: University of Pittsburgh Press, 1976).

Argentina

DESCRIPTION: Large and comparatively prosperous South American nation

SIGNIFICANCE: Argentina once had a tradition of an independent press, but government news censorship became a critical issue during two difficult periods in the late twentieth century

Argentina has long been a nation of many paradoxes. With its prosperous grain and cattle industries, extensive public education system, and traditionally strong and independent press, its cultural and social life compared favorably with that of the United States during the early decades of the twentieth century. During the 1940's and afterward, however, Argentina experienced periods of political stress in which the government restricted freedom of expression in newspapers and news magazines in ways that exceeded even the Red Scare excesses occurring in the United States. The apparent paradox of a nation of literate, cultured people caught up in spasms of press censorship and political repression cast an ominous shadow over the history of mass communications and representative government in South America.

The Perón Era. The regime of Juan Perón (1946-1955) and the military government that preceded it were sensitive to criticism in newspapers and news magazines. The military government established a Subsecretariat of Information and Press as a watchdog agency for the national and regional press. In 1943 the Tucumán newspaper *La Unión* and four newspapers in the province of Mendoza closed under pressure from the national government. The Perón administration also challenged its critics in the national and international arena. *Time* magazine in 1947 featured a cover story of Eva Perón, the president's wife and a formidable political figure in her own right. Objecting to *Time*'s story, Perón blocked the magazine's importation and sale in Argentina through the remainder of his tenure in office.

Perón also faced criticism in the pages of *La Prensa*, a venerable conservative newspaper that had been published in Buenos Aires since 1869. The government attempted to intimidate this newspaper and its owner, Alberto Gainza Paz, by mounting public demonstrations against it, organizing a strike by unionized newspaper distributors, and by limiting its vital supply of newsprint. Finally, in 1951 the Argentine legislature voted to expropriate *La Prensa* and then turned it over to the Perón labor unions (it was returned to Gainza Paz after Perón's overthrow in 1955). All these censorship episodes had a chilling effect on journalists throughout Argentina.

The Dirty War. Censorship of the press returned to Argentina during the 1970's so-called "Dirty War." This civil strife grew out of widespread public disappointment and disaffection when Juan Perón's brief return to the presidency in 1973-1974 brought meager results. Inflated prices and a declining economy continued unabated. Leftists formed urban guerrilla bands, such as the Montoneros, and campaigned to undermine the established order through a variety of techniques, including kidnapping of business and political leaders for ransom. Argentine police and the military responded with repressive measures that often resulted in the seizure, interrogation, and, in many cases, the "disappearance" of young leftists, many of whom had little or no involvement in the guerrilla movements. As many as eight to thirty thousand Argentines disappeared in this period. A private organization, the Argentine Anticommunist Alliance, conducted its own terrorist campaign against suspected leftists in addition to the government's campaign.

Because the Montoneros and other leftist guerrillas used propaganda to build support for their movements, the Argentine military and police forces came to believe that any means of mass communication contained the potential to gain recruits for the radicals. These perceived challenges to political stability and national security led military and law enforcement officials to conclude that censorship of newspapers, news magazines, radio, television, and motion pictures was vital for the government's survival. Convinced that their nation was involved in an Armageddon-like conflict with communists, Argentine law enforcement and military officials cracked down on newspapers and magazines that provided news coverage of, or editorial commentary on, insurgent activity. In the heated atmosphere of what became an urban civil war, government intimidation and censorship of the press acquired a draconian character.

The military government used the conservative press to explain its repressive policies. In 1980 and 1981 General Ramón Camps, the military's specialist on anticommunist strategy and tactics, published a series of articles in *La Prensa* expressing an official interpretation of how Moscow orchestrated the spread of international communism from Cuba in 1959 to the continent in the 1960's and 1970's. Camps claimed that the government's campaign attempted to strike at the radical menace before it developed a large enough following to stage a massive rebellion. This campaign included the leftist press. Only a few editors and reporters were arrested, but their sudden seizure, sometimes by persons not wearing uniforms, badges, or other means of identification, generated intense fear among journalists.

The most notorious case of repressive censorship during that period involved Jacobo Timerman, the editor of the newspaper *La Opinión* from 1971 until his imprisonment in April, 1977. Timerman wanted to report on the fate of the leftists who simply disappeared after being arrested. Right-wing elements within the Argentine military kidnapped Timerman, confined him to a prison cell, and subjected him to brutal interrogations, while physically torturing him. Released in 1979, Timerman was one of the few to return from military incarceration during these years. He described his experience in a book that compared Argentina's repressive tactics to conditions in Nazi Germany.

The *Buenos Aires Herald*, an English-language newspaper that began publication in 1876, also fell victim to government intimidation. The *Herald* covered the urban guerrillas in depth and kept a large file of their literature. In both 1975 and 1977 its managing editor, Andrew Graham-Yooll, and its director, Robert Cox, had their offices raided by police. In the first raid the police detained and questioned Graham-Yooll without formal charges. In 1977 police arrested Cox and ransacked his office. He faced interrogation about his connections with the guerrillas and, although he was not brutalized as Timerman was, his arrest and Graham-Yooll's detention served as ominous reminders that press freedom was severely limited.

Conclusions. These episodes of repressive political censorship reveal the fragility of a free press even in nations with high literacy rates and traditions of free expression of ideological diversity. Although analysts have disagreed on the causes of Argentina's political instability, social divisiveness, and economic distress, it is clear that pressures arising from these conditions contributed to an environment in which the press faced severe challenges to its normal role as a source of information and opinion for the general public.

—*John A. Britton*

See also Chapultepec Declaration; Chilling effect; Falkland Islands War; Journalists, violence against; News media censorship; Timerman, Jacobo.

BIBLIOGRAPHY

A summary of censorship in Argentina can be found in Robert Pierce's *Keeping the Flame: Media and Government in Latin America* (New York: Hastings House, 1979). See also Joseph Page, *Perón: A Biography* (New York: Random House, 1983), Robert Crassweller, *Perón and the Enigmas of Argentina* (New York: Norton, 1987). On the Dirty War era see Jacobo Timerman, *Prisoner Without a Name, Cell Without a Number*, trans. by Toby Talbot (New York; Vintage Books, 1982); Richard Gillespie, *Soldiers of Perón* (Oxford, England: Clarendon Press, 1982); Donald Hodges, *Argentina's "Dirty War": An Intellectual Biography* (Austin: University of Texas Press, 1991); and David Rock, *Argentina, 1516-1982: From Spanish Colonization to the Falklands War* (Berkeley: University of California Press, 1985).

Aristophanes

BORN: c. 450 B.C.E., Athens, Greece
DIED: c. 385 B.C.E., Athens, Greece
IDENTIFICATION: Athenian comic playwright
SIGNIFICANCE: Aristophanes was prosecuted and fined for writing a play critical of Athenian foreign policy

The plays of Aristophanes contained scathing attacks on prominent Athenian personalities, as well as on the state of Athens itself, and were therefore controversial and subjected to censorship. He was a contemporary and, perhaps, a friend of Socrates, although his play *The Clouds* ridiculed Socrates and may have contributed to the philosopher's downfall. His plays, invariably witty, contain an odd combination of political satire, scatology, and sexual humor. In the *Lysistrata*, for example, written during war with Sparta, the women of Athens agree not to have sex with their husbands until the men stop fighting. The plot provides much occasion for sexual innuendo and explicit discussions of sex.

Athenian playwrights enjoyed considerable freedom of speech. The laws did forbid them to be impious, but piety was defined narrowly. Aristophanes was therefore able to poke some fun at the gods. For the Athenians, piety was more cultural than cognitive; one was pious if one respected and participated in the religious life of the city. No one was more patriotic in this respect than Aristophanes himself; *The Clouds* is a virulent indictment of the Sophists, who were notoriously scornful of traditional ways and beliefs. His lowbrow humor was not politically dangerous for him. His plays were probably no more ribald than other comedies of the day. Plato con-

demned comedy, but he also condemned poetry generally. Aristotle thought comedy decidedly inferior to tragedy. Neither singled out Aristophanes as particularly pernicious.

However, Aristophanes carried his political satire too far in *The Babylonians*. Produced while Athens was at war, it portrayed Athenian satellite states as Babylonian slaves. This was quite an embarrassment for Athens, especially since the play was seen by representatives of the subject states. Cleon, a powerful Athenian leader, accused Aristophanes of the crime of "injuring the people." The Athenian Council found him guilty and assessed a large fine. Following this censure, Aristophanes was more careful to stay within the law, but he still fearlessly satirized some politicians. He took on his nemesis Cleon in *The Knights*, for example; Cleon responded by trying—unsuccessfully—to have Aristophanes stripped of his citizenship.

Aristophanes' bawdiness earned him the enmity of some later writers, most famously Plutarch, who condemned the dramatist's supposed coarseness and vulgarity. He found Aristophanes' invective to be mean-spirited and unsubtle, and his puns and double-entendres to be childish.

Because of their shocking form of humor, Aristophanes' plays have through the centuries been subject to various forms of censorship. Although the nineteenth century was a time of great interest in Greek and Roman literature, literal translations of Aristophanes' plays were kept from the general public. Another tactic was to translate freely but put the bawdy parts in Latin. Not until the 1950's were accurate translations of Aristophanes available in the United States.

See also Anaxagoras; Aristotle; Athens, ancient; Democritus; Libraries; Literature; Plato; Socrates.

Aristotle

BORN: 384 B.C.E. Stagirus, Chalcidice, Greece
DIED: 322 B.C.E., Chalcis, Euboea, Greece
IDENTIFICATION: Ancient Greek philosopher
SIGNIFICANCE: Aristotle's metaphysical and natural philosophy was condemned by officials of the Roman Catholic church during the thirteenth century

Aristotle was the most comprehensive and systematic philosopher of Western antiquity. Combining empirical observation and logical analysis, he took the natural world as a starting point to inquire into the causes of various observed phenomena. Beyond the separate sciences that he helped to create, Aristotle speculated on the existence and cause of nature itself. His writings on the nature of a supreme being and the eternity of the world later caused medieval Church authorities to suppress some of his works.

Aristotle's Metaphysics. Metaphysics is the study of being—or of ultimate reality. As such, it is science, or knowledge, in the most complete sense. Aristotle's own doctrine on reality is disarmingly simple. What is ultimately real is "substance" or "primary being." Substance is always a particular thing. For example, a certain pencil, a certain table, or a certain tree is real. Although the pencil and the table are made of wood, they cannot be identified with or reduced to "tree," any more than the tree may be reduced to or generalized as "matter." The pencil, table, and tree exist separately and simultaneously, and are thus equally portions of "reality."

Aristotle acknowledges that in order to know any particular thing it is necessary to have an "idea" or "definition" of it. In this, he agreed with his predecessors Socrates and Plato. However, he denies that these "general" things either exist apart from particular objects, or are more real than these objects. There was not, he thought, a separate, superior realm of ideas which caused the visible, tangible world of particular things. Ideas are fully real only insofar as they are inseparable aspects of the things perceived by ordinary common sense.

Common sense perception, however, does not explain change, especially the fact that every particular thing comes into being and eventually ceases to exist. Each thing is real but impermanent. Thus it may appear that the only "thing" which is eternal is change itself. Aristotle holds that change is eternal, as is what change implies—time. That which changes and moves has two sorts of imperfections. Since it changes, it is only equivocally "eternal." Since it moves, it needs that which moves it. This necessitates an "unmoved mover," which is as eternal as that which it moves—the world of motion and change. It is wholly "actual," meaning complete, perfect, and thus unchanging. It is immaterial, since everything material changes, and it is intelligible, since this is both the opposite of the material, and that which moves both material and other intelligent beings. Thus the unmoved mover is both the first and the final cause and, for the best, intelligent beings, the greatest good.

Christian Problems with Aristotelianism. By Christian standards, there is nothing inherently irreverent or atheistic about Aristotle's doctrines on being. On the contrary: It is easy to understand Aristotle's unmoved mover as God. However, Aristotle's thought presented two serious problems to Christian theologians. First, because Aristotle argues that the world known to common sense is eternal, it cannot be the product of divine creation. Second, Aristotle argues that the natural world is not only eternal, but also good. Each particular thing in it is or contains "being." Intelligent beings, moreover, naturally wish to know the "intelligible itself," which is the unmoved mover understood by them to be the greatest good. Human beings as knowledge-seekers are thus naturally the best among a world of naturally good beings.

This appreciation of an eternal natural world, and especially of human beings, contrasts sharply with Christian doctrines of the Creation and the Fall. The Bible's Book of Genesis describes a world created by God; in it the first man and woman disobey His commandment not to eat of the tree of the knowledge of good and evil and are expelled from Paradise. This deep awareness of Original Sin led the great fifth century Christian theologian and philosopher Saint Augustine to prefer the philosophy of Plato to that of Aristotle. Augustine understood Plato and his followers to argue that the visible, sensible world is an imperfect, somewhat shadowy "copy" of divine ideas existing in the mind of God. These ideas are held to be the cause of the natural world, thus supporting doctrines of both divine creation and natural imperfection. This comprehensive metaphysical/theological understanding was termed "exemplarism": It was the prevailing Roman Catholic doctrine through the twelfth century.

The Suppression of Aristotle. Around 1150 C.E., Aristotle's works became widely available in Christian Western Europe. They added substantially to the philosophical controversies occurring in universities at Oxford and Paris. Aristotelian naturalism was seen as endangering the "Augustinian tradition," a loose combination of neo-Platonism and Christian mysticism. The response of the Church to Aristotelian philosophy was as complex as its own far-flung organizational structure. On one hand, the Provincial Council of Paris banned the teaching of Aristotle's "natural philosophy" in 1210; the University of Paris banned Aristotelian works on metaphysics and natural philosophy in 1215; these prohibitions were renewed in 1263. On the other hand, Aristotle's works on logic and ethics were not prohibited; by the mid-thirteenth century lectures were being delivered in Paris on all known Aristotelian works. The papacy "examined" rather than flatly prohibited Aristotle's thought. In 1231, Pope Gregory IX appointed a commission to "correct" Aristotle's works; and, about 1262, Pope Urban IV was very probably aware that William of Moerbeke was translating Aristotelian texts at the Papal Court.

This mixed response makes it evident that the Church's broad policy was to discover whether Aristotelian philosophy could be incorporated into Christian theology. There were two basic reasons for this response. First, as shown, Aristotle's doctrine of the unmoved mover is compatible with Christian theological and spiritual outlooks. Second, as Aristotelian works were introduced and translated, it quickly became obvi-

Aristotle's philosophical legacy retarded the development of science until the Renaissance. (Library of Congress)

ous that Aristotle was a great philosopher. To ban or even heavily censor his works would have meant that the Church was turning permanently against philosophy.

Saint Thomas Aquinas, a thirteenth century Benedictine (later a Dominican) monk, studied Aristotle in order to grasp the validity and the limits of rational philosophy in relation to revealed Christian doctrine. For Thomas, Aristotle's philosophy was true as far as unaided human reason could go. He concluded that the mind can comprehend "Pure Active Being"—Aristotle's unmoved mover—but cannot grasp creation without material, and so he necessarily holds that the world is eternal. Thus, without divine revelation, the Aristotelian philosophical view is completely plausible; given revelation, belief informs reason. By Augustinian standards, Thomas conceded much to secular philosophy. Portions of his thought were constrained in parts of Christendom. In 1277, the Bishop of Paris and the Archbishop of Canterbury condemned several of his propositions. However, following Thomas' canonization in 1323, these censures were withdrawn. Thomas' thought became Roman Catholic doctrine, thus establishing Aristotle's rational and naturalistic outlook in Western Europe.

—*John F. Wilson*

See also Art; Bacon, Roger; Bible; Christianity; Paris, Council of; Plato; Science; Vatican.

BIBLIOGRAPHY

Aristotle presents his concept of the "unmoved mover" in his *Metaphysics* (Ann Arbor: University of Michigan Press, 1960), which is ably discussed by Sir David Ross in *Aristotle* (rev. ed., London: Methuen, 1964). For a discussion of the Augustinian tradition and the medieval enlightenment, see K. E. Kirk, *The Vision of God: The Christian Doctrine of the Summum Bonum* (abridged ed., London: Hodder & Stoughton, 1966). On the Christian suppression of Aristotelianism, see Frederick C. Copleston, *Medieval Philosophy* (New York: Harper & Row, 1961). Etienne Gilson, *Elements of Christian Philosophy* (New York: New American Library, 1963), contains a good discussion of Saint Thomas Aquinas.

Armbands and buttons

DEFINITION: Items that can be worn to express personal views

SIGNIFICANCE: Armbands and buttons are often quiet symbols of differing or unpopular opinions or philosophies

The wearing of black armbands by men has always indicated mourning, an expression of grief. The grief was not necessarily from a death of a person, but the death of an ideal, a law, or an event. Armbands became very visible in the United States with the passing of *Roe v. Wade*, environmental issues, and restrictive immigration laws. People have been censored by being obliged not to wear certain armbands, buttons, or T-shirts; others have been obliged to wear demeaning insignia.

The wearing of swastika armbands by Nazis affirmed that censorship was a Nazi right. The requirement that Jews wear the Star of David patch or armband was an infringement on their freedom of expression, which includes the right not to wear a given article. On liberation of France at the end of World War II, members of the French underground wore armbands with pride. During the Vietnam War, dissidents wore black armbands as a protest against U.S. involvement. A teacher in New York state wore an armband as a gesture of protest against the Vietnam War, assuming his action would be protected by the First Amendment. The local school board fired him. The case was taken to court and the court upheld the teacher's rights of expression. The wearing of an armband or a button proclaiming personal opinions, a punishable offense in other countries, is a choice to Americans.

Political buttons began as a form of electioneering. American companies found the celluloid pinback buttons a good commercial enterprise and soon expanded from politics to advertising. The early buttons were carefully planned to not offend. They were used to sway the reader to vote or buy certain things, but were not offensive. During the Spanish-American War, buttons with a picture of the U.S.S. *Maine* circled with the phrase "Remember the Maine" were common. During World Wars I and II buttons were used to champion causes. Beginning in the 1960's, buttons, banners, and signs with controversial messages became more common.

In the 1990's, there were fewer armbands and buttons on display. They have been overshadowed by bumper stickers and T-shirts. Such displays of political opinion continue to be frowned upon in various settings, for example, the workplace.

See also Advertising as the target of censorship; Bumper stickers; First Amendment; Marching and parading; National Socialism; Offensive language; Symbolic speech.

Armed Forces Radio and Television Service (AFRTS)

FOUNDED: 1942

TYPE OF ORGANIZATION: Broadcasting service for U.S. military personnel

SIGNIFICANCE: The AFRTS has sought to entertain, educate, and inform members of the military services through broadcasts that are free of criticism of the U.S. government

The Armed Forces Radio Service (AFRS) began in 1942, shortly after the United States entered World War II, at a small station in Alaska that provided music from recordings to military personnel stationed there. Its success encouraged the federal War Department to establish its own broadcasting service. AFRS began as a strictly entertainment service, broadcasting music and radio dramas straight from Hollywood to forty-seven countries. Within a few years, however, the War Department's information and education division insisted on using the service to broadcast educational material as well. These materials included science documentaries and programs designed to promote acceptance of cultural diversity among personnel.

All AFRS broadcasts had to be approved by educational authorities and sociological experts appointed by the War Department, as well as by the Office of War Information. The AFRS was mandated to be totally nonpolitical, dedicated as it was to entertainment and education, and local station operators were free to broadcast anything provided by the AFRS or any wire service. The War Department, however, forbade stations to broadcast their own editorial commentaries or any political speeches, although prepared statements from the State Department were acceptable.

In 1954 the AFRS was renamed the Armed Forces Radio and Television Service (AFRTS) and it continued its policy of controlled information.

See also Military censorship; Radio; Radio Free Europe; Voice of America.

Armenian genocide

DATE: April, 1915-1917
PLACE: Anatolia and Mesopotamia, Ottoman Empire
SIGNIFICANCE: Since attempting to exterminate its Armenian population during World War I, Turkey has denied practicing genocide

In April, 1915, Turkish leaders began taking advantage of the crisis of World War I by accusing Turkey's Armenian subjects of collaborating with the Russian enemy. Armenian intellectuals and soldiers were killed and women and children were deported from the Armenian plateau to the southern interior of the Ottoman Empire, where many perished. Between 1915 and 1917 at least half and perhaps as many as 70 percent of the Armenian population of the empire was exterminated.

Turkish authorities used deception to carry out the Armenian genocide, but foreign diplomats, journalists, and missionaries reported the massacres. By May 24, 1915, Russia, France, and Great Britain denounced the killings and warned of punishment. At the Paris Peace Conference, the victorious Allies decided to remove Armenia from Turkish control. After a political revolution in Turkey, the new government of Kemal Atatürk was granted a revised peace treaty in 1923 that mentioned neither Armenians nor the massacres. In 1939 Adolf Hitler boasted that no one remembered the Armenians.

Western scholars soon contributed to the amnesia by either employing sophistry regarding the Turkish actions or by ignoring the genocide. A book by Lewis V. Thomas and Richard N. Frye, *The United States and Turkey and Iran* (1951), praised the forced "Turkification and Moslemization" in Anatolia for creating a homogeneous Turkish republic. An early work on World War I by C. R. M. F. Cruttwell, *A History of the Great War 1914-1918* (1934), includes only one sentence on the massacres of Armenians in 1915. Even a modern survey of the war by Bernadotte E. Schmitt and Harold C. Vedeler, *The World in the Crucible 1914-1919* (1984) only mentions the Armenian genocide in passing in one paragraph dealing with war propaganda.

After 1923 the Turkish government attempted to undermine any attempts to discuss the Armenian genocide. In 1982 Turkey exerted pressure on Israel to eliminate the topic of the Armenian genocide from the International Conference on the Holocaust and Genocide meeting in that country. In 1983 the American movie company MGM announced plans to produce

To commemorate the anniversary of the genocide that began in 1915, Armenian demonstrators burn a Turkish flag in front Turkey's Athens embassy in 1996. (AP/Wide World Photos)

a film on the Armenian tragedy based on Franz Werfel's novel, *The Forty Days of Musa Dagh* (1933). Turkish pressure caused MGM to cancel the project.

Between 1984 and 1990 Turkish efforts concentrated on preventing the U.S. Congress from passing a resolution establishing a day of commemoration for the Armenian genocide. In 1984 a resolution of the House of Representatives on this issue was met by Turkish pressures on American companies and on U.S. interests in the Middle East. In 1990 a Senate resolution sponsored by Robert Dole that would have established a day of commemoration was defeated by a vote of 51-48. Only the disintegration of the Soviet Union after 1991 resulted in the reestablishment of an independent Armenian republic on Turkey's border.

See also Holocaust, Jewish; Turkey; World War I.

Art

DEFINITION: Works such as paintings and sculpture that are created primarily to give pleasure to the eye

SIGNIFICANCE: The ambiguities of visual communication have caused censorship of the arts to be justified on more abstract grounds than other forms of censorship

After Michelangelo completed *The Last Judgment*, his final fresco for the Vatican's Sistine Chapel, in 1541, the work shocked papal conservatives. It upset them, not only because of the human nudity it depicted, but also because of its portrayals of members of the papal court—including an aide to the pope himself—as damned souls. Seventeen years later Pope Paul IV put a partial end to the controversy by commanding Daniele de Volterra to paint drapery over the exposed genitalia in the painting. For his part in this famous, and enduring, instance of art censorship, Volterra was nicknamed "the britches-maker" by his fellow artists. Nevertheless, his additions to the fresco survived intact until the painting was restored in 1990.

Nudity and papal grudges against the artist were not the only reasons for censoring *The Last Judgment*. The act of draping representations of nudity delivered a powerful political message that a new, conservative day had dawned in the papal court and that Renaissance Humanism, with its twin preoccupations with the human form and individual genius, would no longer be tolerated. Since that time *The Last Judgment* has served not only as model of artistic design and execution, but also as an outstanding example of the peculiar nature of art censorship. Michelangelo's work was censored not for its content, but for ideological implications that were no longer in step with the authority who had commissioned it.

Icon. Visual art is perhaps the oldest aesthetic form to be censored. By the time of its Third Dynasty around 3000 B.C.E., the Egyptian Empire had established a rigid set of conventions for artistic representation. Egyptian artists were compelled to paint in a few standard tones and to present figures in profile. The proscription of art in the ancient world took its most uncompromising form among the Hebrews, whose religion forbade graven images. The iconoclasm of Hebrew culture has continued to influence art censorship in the Judeo-Christian and Muslim worlds.

Often it is artwork's iconic value, as much as its alleged indecency, that has inspired censorship. A classic example is Spanish painter Francisco Goya's *Maja Desnuda* (1800), a study of a reclining female nude based upon a sleeping figure in a painting by Titian. Upon public discovery of the painting in 1814, Goya had to defend his work before the Spanish Inquisition, not simply because his female figure was nude, but also because she was awake—radiating a lack of shame in her femininity and sexuality. Edouard Manet's painting *Olympia* (1863), prohibited from the Paris Salon, stirred a similar controversy when exhibited at the Salon des Refuses because it portrayed a courtesan of the day in the pose of a Renaissance goddess.

The coupling of iconic value with homoerotic content fed the 1991 controversy surrounding an exhibition of Robert Mapplethorpe's homoerotic photographs that was funded by the National Endowment for the Arts (NEA). To present a figure as an icon is not simply to confer on it public acceptance of whatever the figure might symbolize, but also to ground that acceptance in the authority of its model. Hence the angry reactions of cultural conservatives such as North Carolina's Senator Jesse Helms, who punished the NEA by slightly reducing its annual funding.

Iconoclasm. Much like the Soviet dictators of the twentieth century, the ancient Egyptian pharaohs frequently erased hieroglyphic references or obliterated art works that depicted rivals or predecessors. Thutmose III (c. 1400 B.C.E.) ordered the destruction of all artworks depicting his co-regent Queen Hatshepsut. Such wholesale destruction accounts for one of the oldest, and surely the most effective, forms of censorship. The motives behind such acts are best understood when one considers the ideological importance of the artwork destroyed. To destroy a work of art is often to destroy a political and cultural symbol. When the Vandals (whose destructive habits inspired the term "vandalism") sacked Rome in 455 C.E., they destroyed numerous artworks in order to dispirit the Romans. The Paris Communards of 1871, under the leadership of painter Gustave Courbet, demolished the Vendome Column to symbolize the end of the Bourbon dynasty. In 1989 China's communist government sought to quell a prodemocracy demonstration in Beijing's Tiananmen Square by bulldozing its symbol: a hastily constructed statue of Liberty.

The term "iconoclast" derives from an eighth-ninth century party faction the Eastern Orthodox church that—in its zeal to distance itself from the Roman Catholic church—attempted to forbid all holy images and the rituals associated with them (for example, kissing icons). During the Protestant Reformation, Martin Luther specifically targeted what he called the idolatry of the Roman church. Luther's followers destroyed innumerable church artworks (stained glass windows, tapestries, sculptures, carvings, illuminated manuscripts, and relics) as their first order of business in reforming the church. The Catholic church itself practiced iconoclasm against the illustrated Mayan and Aztec codices in their campaign to convert the New World in the sixteenth century.

Organized destruction of artworks has also been undertaken on moral or aesthetic grounds. At times the destruction has

Pope John Paul II celebrates mass in the Sistine Chapel in 1994, shortly after completion of a fourteen-year project to restore Michelangelo's Last Judgment *frescoes to their original, uncensored glory.* (AP/Wide World Photos)

resulted from the indignation of a single offended individual. In 1900 temperance activist Carrie Nation not only smashed the liquor bottles but also a revealing painting of Cleopatra behind the bar in the Hotel Carey in Wichita, Kansas. Adolf Hitler, himself formerly a painter, combined anti-Semitism with an antimodernist aesthetic when he objected to what the Nazis called the degenerate art of 1930's Germany. Three years prior to his final solution for the Jews, Hitler allowed Hermann Göring to "sterilize" German museums and exhibits of all modern art by "un-German" artists.

The Censors. Like most censorship, that of art has been largely reactive. The exceptions to this rule are the totalitarian states (as various as ancient Egypt, seventeenth century France, Adolf Hitler's Germany, and Joseph Stalin's Soviet Union) that have established official boards or academies to inspect and approve all artwork on public display. In nations without prior restraint on art, self-appointed crusaders have often been influential in acts of censorship. Anthony Comstock's late nineteenth century New York Society for the Suppression of Vice, for example, targeted indecent art as well as literature. Comstock established his reputation in 1884 when his testimony helped convict a young shop clerk of violating antiobscenity laws. At issue were reproductions of contemporary French paintings that had recently been displayed in a Philadelphia art museum. By 1913 the vice crusader unwittingly became an enterprising art promoter's best friend when, on a tip from the promoter, he investigated Paul Chabas' *September Morn* (1912). Comstock's campaign helped to make the painting—which featured a girl bathing nude—a *cause célèbre* that eventually sold more than seven million reproductions.

Book Illustrations and Album Cover Art. Book illustrations and record album cover art have led to numerous instances of censorship—even when the contents of the books or records themselves have been deemed harmless. In 1959, for example, the public library in Montgomery, Alabama, removed the children's book *The Rabbits' Wedding* (1958) from open circulation when white patrons objected that the male rabbit was black and his bride was white. In 1964 a Human Relations Council in Lincoln, Nebraska, objected to the stereotyped illustration of black people in the picture-book *Little Black Sambo* (1943) and lobbied successfully to have it removed from the local public school system.

A number of rock music albums have been recalled on the basis of cover art alone. The most famous instance is probably the original cover of a Beatles album, on which the band members posed in butchers' smocks with pieces of raw meat and bloody human dolls. Unlike most art objects, books and records are created for mass reproduction; their censorship usually involves attempts by elites to prevent socially destabilizing information and ideas from reaching mass audiences. However, art objects such as paintings and sculptures have traditionally been unique and solitary creations primarily available to the elite that can afford them.

Although reproductions of classic works of art have been available in the form of black-and-white engravings since the eighteenth century. Inexpensive full-color facsimiles became readily available only in the twentieth century. Even in the nineteenth century, which witnessed the first establishment of public museums, access to original artworks was, by comparison to the twentieth century, severely limited. The arrival of an art-viewing public and the concomitant need to protect them from indecent or aesthetically revolting art did not occur until the mid-nineteenth and twentieth centuries.

Is It Art? The debate over whether an object is a work of art or not has led to notable examples of censorship. A typical reason for censoring something is that it is not "art," but rather trash, pornography, or the like. In 1926 U.S. Customs classified Constantin Brancusi's modernist sculpture *Bird in Space* as a taxable piece of hardware rather than a duty-free art object. The artist brought a lawsuit against the United States and won reclassification in a customs appeal court.

The modernists were not the first to face this most fundamental form of censorship: the denial of an object its status as art. Rebuffed by the state-sanctioned Beaux Arts Academy, the French Impressionists had to coordinate their own salon, the salon of rejects, in order to present their work for the public. Their resulting 1863 show won more opponents than adherents—critics warning that the new style might strike unwitting viewers blind or drive them mad. Manet's *Le Déjeuner sur l'herbe* (1863) was singled out for denunciation, not only because it depicted a shamelessly nude woman in the presence of two fully dressed men, but because of its "amateurish" lack of three-dimensional perspective.

Impressionism remained embattled in the decades that followed. In 1878 the American painter James McNeill Whistler sued English critic John Ruskin for libel. In a London review Ruskin had declared Whistler's *Nocturne in Black and Gold: The Falling Rocket* (1874) a "wilful imposture" of legitimate art. Whistler won a pyrrhic victory; however, his one farthing in damages did little to cover the cost of his suit. Little did such critics as Ruskin know that abstract, abstract expressionist, minimalist, and conceptual art were to come; many have criticized such schools for producing works that are not art.

The question of whether something is art has been raised in connection with performance art, an avant-garde movement that combines conceptualism and multimedia presentation with live drama. On several occasions during a tour of college campuses in the 1980's Vito Acconci was prevented by school authorities from finishing a piece in which he hid under a ramp and masturbated while verbally fantasizing, through a loudspeaker, about members of the audience above him.

Censorship of Reproductions. Artworks, produced for and admired by one culture or era, have been censored when displayed by another. More often than not in such cases, copies, replicas, or facsimiles of original artworks have fallen victim to censors. The best-known victim of modern censorship has probably been Michelangelo's *David*. In response to protests in Orange County, California, a fig leaf was added to a marble replica of the statue at the Forest Lawn Memorial Park in 1937. Three decades later the Beverly Hills vice squad seized a replica without a fig leaf from a local art gallery, and a poster of the statue was removed from a Sydney, Australia, bookstore on charges of obscenity. Some artworks controversial in their original cultures have remained so. Goya's *Maja Desnuda* raised a new volley of protest when it appeared on a Spanish postage stamp in 1930. As late as 1959 the U.S. postmaster generally refused to forward letters with the offending Spanish stamp. An almost life-sized reproduction of Goya's painting was moved, after protest, from the men's room in a hotel restaurant at Los Angeles International Airport to the men's room in the same chain's airport hotel in Honolulu, where a similar controversy arose.

Political Cartoons. Censorship of political cartoons dates back to the eighteenth century, when the first newspapers and regularly published journals appeared. British caricaturist James Gillray was jailed in 1796 for publishing a print that satirized the financial motive behind the Prince of Wales' recent marriage to Caroline of Brunswick. The charges against him were eventually dropped, but his case shows how the threat of prosecution is at times a more effective means of censorship than an outright ban. For example, in the United States, the Sedition Act of 1798, which banned "false, scandalous or malicious criticism" of the government, included political cartoons.

During a politically unstable time in France in 1832, Honoré Daumier was fined five hundred francs and sentenced to six months in jail for drawing a cartoon titled "Gargantua" that depicted King Louis Philippe consuming the nation's wealth while excreting privileges. Charles Philipon, publisher of the weekly *La Caricature*, for which Daumier's drawing was intended, was also fined and jailed, even though the offending cartoon was never printed. The regime then declared an outright ban on all political cartoons that lasted until 1848.

In the United States political cartoons have generally been considered speech that is protected under the First Amendment. This has often led to attempts at censorship that have avoided the word "censorship." In 1870, for example, New York City's corrupt political machine leader William "Boss" Tweed reportedly offered Thomas Nast a million dollars to stop drawing the damaging series of cartoons attacking him. Nast refused and his cartoons helped precipitate Tweed's downfall.

Such methods of persuasion have often taken even more blunt forms. In 1945 General George S. Patton pressured army sergeant Bill Mauldin, whose cartoons in the armed forces newspaper *Stars and Stripes* had received a Pulitzer Prize, to soften his often satirical tone so as not to undermine troop morale. Mauldin resisted, although his work was not protected by the First Amendment because he did his work as a member of the U.S. armed forces. On occasion public figures lampooned in political cartoons have sought recourse in libel suits. President Richard Nixon won such a 1969 suit against a Connecticut student who had published an obscene caricature of him. Normally, however, libel has been difficult to prove in political cartoons. An 1808 decision in an English law court established ridicule as a "fit weapon of criticism."

Public Art. As in the case of *The Last Judgment*, censorship of art has often originated with patrons who have commissioned artworks. Such censorship has been a relatively straightforward affair in privately commissioned work. How-

ever, the public art of the Western democracies, ultimately commissioned by taxpayers, has led to bitter controversies. In 1945, for example, citizens of Kennebunkport, Maine, raised a thousand dollars to commission a new mural by a Maine artist to replace a federally funded work that had been painted in the style of Mexican Diego Rivera. Several murals commissioned by the Federal Art Project of the Works Progress Administration were whitewashed over for similar reasons by unappreciative citizens in cities, such as Columbus, Ohio. In 1955 residents of Los Angeles sought unsuccessfully to remove a Giocometti-inspired sculpture, *The Family*, that had been commissioned for the city's police department headquarters. On the other hand, anticommunists were successful in their efforts to remove murals from San Francisco's Coit Tower that included portraits of resentful workers, one of whom carried a book by Karl Marx.   *—Luke A. Powers*

See also Beatles, the; Caricature; Daumier, Honoré; Degenerate Art Exhibition; *Little Black Sambo*; Manet, Edouard; Mapplethorpe, Robert; Maya books, destruction of; Michelangelo; Mural art; National Endowment for the Arts; Performance art; Postage stamps; Whistler, James Abbott McNeill.

BIBLIOGRAPHY

The most exhaustive work on this subject remains Jane Clapp's *Art Censorship: A Chronology of Proscribed and Prescribed Art* (Metuchen, N.J.: Scarecrow Press, 1972), which provides a simple chronicle. Moshe Carmilly offers a provocative intellectual history in *Fear of Art: Censorship and Freedom of Expression in Art* (New York: R. R. Bowker, 1986). In *Pornography and Obscenity* (Yonkers, N.Y.: Alicat Book Shop, 1948), censored painter and novelist D. H. Lawrence makes a crucial distinction in a classic defense of artistic freedom. Herbert Read's *The Meaning of Art* (Winchester, Mass.: Faber & Faber, 1951) is an accessible introduction on the ideological nature of art, as is John Berger's playful *Ways of Seeing* (London: Penguin, 1972).

Article 19

FOUNDED: 1986

TYPE OF ORGANIZATION: London-based international human rights organization that promotes freedom of expression and information

SIGNIFICANCE: Article 19 has monitored censorship in all forms of media throughout the world

Registered as a charity within the United Kingdom, Article 19 took its name from Article 19 of the United Nations' Universal Declaration of Human Rights, which states:

> Everyone has the right to freedom of opinion and expression; this right includes freedom to hold opinions without interference and to seek, receive and impart information and ideas through any media and regardless of frontiers.

Acting as a watchdog of censorship issues through a worldwide network of correspondents, the organization has brought violations of free expression to the attention of appropriate local officials in various countries, while publicizing such violations worldwide. It has also sent representatives to various councils addressing censorship issues, and it has worked

UNIVERSAL DECLARATION OF HUMAN RIGHTS

In 1948 the General Assembly of the United Nations unanimously adopted the Universal Declaration of Human Rights, a document containing thirty numbered articles spelling out rights that all nations should regard as inalienable. Three of its articles pertain directly to free expression:

Article 18

Everyone has the right to freedom of thought, conscience and religion; this right includes freedom to change his religion or belief, and freedom, either alone or in community with others and in public or private, to manifest his religion or belief in teaching, practice, worship and observance.

Article 19

Everyone has the right to freedom of opinion and expression; this right includes freedom to hold opinions without interference and to seek, receive and impart information and ideas through any media and regardless of frontiers.

Article 20

1. Everyone has the right to freedom of peaceful assembly and association.
2. No one may be compelled to belong to an association.

In 1966 the U.N. General Assembly gave the Universal Declaration of Human Rights the force of law by redrafting it as the International Covenant on Civil and Political Rights (ICCPR). Member states that sign this covenant acknowledge a legal obligation to honor each of its articles. States that sign an optional protocol open themselves to legal action by citizens who claim that their rights under the covenant have been violated. By the early 1990's 92 of the 164 U.N. member nations had signed the covenant and 51 of these had signed the protocol.

Source: Charles Humana, comp. *World Human Rights Guide.* 3d ed. New York: Oxford University Press, 1992.

directly for the release of persons imprisoned or otherwise sanctioned by governmental acts of censorship. The organization publishes *Article 19 Bulletin* and monographs on free speech suppression and censorship in various countries, and it has issued surveys of information freedom and censorship worldwide in regular *Article 19 World Reports.* During the 1990's its *Article 19 Commentary Series* issued a dozen reports each year, prepared on a country-by-country basis matching reports on the same countries by the U.N. Human Rights Committee.

Article 19 has also publicized the detentions of persons peacefully expressing opinions; the torturing, killing, or deportation of journalists; book confiscations; arrests of politicians; and closings of newspapers and broadcast stations. Specific cases have included the death sentence that Iran issued against author Salman Rushdie. Article 19 has also publicized more subtle violations of free expression, such as "standards" effectively censoring information on sex, violence, obscenity, and indecency that range from film classification to outright bans. Other violations that it has exposed include misuses of libel and privacy laws, laws appealing to national security or restricting access to information or limitations silencing government employees, standards of "blasphemy," restrictions on access to radio and satellite bands, wartime military news blackouts, limitations on printing presses and supplies, political embargoes that include bans on the importation of books, denial of food relief to protesting antigovernment minorities, limitations on "hate speech" and terrorist statements, cultures of secrecy that promote self-censorship, and the subtle informal censorship enforced by social ostracism and economic control.

Although dictatorships have often been cited for their use of force and blatant censorship, Article 19 has also drawn attention to the use of immigration law and deportation in the United Kingdom and censorship embodied in flag desecration laws in the United States.

Although support of freedom of expression is a recognized part of international law, including the International Covenant on Civil and Political Rights of the United Nations and the European Convention on Human Rights, the implementation of such rights has varied widely due to varying cultural standards of rights, security, and morals.

See also Blasphemy laws; Classification of information; Flag burning; Free speech; Immigration laws; Police states; Rushdie, Salman; *Spycatcher*; United Kingdom.

Asian Americans

DESCRIPTION: Americans of Asian origin or descent
SIGNIFICANCE: Asian Americans have been subject to many subtle forms of censorship

Throughout much of American history, the silencing of Asian perspectives has been so complete that there have been few occasions for open and official acts of censorship against Asians. Asian Americans have been talked or written about; rarely, until recent times, have they been allowed the opportunity or the means to talk or to write for themselves.

It is true that Asian Americans have always addressed one another, in print as well as in speaking, from the earliest days of Asian immigration. In 1854 Chinese Americans founded the *Golden Hill News*, featuring reports from China. Such forms of expression, however, were of little interest, at that time, to the larger society.

Official, conscious censorship is a form of recognition. It involves recognizing that views are important enough to be banned. Asian Americans, however, have been largely invisible and inaudible in American history. To hear Asian voices, one must turn to sources such as the poems scratched into the walls of detention cells and benches in places such as Angel Island in San Francisco Bay. The censorship of Asian American voices has not, for the most part, involved laws forbidding individual pieces of writing. It has been the consignment of an entire segment of the American population to silence.

On occasion the majority population and the government have taken active steps to take away the voices of the Asian minority. In 1854 the California Supreme Court, in *People v. Hall*, barred Chinese witnesses from giving testimony in court, preventing Chinese from testifying against a white man accused of murdering a Chinese man. The court declared that the Asians were "a race of people whom nature has marked as inferior, and who are incapable of progress or intellectual development beyond a certain point." Since Asian Americans have been such a small and silenced part of the population, there have been only a few occasions in which they have been subject to open censorship. During World War II, it may be argued that Japanese Americans became the most censored segment of the American population in the twentieth century in the United States. Not only were portrayals of Japanese people required to conform to the standards of propaganda, Japanese American publications were subjected to rigorous oversight and the Japanese Americans of the West Coast were placed into camps where censorship was a part of everyday life.

Two topics dominate contemporary issues of censorship relevant to Asian Americans. First, it may be contended that the English-only movement, which seeks to require by law that English be the only officially allowed language for elections and other public events, is actually a form of censorship. Since so many Asian Americans speak languages other than English, this would deprive many of them of the ability to make their voices heard. Second, as a minority group, Asian Americans have an interest in "positive censorship," or efforts to discourage or forbid stereotypical, racist portrayals of minorities.

Japanese in World War II. At the beginning of World War II, Army Chief of Staff George C. Marshall asked the famous Hollywood director Frank Capra to make a series of orientation films for American soldiers. Known as *Why We Fight*, the purpose of the series was to inform the soldiers about the war and to inspire them with a sense of mission. The entire series was under the control of its sponsor, the War Department, and the War Department used its power of censorship to ensure that Capra's films were conveying the desired messages. Each script had to be approved by about fifty military and civilian agencies in Washington, D.C.

The series became popular even in the civilian population. In the first film the Japanese Army was shown as a group of brutal subhumans marching down Pennsylvania Avenue after a Japanese victory. The final film was made after the war in Europe was ending and the U.S. had turned its full attention to the Pacific, but plans for the film had been made as early as 1942. The last film was delayed because of disagreements between the scriptwriters and the army censors about how the Japanese should be portrayed. Many of the scriptwriters favored casting the military leaders of Japan as the real enemy

and presenting ordinary Japanese people in a sympathetic light. The U.S. Army, on the other hand, preferred showing all Japanese as enemies. The War Department rejected script after script as too sympathetic to the Japanese people. In the end, the Japanese were shown largely as stereotyped, mindless masses, subservient to the will of their military overlords. The film, however, was taken out of circulation immediately after it was released. The censors had delayed its making for too long, and shortly after its completion the atomic bombs were dropped on Japan and the war came to an end.

As the American military image of the Japanese changed from one of invading subhumans to one of obedient little brothers under the occupation, the goals of control of expression changed. General Douglas MacArthur's headquarters ordered the film withdrawn from circulation. It did not become public again until the 1970's, when film buffs discovered it.

Internment. During World War II, Japanese Americans became perhaps the most completely censored people in the United States. Part of this censorship was aimed at Japanese language publications in the United States. Under the Espionage Act, which had been passed during World War I, the U.S. Post Office had the power to inspect all materials to be mailed for subversive contents and to reject as unmailable any judged to be unacceptable. Foreign-language publications, especially those published in Japanese, German, or Italian, came under close inspection. In February of 1942, the postmaster of Fresno, California, wrote his superiors to tell them that he was requiring *The Japanese Times of California*, a small Japanese language weekly newspaper, to furnish translations of all articles appearing in each issue. These translations had to be accompanied by a signed affidavit from the editor swearing that the translations were accurate.

Unlike German or Italian Americans, however, Japanese Americans became subject to much wider and more intrusive forms of government control and censorship. Following the attack on Pearl Harbor, Secretary of the Navy Frank Knox claimed, without any evidence, that the success of the Japanese attack had been due to information provided by Japanese Americans acting as spies. The War Department suggested that all Japanese Americans should be interned.

Popular opinion on the West Coast supported the relocation of Japanese Americans. Newspapers, radios, and other forms of media fanned popular anti-Japanese American sentiment. Although government studies of the attitudes of Japanese Americans, such as the Munson Report, indicated that these citizens were overwhelmingly loyal to the U.S. Government, these studies were suppressed. In February, 1942, President Franklin Roosevelt signed Executive Order 9066, which provided for the evacuation and detention of Americans of Japanese ancestry.

In these concentration camps, called "relocation centers," Japanese Americans lived under the complete control of military authorities, and all means of public expression were censored by these authorities. Camp newspapers, such as the *Tanforan Totalizer* at the Tanforan Assembly Center, had to clear all stories before publication. At this same center, when the children of the camp junior high school chose red and white as their school colors, the Federal Bureau of Investigation immediately declared the colors "subversive," since they were the same as the colors in the Japanese flag.

English-Only Movement. The languages of Asian Americans helped to silence their voices during much of American history. In recent years, a movement to make English the only legal language in official American public life has threatened to silence them once again. The 1990 U.S. Census showed that 44 percent of Asian Americans living in New York City did not speak English well. Adoption of an enforced official language can effectively censor such Asian Americans by making it impossible for them to express themselves in a manner that can be heard. In the 1992 presidential election, about 30 percent of Chinese American voters used bilingual ballots in casting their votes. If English were to become the only language allowed for public activities such as voting, many if not all of these voters would have been unheard and the Chinese American vote would have been much less. If languages other than English are forbidden in courtrooms, this could have the effect of the *People v. Hall* decision in nineteenth century California: It could provide a barrier to the participation of Asian Americans in the nation's legal system.

Positive Censorship? Limits on freedom of expression are usually looked upon as undesirable by Americans. However, it may be important to distinguish between truthful expression and false expression, between honest opinions and slander. Freedom of speech is never absolute: those who knowingly publish false and damaging statements about others can be convicted of libel under U.S. law. Moreover, there is a close connection between violence in speech or writing and acts of violence.

During the 1870's, tirades against Chinese immigrants in newspapers and by politicians were followed by widespread acts of assault against these early Chinese Americans, including anti-Chinese riots in San Francisco and in other cities. Contemporary anti-Asian speech and violence has not been as dramatic, but the connection between the two seems to continue to exist. Stereotypes and caricatures of Asians, especially of Japanese, have become more common since the downturn of the American economy in the 1980's. These stereotypical images may, in part, be responsible for the rising level of hate crimes against Asians, which reached about nine thousand reported crimes in 1992, according to statistics compiled under the federal Hate Crimes Statistics Act.

The forbidding of hate speech against Asian Americans, as well as against other groups, has had its critics. One of the most vocal critics of the forbidding of hate speech on college campuses, Dinesh D'Souza, is an Asian American born in India. In his book *Illiberal Education: The Politics of Race and Sex on Campus* (1991), D'Souza accuses universities of censoring speech and writing assumed to be offensive to women and members of racial minorities. This form of political correctness, D'Souza claims, limits free discussion on college campuses and actually makes them more intolerant places.

Among the cases of politically correct censorship described by D'Souza is the case of an Asian American college student, Nina Wu. In 1989 Wu was expelled from her dormitory at the University of Connecticut after she put up a humorous poster on her door listing categories of people who were unwelcome. The poster contained a reference to gay people that the university found unacceptable. Wu was allowed to reenter her dormitory only after she filed suit. *—Carl L. Bankston III*

See also Hate laws; Language laws; Political correctness; Propaganda; Race; Tokyo Rose; World War II.

BIBLIOGRAPHY

Sucheng Chan's *Asian Americans* (New York: Twayne, 1991) gives a good overall history of Asian people in the United States. *Asian Americans and the Supreme Court* (Westport, Conn.: Greenwood Press, 1992), edited by Hyung-Chan Kim, provides major documents dealing with the civil rights history of Asian Americans. Michi Weglyn's *Years of Infamy* (New York: Morrow, 1976) offers the history of Japanese American internment during World War II and a description of life in America's relocation camps. *Language Loyalties* (Chicago: University of Chicago Press, 1992), edited by James Crawford, is a collection of opposing viewpoints on the English-only controversy. Dinesh D'Souza's *Illiberal Education* (New York: Free Press, 1991) presents the view that political correctness on college campuses is a form of censorship. Darrell Hamamoto's *Monitored Peril* (Minneapolis: University of Minnesota Press, 1994) discusses the representation of Asian Americans on American television.

Assembly, right of

DEFINITION: The right of citizens to gather together to express opinions, including protests of government policies

SIGNIFICANCE: The "right of the people peaceably to assemble" is one of the basic freedoms of the First Amendment to the U.S. Constitution

The right of assembly and the companion right of petition are protected by the First Amendment to the U.S. Constitution. Together, they round out the idea of participatory democracy held by the Founders, helping to protect free citizen pursuit of "the redress of grievances."

Initially, the right of assembly could not be applied to actions of states, because the First Amendment limited only Congress from making any law that dealt with the rights of assembly and petition. This situation existed until the post-Civil War passage of the Fourteenth Amendment, which guaranteed that no state could enforce any law that could "abridge the privileges or immunities of citizens of the United States; nor shall any State deprive any person of life, liberty, or property, without due process of law; nor deny to any person within its jurisdiction the equal protection of the laws." It was this provision, part of a cluster of amendments that freed and enfranchised former slaves, that applied the Bill of Rights—and, consequently, the rights of assembly and petition—to the states.

The first judicial enforcement of individual rights to assembly came in the Supreme Court's 1875 decision in *United States v. Cruikshank*. In his opinion, Chief Justice Morrison Waite noted that the right of assembly was, however, restricted by the limitation expressed in the Bill of Rights that an assembly be peaceful and for "lawful purpose."

The notion that constitutionally protected assembly must be peaceable is built into numerous federal and state court opinions; the right to assemble without peaceful intent is not deemed to be absolute. The right to assemble has thus been subject to, among other things, reasonable police regulations. Court actions limiting the behavior of protesters picketing abortion clinics have been upheld by the Supreme Court in *Madsen v. Women's Health Center* (1994).

Most state constitutions have articles that guarantee the right of peaceable assembly and petition. Thirty-eight states guarantee one or more such rights in their constitutions; eight of those states guarantee the right of petition, and one, Maryland, guarantees the right of petition but not that of assembly. Three states, Minnesota, New Mexico, and Oregon, do not prescribe a constitutional right of assembly, peaceable or otherwise, or a right of petition for their citizens. Those states rely on general statements that empower citizens.

See also Demonstrations; First Amendment; Fourteenth Amendment; Free speech; Marching and parading; Picketing.

Associated Press (AP)

FOUNDED: 1848

TYPE OF ORGANIZATION: American news-gathering service that supplies subscribing members with timely coverage of events

SIGNIFICANCE: The universal recognition of the Associated Press has given it the ability to create a news coverage agenda

The number and variety of media outlets (newspapers, broadcast stations, cable channels) leads one to believe that the world has a diverse media system. In fact, much of the news presented on any outlet comes from wire services. In the United States the single largest content provider is the Associated Press (AP). Even competing news services, including those operated by some of the country's largest newspapers and broadcast networks, rely on AP to set the agenda for story prominence.

AP has been the gatekeeper of U.S. news since the mid-1800's. Increased literacy, industrialization, improved communication technology, and a changing definition of news (from partisan content to nonpartisan content) are some of the reasons for the founding of AP. It was to serve as a news gathering cooperative to allow publishers to improve the quality of coverage and reduce news gathering costs. Members received timely coverage of domestic and international stories written in objective language.

AP has increased worldwide information flow. During World War I, AP helped break a news cartel created by France's Havas news agency and Britain's Reuters. (The French government had prohibited distribution of news about German successes in World War I, and that prohibition extended to international clients of Havas.) AP was not, however, established to promote the universal free flow of information. Members have been severely penalized for violating their agreements with AP. Threat of antitrust action from the attorney general forced AP in 1915 to begin allowing members to receive news reports from other wire services.

The governance history of AP suggests that rank-and-file subscribers once had little power. In 1943 a federal district court found that financial investments by ninety-nine of AP's 1,247 members provided them control over the election of AP Board of Directors. Board members' actions reflected the interests of more wealthy members of AP. One notable news dissemination controversy was whether AP should service the new and growing radio industry. Newspapers owning radio stations wanted to receive AP service; stations without radio properties opposed aiding a potential competitor. In turn, AP recognized that radio networks might lead to independent news-gathering organizations in competition with AP. The AP board in 1933 approved radio stations' broadcasting AP news bulletins. Not until 1946 did AP create associate memberships for radio and television stations.

Federal Judge Learned Hand in *United States v. Associated Press* (1943) found the AP in restraint of commerce for prohibiting members from relaying news they collected to parties other than the AP. Hand's decision supported the dissemination of news from as many sources as possible. Broad dissemination of news he concluded was virtually part of the First Amendment.

AP has monitored dissemination of its information to prohibit appropriation by nonmembers, but the prospect of AP's censoring coverage of significant news events is unlikely. AP may be the single largest U.S. news provider but other newspaper and television wire services in the United States and the world zealously cover the news. A multiplicity of news gathering increases the likelihood of newsworthy events receiving coverage.

News reporting, whether done by AP or another news agency, involves critical decision making and perhaps indirect censorship. The act of news reporting requires reporters and editors to make decisions about newsworthiness, including determining not only whether a story is reported but how much time or space a news medium devotes to reporting the story.

See also Cable News Network; Campaign for Press and Broadcasting Freedom; News media censorship; United Kingdom.

Astronomy

DEFINITION: Scientific study of celestial bodies

SIGNIFICANCE: Efforts to impede the progress of astronomy by various kinds of censure and censorship have occurred throughout history, but have seldom been successful for very long and have sometimes even aided astronomy's development

Astronomy has often come into conflict with prevailing religious ideas and has occasionally suffered from attempts to hinder its progress. In the ancient world celestial bodies were often worshipped as deities, and efforts to understand and explain them as natural phenomena were viewed as impious attacks on religion. The medieval synthesis of Christianity with Aristotelian science in the thirteenth century clashed with later innovations in astronomy, leading to theological conflicts with the Roman Catholic church and official censorship.

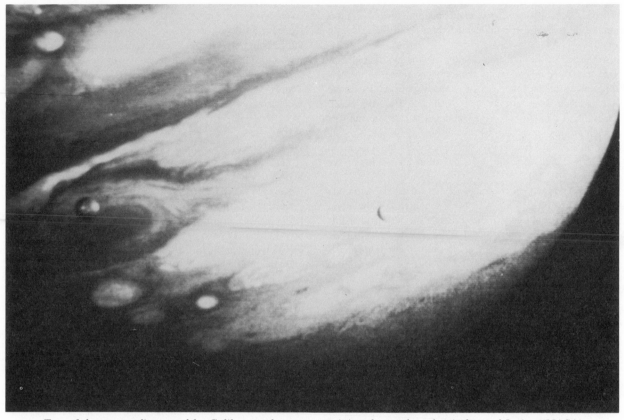

Two of the moons discovered by Galileo can be seen transitting the southern hemisphere of Jupiter. (NASA)

Ancient and Medieval Astronomy. At Athens in the fifth century B.C.E., Anaxagoras taught that celestial bodies were not deities but material objects. He claimed that the moon was made of earth and the sun was a flaming stone, explaining for the first time that the phases of the moon were the result of reflected light from the sun. As a result, he was persecuted for impiety and he was jailed and banished from Athens. Some years later, Meletus accused Socrates at his trial in 399 B.C.E. of teaching that the sun is a stone and the moon is made of earth. In his unsuccessful defense, Socrates credited Anaxagoras with these teachings. Plato was finally able to remove the scandal associated with these ideas and to obtain their general acceptance.

In the third century B.C.E., Aristarchus of Samos taught that the earth revolved around the sun, leading to his later reputation as the Copernicus of antiquity. In his dialogue "On the Face in the Round of the Moon" (in *Moralia*, c. 100 C.E.), Plutarch asserts that Cleanthes, the second head of the Stoic school, thought that Aristarchus ought to be indicted on a charge of impiety for putting the earth in motion. This was contrary to the then-popular geocentric view of the world. Renowned astronomer Nicolaus Copernicus learned of Aristarchus' ideas from this source.

In the thirteenth century, the idea of the permanence and perfection of the heavens was revived within Christendom by the work of Thomas Aquinas in his great synthesis of Aristotelian science with Christian theology. In 1277, at the instigation of Pope John XXI, the Bishop of Paris, Etienne Tempier, issued a blanket condemnation of 219 propositions along with the penalty of excommunication for holding any one of them. Many of the propositions involved Aristotelian science, including: God could not make several worlds, God could not produce something new, God could not make a vacuum, and the elements are eternal. Such ideas impose limits on the absolute power of God. In spite of this condemnation, the influence of Aristotelian science continued for more than three centuries, partly because of the growing acceptance of the Thomistic synthesis by theologians. In fact, the condemnation only applied locally and was finally annulled in 1325. It has been suggested that the condemnation had a positive effect on astronomy because it forced scientists to think in new ways and to entertain possibilities that Aristotelian science had considered impossible, namely, that perhaps God could make several worlds, and so on.

The Scientific Revolution. The demise of Aristotelian science began with the revival of heliocentric theory by Copernicus in the sixteenth century, although more than a century passed before the theory was widely accepted. Copernicus delayed publication of his controversial book until the year of his death in 1543 but experienced no opposition from the Roman Catholic church. In 1559 Pope Paul IV issued the first official *Index Librorum Prohibitorum*, which did not ban any works related to Copernican theory. Pope Pius V established the Congregation of the Index to oversee censorship in 1571, but no Catholic astronomers worked under the formal prohibitions of the *Index* or the Inquisition throughout the sixteenth century.

At the end of the sixteenth century, several natural philosophers came under scrutiny by the Inquisition. One of the few Copernicans at the time was Giordano Bruno, who was the first to teach that stars are suns with their own populated planets, and that the universe contained an infinite number of such worlds spread throughout infinite space. He was arrested in 1592 for his pantheistic ideas by the Inquisition. In 1600 he was burned at the stake and all of his writings were prohibited.

In 1609 Galileo Galilei became the first to use the telescope to study the heavens. His discovery of mountains on the moon and sunspots convinced him that Aristotle was wrong in claiming the perfection of the celestial realm. His discovery of the moons of Jupiter and the phases of Venus supported his growing Copernican convictions. Although these discoveries did not actually prove the heliocentric theory, he began to argue more strongly that the earth moves around the sun. In 1616 Galileo was warned by the Holy Office and the idea of a moving earth was expressly condemned. Copernicus' book, *The Revolutions of Celestial Orbs* (1543), was placed on the *Index*, but Galileo and his works were spared condemnation.

After the election of Pope Urban VIII in 1623, Galileo received permission to write about the motion of the earth as a scientific hypothesis. He submitted his manuscript to the chief censor at Rome in 1630 and was given permission to publish it after several minor revisions. His masterpiece, the *Dialogue on the Two Chief World Systems*, appeared in 1632 with a concluding paragraph, suggested by Pope Urban, that the Copernican theory was neither true nor conclusive. Galileo put these words in the mouth of a character called Simplicio, who represented Galileo's scholastic opposition. Sale of the book was stopped and Galileo was summoned to Rome. After trial by the Inquisition in 1633, he was judged guilty and the book was totally forbidden. On June 22, 1636, at the age of seventy, he was required to kneel before the tribunal and recant his belief in the reality of the Copernican system. He was then sentenced to house arrest at his country estate, with no visitors allowed except by special permission.

As a result of Galileo's conviction, progress in astronomy shifted from Italy to Northern Europe and England. After Isaac Newton and others had confirmed the heliocentric system of the planets, Copernicus' book was removed from the Index of Prohibited Books in 1832 and Catholics were allowed to teach Copernicanism with complete freedom. —*Joseph L. Spradley*

See also Anaxagoras; Aristotle; Censorship; Copernicus, Nicolaus; Galileo Galilei; *Index Librorum Prohibitorum*; Intellectual freedom; Science; UFO evidence.

BIBLIOGRAPHY

Anthony M. Alioto, *A History of Western Science* (Englewood Cliffs, N.J.: Prentice-Hall, 1987), discusses several science-religion conflicts in a balanced way. John William Draper, *History of the Conflict Between Religion and Science* (3d ed. New York: D. Appleton, 1875), and Andrew Dickson White, *A History of the Warfare of Science with Theology* (New York: D. Appleton, 1896), are classics with strongly biased views against religion. David C. Lindberg and Ronald L. Numbers, eds., *God and Nature* (Berkeley: University of California Press, 1986), features excellent scholarship on science-religion issues. Joseph L. Spradley, *Visions That Shaped the Universe* (Dubuque, Iowa: Wm. C. Brown, 1995), emphasizes relations between science and religion.

Atheism

DEFINITION: Conscious disbelief in any sort of gods or supernatural beings

SIGNIFICANCE: Historically subject to censorship, atheism has also been the official creed of totalitarian regimes that have censored religious expression

Blunt professions of atheism emerged in late seventeenth century Europe. Previously, "atheism" also meant "heresy" and served two main rhetorical purposes—either as an expression of theoretical atheism, often mentioned only for subsequent pious refutation, or as an especially freighted invective to hurl at an enemy. A number of early modern cultural factors helped to make atheism intellectually viable. European exploration and trade increased contact with non-European cultures and non-Western religions, familiarizing Europe with radically different systems of belief. This new cosmopolitanism eroded some of the inevitability of believing in God. In addition, the revival and adaptation of ancient materialistic philosophies for scientific purposes provided the means for a nontheological cosmogony. Most important, perhaps, was the Protestant Reformation, which shattered the relative uniformity of religious thought and culture in Europe.

The social and religious discord unleashed by the Reformation promoted vast intellectual and institutional change, not least of which the growth of atheism. Francis Bacon, as early as 1612, recognized the ironic trajectory of the Reformation. He pointed out that, if religion were divided into two or more factions (especially warring factions, as the case was in Europe), some people were bound to renounce both sides. In such a climate, arguments and name-calling wielded against one's religious enemies sometimes served to subvert belief among one's co-religionists.

Religion and Liberalism. The unrest the Reformation wrought upon Europe also changed the political landscape. To contain the disastrous effects of protracted religious conflict, a set of related political ideas gradually took root in Europe. Gradually, it became less frequent that people were put to death for heresy. Philosophers and political theorists developed the concepts of universal political rights and religious tolerance, which eventually culminated in liberalism, with its wall of separation between church and state. Political rights grant protection to citizens regardless of their religious views. Toleration ensures for religious minorities peaceful coexistence. The liberal doctrine of separation of church and state has three elements. The principle of liberty obligates the state to permit the practice of any religion that does not infringe on the other rights the state must protect. The principle of equality prevents the state from favoring one religion over another. Lastly, the principle of neutrality prevents the state from favoring the religious over the nonreligious. These innovations, viewed as needed reforms, were designed to preserve civic concord and prevent baneful conflict while acknowledging religious difference.

Atheism Censored. That these proposed reforms did not secure immediate assent or implementation helps account for the fact that open, avowed atheism did not appear on the European continent until 1770 with the publication of Baron d'Holbach's *System of Nature*, and in England until 1782 with the pseudonymously authored *Answer to Dr. Priestly's Letters to a Philosophical Unbeliever*. Another reason for the slowness of atheism to appear after the events that precipitated it is the near-universal eighteenth century belief that atheism led inexorably to socially pernicious moral license. "Free thought," the common eighteenth century English term to designate all sorts of religious unorthodoxy, including atheism, draws attention to the political and social implications of atheism. Originally, "freethinker" made reference to a general mode of inquiry not bound by scholastic precedent, but by 1700 it came to designate religious views in self-conscious violation of judicial or legislative precedent. To its bearer the term ascribed defiance of the censorship of unorthodox speculation. It advertised liberty of inquiry from both overt state sponsored suppression and the coercion exerted by the boundaries of conventional thought. This term's ubiquity in the eighteenth century attests to the nascent state of liberalism and toleration. Significantly, both the German and the French languages adopted a translated equivalent for "free thought."

Early modern European governments commonly resisted liberal neutrality. In France, freethinkers were often forced to publish in Holland and the atheism of Denis Diderot's *Letter on the Blind* (1749) cost him six months in prison. In England the Act of 1697 "for the effectual suppressing of blasphemy and profaneness" made it criminal to "deny any one of the persons in the holy Trinity to be God, or . . . assert or maintain there are more Gods than one, or deny the Christian religion to be true, or the holy Scriptures of the Old and New Testament to be of divine authority." Thomas Woolston died in prison after prosecution in 1729 for his *Discourses Our Saviour's Miraculous Power of Healing*, which was published in 1730. Designed to promote orthodoxy and aimed primarily at the deists (those who admit a creator deity, but deny God's providence—that is, his control or interest in the physical events or moral affairs of the universe), the Blasphemy Act ironically served to promote atheism. Strong evidence suggests that Richard Carlile, imprisoned in 1823, Jacob Holyoake, who in 1842 was the last individual imprisoned for atheism in Britain, and Charles Bradlaugh, who was charged with atheism in 1868, all, in response to their persecution, either actually became atheists or were strengthened in their atheistic convictions. The same dynamic influenced Britain's most famous atheist, Percy Bysshe Shelley, who while not persecuted by the government, became hardened in his atheism after being expelled from Oxford for having penned *The Necessity of Atheism* (1811).

In twentieth century America, public education has become the arena for conflict about censorship and atheism. In 1963 Madalyn Murray O'Hair, an outspoken atheist, brought suit against the city of Baltimore, charging that required prayer in school violated the constitution's wall of separation. Reaffirming an earlier ruling, the Supreme Court in *Murray v. Curlett* ruled in her favor, citing the first amendment establishment clause (that the government not legislate "respecting establishment of religion"). Since the mid-1970's Christian Fundamentalists have contended that this interpretation of the wall of separation, through the school culture and curriculum which it promotes, in effect violates the principle of neutrality. They characterize the schools as imbued with "secular humanism," an antireligious outlook which arrogates for humanity God's rightful place. Accordingly, they have recently fought to restore a forum for prayer in school and to include creation science (biblical creationism clothed unbecomingly in the protocols of science), in the curriculum.

Atheism Censoring. In the twentieth century governments have actively transgressed the principle of neutrality, not to suppress atheism, but rather to promote it. The Soviet Union makes a case in point. The Bolshevism that emerged dominant after the Russian Revolution subscribed to a version of Marxism that explains religion as an illusion of the oppressed class, fostered by the bourgeoisie. Religion of any kind officially became an obstacle to socialist equality. Early Bolshevik legislation, nevertheless, has a distinctly liberal ring to it. Article 13 of the 1918 constitution of the Russian Soviet Federated Socialist Republic permitted both religious and antireligious propaganda. The same year the Decree on the Separation of Church from State and School from Church was enacted. Within a few years, however, the principle of neutrality was broached. In 1928 the Bolsheviks actually put the Bible itself on trial. The 1929 Law on Religious Associations further eviscerated the earlier liberalism. This legislation forbade religious instruction outside the home to anyone under the age of eighteen, prohibited religious libraries and reading rooms, and suspended the constitutional right to religious propaganda. This latter provision meant that Bibles and religious journals could no longer be published. Through these legal means and through means more covert, the Soviet Union actively suppressed religion throughout its history.

—*Matthew C. Bagger*

See also Bacon, Francis; *Bradlaugh v. The Queen*; Communism; Death; Diderot, Denis; Heresy; Hobbes, Thomas; O'Hair, Madalyn Murray; Reformation, the; Religion; Shelley, Percy Bysshe; Soviet Union.

BIBLIOGRAPHY

John Stuart Mill's *On Liberty* (Indianapolis, Ind.: Hackett, 1978) is the classic statement of liberalism. Michael J. Buckley's *At the Origins of Modern Atheism* (New Haven, Conn.: Yale University Press, 1987) argues that the church employed ill-advised strategies in combatting atheism. David Berman, *A History of Atheism in Britain* (London: Routledge, 1988), contains much useful information. Eugene B. Shirley, Jr., and Michael Rowe, eds., *Candle in the Wind: Religion in the Soviet Union* (Washington, D.C.: Ethics and Public Policy Center, 1989) is a collection of essays published prior to the Soviet Union's collapse.

Athens, ancient

DESCRIPTION: Independent Greek city-state that flourished between the ninth and fourth centuries B.C.E.

SIGNIFICANCE: Although ancient Athens is recognized for encouraging intellectual freedom, it serves as a reminder that perhaps no society can be totally free from censorship

Long credited with being the birthplace of Western democracy, Athens was unique among the city-states of ancient Greece for its commitment to intellectual freedom. European and Asian scholars gravitated to this center of learning to study, teach, and create some of the finest art and literature in the history of Western civilization. Few great artists, philosophers, scientists, and writers of the time did not enjoy the freedom Athens provided. Nowhere else in the ancient world could citizens attend state-sponsored religious festivals in which large parts of comic plays were given over to the lampooning of cherished political institutions and popular political leaders, even in the midst of bitterly fought wars.

Other Greek city-states were not as open-minded. The autocratic city-state of Sparta, for example, banned certain forms of poetry, music, and dance out of fear that they might undermine masculinity and promote a libertine disregard for moral behavior. However, it would be a mistake to regard democratic Athens as a totally nonrepressive society. It was, after all, a jury of Athenians that condemned to death Socrates, the great philosopher who laid the philosophical foundations for Western culture. In 399 B.C.E. Socrates was indicted for impiety—a charge concocted by his political enemies. Probably because blatant censorship would have offended the democratic sensibilities of the Athenian public, no law existed prohibiting the free expression of ideas. So in those rare instances when intellectual censorship was exercised, it was usually under the guise of impiety, a charge for which there was far-reaching precedent.

As far back as Athens' first comprehensive code of law, which had been written in the seventh century B.C.E., piety was required for religious observances. Around the year 438 B.C.E. the Athenian assembly passed legislation forbidding investigation of the heavens, requiring offenders to stand trial for impiety. This law was directed against the scientist Anaxagoras, who had to flee the city to avoid prosecution. About a quarter of a century later, the poet known as Diagoras the Atheist was also forced to flee Athens for mocking the Eleusinian Mysteries, the cult of the city in honor of the "Earth mother." The persecutions of Socrates, Anaxagoras, and Diagoras demonstrate an intolerant streak in what was generally an open and freedom-loving culture.

It is also important to realize that one of the most potent forms of censorship is the silencing of certain members of the population by failing to recognize their right to express ideas and opinions. This was what most Athenians experienced. Only native-born males were considered "citizens." Women, slaves, and resident aliens could never hope to enjoy the full fruits of Athenian freedom. Censorship has been practiced in every society, and ancient Athens was no exception.

See also Atheism; Censorship; Intellectual freedom; Roman Empire; Socrates.

Atomic Energy Act of 1954

ENACTED: August 30, 1954

PLACE: United States (national)

SIGNIFICANCE: This statute regulating all atomic and nuclear-related materials and publications has been used to censor persons who might discover how to build nuclear weapons

The Atomic Energy Act of 1954 was developed as a revision to the 1946 Atomic Energy Act to establish guidelines for atomic energy. Prompted by growing public concern about the safety of atomic energy, one provision in the act allowed the government to block any nuclear-related information from being published if it jeopardized national security. Much controversy arose over what kind of material should be considered dangerous enough to be censored. In addition, the article attempted to block information yet to be discovered from being revealed or published. Critics argued that this provision was too difficult to enforce and contradicted the First Amendment.

In case of *United States v. the Progressive, Inc., et al.*, Howard Morland, an independent physicist, discovered the basic design for an H-bomb, which he proposed to publish in *The Progressive* magazine in early 1979. When news of this reached the government, they sought a temporary restraining order. The government argued that the findings could accelerate the efforts of an individual or other country to develop a weapon and, if the individual or country had the resources, a working weapon could be built and used. Morland's attorneys argued that he had a constitutional right to publish the material.

The court instructed both sides to work together to develop a version of Morland's article that could be published and satisfy both sides. After the parties failed to reach a compromise, the court issued a temporary injunction. This decision centered on the central issue of whether the article in the 1954 Atomic Energy Act listed clear and specific criteria on what type of material posed a serious threat to security. In the court's opinion, Morland's paper clearly violated the 1954 Atomic Energy Act, thereby warranting a temporary injunction.

Although the government temporarily succeeded in preventing Morland's entire article from being published, it could not prevent the central portion of the article from being published. An article containing the same essential information was sent as a letter to the editor of the University of Wisconsin student newspaper, which published it in an edition of several hundred copies. The government then secured another injunction and attempted to recover all the copies, but failed to do so. Since the essential information was now public, Attorney General Benjamin Civiletti eventually decided to drop the case against Morland and *The Progressive*.

See also Classification of information; "H-Bomb Secret, The"; Military censorship; National security; Nuclear research and testing.

Attorney General's Commission on Pornography

DATE: 1986

PLACE: Washington, D.C.

SIGNIFICANCE: Conservatives, feminists, and religious leaders were among those who supported the commission and the creation of a division within the Department of Justice to attack pornography

The Attorney General's Commission on Pornography produced a conservative, procensorship document. Such a result was predictable given the members of the commission. The panel included Fundamentalist Christian psychologist James Dobson, three current or former prosecutors who had specialized in obscenity cases—including Alan Sears, legal counsel for the antipornography group Citizens for Decency Through Law—another law professor whose long-held position was that pornography is not constitutionally protected, two experts on sex offenders whose work had focused on the pornography-sexual violence connection, a child abuse expert, and Father Bruce Ritter, a priest who worked with runaways in New York City (he later left his ministry after being charged with child sexual abuse).

The final report relied on four major points to come to its conclusion that pornography was indeed dangerous and should be subject to additional government prosecution and control. The first point was the testimony of those who had been harmed by the effects of pornography. The second was psychological laboratory research concerning the effects of viewing pornographic materials. The third point was investigation of what was available in adult bookstores. The fourth point was the views toward pornography that the panel members brought with them. Each of these points was challenged by opponents of the report.

The commission held public hearings in six major cities; those opposed to pornography were permitted to dominate the sessions. Those who testified included seventy-four law enforcement representatives, fourteen abused children, ten representatives of religious organizations, nine antipornography groups, seven antipornography feminists, six self-described former porn addicts, and five abused wives. Andrea Dworkin, Catharine MacKinnon, Dorchen Leidholdt, Deborah Chalfie, and Martha Langelan all testified, the last three as representatives of Feminists Against Pornography. Others who gave testimony were Terese Stanton, Judith Reisman, and Linda Marchiano.

The commission had neither the time nor the money to do new empirical psychological research into the effects of pornography on viewers. Despite the many criticisms of existing research, the commission drew only upon extant studies to make its unambiguous claim that sexually violent pornographic material had negative effects on attitude and behavior, and was quite likely to lead to sexual assaults against women. When pornography effects researchers such as Neil Malamuth, Edward Donnerstein, Daniel Linz, Dolf Zillman, and Kathryn Kelley discovered how the commission had used their data, they quickly rushed to disavow any connection with the commission's findings.

In order to determine the extent and types of pornography currently available the commission employed two vice detectives from Washington, D.C., who visited adult bookstores in a small number of major cities. Their findings, and particularly the way they were presented in the report, led to several criticisms that the commission wanted to present erotic materials in the worst possible light. The findings consisted of lists of 2,325 magazine titles, 725 book titles, and 2,370 film titles. At no point was a content analysis done of the films or magazines. Instead, the report simply listed cities in which the following types of pornography could be purchased: depictions of sex between humans and animals; urination and defecation; bondage, rape, and sexual violence; sex with amputees; and simulated child sex. The percentages that each of these categories represented of the available total was never stated.

The commission's tendency to incorporate their own biases and moralize about pornography appears most clearly in its discussion of nonviolent and nondegrading materials—which they argued was a small percentage of the available market in porn in comparison to violent and degrading materials. The commission focused on the fact that these materials were antifamily.

The final report was sharply criticized by civil libertarians and social scientists—and even two commission members—when it was released. Commission members Judith Becker and Ellen Levine criticized the lack of concise definitions of pornography and antisocial behavior. They were particularly disturbed by certain commissioners' desire to include such sexual practices as masturbation, homosexuality between consenting adults, or premarital sex as forms of antisocial behavior.

The final report included eighty-nine suggestions for actions that could be taken by the federal government, state and local governments, and private citizens to restrict the free availability of pornographic materials. These included calls for new statutes, increased law enforcement activities, the use of new forfeiture penalties, citizen boycotts of pornography outlets, and so on. Federal government activities geared toward the elimination of pornographic materials increased significantly after the publication of the report.

See also Censorship; Terrorism.

Australia

DESCRIPTION: Continent in Oceania whose British colonies became a single independent nation in 1901

SIGNIFICANCE: Australia's history of freedom of speech and censorship has many parallels with those of the United States and Great Britain

Australia was first colonized by Great Britain in the late eighteenth century, when the British founded a penal colony at Botany Bay. Eventually, the continent, along with the neighboring island of Tasmania, was divided into seven British colonies. Australia remained sparsely populated, however, until after the gold rush of 1851. When the Australian colonies separated from British rule in 1901, they unified under a parliamentary democracy, following the ideals incorporated in English common law, and incorporating the guarantees embodied in the U.S. Constitution. Partly for these reasons, Australia's subsequent experience with censorship has been similar to that of Great Britain and the United States.

Censorship of film, for example, has been controlled by the Commonwealth Film Censorship Board that was established in 1917. This board classifies films in a manner similar to that of the Motion Picture Association of America. The classifications include G, for general audiences; NRC, no one under age twelve admitted; M, age fifteen and over only; and R, no one between ages two and eighteen admitted. Only the R rating is a prohibition governed by law; the other ratings are advisory. Films may also be refused licenses due to their indecency or obscenity; potential to incite crime or undermine morality; or their possible offensiveness to an ally of Australia or to the people of any nation which—like Australia—recognizes the British monarchy as its head of state. Only about 2.5 percent of films are refused licenses—most of them for obscenity.

Australia's Queensland state, in the northeast, has added its own regulations to the national film regulations. The state has a film review board that reviews all complaints against films. As a result, many R-rated movies are not distributed in Queensland.

In 1982 Australia's parliament passed a Freedom of Information Act modeled on that of the United States that gave citizens and reporters access to documents and incorrect government records. However several significant areas were exempted from the act, including national security and defense documents, documents related to international relations, internal cabinet documents, and documents made prior to the passage of the bill.

Obscenity restrictions are handled by both the national government and the states. The Commonwealth deals with imported materials and prohibits the importation of materials that are blasphemous, indecent or obscene, or which unduly emphasize sex, horror, violence, or crime. The state governments handle the publication, advertising, and distribution of materials produced domestically, and regulations vary significantly from state to state.

In general, Australia has had a free press, but with limitations in two areas. The police have the power to request a suppression order against the publication of court evidence, which some believe can be used to limit genuine grievances against the government. Also, a few powerful people dominate the commercial networks, sometimes called a "government-sanctioned oligopoly." The newspaper industry has had a similar limitation, in that one corporation has controlled 50 percent of national newspaper circulation.

In May, 1993, the Conservation Council of Western Australia, a coalition of sixty-seven environmental groups, accused the Department of Conservation and Land Management of using the peer review process to censor and suppress papers critical of the government's management of the region's forests. The government has denied these charges and pointed to significant papers that were published that contradicted the government's policies.

See also Blasphemy laws; Courtrooms; Film advisory board; Film censorship; Freedom of Information Act.

Automobile safety news

DEFINITION: Media attention directed toward the safety of automobiles

SIGNIFICANCE: Automobile manufacturers have attempted to censor potentially damaging information regarding automobile safety

Drivers ignoring unsafe conditions in a central California dust storm contributed to a mass collision involving more than a hundred vehicles in November, 1986. (AP/Wide World Photos)

Knowing which automobiles have serious defects is important to consumers and is newsworthy information. The automobile industry is a major American institution having almost iconic status during most of its history. The industry has campaigned since its beginning to persuade consumers that its automobiles are of the highest quality and safe. Not until the mid-1960's, with the publication of Ralph Nader's *Unsafe at Any Speed* (1965) did the self-protection capabilities of the auto industry become apparent. Nader's premise was that the industry is indifferent to public safety. During congressional hearings, the General Motors Corporation admitted having hired investigators to harass and intimidate Nader. Nader was nevertheless instrumental in increasing consumer rights, actively supporting the passage of the National Traffic and Motor Vehicle Safety Act (1966). Since the 1960's, the media have become very effective in influencing consumer behavior. In the mid-

1980's, Columbia Broadcasting System's news show *60 Minutes* raised concerns about the Audi 5000 and its possible unintended acceleration problems. Audi's sales plunged after the broadcast and never fully recovered.

The automobile industry has used various means to censor damaging information, including filing lawsuits and lobbying lawmakers. To avoid public trials, the industry has paid large sums of money to people injured in automobile crashes. To avoid public hearings, the industry has also negotiated expensive settlements with the National Highway Traffic Safety Administration (NHTSA), the organization responsible for monitoring automobile safety and recommending vehicle recalls as defects become known.

Auto manufacturers have complained that fraudulent reporting harms their ability to sell automobiles. In the early 1990's, for example, National Broadcasting Company (NBC) televised a segment on General Motors' pickup trucks manufactured between 1973 through 1987. The news show *Dateline NBC* presented images of the truck erupting into flames as another vehicle struck its side. They claimed that the gas tanks were mounted in the wrong place, causing explosions upon impact. *Dateline* failed to mention that the fire was caused by an explosive device placed against the tank by the consultants performing the test. General Motors filed a defamation suit and withdrew it after NBC made a public apology. Thus, the industry has also been the victim of news organizations intent on obtaining a leading story.

The auto industry has gone, however, to great lengths to censor public access to safety information. In the early 1990's, the NHTSA accused Toyota of violating a federal law. Toyota's Land Cruiser model may have had problems with a part inside the fuel tank breaking off and punching holes in the tank. The NHTSA accused Toyota of quietly repairing some vehicles under a secret warranty program, without giving the notification required by law. When the NHTSA decided to hold public hearings regarding 1973 to 1987 pickup trucks, General Motors settled with the government for $51 million. A term of the settlement was for the government to close its investigation without holding public hearings. Ford's Pinto model was a popular economy car until an investigation stemming from a lawsuit revealed that the company was aware of the potential hazard in the placement of the car's gas tank.

See also Advertising as the target of censorship; Airline safety news; Bumper stickers; Nader, Ralph.

B

Babel, Isaac Emmanuilovich

BORN: July 13, 1894, Odessa, Ukraine, Russian Empire
DIED: March 17, 1941, Siberia, Soviet Union
IDENTIFICATION: Russian short-story writer and playwright
SIGNIFICANCE: After being persecuted for his artistic integrity, Babel was liquidated during Joseph Stalin's reign of terror

A leading Russian short-story writer during the 1920's, Babel became a suspect in the eyes of the Soviet police after publishing *Red Cavalry* (1926), a collection of stories about the Russian civil war. Although he had joined the Bolsheviks during the revolution, his stories presented the revolution and civil war as he saw them—an orgy of barbarous actions perpetrated by all sides. Publication of that book marked the beginning of official distrust that shadowed Babel through the rest of his life. The fact that he was Jewish contributed to this distrust, although the new Soviet regime officially outlawed anti-Semitism. However, Babel was not a stranger to religious persecution; as a child his family was subjected to a pogrom in which he was almost killed.

When Joseph Stalin consolidated his power and introduced the First Five-Year Plan, establishing his total control over Soviet life, Babel refused to write on demand in support of the regime. He then had difficulties publishing his own work; he was criticized not only for writing "antirevolutionary" stories, but for not writing enough that followed the tenets of Socialist Realism.

During the 1930's Babel wrote constantly, but published little, while making his living writing film scenarios. He avoided politics and lived in constant fear of being arrested for his views on recent history and literature. Because of this fear, he refused to help others threatened by the police and might have thereby even unwittingly contributed to their plights. His family emigrated to Belgium, but he refused to leave the Soviet Union. After he had an affair with a Russian woman from the Far East, he was unjustly accused of being a spy for Japan. When the secret police arrested him in May, 1939, his neighbors heard him mutter, "They didn't let me finish." He was sent to a concentration camp, where he perished in 1941. His death was not announced until fifteen years later, with a brief explanation that he was the victim of the "personality cult"—a current euphemism for Stalin's dictatorial rule.

Many of Babel's confiscated manuscripts have never been located; most likely they were burned by the secret police in December, 1941, during preparations for retreat before the German invasion. Babel's literary rehabilitation was slow, but eventually he received his due as one of the best stylists in Russian literature and as one of the premier short-story writers in the world.

See also Communism; Police states; Russia; Socialist Realism; Soviet Union; Stalin, Joseph; Zhdanov, Andrei.

Babeuf, François Noël

BORN: November 23, 1760, Saint-Quentin, France
DIED: May 27, 1797, Vendôme, France
IDENTIFICATION: French revolutionary leader
SIGNIFICANCE: After contributing to the success of the French Revolution, Babeuf was executed because of his outspoken criticism of the new regime

A visionary and agitator who wished to establish a communist republic of equals in France, Babeuf witnessed the storming of the Bastille. He eagerly embraced the aspirations of the revolutionaries of 1789 and drafted an article demanding the abolition of feudal rights. As the Revolution deepened, Babeuf's commitment became more radical and increasingly at odds with public authorities. He established a journal known as *The Tribune of the People*, in which he attacked the leaders of the Reign of Terror and the economic outcome of the Revolution. The vigor of his condemnation of the Thermidorians, who ended the Terror, led to his arrest and the suppression of his journal. While he was in jail, his young daughter died of starvation, and he emerged from prison a confirmed communist.

To promote his radical ideals Babeuf founded a political club known as the Society of Equals, which was suppressed. His goal was the creation of a new regime that would provide the necessities of life to all. He proposed that the state guarantee the well-being of young children and provide equal education for all. On the eve of a projected uprising, Babeuf and several followers were arrested. He was made a public example by being taken to prison in a cage. At his trial Babeuf defended himself and his ideas eloquently, but his defense failed and he was beheaded.

See also Death; Diderot, Denis; France; Rousseau, Jean-Jacques.

Bacon, Francis

BORN: January 22, 1561, London, England
DIED: April 9, 1626, London, England
IDENTIFICATION: English philosopher, essayist, lawyer, and statesman
SIGNIFICANCE: Bacon's works criticizing the dogmatic and deductive methods of Scholasticism were banned by the Roman Catholic church

A noted lawyer and statesman of Renaissance England, Bacon defended the prerogatives of the crown and endorsed the divine right theory of monarchy. In a rapid rise to power, he became England's attorney-general in 1613 and lord chancellor in 1618. In 1621, however, his political career ended when he was convicted of taking bribes from litigants while their cases were pending. Forced into retirement, Bacon spent the remainder of his life writing on philosophy and literature. The most influential of his thirty works included *The Advancement* of Learning (1605, expanded in 1623), *The New Organon and Related Works* (1622), *The New Atlantis* (1626), and several volumes of essays.

Although Bacon was not a practicing scientist, he is considered one of the prophets of modern science because of his popularization of the inductive method in research. In place of speculation and the deductive logic emphasized by the Scholastic philosophers, he proposed a "new method of reasoning" that derives general principles from the study of particular facts or instances, with the use of experiments when possible. While he remained a faithful member of the Church of England, he taught that scientists should assume the existence of a mechanistic and materialistic universe, and he proclaimed a sharp separation between scientific knowledge based on empirical methods and religious faith based on divine revelation.

By teaching that scientists should pursue truth without the "idols" of traditional assumptions, Bacon encouraged skepticism and rejection of religious censorship, at least in the realm of empirical science. Bacon's writings later inspired and influenced Denis Diderot and other liberals of the Enlightenment. Although Bacon has been held in high esteem by twentieth century philosophers, they typically argue that he did not pay sufficient attention to the necessity of using deductive logic and theoretical hypotheses in guiding research.

Since Bacon was a contemporary with Giordano Bruno and Galileo, conservative Roman Catholic theologians were naturally alarmed by the implications of his method. The Roman Catholic church also disliked his strong criticisms of medieval philosophy, as well as his tendency toward materialism. In 1640, all of his works were proscribed by the Spanish Inquisition, and they were also placed on Sotomayor's *Index*. In 1668, *The Advancement of Learning* was placed on the Vatican's *Index Librorum Prohibitorum*, where it remained as late as 1948. Bacon was commonly classified with Thomas Hobbes as a materialist, although Bacon does not appear to have been an atheist or a consistent proponent of materialism.

See also Bruno, Giordano; Diderot, Denis; Galileo Galilei; Hobbes, Thomas; *Index Librorum Prohibitorum*; Science; Spanish Inquisition.

Bacon, Roger

BORN: c. 1213, Ilchester, Somerset, England
DIED: c. 1292, probably Oxford, England
IDENTIFICATION: English cleric, philosopher, and scientist
SIGNIFICANCE: Bacon's books were censored and he was imprisoned for his revolutionary ideas about science
After attending the universities of Oxford and Paris, Bacon taught for a time at the University of Paris, then the leading center for the study of the works of the Greek philosopher Aristotle. It was probably there that he developed his life-long interest in Aristotle's natural science. However, he soon returned home to England and became a Franciscan monk at Oxford. There he studied and taught Aristotelian science, and undertook scientific experiments, subjecting the ancient philosopher's observations of the natural world to concrete tests.

At the request of his friend Pope Clement IV, Bacon wrote his *Opus Majus* (1268), an encyclopedic work encompassing

discourses on philosophy, grammar, logic, mathematics, physics, and experimental research. Strongly critical of the scientific learning of the time, this work called for a reformation in the way that science was taught and practiced. Because Clement died shortly after the book's completion, the work had little impact during Bacon's lifetime. However, Bacon's call for empirical testing would be heard by future scholars and used to undermine the authority of many ancient texts—including those of Aristotle.

Though a pioneer of experimental science, Bacon was not completely free of the pseudosciences widely accepted in his day. He was especially fascinated with alchemy, which combined cosmology (the study of the origin and nature of the universe) with chemical experiments. Medieval alchemists attempted to isolate the prime matter out of which they believed all objects of the physical world could be created, including gold. Although Bacon never found the coveted philosopher's stone (the hypothetical substance that could turn base metals into gold), he is credited with many inventions and scientific contributions.

At one time, it was commonly believed that it was Bacon who discovered that the mixture of sulfur, saltpeter, and charcoal produced gun powder. Only later was it learned that he had obtained the formula from Arab sources. However, he did invent a camera obscura for observing solar eclipses, he provided new and ingenious insights on refraction, and he explained why the sun and moon appear to increase in size when they are viewed on the horizon of the earth.

Instead of fame, Bacon's revolutionary scientific ideas brought him disgrace and condemnation. In 1278, his books were banned by the minister general of the Order of Franciscans—who later became Pope Nicholas IV—and Bacon was confined for ten years on suspicion of heresy. After his release, he returned to Oxford, where he taught and wrote until his death. Because of his extensive knowledge, he is known to posterity as Doctor Mirabilis—"Wonderful Teacher."

See also Abelard, Peter; Aristotle; Heresy; Science; Vatican.

Baez, Joan

BORN: January 9, 1941, Staten Island, New York
IDENTIFICATION: American folksinger and civil rights activist
SIGNIFICANCE: Because of Baez's opposition to the Vietnam War, she was not allowed to perform at Constitution Hall in Washington, D.C.
During the early 1960's, Baez established herself as one of America's most poignant and successful folksingers. As a civil rights activist, she participated in numerous political rallies and marches that were held in support of minority causes, including Berkeley's Free Speech Movement. Outraged by U.S. involvement in the Vietnam War, she refused to pay 60 percent of her federal income tax in 1964 to protest the tax money used for military armaments. She believed that nonviolence should be used whenever possible to resolve disputes. In 1965 she founded the Institute for the Study of Nonviolence.

In 1967 the Daughters of the American Revolution (DAR) refused to allow Baez to give a concert at Constitution Hall in Washington, D.C., because of her outspoken opposition to the

Folksinger Joan Baez performs in 1966, at the height of her fame. (AP/Wide World Photos)

Vietnam War. After it became publicly known what the DAR had done, Secretary of the Interior Mo Udall gave Baez permission to perform at the base of the Washington monument. Approximately thirty-thousand people attended this outdoor concert. Baez continued forcefully to voice her opposition to the war and was arrested for opposing the military draft. Baez was willing to suffer the consequences of her convictions. Always a strong voice for social justice, she afterward remained true to her beliefs.

See also Daughters of the American Revolution; Draft-card burning; Folk music; Free Speech Movement; Protest music; Seeger, Pete; Vietnam War.

Bakunin, Mikhail Aleksandrovich

BORN: May 30, 1814, Premukhine, Tver, Russia
DIED: July 1, 1876, Bern, Switzerland
IDENTIFICATION: Russian anarchist
SIGNIFICANCE: Bakunin's advocacy of revolutionary violence resulted in his persecution in many European countries; even Karl Marx tried to suppress his ideology

If Pierre-Joseph Proudhon provided many of the basic ideas of nineteenth century anarchism, Mikhail Bakunin gave anarchism its doctrine of action. He equated violence with virtue, defining terrorism in *God and State* (1871) as a weapon to produce nothing less than "the annihilation of everything as it now exists." Bakunin's writings, the man himself, and the movements he helped found were vigorously persecuted.

Bakunin grew to adulthood hostile to his provincial noble family's values. Dissatisfied with his career as a military offi-

cer, he moved into the radical literary circles of Vissarion Belinsky and Ivan Turgenev. In 1840 he traveled to Paris and entered radical intellectual circles, meeting both Proudhon and Marx. In 1847 Bakunin was expelled from Paris after urging Poles to overthrow czarist control in a meeting before a Polish refugee association. He then went to Prague, where he urged the Slavs to destroy the Austro-Hungarian Empire in order to pave the way for the emergence of a virtuous society. His activities gained him permanent listing by international police authorities. While in Dresden in 1849, Bakunin mounted the barricades during the German city's brief revolution, and was promptly sent to prison. After being returned to Russian authorities in 1851, he spent six years in a Russian prison. In 1857 he was banished to Siberia. He escaped in 1861 and made his way to London, where he lived with the famous Russian exile Alexander Herzen and often met with Karl Marx.

Bakunin went to Italy in 1865, during a critical period in Italian unification, and won many young disciples to anarchism in Naples. This experience also convinced him that revolution would first take place in nonindustrial areas, such as Naples and his native Russia, where people were "socialist by instinct and revolutionary by nature." To this end, he founded his first anarchist organization, the International Brotherhood.

In 1867 Bakunin moved to Switzerland. There he worked with Sergei Nacheev, a young Russian exile, to write manifestos advocating bold acts of terrorism to destroy existing society; these manifestos greatly influenced future generations of anarchists. Bakunin was able to make converts out of rural Swiss watchmakers, elite artisans who knew how to make powerful bombs. By 1868 he founded the International Social Democratic Alliance, which he joined to Marx's International. In later years Bakunin organized strong anarchist organizations in Lyon, Marseilles, Madrid, and Barcelona.

Bakunin's stress on violence and his hostility to Marx's ideas about state communism and mass class consciousness led to bitter quarrels. At the Hague Conference in 1872, Bakunin and his fellow anarchists were expelled from the International. After participating in Bologna's abortive 1874 uprising, Bakunin fled to Switzerland.

Bakunin died in Bern two years later, leaving his scattered writings for future editors to compile. Although he created no coherent body of doctrine, his ideas about violent propaganda inspired many political assassinations and bombings, from the 1880's until well into the twentieth century. Not only Bakunin's writings, but his very ideas were vigorously suppressed in most Western nations. Because of his legacy, many socialist and labor organizations in the United States were later branded as subversive merely because they were believed to be anarchistic.

See also Communism; Goldman, Emma; Kropotkin, Peter; Marx, Karl; Russia; Terrorism.

Baldwin, James

BORN: August 2, 1924, New York, New York
DIED: November 30, 1987, St. Paul de Vence, France
IDENTIFICATION: American author

SIGNIFICANCE: Censors have repeatedly attacked Baldwin's works, both before and after their publication

Prior to publication of Baldwin's first short story, "Previous Condition" in *Commentary* in 1948, a number of words were deleted because his editor feared that they would violate obscenity laws. Thus began Baldwin's struggle against censorship. Most of his subsequent work was affected by censorship either before or after publication. Alfred A. Knopf agreed to publish his first novel, *Go Tell It on the Mountain* (1953), but after suppressing several passages that his editor deemed obscene. Baldwin acquiesced, but later regretted doing so and determined to fight harder against expurgation in the future.

When Baldwin submitted his second novel, *Giovanni's Room* (1956), to Knopf, it was rejected. His editors feared the possibility of facing legal action if they published a novel that treated homosexuality openly. They warned Baldwin that he would never be able to publish his work anywhere without subduing its homosexual content. Baldwin's agent, Helen Strauss, even suggested that he burn his manuscript. Instead, Baldwin took the novel to Michael Joseph in London, who agreed to publish not only it, but anything else that Baldwin wrote. Following the novel's acceptance for publication in England, Dial Press contracted with Baldwin to publish the book in the United States, where it actually appeared earlier than in England.

In 1960 *Partisan Review* contracted with Baldwin to publish excerpts from the novel on which he was then working, *Another Country* (1962). William Fitelson, the magazine's attorney, warned its editors that they would risk prosecution by printing obscene words. After replaced the allegedly obscene words in Baldwin's story with asterisks, Baldwin was so furious that he maintained he would have taken the material back, had he known the journal's intentions. When the novel was published in book form, most of its obscene language was omitted entirely—apparently under the direction of editors.

Reviews of *Another Country* were mixed. Some critics gave it high praise; others called it a failure. Several critics called it degrading, pornographic, even though most acknowledged its power. It became a best-seller and quickly attracted the attention of the Federal Bureau of Investigation (FBI), which regarded it as similar to Henry Miller's *Tropic of Cancer*. FBI director J. Edgar Hoover examined *Another Country* personally. Although the FBI determined that legal action against the novel was unnecessary, the bureau compiled an extensive file on Baldwin over the next twelve years. Included in the file were data on various unsuccessful attempts to censor the novel.

In the 1990's censors continued to attack Baldwin's works, including his later novel, *If Beale Street Could Talk* (1974), and tried to remove them from schools and libraries. In addition to making general charges of obscenity and immorality, critics claimed the works were offensive in their presentation of religion and sex and in their promotion of secular humanism.

See also African Americans; Federal Bureau of Investigation; Homosexuality; Hoover, J. Edgar; Literature; Miller, Henry; Offensive language; Secular humanism.

Balzac, Honoré de

BORN: May 20, 1799, Tours, France
DIED: August 18, 1850, Paris, France
IDENTIFICATION: French novelist, poet, and playwright
SIGNIFICANCE: All of Balzac's novels and collections of short stories were placed on the *Index Librorum Prohibitorum* and many have been banned in Russia, Canada, the United States, and Spain

As a young man, Balzac attended the Sorbonne, where he acquired a life-long and passionate devotion to literature. He published his first successful novel, *Les Denier chouan*, in 1829. This event marked the beginning of an extraordinarily prolific literary career in which he produced over ninety novels and short stories. His masterpiece was *La Comédie humaine*, a long series of novels that contained many of his finest works, such as *Eugénie Grandet* (1833) and *Le Père Goriot* (1834). He also wrote and produced plays, several collections of poems, and several works of literary criticism. Early in his career, Balzac produced a number of sensational novels under pen names. Although he could never be described as a subtle or delicate novelist, his heavy use of tiny details helped to portray the lives of ordinary people realistically. Attention to detail, combined with his unbounded energy and passion for life, allowed Balzac to create a vast and exciting panorama of life in early nineteenth-century France in his novels.

Embedded in this panorama was Balzac's determination to expose the evil and venality that he believed permeated French society during the early nineteenth century. He was never troubled by censorship during his lifetime—largely because his political views did not conflict with those of the various regimes that held power—however, his realistic exposure of human foibles upset the guardians of public morality of the late nineteenth century. The Roman Catholic church placed his complete works on the *Index Librorum Prohibitorum*, despite the fact that Balzac had never been as hostile toward organized religion as many of his French and European literary contemporaries. In fact, he regarded organized religion as necessary to hold society together, and criticized it in his work only when he believed that it failed to meet his exalted standard. In the late nineteenth and twentieth centuries the governments of many countries, including Russia, Canada, the United States, and Spain temporarily banned selected titles from his long list of novels. Explicit sexual content and overt political criticism in his work did not prompt these actions. It was Balzac's frequently unflattering portrayals of the upper echelons of French society that upset his various censors.

See also Baudelaire, Charles; Dumas, Alexandre, *père*; Flaubert, Gustave; France; Gautier, Théophile; Hugo, Victor; *Index Librorum Prohibitorum*; Sand, George; Stendhal.

Banned Books Week

DEFINITION: Annual event held every September since 1981
SIGNIFICANCE: Designed to celebrate the freedom to read, this event has served to raise public awareness of censorship

Banned Books Week is sponsored by the American Library Association, the American Booksellers Association, the American Society of Journalists and Authors, the Association of American Publishers, the National Association of College Stores, and the American Association of University Presses. It is observed in schools, libraries, and bookstores throughout the United States through displays of challenged and censored books, lectures, banned-book readings, and editorials.

Events during Banned Books Week are designed to demonstrate the diversity of books that are challenged and the reasons behind the challenges. For example, PEN Center USA, an organization of writers and editors, and the Southern California Booksellers Association have collaborated at several annual celebrations by assembling celebrities, authors, and booksellers in order to attract the general public to readings and to educate about censorship and the wide variety of people and books it affects.

By making the public aware of the types of work censored, and the people or organizations who challenge materials, organizers of Banned Books Week hope to help preserve First Amendment rights and the freedom for all to read. Maintaining these rights assures that no one person or group dictates what the rest of the public may read. A common theme during the annual event has been that all reading material is offensive to someone; if everything challenged were removed, nothing would be left.

The professionals of schools, libraries, and booksellers that celebrate Banned Books Week have included many who have encountered censorship issues as a part of their work. Library collection-development and school book-selection policies have often included statements regarding procedures for handling challenges from concerned citizens, along with other information on how materials are selected.

Well-known and classic books that have been celebrated during Banned Books Weeks have included the Bible; Brothers Grimm fairy tales, which were challenged in Kyrene, Arizona, because of their violent content, negative portrayals of women, and anti-Semitic allusions; *The American Heritage Dictionary*, challenged in Nevada for objectionable language; L. Frank Baum's *The Wizard of Oz*; Mark Twain's *Adventures of Huckleberry Finn*; Joseph Heller's *Catch 22*; John Stein-

Attempts to Ban Books from U.S. Schools in 1993-1994

The 1993-1994 school year saw a record number of efforts to ban books from U.S. schools. This map summarizes the number of such attempts in each state.

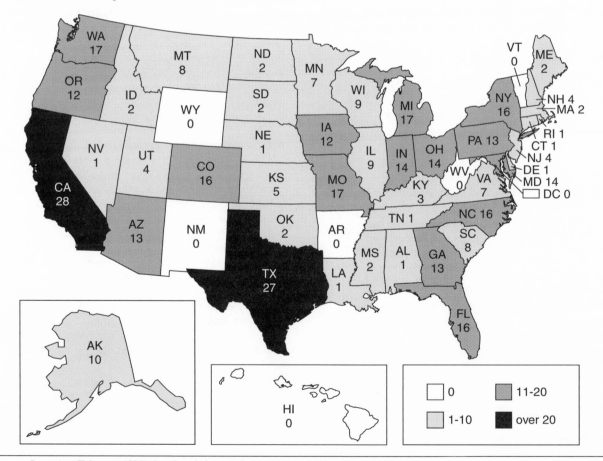

Source: Parenting (February, 1995), based on information from People for the American Way.

In 1982 New York University's book store marked Banned Books Week with a window display depicting banned authors and literary characters behind prison bars. (UPI/Corbis-Bettmann)

beck's *The Grapes of Wrath*; and books by such popular children's authors as Laura Ingalls Wilder and Judy Blume.

See also *Adventures of Huckleberry Finn*; Dictionaries; Freedom to Read Week; *Grapes of Wrath, The*; *Little House on the Prairie*.

Barnett, Ross Robert

BORN: January 22, 1898, Standing Pine, Mississippi
DIED: November 6, 1987, Jackson, Mississippi
IDENTIFICATION: Governor of Mississippi (1960-1964)
SIGNIFICANCE: An inflexible segregationist, Barnett promoted censorship and sacrificed civil liberties in order to maintain the racial status quo

In January, 1962, Governor Barnett asked Mississippi's legislature to outlaw the Communist Party, pass an enforceable sedition act, and compel state employees to take an oath of allegiance to the United States and Mississippi. He also supported efforts of the Daughters of the American Revolution in Mississippi to purge grammar and high school textbooks because they did not teach states' rights, racial integrity, free enterprise, and "Americanism." The justification for his actions was to ensure that Mississippi's children would be truly informed about the Southern way of life.

In 1963 the Citizens' Education Association formed to combat subversive ideas in Mississippi textbooks and to eliminate standard guidance and testing programs. Barnett, who previously chaired his state's textbook committee, invited members of the new association to testify before the state committee about textbooks being used in the public schools.

Association members claimed that their children were being brainwashed by textbooks that preached that prejudice was wrong. They also claimed that the textbooks tried to further a belief in the brotherhood of all people and advocated plans for a world government. Although Barnett sided with the Citizen's Education Association, a majority of the committee members voted against immediately purging textbooks.

See also Civil Rights movement; Communist Party of the U.S.A.; King, Martin Luther, Jr.; Loyalty oaths; National Association for the Advancement of Colored People; Race; Textbooks.

Basic Instinct

TYPE OF WORK: Film
RELEASED: 1992
DIRECTOR: Paul Verhoeven (1938-   )
SUBJECT MATTER: An emotionally troubled detective becomes involved with a bisexual murder suspect
SIGNIFICANCE: This controversial film was criticized by gay groups because of its portrayal of lesbian and bisexual murderers; it gained further notoriety when several scenes of sex and violence were cut prior to its release

Basic Instinct generated most of its controversy even before it was released. During the filming of this psychosexual thriller, gay groups publicly objected to what they viewed as homophobic elements in the script, particularly its characterization of two lesbian or bisexual murderers. When groups such as Queer Nation disrupted filming, restraining orders were issued against the protesters. Screenwriter Joe Eszterhas suggested

Murder suspect Catherine Tramell (Sharon Stone) holds an ice pick as a detective (Michael Douglas) watches in Basic Instinct. *(Museum of Modern Art/Film Stills Archive)*

modifications based on recommendations from the Gay and Lesbian Alliance Against Defamation and other groups, but director Paul Verhoeven and producer Alan Marshall rejected the changes. Executives of the production company accused the demonstrators of "censorship by street action."

Further controversy arose when the Motion Picture Association of America's ratings board demanded that the film be cut if it was to receive an R rating. Previous Verhoeven films, such as *Flesh and Blood* (1985) and *Robocop* (1987) had also been trimmed for R ratings, but the proposed cuts to *Basic Instinct* were both more extensive and more widely publicized. The film's sex and murder scenes were toned down by cutting footage or by substituting less graphic shots. Following the film's R-rated theatrical run and initial video release, a fully restored and unrated version was released on video.

See also Film censorship; Homosexuality; Motion Picture Association of America; Pressure groups; Sex in the arts.

Basque separatism

Date: 1980's

Place: Spain

Significance: The Basque population in Spain have continued to agitate for either independence or greater political autonomy and the preservation of their culture and language

The Basque provinces of Álava, Guipúzcoa, Vizcaya, and Navarra form Spain's northwest border along the Pyrennes with France. The Basque homeland, in Basque Euzkadi, is distinguished by a language unlike Europe's Romance or Germanic tongues. For centuries the Basque people have fought to maintain their culture and traditions against the centralizing authority of Spain's central government. During the rule of Francisco Franco (1939-1975) the Basque people's nationalistic aspirations led to nighttime raids, torture, the loss of government moneys, and extensive press censorship. It was illegal in Franco's Spain for Basques to speak their language, maintain their own schools, or to fly the Basque flag.

With the resumption of the monarchy in 1975, Spain began a slow but methodical transition to the restoration of democratic government. In 1978 a new constitution was promulgated for Spain, institutionalizing the monarchy, guaranteeing civil rights, and guaranteeing the right of recognized nationalities within Spain to seek local autonomy. Article 20 of Spain's constitution provides for the right to freely express and disseminate thoughts, ideas, and opinions by word, in writing, or by any other means of communication. These rights cannot be restricted by any form of prior censorship and the confiscation of publications and recordings and other information media can be carried out only with a court order. Article 143 of Spain's constitution provides the procedure for provinces—such as the Basque region—with common historic, cultural, and economic characteristics to accede to self-government, form self-governing communities, and establish regional control over economic development, banking, law and order, education, and social welfare.

In December, 1977, Spain issued a pre-autonomy decree for the Basque provinces of Álava, Guipúzcoa, and Vizcaya; Navarra chose to become a separate autonomous region in 1980. It was the intent of the Spanish government to defuse the tense situation in the Basque countries, which had been kept under control by government repression, by the grant of autonomy within a democratic Spain. Among Basque's regional parties, the Basque Nationalist Party (PNV), Euzkadiko Ezberra (EE), Herri Batasuna (HB), and Euzkadi Ta Askatasuna or Basque Fatherland and Liberty (ETA), only the ETA continued violent acts, usually the assassination of military or police personnel, to seek complete independence.

During the closing months of the Franco regime, new antiterrorist laws were approved granting the death penalty for the killing of any police, security, or military person and making it a crime to condone, defend, or criticize acts of terrorism or sentencing, calling for solidarity with terrorist organizations, and insulting the armed forces. Between 1978 and 1981 prominent newspaper and magazine writers and publishers were arrested within Spain and the Basque region for discussing Franco-era repression, reporting unrest within the armed forces, and publishing previously classified internal government reports. These cases revealed a gap, since closed, between Spain's 1978 constitutional grant of civil liberties and the still-repressive and functioning Francoist courts and penal system.

For most of the decade of the 1980's the Spanish press has freely published information about the Basque region. The

Spanish police cut the chains of people demonstrating for Basque separatism outside a Madrid building where the European Security Conference was meeting in 1980. (AP/Wide World Photos)

only press restrictions surround secret government talks with the ETA, ongoing military operations against Basque terrorism, and the disclosure of secret government expenditures to fund antiterrorist activities within the Basque provinces.

See also Armenian genocide; Terrorism.

Baudelaire, Charles

BORN: April 9, 1821, Paris, France
DIED: August 31, 1867, Paris, France
IDENTIFICATION: French poet
SIGNIFICANCE: Baudelaire was prosecuted for offending public morals when he published a collection of poems that expanded the thematic range of poetry and foreshadowed the development of twentieth century poetry

On June 25, 1857, Baudelaire's volume of poetry *Les Fleurs du mal* (*Flowers of Evil*, 1909) went on sale. Some of its poems had been published years earlier in periodicals, but the full impact of what Baudelaire was attempting to do with verse was not felt until the collection was published as a whole. With this book Baudelaire boldly professed that it was possible for something beautiful to be a product of evil, and that so-called perverse topics, such as lesbianism, could be molded into poetic eloquence. Although Baudelaire understood that some conservative literary critics—possibly even the French government—would find parts of *Flowers of Evil* offensive, he was confident that ultimately vindication would be his.

Within a few weeks of the book's going on sale, Baudelaire and his publisher, the partners Auguste Poulet-Malassis and Eugène de Broise, were indicted for offending religious morality, and copies of *Flowers of Evil* were confiscated by the French government. In January, 1857, similar charges had been brought against Gustave Flaubert's novel *Madame Bovary*. After Flaubert was found innocent, the government risked another embarrassment by prosecuting Baudelaire. On August 20, 1857, Baudelaire appeared before the sixth court of the Tribunal de la Seine. His attorney, Gustave Chaix d'Est-Ange, argued that Baudelaire intended through the poems of *Flowers of Evil* to illustrate his contempt of evil. The judges dropped the charge of offending religious morality but found Baudelaire guilty of the lesser charge of offending public morality and fined him three hundred francs. The publishing partners were fined 100 francs each. The judges also decided to suppress six poems from the collection.

Although Baudelaire did not receive a prison term, he was deeply saddened by the verdict; he died ten years later. It would not be until 1949 that the judgment against him was officially reversed by the French government and the six suppressed poems were legally included in a French edition of *Flowers of Evil*.

See also Balzac, Honoré de; Dumas, Alexandre, *père*; Flaubert, Gustave; France; Gautier, Théophile; Hugo, Victor; Poetry.

Bauhaus, the

FOUNDED: April 20, 1919

TYPE OF ORGANIZATION: German school of experimental, avant-garde design and architecture

SIGNIFICANCE: The Bauhaus made an indelible mark on modern industrial design and architecture, but under the repressive government of Germany's National Socialist Party the school lasted only fourteen years

The Bauhaus was the creation of Walter Gropius, a German architect who had achieved a reputation for innovative architecture using steel framing and curtain walls. Gropius was disturbed by what he saw as a growing rift between the arts and crafts on the one hand and science and technology on the other.

His opportunity came in 1919, when he was appointed director of the school of fine arts and the school of arts and crafts in Weimar Germany. He combined the two disciplines and named the new school the Bauhaus, literally, "house of constructions." Gropius assembled as faculty some of the greatest names in modern art—Lyonel Feininger, Paul Klee, Oskar Schlemmer, Wassily Kandinsky, and others—thereby assuring the school's success. Training—in a series of fields from pottery and furniture design to dance and theatrical production—was divided into two parts, one under artists, the other under craftspersons, with the objective of having students become adept in both areas. Guiding principles were that form follows function and that production is coordinated with technology.

From the beginning the conservative citizens of Weimar were hostile to the work of the Bauhaus. Since it was state-supported, they tried to censor it by shrinking its financial support. Criticism became so intense by 1926 that Gropius moved the school to Dessau, an industrial city south of Berlin. He designed a complex of buildings that embodied the idea of the unity of art, craft, and technology contained in its unifying element, the building.

During its Dessau years the Bauhaus produced memorable designs, such as tubular steel furniture, with Gropius steering a middle course between public taste and artistic innovation. Attacks from the Right, especially from Adolf Hitler's growing Nazi Party, continued. As at Weimar, censorship took the form of cutting off public funds. Weary of handling purely administrative details, Gropius resigned in 1928.

Gropius' successor made no attempt to curb either the leftist activities of students and faculty or the growing abstraction of their design work. The fate of the Bauhaus was sealed. In 1930 the director was dismissed to be replaced by the architect Ludwig Mies van der Rohe. Mies tried to follow Gropius' strategy, but it was too late. Modern architecture and design had by then become identified in Germany with unacceptable leftist political views.

In 1932 the National Socialist Party came to power in Dessau. The new government dismissed the faculty and closed the Bauhaus. Mies tried to continue the Bauhaus in Berlin as a private school. In 1933 the Nazis took control of the national government. The school was permanently closed on April 11, 1933, never to reopen. Its designs and archives, however, remained a major resource for modern industrial design and architecture.

See also Art; Degenerate Art Exhibition; Germany; Intellectual freedom; National Socialism.

Bay of Pigs invasion

DATE: April, 1961

PLACE: Bay of Pigs, Cuba

SIGNIFICANCE: The administration of U.S. president John F. Kennedy applied pressure to keep the news of preparations for an invasion of Cuba secret from the American public

In January, 1961, President Kennedy ordered the Central Intelligence Agency (CIA) to train a force of anti-Fidel Castro exiles to invade Cuba. Concerned with protecting the invasion plans and preserving the prestige of his young administration, Kennedy quietly counseled the American press to maintain secrecy in the name of national security. When *The New York Times* reporter Tad Szulc submitted a story documenting CIA recruitment of Cubans in Miami and hinting that an invasion of the island was imminent, *The New York Times* Washington bureau chief James Reston, at the behest of the White House, advised against publication, and when the article did appear all references to CIA participation were deleted.

The failure of the invasion, which began on April 17, 1961, apparently forced Kennedy to revise his position. Two weeks later he told *The New York Times* managing editor Turner Catledge that had his paper printed more information about the invasion plans it would have prevented a catastrophe for American foreign policy. Reston, ironically, disagreed. The plans were too far along, and Kennedy himself too much committed, to believe that the invasion would have been canceled simply because a newspaper chose to publish a few more details about American involvement.

See also Central Intelligence Agency; *CIA and the Cult of Intelligence, The*; Cuba; Grenada, U.S. invasion of; National security; *New York Times, The*.

Beach Boys, the

DATE: Spring, 1983

PLACE: Washington, D.C.

SIGNIFICANCE: The members of this rock band became the center of national attention when a federal cabinet secretary banned them from performing in a government-sponsored Fourth of July celebration on the Washington Mall

In April, 1983, President Ronald Reagan's secretary of the interior, James Watt, announced that the Beach Boys would be banned from participating in the annual Fourth of July celebration on the Washington Mall. After more than two decades of performing and recording, the band remained one of rock 'n' roll music's most popular and enduring groups.

Citing a connection between rock music, drug abuse, and alcoholism, Watt explained that his decision to exclude the band was a statement for "wholesomeness" because the Beach Boys would attract the wrong element to the Independence Day celebration. More wholesome entertainment would instead be supplied by Las Vegas casino singer Wayne Newton.

Watt's decision earned for him almost universal public and

official derision. Even the president's wife Nancy Reagan rushed to the defense of the Beach Boys, saying that her children had grown up on their music. Vice President George Bush added that he counted the Beach Boys among his friends and that they had performed at a fund-raiser for him. President Reagan presented Watt with a plaster cast of a foot with a bullet hole in it to symbolize the latter's gaff. Faced with such strong opposition, Watt rescinded his ban and the Beach Boys later performed on the mall.

See also Beatles, the; Bush, George; Jackson, Michael; Music; Reagan, Ronald; Rock 'n' roll music; Rolling Stones, the.

Beardsley, Aubrey

BORN: August 21, 1872, Brighton, England
DIED: March 16, 1898, Menton, France
IDENTIFICATION: British illustrator
SIGNIFICANCE: Beardsley's association with Oscar Wilde led to his dismissal as a magazine art editor and may have contributed to shortening his career

A gifted young artist and member of the English Aesthetic Movement, Beardsley first met Oscar Wilde in 1891. However, the two were not publicly associated until 1893, when Beardsley was commissioned by publisher John Lane to illustrate the English translation of Wilde's play *Salomé* (1894). Beardsley's drawings were grotesque, satirical, and on the verge of indecency. Several were expurgated prior to the book's publication.

In early 1894 Beardsley and writer Henry Harland conceived of a new quarterly magazine, *The Yellow Book*, also published by Lane. The first issue, which appeared in April, had a yellow and black hard cover, similar to risqué French novels of the day. Among its contributors were established artists and writers, such as Sir Frederic Leighton and Henry James, and modern irreverents, such as Arthur Symons, Max Beerbohm, and Beardsley himself. The magazine's premise, "art for art's sake," was a challenge to Victorian conservatism.

Wilde's name and writing were noticeably absent from *The Yellow Book*, which sought a level of respectability from the beginning. Unfortunately, on April 5, 1895, as the magazine's fifth issue was going to press, Wilde was arrested on a morals charge. As he was led away by the police, he was reported to be carrying a copy of *The Yellow Book*. (It was later learned that he was in fact carrying a yellow-covered French novel.) A mob gathered and stoned Lane's bookshop. Beardsley was summarily fired as art editor and all traces of his work were removed from the publication. His previous collaboration with Wilde and the erroneous press reports had made him guilty by association.

The Yellow Book lost much of its cachet after Beardsley's dismissal; it died quietly in 1897, having ceased to stir controversy. Beardsley and Symons went on to edit another magazine called *The Savoy*, which they launched in January, 1896. This periodical lasted only eight months, however, fading along with Beardsley's health. Beardsley died of tuberculosis at the age of twenty-five, three years after the *Yellow Book* uproar.

See also Art; Caricature; Whistler, James Abbott McNeill; Wilde, Oscar.

Beatles, the

FORMED: 1959
IDENTIFICATION: British rock band
SIGNIFICANCE: Members of the band were censored for their comments on religion, the Vietnam War, and artistic choices

From 1963 until their breakup in 1971, the Beatles were an international musical phenomenon whose recordings, films, and views influenced an entire generation of young people. As cultural icons and trendsetters, the Beatles had an influence that long outlived their collaborative efforts, retaining their importance as individual musicians and cultural spokesmen decades after the demise of the band itself.

In 1966 Capitol Records, the Beatles' American label, suppressed group leader John Lennon's "butcher boys" cover design for the America-only *Yesterday . . . and Today* record album. The cover showed the members of the group in white butcher outfits surrounded by bloody dismembered human dolls. The photograph was intended to protest the Vietnam War. (Unsubstantiated rumors circulated that Lennon was also protesting Capitol's policy of "butchering" the content of Beatles albums.)

Also in 1966, Lennon aroused public outcry with his com-

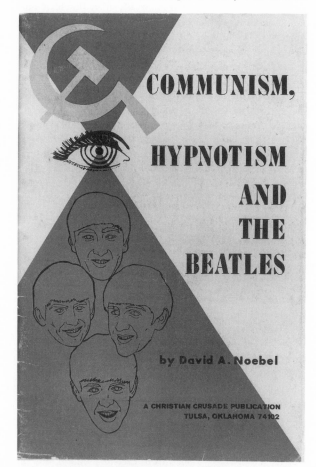

This anti-Beatles tract reflected the right-wing and Christian Fundamentalist hysteria that greeted early rock 'n' roll music. (Robert McClenaghan)

ments published in the British *Evening Standard*. In an interview with Maureen Cleave, Lennon said that "Christianity will go. It will vanish and shrink. . . . We're more popular than Jesus now; I don't know which will go first—rock 'n' roll or Christianity. Jesus was all right but his disciples were thick and ordinary. It's them twisting it that ruins it for me." Lennon's remarks raised little interest in England, but a reprint of his interview in the American teenage magazine *Datebook* prompted American clergy, the Ku Klux Klan, and conservative radio stations to sponsor mass bonfires of Beatle records and memorabilia in Tennessee, Alabama, Georgia, and Texas during the group's August tour of the United States. An estimated thirty-five radio stations, from New York to Utah, banned Beatle records. The Vatican issued a protest, South Africa banned Beatle records, and the Spanish government publicly censured Lennon's remarks.

Under pressure, Lennon made a public apology at a Chicago press conference in August, saying that he had used the Beatles only as an example of how popular culture was replacing religion in young people's lives, particularly in Britain. "I'm not saying that we're better or greater, or comparing us with Jesus Christ as a person or God as a thing or whatever it is." Although the controversy quickly died down, it later caused the Beatles to delete figures of Christ, Adolf Hitler, and Mohandas Gandhi from the collage cover of their 1967 album *Sgt. Pepper's Lonely Hearts Club Band*. In February, 1972, former Beatle Paul McCartney rush-released the single "Give Ireland Back to the Irish" in response to the January massacre of thirteen Irish civilians by British police in Londonderry. The British Broadcasting Corporation immediately banned the song. In protest, McCartney issued an innocuous single, "Mary Had a Little Lamb," which McCartney claimed was deliberately banal in order to avoid censorship.

See also Beach Boys, the; Free speech; Ku Klux Klan; Lennon, John; Music; Protest music; Radio; Recording industry; Rock 'n' roll music; Rolling Stones, the; Vietnam War.

Beaumarchais, Pierre-Augustin Caron de

BORN: January 24, 1732, Paris, France
DIED: May 18, 1799, Paris, France
IDENTIFICATION: French dramatist, social critic, and pamphleteer
SIGNIFICANCE: Beaumarchais' plays were suppressed for their criticism of aristocracy, and he himself promoted the burning of two books that attacked the French monarchy

At age twenty-three, Pierre-Augustin Caron abandoned the clockmaking trade to take up a minor office he had purchased in the court of French king Louis XV. He rapidly became a favorite of the royal princesses, rose to the position of secretary to the king, and added "Beaumarchais" to his name. During the 1760's, Beaumarchais acquainted himself with classical and French literature and began writing plays. His *Eugénie*, an attack on social privilege, was licensed in 1767, after its setting was changed from Paris to London; and his *Two Friends*, a melodrama about a silk-merchant and a tax-collector, had its first performance in January, 1770. Neither play was a commercial success, however.

In January, 1773, Beaumarchais finished a preliminary version of his first major work, *The Barber of Seville*. The play was passed by the government censor in February, 1773, but the license to stage the play was withdrawn when the sentence of *blâme*, which entailed a deprivation of all civil rights, was pronounced against Beaumarchais for his part in a brawl. Beaumarchais' defense of his case in four pamphlets won him wide sympathy, including Voltaire's, but failed to reverse the official judgment against him: by order of the Parliament of Paris, the pamphlets were burned in March, 1774. In the hope of rehabilitating himself, Beaumarchais traveled under the name of "Le Chevalier de Ronac" to London in the king's service in April, 1774, to negotiate terms with exile Théveneau de Morande, who threatened to distribute an exposé of the life of Mme du Barry. A payment of 32,000 livres was agreed to, and Beaumarchais oversaw the burning of all copies of Morande's *Memoires secrets d'une femme publique*. Two months later, Beaumarchais arranged for the destruction of a pamphlet that attacked the character of Marie-Antoinette and her mother, the Empress Maria Theresa. Authorization to perform *The Barber of Seville* was granted in February, 1775. Full civil rights were restored to Beaumarchais in September, 1776, in recognition of his service in supplying arms to the revolutionaries against the English crown in America.

The lifting of *blâme* from Beaumarchais, however, did not assure royal approval of his next play, *The Marriage of Figaro*, which he originally completed in 1778, on "the ignorance and the baseness of the great." In 1782, after Louis XVI read *The Marriage of Figaro* in manuscript, he forbade its performance on the stage. "The author," he observed, "mocks everything which ought to be respected in a Government." However, the championing of Beaumarchais' cause by Marie-Antoinette and the Comte d'Artois persuaded the king to allow a private performance of *The Marriage of Figaro* in 1783. Approval by five of the six censors who reviewed the play within the months that followed led to the granting of a license for its public performance. In March, 1784, *The Marriage of Figaro* opened at the Comédie-Française, where it ran for one hundred performances. In 1785 Marie-Antoinette herself played the part of Rosine and the Comte d'Artois played Figaro in a performance of *The Barber of Seville* with the king and Beaumarchais in attendance. Beaumarchais' *Tarare*, a play representing the overthrow of tyranny by the common man, was first staged in 1787.

See also Drama and theater; France; Literature; Opera; Voltaire.

Beavis and Butt-head

TYPE OF WORK: Television program
FIRST BROADCAST: 1992
CREATOR: Mike Judge (1963-   )
SUBJECT MATTER: Animated characters parody the gross speech and behavior of modern adolescent boys
SIGNIFICANCE: This popular cartoon show heightened the debate over violence on television when it was blamed for inciting children to imitate dangerous behaviors that it depicted

Beavis and Butt-head was the highest rated program on the Music Television (MTV) network almost as soon as it began in 1992. It was also the most controversial. Some critics praised its satire; others reviled its crudeness. Many were shocked by its violence, profanity, and sexual and scatological humor. The first serious attempt to force *Beavis and Butt-head* off the air began when retired broadcasting engineer and lottery winner Dick Zimmerman attributed the death of a cat that had been killed by a firecracker to the broadcast five days earlier of a *Beavis and Butt-head* episode in which the characters had discussed cats and firecrackers. Zimmerman offered a five-thousand-dollar reward for the capture of the cat killers, and he started a letter-writing campaign against the program. MTV pulled the cat episode from the air, along with three other controversial episodes.

The best-known incident involving *Beavis and Butt-head* was reported in October, 1993, when an Ohio woman said that her five-year-old son set a fire that killed his two-year-old sister after he had watched Beavis and Butt-head set fires on their television show. MTV responded to the controversy by banning references to setting fires from the program. It also moved the show's broadcast time to late evening, and began running disclaimers before each episode.

See also Cable television; Copycat crime; Crumb, Robert; Music TeleVision; Television; Violence.

Bentham, Jeremy

Born: February 15, 1748, London, England
Died: June 6, 1832, London, England
Identification: English legal and social reformer, philosopher, and pamphleteer
Significance. Bentham's many published attacks on censorship inspired a school of followers who denounced censorship long after his death

An influential critic of the English legal system, society, and government, Bentham founded the Utilitarian school of philosophy, which sought to place social theory and reform on a commonsense basis and to extend the benefits of an organized political community to all classes of society. Bentham was also a lifelong supporter of freedom of the press as a check on governmental abuse of power, and as an indispensable link between people and government. In his first published work, *A Fragment on Government* (1776), he wrote of the free press that through it "every man, be he of one class or the other, may make known his complaints and remonstrances to the whole community." Bentham was also the intellectual—and formally designated—godfather of John Stuart Mill, whose *On Liberty* (1859) included an impassioned case against stifling free expression through censorship or other means.

The full significance of Bentham's attacks on censorship was only apparent, however, after the close of the struggle with France in 1815. Thereafter the democratic implications became manifest of Bentham's belief that the welfare of the lowest pauper should count as much to society as the happiness of the highest prince. As a full-blown democrat, Bentham set to work out reform proposals and policies that would put into practice his view that "the more closely we are watched, the better we behave." Bentham had already put that philosophy to practice in his plans for a new kind of prison architecture and management in which inmates could be constantly watched. In the new democratic world of democracy that he envisaged, the "watchdog" function took a new form. Since governments tend constantly to abuse their power, the democratic public must have the means to expose government's misdeeds. That means was a free and active press, which could inform an equally active and censorious public opinion.

The ultimate sanction against a corrupt or abusive government was elections that removed wrongdoers from office. However, as Bentham suggested in his pamphlet *On the Liberty of the Press* (1823), a free press is an essential tool for a democratic citizenry. Press freedom is not just a question of what Bentham called "securities against misrule." Democratic liberty exists in part when government has sufficient power to carry out the popular will; but democratic government is also to be responsive to public demands and complaints. An unfettered press is a principal means of transmitting public sentiment between elections as well as informing an attentive public of government behavior.

Allied to Bentham's opposition to formal press censorship was his hostility to libel law which had the effect of self-censorship and public silence on key issues. Libel law included "seditious libel," in which the state itself is attacked as well as blasphemous libel. These laws were used repeatedly in England and on the continent to suppress political dissent. In his *Letters to the Spanish People* (1820), for example, Bentham denounced the use of libel to suppress criticism of the Madrid police and of a proposed law against political meetings. He called instead for freedom for fulsome attacks on public officials without hindrance of libel accusations. In so doing, he looked forward to the landmark U.S. Supreme Court case *New York Times Co. v. Sullivan* (1966), which established just such a freedom. Indeed, Bentham held up American libel law of his day as shining evidence that public tranquillity and freedom of the press were thoroughly compatible.

See also Democracy; Free speech; Libel; Mill, John Stuart; *New York Times Co. v. Sullivan*; Prisons.

Berrigan, Daniel

Born: May 9, 1921, Virginia, Minnesota

Berrigan, Philip Francis

Born: October 5, 1923, Two Harbors, Minnesota
Identification: American Roman Catholic priests and social activists
Significance: Dubbed the Berrigan Brothers by the media, these men were prosecuted for their anti-Vietnam War activities

Leading figures of the anti-Vietnam War "New Catholic Left" movement, the Berrigans were both central figures in American trials for their nonviolent but dramatic actions against U.S. government policies. They had long been interested in civil rights issues when they came to national prominence. In May, 1968, they were arrested for pouring blood on Baltimore draft board records, and for burning similar documents in Catonsville, Maryland, with homemade napalm. During the ensuing trial of the "Catonsville Nine," a group of defendants that included the Berrigans and seven other war protesters, photos and posters of the brothers in priests' collars, manacled in handcuffs while holding up the two-finger "peace sign," became well-known symbols of the antiwar movement.

The Berrigans were sentenced to six years in federal prison, but Daniel Berrigan went underground for four months, exasperating federal authorities by making brief public appearances before disappearing again. He was eventually caught and joined his brother serving his sentence in the federal prison at Danbury, Connecticut, where they led a hunger strike among prisoners in August, 1971.

In January, 1971, Philip, five fellow clergy members, and a Pakistani college professor were indicted as the "Harrisburg Seven" for allegedly plotting to raid government offices, kidnap presidential advisor Henry Kissinger, and blow up heating ducts in the Pentagon Building. The government's case, built around Boyd Douglas, an unreliable and compromised Federal Bureau of Investigation (FBI) informant, failed, although the defense team led by former U.S. attorney general Ramsey Clark presented no case on its own behalf. The prosecution, led by veteran District Attorney William Lynch, succeeded only in convicting Philip Berrigan for smuggling love letters to Sister Mary McAllister, a fellow defendant.

During their trials at both Catonsville and Harrisburg, Pennsylvania, the articulate and charismatic brothers were sup-

Shortly after this picture was taken Philip F. Berrigan (center) and his brother Daniel Berrigan (right) were arrested for helping to burn draft records in Baltimore in 1968. (AP/Wide World Photos)

ported by large-scale propaganda machines on a level similar to major political campaigns. This was particularly true for the Harrisburg Seven trial, in which the government's case became increasingly embarrassing to FBI director J. Edgar Hoover and the Nixon Administration. Daniel Berrigan's reputation was augmented by his speeches and writings, notably his play, *The Trial of the Catonsville Nine*, performances of which began in New York City in the fall of 1971, and his autobiography, *The Dark Night of Resistance*, which won the Thomas More Medal. (He has also published three volumes of poetry, commentary on the Roman Catholic church, and essays on humanity's responsibilities in the nuclear age.)

After 1979 Philip Berrigan continued his antiwar activities while working in two groups, the New York ecumenical organization "Kairos" and "Plowshares," which have performed at least thirty demonstrations including damaging two unarmed warheads at a General Electric plant in King of Prussia, Pennsylvania. These actions led to repeated jail sentences for Philip. Another notable incident was an April, 1992, sentence in Ellicott County, Maryland, for five years resulting from his involvement with seven other activists who trespassed into the Johns Hopkins Applied Physics Laboratory in Columbia, Maryland.

See also Criminal trials; Draft-card burning; Draft resistance; Religion; Vietnam War.

Bhopal disaster

DESCRIPTION: Chemical plant accident that caused thousands of deaths

DATE: December 3, 1984

PLACE: Bhopal, India

SIGNIFICANCE: The Union Carbide Company has been accused of covering up the "worst industrial disaster in history" after an accident at its chemical plant in Bhopal caused at least 2,500 deaths and injured hundreds of thousands more

During the morning of December 3, 1984, forty tons of methyl isocyanate (MIC) released from Union Carbide's Bhopal chemical factory drifted over the northern India city, causing thousands of residents to suffocate on the deadly gas and try to flee through the dark streets. No alarm was sounded and no evacuation plan had been prepared. The official body count was 2,500, but unofficial estimates range as high as ten thousand. Several hundred thousand more people filed damage claims for personal injuries and economic losses. Many of these people still suffered from breathlessness, chest pain, blindness, hypertension, anxiety, and depression a decade later.

Union Carbide has been accused of trying to downplay the effects of the gas leak to avoid taking responsibility and paying compensation. For example, right after the accident, the company claimed that MIC was only a mild irritant even though its own safety manual emphasized that the chemical was "deadly even in very small doses." According to *Scientific American* (June, 1995), the lack of information provided on MIC by the company hindered the effective treatment of survivors.

Union Carbide also shifted the blame from itself when, in 1985, its media relations manager stated to the press that the leak had been caused by a "disgruntled worker." That unnamed

A Bhopal slum dweller collects water near the Union Carbide chemical plant, whose toxic gas leak killed thousands two months earlier. (AP/Wide World Photos)

person was accused of purposely contaminating a storage tank by attaching a water line to the tank that caused the gas leak. The theory that one disgruntled worker caused the leak is referred to as the "sabotage theory." This view tended to support the negative media image of workers which made the management of the company look faultless. However, the company never explained how such an act could have occurred or why there was a lack of safety measures. Union Carbide also failed to admit to documented hazardous operations.

Also, Union Carbide dismissed Bhopal as an isolated incident. According to *The Economist* (December 3, 1994), in early 1985 Union Carbide told West Virginia residents who lived near two similar Union Carbide MIC plants, that accidents such as Bhopal could not happen in West Virginia. A few months later there was a leak at one plant and 145 people needed hospital treatment. Later, in the midst of protests in the streets of India and pending court cases, Union Carbide announced to its shareholders that "the disaster was behind them."

See also Classification of information; India; Pesticide industry; Press conferences; Toxic waste news.

Bible

TYPE OF WORK: Book
WRITTEN: c. Third century B.C.E.—first century C.E.
AUTHORS: Multiple scribes
SUBJECT MATTER: Sacred text of Christianity
SIGNIFICANCE: Because the Bible is the sacred book of Christianity, it has frequently been the object of censorship in struggles to control religious belief and practices among Christians

The Bible contains books that are sacred in both Judaism and Christianity. The first portion, called by Christians the Old Testament, elaborates God's dealings with his chosen people, the Jews, and is sacred to Judaism and Christianity. The second portion, referred to by Christians as the New Testament, describes events associated with the life of Jesus, whom Christians called Christ, and the early church and its teachings. This latter portion is not accepted as scripture by Judaism. Some Christians view certain other books known as the Apocrypha as an integral part of the Bible. The Bible has been a frequent target of censorship efforts, both among Christians themselves, who sometimes disagreed vehemently over its proper interpretation, and by government authorities hostile to Christian faith and thus hostile to its central sacred text.

The Bible and the Vernacular. Christians themselves have sometimes been ready to censor certain forms in which the Bible has been made available to lay Christians. In the decades immediately prior to and following the Protestant Reformation, Roman Catholic authorities were often vigorous opponents of attempts to make the Bible available in the vernacular, that is in a tongue readily accessible to lay readers, unlike Hebrew, Greek, or Latin. Medieval church authorities widely agreed that giving common people access to the sacred Scriptures was the equivalent of casting pearls before swine. Ordinary men and women needed most to listen to the learned teach about the Scriptures, rather than read the Scriptures themselves. For centuries, the learned had no problem enforcing their preferences in this regard, as only they knew how to translate the Hebrew or Greek or Latin texts. Shortly before the Protestant Reformation in the sixteenth century, a handful of scholars became convinced that common people would benefit from reading the Scriptures themselves, in their own tongues. William Tyndale, for example, partially completed translating the Bible into English, with the aim of allowing "the boy that driveth the plough" to understand its words and teaching. Opponents of Tyndale's enterprise ultimately captured him, however, and had him strangled and burned at the stake in 1536. With the advent of the Reformation, the numbers of those committed to the work of translation swelled, and their efforts began to produce one after another translations of the Bible into languages that ordinary men and women could read. Where the Roman Catholic church still held political power, however, it frequently used this power to staunch the ever increasing current of vernacular translations. In many places mere possession or publication of a vernacular translation was a crime punishable by death.

The Bible and Indecency. Long after vernacular translations of the Bible had become commonplace, a new crop of censors arose who feared that the Bible might be too much for some souls to handle. Beginning around 1830, a steady stream of "family" Bibles began to appear, in which indelicate passages had been excised or dislocated from the main body of text to facilitate the public reading of the Bible in mixed company. The most famous of these attempts to make the sacred scriptures of Christianity fit for ordinary consumption was that undertaken by the great American lexicographer, Noah Webster. Webster produced his version of the Bible in 1833. In some respects this version, *The Holy Bible, Containing the Old and New Testaments, in the Common Version, with Amendments of the Language*, simply revised the text of the ever popular but seriously dated King James Bible to make its language conform more closely to usage of that era. However, Webster also made changes in the text with an eye to cloak what he viewed as indecent matters in either obscurity or euphemism.

Modern Political Correctness. Less concerned with indelicacy than sexism and racism, some modern translators of the Bible have launched efforts to purge it of its perceived male chauvinism and racially offensive language. In 1995 the prestigious Oxford University Press introduced *The New Testament and Psalms: An Inclusive Version*. The "inclusion" that this version achieves is purchased at the price of excluding the male-specific and patriarchal language of the original text of the Bible. Biblical references to God as "Father" are replaced by references instead to "the Father-Mother." Concern for anti-Semitic overtones strips references in the Gospels of their finger-pointing at the Jews for having killed Jesus in favor of an indefinite pronoun. Whereas the original text of the Bible asks what fellowship hath Light with Darkness, the editors of the inclusive version ask instead what fellowship hath Day with Night.

The Bible in Public Schools. The establishment clause of the First Amendment to the U.S. Constitution forbids government from making laws "respecting an establishment of religion." Applying this clause, the U.S. Supreme Court has held that public schools cannot sponsor devotional religious exercises or otherwise attempt to advance the cause of religion in the public schools. For example, the Court held in *Stone v. Graham* (1980) that a school may not post a copy of the Ten Commandments from the Bible on a wall, even if for the alleged purpose of informing the students of an important source of the Western legal tradition. Nevertheless, the Court has also declared that the establishment clauses poses no barrier to the objective study of the Bible for its literary or historical significance.

School officials have sometimes demonstrated uncertainty about the place of student-initiated study of the Bible in light of the Supreme Court's establishment clause holdings. Apparently, prior to the mid-1980's, some school officials viewed the Court's decisions as requiring that school officials prevent any religious use of the Bible by students at school, even in clubs and informal gatherings not sponsored by the school itself. In 1984 Congress acted to abolish these attempts by school officials to censure private student-initiated Bible study and religious fellowship by passing the Equal Access Act. This law provides that religious students in secondary schools must be given the same right to Bible study, or other forms of religious fellowship, as are accorded other noncurriculum student clubs to pursue their chosen interests. *—Timothy L. Hall*

BIBLIOGRAPHY

Anne Lyon Haight's *Banned Books: 387 B.C. to 1978 A.D.* (rev. ed. New York : R. R. Bowker, 1978) includes a section concerning censorship of the Bible. For a somewhat older, but still useful history of the Bible since the Protestant Reformation, see *The Cambridge History of the Bible: The West from the Reformation to the Present Day*, edited by S. L. Greenslade (Cambridge: Cambridge University Press, 1963). David Lawton's *Faith, Text, and History: The Bible in English* (Charlottesville, Virginia: University of Virginia Press, 1990), contains an account of the medieval opposition to translation of the Bible into vernacular tongues. Jaroslav Pelikan's *The Reformation of the Bible/The Bible of the Reformation* (New Haven: Yale University Press, 1996) focuses attention of the rise of vernacular translations during the Reformation. Robert M. O'Neil discusses the problem of erroneous attitudes about the inclusion of literary and historical study of the Bible in public schools in his essay, "The Bible and the Constitution," in *Censored Books: Critical Viewpoints*, edited by Nicholas J. Karolides, Lee Burress, and John M. Kean (Metuchen, N.J.: Scarecrow Press, 1993).

See also Abridgment; Christianity; Dead Sea Scrolls; James I; Jeremiah's Book of Prophesies, burning of; Koran; Printing; Reformation, the; Talmud; Webster, Noah.

Biddle, John

BORN: 1615, Wotton-under-Edge, England

DIED: September 22, 1662, London, England

IDENTIFICATION: English religious writer

SIGNIFICANCE: Instrumental in founding England's Unitarian church, Biddle stood firm in his religious beliefs though it meant the loss of his liberty and life

An English scholar of high ideals and the master of the Crypt School in Gloucester, Biddle began to question the validity of the Trinity while studying the New Testament. After concluding that the Three Persons of the Trinity were unequal and did not embody a single God, he asserted that the Holy Spirit was an intellect separate from God. In 1644 he drew up a series of arguments on this premise, substantiated by biblical passages. After presenting his theory to friends, one confidant reported him to authorities who charged him with heresy.

Jailed for various periods during his life, Biddle sought public acknowledgement in 1647 by publishing his *XII Arguments* in a pamphlet. Despite public burnings of his tract and publication of books refuting his theory, Biddle's fame spread and a second edition of his work soon appeared. Responding to a 1648 declaration making it a capital offense to deny the Trinity, Biddle wrote two more books on the subject. A new controversy arose in 1654 when he launched wider attacks on Christian doctrines in *A Two-fold Catechism*. Arrested, released, saved from death by Oliver Cromwell, and exiled to the Scilly Isles, Biddle returned home in 1662 only to be imprisoned in London, where he died five weeks later.

See also Book burning; English Commonwealth; Heresy.

Billboards

DEFINITION: Large advertising signs, usually erected outdoors

SIGNIFICANCE: While representations made in billboard advertisements have achieved greater legal protection, society has developed more sophisticated and judicially acceptable methods of controlling their display

Effective and comparatively inexpensive forms of advertising, billboards have publicized such wide-ranging products as food, clothes, fertilizer, alcohol, cigarettes, topless clubs, churches, museums, and cultural events. Often they have caused serious controversy because of their public nature and the tendency of advertisers to get people's attention through provocation and shock techniques—such as eye-catching images and sensational language. Prior to the 1960's, all levels of government in the United States could exercise great discretion over billboards. Commercial speech did not garnish any form of protection under the First Amendment. Even with such government freedom to regulate, however, billboard proliferation dominated early America. In the mid-1960's, Lady Bird Johnson, the wife of President Lyndon Baines Johnson, promoted passage of the Highway Beautification Act, a law that allowed municipalities to remove unwanted billboards considered aesthetically unpleasant. However, the law required municipalities to reimburse billboard owners at a current multiple of their annual revenues. This proved to be expensive, and most municipalities had limited resources.

During the mid-1970's, the courts began searching for forms of protected speech within commercial advertisements. By nature laws tend to be discriminatory. It is the depth of such discrimination that is the basis for constitutional analysis. The courts began testing to see if the burden on advertisers' First Amendment rights of expression outweighed government's right to regulate.

In 1963 the ultra-right wing John Birch Society used billboards along busy highways to wage a campaign against the chief justice of the United States. (AP/Wide World Photos)

The federal government obtains its power to regulate billboards through the Constitution's interstate commerce clause. The right of local government to regulate for the health and safety of its citizens is limited by the First Amendment's free speech clause. The First Amendment is implicitly brought to bear upon municipalities by the Fourteenth Amendment. If protected speech exists in a billboard message, then courts apply a strict scrutiny test under which few laws can survive.

To avoid free speech problems, many practical ways of billboard censorship have evolved. For example, municipalities may regulate billboards to prevent public displays of obscenity, to provide for their proper placement, and to protect the aesthetics of a community through zoning laws. The subjectivity involved in determining obscenity has made many obscenity laws ineffective. However, commercial messages that constitute public nuisances and affect public safety, such as nudity on billboards near busy intersections, can be successfully regulated. By the early 1980's, the most effective way to regulate billboards was through the use of zoning laws. Communities began designing master plans to control neighborhood development. Zoning allows for the collection of fees and taxes, and the establishment of time-consuming approval processes. Zoning can ban billboards from areas near schools, child-care centers, and predominantly poor or ethnic neighborhoods. Moratoriums temporarily stop the propagation of billboards while communities analyze their zoning potential. Moratoriums can be extended many times for various reasons.

By the mid-1980's, municipalities throughout the United States were significantly reducing the number of billboards without having to worry about improper content-based censorship. The cities of Hurst and Grand Prairie, Texas, for example, completely halted all new billboard construction. The city of Fort Worth, while not banning them, did reduce the number of old billboards by 438, while limiting new billboards to only twenty-seven.

See also Advertising as the target of censorship; Alcoholic beverages; Nudity; Obscenity: legal definitions; Smoking; Unprotected speech.

Biography

DEFINITION: Narratives—usually book-length—of human lives

SIGNIFICANCE: Efforts to distort or protect the reputations of important or famous persons have made biographies the objects of censorship and suppression

As a literary genre biography is largely the product of the eighteenth century and of one seminal work in particular: James Boswell's *Life of Samuel Johnson* (1791). Biographies had appeared earlier, however, including several by Samuel Johnson himself, and the idea of biography extends back to the writing of the lives of medieval saints and to the second century Roman writer Plutarch, whose *Parallel Lives* exerted an enormous influence on the later development of biography writing. However, it was Boswell's innovations that revolutionized the genre and made it the target of suppression and censorship. He sought not only to memorialize the greatness of his subject, but to reveal his flaws. Boswell reported long passages from Johnson's actual conversations, noted his mannerisms, and in general presented an intimate picture such as no biography had ever before dared to attempt.

Because Boswell was Johnson's friend, and because Johnson had sanctioned this minute attention to his life and believed in the superiority of biography as a genre, Boswell escaped becoming the target of censorship himself. However, biographers since Boswell's time have confronted many efforts to discourage, censor, and even legally ban their books. Biographers themselves have colluded in censorship, and their subjects have often destroyed papers and mobilized friends and families to thwart their biographers' investigations.

Nineteenth Century Biography. After Boswell, there was a retreat from his bolder innovations which amounted to self-censorship on the biographers' part. In his *Memoirs of the Life of Sir Walter Scott* (1837-1838), for example, John Gibson Lockhart explicitly eschewed Boswell's intimate focus. As Scott's son-in-law, Lockhart wanted to preserve both a relative's and a great man's dignity; he became, in Ian Hamilton's words, a "keeper of the flame," the one anointed to protect the hero's reputation.

Nineteenth century biography is replete with examples of similar self-censorship. Lord Byron's biographer, for example, burned Byron's memoir lest it disgrace his subject. Henry James attempted to fix his own posthumous reputation by burning many of his papers and letters and writing fiction that denigrated the snooping biographer. Thomas Hardy tried to forestall other biographers by writing his own biography, while attributing it to the pen of his second wife, Florence Emily Hardy. Mrs. Gaskell, Charlotte Brontë's biographer, ruthlessly suppressed evidence that might show Bronte to be anything other than a conventional nineteenth century woman. Sir Richard Francis Burton's widow burned many of his unpublished translations of erotica and then wrote a bland biography of him herself. When Thomas Carlyle's biographer, James Anthony Froude, braved this trend against truth and allowed his subject's dark side to show, he was vilified in the press.

The preferred form of biography was not only sanitized, it allowed biographers virtually no leeway to interpret their subjects. Instead they presented documents with narratives that loosely linked them together, giving accounts of their subjects' times. These multivolume life-and-times biographies encased their subjects in piety and euphemism. In 1912 Mark Twain's official biographer, Albert Bigelow Paine, published a three-volume biography that carefully avoided unsavory episodes and dark issues in his subject's life. Paine dedicated the biography to Mark Twain's only surviving daughter with the ironic inscription: "To Clara Clemens Gabrilowitsch, Who steadily upheld the author's purpose to write history rather than eulogy as the story of her father's life."

Twentieth Century Biography. In *Eminent Victorians* (1918) Lytton Strachey shattered the nineteenth century tradition of reverence, censorship, and suppression. Instead of the traditional lengthy tome, he wrote essays questioning the probity of public figures, such as Cardinal Manning and General Gordon. He skewered his subjects by pointing to telling psy-

chological details. Above all, he offered his own interpretations, eschewing long quotations from documents or deference to any authority other than his own.

Since Strachey, twentieth century biographers have had to ask how much of their subjects' private lives should be told. No self-respecting biographer could merely cede control to a subject's friends and family. However access to a subject's papers and the right to quote from published and unpublished work still resided with families, friends, and literary estates. If biographers want full cooperation from them, they can seek "authorization." However, authorization may require a biographer to adhere to a view of the subject pleasing to a literary executor. Executors can help biographers get publishing contracts; they can also threaten publishers, refuse to make material available to a biographer, or even sue a biographer and publisher over matters of libel, invasion of privacy, and copyright infringement. Even when no legal action is taken, a literary estate can poison the atmosphere in which biographers work—a fact well documented in Janet Malcolm's account of Sylvia Plath's biographers in *The Silent Woman* (1994).

A modern technique for censoring or suppressing an unauthorized biography is by carefully rationing or withholding permissions to quote from the published and unpublished work of biographical subjects. A famous case involves Ian Hamilton's biography of J. D. Salinger, author of *The Catcher in the Rye* (1951). After Hamilton sent Salinger a prepublication copy of his book, Salinger took him to court, alleging that he had infringed Salinger's copyright by quoting certain unpublished letters. In fact, Hamilton had quoted only modest portions of those letters in accord with his understanding of what is deemed "fair use,"—a legal doctrine that allows writers to quote from published and unpublished work without securing permission to do so. The judgment against Hamilton and his publisher, Random House, which forced them to reset the book and eliminate all quotations from unpublished letters, had a chilling effect on the publishing industry.

In another instance, Louise DeSalvo, the author of a controversial unauthorized biography of novelist Virginia Woolf, was limited to quoting no more than one hundred words from Woolf's voluminous unpublished writings. Carl Rollyson, the author of an unauthorized biography of journalist and novelist Martha Gellhorn, was threatened with legal action by Gellhorn, whose publisher allowed him to quote nothing from Gellhorn's unpublished papers. Biographers of other controversial figures, such as L. Ron Hubbard, founder of the Church of Scientology, have also been taken to court. Margaret Walker, biographer of novelist Richard Wright, was sued for quoting from letters Wright sent to her. In these two cases, biographers prevailed in court and their books were not suppressed or censored. But the damage was already done, for it made publishers much more wary of publishing unauthorized biographies.

Political Biographies. Censorship involving political figures has tended to be far less prevalent because the law regards them as public figures, and it is much more difficult to sue biographers for invasion of privacy, libel, or copyright infringement. Powerful figures, such as urban planner Robert

Moses, have tried to stop biographers. However, the realm of the politician is so much larger and harder to control that aggressive unauthorized biographers such as Robert Caro have been able to acquire access to the essential evidence. Pressure can, however, be brought to bear by powerful families. The Kennedy family, for example, attacked William Manchester's biography of John F. Kennedy, making it difficult—but not impossible—for him to publish *The Death of a President* in 1967.

Recent court decisions and a congressional amendment clarifying that fair use applies to unpublished as well as published work has eased the problem of censorship for biographers. But wherever prominent persons' papers are in the hands of estates holding power to give or withhold permission to quote from published and unpublished work, biographers may be in the position of negotiating the truth, of deciding what can be left in or out of their biographies to satisfy the keepers of the flame.   —*Carl Rollyson*

See also Book publishing; Chilling effect; Copyright law; *Death of a President, The*; Euphemism; Franklin, Benjamin; Libel; Obituaries; Privacy, right to; Twain, Mark.

BIBLIOGRAPHY

Ian Hamilton, *Keepers of the Flame: Literary Estates and the Rise of Biography from Shakespeare to Plath* (Boston: Faber & Faber, 1994), and Michael Millgate, *Testamentary Acts: Browning, Tennyson, James Hardy* (New York: Oxford University Press, 1992), are key works for studying censorship in biography and the biographer's relationship with literary estates. See also Ian Hamilton, *In Search of J. D. Salinger* (New York: Random House, 1988), and Janet Malcolm, *The Silent Woman* (New York: Alfred A. Knopf, 1994). Steve Weinberg, *Telling the Untold Story: How Investigative Reporters Are Changing the Craft of Biography* (Columbia: University of Missouri Press, 1992), provides many examples of censorship in biography, including his own battle to publish a biography of magnate Armand Hammer.

Birth control education

DEFINITION: The teaching of practical methods for preventing pregnancy

SIGNIFICANCE: In the nineteenth century contraceptive information was classified as obscene; it took the efforts of organized birth control movements in the twentieth century to legalize and spread birth control information

Information on birth control has been available in various forms since the beginning of history. Transmitted by word of mouth, it has been difficult to censor; however, information spread by word of mouth is often inaccurate and unreliable. Condemned by churches as sinful, contraception information was spread informally and was often ineffective. The nineteenth century rise in literacy and mass publication in Western nations made reliable contraceptive advice more readily available.

The Nineteenth Century. Freethinkers and other radicals were the first to spread contraceptive information. In 1823 Francis Place, a British political activist, distributed instructive handbills to members of the working class. In the United States, Robert Dale Owen, a utopian freethinker, published

Moral Physiology in 1831; Charles Knowlton, a Massachusetts physician, published *Fruits of Philosophy* a year later. Both books argued for limiting family size and provided practical instructions. Knowlton was indicted several times for obscenity and twice found guilty during the early 1830's.

Despite the scandals following publication of these books, birth control proved a popular subject. Not only were self-help books on contraception and physiology available, but the mid-century saw an explosion of advertisements for contraceptive devices, techniques, and information. Many products were fraudulent and the techniques bizarre and sometimes dangerous; others honestly represented the latest advances in technology. In addition lecturers in physiology traveled giving speeches on contraceptive practice. One speaker, Frederick Hollick, was arrested twice during the 1840's, once for publication of *The Origins of Life* (1845) and again for his birth control lectures.

Censorship During the 1870's. The increased availability of contraceptive information drew a counterattack, especially in the United States. During the 1870's there was increasing concern over declining birthrates among native-born, white, middle-class Americans, new patterns of immigration, and the easy availability of sexually explicit materials. Opponents linked contraceptives to the rising numbers of immigrants and nonwhite Americans. Others feared the impact that sexual intercourse without pregnancy might have on the moral behavior of women.

In the United States, antivice crusader Anthony Comstock pushed through an 1873 federal law that criminalized the distribution of contraceptive information and ruthlessly pursued violators. Among his victims was Edward Bliss Foote, a civil libertarian and physician who had made his living selling contraceptive information and devices before 1873. Foote was arrested in 1876 for violating the Comstock Act of 1873 by mailing contraceptive advice. Despite his medical credentials, Foote was convicted and fined three thousand dollars. After this case, many physicians retreated from providing birth control education, leaving the shrinking field to nonprofessional vendors. Despite the risk of arrest, mail-order businesses and drug stores continued to sell condoms, diaphragms, chemical solutions, and other goods. Newspaper and magazine advertisements for such products were censored, but advertisers often got away with disguising contraceptives as "feminine hygiene" products.

American censorship of birth control became formalized in law. European censorship more often took the form of occasional prosecutions for obscenity based on the nature of the information or the audience intended. In Great Britain, for example, Annie Besant and Charles Bradlaugh were convicted for reprinting Knowlton's *Fruits of Philosophy* in 1877. Their trial was well publicized and stimulated the foundation of the Malthusian League, the first organization dedicated to promoting contraception. In 1916 socialist Guy Aldred was prosecuted for selling a British version of Margaret Sanger's *Family Limitation* pamphlet aimed at a working-class audience. Two years later, Marie Stopes's *Married Love*, designed for middle-class readers, went unprosecuted. In other areas of Europe, the

Netherlands and Germany in particular, governments paid little heed to contraception and physicians developed new contraceptive devices.

In Britain and the United States physicians were often among the most vocal opponents of birth control education. Insistent on professionalizing medicine, doctors launched campaigns warning of the physical dangers of contraception and supported efforts to criminalize it. Doctors often denied women's requests for birth control education because the idea offended their notions of women's dependency and passive sexuality. Although many middle- and upper-class women could persuade doctors to help them, among the working class, access to reliable contraceptive information became more difficult, although declining birthrates among the middle class, not the poor, were the source of societal fears about birth control.

Efforts to Repeal Censorship. By the mid-1910's feminist leaders Emma Goldman and Margaret Sanger began challenging birth control prohibitions. Goldman spoke on birth control from 1910-1917, distributing a pamphlet titled *Why and How the Poor Should Not Have Many Children*. Before she was deported for her radicalism in 1917, she was arrested in 1916 and briefly jailed for distributing contraceptive information. Sanger, a practical nurse, became the leading birth control advocate in the United States. She organized legal challenges to the Comstock Act in 1914, 1916, 1917, and 1936 that resulted in the exemption of physicians from prosecution for importing and distributing contraceptives.

In the years following World War I, organized birth control leagues were founded in Europe and America. These organizations shared information and techniques at conferences and by published reports. During the 1930's opposition to birth control education generally declined. In 1937 the American Medical Association ended its long opposition to the practice. By then, too, most religious groups supported birth control. In 1930, for example, the British Lambeth Conference of Anglican Bishops endorsed birth control, and the Federal Council of Churches of Christ in America followed suit in 1931. The Roman Catholic church, however, refused to endorse birth control; in 1930 Pope Pius XI reaffirmed his opposition.

While birth control was becoming more readily available in most countries by the 1930's, in Germany it was repressed. In 1933 Adolf Hitler's new National Socialist government closed down birth control leagues and arrested their leaders because the Nazi Party wanted German women to have high birthrates. In 1941 Germany made it illegal to import, produce, or sell birth control devices (except condoms); by 1943 offenses were punishable by death. Germany did not legalize birth control again until after World War II.

After World War II increased numbers of birth control clinics and widespread discussion of sex helped spread birth control information. A series of court decisions broadened legal use of contraceptives in the United States. In *Griswold v. Connecticut* (1965) the U.S. Supreme Court held that use of birth control techniques by married couples was not obscene. In 1971 Congress repealed most of the provisions of the Comstock Law. In 1972 the Supreme Court's *Eisenstadt v. Baird* decision held that unmarried couples had the same right to use contraceptives as married couples. With its *Carey v. Population Services International* decision in 1977, the Supreme Court upheld the rights of lay providers to supply contraceptive education to minors and legalized birth control advertisement.   —*Cathy Moran Hajo*

See also Books and obscenity law; *Bradlaugh v. The Queen*; Comstock Act of 1873; Goldman, Emma; Sanger, Margaret; Sex education; Sex manuals; Stopes, Marie.

BIBLIOGRAPHY

Angus McLaren's *A History of Contraception: From Antiquity to the Present* (New York: Basil Blackwell, 1990) provides an overview of birth control distribution. For more detail on censorship efforts in America, including the Comstock Act, see Janet Farrell Brodie, *Contraception and Abortion in Nineteenth-Century America* (Ithaca, N.Y.: Cornell University Press, 1994). Linda Gordon's *Woman's Body, Woman's Right: A Social History of Birth Control in America* (New York: Penguin, 1976) carries the American story to the 1970's, including further detail on Margaret Sanger's career. For studies of European birth control education see Atina Grossmann's *Reforming Sex: The German Movement for Birth Control and Abortion Reform, 1920-1950* (New York: Oxford University Press, 1995), and Angus McLaren's *Birth Control in Nineteenth Century England* (New York: Holmes & Meier, 1978).

Birth of a Nation, The

TYPE OF WORK: Film
RELEASE DATE: 1915
DIRECTOR: D. W. Griffith
SUBJECT MATTER: An epic saga (1875-1948) depicting the South's rebirth during Reconstruction after the Civil War
SIGNIFICANCE: The most censored work in film history, this film portrays African Americans as buffoons and thugs and glorifies the Ku Klux Klan as an organization that saved the South

A three-hour film by David Wark Griffith, *The Birth of a Nation* took its story from two books by a fundamentalist preacher who was the grandson of a Ku Klux Klan member, Thomas Dixon. Adapted from Dixon's novels *The Clansman* (1905) and *The Leopard's Spots* (1902), Griffith's film was originally released as *The Klansman* in Los Angeles on February 8, 1915. Dixon suggested changing the title to *The Birth of a Nation* for its New York release later that year. Dixon sought an endorsement for the film's historical authenticity from his former classmate President Woodrow Wilson, whose commentaries are interspersed throughout the silent film's title cards. Despite the film's acclaim as a cinematic masterpiece, *The Birth of a Nation* is best remembered for its portrayal of Southern African Americans in the Reconstruction era and its glorification of the Ku Klux Klan. The film's success inspired the Klan, which had disbanded during Reconstruction, to establish a new charter in late 1915.

Several weeks after the film's opening, the U.S. Supreme Court introduced government censorship to the motion picture industry in *Mutual Film Corporation v. Industrial Commission of Ohio*, a case unrelated to *The Birth of a Nation*. The court defined the fledgling industry as a business, therefore depriv-

The many objections that African Americans had to The Birth of a Nation *included D. W. Griffith's use of white actors in blackface to portray African Americans, as in this lynching scene.* (Museum of Modern Art/Film Stills Archive)

ing it of the constitutional guarantees of freedom of speech and press because the industry was "capable of evil" through its "attractiveness and manner of exhibition." The decision was not overturned for thirty-five years.

Griffith's work became the most banned film in history, experiencing more than a hundred incidents of censorship in and out of court—a third of which occurred immediately after the film's release. The 1915 release was originally banned in Minneapolis, Minnesota; Chicago, Illinois; Pittsburgh, Pennsylvania; Denver, Colorado; St. Louis, Missouri, and the entire state of Ohio. The Minnesota banning inspired a court case, *Bainbridge v. the City of Minneapolis* (1915), when Minneapolis Mayor W. G. Nye threatened to revoke a theater's license for showing the film. The exhibitor took the case to court but lost in both a district court and in the state's supreme court, which upheld the mayor's power to revoke a license issued by the city council. After O.J. Simpson's 1995 acquittal on murder charges, Turner Classic Movies cancelled its planned showing of the film, considering racial tensions at that time too strained.

Showings of *The Birth of a Nation* have undergone a series of legal challenges from the National Association for the Ad-vancement of Colored People, which attacked the film by relying on local ordinances that kept it from being shown. These efforts met with only moderate success. Despite its racial overtones, however, Griffith's film is often studied on college campuses as a classic example of cinematic technique.

See also African Americans; Civil War, U.S.; Film adaptation; Film censorship; Ku Klux Klan; National Association for the Advancement of Colored People; Political correctness; Simpson, O. J., case.

Black, Hugo

BORN: February 27, 1886, rural Clay County, Alabama
DIED: September 19, 1971, Washington, D.C.
IDENTIFICATION: U.S. Supreme Court justice (1937-1971)
SIGNIFICANCE: With Justice William O. Douglas, Black was one of the two justices who interpreted the First Amendment as prohibiting almost all forms of censorship of free speech and press

In 1937 U.S. President Franklin D. Roosevelt made Senator Hugo Black of Alabama his first nominee to the U.S. Supreme Court. Roosevelt had been frustrated by Supreme Court decisions invalidating his economic program to end the Great Depression that were made by old and conservative members who would not resign. He chose Black as one of his loyal supporters. After Black's quick confirmation, a sudden uproar erupted over Black's brief past membership in the Ku Klux Klan (KKK), a notoriously antiblack organization. Black's defense was that any successful Alabama politician had to be part of the KKK, and that his Senate voting record showed he was not beholden to the Klan. He went on to be one of the strongest supporters of free expression and racial justice.

On free expression, Black was a strong opponent of censorship who believed that the First Amendment's words, "Congress shall make no law . . . abridging freedom of speech or the press" should be taken as absolute. Other justices favored using a balancing test to decide whether free speech was more valuable than government regulations for some presumably good purpose. Black's position was that the only balancing needed had been done when the First Amendment's Framers had set the balance entirely in favor of free speech and press. He dissented in cases upholding the convictions of communists during the Red Scare, and he wrote a stirring defense of free press in the Pentagon Papers case—his last opinion before his death. He also declined to censor pornography, although he personally abhorred it.

Despite Black's long support of free speech and press, he did not agree that protections of speech and press automatically extended to actions. He particularly did not hold that

Associate Justice Hugo Black was one of the Supreme Court's strongest defenders of free speech. (Library of Congress)

demonstrations were protected as fully as speech and press. Black upheld an absolute right of people to write and speak because he was a literal textualist in interpreting the Constitution. He also held that assemblies had to be peaceable, because the First Amendment protects only the right "peaceably to assemble." When he voted to oppose convictions of groups violating various laws governing demonstrations, he was being consistent with a larger understanding that the Constitution should be read for the exact meaning of its words whenever possible.

Many constitutional scholars have described Black's method of constitutional interpretation as "textualism," meaning that the constitution's words should be followed exactly whenever possible. Black's position on assembly would thus be consistent, because the word "peaceably" appears before the word "assemble" in the First Amendment, allowing prior restraints to be applied to assemblies. Black also opposed expanding speech to include actions that have been called "symbolic" speech.

See also Assembly, right of; Courts and censorship law; Douglas, William O.; First Amendment; *Pentagon Papers, The*; Prior restraint; Symbolic speech; Warren, Earl.

Black Like Me

TYPE OF WORK: Book
PUBLISHED: 1961
AUTHOR: John Howard Griffin (1920-1980)
SUBJECT MATTER: Memoir of a white man's experience traveling through the Deep South disguised as a black man
SIGNIFICANCE: The passionate racial feelings that this book aroused among white Americans have made it one of the country's most frequently banned books

One of the books referred to as the "dirty thirty" by a number of scholars, *Black Like Me* has ranked among the thirty books most frequently attacked after 1965. It was one of eleven on the list that dealt with non-Anglo-Saxon whites. The Southern racial climate of the 1950's and the 1960's Civil Rights movement tended to indicate to many that censorship of these eleven books was based on racial motivations.

Griffin's initial intention in writing *Black Like Me* was simply to research the conditions of African Americans in the South. After he began, however, he realized that to get inside the "skin" of an African American and to experience their suffering, he had to become one. He then artificially changed his skin coloring to brown and traveled through the South as a black man. His book recounts his treatment at the hands of both white and black people.

Criticized as not reflecting a true portrait of Southern society, *Black Like Me* was also praised by supporters as having removed the pretensions that existed in America. In 1966 a renewed attack was made on the publication of a paperback edition, which was deemed unfit for children.

See also African Americans; Race.

Blacklisting

DEFINITION: Specifying persons or groups to be punished or denied employment on the basis of their beliefs or associations

SIGNIFICANCE: Blacklisting has been used as a device to isolate, ostracize, and deny employment to dissenters from the popular consensus

Blacklisting reached its height during the Cold War in the United States, but it has historically been used by governments, churches, and businesses to target dissidents. During World War I the U.S. government blacklisted businesses with suspected subversive connections. In 1947 the administration of President Harry S Truman blacklisted ninety supposedly disloyal businesses as part of a "get tough with Russia policy" designed to halt communism. Truman's Loyalty Review Board investigated three million federal employees, three thousand of whom resigned or were dismissed.

The 1950's Red Scare, reminiscent of the 1919-1920 Red Scare, linked political radicalism with suspected foreign conspiracies. Conservatives, fearing that American communists (numbering about eighty thousand during the 1940's) were conspiring to overthrow the government, united to blacklist suspects.

The 1950's Hollywood blacklist originated during an industry-wide meeting in New York City on November 24-25, 1947. Bowing to political and economic pressure, film studios fired a group of allegedly procommunist employees and implemented the blacklist, a self-policing strategy to prevent government control and to avert costly public boycotts.

The House Committee on Un-American Activities (also known as the House Un-American Activities Committee, or the HUAC) targeted Hollywood because it considered movies, disseminated to millions, an ideal vehicle to spread subversive ideas among the American public. Hollywood developed the largest blacklist in America, eventually barring 212 employees, some with only a slightly suspicious past. Blacklists targeted those who refused to sign a loyalty oath, those who invoked the Fifth Amendment, and those who refused to appear before the HUAC. People knew they were blacklisted when jobs disappeared, income dropped, and friends evaporated. Removal from the blacklist required a degrading ceremony, in which one renounced communism and named other former communists. The pressure to recant was constant and unrelenting; the alternative—social and financial ostracism—was devastating.

Blacklisting repressed information as well as people. The *Index Librorum Prohibitorum* blacklisted books that the Roman Catholic church believed damaged faith or morals. The U.S. Customs banned books, beginning in 1842. Modern American churches, libraries, and schools have blacklisted literature, removing materials disapproved of by interest groups. Films have been banned because of their subject matter or the suspected radicalism of the actors.

Blacklisting gradually eroded during the 1960's. Dalton Trumbo, nominated under a pseudonym for an Academy Award, struck a blow against blacklisting by publicly accepting the award in his own name. The HUAC blacklisted former communists without such constitutional safeguards as an impartial trial, the right to cross examination, and the exclusionary rule. Informers became role models, honored with jobs, prestige, and media praise.

Blacklisting had immense social costs, damaging government credibility and faith in freedoms guaranteed by the United States Constitution. Fear, suspicion, and betrayal destroyed community trust. Film content became extremely conservative, avoiding controversial subjects. Blacklisting, by tampering with ideas and information, changed and corrupted history.

See also Boycotts; *Front, The*; Hollywood Ten; House Committee on Un-American Activities; *Index Librorum Prohibitorum*; Seeger, Pete; Trumbo, Dalton.

Blackstone, William

BORN: July 10, 1723, London, England
DIED: February 14, 1780, London, England
IDENTIFICATION: English jurist best known for his writings on common law
SIGNIFICANCE: Blackstone's views on the nature of freedom of expression influenced early American discussions on this subject

Blackstone's *Commentaries on the Laws of England* (1765-1769) influenced the early development of the American commitment to freedom of speech and press. During both the colonial and revolutionary eras American lawyers relied heavily on Blackstone's work as the most authoritative treatise on British common law because it specifically addressed the contours and limits of freedom of speech and press.

For Blackstone, freedom of expression was essential to free government, but he thought that this freedom consisted simply in freedom from prior restraints of speech. A prior restraint prevents the initial dissemination of speech, most commonly by requiring speakers or printers to obtain licenses before speaking or publishing. According to Blackstone, government might punish various kinds of objectionable speech without infringing on freedom of speech, so long as it took no steps to restrain such speech before it was uttered. It has long been unclear whether the framers of the U.S. Constitution's Bill of Rights incorporated Blackstone's views about freedom of speech into their own understandings of the First Amendment. Ultimately, the U.S. Supreme Court determined that the First Amendment's protection of speech and press is more expansive than what Blackstone had envisioned by interpreting the amendment's freedoms to embrace more than simply freedom from prior restraints.

See also Constitution, U.S.; Courts and censorship law; First Amendment; Jefferson, Thomas; Madison, James; Prior restraint.

Blasphemy laws

DEFINITION: Blasphemy is irreverent or contemptuous expression about God or something held sacred
SIGNIFICANCE: Blasphemy continues to be a justification for censorship, even for the death penalty

Blasphemous remarks are, according to the Mosaic law of the Hebrew Bible, punishable by death. The crime of blasphemy was incorporated into the Roman emperor Justinian's sixth century great codification of Roman law. In medieval Europe, blasphemy was included in canon law and was generally punishable by death.

Writing in Europe was for centuries subject to prior censorship; this prior reading before publication or performance was intended, among other things, to prevent blasphemy. Blasphemy was typically prosecuted in ecclesiastical courts, which usually condemned the convicted to burning at the stake. In seventeenth century England, blasphemy was treated as a political crime by the Star Chamber, which was a committee with broad powers of prosecution, so named because the hall in which it met had stars painted on the ceiling. With the demise of Star Chamber proceedings, blasphemy became an offense of common law in 1675 on the grounds that it "tended to the subversion of all government." Later in the century a Blasphemy Statute was enacted—which has never been repealed—that became the basis for self-censorship and for numerous prosecutions when deterrence failed. Scottish law also punished blasphemy, originally by death, but after 1825 by fines and imprisonment.

In other parts of the English-speaking world, such as the United States and Australia, both common and statute law made blasphemy punishable with fines and imprisonment. In Australia, resistance to prior censorship began in earnest in the 1870's. In 1871 one William Jones was prosecuted and sentenced in New South Wales to two years imprisonment, and he was fined a large sum for denying the main tenets of Christianity and for declaring the Bible "the most immoral book ever published." Opposition to the sentence was so great that he was released after four months. Resistance to similar charges continued for the remainder of the nineteenth century. Authorities of various English-speaking nations attempted to silence offensive publications but in the end failed.

In the twentieth century efforts to enforce censorship of religiously objectionable material diminished but did not disappear. In Australia, attempts were made to ban an Italian socialist magazine in 1911, and several years later issues of another offending magazine were destroyed.

In England one W. J. Gott was sentenced in 1922 to nine months at hard labor for distributing blasphemous pamphlets and died shortly after being released. For the next half century, although the law was still on the books, blasphemy prosecutions in England ceased. In 1977, however, the editor and publishers of the London newspaper *Gay News* were tried, convicted, and fined for a crime of blasphemous libel for publishing a poem.

In the United States the legal definition of blasphemy has included "fighting words," or speech so offensive as to incite violence. In *Chaplinsky v. New Hampshire* (1942) and in other cases involving offensive speech of Jehovah's Witnesses, the U.S. Supreme Court recognized fighting words as impermissible speech, but the Court made clear that the deciding issue was not the words themselves but the "clear and present danger" that the words would cause a breach of the peace. Later, the requirement was softened to "clear and probable danger" of a breach of the peace. Speech itself, however offensive, including speech that would in earlier times be outlawed as blasphemous, is, however, protected. The United States in the twentieth century witnessed the growth of a veritable industry of censorship attempts, many successful, against school text-

books and school libraries; these attempts were often led by Fundamentalist Christians who considered various books or passages within books blasphemous.

A notorious example of an attempt to punish a writer for blasphemy began in 1989, when a powerful Iranian cleric, the Ayatollah Ruhollah Khomeini, issued a *fatwa* (legal opinion) declaring British writer Salman Rushdie's novel *The Satanic Verses* blasphemous and offering a large reward for his murder. Rushdie went into hiding and, to safeguard his life, he was rarely seen thereafter. The Rushdie case became an international *cause célèbre*.

See also Australia; Bible; Christianity; Clear and present danger doctrine; Death; Fighting words; Heresy; Iran; Islam; Jehovah's Witnesses; Religion; Rushdie, Salman; Secular humanism.

Blue Book of 1946

TYPE OF WORK: Government report
RELEASED: March, 1945
AUTHORS: Officers of the Federal Communications Commission (FCC)
SUBJECT MATTER: Critical evaluation of the failure of American broadcast licensees to meet their obligations to provide public service programming
SIGNIFICANCE: Members of the broadcasting industry denounced this report as an attempt at anti-American censorship and rendered its recommendations ineffective by their resistance

During the late 1930's and early 1940's the FCC received many complaints about the wide discrepancies between what broadcast licensees had promised to broadcast in their license applications and what they were actually broadcasting. Concerned that broadcasters were not living up to their public service obligations, the FCC hired a former British Broadcasting Corporation executive, Dr. Charles Siepmann, to direct a study of the problem and to make recommendations on improving its program evaluation service.

In March, 1945, the FCC released Siepmann's formal report, *Public Service Responsibility of Broadcast Licensees*—which became known as the "Blue Book" after the color of its cover. Focusing on a selected group of licensees, the report charged American broadcasters generally with failing to provide enough programming on local public affairs or public service issues, and with airing excessive numbers of commercials. The report advised the FCC to use its licensing powers to ensure that stations adhere to certain broad guidelines in order to meet their public service obligations, and it recommended that the commission review stations' past records at license renewal time.

The Blue Book proposed an unprecedented policy for the FCC, which for the first time would take into account the programming records of mainstream broadcasting stations when issuing their licenses. The National Association of Broadcasters immediately began attacking the FCC and its members, however, charging them with trying to interfere with the First Amendment rights of member stations. The unexpected intensity of these attacks—which were supported by some members of Congress—caused the FCC to back off from the Blue Book's recommendations. Although the FCC never officially rescinded this report, broadcaster resistance rendered its directives largely ineffective.

See also Broadcast media; Fairness doctrine; Federal Communications Commission.

Blue Velvet

TYPE OF WORK: Film
RELEASED: 1986
DIRECTOR: David Lynch (1946-   )
SUBJECT MATTER: When a young man and woman undertake to investigate a crime, they become involved with a sexually abused nightclub singer and a sadistic killer
SIGNIFICANCE: Described by one reviewer as "The Hardy Boys in Hell," *Blue Velvet* challenged the limits of the Motion Picture Association of America's rating system and divided critics between those praising it as a brilliant work of art and those dismissing it as pornographic trash

Blue Velvet contains frontal nudity and simulated sexual activity, but it was the violent sexual assaults of the villain—chillingly played by Dennis Hopper—that shocked and outraged audiences and sent many people scrambling for theater exits to demand their money back. *Blue Velvet* mixes the conventions of *film noir*, the "coming-of-age" story, soft-core pornography, and gothic horror so expertly that reviewers split between those who loved it and those who hated it. For example, James M. Wall, writing in *Christian Century*, called it the best film of 1986 for its exploration of human evil, while John Simon blasted it in *The National Review* as "true pornography" and "mindless junk." David Lynch, who was nominated for an Academy Award for his direction of the film, has called it "a trip beneath the surface of a small American town" and a "probe into the subconscious of a place where you face things that you don't normally face."

See also Film censorship; Motion Picture Association of America; *Natural Born Killers*; Sex in the arts; Violence.

Blume, Judy

BORN: February 12, 1938, Elizabeth, New Jersey
IDENTIFICATION: American writer of fiction for juveniles and young adults
SIGNIFICANCE: Blume has been one of the most frequently censored writers for young readers largely because of her honest portrayals of teenage sexuality

Blume has written frank, cutting-edge books that are loved by many young readers but often loathed by parents, school officials, and watchdog groups. Her detractors have objected to

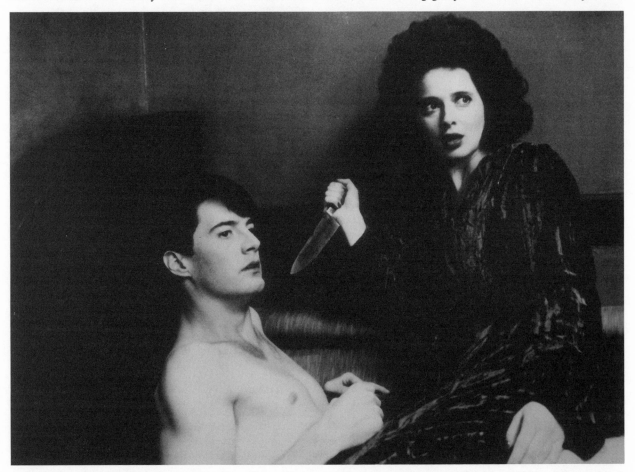

Isabella Rossellini and Kyle MacLachlan play ill-fated lovers in Blue Velvet. *(Museum of Modern Art/Film Stills Archive)*

Judy Blume and George Cooper at a Chicago banquet where Blume received a Freedom to Read award in November, 1984—a week after three of her books were banned from school libraries in Peoria, Illinois. (AP/Wide World Photos)

children reading about such topics as the development of sexual awareness during the teen years, menstruation, masturbation, and premarital sex. According to People for the American Way, Blume authored more of the books for young people that were banned between 1982 and 1992 than any other writer.

One of Blume's early efforts, *Are You There, God? It's Me, Margaret* (1970) acted as a magnet, attracting young readers and censors alike in 1970. Written in the form of nighttime prayers, the story is about a girl named Margaret, who agonizes over being a new girl in town, her parent's mixed-faith religions, her small breasts, her late menstruation, and other matters. Told with great restraint and humor, the book immediately stirred controversy, and never appeared on many school library shelves. The next year, *Then Again, Maybe I Won't* (1971) met with even stronger opposition, because it dealt with the problems of a teenager named Tony, who, like Margaret, worries about his developing body. Censors charged that Blume's book promoted voyeurism, shoplifting, and dealt with unsavory subjects such as alcohol abuse, masturbation, and the fear of unexpected erections.

Candid depictions of female masturbation in *Deenie* (1973) and the "naughty" language that children use in *Blubber* (1974) brought forth more denunciations and were banned in many middle schools. The most controversial and most widely banned of all Blume's books is *Forever* (1975). It tells the story of Katherine, a champion high school tennis player, who

narrates her experience of first love, which develops into an unexpected sexual encounter. Censors deemed the book pornographic in its detailed sexual descriptions and inappropriate in its use of four-letter words and its discussion of birth control and disobedience to parents.

Strangely, both conservative and liberal groups attack Judy Blume. Conservative organizations such as the Moral Majority, Eagle Forum, and National Association of Christian Educators aid parents and school officials in ferreting out Blume's books because, these protestors believe, the books titillate and sexually stimulate children. Liberals, on the other hand, label Blume a racist because her characters—drawn mainly from her own childhood experiences in all-white neighborhoods—are not racially diverse; moreover, liberals condemn Blume for lacking "a feminist's perspective," in that her books often feature housewives rather than career women.

Blume defends her novels, believing them to be moral, since they really support traditional values. She has fought attempted censorship over the years, often appearing on talk shows to discuss the issues. The continued popularity of Blume's works among young readers attests to her accuracy in portraying teenagers' concern with sexual development. To Blume, "puberty" is not a dirty word.

See also Banned Books Week; Books, young adult; Libraries, school; People for the American Way; Sex in the arts.

Blyton, Enid

BORN: August 11, 1897, East Dulwich, London
DIED: November 28, 1968, Hampstead, England
IDENTIFICATION: English author of children's fiction
SIGNIFICANCE: Blyton's easy-to-read books received much controversy and criticism and were banned by many educators and librarians

A best-selling children's author in Great Britain, Enid Blyton (who also wrote as Mary Pollack), began her writing career in 1922 with the publication of *Child Whispers*, a book of poetry. Before becoming a prolific writer, Blyton served as an editor of *Sunny Stories* magazine and compiled a children's encyclopedia. Until her death she wrote as much as one book a month, finishing hundreds of books for children ages five through fifteen. Her most famous works were *Noddy* books, the *Famous Five*, and *Secret Seven* series.

Although her works set in idyllic rural England enjoyed great popularity, were translated into many languages— including Russian and Swahili—and sold in the millions yearly, they also received repeated complaints from teachers and public librarians. Disputes centered on the overly limited vocabulary that she used, her use of racial and gender stereotypes, and her predictable plots. As a former teacher, Blyton believed that her young readers needed simplicity and familiarity.

Supporters of Blyton's works argued that her writing inspired development of early reading, but librarians refuted such assertions and removed her books from library shelves. Despite this, Blyton's popularity continued; more than three hundred of her books remained in print at the end of the 1980's.

See also Books, children's; Libraries, school; Race.

Boccaccio, Giovanni

BORN: June or July, 1313, Florence or Certaldo, Italy
DIED: December 21, 1375, Certaldo, Italy
IDENTIFICATION: Italian storyteller, poet, and humanist
SIGNIFICANCE: Boccaccio's secular masterpiece, the *Decameron*, has historically been a major target of censors objecting to its salacious and anticlerical content

Boccaccio was a scholar whose voluminous works included romantic novels, epic poems, biographies, and collections of myths and legends. His most famous work—and the one most often censored—is the *Decameron*, a collection of one hundred tales that appeared from 1349 to 1351. Although Boccaccio had probably collected the tales over many years, his introduction to the work explains that seven young ladies and three young men entertained each other with the stories for ten days while the bubonic plague ravaged Florence in 1348. Both charming and humorous, the stories deal mostly with themes of love and sex—often in a lascivious fashion. Although Boccaccio appears to have been a practicing Roman Catholic, he used the stories to poke fun at the moral laxity of the priests and monks of his time.

From an early date, pious critics were shocked by the salacious and ostensibly anticlerical aspects of the *Decameron*. In 1497 Girolamo Savonarola, the prior of Florence's St. Mark's Cathedral, burned the work as a part of the "bonfire of the vanities." In 1559 the *Index Librorum Prohibitorum* of Pope Paul IV condemned the book; however, in 1573 Pope Gregory XIII allowed publication of an expurgated edition that retained the licentious parts but removed portions considered disrespectful of the Church and tainted by heresy. Fourteen years later, Pope Sixtus V proscribed all editions of the work. Around 1600 Boccaccio's book was condemned by both the Sorbonne and the French Parliament, and a French law of 1819 required officials to ban it and similar works as harmful to religion and public morality.

In the United States, moral crusaders have frequently attacked the *Decameron* as lewd and pornographic. Authorities who enforced the Comstock Act of 1873 used the Hicklin rule to proscribe it and other risqué classics from the mails. Anthony Comstock was willing to allow such classics to be sent to select libraries where they could be examined by mature scholars, but he did not want them sent to private individuals who might allow young people to read them. In 1922, a federal district judge fined a bookseller one thousand dollars for sending an expurgated edition of the book through the U.S. mails. Under the Tariff Act of 1930, the *Decameron* was one of the books automatically confiscated by customs, although the federal customs office allowed the book to enter the country the next year. During the 1930's, the courts of New York and most other states ruled that the *Decameron* was not obscene. As late as 1934, however, police in Detroit continued to seize the book, and in 1935 it was still banned by the Boston Watch and Ward Society.

In Great Britain, legal prosecution of the *Decameron* did not end until the mid-1950's. A 1953 list included the book as one of seven hundred titles to be destroyed by local British magistrates. The last major attempt to ban the book occurred in Swindon, England, where local justices of the peace in 1954 ordered confiscated copies to be burned; however, an appeals court, finding that a copy was already in the local library, reversed the order. The abandonment of the Hicklin rule made it increasingly difficult for authorities to censor recognized classics such as the *Decameron*.

See also Books and obscenity law; Boston Watch and Ward Society; Comstock, Anthony; Comstock Act of 1873; Customs laws, U.S.; Hicklin case; *Index Librorum Prohibitorum*; Italy; *Oh, Calcutta!*; *Roth v. United States*; Vatican.

Bolles, Donald F., Jr.

BORN: July 10, 1928, Milwaukee, Wisconsin
DIED: June 13, 1976, Phoenix, Arizona
IDENTIFICATION: American investigative reporter
SIGNIFICANCE: Bolles was killed by a car bomb, the first time in fifty years that murder had been used to prevent an American newspaper reporter from pursuing a story

Don Bolles joined the *Arizona Republic* in 1962 after nearly nine years as a reporter and editor with the Associated Press. He quickly established a reputation as a tireless investigative reporter, earning a Pulitzer Prize nomination in 1965 for stories exposing bribery and kickbacks in the Arizona state government. In 1967 he exposed land fraud in the state and in 1973 exposed Mafia infiltration of legitimate businesses.

On June 2, 1976, a bomb exploded under Bolles's car at a Phoenix hotel where he had gone to meet a man linked to organized crime and a sports concessions firm. Fatally injured, Bolles died eleven days later. Police arrested the man Bolles was to meet, who later pleaded guilty in the slaying, implicating two others as well. The convictions of all three were overturned by the Arizona Supreme Court in 1980, but retrials also resulted in convictions in Bolles's death or related cases.

The murderous effort to silence Bolles drew the wrath of journalists across the nation. In an unprecedented move, the organization Investigative Reporters and Editors, which had been founded the previous year, assembled a team of nearly forty print and broadcast journalists for what became known as the Arizona Project. Their goal was to continue Bolles's work and show that violence would not deter journalists. After four months of probing corruption in Arizona, the team produced a series of twenty-three articles totaling some eighty thousand words. It appeared in newspapers in March and April, 1977. Bolles became the best-known martyr to American journalism since Elijah Lovejoy.

See also Death; Journalists, violence against; Lovejoy, Elijah Parish.

Book and Periodical Council Statement on the Freedom of Expression and the Freedom to Read

TYPE OF WORK: Tract
PUBLISHED: 1978
AUTHORS: Members of Toronto's Book and Periodical Development Council
SUBJECT MATTER: One-page statement denouncing censorship

SIGNIFICANCE: This tract expresses the anticensorship position of a coalition of Canadian organizations representing authors, librarians, publishers, and book and magazine distributors

Originally established in 1975 as the Book and Periodical Development Council, the Book and Periodical Council is an umbrella organization for some twenty-four associations involved in the writing, editing, publishing, manufacturing, distribution, selling, and lending of books and periodicals in Canada.

In 1978 the council published a statement setting forth its basic tenets regarding freedom of expression and the freedom to read. Concerned about growing efforts to censor printed materials and their creators, council members wished to "assert the public interest in the preservation of the freedom to read." In concluding its statement, the council affirmed its "absolute commitment to combatting, in whatever form it takes, the suppression of books and periodicals because we believe that the written word is the ultimate mode of free expression." Since 1984 the Book and Periodical Council, through its Freedom of Expression Committee, has sponsored a national "Freedom to Read Week" in February to focus public attention on intellectual freedom.

See also Advocacy; Canada; Canadian Library Association Statement on Intellectual Freedom; Chapultepec Declaration; First Hemispheric Conference on Free Expression; Freedom; Freedom to Read Week; Intellectual freedom; Library Bill of Rights; School prayer.

Book burning

DEFINITION: Deliberate physical destruction of printed texts with fire

SIGNIFICANCE: Book burnings have occurred as an extreme form of censorship for thousands of years

Books are often burned on the grounds that they contain subversive political or religious ideas, or include language and material not appropriate for young readers. Governments and organizations wishing to repress certain thoughts and ideas have faced a problem in censoring material that already has been printed. One solution has been the physical destruction of the printed matter, usually by fire. Books have also been deliberately ruined by water. The public burning of books often does more than merely destroy unwanted material, however, it can serve as an impressive expression of the power of the state, and as a unifying and exciting experience for the crowds that participate in the burnings.

Records of book burning date back thousand of years. Unhappy with the prophecies of Jeremiah, King Jehoiakim burned the first book of the prophet in 605 B.C.E. Jeremiah promptly rewrote the book. Another instance of mass book burning occurred in the third century B.C.E. in China. The first emperor of the Ts'in Dynasty ordered the works of Confucius destroyed. Less than thirty years later, the Emperor Shih huang-ti ordered all printed works in his empire destroyed except for those containing practical information, which would be housed in the Imperial Library. He hoped that the destruction of historical records would hamper the efforts of

contenders to the throne. Although neither emperor was completely successful in his efforts, the possibility of losing the works of Confucius so frightened later Chinese rulers that they ordered the philosopher's works carved on enormous stone tablets, impervious to flame.

Religious Burnings. Books condemned as heretical by various churches often have been burned. The Book of Acts in the Bible states that after hearing the ministry of Paul, the Ephesians burned books of "curious arts," or magic, worth fifty thousand pieces of silver. The Christian church often targeted the works of other religions for burning. Monastic orders commanded the burning of Hebrew books in Egypt in 1190; the destruction of Hebrew books by Christian religious authorities continued for centuries. In Paris fifty years later the Talmud and other Hebrew works were denounced as blasphemous. Twenty-four carts were required to haul the condemned texts to the public burnings. In Florence in 1497 the cleric Girolamo Savonarola ordered the burning of the vanities, which included playing cards, dice, works of art, and the works of celebrated authors such as Dante Alighieri and Giovanni Boccaccio. Savonarola and his works, in turn, were destroyed by fire the following year when the church condemned him as a heretic.

The works of Martin Luther were burned in St. Paul's churchyard in England in 1521. Four years later copies of William Tyndale's translation of the New Testament were denounced and burned, making Tyndale the first Englishman to have his work destroyed on British soil. Luther's translation of the Bible was denounced by the papacy and burned in Germany in 1624. During the years of the English Revolution, when Puritans controlled the British government, numerous religious tracts and pamphlets were publicly burned as heretical.

Puritan values also reached across the Atlantic. The first publicly burned book in North America was William Pynchon's *The Meritorious Price of Our Redemption* (1650). Pynchon was among the leading citizens of the Massachusetts Bay Colony, which was founded on the principles of Puritanism. Originally published in London, Pynchon's pamphlet contained theological arguments that deviated from Puritan orthodoxy. When copies became available in Massachusetts, the General Court condemned the work as heretical. Copies were burned in the Boston marketplace on October 20, 1650. Pynchon soon departed for England.

Political Burnings. Burnings also occur in the context of military conquest or political revolution. The new ruler destroys the remnants of the old regime in order to eradicate possible subversive influences and to display the power of the new state. In the early years of the French Revolution the books of the monasteries were gathered and destroyed; estimates for those burnings run as high as four million books and twenty five thousand manuscripts. Governments have also destroyed pamphlets and manuscripts that question their legitimacy. During the sixteenth and seventeenth centuries England witnessed a number of burnings as the kings and queens of that nation burned material that criticized the monarchy. In 1614 King James I ordered Sir Walter Raleigh's *History of the World*

(1614) burned for "being too saucy in censuring princes." During the Restoration several authors, including John Milton, had their political tracts burned by the command of King Charles II.

The Spanish military conquest of the Yucatan Peninsula met with resistance and revolts. Determined to force the Maya to convert to Christianity and obey Spanish rule, the Spanish proceeded to annihilate the remnants of Mayan culture. The Spanish targeted the sacred books of the Jaguar Priests, which were actually deerskin and bark inscribed with hieroglyphics. Bishop Diego de Landa enacted a policy of burning the sacred texts. While historians debate the veracity of the tale of a massive book burning directed by Landa in Mani in 1562, they agree that Landa participated in many burnings. Landa condemned the sacred texts as the work of the devil and reported that their destruction caused great dismay among the Maya.

The Nazi Burnings. In May, 1933, four months after the Nazis came to power, huge bonfires burned thousands of books in cities throughout Germany. The new regime had announced that only "good art," art that served the people, would be tolerated. In response to this pronouncement, the German Student's Corporation planned the mass book burnings. The largest was a well-organized event held in Berlin. A torchlight parade of five thousand students marched into the Franz Joseph Plaza and ignited a huge mound of wood. Trucks and oxcarts hauled the condemned books into the plaza, where crowds of enthusiastic students pitched them into the bonfire. Nearly forty thousand people assembled to watch the burning. At midnight Nazi official Joseph Goebbels spoke to the crowd and announced that Germany had been cleansed and that a new era had begun.

Burned books included works by the German authors Karl Marx, Thomas Mann, and Erich Maria Remarque. Works by foreign corrupters such as Ernest Hemingway, André Gide, Jack London, Upton Sinclair, and Margaret Sanger were thrown into the flames. Smaller book burnings continued throughout Germany. After the Germans conquered Austria in 1938, the libraries in that nation were stripped of controversial works, which were then burned.

In the repressive atmosphere of the Third Reich the burnings generated no strong criticism. Many professors supported the burnings, and at most Germans rationalized the burnings as the work of overzealous students. However, intellectuals and authors recognized the ominous overtones of the incidents and began leaving Germany in large numbers during the 1930's. Reaction in the United States was much stronger. The Berlin

Young German supporters of Adolf Hitler's National Socialist Party collect "un-German" books and pamphlets to burn. (National Archives)

fires became front-page news, and one hundred thousand people marched in a New York protest parade. Editors and intellectuals condemned the burnings and denounced Germany as "insane" or "neurotic." At the conclusion of World War II many people recalled the words of the nineteenth century poet Heinrich Heine, who wrote that "where books are burned, in the end people will be burned," a warning that came true during the Nazi era.

The Nazi bonfires raised new doubts about the legitimacy of book burning. When the public library in St. Louis ordered the burning of John Steinbeck's *The Grapes of Wrath* (1939), an appeal from the National Council on Freedom from Censorship had the order weakened and the book was placed on the "Adults Only" shelf. Before the 1930's the practice of book burning had been strongly criticized; but after World War II book burning was feared as the first step toward totalitarianism. Even during the tense ideological battles of the Cold War, most Americans refused to countenance book burning. In 1953 Senator Joseph McCarthy's investigation into the holdings of American-supported overseas libraries led to directives ordering the removal of controversial authors. This decision led to a national outcry against censorship which intensified when it was reported that government officials had burned some books. The early reports were exaggerated; apparently only a dozen or so books were burned because the librarians did not know what to do with them. The reports of book burning nevertheless distressed Americans, many of whom could remember the Nazi outrages.

Fundamentalism. The disturbing features of book burning, however, did not end the practice. While the United States government did not sanction book burning, individuals and groups continued to burn books they found objectionable. The conflict shifted from national governments to school boards as most of the burned books came from public school libraries. With the rise of Fundamentalist religious groups in the twentieth century, books were often condemned as blasphemous or immoral, often on the grounds that they contained obscene language or inappropriate sexual content.

One case that garnered national attention occurred in 1974 in Drake, North Dakota. A high school English teacher assigned Kurt Vonnegut's *Slaughterhouse-Five* (1969), James Dickey's *Deliverance* (1970), and a short-story anthology. The school board pronounced the books dirty, fired the teacher, and ordered the books burned. The public burning of *Slaughterhouse-Five* generated so much negative publicity that the school board rescinded the order. The school superintendent claimed that the school board's actions had been proper. The teacher filed a lawsuit and won an out-of-court settlement.

Despite the reaction to the Drake burning, the destruction of books continued in the United States. In 1977 John Steinbeck's *Of Mice and Men* (1937) was burned in Pennsylvania, and in 1981 copies of *National Geographic* magazine and several comic books were burned in Omaha, Nebraska. The children's books *Cinderella* and *Snow White and the Seven Dwarfs* were reported burned in Louisiana in 1982 because they contained references to witches. In 1993 a crowd assembled on the steps of the school district building in Kansas City

and burned a single copy of a juvenile book that offered a positive portrayal of lesbianism. A telephone poll conducted after the burning revealed that 50 percent of the respondents approved of the incident. However, many high school students protested the event by checking thousands of books out of school libraries to illustrate how empty library shelves would be if controversial books did not exist.

Fundamentalist book burnings are not merely an American phenomenon. After the Ayatollah Ruhollah Khomeini condemned Salman Rushdie's *The Satanic Verses* (1988) and called for Rushdie's assassination, Islamic fundamentalists in the British town of Bradford burned copies of the novel in the streets in early 1989.   —*Thomas Clarkin*

See also Alexandria library; Confucius; Democritus; Heine, Heinrich; Jeremiah's Book of Prophesies, burning of; Luther, Martin; Maya books, destruction of; National Socialism; Pascal, Blaise; Puritans; Raleigh, Sir Walter; Rushdie, Salman; Savonarola, Girolamo; Spanish Empire; Talmud.

BIBLIOGRAPHY

A comprehensive survey of book burning as a form of censorship remains to be written. Readers interested in the topic should refer to works on banned literature for chapters or articles on book burning. Some works that include material on book burning include Anne Lyon Haight's *Banned Books: Informal Notes on Some Books Banned for Various Reasons at Various Times and in Various Places* (New York: R. R. Bowker, 1970). Marc Drogin's *Biblioclasm: The Mythical Origins, Magic Powers, and Perishability of the Written Word* (Totowa, N.J.: Rowman and Littlefield, 1989) contains a short chapter on book burning. For China in the eighteenth century, see Luther Carrington Goodrich's *The Literary Inquisition of Ch'ien-Lung* (New York: Paragon Book Reprint, 1966). On English book burnings, see Charles Ripley Gillett's *Burned Books: Neglected Chapters in British History and Literature* (Port Washington, N.Y.: Kennikat Press, 1964).

Book publishing

DEFINITION: The mechanical reproduction and distribution of the printed word, in compact forms designed to ensure durability and ease of use

SIGNIFICANCE: As major book publishers have come to control both networks of production and distribution, they have become a bottleneck through which written ideas must pass

The old newspaper reporter's adage has it that freedom of the press extends only to those people who own one. The material philosophy that leads to this conclusion can also be applied to the business of book publishing. Newspapers are intended to be ephemeral products, lasting only a day or two before they are discarded. Books are designed to be more permanent, lasting through a few readings, in the example of mass market paperbacks, to texts designed to last for centuries, as in the case of volumes intended for libraries. As such, books require larger capital investments to produce than do more short-lived forms of information.

Because of the size of investment necessary to produce and distribute books, strict editorial policies direct most publishing houses. As competition has increased over the years, theory would have it that a freer range of ideas should be the result, expressed by the metaphorical phrase "the marketplace of ideas." That the opposite is the case has been noted by many critics of the modern publishing industry, and many have equated the current trend toward fewer and fewer publishing outlets as a form of censorship exercised by the multinational corporations that own most of the major European and American publishing companies.

History of Book Publishing. Although the Romans utilized slave labor to underpin a thriving market for hand-copied books, book publishing in its present form became possible only after the invention of movable type by German printer Johann Gutenberg in the early fifteenth century. Movable type soon led to an explosion of book publishing and the dissemination of ideas that were perceived as dangerous in some quarters. An early best-seller, *Gargantua and Pantagruel*, written by a former monk and medical doctor, François Rabelais, lampooned the medieval Roman Catholic church for its strict adherence to rigid doctrine. The satire led to the book's being banned in parts of Europe, and Rabelais' near arrest. A popular book published by Galileo, *A Dialogue Concerning Two Planetary Systems*, which challenged the Church doctrine concerning an earth-centered universe, led to his imprisonment in his own home, and to the book being banned by the Church. In the early days of book publishing, popularity did not always ensure personal safety for authors.

Other factors worked against the spread of book publishing. The absence of laws regarding copyright made plagiarism and piracy of written works a common practice. Draconian libel laws in England worked against the publication of many works, leading to either self-censorship or outright repression. Seventeenth and eighteenth century English laws meted out stiff punishments for anyone found guilty of making false statements in print about another's character. Strangely enough, the punishment was usually doubled if the statements were found to be true, as the crime was then deemed to be defamation of character. Not surprisingly, fiction, plays, and poetry came to be the publishing genres of choice, for few publishers were willing to risk imprisonment through the publication of a controversial work of nonfiction.

One publisher who came to have a reputation for "libeling and lampooning" was also the first important book publisher in the North American colonies, and subsequently in the newly founded United States: Benjamin Franklin. Franklin describes the perils of book publishing under colonial rule in his autobiography. Franklin's writing career began during his early teenage years, after his brother was arrested and forbidden from publishing his Boston area newspaper. Franklin later found the publishing climate much friendlier in Philadelphia, and produced books there in both English and German. He also describes in detail the difficulties he encountered while trying to raise the capital necessary to get started in the business.

The invention of automatic typesetting in the late nineteenth century and the adoption of an international copyright convention during the same period made the production of cheap mass-market books a profitable enterprise. Through this advance in technology books became much more widely available and accessible, but the discounted prices were primarily the result of economies of scale. The ever-increasing cost of production and distribution created an even newer form of censorship, as the demand for profitability became the yardstick against which all other textual qualities paled.

Commodification and Media Ownership. Although the twentieth century has witnessed numerous examples of outright suppression of book publishing, such as the banning and burning of books in Nazi Germany, Fascist Italy, and the Stalinist Soviet Union, these forms of censorship proved to be at best temporary stops against the free expression of ideas in printed form. A more significant phenomenon has been the century-long trend toward the consolidation of media outlets into fewer and fewer hands, and even by the absorption of book publishers into manufacturing conglomerates that have little or no history, or even interest, in the written word—at least outside of the context of profitability. This phenomenon is often referred to as "commodification," the process through which an item that has often been seen as having unique distinguishing characteristics is turned into a parcel of homogenized commerce.

Commodification takes place when the exchange value, or unit cost and profitability of an item, comes to be perceived as more important than the use value, or long-term usefulness, of the same. An economy, such as those of most of the major manufacturing countries, which is based on short-term profitability instead of long-term gain, is particularly susceptible to the commodification of its cultural products. A book, which is traditionally viewed as a vessel holding ideas, is instead turned into another product of the entertainment industry; or even more likely, as just another consumer product, on the same level as a candy bar or a cosmetic product. Values such as the indeterminate and subjective "intrinsic literary merit" are given little room on the spreadsheet of the multinational corporation.

Even less likely to reach printed form in such an economy are those ideas deemed to be critical of, or even dangerous to, the operation of such a system of profit and loss. Linguist Noam Chomsky refers to this system of publishing as a "propaganda" system and maintains that only those messages which reinforce the publishing hierarchy are ever likely to find their way into the popular press. A case in point is the nonpublication of African American writer Richard Wright's second autobiography, *American Hunger*, which he wrote during the 1940's, shortly after the publication of his acclaimed and popular first volume of his life story, *Black Boy*—which was denounced in Congress by Southern legislators appalled by its cruelly accurate portrait of life in the American South. Wright's publisher deemed *American Hunger* to be too incendiary to print in the 1940's, and its message of civil rights and economic justice was not made available to the reading public until 1977, many years after Wright's death.

Two individuals have been given a great deal of credit for the construction of the modern publishing system: Australian-born publisher Rupert Murdoch and German media tycoon Reinhardt Mohn. Murdoch began his career as a publisher of tabloid newspapers, then branched out into other media enterprises, such as the Fox television network, and book publishing. He eventually purchased the venerable American publishing house of Harper & Row, which in its most recent incarnation is known as HarperCollins. HarperCollins soon enough became a venue for works of a markedly right-wing persuasion, such as the one written by Speaker of the U.S. House of Representatives Newt Gingrich, *To Renew America* (1995). Coincidentally, perhaps, legislation favored by Murdoch, which has allowed for the further unrestricted growth of his empire, has won support in Congress.

Mohn has taken a different approach to the consolidation of publishing enterprises. Mohn came to admire the American system while being held as a prisoner of war in the United States during World War II. Mohn favored a direct approach to marketing, the book club approach, and following his successes he and his fellow German businessmen were able to purchase many famous literary publishing concerns. American literary giants Farrar, Strauss & Giroux, whose list has included the works of many Nobel Prize winners, and Henry Holt, are both now under German ownership. The publishing industry worldwide has been hit by many cutbacks because of these consolidating practices, mainly in the areas of literary publication.

Vertical Integration. Vertical integration is the ownership of the means of production and distribution by a single individual or entity. In book publishing, vertical integration can take two forms. In its simplest form, the publisher can open up a mail-order division to market products. By avoiding the normal mode of distribution through wholesalers and independent book dealers, such publishers can achieve much higher margins of profit. Not coincidentally, this system of integration also gives the publisher greater control over the contents of the books published. Once a target audience has been established, the publisher can give readers what they want, based on their past purchases—which are typically entertainment and diversion books—and can even influence its tastes. If the enterprise becomes large enough, as it has with some of the larger book clubs, it can begin to affect the editorial policies of an entire industry and function as a means of book advertising as well as merchandising.

The second form vertical integration may take is that of the "superstore," or mass retailer, a department store of books. Many giant booksellers, such as Barnes & Noble, are affiliated with publishing conglomerates. The books found in these superstores tend to be narrowly chosen for target audiences, and thus the range of expression found in such stores is limited by concerns of marketing. Additionally, regional differences are erased by such conglomerations of texts, and a superstore in Tacoma, Washington, for instance, may very well contain essentially the same books as one located in Huntsville, Alabama—much as grocery stores are the same throughout the country. Again, because of the economic relationship with the publisher, superstores can offer books for sale at greater discounts than can independent booksellers, who must go through wholesale suppliers. Independent booksellers, who have long been regarded as the primary means of ensuring the free expression and dissemination of ideas, face an ever grim-

mer economic prospect because of the practices of corporate book publishers and corporate booksellers, who have increasingly come to be one and the same. *—Jeff Cupp*

See also Abridgment; Book burning; Books, children's; Books, young adult; Books and obscenity law; Chomsky, Noam; Copyright law; Intellectual freedom; Lord Chamberlain; Magazines; Newspapers; Propaganda.

BIBLIOGRAPHY

Two works by Raymond Williams serve as useful introductions to the larger social forces that influence book publishing: *Culture and Society* (New York: Oxford University Press, 1956) examines how the products of culture (the book being an emblematic example) came to be thought of differently over the centuries and how the meaning of both words in some ways reflects the relationship between "cultural" products and the larger society. Williams' *Keywords* (New York: Oxford University Press, 1976) presents short, useful discussions of the ever-changing meaning of bookish words such as "literature," "fiction," and "novel." Part one of *The Autobiography of Benjamin Franklin* (1818), edited by William Temple Franklin, gives a fascinating insider's account of the rise of book publishing in the United States. *Friction with the Market* (New York: Oxford University Press, 1986) by Michael Anesko gives a detailed account of the birth of mass publishing in the late nineteenth century through an examination of the publishing history of the works of one writer, American novelist Henry James. An omnibus examination of the often adversarial relationship between women writers and publishers is found in *Women in Print*, edited by Joan E. Hartman and Ellen Messer-Davidow (New York: MLA, 1982).

Books, children's

DEFINITION: Books made expressly for children—almost always by adults

SIGNIFICANCE: Because children are considered to be especially vulnerable to harmful ideas, books written for them have always experienced strong censorship pressures

What children read affects their perceptions of the world and helps to form the attitudes that will govern their behavior as adults. This basic concept helps explain why educators, parents, and society at large have concerned themselves with the content of children's books. Whenever books for children present ideas and material that a group of adults, or even a single parent or teacher, thinks is inappropriate, the possibility of censorship arises.

The very concept of children's literature itself implies a kind of censorship. The first children's books were adaptations of adult literature and oral traditions that originally addressed a wide range of ages. Children were reared on such works as the Bible, which is full of violence. Books that were published specifically for children might be abridged to eliminate scatological material or other content deemed inappropriate for younger readers, as happened to children's editions of Jonathan Swift's *Gulliver's Travels* (1726), originally published as a political satire for adults.

Once books began to be written specifically for children, self-censorship prevented most writers from including anything that adults thought would be offensive to the young. Insofar as a book is directed specifically at children, some degree of censorship has, in such a process, already occurred before the book is printed.

Censorship of adult books is typically directed against graphic sex, ideas offensive to a dominant religion, or political thought opposed to existing authorities. Potential censors have claimed to find all three categories in children's literature, but few children's books deal with politics in a way likely to trigger government censorship or are sufficiently explicit to be found legally obscene. Nevertheless, children's books have experienced some form of censorship since they first began to appear.

Early Children's Books. The few books written for children before 1700 were intended to provide moral instruction, not entertainment. Children's literature emerged during the eighteenth century, heavily influenced by the English philosopher John Locke, who argued that children's reading should entertain as it taught. But Locke's thinking also contained the seeds of censorship. Locke argued that children should be isolated from superstition, which bred fear and other dangerous habits of thinking; instead, they should read only about what was provably true.

For most of the subsequent history of children's books, a tension between entertainment and instructional values has operated to shape the stories offered to children. John Newbery, considered the first children's publisher and Locke's disciple, avoided heavy-handed didacticism but also eliminated material that would trouble young minds. Locke's injunction against teaching of false information was used to suppress chapbooks, inexpensive publications filled with fairy tales and adventure stories and sold by traveling peddlers. Newbery appropriated fairy tales for his books, altering them to make them more "wholesome" and often didactic. Other followers of Locke, however, specifically warned against letting children read fairy tales.

While chapbooks and fairy tales caused some concern, few "serious" children's books drew the attention of would-be censors before the 1860's. Early nineteenth century writers, parents, teachers, and publishers were all of one mind about what children needed: moral, consciously didactic tales meant to instill proper social behavior and religious belief.

Didacticism declined and more entertainment values appeared in children's books in the last half of the nineteenth century, following the publication of Lewis Carroll's *Alice's Adventures in Wonderland* (1865). A distinction remained, however, between "serious" children's books, which experienced few external censorship pressures, and "trash literature" such as the dime novels, mostly western and detective stories, that had succeeded chapbooks as cheap reading for youth, especially in the United States.

Antipornography crusader Anthony Comstock waged a public campaign in the 1880's against dime novels, claiming that they lured young readers into delinquency and crime. He succeeded in getting state laws passed to limit children's access to such works. Following Comstock's arguments, and out of a conviction that cheap literature corrupted children's read-

ing tastes, many librarians also banned dime novels from the early children's collections. Such works as Mark Twain's *The Adventures of Tom Sawyer* (1876) and *Adventures of Huckleberry Finn* (1884), which superficially resembled the dime novels in some respects, were also banished from some children's libraries.

In the early twentieth century, librarians continued to ban certain kinds of "low" reading, notably series books, pulp magazines, and comic books—the descendants of the dime novels. These cheap forms drew censors' attentions. In the late 1940's, Frederic Wertham attacked comic books as fostering juvenile delinquency and doing little to develop children's reading. Although his main target was lurid detective and horror comics, he also found implicit homoeroticism in some superhero comics, which he claimed promoted homosexuality. Under threat of external censorship, the comics industry established a voluntary code of ethics, banning graphic crime and horror stories. Voluntary enforcement of the code reduced comic-book violence and diminished criticism.

The Late Twentieth Century. Prior to the 1960's, most censorship affected cheaper "nonliterary" types of children's reading. Social change in that turbulent decade, however, led writers to break former taboos on the depiction of sexual, racial, and violent themes in mainstream children's books. In the late 1960's and 1970's, realistic children's fiction began to reflect larger social problems and the emerging realization among adults that older children, at least, were trying to work out the meaning of their newly emergent sexual impulses.

Books such as Judy Blume's *Are You There, God? It's Me, Margaret* (1970), which deals with a sixth-grade girl's anxieties about menstruation and breast development, or Robert Cormier's *The Chocolate War* (1974), about peer pressure and intimidation in a boys' high school, present a different image of childhood than does previous children's literature. To many adults, such books violate the social myth of childhood innocence, an active force in Western culture since the eighteenth century, and censorship attempts reflected a defense of this social idea.

Defenders of realism in children's books have argued that the books offered young readers a gritty realism that addressed their innermost fears and concerns. Opponents saw the books themselves as creating those fears and concerns. The realistic children's books were controversial enough when they appeared on publishers' lists; they became the focus for censorship wars when they were purchased by libraries for children's and young adult collections, or assigned by middle school and high school teachers for classroom reading. Concerned parents and others complained that the sexual and violent content of some children's books were disturbing to their children.

Many of Judy Blume's books have been attacked for their frank presentation of adolescent sexuality. Also frequently opposed are books that cast doubt on adult authority, as Cormier's *The Chocolate War* does, or that depict children using foul language, as does the central character of Katherine Paterson's *The Great Gilly Hopkins* (1978). Paterson's response to complaints about her character's language illustrates a chief argument against children's book censorship. She points out that Gilly engages in a number of antisocial behaviors, so that her language is appropriate to her character; furthermore, she learns over the course of the book that her prejudice is misdirected and her antisocial behavior is most injurious to herself. Opponents have taken selected elements out of context; the book as a whole does not condone the disputed behavior and in the eyes of many readers presents a strong moral tale that would be unrealistic and unbelievable were the offensive language purged.

A second defense of challenged books questions the adult challengers' implicit belief that child readers are innocent of knowledge of the particular social ills, sexual impulses, or violent experiences that the books depict. Supporters of the literature argue that children are in fact more complex and less naturally innocent than the censorious arguments suggest, and that realistic children's fiction simply lays bare in print the emotions and experiences that many children already have.

Two other categories of children's books have also been the targets of censorship in contemporary society: fantasy and school textbooks. Objections to textbooks tend to follow lines similar to those for realistic fiction: inappropriately sexual or social content in literature anthologies, or negative portrayals of minority groups. Additional concerns have also been raised, however, about the relationship between what is taught in textbooks and religious beliefs, and about the portrayal of American history.

Conservative parents and educators sometimes object to textbooks that contain writings hostile to their religious beliefs or supportive of other religious beliefs—in particular, the inclusion of non-Western folkloric material that they see as satanic or anti-Christian. On the other hand, liberal parents and educators may oppose old-fashioned textbooks that adopt an inherently Christian viewpoint without acknowledging it as such, or that fail to include other cultural groups within their scope.

Fantasy, whether in the form of traditional folklore or in modern dress as fantasy novels, has been viewed with suspicion since Locke's time. While some observers celebrate the role of fantasy in unlocking the imagination, others argue that fantasy undermines children's developing understanding of the world as it is. In the late twentieth century, fairy tales and fantasy have also been the subject of censorship attempts because they may depict witches and other supernatural creatures that some associate with satanic beliefs and antireligious values.

The upsurge in censorship of children's books during the 1970's came from conservative parents, often based on religious beliefs that were offended by many of the issues raised by the new realism. Censorship efforts also came from the Left. Concern had already been raised about books such as *Adventures of Huckleberry Finn*, which disturbed some black readers and liberal parents by its depiction of black slaves, and in particular for its use of the word "nigger." As educators became sensitive to cultural representations of minorities, thanks in part to the activities of the Council on Interracial Books for Children, however, more books that appeared to present racial and religious minorities and women in negative

ways became targets as well. The defense against left-wing censorship attempts has been similar to that for censorship from the Right: to argue for the essential realism of the writing and to oppose taking isolated language or scenes out of context.

Book challenges are successful in about 40 percent of all cases—too many for those who oppose censorship of children's books, too few for those who bring the challenges. To ensure victory, would-be censors in the 1990's began to employ a new strategy: silent removal of offending materials from library shelves, by checking out or removing books and not returning them. This effectively prevents children and anyone else from having access to the material and, in an era of declining budgets, such silently censored books may not be replaced. —*A. Waller Hastings*

See also *Alice's Adventures in Wonderland*; Books, young adult; Fairy tales; Horror series controversy; Libraries, school; Locke, John; McGuffey Readers; Paterson, Katherine; Twain, Mark.

BIBLIOGRAPHY

In *Suitable for Children?: Controversies in Children's Literature* (Berkeley: University of California Press, 1976) Nicholas Tucker compiles historical documents and modern scholarship about children's book censorship. Mark I. West's *Children, Culture, and Controversy* (Hamden, Conn.: Archon Books, 1988) provides a historical overview connecting censorship of children's reading to concepts of childhood innocence. Lee Burress' *Battle of the Books: Literary Censorship in the Public Schools, 1950-1985* (Metuchen, N.J.: Scarecrow Press, 1989) identifies factors contributing to increased censorship since 1950. James Moffat's *Storm in the Mountains: A Case Study of Censorship, Conflict, and Consciousness* (Carbondale, Ill.: Southern Illinois University Press, 1988) presents a wide spectrum of viewpoints via a detailed examination of the 1974 textbook controversy in Kanawha County, West Virginia. Henry Reichman, in *Censorship and Selection: Issues and Answers for Schools* (Chicago: American Library Association, 1988), outlines the major arguments about and causes of children's book censorship. In addition, recent censorship activities are frequently discussed in professional library and education journals such as *School Library Journal* and *The New Advocate*.

Books, young adult

DEFINITION: Books intended for teenage readers

SIGNIFICANCE: Young adult books have been censored for themes of suicide, drugs, teenage pregnancy, obscenity, and sexuality

Before the invention of movable type in the fifteenth century, books for children were lesson books in Latin for the upper class. These early texts set the tone for children's literature as works that should present models of moral instruction.

Historical Antecedents. The expanded use of movable type resulted in increased literacy. As the middle class became concerned with educating their children, distinctions were made between literature for adults and literature for children. In colonial America, the Puritans assumed that the moral redemption of their children was a parental obligation. Books for children, then, were religious and highly moralistic.

During the seventeenth and eighteenth centuries, some books began to bridge the gap between literature for adults and literature for children. Daniel DeFoe's *The Life and Strange Surprising Adventures of Robinson Crusoe* (1719) and Jonathan Swift's *Gulliver's Travels* (1726) are two. In 1744 John Newbery began to publish books specifically intended for children, many of which were deliberately written for enjoyment. The preachy *Little Goody Two-Shoes* (1765) may be cited as the first short juvenile novel.

During the nineteenth century, children were viewed as winsome innocents lacking adult hypocrisy. Children's classics such as Louisa May Alcott's *Little Women* (1867) and Lewis Carroll's *Alice's Adventures in Wonderland* (1865) were widely read and contrasted with the popular domestic novel. Written primarily for older girls and women, domestic novels promoted acceptable social values and traditional morality. Boys and men read dime novels, adventure novels that contained rugged male protagonists in unrealistic adventures. These books were suspiciously regarded by the clergy, teachers, and many parents. As the nineteenth century closed, distinctions had been made between classics and nonclassics and between boys' books and girls' books. Furthermore, many works for young people had been attacked by adults.

Trends in the Twentieth Century. The concept of adolescence as a separate stage of life had evolved during the nineteenth century and was defined by G. Stanley Hall in 1905. Literature for young adults thus began to reflect this life period more definitively. Books of the early twentieth century included Booth Tarkington's *Penrod* (1914), which deals with the comical adventures of a twelve-year-old male protagonist. Eleanor Porter's *Pollyanna* (1913) portrays an early adolescent female coping with growing up.

During the 1930's, the term "junior books" came into use. Publishers soon formed junior book divisions and for the next three decades, authors such as Henry Gregor Felsen, James Summers, and John Tunis were popular with boys, and Janet Lambert and Maureen Daly were read by girls. During this period, the characteristics of the young adult novel were established: about 200 pages in length, immediate reader entry into the novel, realistic dialogue, and adolescent characters in relevant settings and situations.

During the 1960's, adult books such as *The Catcher in the Rye* (1951) and *Lord of the Flies* (1954) became popular reading for adolescents. At the same time literature written for adolescents began to reflect changing mores of society and new conflicts for the young adult. S. E. Hinton's *The Outsiders* (1967) deals with the problems of gangs. Paul Zindel's *The Pigman* (1968) portrays a male and female protagonist. African American characters are important in works such as Nat Hentoff's *Jazz Country* (1965) and Robert Lipsyte's *The Contender* (1967).

As books for adolescents became more realistic about many adolescents' lives, they became more controversial. Robert Cormier's *The Chocolate War* (1974) includes violence and a corrupt adult world. Katherine Paterson's *The Great Gilly Hopkins* (1978) deals with an eleven-year-old female protagonist who regularly uses profanity. *The Catcher in the Rye* has been censored for profanity as well, even though its protagonist mentions profanity only to disparage it. The novels of Judy Blume deal with emerging sexuality. Robert Peck's *A Day No Pigs Would Die* (1972) graphically portrays the birth of a cow. Controversial issues continued with exemplary works such as Walter Dean Myers' *Fallen Angels* (1988), the raw story of an older adolescent in the Vietnam War, and Bette Greene's *The Drowning of Stephan Jones* (1991), which portrays a male homosexual couple. As young adult books increasingly portrayed such controversial issues as suicide, alcoholism, teenage pregnancy, violence, sexuality, and racial issues, moves to censor such books escalated.

Young adult books have roots in moral instruction; some adults believe that adolescents should be reading time-honored works of literature in order to learn traditional moral qualities and engage in culturally accepted ideas. Adults having this perspective also tend to view a text as having one specific meaning for all readers. Many censors also believe that reading may effect change in attitude and behavior; that is, if profane language occurs throughout a work, this use increases profane language use in the reader. In September, 1990, for example, parents in Bluffton, Ohio, challenged *Fallen Angels* on the grounds of its containing obscene language, which they said violated school rules.

Schools and schoolbooks are often blamed for the maladies of society. Adolescent readers are often seen as submissive and impressionable people who have not developed their own values and thus need the protection of adults. Madeleine L'Engle's *A Wrinkle in Time* (1962), for example, has been attacked as fostering New Age religion. Zindel's *The Pigman* has been challenged on the grounds that it deals with the topics of death, dismemberment, witchcraft, torture, and masturbation. Complaints against Judy Blume's *Then Again, Maybe I Won't* (1971) include voyeurism, masturbation, and alcohol abuse. Would-be censors believe that such themes pollute the minds of young adults.

Young adult books that reflect a diversity in racial and ethnic identity and customs may find themselves opposed by various groups. For example, parents in Bremerton, Washington; Benning, California; and Pleasanton, California, have challenged Maya Angelou's autobiographical *I Know Why the Caged Bird Sings* (1969) for its sexually explicit passages, even calling her description of her childhood rape pornographic.

Records of challenges reported to the Office of Intellectual Freedom between 1979 and 1986 and to the People for the American Way from 1982 to 1987 reveal that the objectionable books portrayed adolescents acting realistically. Oppositions to such books, therefore, reflect a basic suspicion of the adolescent stage of development, particularly the searching for self-definition and experimentation that are characteristic of young adults.

Who Challenges Young Adult Books? Since the 1960's, groups from the religious right have attacked public schools in general and language arts departments in particular. These conservative Protestants believe in the absolute authority of the Bible and salvation through belief in Christ. Christian news shows charge educators with diluting academics, condoning homosexuality, and generally opposing Christian principles. The term "secular humanism" is used to confront texts that are viewed as opposing God, Christianity, and patriotism. New Age religion, it is alleged, teaches that humans must save themselves and reject theism.

Fantasy books are particularly susceptible to the secular humanism charge because of witches, fairies, and other chimerical characters. Katherine Paterson's *Bridge to Terabithia* (1977), for example, has been challenged on the basis of containing New Age religion and inappropriate use of God's name. Roald Dahl's *The Witches* (1983), popular with upper elementary and middle school children, has been accused of teaching witchcraft and Satanism.

Radicals and feminist activists have also challenged young adult books, showing that censorship comes from the Left as well as the religious right. In LaGrange, Kentucky, a challenge to *The Witches* came from members of the Wiccan religion, who maintained that witches in the book were negatively depicted. A parent in Louisville, Kentucky, challenged Judy Blume's *Blubber* (1974) because of characters who speak racial slurs. Challenges regarding racism and sexism present complex questions since people disagree about what constitutes racism or sexism and its influence on the reader. Recurrent battles concerning *Adventures of Huckleberry Finn* (1884) are examples.

Defenders of Young Adult Books. Until the 1969 Supreme Court decision in *Tinker v. Des Moines Independent School District*, students were viewed as having no rights. Justice Abe Fortas affirmed the constitutional right of students and teachers in the context of the school. The case of *Board of Education, Island Trees Union Free School District v. Pico* in the early 1970's declared that First Amendment rights had been violated by removal of several young adult books from the school library. During the 1980's, however, the Supreme Court seemed to curtail the rights of the student reader. In the 1988 *Hazelwood School District v. Kuhlmeier* decision, the Court supported the final authority of school administrators, including building principals, to make curricular decisions necessary for the mission of the particular school.

Language arts teachers deal with challenges to young adult books by developing rationales for teaching particular works. In addition, teachers focus on district support of academic freedom and communicate with members of the community about the literature program. Formal policies are also implemented to handle challenges and are followed when such challenges are presented. National professional organizations such as the American Library Association, the National Council of Teachers of English, and the International Reading Association have all taken a strong position against censorship. Rationales for works taught in English and language arts are available through Support for the Learning and Teaching of English (SLATE) and the National Council of Teachers of English (NCTE). Rationales are also available for frequently challenged young adult books. *—Helen O'Hara Connell*

See also *Adventures of Huckleberry Finn*; *Alice's Adventures in Wonderland*; American Library Association; Andrews, V. C.; Banned Books Week; Books, children's; *Catcher in the Rye, The*; *Diary of Anne Frank, The*; *I Know Why the Caged Bird Sings*; Libraries, school; *Lord of the Flies*; Suicide; Textbooks; Tolkien, J. R. R.; *Wrinkle in Time, A*.

BIBLIOGRAPHY

Lee Burress' *Battle of the Books: Literary Censorship in the Public Schools, 1950-1985* (Metuchen, N.J.: Scarecrow Press, 1989) surveys censorship situations and discusses secular humanism. William Gribbin's "Religious Conservatives and Public Schools: Understanding the Religious Right," in *English Journal* (84, no. 5, 1995), defines the term "religious Right" and identifies its membership. Edward B. Jenkinson, *Censors in the Classroom: The Mind Benders* (Carbondale, Illinois: Southern Illinois University Press, 1979), discusses the problems of censorship in materials for young people, including important challenges of the 1970's. Henry Reichman's *Censorship and Selection: Issues and Answers for Schools* (Chicago: American Library Association, 1988) includes major court cases related to censorship. Controversial issues such as obscene language and sexuality in young people's literature are dealt with. John S. Simmons, ed., *Censorship: A Threat to Reading, Learning, and Thinking* (Newark, Del.: International Reading Association, 1994), surveys several dimensions of the problems of censorship of school texts. Julian Thompson's "Defending YA Literature against the Pharisees and Censors: Is It Worth the Trouble?" in *ALAN Review* (18, no. 2 Winter, 1991) defends the author's own writing and all young adult novels considered controversial.

Books and obscenity law

DEFINITION: Laws intended to censor obscene books

SIGNIFICANCE: The application of obscenity law to books has often resulted in the banning of titles, but the courts have also cleared the way for inclusion of titles in libraries

Through most of the world's history, there was little concern for censorship of obscene materials. Instead, the focus of censors was on political and religious ideas. Rigorous campaigns, with or without the benefit of law, were launched against people labeled heretics or revolutionaries. Obscene material was sometimes attacked as so immoral as to be heretical; the Marquis de Sade's writings describe themselves as such. It was not until the nineteenth century that great attention was directed toward obscene materials.

Obscenity Law Abroad. Great Britain enacted obscenity laws in 1857, 1959, and 1964 with each one seeking to tighten loopholes that existed in preceding laws, but in Great Britain and in other countries, a central problem rested in trying to establish any solid definition of what constitutes obscenity. Before the 1960's, Denmark had obscenity laws in place. The laws were difficult to interpret or enforce, and in 1964 the country became characterized for its lack of obscenity law. Since that time, the obscenity law has centered on the illegality of selling pornographic pictures to minors or distributing such materials in public.

France and Germany have taken the position of allowing

adults to read what they please, but publishers are prohibited from producing and selling books going beyond the generally accepted standards of society. Protection of minors from pornographic materials remains a provision of law in these countries and in most of the world.

United States Obscenity Law. Early censorship laws in the United States focused primarily on sexually explicit materials, and legislation in that area was left to the individual states until the middle of the nineteenth century. Massachusetts tried to prohibit the distribution of *The Memoirs of Fanny Hill* (1748) by John Cleland in 1821. The result was that the book was declared obscene.

In 1842 Congress passed legislation banning the importation of obscene materials into the United States, and during the Civil War, Congress acted further by prohibiting the sending of obscene materials through the mails. Soldiers during the Civil War kept images of naked women made with the then-new photographic technology.

A campaign for strict obscenity laws was launched by Anthony Comstock, resulting in the passage of the federal Comstock Act of 1873, which prohibited the importation or mailing of obscene or lewd material. The U.S. Supreme Court eventually changed the grounds on which a book could be declared obscene, and in 1933 a federal court decision allowing James Joyce's *Ulysses* (1922) to be imported into the United States loosened the hold of censorship laws.

Obscenity law in the United States was molded through the 1957 Supreme Court case *Roth v. United States*, which established a three-part test for obscenity: The material as a whole must appeal to a prurient interest, it must be offensive on the basis of contemporary community standards, and it must be utterly without redeeming social value. In the 1973 case of *Miller v. California* it was decided that determination of obscenity would rest with these guidelines: whether the average person, applying contemporary community standards, would find the work, taken as a whole, appeals to a prurient interest, whether the work depicts or describes, in a patently offensive way, sexual conduct specifically defined by the applicable state law, and whether the work, taken as a whole, lacks serious literary, artistic, political, or scientific value. Also, it was ruled that local rather than national community standards would apply. The Miller test is applied in determining whether a particular book is obscene and therefore not protected by the First Amendment. In applying the Miller Test, the courts may reach differing decisions on the same book, depending on the geographical location involved in a case.

Major Court Cases. Court cases in the United States illustrate how unevenly obscenity trials have been decided. In *United States v. Kennerley* (1913), Michael Kennerley was convicted of sending obscene materials through the mail. The material in question was a book that censors had labeled obscene. Another obscenity case in 1953, *New American Library of World Literature, Inc. v. Allen*, was decided against the censor, a police chief in Youngstown, Ohio. The police chief attempted to ban the sale of 108 books he considered obscene, and the New American Library of World Literature, one of the publishers involved, brought suit. Allen said he based his

objections to the material on the cover illustrations of the books, tying those objections to a city ordinance. A federal judge ruled that the chief of police had no legislated authority to ban books.

A reversal in judicial rulings occurred in the case of *Sunshine Book Company v. Summerfield* (1957). A nudist magazine, *Sunshine and Health*, was ruled obscene because the publishers were promoting lust, in the opinion of lower courts. In 1958 the decision was reversed by the U.S. Supreme Court when the Roth standard was applied.

Local ordinances in Los Angeles, California, were applied in the conviction of Eleazer Smith, a bookstore owner, in *Smith v. California* (1959). The book in question would have been judged obscene under the Roth standard, but the U.S. Supreme Court found Smith innocent, emphasizing that book dealers cannot be held liable for not knowing (Smith claimed he had not read the book) the contents of books in their inventories.

In Rhode Island, the legislature created a commission designed to protect youth from obscene materials, but it also had the effect of restricting adult reading in the state. The commission established a long list of books unsuitable for youth and informed book dealers they would be prosecuted if they offered the listed books for sale. In *Bantam Books v. Sullivan* (1963) the U.S. Supreme Court ruled the Rhode Island restrictions in violation of the U.S. Constitution. The commission had, in effect, ruled materials obscene without benefit of a court trial. They could not restrict the sale of materials that had not been legally judged obscene.

Pico v. Board of Education, Island Trees was a court battle that resulted from the school board's removal of nine books from library shelves in 1976 in a school district in Long Island, New York. A district court ruled in favor of the school board in 1979, but a court of appeals reversed the decision in 1980, citing violation of First Amendment rights. The U.S. Supreme Court reviewed the case in 1982, and, in a narrow ruling, opposed suppression of ideas in high school libraries.

—*Harlan R. Johnson*

See also Censorship; Communist Party of the U.S.A.; Free speech; Intellectual freedom; *Miller v. California*; Obscenity: legal definitions; *Roth v. United States*.

BIBLIOGRAPHY

Haig Bosmajian's *Censorship, Libraries, and the Law* (New York: Neal-Schuman, 1983) has detailed information on a large number of censorship cases. Joseph E. Bryson and Elizabeth W. Detty's *The Legal Aspects of Censorship of Public School Library and Instructional Materials* (Charlottesville, Va.: Michie Company, 1982) addresses the literature of censorship and the law, academic freedom, religious freedom, parents' rights, legal definitions of obscenity, and court decisions. Donna A. Demac's *Liberty Denied: The Current Rise of Censorship in America* (New Brunswick, N.J.: Rutgers University Press, 1990) covers a wide variety of topics related to censorship and the law, including bureaucratic restrictions, government control of the press, and the foundations of free expression. Herbert N. Foerstel's *Banned in the U.S.A.: A Reference Guide to Book Censorship in Schools and Public*

Libraries (Westport, Conn.: Greenwood Press, 1994) surveys major book banning incidents, the law on book banning, and the most frequently banned books of the 1990's.

Boston

DESCRIPTION: Among the oldest cities in the United States, Boston is the state capital of Massachusetts

SIGNIFICANCE: Boston has a long reputation of controlling the reading and viewing fare of its citizens

Founded by John Winthrop in 1630 as the main colony of the Massachusetts Bay Company, Boston became the center of American Puritanism and quickly developed into New England's largest city. Its early leaders championed a strong intellectual life and were uniformly theocratic. They helped to establish the Boston Latin School in 1635, and Harvard University was founded in Cambridge, across the Charles River, in 1636. By 1653, Boston had one of North America's earliest public libraries.

As a center of trade, Boston early vied with New York as the preeminent American city. Following the Revolutionary War in 1776, it entered a period of unparalleled prosperity that continued into the nineteenth century. Families made rich by the international trade that flowed through the port of Boston and by the textile mills flanking its rivers demanded strong intellectual resources, including a strong library system. The Boston Public Library, which opened in 1854, represented a new concept in libraries by catering to the general public.

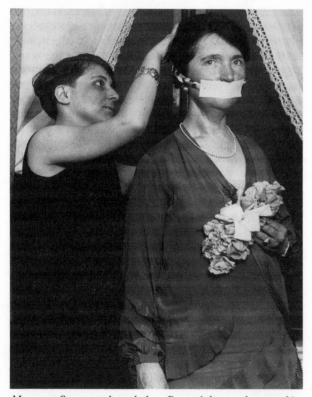

Margaret Sanger acknowledges Boston's ban on her speaking on birth control by having her mouth taped shut before appearing at a public meeting in 1929. (UPI/Corbis-Bettmann)

Excellent museums proliferated in the city, but their displays were stringently censored.

Despite Boston's intellectual and cultural preeminence, its earliest libraries were established specifically to promote specific religious ideologies and to provide materials to promote the conversion of Native Americans to Christianity. Women generally were not permitted to use the early libraries or—as late as the 1850's—even to work in them. It was believed that the presence of women might embarrass male patrons and that women should be protected from anything but the most polite and morally uplifting literature.

As Boston's library system grew, the censorship that it most frequently practiced was one of exclusion. A protective paternalism characterized the Boston Public Library, which refused to make available to its constituency books that it considered offensive. Excluded were works by such authors as Arnold Bennett, Joseph Conrad, Gustav Flaubert, Thomas Hardy, Aldous Huxley, James Joyce, D. H. Lawrence, John Masefield, George Meredith, Carl Sandburg, H. G. Wells, Hugh Walpole, and Émile Zola.

A survey by the *Boston Evening Transcript* revealed that Boston's libraries had few of the eighty-four books reviewed by *The Nation*. Of the twenty-two works considered of permanent literary significance, Boston libraries had three. Of forty-eight classified as distinguished, Boston had thirteen. Of eighteen characterized as colorless or innocent, however, Boston had ten. Of the ten novels listed as essential for serious readers, Boston had none.

The City of Boston has banned books from public sale, including such works as James Joyce's *Ulysses*. It long controlled both public speakers and theatrical productions by requiring a public speaking permit, which, although an unconstitutional prior restraint, was upheld by the Supreme Court in *Davis v. Massachusetts* (1897). It occasionally required playwrights to rewrite portions of plays deemed offensive and sometimes banned total productions by playwrights such as Eugene O'Neill.

See also Books and obscenity law; Boston Watch and Ward Society; Libraries; O'Neill, Eugene; Prior restraint; Women.

Boston Watch and Ward Society

FOUNDED: 1873

TYPE OF ORGANIZATION: New England-based procensorship body

SIGNIFICANCE: This organization became infamous for strict censorship and helped to inspire the phrase "banned in Boston"

After the Civil War Boston religious leaders wanted to watch out for immigrants and rural farmers coming to the city and ward them away from urban vices. Influenced by the Comstock Act of 1873 and the New York Society for the Suppression of Vice, Episcopal priest Frederick B. Allen gathered reformers at Boston's Park Street Church in late 1873 to establish the New England Society for the Suppression of Vice. It was soon renamed the New England Watch and Ward Society, or locally, the Boston Watch and Ward Society. More clerical than its New York predecessor, the society was widely supported by Puritan Bostonians. Its officers included Trinity Church rector Phillips Brooks, Unitarian divine Edward Everett Hale, and the presidents of six New England colleges, including Dartmouth and Yale. Henry Chase conducted routine business. The influential Boston newspaper the *Transcript* endorsed the group.

Early Watch and Ward campaigns used legal pressure and subtle coercion techniques to combat vulgar magazines such as the *Police Gazette*, to rid railroad stations of vagrants, and to ban the sale of obscene materials at newsstands. In 1880 the Massachusetts legislature passed a society-sponsored bill prohibiting the sale of pornography. After this law proved effective, it was extended in 1886 to include crime and police report publications and to prohibit publicly displaying obscene items. In 1892 these changes were used to convict Boston and Lowell booksellers of exposing youths to questionable materials.

In 1915 the society joined forces with Boston's Old Corner Bookstore to establish the Boston Booksellers Committee. Novels that the Committee judged obscene were removed from stores, and newspapers and magazines were kept from advertising or reviewing such books. During the 1920's new publishing houses competing with established firms printed more objectionable manuscripts. The committee repeatedly barred such works from sale, and "banned in Boston" became a common phrase.

The society weakened when Chase became its leader after Allen's death in 1925. In September of that year H. L. Mencken's *American Mercury* published "Keeping the Puritans Pure," an essay attacking Chase, the Watch and Ward, and the Boston Booksellers Committee. When Boston banned the April, 1926, issue of *American Mercury* containing Herbert Asbury's "Hatrack," Mencken went to Boston with his lawyer, Arthur Garfield Hays, and publicly sold Chase a copy. National attention from Mencken's arrest harassed the society.

In April, 1927, booksellers protested the banning of Sinclair Lewis' *Elmer Gantry*. Later that month, publisher Horace Liveright's representatives intentionally sold Theodore Dreiser's *An American Tragedy* to society members. The following month Upton Sinclair visited Boston when his novel *Oil!* was banned. That summer, local newspapers and academics abandoned Chase. By December businessmen suffered financial losses because people traveled elsewhere to buy books. The 1927-1928 legislative session proposed looser censorship laws, but disagreements over definitions of "obscenity" prevented action.

On April 16, 1929, seven hundred people, including Harvard professor Arthur M. Schlesinger and lawyers Hays and Clarence Darrow, rallied at "The Ford Hall Frolic" to support the liberal Massachusetts Library Club Bill, which was defeated. When the Watch and Ward prosecuted Dunster House Bookshop later that year for selling *Lady Chatterley's Lover*, the *Herald* declared the society obsolete. In March, 1930, passage of the Weeks Bill relaxed Boston's obscenity laws. The Watch and Ward dissolved after its last president, Raymond Calkins, resigned in 1931.

See also Books and obscenity law; Boston; Censorship; *Lady Chatterley's Lover*; Lewis, Sinclair; Mencken, H. L.; Sinclair, Upton; Society for the Suppression of Vice, New York.

Bowdler, Thomas

BORN: July 11, 1754, Ashley, Somerset, England
DIED: February 24, 1825, Rhydding, Glamorganshire, Wales
IDENTIFICATION: English censor of William Shakespeare's plays
SIGNIFICANCE: Bowdler's efforts to purify Shakespeare's works for family reading were so thorough that his name has become synonymous with prudism in literary censorship

Bowdler's *The Family Shakspeare* (1818) made Bowdler famous and made his name synonymous with the practice of censoring literary texts by omitting verbal vulgarity. Modern research has found that his purification of Shakespeare was initially a collaborative effort and that his sister Henrietta should be given primary responsibility for the 1807 abbreviated edition that was published in four volumes in the city of Bath. But it was Thomas Bowdler himself who took over the project, expanded it to encompass the full Shakespeare canon, and produced the ten-volume London version that became a nineteenth century bestseller, with thirty printings.

The principles of "bowdlerism" had their roots in the nineteenth century practice of reading literature aloud in family circles. In Henrietta Bowdler and Thomas Bowdler's family, their father read with such delicacy and discretion that (as Thomas later wrote) "his family listened with delight to hear, Hamlet and Othello, without knowing that those matchless tragedies contained words and expressions improper to be pronounced." It was with this childhood experience in mind that Henrietta and Thomas set out to produce an edition of Shakespeare fit for the nineteenth century reading public "in which nothing is added to the original text, but those words and expressions are omitted which cannot with propriety be read in a family."

In practice the Bowdlers' revisions entailed combinations of deletion and substitution exercised in passages whose sexual content they considered too strong, or in which the name of the deity was taken in vain. For example, where Hamlet says "Nay, but to live/ In the rank sweat of an enseamed bed/ Stewed in corruption, honeying and making love/ Over the nasty sty!" Bowdler leaves only "Nay, but to live/ In an incestuous bed." "God" is left intact when it occurs in prayers but is deleted from oaths, with "Heaven" as a frequent substitute. There is, however, a random quality to many of Bowdler's choices. Among terms for prostitute, *bitch* and *punk* are removed, but *harlot*, *baggage* and *quean* remain. The prostitute Doll Tearsheet disappears entirely from *Henry V*.

Despite the diligence of the Bowdlers, some of Shakespeare's plays resisted "bowdlerization," a fact that Bowdler felt obliged both to explain and to apologize for. Doll Tearsheet may have been expendable, but Falstaff clearly was not. *Othello* posed the greatest challenge to Bowdler's method, for Bowdler could not "erase all the bitter terms of reproach and execration . . . expressed by the Moor, without altering his character . . . and . . . destroying the Tragedy."

Bowdler died in 1825, leaving for posthumous publication his revised edition of Edward Gibbon's *The History of the Decline and Fall of the Roman Empire* (1776-1788) based on the same principles as *The Family Shakspeare*. That publication disappeared after failing to sell out its first printing.

"Bowdlerize" seems to have made its first appearance as a verb about ten years after Bowdler's death, and it has remained in use to the present day.

See also Abridgment; Bible; Gibbon, Edward; Literature; Shakespeare, William.

Boycotts

DEFINITION: A group's refusal, as a form of protest, to buy a product or service

SIGNIFICANCE: Boycotts can work as a censorship force

Named after Charles C. Boycott, a land agent who was shunned for refusing to reduce his rents, boycotts, when effectively employed by a collective, can effectively impose penalties on businesses, countries, and organizations. Sellers can also boycott, as for example if a group with a critical resource (oil, or atomic weapons technology) decides not to sell that resource to another party.

Boycotts or economic sanctions can work as censorship forces when collectives join together and refuse, for example, to buy any books that a company has published because one book that the company has published offends them. The purpose of severing the established relationship between the collective and the designated entity is to punish the concern in order to bring about practices that conform to the group's interests.

Consumers have used boycotts when they have been interested in persuading businesses to improve their labor practices. Boycotts have been employed when strikes failed to bring about meaningful changes in work conditions, salaries, and other job-related benefits. The economic conditions that limit the effectiveness of strikes are numerous. Boycotts have been the preferred method used by consumers to demonstrate their disapproval of businesses when the labor market is saturated with a high percentage of unemployed workers, thereby limiting the success of strikes. When this occurs, boycotts, when properly organized and implemented, have been successful alternatives to other efforts on the part of labor.

Economic sanctions are effective political measures that restrain trade and may even destroy a targeted business if they are instituted with widespread support. Consumers, supporting labor, have made boycotts formidable censorship forces against businesses when the following elements are addressed. First, there must be solidarity among workers and all consumers who intend to participate in the boycott. Second, organizers must ensure that the boycott has received adequate publicity to garner support from appropriate segments of the population. Finally, all participants (producers and consumers) in the boycott are expected to have a common political identity. Hence, they expect that using their purchasing power will have a significant impact on the businesses' labor practices. In some cases fines and other negative sanctions have been imposed on consumers to ensure compliance with the boycott.

Minority groups, such as African Americans, have used boycotts or the use of economic sanctions against businesses to improve their participation in companies that have restricted their participation through legislation, policy and force. For example, African Americans and other civil rights activists employed boycotts successfully on a large scale during the Civil Rights movement. Recognizing the importance of boycotts as censorship forces, civil rights activists effected social change by collectively refusing to patronize businesses that had established discriminatory practices. Such boycotts brought about an end to discrimination in public transportation and in public facilities and a decrease in overt discrimination in employment. Because of the successful use of boycotts during the Civil Rights movement, they have been employed subsequently by African Americans to increase their purchasing power, improve their economic status, and to enhance employment opportunities, particularly in the private sector.

Countries have also used boycotts as a means of collectively expressing their disapproval of another country's actions. When countries apply economic sanctions against a designated country it is generally argued that denying resources to the targeted country is employed to encourage compliance with a covenant. For the most part, while boycotts have proven to be an effective means of improving labor relations, their success has been credited to sanctions as well as solidarity.

See also Alcoholic beverages; Censorship; Civil Rights movement; Labor unions; Pressure groups; Smoking.

Bradlaugh v. The Queen

COURT: Court of Queen's Bench, Great Britain

DECIDED: June 18-22, 1877

SIGNIFICANCE: Great Britain's last serious legal challenge to birth control publications, this case had the effect of increasing public interest in contraception, thereby contributing to a decline in the birth rate

In 1877 plainclothes British detectives entered a London bookshop and purchased a copy of *The Fruits of Philosophy* (1832), a sober book on birth control by American physician Charles Knowlton. They then arrested the shop's proprietors, Charles Bradlaugh and Annie Besant, well-known radical secular atheists. Bradlaugh and Besant welcomed the opportunity to test the rights of a free press in light of the Obscene Publications Act of 1850.

For two decades before this incident occurred, Knowlton's book had sold about a thousand copies a year in Britain without incident. Meanwhile, Henry Cook, who operated a freethought bookshop in Bristol, had altered the book by adding two illustrations considered shocking to Victorian sensibilities. Partly because of these illustrations, the criminal indictment against Bradlaugh and Besant charged them with "unlawfully and wickedly devising, contriving, and intending" to corrupt the morals of youth, as well as inciting and encouraging people "to indecent, obscene, unnatural, and immoral practices." The indictment described Knowlton's book as "indecent, lewd, filthy, bawdy, and obscene" and alluded to obscene language that it contained. The party who brought the complaint to the criminal court was never identified.

The case was assigned to the Queen's Bench, with Lord Chief Justice Alexander Cockburn presiding and the Crown's solicitor general, Sir Hardinge Gifford, serving as prosecutor. While Bradlaugh and Besant defended themselves during the five-day trial, as many as twenty thousand people supported them from the streets outside the Westminster Hall courtroom. The defendants argued that offensive language cited in the indictment was not identified and that the book in question was a serious work on medicine and political economy. Justice Cockburn noted that the offending language was not explained, but said that it would be an issue for the Court of Error to decide. A jury then returned a puzzling verdict: "We are unanimously of opinion that the book in question is calculated to deprave public morals, but at the same time we entirely exonerate the defendants from any corrupt motives in publishing it."

Bradlaugh and Besant then took their case to the Court of Error, where they won their appeal. Their original indictment was found to be defective, and the court noted that their appeal was being decided on "a dry point of law, which has nothing to do with the actual merits of the case." The defendants used speeches, articles in Bradlaugh's secularist weekly, *The National Reformer*, and demonstrations to keep their cause before the public.

Over the next three years *The Fruits of Philosophy* sold more than 200,000 copies in Britain, precipitating a decline in the English birth rate. Burdened with a flawed case, the Crown's litigation ironically served to disseminate contraceptive information and awareness even more widely in the populace, demonstrating the risks of challenging the public's perceived needs and interests.

See also *Arabian Nights, The*; Birth control education; Books and obscenity law; Courts and censorship law; Free speech; Intellectual freedom; Morality; Obscene Publications Acts.

Brazil

DESCRIPTION: Largest country in South America
SIGNIFICANCE: As with many of its South American neighbors, Brazil has experienced a gradual change in censorship since the late 1970's

Brazil was colonized by the Portuguese, starting in the middle of the sixteenth century. As was typical of the era, education, press, and politics were dominated by the Roman Catholic church and the Portuguese state. This pattern continued after Brazil gained independence in 1822. Over the next 140 years, by fits and starts, Brazilians in general, and the media in particular, came to enjoy a substantial amount of freedom, except in the fields of entertainment. The role of the Catholic church in Brazilian society, and its moral code, explains governmental actions in this area.

The first law to censor films was passed in 1932, followed by the creation of the Department of Press and Propaganda in 1939 (which required reservation of a certain amount of exhibition time for Brazilian produced films). The Public Entertainment and Censorship Service was created in 1946, with the power to prohibit the exhibition of any film "offensive to public decency," depicting or encouraging criminal acts or evil

intent, and with the additional power to cut, or place age restrictions on all films (a practice that continued into the 1980's).

The period of relative improvement in freedom of speech was interrupted by the military coup of 1964. This takeover, which military leaders called a "revolution" against communism, quickly led to severe restrictions on the press, on free speech, on entertainment, in education (supposed leftists were purged from university faculties), and on political opposition. All speech regarded as encouraging war or subversion, undermining national security or confidence in national institutions was strictly forbidden. Live broadcasts on television (except news programs) were outlawed. All books had to be submitted to the Ministry of Justice and Internal Affairs for review twenty days before publication, and all magazines had to be submitted for review forty-eight hours before publication. University curricula and courses were examined for ideological acceptability.

Starting in the 1970's, censorship was relaxed, allowing criticism of policies and measures, though not of the revolution itself, or any speech labeled subversive or detrimental to national security. *Abertura*, or "opening," was the name for the policy of liberalization which gained momentum starting in 1979, as before-the-fact censorship was suspended. Opposition parties were allowed to organize, and dissidents were allowed to return from exile. In March of 1985, all constraints on political speech were removed, and virtually all forms of media control were banned under the 1988 Constitution. In 1992 President Fernando Collor de Mello was forced to resign, largely due to pressure brought to bear by media investigations, investigations which proceeded despite significant governmental pressure to ease off.

Despite these improvements, violence continued—conducted largely by private groups tolerated by the government—against certain groups, such as environmentalists in the Amazon rain forest, union organizations, and the homeless.

See also Journalists, violence against; National security; News media censorship; Police states; Prior restraint; South America.

Brecht, Bertolt

BORN: February 10, 1898, Augsburg, Germany
DIED: August 14, 1956, East Berlin, East Germany
IDENTIFICATION: German dramatist, poet, and philosopher
SIGNIFICANCE: A Marxist writer who spent fourteen years in exile, Brecht had a significant influence on late twentieth century Western theater

During the 1920's Brecht established his reputation in Berlin with a series of popular political plays that attacked capitalism. These included *The Threepenny Opera* (1928) and *The Rise and Fall of the City of Mahagonny* (1930). As the National Socialist (Nazi) Party rose to power, he began writing openly Marxist plays, such as *The Mother* (1932). After Adolf Hitler became chancellor of the country in 1933, Brecht fled to Denmark. In Germany his writings were burned and his citizenship was withdrawn. Although he was a Marxist, Brecht did not join the Communist Party because he disagreed with the official aesthetic of Socialist Realism and he felt betrayed by the Soviet Union's intraparty purges.

As German military power grew, Brecht fled again in 1939—first to neutral Sweden, later to Finland. He remained in Finland until 1941, when his family fled to the United States. During his exile years Brecht wrote anti-Nazi plays, such as *The Private Life of the Master Race* (1945), and drafts of several of his most important works, including *Mother Courage and Her Children* (1941) and his anticensorship play, *The Life of Galileo* (1943).

Brecht spent the war years with German compatriots in California, writing for Hollywood, but without significant success. These efforts focused on adapting an English version of *The Life of Galileo* for actor Charles Laughton and in drafting *The Caucasian Chalk Circle* (1948). After the war Brecht was summoned before the House Committee on Un-American Activities (HUAC), because of his association with a known communist agent. When he appeared before HUAC in October, 1947, he appeared congenial, answering honestly that he had never been a member of the Communist Party, and he clarified some misconceptions about his writings. The committee thanked him for being "a good example." However, after spending fourteen years in political exile, Brecht decided not to risk further trouble, so he left for Switzerland the next day.

Brecht ultimately established his own theater, the Berliner Ensemble, in East Berlin, where he continued to write and produce politically oriented plays. From 1953 until his death he was again a center of political controversy because he openly supported East German communist leader Walter Ulbricht. Brecht remained a target of political censorship even after his death. After the Berlin Wall was erected in 1961 there was an unsuccessful, short-lived effort to remove his works from the repertories of Western European theaters.

In Brecht's play *The Life of Galileo* the Italian scientist Galileo represents Brecht's own views regarding censorship. Galileo's findings were suppressed by the Roman Catholic church as potentially faith-shaking for the masses. Brecht explained that his play was not about religious oppression, but showed that the victory of authority over the individual was temporary and that it was impossible to restrain truth.

See also Blacklisting; Book burning; Communism; Denmark; Drama and theater; Galileo Galilei; Germany; Heresy; Hollywood Ten; House Committee on Un-American Activities; National Socialism; Socialist Realism; World War II.

Brennan, William J., Jr.

BORN: April 25, 1906, Newark, New Jersey

DIED: July 24, 1997, Arlington, Virginia

IDENTIFICATION: Associate justice of the U.S. Supreme Court (1956-1990)

SIGNIFICANCE: After crafting a modern definition of obscenity, Brennan later departed from it when he became convinced that it produced a chilling effect on treatments of sex in art, literature, and science

As a Supreme Court justice Brennan grappled with censorship issues many times during thirty-four years on bench. His decisions in obscenity cases had a profound influence on the arts, literature, and science. During his first term on the Court in the late 1950's, he was assigned to draft a new definition of obscenity. Until then, obscenity laws had been based extensively on a nineteenth century British doctrine called the Hicklin rule, which provided little protection for expression and opened the door for widespread censorship of sexual materials.

The Hicklin rule punished even isolated sexual passages that might "deprave and corrupt those whose minds are open to such immoral influences." Brennan wanted to ensure that not all communications concerning sex would be deemed obscene. Any contrary ruling would restrain publication of legitimate discussions of sexuality. After New York book distributor Samuel Roth was convicted of mailing obscene materials, Brennan had his chance in 1957.

In *Roth v. United States*, the Supreme Court announced a new obscenity definition that looked at the dominant theme of whole works—rather than isolated passages—from the average person's perspective of contemporary community standard, in order to determine if the works appealed to "prurient" interest. The new Roth test expanded First Amendment protection for serious artists and writers by removing a censorship cloud that had loomed over them under the Hicklin rule. Brennan ruled that the portrayal of sex in art, literature, and science deserved First Amendment protection.

Before long, however, the Roth test posed its own problems, and the Supreme Court was criticized for taking on a censorship role. Brennan was bothered by that characterization and in *Jacobellis v. State of Ohio* said he did not "understand why the Court's performance of its constitutional and judicial functions in this sort of case should be denigrated by such epithets as 'censor' or 'supercensor.' " Indeed, in *Jacobellis*, the Court reversed an Ohio court's finding that the French film *Les Amants* (1958) was obscene. The state's case was grounded in one explicit love scene. Nevertheless, Justice Potter Stewart, who agreed with Brennan's remark, lamented that he could not "intelligibly" define obscenity, but that, "I know it when I see it." Stewart's frustration illustrated the Roth test's ambiguity. As more such cases came to the Supreme Court, Brennan recognized that despite his efforts, censorship was still a real threat. He made an attempt to clarify the definition in *Memoirs v. Massachusetts* (1966) by reminding lower courts that they must consider "all possible uses" of material before they can deem it "utterly without redeeming social value" and thus obscene.

This clarification did little to halt the flow of obscenity cases to the Supreme Court. In the early 1970's, Brennan abandoned the standard he had articulated some sixteen years earlier. He was convinced that this area of First Amendment law was "resistant to the formulation of stable and manageable standards." Attempts to define obscenity would only further the course of censorship. Brennan's departure from the obscenity doctrine also met resistance, principally from Chief Justice Warren Burger, who wanted to redefine obscenity. What most concerned Brennan was Burger's lack of concern for the legitimate artists who might be unfairly swept into any broad definition of obscenity. Burger nevertheless prevailed, and the result was the three-part obscenity test articulated in *Miller v. California* in 1973.

See also Black, Hugo; Courts and censorship law; Douglas, William O.; Hicklin case; *Miller v. California*; Obscenity: legal definitions; *Roth v. United States*; Warren, Earl.

British Board of Film Censors

FOUNDED: 1912

TYPE OF ORGANIZATION: Film censorship body

SIGNIFICANCE: The board deeply influenced British filmmakers

That cinematographic exhibition could pose a threat to public safety and morality was a concern from the earliest days of film production in Great Britain. The Cinematograph Act of 1909 granted local authorities the right to control film exhibition, which was recognized by most cinematographic companies as a form of censorship. In order to forestall the possibility of national control of film exhibition and content, the film industry agreed, in consultation with Reginald McKenna, the home secretary, to develop a self-regulating board to monitor the content of films. The British Board of Film Censors (BBFC) was thus constituted in 1912. Each cinematographic company submitted their finished films to the board, which was responsible for granting a licensing certificate. The U certificate meant the film was appropriate for universal exhibition, while an A certificate meant a film was suitable only for adult audiences. Imported films would also have to pass through the BBFC film censors before being issued a certificate. By the 1930's the BBFC also was examining film scripts prior to production, which they used as a means of controlling film content. Thus the British film industry developed a system of self-regulation more than twenty years before the creation of the Hays office in Hollywood.

In theory the BBFC was intended to define the acceptable audience for each film. In practice, however, it acted as a conservative institution attempting to expunge radical content. Although the BBFC claimed in 1938 that it had removed anything to do with political thought from films, a more accurate appraisal was that the political content was kept in line with the conservative British establishment.

During World War II, however, British film content was liberalized. For example the script for *Love on the Dole* (1941), which described the poverty of the Depression-era working class, was too controversial for the prewar BBFC but

The scene in which James Cagney pushes a grapefruit into Mae Clarke's face in Public Enemy *(1931) raised objections from American women's groups because it depicted physical abuse of women; however, when the film was released in Great Britain, the British Board of Film Censors ordered the scene cut because its unmarried characters were wearing pajamas. (Arkent Archive)*

was passed for production during the war. In addition the Hollywood film *Mission to Moscow* (1944), a pro-Soviet film whose grasp of reality was less than perfect, was passed by the BBFC despite intense conservative opposition. During the war one of the greatest debates over film censorship developed around *The Life and Death of Colonel Blimp* (1943). The film caricatured the innate conservatism, or "Blimpishness" as David Low called it, of the British military. Winston Churchill argued that the film was "detrimental to the morale and discipline of the army" and wanted to have the film censored. Unable to convince his own Ministry of Information, or the BBFC, to ban the film, he was, however, able to force its cutting for export (from 163 minutes to ninety minutes).

The postwar BBFC continued to issue certificates, with standards that were more liberal. In particular the 1950's and 1960's, the so-called permissive decades, witnessed the production of numerous films with overt sexual and radical political messages.

See also Cinematograph Act; Film censorship; Hays Code; *Life and Death of Colonel Blimp, The*; United Kingdom.

British Broadcasting Corporation (BBC)

Founded: 1927

Type of organization: Radio and television association

Significance: The BBC, accountable to the British government, has practiced censorship as policy; the BBC has also earned wide respect for its news service

After a variety of commercial experiments in the years after World War I, British broadcasting effectively began in 1922 with the establishment of the British Broadcasting Company, a private corporation. Almost immediately questions were raised regarding the issue of the responsibility of such a corporation to the general public. A parliamentary committee conducted an investigation and in 1925 recommended that the company be dissolved and a public corporation responsible to parliament be established.

In 1927 the British Broadcasting Corporation came into existence, and John Reith, general manager of the original company, became the director general, a position he held until 1938, when he left to enter politics. Reith, known as the father of the BBC, developed and expanded broadcasting throughout the United Kingdom and in 1932 established the BBC's World Service, the most listened-to shortwave broadcast service in the world. In contrast to the Voice of America, its nearest competitor, with 90 million listeners, the World Service claims some 140 million listeners tuning in to its weekly broadcasts from London. Its standard programming includes music and book reviews as well as domestic and world news, presented in English and in forty-three languages. Almost from its inception the World Service has maintained an international reputation for truth and impartiality that is generally considered unassailable. In 1936 the BBC developed the first regular television service in the United Kingdom, and in 1967 the first color television service in Europe.

Governance of the BBC. As a public corporation, the BBC is prohibited by its royal charter from advertising and from broadcasting sponsored programming. Financed by license fees remitted annually by owners of radio and television receivers, the BBC provides its subscribers with four radio program choices and two television channels. For more than thirty years the corporation maintained a monopoly of broadcast services in Great Britain until the establishment of the Independent Broadcasting Authority (IBA) in 1954. Although the BBC had become a venerable and respected institution in British life, growing public protest to what was perceived as an unresponsiveness to changes in public taste made broadcast choice and diversity an issue whose time had come. The IBA offered the first commercial television channel to the British public, and by 1974, the government had licensed several commercial radio stations, ending the BBC's radio monopoly as well. In 1982 the government sanctioned the introduction of a second commercial television channel.

In its daily operations, the control of BBC programming rests in the hands of the producers, whose decisions and choices are guided by a series of restrictive codes. These codes include a 1973 mandate from the board of governors on taste and standards in the BBC and another in 1979 offering guidance on the portrayal of violence. There is also a list of topics that are not to be discussed, which include the royal family and the Church of England. These and other prohibited items first appeared in the notorious Green Book, or more formally the Policy Guide for Writers and Producers, introduced by Reith in the early days of his directorship. The Green Book governed BBC programming until it was finally withdrawn in 1963. It generally prohibited anything that might be considered crude or sexually suggestive. References either oblique or direct to homosexuality, excessive drinking, women's underwear, and religion were banned. Even politics, generally considered a mainstay of media humor, good-natured and otherwise, was severely restricted. Mild critical comment on the government was occasionally acceptable, but personal ridicule of a particular politician was not. Despite the demise of the Green Book, many of its basic principles and tenets remained in effect.

BBC producers are directly responsible to the director general and the board of governors for following these edicts. The director and the board are in turn ultimately responsible to the Home Secretary, who has the power, presumably in extreme cases, of revoking the BBC's operating license and (with parliamentary review and approval) abolishing its royal charter. Section thirteen of the charter provides the Home Office with the right to prohibit arbitrarily the broadcasting of any material deemed unsuitable, even in situations where the issue of what is suitable is not defined by the restrictive codes. In 1964 the BBC Board of Governors, in an attempt to clarify its role as the guardian of the national culture, defined its responsibility as one that would safeguard the presentation of programs that would "not offend against good taste or decency, or be likely to encourage crime or disorder, or be offensive to public feeling." Matters such as "taste" are subjectively defined and generally unclear; potential penalties for infractions are less equivocal. Broadcasters who might persist in a basic right to freedom of expression or "artistic license" are liable for criminal prosecution on statutory charges of "conspiracy to corrupt public morals" or "conspiracy to outrage public decency." In the most extreme cases, section nineteen of the charter provides the Home Office with the power to dispatch troops to seize control of the BBC on the behalf of the crown and "the public interest."

Politics and Foreign Policy. Although generally compliant with government restrictions on programming that raises questions concerning "good taste" and "decency," the BBC has provoked the greatest controversy in its handling of politics and foreign policy. In the 1982 military conflict between Great Britain and Argentina over the Falkland Islands, the BBC uncharacteristically refused to stay within the limits of government-prescribed coverage, and were duly reprimanded by the Tory government's media committee.

In the prolonged conflict between Catholics and Protestants in Northern Ireland, however, the BBC has, under legal duress, adhered closely to government restrictions on domestic broadcasting. Official censorship of any coverage of that prolonged conflict is based on two laws passed in the late 1970's. The Prevention of Terrorism Act (1976) requires British subjects to provide legal authorities with any information that might lead to the prevention of a terrorist act or lead to the arrest and conviction of anyone involved in terrorist activities. Television journalists who interview members of the Irish Provisional Army or who have pursued leads from informants are required by law to cooperate with authorities and provide all information related to such investigations. The 1978 Emergency Provisions Act governing Northern Ireland provides a form of prior restraint, impeding investigative journalism by forbidding the collecting and recording (either audio or video) for television or radio broadcast of any information concerning the military, courts and court officials, police or prison officials that might be used by terrorists. In October, 1988, government censorship went even further. Home Secretary Douglas Hurd officially banned all interviews by the BBC and the IBA with any representatives of Northern Ireland political groups that appeared on a government list of subversive organizations.

In 1996 a proposed restructuring of the BBC that would include consolidation of the World Service with domestic operations was met by strong objections around the world. South African archbishop Desmond Tutu voiced his objections to any changes in the news operation, citing the potential loss of the objectivity and impartiality that has distinguished the BBC's reporting of international news from the reporting of other networks. The Dalai Lama, exiled from Tibet following China's occupation of that country, protested the "dismemberment" of the World Service. In a controversial decision, BBC top management did not permit the Tibetan spiritual leader's views to air on the World Service.   *—Richard Keenan*

See also British Broadcasting Standards Council; Broadcast media; Canadian Broadcasting Corporation; Irish Republican Army; Northern Ireland; Television networks; United Kingdom.

BIBLIOGRAPHY

Two books by Asa Briggs, *A History of Broadcasting in the United Kingdom: The Birth of Broadcasting* (vol. 1, Oxford, England: Oxford University Press, 1961, 1995) and *A History of Broadcasting in the United Kingdom: The BBC: The First Fifty Years* (vol. 2, Oxford, England: Oxford University Press, 1985), offer sound and eminently readable detail of the BBC's early years, but are a bit more laudatory than objective. Roger Milner's *Reith: The B.B.C. Years* (Edinburgh: Mainstream, 1983) objectively balances the puritanical conservatism of the first director general with his very solid accomplishments, particularly in the years prior to World War II. The BBC's alternating struggle and compliance with government censorship is effectively detailed in Tom O'Malley's *Closedown?: The BBC and Government Broadcasting Policy, 1979-1992* (London: Pluto Press, 1994).

British Broadcasting Standards Council (BBSC)

FOUNDED: 1990

TYPE OF ORGANIZATION: British television and radio monitoring body

SIGNIFICANCE: The council is a statutory organization that monitors radio and television broadcasts in Great Britain

Created under the terms of Great Britain's Broadcasting Act of 1990, the Broadcasting Standards Council has a chairperson and seven members who are appointed by the government. Funded by the government, the council investigates complaints from viewers and listeners in matters of taste and decency; these include portrayals of violence, sex, swearing, and blasphemy.

The council considers only complaints about programs that have already been broadcast; it has no power to adjudicate on programs prior to broadcast. The council is helped by a complaints committee, which initially considers complaints. If a complaint is judged worthy of further consideration, the council may require broadcasters to explain themselves. If a complaint is subsequently upheld, the broadcasters may have to state this fact on air and may also be required to apologize to their audiences.

The council has published its findings in monthly and annual reports. It has also issued a Code of Practice that, under the terms of the Broadcasting Act, broadcasters must reflect in their own codes of conduct. The council also publishes guidance on how to complain and undertakes research. In 1994 the government announced its intention to merge the council with the Broadcasting Complaints Commission, which was set up in 1981 and has responsibility for monitoring biased reporting and invasions of privacy.

See also British Broadcasting Corporation; Broadcast media; Campaign for Press and Broadcasting Freedom; United Kingdom.

Broadcast media

DEFINITION: Radio, television, and cable communications

SIGNIFICANCE: The most pervasive form of communications in the late twentieth century, the broadcast media have been the target of numerous efforts to regulate content

The United States government played a pivotal role in the birth of radio, television, and cable broadcasting and took a paternalistic interest in their growth and development. From an economic and technological standpoint, the government's role in promoting these new industries was beneficial and served the national interest. From a First Amendment perspective, however, unwarranted governmental censorship of broadcasting poses a serious and persistent threat to freedom of expression.

Fairness. In 1964 a Pennsylvania radio station, WGCB, carried a fifteen-minute broadcast, the "Christian Crusade," in which the Reverend Billy James Hargis accused Fred J. Cook, author of *Goldwater—Extremist on the Right*, of working for a communist affiliated publication and of sympathizing with Alger Hiss. Invoking the personal attack rule contained in the Communications Act of 1934, Cook demanded and was denied free reply time. When the Federal Communications Commission (FCC) concluded that the station had failed to meet its obligations under the Fairness Doctrine, WGCB went to court.

Ultimately, in *Red Lion Broadcasting Co. Inc. v. Federal Communications Commission* (1969), the U.S. Supreme court, in a unanimous opinion, held that the personal attack aspect of the Fairness Doctrine did not abridge the freedoms of speech or press. The Court found that the Fairness Doctrine was an "obligation whose content has been defined in a long series of FCC rulings in particular cases, and which is distinct from the statutory requirement of Section 315 of the Communications Act that equal time be allotted all qualified candidates for public office." The Court articulated the often-repeated public interest standard in justifying government regulation of broadcasting content. "In light of the fact that the 'public interest' in broadcasting clearly encompasses the presentation of vigorous debate of controversial issues of importance and concern to the public . . . we think the fairness doctrine and its component personal attack and political editorializing regulations are a legitimate exercise of congressionally delegated authority." Adopting the view that spectrum scarcity (there are only so many broadcast frequencies available; therefore issues of public interest can influence private use of said frequencies) also justified government regulations, the Court observed that "licenses to broadcast do not confer ownership of designated frequencies, but only the temporary privilege of using them."

Critics of the *Red Lion* decision argue that neither the public interest nor spectrum scarcity rationales justify less First Amendment protection for radio and television broadcasting than the print media. The value of "vigorous debate of controversial issues of importance and concern to the public" is not unique to broadcasting. Newspapers, magazines, books and films also serve that purpose, yet few, if any, would tolerate government-imposed standards of "fairness" on those forms of expression.

Likewise, the notion that since there are only a limited number of radio and television frequencies available, the government must allocate them in such a manner as to ensure a "diversity of viewpoints," has been criticized as scientifically flawed and unwise public policy. Technically, critics argue, there is no spectrum but only transmitters and receivers of electromagnetic energy. Signals do not interfere with each other in space, they interfere with each other in receivers, which have limited capacity to differentiate between modulations. As technology becomes more sophisticated, the number of channels expand, thereby enlarging the so-called spectrum, allowing for diversity to emerge naturally, not by government fiat.

Furthermore, critics of the spectrum scarcity argument point out that taken to its logical conclusion, scarcity could be used to justify the censorship of the print media as well. Newsprint, presses, distribution trucks, newsstands, and so on are by one standard or another scarce, as are bookstores and movie theaters. If limitations on the delivery or transportation of a means of expression can thereby justify greater government regulation, all media is in jeopardy.

Thus, issues of censorship relating to the broadcast media are seen as part and parcel of broader censorship issues. Precedents established in one area can bleed over into another. Telecommunications technologies involving computers have merged the print and electronic media. Many newspapers are now transmitted by satellite. The Court has decided little on which First Amendment model will prevail in such cases. There is the print model, affording maximum protection for freedom of expression, and there is the broadcast model, allowing for greater government regulation.

Seven Dirty Words. On the afternoon of October 30, 1973, New York radio station WBAI, owned by the Pacifica Foundation, broadcast George Carlin's "Filthy Words" monologue. A few weeks later a listener who said he heard the program while driving with his young son wrote a complaint to the FCC. On February 21, 1975, the FCC issued a declaratory order granting the complaint. The order became part of the station's license file. The FCC stated: "We therefore hold that the language as broadcast was indecent and prohibited by 18 U.S.C. [Section] 1464." The FCC decision was reversed by the Court of Appeals for the District of Columbia. Each of the appellate judges wrote separately. Judge Tamm concluded that the order represented censorship and was prohibited by the Communications Act, Section 326. Judge Bazelon rested his view on the Constitution. Judge Leventhal, in dissent, emphasized the interest in protecting children and said that the FCC had correctly condemned the daytime broadcast as indecent. The Supreme Court, in a 5-4 opinion, ruled for the FCC.

The Court's review was limited to the FCC's determination that the Carlin monologue was indecent as broadcast within the meaning of 18 United States Code, Section 1464, which bars the broadcast of "any obscene, indecent, or profane language." Addressing the Communications Act's prohibition of program censorship (a different law, 47 United States Code, Section 326), the Court said that the FCC is barred from editing a proposed broadcast in advance, but that the law had never been construed to deny the commission the power to review the content of completed broadcasts in the performance of its regulatory duties. The Court found the content of the monologue to be vulgar, offensive, and shocking and argued that the commission's order was not unconstitutional under the First Amendment, either because of being overly broad or because the monologue was not obscene. On the question of whether a broadcast of patently offensive words dealing with sex and excretion may be regulated because of its content, the Court said that case law showed that obscene materials had been denied protection because their content is "so offensive to contemporary moral standards." It noted that because of its characteristics of being received in the home, broadcasting had traditionally received the least First Amendment protection of all media. "Patently offensive, indecent material presented over the airwaves confronts the citizen, not only in public, but also in the privacy of the home, where the individual's right to be left alone plainly outweighs the First Amendment rights of an intruder. The ease with which children may obtain access to broadcast material . . . amply justifies special treatment of indecent broadcasting." The Court concluded: "We simply hold that when the Commission finds that a pig has entered the parlor, the exercise of its regulatory power does not depend on proof that the pig is obscene."

Separately, Justice Lewis Franklin Powell, Jr., joined by Justice Harry Andrew Blackmun, concurred but disagreed with the plurality that Supreme Court justices were free to decide on the basis of content which protected speech was deserving of more or less protection. "The result turns instead on the unique characteristics of the broadcast media, combined with society's right to protect its children from speech generally agreed to be inappropriate for their years, and with the interest of unwilling adults in not being assaulted by such offensive speech in their homes."

In dissent, Justice William J. Brennan, Jr., joined by Justice Thurgood Marshall, stated that such factors—intrusiveness and children in the audience—"simply do not support even the professedly moderate degree of governmental homogenization of radio communications—if, indeed, such homogenization can ever be moderate given the pre-eminent status of the right of free speech in our constitutional scheme—that the Court today permits." Also dissenting, Justice Potter Stewart, joined by Brennan, Marshall, and Byron White, expressed the view that, since the monologue was not obscene, the FCC lacked statutory authority to ban it.

The Right to Editorialize. In 1984 First Amendment protection for political speech proved strong enough to defeat a Congressional effort to ban editorializing by public broadcasting stations. At issue was Section 399 of the Public Broadcasting Act of 1967 forbidding any noncommercial educational station that received funding from the Corporation for Public Broadcasting to "engage in editorializing." The Pacifica Foundation, which owned five such stations, joined by the League of Women Voters of California and Congressman Henry Waxman, filed a legal challenge to Section 399. The U.S. Supreme Court found the law unconstitutional in *Federal Communications Commission v. League of Women Voters* (1984).

According to Justice John Paul Stevens: "Pacifica wants to broadcast its views to Waxman via its radio stations; Waxman wants to listen to those views on his radio; and the League of Women Voters wants a chance to convince Pacifica to take positions its members favor in its radio broadcasts."

Justice Brennan wrote the Court's 5-to-4 majority decision. He noted that Section 399 appeared to restrict precisely that form of speech that the framers of the Bill of Rights considered "indispensable to the discovery and spread of political truth." He reiterated that, because of spectrum scarcity (the viability he elsewhere questioned), those who are awarded a broadcast license can be required to provide programming that serves the public interest. Given the fact that there are hundreds of public radio and television stations throughout the country, "it seems reasonable to infer that the editorial voices of these stations will prove to be as distinctive, varied, and idiosyncratic as the various communities they represent. Accordingly, absent some showing by the Government to the contrary, the risk that local editorializing will place all of public broadcasting in jeopardy is not sufficiently pressing to warrant Section 399's broad suppression of speech."

In dissent, Justice William H. Rehnquist, joined by White and Warren Burger, said that Congress had not violated the First Amendment when it decided that public funds shall not be used to subsidize noncommercial, educational broadcasting stations that engage in editorializing or endorse or oppose any political candidate. It is impossible to separate programming expenses from other expenditures, so Justice Rehnquist said that the only effective means of preventing the use of public moneys to subsidize the airing of management's views is for Congress to ban a subsidized station from all on-the-air editorializing. Justice Stevens, in a separate dissent, said that the statute was proper because of the overriding interest in forestalling creation of propaganda organs for the government. "One need not have heard the raucous voice of Adolf Hitler over Radio Berlin to appreciate the importance of that concern."

New Technologies. The Communications Decency Act of 1996 prohibited the transmission by any means of telecommunications of obscene or "indecent" material to anyone under eighteen years of age or the use of interactive computer services to display "in a manner available" to a person under 18 years of age, any material that "depicts or describes, in terms patently offensive as measured by contemporary community standards, sexual or excretory activities or organs." The act was immediately challenged in court on the grounds that the terms "indecent" and "patently offensive" are unconstitutionally vague and improperly sweep a wide variety of protected speech within their prohibitory scope.

Broadcasting is an easy target of censorship since there is already in place an established bureaucracy capable of enforcing any regulation enacted by Congress. Whether broadcasting will escape censorship depends on whether Congress and the courts apply broad First Amendment principles developed for the print media, such as books, newspapers, and magazines, or more limited protections which treat radio and television.

—Stephen F. Rohde

See also Action for Children's Television; Carlin, George; Communications Act of 1934; Fairness doctrine; Federal Communications Commission; Radio; Stern, Howard; Television; Television, children's.

BIBLIOGRAPHY

A fine comprehensive overview of broadcast media is F. Leslie Smith's *Perspectives on Radio and Television: Telecommunications in the United States* (New York: Harper & Row, 1985). Edwin Diamond, Norman Sandler, and Milton Mueller's *Telecommunications in Crisis: The First Amendment, Technology, and Deregulation* (Washington, D.C.: Cato Institute, 1983) contains a useful series of essays promoting the deregulation of radio and television broadcasting. The authors debunk various rationales for government control of the media, including spectrum scarcity and regulatory obsolescence, and briefly cover low-power television, cable television, satellites, direct broadcast service, cellular radio, and home video. Richard Hixson's *Mass Media and the Constitution: An Encyclopedia of Supreme Court Decisions* (New York: Garland, 1989) summarizes more than two hundred U.S. Supreme Court decisions in the areas of broadcasting, business, censorship, commercial speech, copyright, fair trial, the Freedom of Information Act, free speech, libel, news gathering, obscenity, and privacy. Each entry summarizes a case, its circumstances, key holdings, and important precedents cited in the decision, and it offers references for further reading. Among the First Amendment issues discussed in Rodney A. Smolla's *Free Speech in an Open Society* (New York: Alfred A. Knopf, 1992) are the challenges of new technologies.

Broadcast Music, Inc. (BMI)

FOUNDED: 1939

TYPE OF ORGANIZATION: One of three major performance rights organizations

SIGNIFICANCE: Responsible for breaking the monopoly held during the early part of the twentieth century by ASCAP, the first major performance rights organization, which had effectively limited the broadcast possibilities of certain kinds of music

Founded in 1939, the National Association of Broadcasters was created to compete with the American Society of Composers, Authors & Publishers (ASCAP), which then held a virtual monopoly of the business of collecting performance fees for musicians, songwriters, and music publishers. The National Broadcasting Company and Columbia Broadcasting System were major stockholders in BMI by 1940. Because ASCAP had exclusive arrangements with many music interests to collect performance fees owed them from broadcasters and other sources, BMI initially had to make its collection arrangements with the musical interests ASCAP had shunned: blues, country, and, eventually, rock music. ASCAP's refusal to allow music interests in these areas to become members of its organization had the effect of limiting the broadcast avenues for this music. BMI's entry into the business thus created broadcast opportunities for these forms of music. Television networks had a major stake in BMI, so they used their programming power to encourage the performance of music licensed by BMI and to discourage giving air time to music licensed to ASCAP.

See also American Society of Composers, Authors & Publishers; Music; Recording industry.

Bruce, Lenny

BORN: October 13, 1925, Mineola, New York

DIED: August 3, 1966, Los Angeles, California

IDENTIFICATION: American comic and social critic

SIGNIFICANCE: Bruce's stand-up comic routines included social satire and frank language that provoked continual police harassment and criminal prosecution

From 1961 until 1966 comic Lenny Bruce was caught up in a net of police harassment and criminal prosecutions for his on-stage satiric monologues, which included controversial commentaries on drug use, sexuality, politics, and religion. However, his performances gained national notoriety more for their frequent use of offensive language than for the issues that they addressed. Bruce considered himself a conservative social critic, but got most of his support from civil libertarians, who usually portrayed him as a martyr for the right of free speech.

Bruce's first arrest for obscenity came after he performed at a San Francisco jazz festival in October, 1961. He won that case, but was soon arrested in Beverly Hills, California. In February, 1963, his jury in that case deadlocked. Three days

A week after Lenny Bruce arrived in London in April, 1963, Great Britain's home secretary ordered him to leave the country "in the public interest." (AP/Wide World Photos)

later his third obscenity trial began in Chicago, Illinois. After attempting to defend himself, Bruce was convicted on February 28, 1963. While lawyers began his appeal on the Chicago conviction in the summer of 1964, Bruce was arrested in New York City for giving obscene performances at a coffee house; he particularly rankled local Roman Catholic leaders with his comments on the pope.

By the following winter, Bruce was under a nationwide performance lockout—except in San Francisco, where he was protected because of his earlier court win. However, he was still under constant police surveillance and was subjected to numerous police narcotics raids. In late 1964, he asked attorney Edward de Grazia for help after de Grazia had successfully defended Henry Miller's *Tropic of Cancer*. The landmark Miller case would have assisted Bruce if not for Bruce's own increasingly erratic behavior.

Bruce's inability to work reliably and his contentious relationships with his lawyers complicated his legal defense, but his fellow defendant, the coffee house owner Herbert Solomon, was acquitted of the charges against him. Bruce blamed his attorneys for his own troubles and sent them a series of incomprehensible petitions, letters, transcripts, and tapes. In New York he filed for damages because of his inability to work, and filed an appeal with the state's supreme court against the restraining order that prevented him from performing.

In December, 1964, Bruce lost his New York appeal in a legally controversial decision and was sentenced to four months in prison. After jumping bail, he returned to San Francisco disillusioned. In a state of delirium, he leaped out of a hotel window the following March. Because of his obsession with the law, his subsequent comedy routines declined in quality until he took a narcotics overdose that ended his life in August, 1966. In 1968 his former New York co-defendant, Solomon, filed a posthumous appeal on his behalf, and won after New York prosecutors admitted they had hounded Bruce into poverty and suicide.

A 1966 survey of American libraries found that most determined Bruce's autobiography, *How to Talk Dirty and Influence People* (1965) was unsuitable for their shelves, and the book was banned in Great Britain, from which Bruce had been expelled in 1963.

See also Carlin, George; Criminal trials; De Grazia, Edward; Obscenity: legal definitions; Offensive language; *Playboy*; Sahl, Mort.

Bruno, Giordano

BORN: 1548, Nola, near Naples, Italy
DIED: February 17, 1600, Rome, Italy
IDENTIFICATION: Italian philosopher
SIGNIFICANCE: To the Roman Catholic church and the Inquisition, Bruno was more than a heretic; he was a dangerous person capable of creating a cult following and who had to be executed for his opinions

Bruno entered the Roman Catholic church's Dominican order in Italy at the age of eighteen. As his thinking developed, it deviated from the norm. In 1576 he was indicted for heresy, but he escaped and spent sixteen years traveling throughout

The heresies expressed in Giordano Bruno's books moved the Inquisition to burn him at the stake in 1600. (Library of Congress)

Europe. Meanwhile, he attracted wide attention for his philosophical positions. Bruno was an original thinker, capable of influencing in later years not only Baruch Spinoza but also German philosophers, such as Friedrich Jacobi, Friedrich Schelling, and Georg Hegel.

Bruno was a philosopher of nature, part of the movement away from the domination of Aristotle. He embraced the Copernican system and developed it in metaphysical terms. For example, he held that God is infinite and unitary substance, while the effects of this substance (like people) are merely accidents. In this view, he anticipated Spinoza. Bruno concluded that there is an infinite number of worlds. Bruno's hylomorphism was seen, variously, as pantheism and as materialism. Bruno was also fascinated by magical matters and the Hermetic cult of ancient Egypt. For example, he was famous for his mnemonics, which incorporated the mysticism and magic of Raymond Lull.

During the sixteenth century the Roman Catholic church was under attack by the growing Protestant Reformation. In 1591 Bruno was arrested by the church's Venetian Inquisition. The burden was on him to prove his innocence, with no right to cross-examine witnesses. Some charges against Bruno were doctrinal, such as his alleged denial of transubstantiation; others concerned philosophical positions. In 1593 he was transferred to the Roman Inquisition. Fragmentary records make it impossible to know how Bruno was treated during his imprisonment, but by 1599 he had ceased to be cooperative. He denied that his opinions were heretical.

Part of Bruno's defence before the Inquisition was his appeal to the doctrine of the Two Truths, a doctrine advanced by William of Ockham and John Duns Scotus that had not yet been condemned by the church. Bruno argued that he was a philosopher, and that he could follow philosophical truth wherever it leads, so long as he did not contradict any of the truths of theology. There were, he held, two sets of truths—those of philosophy and those of theology. The Inquisition disagreed. When he was sentenced to death, Bruno told his judges that perhaps they had greater fear in passing the sentence than he had in hearing it. His judges refused the reduced severity of garroting before he was burned to death in Rome and his ashes were thrown to the winds. In 1603 his books were added to the *Index Librorum Prohibitorum*.

In 1889 a statue to Bruno's martyrdom was erected in the same Roman marketplace where he was burned. It still stands as silent testimony to Bruno's courage in his convictions.

See also Death; Galileo Galilei; Spanish Inquisition; Spinoza, Baruch.

Bryant, Anita

BORN: March 25, 1940, Barnsdall, Oklahoma

IDENTIFICATION: American pop singer and entertainer

SIGNIFICANCE: A professed Christian, Bryant undermined her success as a singer and spokesperson for the Florida Citrus Commission by speaking out against equal rights for homosexuals

Bryant got her first taste of the entertainment business when she performed in a high school operetta while only in first

Anita Bryant sings with her Florida pastor, William Champan, shortly after her "Save Our Children" organization helped defeat a Miami gay rights ordinance in 1990. (AP/Wide World Photos)

grade. Loving everything about the stage, she vowed to become a star someday. She performed on local radio and television stations during her teen years. When she graduated from high school she lacked the funds for college, so she entered a Tulsa, Oklahoma, beauty pageant. She went on to become Miss Oklahoma and second runner-up for Miss America. Her fresh good looks and Christian values helped to win her a place as America's sweetheart.

Later Bryant recorded several gold records and wrote a best-selling book. She tried to give up her career for marriage, but was unhappy without her work. Her husband became her manager and scheduled performances at the White House, the Democratic and Republican conventions in 1968, the Orange Bowl, and Super Bowl. President Lyndon Baines Johnson even asked Bryant to sing at his funeral. Despite these successes, Bryant's outspokenness about her personal beliefs eventually led to her downfall. She lost her lucrative job as Florida's Citrus Spokesperson after leading a 1977 campaign to repeal a Dade County, Florida, law prohibiting discrimination against homosexuals in housing and employment.

See also Advertisers as advocates of censorship; Homosexuality; Political correctness.

Buddhism

DEFINITION: A major Eastern religion emphasizing ways to end worldly suffering by mental and moral self-purification

SIGNIFICANCE: Buddhism's democratic and pacific teachings have often led to its repression by various governments

Buddhism is one of the major religions of the world, with an estimated 300 million believers, most of them in Asia. The religion was founded in the sixth century B.C.E. by Siddhartha Gautama, a young prince who left his family in search of enlightenment. He subsequently spent his remaining years as a teacher, wandering throughout northern India to spread his views.

Buddhist teaching seeks a "middle path" between luxury and self-denial. Buddhism believes that suffering is inherent in a person's life, and that such suffering is caused by desire. Therefore, one must eliminate such wants before it is possible to relieve the suffering.

Buddhists advocate the noble Eightfold Path as leading to enlightenment—right views, right intentions, right speech, right conduct, right livelihood, right effort, right awareness, and right meditation. When people free themselves from desire by following the eightfold path, they bring an end to the eternal suffering caused by reincarnation. The state of being free from the reincarnation caused by continued desire is called nirvana. The term "buddha" means "enlightened one," and was originally applied to Siddhartha Gautama. The term is not a proper noun, however, and can refer to anyone who acquires enlightenment by following the noble Eightfold Path. Although Buddhism lacks a central, all-encompassing book of its beliefs, most groups use some form of the "Tripitaka," or "three baskets." This is an anthology of sayings and words of conduct for Buddhist worshippers. There are a number of other works revered by Buddhists, though they vary widely according to sects.

Despite its roots in India, modern Buddhism has been strongest in such Asian countries as Thailand, Burma (now Myanmar), Cambodia, Sri Lanka, Mongolia, and Japan. There are also significant Buddhist populations in China, Laos, Vietnam, and Korea. Buddhism was persecuted, which involved censorship, in its native India, although King Asoka the Great made it the official religion of his territory in the third century B.C.E. As centuries passed, Buddhism in India declined as a result of sectarianism, hostility from the Hindu Brahmans (who considered Buddhism's antielitism and democratic spirit heretical), and persecutions from Islamic conquerors.

Early Buddhism was at times an official religion in various parts of Asia ruled by emperors who claimed adherence to the teachings of Buddha. In Korea, the Shilla Dynasty made Buddhism the state religion from 668-935, and in the Koryo Dynasty (935-1392), the government sponsored extensive construction of monasteries. In the eleventh century, Buddhist kings ruled in Burma, Cambodia, and Vietnam. This sometimes led to the censoring of documents that embraced other religions. Buddhism has been suppressed by many governments that saw the religion as a challenge to state control. In Tibet, King Glandarma (838-842) seized numerous properties from the Buddhists, claiming monastic orders were becoming wealthy from hiding behind their tax-exempt arrangement with the monarchy. In Korea, the Yi Dynasty (1392-1910) endorsed Confucianism over Buddhism, and Buddhists were greatly persecuted.

Buddhism came under increasing attack after World War II, particularly with the spread of communism throughout Asia. In China, Mao Zedong launched the Cultural Revolution in 1966. Temples and monasteries were attacked and often leveled, Buddhist books were destroyed, and scores of Buddhists were killed, tortured, or sent away for re-education. In Cambodia, Pol Pot, mimicking Mao, followed policies that were, if possible, even more cruel from 1975 to 1979. In Myanmar, which has a rich tradition of Buddhism, Buddhist scholar and Nobel Peace Prize winner Aung San Suu Kyi was placed under house arrest in 1989 for her advocacy of democracy and religious freedom.

See also Burma; Censorship; Christianity; China; Civil Rights movement; Islam; Japan; Labor unions; Religion; Vietnam.

Bulgakov, Mikhail Afanasyevich

BORN: May 15, 1891, Kiev, Ukraine, Russian Empire
DIED: March 10, 1940, Moscow, Soviet Union
IDENTIFICATION: Russian novelist and playwright
SIGNIFICANCE: Bulgakov's writing career was shortened by censorship, which prevented the full development of his potential

As a young man Bulgakov lived through Russia's revolution and civil war without taking sides. When he began publishing in the mid-1920's, he took an objective view, as in his novel *The White Guard* (1926), later adapted for stage as *Days of Turbins*. Both works were very popular, a fact that led eventually to Bulgakov's ostracism. All of his works take satirical views of the changed state of affairs in the Soviet Union. His

play *Zoyka's Apartment* (1926), which satirizes the housing problems, as well as the new Soviet philistines, had to be withdrawn. Another of Bulgakov's plays, *Molyer; A Cabal of Hypocrites* (1936), uses the struggle that the French playwright Moliere waged against critics—whom he often pilloried—in order to symbolize his own plight within modern Soviet society.

Perhaps the greatest satire of the Soviet system is to be found in Bulgakov's novel *The Master and Margarita* (written in the 1940's but not published until 1967). It challenges the very basis of the Soviet system by posing age-old questions about the truth, reality, and sanctity of materialistic philosophy. For all these reasons Bulgakov was severely censored and prevented from publishing and developing his full potential as a writer in a police state.

See also Akhmatova, Anna; Babel, Isaac Emmanuilovich; Drama and theater; Mayakovsky, Vladimir; Pasternak, Boris; Police states; Russia; Socialist Realism; Soviet Union; Stalin, Joseph; Zamyatin, Yevgeny Ivanovich.

Bumper stickers

DEFINITION: Small printed signs on which brief messages are affixed to cars and other vehicles
SIGNIFICANCE: Trends toward uninhibited expression on bumper stickers have led to calls for legislation restricting what words may be displayed on vehicles

Bumper stickers have long been a popular form of political expression in the United States; during election years campaign slogans and candidates' names can be seen on countless vehicles. Since the 1960's the subject matter appearing on bumper stickers has diversified greatly. Since then millions of stickers have expressed the views of vehicle owners not only on politics, but on religion, sports, music, drugs, the environment, and other issues. The proliferation of such stickers has introduced new clichés into the language and inspired conscious efforts at humor and parody. For example, a popular retort to such stickers as "Save the Whales" and "Abolish Nuclear War" has been "Nuke the Whales!"

The general relaxation of American obscenity laws since the 1960's has fostered increasingly uninhibited expression in bumper stickers—many of which contain words once regarded as legally "obscene." As a consequence, many states—including Alabama, Florida, Louisiana, Missouri, North Carolina, South Carolina, and Washington D.C.—have specifically outlawed the display of "obscene" bumper stickers. A law enacted in Alabama in July, 1987, is typical in making it "unlawful for any person to display in public any bumper sticker, sign or writing which depicts obscene language descriptive of sexual or excretory activities."

After Alabama's law was passed, a motorist named Wayne Baker put a sticker on his truck with the words "How's My Driving? Call 1-800-EAT-SHIT!," spoofing signs such as "How's My Driving? Call 1-800-2-ADVISE," which are commonly seen on commercial vehicles. Soon afterward Baker was stopped by a police officer who informed him that this bumper sticker violated state law. The officer threatened Baker with a fine unless he removed the sticker's last two words, and warned him that words such as "crap" and "doo-doo" would also violate state law. Baker agreed to scratch out the offending language but later filed suit in federal district court claiming that his First Amendment rights had been violated. The court agreed and struck down Alabama's law in 1991.

See also Alabama; License plates, customized; Obscenity: legal definitions; Police.

Burlesque shows

DEFINITION: Variety entertainments typically featuring comedy acts and exotic striptease dancing

SIGNIFICANCE: Once considered a harmless form of amusement, burlesque shows were eventually condemned and marginalized

Early nineteenth century burlesque shows, such as those at New York's Olympic Theater under William Mitchell, mocked fashionable drama, events, and people. During the mid-nineteenth century burlesque shows increasingly featured female entertainers. In actress and manager Laura Keene's *Seven Sisters* (1860), for example, almost all roles were played by women dressed in costumes considered highly revealing at the time. This evoked criticism, which increased in 1868, when Lydia Thompson brought her troupe, the British Blondes, to New York to present *Ixion*, generally considered the first modern burlesque show.

Initially favorable reviews gave way to condemnation when Thompson's show moved to New York's fashionable Niblo's Gardens. Newspaper editors, members of the clergy, legislators, and women's rights advocates were disturbed by the show's suggestive language, impudent interaction among performers and audience, music associated with African American culture, and abundant displays of female bodies. The women performers were condemned as unnatural. When Thompson's group went on tour, the criticism published by the *Chicago Times* was so vicious that Thompson and members of her troupe horsewhipped the newspaper's editor.

Controversies such as that apparently helped burlesque to gain in popularity. Variety show entertainments (later known as vaudeville) that were developing during the same period attracted increasingly middle-class audiences. Burlesque shows—which by the 1870's were often using the format of the minstrel show and the earthy material of the concert saloon—appealed more to the urban working class and poor. "Clean" burlesque continued, especially with such performers as Joe Weber and Lew Fields, and regained some popularity during World War I.

By the 1890's, however, burlesque was usually as "hot" as local law enforcement allowed, especially after cooch dancing—the forerunner of the modern striptease—was borrowed from the Chicago Columbian Exposition of 1893. Herbert, Billy, Abe, and Morton Minsky—the most famous early twentieth century burlesque producers—introduced a signal system to warn performers of the presence of police in audiences so that they could switch to their clean material. Police raids were frequent. The most famous occurred on April 20, 1925, after a complaint by John Sumner, secretary for the New York Society for the Suppression of Vice. (It became the basis

for a 1967 novel by Roland Barber and the 1968 film *The Night They Raided Minsky's*.)

The 1920's brought increasing regulation. After the 1929 stock market crash and subsequent Depression, many legitimate theaters failed. As burlesque moved into empty Broadway theater buildings, property owners, fearful of declining values, joined religious forces and legislators in attacking burlesque and blaming it for Times Square sex crimes. New York City banned strip acts in 1933. The Minskys' establishment closed in 1935; they reopened temporarily after an appeal, but that same year managers had to sign an oath, promising to refrain from indecency. Finally, on May 2, 1937, New York City refused to renew the licenses of the city's fourteen burlesque houses. Legal appeals failed.

Burlesque vanished from New York. Elsewhere it remained marginalized as questionable entertainment and eventually was best known through reviews and revivals featuring striptease artists, such as Gypsy Rose Lee's appearance in Mike Todd's 1942 *Star and Garter*, Ann Corio's 1962 *This Was Burlesque*, and Tempest Storm's 1973 Carnegie Hall performance.

See also Drama and theater; Nude dancing; Nudity; Society for the Suppression of Vice, New York; Sumner, John.

Burma

DESCRIPTION: Known as Myanmar since 1989, Burma is a Southeast Asian nation that was once ruled as part of British India

SIGNIFICANCE: Burma has had one of the most repressive governments in post-World War II Asia

Burma's history of censorship started at least as early as the late 1840's when Buddhist officials in Rangoon allegedly forbade the importation and distribution of Bibles by the American Baptist Missionary Society. This prohibition helped provoke the Second Anglo-Burmese War, which ended in 1852 and resulted in the loss of Pegu Province, at the mouth of the Irrawaddy River, to the British, leaving Burma a landlocked nation.

As a colonial power over the next century, Great Britain applied censorship as it monitored the vernacular newspapers and nationalist movements. George Orwell's first novel *Burmese Days* (1934) is based on his experience as a colonial policeman in Burma. He later wrote *Nineteen Eighty-Four* (1949), in which he coined expressions such as "newspeak" and "newthink," which, though more akin to fascism and communism, may have had some Burmese associations.

During the 1950's Burma's free press included more than thirty daily newspapers, including six in Chinese and three in English, but that number has since been severely reduced. Creeping censorship began in the early 1950's under such agencies as the Press Review Department, the 1950 Emergency Provisions Act, and the 1962 Printers and Publishers Registration Law. The suspension of newspaper publication and the detention of editors occurred during the 1960's.

Burma has a Press Scrutiny Board. In 1975 the Ministry of Home and Religious Affairs issued guidelines including prohibitions on "any incorrect ideas and opinions which do not

Muslims fleeing Burma's repressive regime land in Bangladesh in 1992. (AP/Wide World Photos)

accord with the times" and "descriptions which, though factually accurate, are unsuitable because of the time or the circumstance of their writing." The most notorious censorship occurred after September, 1988, when the State Law and Order Restoration Council (SLORC) assumed power in a bloody military coup. The repressiveness of the government was dramatized by Daw Aung San Suu Kyi, who won the Nobel Peace Prize in 1991. The daughter of Aung San, a leading nationalist assassinated in 1947, she has been an outspoken democratic constitutional opponent to the military rule of General Ne Win and his various successors. She told an American Congressman, "I've always said that the only answer to Burma's problems is dialogue. . . . I'm ready at any time, but they [SLORC] seem not terribly keen." She was placed under house arrest in July, 1989, but her restrictions were somewhat eased in August, 1995.

Burma's censorship in the Ministry of Thought has relied on self-censorship and the threat of economic ruin and imprisonment. Much Burmese literature has had to be presented to the ministry after it was published, and has had to be passed as fit for the public before it could be distributed and the publishers' investments recouped. Illegal distribution of literature has resulted in twenty-year prison sentences. This has inhibited the style and freedom of expression of Burma's writers. Paper has been government rationed and expensive. In the early 1990's

at least twenty government censors worked in the same building that had housed the Japanese secret police during the Japanese occupation in World War II.

While the reading public is the major literary victim of censorship, in Burma, students, writers, and editors have been physical victims, sometimes being killed in demonstrations or dying in incarceration. The 1995 film *Rangoon* is a cinematic version of conditions under the SLORC regime.

See also Buddhism; China; Colonialism; India; Japan; Orwell, George; Pakistan; Police.

Burton, Richard Francis

BORN: March 19, 1821, Torquay, Devonshire, England
DIED: October 20, 1890, Trieste, Italy
IDENTIFICATION: English literary scholar and explorer
SIGNIFICANCE: A true Renaissance man, Burton risked criminal prosecution in order to translate volumes of classic Asian and Arabian erotica

In 1863 Burton helped to establish the Anthropological Society of London, which would later become the Anthropological Society of Great Britain and Ireland. He hoped that this society would publish scholarly discussions of sexual matters without hesitation, but the society instituted rules concerning "respectability" and "propriety" that frustrated Burton's efforts to publish sensitive material. With or without the support of scholarly societies, he published learned books that dealt with the sexual habits of various non-Western peoples. Although these studies met with some criticism, there was a certain amount of toleration throughout British society for discussions of people whom the public considered mere "savages." Over the years though, Burton became frustrated with his prudish editors, who censored many of his descriptive footnotes.

In 1872 Burton and his wife, Isabel, took up residence in Trieste, Italy. This would turn out to be Burton's last British consul post. During his years there, he focused on literary matters. It was his wish that the erotica that he had collected from various parts of the world be made available to an English-speaking audience. In translating the ancient love manuals of India and Arabia, Burton and his collaborators had to be careful. If the translations were not handled properly, Burton could be prosecuted under the Obscene Publications Act of 1857. It was necessary to publish the translation of the ancient erotic Indian classic, the *Kama Sutra* under the imprint of an imaginary publishing firm, the "Kama Shastra Society of London and Benares." Burton collaborated with Foster Fitzgerald Arbuthnot on the translation projects *The Kama Sutra of Vatsyayana* (1883) and the *Ananga Ranga* (1885).

Burton's translation of *The Kama Sutra of Vatsyayana* soon became one of the most pirated books in the English language. It could not be officially published in England or the United States though until 1962. Burton published his translation *The Perfumed Garden of the Cheikh Nefzaoui: A Manual of Arabian Erotology* in 1886. He also published a remarkable unexpurgated translation *The Book of the Thousand Nights and a Night: A Plain and Literal Translation of the Arabian Nights Entertainments* (16 vols., 1885-1888). Burton took great care in his translations not to use language that could be considered obscene. After his death in 1890, his wife destroyed his revised edition of *The Perfumed Garden* and many other manuscript diaries and notes that she believed to be obscene.

See also *Arabian Nights, The*; *Kama Sutra*; Obscene Publications Acts; Sex in the arts; Sex manuals; Translation.

Bush, George

Born: June 12, 1924, Milton, Massachusetts

Identification: Forty-first president of the United States

Significance: As president, Bush continued the censorship and secrecy policies of President Ronald Reagan and he proposed amending the Bill of Rights

After serving as a Navy pilot in World War II, Bush returned to Yale University, graduating Phi Beta Kappa in 1948. With the assistance of his wealthy family, he entered the oil business in Texas; by 1966 he had become a millionaire in his own right. In 1966 and 1968 he won elections to the U.S. House of Representatives from Houston, Texas. After he lost a race for the Senate in 1970, President Richard Nixon appointed him U.S. ambassador to the United Nations. In November, 1972, Nixon asked Bush to chair the Republican national committee, and Bush loyally defended Nixon during the subsequent Watergate affair. Under President Gerald Ford, Bush served as U.S. envoy to China (1974-1975) and as director of the Central Intelligence Agency (1975-1976).

After Ronald Reagan defeated Bush for the Republican presidential nomination in 1980, he chose Bush as his vice president. Bush faithfully supported Reagan's initiatives, including the latter's moves to restrict public access to information, but when the Iran-Contra scandal broke out in late 1986 Bush insisted that he himself knew nothing of the affair.

Elected to the presidency in his own right in 1988, Bush showed comparatively little interest in domestic affairs, leaving domestic policy statements to his cabinet members. However, when the U.S. Supreme Court ruled in *Texas v. Johnson* (1989) that burning the United States flag was political free speech protected by the First Amendment, Bush demanded that Congress pass a constitutional amendment modifying the Bill of Rights. Congress did not agree.

Meanwhile, Bush concentrated on foreign diplomacy, in which he preferred to act as quietly and secretly as possible. He was reluctant to articulate publicly his policy; the more he told the public, the less freedom of maneuver he had in the personal diplomacy he enjoyed with other heads of state. For example, when the Chinese government forcefully cracked down on dissidents at Tiananmen Square in 1989, Bush publicly condemned them, while secretly sending envoys conveying his personal understanding and respect.

Bush privately told friends that the only mistake that the U.S. government made in the Vietnam War was failing to muzzle the press and throw overwhelming force into the battle; he would not make the same error himself. When he could not negotiate an agreement with Panamanian dictator General Manuel Noriega, he launched a massive invasion to capture and remove Noriega.

Iraq's invasion of Kuwait in August, 1990, brought forth a vigorous international response. Bush used personal diplomacy to forge a multinational coalition that put several hundred thousand troops in Saudi Arabia, while he publicly insisted that these moves were purely defensive. When Bush finally ordered the armies to attack, he followed the censorship precedents Reagan had set in the Grenada occupation. Reporters were strictly limited in what they could observe, only pool coverage of the war was permitted, and carefully prepared news conferences flooded television with the images that the Bush Administration wanted the public to see.

See also Central Intelligence Agency; Flag burning; Iran-Contra scandal; Panama, U.S. invasion of; Persian Gulf War; Presidency, U.S.; President's Commission on Obscenity and Pornography; Reagan, Ronald; *Texas v. Johnson*; Tiananmen Square; Watergate scandal.

Butler v. The Queen

Court: Supreme Court of Canada

Decided: February 27, 1992

Significance: Feminist efforts to have pornography restricted on the grounds that it degrades and dehumanizes women failed in the United States, but succeeded in Canada in this case

In early 1992 the Supreme Court of Canada issued an unprecedented decision in *Butler v. The Queen*, holding that sexually explicit books, films, magazines, and videos portraying women in a "subordinating" or "degrading" manner violated the country's obscenity laws. The decision exposed publishers, producers, and distributors of pornographic materials to criminal penalties. The high court's decision added, however, that for material to be obscene, it had to be judged as a whole; it could not be declared obscene if it had artistic purpose or was part of the serious treatment of a sexual theme.

American feminist Catharine MacKinnon hailed the Canadian court's ruling as "a stunning victory for women . . . of world historic importance." Andrea Dworkin called it "probably the best articulation of how pornography, and what kinds of pornography, hurt the civil status and civil rights of women." However, other feminists disagreed. Writer Pat Califia declared that "Dworkin has done more damage to women's culture in her tenure as darling of the media than anyone who is a leader of the right wing." Liz Czach, a member of the feminist caucus of the Ontario Coalition Against Film and Video Censorship, declared that the *Butler* decision "isn't protecting us; it's silencing us."

Enforcement of Canada's antiobscenity laws after the *Butler* decision fueled criticisms of MacKinnon and Dworkin. According to the Canadian publication *Feminist Bookstore News* (Spring, 1993), the decision was being used "only to seize lesbian, gay and feminist material." During the first year and a half after the ruling, more than half of all Canadian feminist book stores had materials confiscated or detained by customs.

Butler also had other results not anticipated by its proponents. It has been used to justify the suppression of material allegedly degrading to men, not women. For example, *Weenie-Toons! Woman Artists, Mock Cocks* was seized by Canadian Customs because of its alleged "degradation of the male penis." An outspoken lesbian comic magazine, *Hothead Poison*, featuring the exploits of a lesbian terrorist taking revenge on misogynist males, was banned by customs. It depicted no sexual activity, but was judged "sexually degrading to men." Canadian Customs also banned *Hot, Hotter, Hottest* until they realized that it was an ordinary cookbook featuring spicy food.

On a more serious level, Canadian Customs raided the home of retired psychologist Robert Lally in 1993 and seized the only copies of his manuscript for an untitled novel about pedophiles, which was based on composites of his patients. The author claimed that he intended the work "to disgust people and frighten the hell out of them" so they would take action against pedophiles.

In perhaps the most ironic enforcement of the *Butler* decision, two of Dworkin's own books, *Pornography: Men Possessing Women* and *Woman Hating* were seized at the U.S.-Canadian border on the grounds that they "illegally eroticized pain and bondage." To condemn sexually explicit descriptions of men committing violence against women, Dworkin had excerpted the worst examples she could find. But under her own theory, adopted in *Butler*, the redeeming political nature of her work could not save it from suppression.

See also Canada; Customs laws, Canadian; Dworkin, Andrea; MacKinnon, Catharine A.; Women, violence against; Women Against Pornography.

C

Cabell, James Branch

BORN: April 14, 1879, Richmond, Virginia
DIED: May 5, 1958, Richmond, Virginia
IDENTIFICATION: American author and literary editor
SIGNIFICANCE: Haunted during his professional life by accusations of homosexuality, Cabell was subjected to censorship for a satiric novel alleged to violate New York State's antipornography laws

A brilliant student born into an elite Virginia family, Cabell was destined both in his personal life and in his writings to challenge staid visions of sexuality and sexual taboo. Among the controversial aspects of his fiction were his interest in the occult and his parodies of modern Southern aristocracy. The latter were often comic treatments of upper-crust society thinly disguised in sexually suggestive allegories of life in the Middle Ages or as refashionings of classical myths. Cabell taught French and Greek and worked in journalism, as a genealogist, and briefly, as a coal miner, before he married Priscilla Bradley Shepherd in 1913.

Cabell became internationally known amid the uproar that followed the publication of his novel *Jurgen* (1919), a bawdy tale of medieval romance. Cabell and his publisher were placed under indictment by the New York Society for the Suppression of Vice in January, 1920, for alleged violation of New York's pornography laws. The case was decided in Cabell's favor on October 19, 1922. Meanwhile, the publicity and debate engendered by the case made Cabell a central figure of the 1920's American literary avant garde, with its advocation of freer sexuality and the testing of conventional social boundaries combined with wit and urbane sophistication.

The author of over fifty books, Cabell was also an editor of the Richmond literary *Reviewer* in the 1920's and, with Eugene O'Neill, Sherwood Anderson, and others, of the *American Spectator* during the early 1930's.

See also Censorship; Literature; Morality; O'Neill, Eugene; Sex in the arts; Society for the Suppression of Vice, New York; Sumner, John.

Cable News Network (CNN)

FOUNDED: June 1, 1980
TYPE OF ORGANIZATION: Television news broadcaster
SIGNIFICANCE: Court orders preventing the publication of information by the media are a clear form of government censorship; CNN was the subject of such an order in 1990

Cable News Network, an around-the-clock news channel that came of age in the 1980's, is now a worldwide source of news and information. In the 1990's it was also the subject of a governmental prior restraint that set the stage for discussions about government censorship of the news-gathering process.

CNN obtained from an undisclosed source audio tape recordings of telephone conversations between imprisoned Panamanian leader General Manuel Noriega and his attorney while Noriega was waiting trial in Miami, Florida, on drug-trafficking charges. The U.S. government had allegedly recorded the conversations. CNN wanted to broadcast the recordings, but was ordered not to do so by a U.S. district court in Miami. Despite the court's order, the network broadcast portions of the tapes on November 10, 1990. Meanwhile, it also filed an emergency motion asking the federal court to lift the ban on their broadcast.

The court was concerned about Noriega's claim that the recorded conversations were cloaked in attorney-client privilege and thus not admissible in the criminal case being brought against him. The tapes might also divulge the defense's strategy. In order to determine if the conversations were entitled to protection as privileged information, the court wanted to listen to them, but CNN refused to turn them over, arguing the court could obtain the tapes from the government itself.

CNN's refusal to cooperate troubled the court. Saying that the news network had "shackled" it, the court also pointed out what it perceived as an irony: "While appealing to our nation's judicial system for relief, CNN is at the same time defiant of that system's reasonable directions." CNN finally turned over the tapes on November 20, 1990, ten days after it had broadcast them. The court found only two of the tapes were protected by attorney-client privilege, and that the broadcast of those conversations did not jeopardize Noriega's rights. The ban was then lifted.

Nearly four years later, however, the U.S. attorney charged CNN with criminal contempt for having willfully violated the court's order not to broadcast the conversations. In the ensuing court proceedings, Judge William M. Hoeveler found the network guilty of contempt. The original order, according to the judge, was specific enough to let the network know what it could not broadcast. The judge pointed out that on the day that the order was issued, the network had aired a story that included its details. The fact that CNN aired the tapes on the advice of its own lawyers was not enough to defeat the requirement that the violation was willful.

The sentence for criminal contempt was an $85,000 fine and a public apology, which the network agreed to broadcast. Included in the statement of apology was an admission that "CNN realizes that it was in error in defying the order of the court and publishing the Noriega tape while appealing the court's order."

See also Cable television; Metzger, Tom; Music TeleVision; News media censorship; Panama, U.S. invasion of; Prior restraint; Privileged communication; Talk shows.

Cable television

DEFINITION: Nonbroadcast U.S. telecommunications medium
SIGNIFICANCE: U.S. courts have viewed cable television differently from broadcast television in decisions involving censorship attempts

Cable television in the United States, created during the late 1940's to improve reception, expanded its services by the mid-1970's to include distant television stations, advertiser-supported networks, pay-cable, and local community offerings. With its diverse programming, cable television created tensions between broadcasters advocating free expression and those demanding censorship of programs deemed obscene or indecent. Over the years, broadcasters have usually won court battles involving obscenity charges and threats of censorship on grounds that First Amendment rights to free speech were violated. For example, during the 1980's the courts found a restrictive Miami cable ordinance and three Utah cable statutes in violation of the First Amendment; likewise a Puerto Rican case involving the Playboy Channel in the 1990's. The courts have viewed the cable industry differently from broadcast television because cable involves voluntary agreements between subscribers and service providers, based on monthly payments that may be canceled by subscribers if so desired.

In spite of court decisions favoring free expression, Congress and governmental agencies have continued to formulate policies restricting obscenity and indecency on cable systems. For example, the Cable Communications Policy Act of 1984 encouraged local authorities to stipulate in contracts with cable franchisers that they not broadcast indecent or obscene materials. The same act required a percentage of channels on each system to be set aside as public service access channels to encourage program diversity for different ethnic and ideological viewpoints. By encouraging unconventional programming, the act set in motion possible obscenity problems and raised the specter of censorship.

The 1984 law also required cable operators to make available to customers, on request, "lockboxes" to prevent children from viewing objectionable programs. Subscribers use these to activate traps behind their television sets to block out objectionable programs. The courts have approved such devices, reasoning that they provide a practical way of preventing indecent language or sexually explicit acts from entering the objecting homes while allowing others access to such programming.

The 1980's promise of cultural diversity on cable systems turned empty in the 1990's with the megamergers of telecommunication empires which blended audio, video, computers, and data services into an almost monolithic structure. Also, the Telecommunications Act of 1996 allowed giant corporations to own more media outlets. Critics charged that by the mid-1990's only twenty corporations owned most U.S. media outlets, thereby setting the news agenda to influence public opinion on critical issues. For example, critics cited the proposed 1993 health care plan in which the controlled media chose to focus on one favored plan and ignored others, causing the public to be ignorant of alternatives. Critics contended that the reduction of news outlet owners and the elimination of diverse viewpoints and programming amounts to hidden censorship.

Like the United States, Canada is densely cabled and has found itself facing similar issues related to censorship. Unlike the United States, Canada has relied more on the government to regulate content to protect its cultural values against such international cable encroachments as Hollywood violence, sex, and foul language. Some Canadians resent American courts for making "freedom of speech" paramount in rendering judgments on decency matters in programming; ironically, they consider the American courts to have an unrealistic "absolutist position."

See also Communications Decency Act; First Amendment; Shakur, Tupac.

Caldwell, Erskine

BORN: December 17, 1903, White Oak, Georgia
DIED: April 11, 1987, Paradise Valley, Arizona
IDENTIFICATION: American writer
SIGNIFICANCE: Caldwell's novels and the films and plays adapted from them were often attacked by censors for their perceived obscenity

The son of a Southern Associate Reformed Presbyterian minister, Caldwell wrote novels that were felt by some to be obscene. His were the kinds of books sold with sexually provocative covers and, after purchase, hidden away. Because his stories were so widely disseminated through millions of paperback reprints as well as adaptations for stage and screen, he may have spent more time combatting censorship than any other American author.

Caldwell's first encounter with censorship occurred when he tried to sell his first novel, *The Bastard* (1929), in a Portland, Maine, bookshop. The local district attorney called it "obscene, lewd, and immoral" and threatened to arrest Caldwell unless all copies of the book were returned to the publisher in New York. Caldwell wrote an impassioned defense of his novel, denouncing New England Puritanism, and justifying his working-class subject matter and frank treatment of sexuality.

Caldwell's masterpiece, *Tobacco Road* (1932), caused an outcry in his native South. Many felt that the book's impoverished and morally degraded Lester family was a slanderous portrait of sharecroppers and the South in general. After the novel was made into a successful Broadway play, traveling productions met with censorship throughout the United States. A Chicago production was opposed by the Roman Catholic church and Mayor Edward F. Kelly, who called the work "a mess of filth and degeneracy." In Washington, D.C., Congressman Braswell Deen of Georgia denounced the play from the floor of Congress. In thirty-six other cities the work was officially condemned.

God's Little Acre (1933) also prompted censorship, this time from the New York Society for the Suppression of Vice, which took Caldwell's publisher, Viking Press, to court. Many literary figures, including H. L. Mencken, Sinclair Lewis, and Sherwood Anderson, supported Caldwell. In a decision that vindicated both author and publisher, a New York magistrate argued that single passages of a sexual nature did not constitute sufficient evidence to condemn a book and that any successful argument for censorship must show that the tendency of the book as a whole was to inspire impure thoughts and desires.

These cases had a mixed effect on Caldwell's publishing future. His next novel, *Journeyman* (1935), was limited to an edition of only 1,475 copies because Viking feared new legal challenges. Over the long run, however, the publicity enhanced Caldwell's book sales. In the 1940's and 1950's, millions of copies of his books were published in cheap paperback editions, whose lurid covers attracted huge readerships. Caldwell's fame also attracted the notice of Hollywood, which made films of *Tobacco Road* (1941) and *God's Little Acre* (1958). Both stories' sexual content and leftist political messages were effectively muted, however. Caldwell called *Tobacco Road* "one of the most conspicuous failures in cinematic history," a failure that he attributed to its being produced during a time of "unrestrained censorship."

Amid the controversy surrounding him, Caldwell's artistic accomplishments were often ignored. Partly because of the lingering feeling that he was a writer of trash, literary critics did not treat him with the respect that other writers of his generation received. Only since his death have thorough studies of his work and life been undertaken.

See also Cover art; Film adaptation; Literature; Obscenity: legal definitions; Society for the Suppression of Vice, New York.

Caligula

TYPE OF WORK: Film
RELEASED: 1980
DIRECTOR: Tinto Brass (1933-   )
SUBJECT MATTER: Cinematic attempt to depict the mad behavior of the first century C.E. Roman emperor Caligula
SIGNIFICANCE: Widely condemned as obscene, this film received an X rating that limited its distribution

A serious attempt to depict one of history's most controversial figures, *Caligula* was commercially ruined by the adults-only rating that it received. The film had a primarily British all-star

British actor Malcolm McDowell plays the Roman emperor Caligula. (Museum of Modern Art/Film Stills Archive)

cast featuring Malcolm McDowell in the title role. Produced by *Penthouse* magazine, it was shot largely on studio locations. Much of the film consists of long monologues by Caligula, whose historical antecedent was known for his brutality and deviant sexual behavior.

The challenge facing director Tinto Brass was to capture Caligula's mad ravings and actions in such a way so as to give the film a chance to achieve a wide distribution, particularly in the United States. However, the film never succeeded commercially. Its depictions of sex, and not its bloodletting and gore, got it into trouble. Particularly problematic was the incestuous relationship between Caligula and his sister (Teresa Ann Savoy)—who is almost continuously disrobed throughout the film. The love scenes between Caligula and his sister were exceptionally graphic for a commercial film of its time, and another controversial scene has Caligula sodomizing a soldier.

The Motion Picture Association of America (MPAA) effectively killed the film's distribution by giving it an X (adults only) rating. Although a few films had previously survived that rating, it had doomed most serious films.

See also Motion Picture Association of America; Obscenity: legal definitions; *Penthouse*; Roman Empire; *Satyricon, The*; Sex in the arts; Violence.

Call-in programs

DEFINITION: Radio and television talk shows that feature telephone conversations with audience members
SIGNIFICANCE: No-holds-barred attitudes among hosts and callers have combined with relaxed government regulations to create unprecedented freedom of expression in broadcast media

Talk radio featuring audience participation began in 1933 with a Columbia Broadcasting System program called *Voice of Experience*, on which listeners contributed to a fund for the "less fortunate." By the late twentieth century the format was a major growth area for radio stations—particularly AM radio stations, whose music formats could not compete with those of FM stations, which have better quality broadcast signals. Broadcasters have found such shows unusually profitable: Though inexpensive to produce, they bring in high ratings and more advertising revenue.

Individual call-in shows have tended to focus on narrow subject areas, such as news, music, sports, and personal and social issues. Many listeners are attracted by the excitement of being heard on the air and conversing directly with famous hosts. The shows thrive on controversy and unpredictability. Hosts such as Howard Stern, who has become noted for pushing the limits of what is considered indecent and obscene, have become known as "shock jocks." Stern's broadcast company was even willing to pay large fines to the Federal Communications Commission because of the increased ratings for the stations that aired his controversial call-in show.

Although stations monitor calls to screen out libelous remarks and obscene language, callers can still say almost anything. Broadcasts are delayed about seven seconds by digital recording devices that enable hosts to stop profanity and libelous statements from reaching the air. However, the imperfection of broadcasting safeguards fosters audience perceptions that outrageous remarks might be uttered at any moment.

Talk show hosts and "screeners," who are the first people to answer telephone calls from audience members, determine who has access to the airwaves. The screeners typically block calls from people who are confused or inarticulate, those with strong accents or who sound very old, and those who seem dangerously hostile or contrary. Studies have indicated that less than 3 percent of call-in show listeners get on the air.

Controls on the content of call-in-shows come primarily from the policies of the broadcasting networks. Sun Radio Network, for example, has not permitted discussion of controversial political topics or the promotion of causes. Within the United States, government controls have focused on obscene language, particularly during hours that children may listen. The demise of the Federal Communications Commission's Fairness Doctrine after 1987 made it easier for programs to discuss controversial issues. Government efforts to extend limits on obscene programming have generally been rejected by the courts. New technologies such as cable and satellite transmission are not covered by the same regulations as over the air stations. The satellite delivered messages of Digital Audio Broadcasting would be outside government control.

See also Broadcast media; Fairness doctrine; Limbaugh, Rush; Obscenity: legal definitions; Stern, Howard; Talk shows; Tape-delay broadcasting.

Calvin, John

BORN: July 10, 1509, Noyon, Picardy
DIED: May 27, 1564, Geneva
IDENTIFICATION: Protestant reformer
SIGNIFICANCE: Calvin was perhaps the ablest systematizer of Protestant Reformation theology, and there were powerful efforts to suppress his writings

Calvin's most famous work, the *Institutes of the Christian Religion*, first appeared in 1536 and went through several editions until 1559. The Roman Catholic church immediately perceived that Calvin's book struck at the very heart of its theology, and responded by not only banning Calvin's books but burning them at the Sorbonne of Paris and other places. Roman Catholic authorities correctly sensed that Calvin's ideas, especially his repudiation of the Mass, struck at the heart of Catholic doctrine and papal authority. From the church's vantage point Calvin was a dangerous heretic who, if unchecked, might destroy the true Church as its leaders understood it. As a result, Calvin was forced to spend the greater part of his life in exile: first in Geneva, then in Strasbourg, and back to Geneva, to avoid arrest and prosecution by church authorities.

Calvin was clearly a victim of censorship. Ample evidence attests the fact that he also could give as good as he received. There were several occasions on which he practiced censorship. For example, shortly after he returned to Geneva from Strassburg, he established an ecclesiastical constitution that gave magistrates power to punish both civil offenses and a wide-ranging assortment of religious offenses, such as blasphemy and heresy. One of the first to feel the brunt of this power was Jêróme Hermès Bolsec, who was banished from Geneva in 1531 because he challenged Calvin's own doctrine of predestination.

In 1558 John Knox wrote a book challenging the legitimacy of all female rulers. Calvin quickly responded by having Knox's book banned and by writing to various English exiles to dissociate himself from Knox's opinions. Coming in the year in which Elizabeth I became queen of England, Knox's opinion was an especially sensitive one.

For Calvin any deviation from his opinions about Scripture meant denying the word of God. Hence he could condemn Miguel Servetus to be burned at the stake for heresy, and prevent Sébastion Castellio from receiving a pastoral charge in Geneva because the latter questioned the inspiration of the Song of Solomon and the statement in the Apostles' Creed, "He descended into Hell." Some would say that the man who had so fiercely denounced the tyranny of the pope became the tyrant of Geneva.

See also Heresy; *Index Librorum Prohibitorum*; Knox, John; Luther, Martin; Puritans; Reformation, the; Vatican.

Campaign for Press and Broadcasting Freedom (CPBF)

FOUNDED: 1979
TYPE OF ORGANIZATION: British group supporting democratically accountable and open media
SIGNIFICANCE: This group has worked against bias and censorship in large, privately owned broadcasting organizations

The Campaign for Press Freedom (CPF) was set up at a meeting at Great Britain's Trades Union Congress (TUC) Annual Conference in 1979. The body's primary concern was to counter and expose what it saw as right-wing biases in the reporting of industrial disputes by the British national press. Three years later it broadened its name—and its focus—to the Campaign for Press and Broadcasting Freedom (CPBF). Since then the organization has aimed to ensure that the news media maintain high standards and offer a diversity of voices. To uphold the latter aim the CPBF has opposed the concentration of media ownership in a few hands and has promoted nonprivate ownership of newspapers. It has also defended public service broadcasting, and has opposed racism, sexism, and incitements to violence in the media.

The CPBF has listed among its aims support for the right to know; the right to fair representation, access and accountability; workers' participation; the right to make contact; freedom of the airwaves; facilities for all; and the right to reply. To help achieve these aims, it has allied with other pressure groups.

In 1995 the CPBF had about fifteen hundred individual and institutional members. It publishes a regular journal, *Free Press*, as well as books and pamphlets.

See also First Hemispheric Conference on Free Expression; Pressure groups; Reporters Committee for Freedom of the Press; Right of reply; United Kingdom.

Campus speech codes

DEFINITION: Restrictions on speech adopted by colleges and universities to combat hate speech

SIGNIFICANCE: Such policies challenge traditional interpretations of the free speech clause of the First Amendment

Speech codes generally prohibit derogatory or pejorative remarks made on college or university campuses that are aimed at historically disadvantaged groups. Campus speech codes are a reaction to hate speech—demeaning words directed at members of historically disadvantaged groups, including racial, ethnic, and religious minorities, women, homosexuals, and the handicapped. Hate speech, it is argued, is assaultive because it is directed intentionally to group characteristics. Hate speech is said to injure self-esteem, undermine self-confidence, alienate victims from their campus communities, and make it more difficult for victims to learn.

Rationale. Under this view, hate speech is not merely offensive but also psychologically and physically traumatic: It further oppresses disadvantaged groups and underscores their systematic subordination. Advocates of campus speech codes criticize absolutist legal protection of speech made without acknowledgment of historical context or widely disparate power relations in society. They argue that hate speech embodies a persecutory message of racial inferiority, directed against a historically oppressed group. Moreover, hate speech does not honor the primary purpose of the First Amendment, which is to facilitate the greatest amount of speech.

Instead, hate speech injures its victim, stops dialogue, and reinforces harmful social inequalities. As such, hate speech is not predominantly speech but conduct as harmful as a physical assault: Victims experience it as a blow that generates rage, fear, shock, and flight. Accordingly, advocates of campus speech codes argue that legal doctrine should either carve out a hate speech exception to the protections of the free speech clause of the First Amendment or adopt a contextual analysis that balances the harm hate speech inflicts on disadvantaged groups and the value of freely expressing all ideas, however distasteful.

Opponents of campus speech codes argue that censoring speech will not curtail racism or sexism. Moreover, they claim that such codes undermine the primary purpose of institutions of higher learning, which is to encourage wide intellectual freedom and open discussion of ideas.

Court Cases. In *Chaplinsky v. New Hampshire* (1942), the U.S. Supreme Court held that "fighting words which by their very utterance inflict injury or tend to incite an immediate breach of the peace" did not merit First Amendment protection. But in *UWM Post v. Board of Regents of University of Wisconsin* (1991), the court noted correctly that after the Chaplinsky decision "the U.S. Supreme Court has narrowed and clarified the scope of the fighting words doctrine to include only words which tend to incite an immediate breach of the peace."

Courts invariably have viewed campus speech codes suspiciously. In *Doe v. University of Michigan* (1989), the United States District Court for the Eastern District of Michigan applied the free speech clause of the First Amendment to the University of Michigan's hate speech restrictions. In response to an increase in racial intolerance and harassment, the University of Michigan prohibited individuals, under the penalty of sanctions ranging from formal reprimands to expulsion, from "stigmatizing or victimizing" individuals on the basis of race, ethnicity, religion, sexual orientation, gender, and a host of other categories. Administrative memos established that this policy was designed to sanction any remarks that seriously offended many individuals beyond the immediate victims and that thereby jeopardized the education climate of the campus.

The court acknowledged the state's extensive power under the First Amendment to regulate discriminatory conduct, but reaffirmed long-standing doctrine that the state's power to regulate pure speech is far narrower. Only "the lewd and obscene, the profane, the libelous, and the insulting or 'fighting words'" are legitimately subject to state regulation. While conceding that some racial epithets might fall under this domain under certain circumstances, the court held that the university could not sanction speech merely because a large number of people were seriously offended by it. After analyzing the University's response to three complaints against students under its hate speech policy, the court held that the policy was overbroad in that it swept serious classroom comments made without malevolent intent under its domain. Moreover, the policy was unconstitutionally vague because its requirement that speech must "stigmatize or victimize" individuals on the basis of listed characteristics resisted precise definition. Accordingly, the Court held that the policy violated the free speech clause of the First Amendment and the due process clause of the Fourteenth Amendment.

Most campus speech codes prohibit only a select class of fighting words: Insults aimed at sex, race, nationality, handicaps, or sexual orientation. In *R.A.V. v. City of St. Paul* (1992), the U.S. Supreme Court held that such subcategories can be proscribed when the regulations pertain to conduct. The Court held, however, that the St. Paul ordinance was not aimed at conduct but at speech. A majority of the justices noted that the ordinance could still be constitutional if St. Paul could show that the ordinance was grounded on a compelling governmental interest and the content-based restriction on expression was necessary to further that compelling interest. Although the Court held that the ordinance was grounded on the compelling interest of protecting individuals from hateful discrimination, it also found that the means used were neither necessary nor the least restrictive way to serve that interest.

In *Robert J. Corry v. Leland Stanford Junior University* (1995), a California Superior Court declared the Stanford University speech code unconstitutional and issued a preliminary injunction against its enforcement. Although Stanford argued that its speech code did not prohibit ideas, the Court held that the speech code wrongly prohibited words that would only cause people to feel insulted and stigmatized.

Courts have thus legally tolerated hate speech as a cost society must endure to protect valuable speech from constitutional attack. Thus, campus speech codes invariably have been found to be unconstitutional at public institutions. Universities have turned to other means to discourage hate speech: stricter penalties for violations of student conduct regulations that are motivated by racism or bigotry, educational efforts aimed at greater mutual tolerance, and increased awareness of the effects insulting and stigmatizing speech have on victims.

—*Raymond A. Belliotti*

See also Defamation; Fighting words; First Amendment; Hate laws; Homosexuality; Political correctness; Race; Symbolic speech.

BIBLIOGRAPHY

Words That Wound, by Mari Matsuda et al. (Boulder, Colo.: Westview Press, 1993) provides an accessible introduction written explicitly from the perspective of victims of hate speech. Amy Gutmann argues in *Democratic Education* (Princeton, N.J.: Princeton University Press, 1987) that a private university has associational freedom to shape and define its communal life. Campus speech codes may be consistent with that freedom. Lee Bollinger's *The Tolerant Society* (New York: Oxford University Press, 1986) argues that legal protection of hate speech reinforces public commitment to tolerance, which strengthens individual and social character. Arati R. Korwar's *War of Words: Speech Codes at Public Colleges and Universities* (Nashville, Tenn.: Freedom Forum First Amendment Center, 1994) examines campus speech codes across the United States and argues on practical and theoretical grounds against them.

Canada

DESCRIPTION: Northern neighbor of the United States; an independent nation occupying the bulk of the North American continent

SIGNIFICANCE: Censorship issues, which have long been important in Canada, have often arisen from issues relating to differences between Canada and the United States

In contrast to the United States, Canada has historically emphasized group rights over those of individual citizens. This in turn has often led to justifying incidents of government censorship by claiming that they have served the greater good of society as a whole. In fact, the Supreme Court of Canada used such a justification in two prominent rulings in the 1990's. Canadian censorship has also tended to be top-down censorship directed by institutions of the state. Grass-roots censorship sparked by religious groups and other organizations, although not unheard of, has not occurred as frequently as in the United States.

Canada's Constitution. Canada's history of free speech traditions aligns it more closely with the United Kingdom than with the United States. For much of its past, Canada had no legal guarantee of freedom of speech, unlike the First Amendment protections of the U.S. Constitution. Canada's founding constitution, the British North American Act (BNA)—which became the Canada Act in 1982 when it was repatriated from the United Kingdom—contains no references to protection of freedom of speech and expression. In fact, the act specifically allows the federal government to make laws in order to ensure "peace, order, and good government." The promotion of such values speaks to the collectivist approach of Canadian society, in contrast to an emphasis on individuality in the United States.

British Tradition and World War I. The British tradition in Canada has often led to an emphasis on competing values of liberty and order. Liberty was promoted as being the British way, but so was the maintenance of an orderly society, even if this required censorship. Widespread use of censorship in Canada has occurred most frequently during times of social disorder, such as wars or political turmoil. World War I was the first example of comprehensive government censorship in Canada. During that conflict censorship was conducted under the War Measures Act, which was quickly passed after the outbreak of the war by the Conservative government of Prime Minister Robert Borden. This legislation remained on the books until the 1980's; meanwhile, it was used during World War II and during the 1970 "October Crisis" in the province of Quebec.

To restrict the flow of information, one clause of the War Measures Act provided Canada's federal government with complete control over "censorship and the control and suppression of publications, writings, maps, plans, photographs, communications and means of communications." An official censor was also appointed by the federal government whose job was to ensure that newspapers and other publications did not carry stories which might injure Canada's security or war effort. Lower level censors even restricted the free flow of mail. The response of Canadian citizens to the War Measures Act was typical of their responses to most acts of censorship: little or no public protest against infringements on civil liberties.

The Interwar Period. The aftermath of the war, coupled with the Bolshevik Revolution in Russia and fears of its spread, led to wide-ranging censorship in Canada. Many non-English publications were banned outright. To deal with political radicalism, the federal government introduced an amendment to the Criminal Code of Canada that later effectively outlawed the Communist Party of Canada and permitted the widespread censorship of materials determined subversive by the government. The law also allowed for twenty-year prison terms for anyone who acted as an officer of any unlawful association, or who sold, spoke, wrote, or published anything representing an unlawful association.

Another clause of the Criminal Code called for twenty-year prison sentences for anyone "who prints, publishes, edits, issues, circulates, sells, or offers for distribution any book, newspaper, periodical, pamphlet, picture, paper, circular, card, letter, writing, print, publication or document of any kind, in which is taught, advocated, advised or defended . . . as a means of accomplishing any governmental, industrial or economic change." Even the importation of restricted material or its circulation through the mail could lead to twenty-year sentences. Civil liberties organizations repeatedly attacked this legislation as being undemocratic and draconian until it was repealed in 1936.

In the 1920's radicalism, which was most often associated with non-Anglo Saxon Canadians, sparked many blatant incidents of government censorship. During this period the city of Toronto passed a bylaw forbidding public speeches in languages other than English. Sixty-eight University of Toronto professors signed a letter to a local newspaper attacking the law as an infringement on freedom of speech.

World War II. World War II brought back forms of censorship that had been used during the earlier world war. A censorship coordinating committee was established under the leadership of a former journalist. In addition, twelve regional censorship bodies were created to monitor the content of newspapers. The federal government also introduced two additional pieces of legislation in order to provide itself with even more power. The Official Secrets Act—which stayed in effect after the war—was directed at inhibiting the flow of any information deemed sensitive by those in power. The Defence of Canada Regulations, passed on September 3, 1939, by Liberal Party leader and Prime Minister William Lyon Mackenzie King, gave the government even more power over the civil liberties of Canadians. Two of its clauses designed for the "control of means of communication" allowed the government to restrict any form of communication, including the written word, film and sound, if deemed prejudicial to the war effort.

Cultural Censorship. One of the earliest film censorship bodies in North America was the Ontario Film Review Board, which was created in 1913 with the powers of classification and censorship. Its censorship choices reflected both moral and political concerns. For example, it censored kisses from films for a period, but also scenes of waving American flags, since part of its mandate was to promote Canadian patriotism through the restriction of foreign propaganda. Throughout its existence the Ontario Film Board has faced charges of censorship. The most famous example occurred in the mid-1970's when it banned *Pretty Baby*, an American film which included depictions of child prostitutes, and *The Tin Drum*, a German film containing a scene of a child exposed to adult sexuality. Since that period, the board has become more liberal and has allowed the viewing of sexually explicit films, although it has continued to review each film allowed into the province. All other Canadian provinces, with the exception of Manitoba, have similar bodies, and their decisions are often influenced by those made by the Ontario board.

Books have often come under attack from both government and nongovernment censors. The most frequent examples of this type of censorship have involved bannings of books by school boards because of the religious or sexual material, racist stereotyping, and even excessive American content. A powerful tool of state censorship in this area has been Customs Canada—the government body that monitors importation of goods into Canada. In 1949 Customs banned importation of more than a hundred foreign publications based on different criteria, including moral and political content. By 1971 that number had grown to 4,461 publications banned because they contained immoral or indecent content, and two that were banned because of their seditious or treasonable material. Gay and lesbian publications entering the country have often been seized by customs officials, prompting calls of censorship.

Political and Constitutional Change. Infringements on civil liberties during wartime made many Canadians realize that the lack of constitutional guarantees of civil liberties was dangerous. Conservative party leader John Diefenbaker, who served as prime minister from 1957 to 1963, passed a federal

Canadian prime minister Jean Chretien during a 1994 visit to Beijing, China. (AP/Wide World Photos)

bill of rights through parliament in 1960. It guaranteed freedom of speech and freedom of the press among other rights. Critics quickly pointed out, however, that the legislation was nonbinding because it was only a statute of parliament, and was not enshrined in the constitution.

The pivotal year in Canada's constitutional evolution was 1982. In that year the Liberal government of federal prime minister Pierre Trudeau, and the governments of nine of the ten Canadian provinces (only Quebec refused to participate) repatriated the country's constitution from Britain and enacted the Canadian Charter of Rights and Freedoms. Section two guaranteed as fundamental freedoms "freedom of thought, belief, opinion and expression, including freedom of the press and other media of communication." Even then, however, such rights were not unlimited, since the previous clause, under the title of "Guarantee of Rights and Freedoms," noted that the charter guaranteed "the rights and freedoms set out in it subject only to such reasonable limits prescribed by law as can be demonstrably justified in a free and democratic society."

A further limitation on the rights protected by the charter related to the nature of the Canadian political system. Unlike the United States, Canada has a parliamentary system that emphasizes the supremacy of parliament as a body. Several provincial governments were unwilling to support the constitutional change of the early 1980's without some recognition of the supremacy of the legislative body. Thus a "notwithstanding" clause was included in the Canadian Constitution of 1982. This allowed either federal or provincial governments to declare specific pieces of legislation to be exempt from, or "notwithstanding," the Charter of Rights. Such a decision was subject to renewal after five years. Civil libertarians have long argued that the "notwithstanding" affords too much power to the state. However, it is in keeping with Canadian tradition.

Such a power has been used. In the aftermath of a Supreme Court ruling that a Quebec provincial law banning use of English on outdoor signs was unconstitutional, Quebec's provincial government declared the legislation as "notwithstanding the Charter of Rights" or, in other words, exempt from being overturned because it violated any of the rights protected under the charter. With its large French-speaking population in the midst of a largely English-speaking nation, the province of Quebec justified such legislation as being for the protection of minority group rights, although at the expense of individual rights because it infringed on freedom of speech and expression and led to the censoring of signs.

The Supreme Court of Canada used a similar rationale in two prominent decisions made after the passing of the charter. In upholding federal hate-law legislation the court ruled that infringements on freedom of speech contained under this legislation were necessary for the greater good of society since the law mitigated against attacks on minority groups. In 1992 the court ruled in *Butler v. The Queen* that the rights of women and children to protection from the negative effects of pornography were more important than the freedom of individual citizens to create and distribute such material. In essence, the Court decided that in keeping with Canadian tradition, or at least the perception of that tradition, collectivity was more important than individuality. —*Steven R. Hewitt*

See also *Butler v. The Queen*; Canadian Access to Information Act; Canadian Broadcasting Corporation; Canadian Library Association Statement on Intellectual Freedom; Canadian Radio-Television and Telecommunications Commission; Child Pornography Law; Customs laws, Canadian; Freedom; Hate laws, Canadian; Impressions reading series; Judicial publication bans; Libraries, Canadian; Official Secrets Act (Canada); Project Censored Canada; United Kingdom; United States; Yaqzan, Matan, affair.

BIBLIOGRAPHY

Allan Borovoy's *When Freedoms Collide: The Case for Our Civil Liberties* (Toronto: Lester & Orpen Dennys, 1988) offers a detailed analysis of issues pertaining to civil liberties in Canada. Bill Waiser and Dave De Brou, eds., *Documenting Canada: A History of Modern Canada in Documents* (Saskatoon, Saskatchewan: Fifth House Publishers, 1992), offer the text of several documents pertaining to issues of Canadian censorship. The Ontario Law Reform Commission's *Report on the Powers of the Ontario Film Review Board* (Toronto: Government of Ontario, 1992) examines one significant instrument of government censorship in Canada, the Ontario Film Review Board. In *Freedom of Expression and the Charter* (Toronto: Thomson Professional Publishing Canada, 1991) David Schneiderman has collected essays by prominent scholars on the impact of the Canadian Charter of Rights on freedom of expression.

Canadian Access to Information Act

ENACTED: 1983

PLACE: Canada (national)

SIGNIFICANCE: This federal law governs the release of all documents and material held by government departments and agencies; individual provinces have similar laws

The Access to Information Act was introduced and passed by the Liberal government of Prime Minister Pierre Trudeau. Prior to its passage Canada's federal government had no concrete rules governing release of documents and other materials; each department and agency had its own idiosyncracies. The new act provided systematic rules for the release of all federal government-controlled information, regardless of its age. It required individuals or agencies wishing access to federal government materials to complete application forms and pay nominal fees. However, it placed no limit on the additional costs that could be incurred by persons making such requests.

The law defined three categories of information that could be exempted or censored. These included details of a personal nature relating to living persons and those who have been dead less than twenty years, and information received from external agencies, such as the U.S. Federal Bureau of Investigation. The broadest exemption covered information that might threaten national security. All these restrictions have generated considerable criticism and controversy since the law was enacted.

See also Canada; Freedom of Information Act; Privacy, right to.

Canadian Broadcasting Corporation (CBC)

FOUNDED: November 2, 1936

TYPE OF ORGANIZATION: Government owned and operated broadcasting organization

SIGNIFICANCE: A primary reason for the CBC's existence has been to reduce the amount of U.S. programming that is broadcast in Canada

The CBC operates national radio, FM stereo, and television networks that broadcast in English and French. It also provides regional and local radio and television programming in both official languages; broadcasts locally produced programs in English and Native American languages for people living in the Far North; runs a multilingual shortwave service for listeners overseas; and televises the proceedings of Canada's House of Commons via cable.

The Canadian federal government established the CBC as a Crown corporation in 1936. At that time privately owned Canadian broadcasting stations were falling into American hands and seemed incapable of providing adequate Canadian alternatives to the American programming already flooding across the border. The moving force within the commission that recommended creation of the CBC was Charles Bowman, editor of the *Ottawa Citizen*. Bowman was convinced that public ownership of broadcasting was necessary to protect Canada against being overwhelmed by American cultural penetration.

Maximum Canadian content and protection against the onslaught of American culture became a permanent goal of the

CBC. On November 23, 1995, Perrin Beatty, the head of the CBC, announced that as of the fall of 1996 all U.S. programming was to be removed from the English-language television network's prime-time schedule. The money spent on U.S. programs was to be redirected to support Canadian producers, writers, and performers.

Wayne Skene's book *Fade to Black: A Requiem for the CBC* (1993) criticized the CBC for becoming virtually indistinguishable from commercial Canadian and U.S. networks. Skene argues that this state of affairs was a product of single-year funding, which resulted in a lack of culturally important programs, such as Canadian stage plays, reviews of books and literature, dance, performance, music, historical documentaries and drama, and regional drama. It has also created shallow news and current affairs programming, which too often relies on the glib and insubstantial, as the CBC tries to balance its books every twelve months. Skene recommends replacing the corporate structure with a decentralized organization allowing for more purely Canadian programs.

See also British Broadcasting Corporation; Broadcast media; Canada; Canadian Radio-Television and Telecommunications Commission; Project Censored Canada; Television networks.

Canadian Library Association Statement on Intellectual Freedom

DATE: 1974

PLACE: Hamilton, Ontario

SIGNIFICANCE: Similar to the American Library Association's Library Bill of Rights, this statement affirms the right of Canadians to have access to knowledge, for their own good and that of the nation

The Canadian Library Association (CLA) is a nonprofit voluntary organization founded in 1946 by Elizabeth Homer Morton to help develop high standards of librarianship and library and information services. The organization's Statement on Intellectual Freedom was adopted in June, 1974, by its executive council, which revised it in 1983 and 1985. In 1987 the CLA had approximately 3,500 individual and 800 institutional members. The body's five divisions represent the various interests of public, special, school, and college and university libraries, and library trustees.

In 1968 the CLA became a unilingual association, leaving representation of Canada's francophone libraries to ASTED (Association pour l'avancement des sciences et des techniques de la documentation). Open to anyone with an interest in libraries, the CLA is governed by an elected council and a board of directors. Its council is composed, in part, of representatives from provincial library associations. The CLA maintains active publication and seminar and workshop programs, and it speaks for librarian's concerns at the national level by making representations to government and official commissions.

See also Book and Periodical Council Statement on the Freedom of Expression and the Freedom to Read; Chapultepec Declaration; First Hemispheric Conference on Free Expression; Expression and the Freedom to Read.

CANADIAN LIBRARY ASSOCIATION STATEMENT ON INTELLECTUAL FREEDOM

- All persons in Canada have the fundamental right, as embodied in the nation's Bill of Rights and the Canadian Charter of Rights and Freedoms, to have access to all expressions of knowledge, creativity and intellectual activity, and to express their thoughts publicly. The right to intellectual freedom, under the law, is essential to the health and development of Canadian society.

- Libraries have a basic responsibility for the development and maintenance of intellectual freedom.

- It is the responsibility of libraries to guarantee and facilitate access to all expressions of knowledge and intellectual activity, including those which some elements of society may consider to be unconventional, unpopular or unacceptable. To this end, libraries shall acquire and make available the widest variety of materials. It is the responsibility of libraries to guarantee the right of free expression by making available all the library's public facilities and services to all individuals and groups who need them.

- Libraries should resist all efforts to limit the exercise of these responsibilities while recognizing the right of criticism by individuals and groups.

- Both employees and employers in libraries have a duty, in addition to their institutional responsibilities, to uphold these principles.

Canadian Radio-Television and Telecommunications Commission (CRTTC)

FOUNDED: 1968

TYPE OF ORGANIZATION: National broadcasting regulatory body

SIGNIFICANCE: The CRTTC has primary control over radio and television broadcasting throughout Canada

In 1976 the Canadian Parliament transferred to the CRTTC the jurisdiction over federally regulated telecommunications companies formerly exercised by the Canadian Transport Commission, changing its name to the Canadian Radio-Television and Telecommunications Commission. Since then the CRTTC has decided on the issuance and renewal of licenses for all broadcasting undertakings, including networks and cable systems. It may attach conditions to licenses and makes regulations respecting broadcasting. It may also revoke any license, except one issued to the Canadian Broadcasting Corporation (CBC). The full commission makes decisions involving the revocation of licenses, general broadcasting policies, and regulations and rules of procedure. Public consultation, through written notice and comment or public hearings, is a general practice. Among the important early decisions of the

CRTTC were a provision for a minimum level of Canadian music on the air; rules respecting amounts of Canadian content in television schedules; licensing of third television networks in Ontario and Quebec; and the wide licensing of cable systems that would carry American programming directly to areas beyond the broadcasting range of U.S. stations. A 1988 CRTTC decision prohibited access to any local television advertising market unless broadcasters provided a local program service in that market.

The 1970 Report of the Special (Canadian) Senate Committee on the Mass Media, the so-called Davey Report (after its chair, Senator Keith Davey), helped focus light on the state of Canadian mass media. The section of the report on broadcasting helped provide much of the framework for the 1974 CRTTC hearings on the renewal of broadcast licenses. The briefs presented to the CRTTC were overwhelmingly in support of public broadcasting.

The fifteen-member Senate Committee report began by calling broadcasting "The Beast of Burden"—an institution saddled unlike any other medium with responsibility for holding the country and its culture together. It immediately took a jab at private broadcasters, pointing out that they, too, were expected to share the burden. The report added that the 1968 Broadcasting Act had declared the airwaves to be public, not private property and that "Canadians had a right to expect that broadcasters would use that public property to strengthen our culture, rather than dilute it." This Senate committee thought that the CBC was "a national institution in a country that lacks national institutions." It was a unique institution, made vulnerable by an unfortunate reliance on commercial revenue and annual appropriations from Parliament.

See also British Broadcasting Standards Council; Canada; Canadian Broadcasting Corporation; Federal Communications Commission.

Caricature

DEFINITION: Artistic exaggeration—usually through drawings—of the physical or moral characteristics of persons being held up for ridicule

SIGNIFICANCE: One of the oldest forms of political satire, caricature has long attracted harsh censorship from the authority figures whom it has attacked

Drawings were especially dangerous, the French interior minister warned his subordinates in 1829, because they "act immediately upon the imagination of the people, like a book . . . read with the speed of light." Referring to French laws requiring prior restraint of drawings and caricatures, he added: "It is then extremely important to forbid all which breathes a guilty intention in this regard." The views of the French minister have been widely shared by repressive regimes throughout history. Often the potential impact of political drawings has been feared far more than that of the written word, as is clearly evident, for example, from the fact that in many countries of nineteenth century Europe, including France, Russia, and Portugal, prior censorship was required for political caricatures long after such controls were abolished for the written word. Thus, in France, prior censorship of the printed word was

abolished in 1822, but was maintained, with a brief interruption, for drawings until 1881.

The Fear of Caricature. Political caricatures have been especially feared because the impact of drawings has been seen as not only more immediate but also more visceral than that of the printed word. In 1835, for example, the French legislature considered reintroducing prior restraint of political caricature, despite the constitutional charter of the 1830's banning all forms of censorship. Prior restraint was reestablished, ending the brief interruption of such censorship in nineteenth century France. The rather sophisticated reasoning for reinstatement of censorship was that writing speaks to the mind, but cartoons and caricature speak directly to the senses.

In addition to the perception that the impact of caricatures is extraordinarily immediate and powerful, political authorities have especially feared them because drawings can be understood even by the dreaded and often illiterate poor, who can understand political illustrations. In the United States, political boss William Tweed, who was repeatedly targeted by the brilliant caricaturist Thomas Nast, declared, "Those damned pictures: I don't care so much what the papers write about me—my constituents can't read, but damn it they can see pictures!"

Caricature Censorship in Operation. Almost everywhere that political caricatures have been subject to governmental controls, the result has been a kind of guerrilla war between the authorities and caricaturists who have sought to evade, outfox, or outright defy their influential targets. Means of resistance include ignoring requirements to submit drawings for censorship approval, expressing opposition to censorship by leaving blank spaces where censored drawings were to have appeared, and political criticism in veiled references. A famous example is the portrayal of French king Louis-Philippe as a pear during the 1830-1835 period in France. Of all of the caricaturists in nineteenth century France, probably the most brilliant and effective was André Gill (Gosset de Guines, 1840-1885), who was credited with helping to bring down two regimes, despite censorship bans on dozens of his drawings. But such tactics have often carried a high price. In France, from 1815 to 1914, about twenty caricature journals were directly suppressed or indirectly forced to close as a result of government reprisals. More than a score of caricaturists and their publishers and printers were jailed. Thus, Honoré Daumier, perhaps the most famous caricaturist in world history, was jailed for six months in 1832 for a disguised portrayal of King Louis-Philippe seated on a toilet throne, receiving tribute from the poor while excreting graft into the hands of his wealthy supporters. In Japan, where until late in the nineteenth century all depictions of current events and all portrayals of the country's top rulers for the past five centuries were forbidden, one of the most famous producers of woodblock prints, Kitagawa Utamaro, was sentenced to two months in jail and house arrest in 1804 for depicting the warlord who had been treacherously overthrown two hundred years earlier by the progenitors of the ruling Tokugawa regime. In the years 1985 to 1995, a Palestinian cartoonist was assassinated in London, an Iranian caricaturist and his editor were sentenced to long jail terms for a drawing that supposedly resembled Ayatollah

In 1873 caricaturist André Gill drew the cartoon at the left, depicting France's recently deposed president, Adolphe Thiers, being carried off in a barrel labeled "forgetfulness" because his services to the country were being forgotten. Government censors forced the journal L'Eclipse *to remove Thiers's image, however, leaving the published picture on the right pointless.* (Robert J. Goldstein)

Ruhollah Khomeini, a Turkish editor was jailed for sixteen months for publishing a caricature of his country's president, and numerous Burmese caricaturists were jailed or forced into exile.

Political caricatures have been so hated by repressive regimes that frequently such governments have not only censored their own press but also banned the importation of foreign caricatures and lodged diplomatic protests against the publication of critical caricatures in other countries. For example, in 1934, the Nazi government protested the exhibit of anti-Hitler caricatures in Prague (produced by German caricaturists forced into silence or exile), a display that a Czech painter praised as "an extraordinarily important artistic anti-Fascist manifestation." Even in relatively democratic countries, political caricatures have sometimes been subjected to harsh controls or reprisals. For example, India, which has had a generally good record for press freedom since independence (although the prior British colonial regime strictly controlled caricatures while boasting of press freedom at home) censored the written and the illustrated press during the 1975-1977 state of emergency declared by Prime Minister Indira Gandhi. In the United States radicals were prosecuted on at least two occasions for political caricatures around the time of World War I, and the San Francisco police chief was dismissed in

1992 for ordering the seizure of a newspaper that published a hostile caricature of him.

Caricature censorship often illuminates with great precision what the regimes involved fear most. A careful study of which drawings are censored and which are approved provides a valuable indicator of the preferences and intentions of those who have the control. The French caricature journal *L'Eclipse*, often the target of censorship bans, observed on September 20, 1874, that "one could, one day, write an exact history of the liberty which we enjoy during this era by writing a history of our caricatures."   —*Robert Justin Goldstein*

See also Art; Beardsley, Aubrey; Daumier, Honoré; *Doonesbury*; *Far Side, The.*

BIBLIOGRAPHY

There is no general study of caricature censorship. For a survey of nineteenth century European caricature censorship, see the appropriate chapter in Robert Justin Goldstein, *Political Censorship of the Arts and the Press in Nineteenth-Century Europe* (New York: St. Martin's, 1989). For studies of particular countries, see, by the same author, *Censorship of Political Caricature in Nineteenth-Century France* (Kent, Ohio: Kent State University Press, 1989); David King and Cathy Porter, *Images of Revolution: Graphic Art from 1905 Russia* (New York: Pantheon, 1983); and Sarah Thompson and

H. D. Harootunian, *Undercurrents in the Floating World: Censorship and Japanese Prints* (New York: Asia Society Galleries, 1991).

Carlin, George

BORN: May 12, 1937, Bronx, New York

IDENTIFICATION: American stand-up comedian

SIGNIFICANCE: In 1979 the U.S. Supreme Court ruled that George Carlin and the Pacifica Foundation could be fined because of the airing of Carlin's "filthy words" routine

Carlin has been known since the early 1970's for his irreverent and often obscene monologues. He has had a number of specials on television, but they have invariably only appeared on cable channels on which obscenity is permitted to some extent; when these shows have been repeated on network television or transferred to videotape, the forbidden words have generally been deleted.

Carlin's political stance has been generally anti-establishment, and this has earned him regular attacks from various conservative groups. One particular incident stands out because of its deep ramifications in federal law. In the early 1970's Carlin developed a routine generally referred to as "filthy words." According to Carlin, these words could not be uttered on radio: "shit," "piss," "fuck," "cunt," "cocksucker," "motherfucker," and "tits." In 1973 Carlin's routine aired on WBAI, an FM radio station in New York City affiliated with the Pacifica Foundation. The Federal Communications Commission (FCC)

George Carlin performs in New York City in 1992—more than two decades after broadcasting the "seven words you can't say on radio." (AP/Wide World Photos)

threatened to fine Carlin and Pacifica. Its ruling was upheld by the Supreme Court in 1979.

The Court justified censoring broadcasts more strictly than the print media because broadcasts were more accessible to the public, including children. The Court's majority opinion stated that while printed materials could be kept out of children's hands with relative ease, radio and television programs could not easily be kept away from minors.

See also Bruce, Lenny; Federal Communications Commission; Murphy, Eddie; Pacifica Foundation; Radio; Sahl, Mort; Television.

Carnal Knowledge

TYPE OF WORK: Film

RELEASED: 1971

DIRECTOR: Mike Nichols (1931-   )

SUBJECT MATTER: Two college roommates pursue the "ideal woman," engaging in plenty of sexual experimentation along the way

SIGNIFICANCE: This acclaimed film was the basis of the 1974 *Jenkins v. Georgia* case, in which the U.S. Supreme Court found that nudity alone does not make material legally obscene

Carnal Knowledge, directed by Mike Nichols and written by Jules Feiffer, who also wrote the play on which the film was based, appeared in 1971 to critical acclaim and box office success. Ann-Margret was nominated for an Academy Award for best supporting actress, and the film's other stars included Jack Nicholson, Candice Bergen, Art Garfunkel, and Rita Moreno. The film, which covers the period from the late 1940's to the sexually liberated 1960's, contains some nudity and sex, including, at the end of the movie, a depiction of fellatio.

It was presumably the sexual nature of the film that led police in Albany, Georgia, to seize the film and arrest Billy Jenkins, the manager of the theater where it was being shown. The charge was distributing obscene material, and Jenkins was convicted by a jury in the Superior Court of Dogherty County. After the Supreme Court of Georgia refused to overturn the verdict, the case went to the U.S. Supreme Court.

In considering the case, the Court would confront two earlier Supreme Court rulings: *Paris Adult Theatre I v. Slaton* (1973), in which the Georgia Supreme Court had supported the Atlanta district attorney's petition to prevent two "adult" theatres from showing allegedly obscene films, and *Miller v. California* (1973). The pro-censorship rulings in these cases had caused concern on the part of the motion picture industry, which feared that even artistically responsible films with sexual content would be attacked by local pressure groups. Jack Valenti, president of the Motion Picture Association of America, accordingly supported Jenkins' case, which was argued by the famed attorney Louis Nizer. Rather than making a case for total freedom of expression in all films, Nizer argued that *Carnal Knowledge* was not hard-core pornography, and that the merit of a film should not be decided by whether or not it met community standards of decency.

The Court ruled that *Carnal Knowledge* did not present sex in the patently offensive way described in *Miller*, since the

Rita Moreno plays a hooker servicing Jack Nicholson in Carnal Knowledge. *(Museum of Modern Art/Film Stills Archive)*

camera did not focus on the bodies of the actors in sexual scenes. The Court found that while there was some nudity, nudity alone does not legally constitute obscenity, and therefore the film came under the protection of the First and Fourteenth amendments. The problem of freedom of expression for all films, however, remained unresolved. The Court was not ready to reverse the *Miller* decision, and what emerged from the *Carnal Knowledge* case was a modification of the earlier ruling. Supreme Court justice William Rehnquist wrote that only explicit displays of patently offensive sexual conduct could be ruled obscene by local judges.

See also Film censorship; *Miller v. California*; Motion Picture Association of America; Nudity; Pornography; Sex in the arts.

Casanova, Giovanni Giacomo

Born: April 2, 1725, Venice, Italy

Died: June 4, 1798, Dux, Bohemia (now Duchcov, Czech Republic)

Identification: Eighteenth century European notable and writer

Significance: Casanova's published memoirs, which earned him a reputation as an uninhibited lover, have been widely banned and censored

During his long career Casanova was a military officer, priest, lawyer, mining consultant, poet, author, playwright, theatrical director and producer, lottery organizer, spy, gambler, banker, mathematician, freemason, cabalist, con man, police agent, magician, abortionist, cook, violinist, philosopher, dancer, silk manufacturer, and nunnery administrator. He is known to have met and conversed with many of the great literary and political figures of his time. He also was a name-dropper, storyteller, and opportunistic scoundrel. Casanova's claim to have had sexual intercourse with several hundred women is probably as good an estimate as is available, and he is known to have had at least eleven episodes of venereal disease.

Although Casanova published at least twenty books, his reputation rests almost entirely on his memoirs. His original twelve-volume manuscript, *Histoire de ma Vie, jusq'à l'an 1797*, was sold to the Leipzig publisher, F. A. Brockhaus, for two hundred thalers (about eighteen dollars) in 1820. Brockhaus then published a German translation between 1822 and 1828. In order to counter pirated French translations, Brockhaus commissioned Jean Laforgue to edit the original manuscript. The fact that Laforgue's edited version, *Memoires de Jacques Casanova de Seingalt, écrits par lui meme* (1826-1838), was published in segments, in Leipzig, Paris, and Brussels may reflect objections from the authorities. Brockhaus then sequestered the manuscript, as controversy and unscrupulously altered pirated versions of the published text proliferated. As a consequence, some modern scholars theorized that the book was a hoax and that Casanova himself never existed. Publication of the complete French text in 1960, with footnotes and comments followed by a definitive English translation, revealed the deficiencies in Laforgue's work. Laforgue altered Casanova's literary style, deleted passages that he considered obscene or otherwise objectionable, put words in Casanova's mouth, and inserted his own political and religious opinions.

Casanova's memoirs and, to a lesser extent, his other works have been censored for their anticlericalism, republicanism, and, most notably, for immorality. His memoirs were listed in the Roman Catholic *Index Librorum Prohibitorum* of Pope Gregory XIV in 1834, remaining for all subsequent revisions and editions. The French government of Louis Napoleon banned his memoirs in 1863, the government of the Republic of Ireland banned them in 1934, and Benito Mussolini's Italian government banned them in 1935. The memoirs did not become generally available in the United States until after 1929 and have since frequently been targeted by local censors. For example, the Detroit police department seized the book in 1934.

See also Abridgment; France; Harris, Frank; *Index Librorum Prohibitorum*; Slander.

Catcher in the Rye, The

Type of work: Book

Published: 1951

Author: J. D. Salinger (1919-   )

Subject matter: Novel about an alienated teenager struggling with the conflicts of growing up and coping with life's meaning and complexities

Significance: Salinger's only full-length novel has consistently been both one of the most widely taught books in American literature courses and one of the most frequently attacked books of all types

Published in 1951, *The Catcher in the Rye* was an immediate best-seller and a Book-of-the-Month-Club selection. The controversy surrounding it began almost simultaneously with its publication. The complaints against this book have been steady throughout the years, beginning in 1954 in California's Los Angeles and Marin counties. Surveys taken in the early 1960's indicated that the book was one of the most often banned selections, as well as one of the most frequently taught books in schools. Two decades later its rankings in both categories remained essentially unchanged. The book has been a target of censorship by critics who have found its central character, Holden Caulfield, a poor "role model" who uses foul language, among other things. Those who defend the book, however, maintain that its multidimensional qualities justify teaching it in literature courses at all educational levels.

The Storyline. As the narrator of *The Catcher in the Rye*, Caulfield describes the two days that he spends roaming New York City because his "nerves were shot." He uses this trip as a temporary escape before his parents learn that he has been expelled from yet another prep school. During this adventure, Caulfield makes both an actual and symbolic journey. In New York, he not only finds diversion from the problems he is having at school, but he immerses himself in the place that he finds most confusing—the adult world. As he wanders the city, he visits bars, encounters a prostitute, calls an old girlfriend, helps several nuns, and sneaks home for a brief visit with his kid sister, Phoebe, whom he dearly loves.

Caulfield discloses both the concrete details of his excursion to New York and the intimate details of his inner self. As an antihero, Caulfield finds it difficult to function in a system where nothing seems to be done for its own sake. Instead he sees people behaving primarily to satisfy others' expectations. Although he strives for a sense of normalcy, he knows that he will never attain it. He remains a tortured adolescent; unable to understand life, he dismisses all adults as "phonies" and regards life as an unevenly matched game.

Procensorship Arguments. Caulfield's poor attitude about life is only a minor point for those who have tried to censor this book. A 1991-1992 study by the People for the American Way found that this novel was among those most likely to be censored on the grounds that it is "anti-Christian," or opposed to a censor's religious convictions. Throughout the United States, parents have objected to the teaching of the book to their children in the public classroom because of its sexual content, references to drinking, rebellion, profanity, vulgarity, and prostitution. Other charges leveled against teaching the book have included its portrayal of an allegedly immoral figure who is a poor role model for youths, its negative depictions of adults, and its lack of literary value. Some who have fought to censor this novel have taken a middle ground, claiming that the book should not be read by high-school-age students because it contains primarily adult themes. In 1991, for example, an organization called Concerned Citizens of Florida wanted to remove the book from a high school library, charging that its content was "immoral" and had "no literary merit."

The language that Caulfield uses to tell his story is another broad basis of contention for censors. Some parents who have formally complained about the teaching of the book have counted hundreds of "vulgarities," such as "damn," "Chris-sakes," "horny," "hell," "crap," and "bastard."

Anticensorship Arguments. Those who have taught *The Catcher in the Rye*, or have advocated teaching the book, have generally emphasized its literary value and have objected to the idea of censorship in general. Supporters have argued that if the book were removed from classrooms or libraries because of the objections of a few parents, all children would be harmed by such censorship. Those who have taught the book point out that it is much more than the tale of a misfit teenager. In using the antihero device, Salinger created a character with whom young readers can easily identify. However, this is exactly what has alarmed those who have wished to censor the book. Supporters of the book argue that those who call Caulfield a poor role model forget that he does want to become a hero to children. Indeed, the title of the book derives from a dream in which he stands in a rye field next to a cliff. As children run toward him, he catches them before they fall over the edge of the cliff. Symbolically, Caulfield is saving these children from becoming adults. He does not want himself or any children to fall into the adult world. For those who teach the novel, this is why they teach it—its thought-provoking theme of passing from a child's to an adult's world without hope of turning back. For those against it, this represents just another negative characterization of adults, and that when coupled with the foul language and suggestive scenes also in the novel, it is inappropriate material to be taught in schools.

—Andrea D. Cardwell

See also Banned Books Week; Biography; Books, young adult; Freedom to Read Foundation; Libraries, school; People for the American Way.

BIBLIOGRAPHY

Salinger's reclusiveness since the early 1950's has impeded scholarship on his work. The only full-length biography yet published is Ian Hamilton's *In Search of J. D. Salinger* (1988); however, its value is limited because Salinger's lawyers forced Hamilton to cut much of its text before it was published. There is, nevertheless, a comparatively large amount of published criticism of Salinger's work, including a number of books focusing on *The Catcher in the Rye*. These include Malcolm M. Marsden, ed., *"If You Really Want to Know": A "Catcher in the Rye" Casebook* (Boston: Scott, Foresman, 1963); Harold Bloom, ed., *Holden Caulfield* (New York: Chelsea House, 1990); Joel Salzberg, ed., *Critical Essays on Salinger's "The Catcher in the Rye"* (Boston: G. K. Hall, 1990); and Jack Salzman, ed., *New Essays on "The Catcher in the Rye"* (Cambridge, England: Cambridge University Press, 1991). The novel is also the subject of a monograph by Sanford Pinsker, *"The Catcher in the Rye": Innocence Under Pressure* (New York: Twayne, 1993).

Caxton, William

BORN: c. 1422, Kent, England
DIED: c. 1491, London, England
IDENTIFICATION: Printer, publisher, translator, and editor

Significance: After introducing printing to England, Caxton helped to standardize the English language and saw the first government attempts to control book publication

Apprenticed to a London silk merchant, Caxton went to Bruges in the 1440's, where he engaged in wool trading. After he saw an early printing press in Cologne decades later, he established his own press in Bruges. His book translation *The Recuyell of the Historyes of Troy* (1475) was the first book printed in the English language. After returning to England, Caxton founded a press in Westminster in 1476. Over the next fifteen years, he printed nearly one hundred works, including Geoffrey Chaucer's *The Canterbury Tales* (1478), his own translation of the German classic *Reineke Fuchs* as *Reynart the Fox* (1481), and Sir Thomas Malory's *Morte d'Arthur* (1485). Literacy increased as English books replaced the Latin of the medieval manuscripts. Caxton published the first English illustrated book, and his publication of Malory popularized the romances of King Arthur and Camelot.

Early in Caxton's career as a printer there was an appreciation of the potential power of the press. In 1476, the English government prohibited printing anything without royal permission. Prelicensing continued into the seventeenth century, eliciting John Milton's essay *Areopagitica* (1644). Caxton himself was aware of the press's power. He divided Malory's *Morte d'Arthur* into chapters, tightened its language, and set a model for English vocabulary and pronunciation. Standard English became that of Caxton's London and southeast England, flavored with French that he acquired on the Continent.

See also *Areopagitica*; Book publishing; Henry VIII; Printing; Prior restraint; United Kingdom.

Censor

Definition: One who removes or suppresses, usually from written or visual material, what is considered morally, politically, or otherwise objectionable

Significance: Censorship does not happen without censors, who may be officials or self-appointed

In Rome in 443 B.C.E., two censors were elected to office. Their primary responsibilities were three. First was census taking of the Roman citizens. The census was the basis for civic life to the Romans; it formed a foundation for taxation, voting, and conscription to military service. Their second responsibility was evaluating property. Assessing the citizens' property was critical to the maintenance of the Roman state. Romans believed that the greater one's possessions, the more one owed to the state and hence, the more one had to say in state matters. Their third responsibility was managing public commerce and overseeing public morals. Because censors assigned state contracts and maintained the census lists, they eventually assumed the responsibility of overseeing public morality.

Many censors have plied their skills since the fall of Rome. In times of war, governmental bodies often establish official censors. At other times, censors are appointed but without the now-stigmatized title. During wartime it is the censors' job to inspect any and all forms of communication entering or leav-

During World War I French newspapers often replaced censored stories with caricatures of the censors themselves. (Ross Collins)

ing the country. Censors remove, change, or destroy any information that might endanger the security of the state.

Religious organizations have instituted official censors, especially in periods of suspected moral decay. It was their role to list as objectionable any types of literature, film, or photographs they found to be morally offensive.

See also Censorship; *Index Librorum Prohibitorum*; Lord Chamberlain; Prior restraint; Roman Empire.

Censorship

Definition: Placing restraints upon the distribution, dissemination, or production of books, films, plays, speeches, television programs, works of art, or other forms of expression

Significance: Censorship ostensibly seeks to protect people from dangerous materials

For as long as human beings have banded together in groups, a tension has existed between the right to exercise personal freedom and the need to protect and preserve the general welfare. Censorship may seem reasonably in many cases as a form of protection against harm to the public welfare, but it raises the question in free societies of how competent the censors are to arrive at correct judgments regarding what is harmful and what is not. Archaeologists and anthropologists have unearthed evidence that in most prehistoric societies some behaviors were prohibited. Taboos relating to every aspect of human interaction existed among the earliest people. The elders quickly ingrained them in the young.

Taboos frequently had to do with sexual conduct and obedience to authority. Much modern censorship is concerned with similar issues. Taboos were also concerned with economic matters, with the distribution of limited resources usually based upon some established hierarchical order. Such ceremonies as tribal initiation rites marked the passage of children into the stage of life at which sexual activity and the responsibilities that accompany parenthood and full tribal membership removed some of the constraints that applied to them during childhood.

The Roman Censors. In ancient Rome, censors, generally elected by the people and serving terms that ranged, at different times in Rome's history, from eighteen months to five years, were in charge of the census. They kept track of the population and of citizens' assets, which had to be carefully tallied for purposes of taxation and the determination of military obligations.

The first Roman census is thought to date to the reign of Servius Tullius in the sixth century B.C.E. At this time, responsibility for the census fell to the ruler. Records reveal that the first people specifically designated to be census takers were elected by the citizenry in the middle of the fifth century B.C.E. In 443 B.C.E. two censors were elected, each holding veto power over the other. Roman censors were typically ex-consuls and, at first, had to be patricians. Within a century, however, a plebeian was elected censor; by 339 B.C.E. public law mandated that one censor must be a plebeian.

In addition to keeping records about the population from whom they collected taxes, the censors were specifically charged with upholding the morality of the community. It was within their considerable power to revise the list of Roman senators at any time and to remove any senator who had breached the law or whom they considered morally deficient. Because the censors answered to no one, they had tremendous power, which eventually became so great as to necessitate strict regulation in their selection. By the first century C.E. the powers of the censors were eventually curtailed and, by the time Emperor Domitian (81-96 C.E.) became a censor for life, the post was severely weakened.

Modern Censorship. Considerable official censorship is directed at the written or spoken word. In societies that were largely illiterate, which was the case in most of Europe until the invention of the printing press in the last half of the fifteenth century, direct control of ideas was usually enforced by rulers with limited spheres of influence.

Once it became possible to mass produce written documents and distribute them within a population that was growing steadily more literate, the rulers and clerics, who had enjoyed an authority seldom publicly contested by their social inferiors, had cause to feel threatened. The vulgar-language Bible, for example, was sometimes more censored than equivalents of the trashy novel, because Church authorities feared, with reason, that as the Bible became widely read, a wide divergence of biblical interpretation would bring disorder to society. The masses became their own interpreters of the ideas that began to fill the increasingly available books and broadsides.

Martin Luther, excommunicated by the Roman Catholic church in 1521, four years after he had publicly posted his objections to many church practices, translated the New Testament into German and urged his followers to become literate so that they could read and interpret Scripture on their own. He thereby endorsed the notion of universal literacy. Societies that had functioned under established rulers whose authority was absolute, now began to move toward the sort of questioning of authority that distinguishes free societies.

While personal freedom for the common person generally did not exist during most of the Middle Ages, with the dissemination of new and radical political and religious ideas made possible by the printing press, traditional authority began to crumble. In Britain, the House of Commons gained the considerable power and influence that made possible the Cromwellian Rebellion and the seizing of much of the power of the Crown, a situation that lasted from 1649 until the restoration in 1660. During the Interregnum, as this period is known, the Puritans attempted to curtail many freedoms.

Between the middle of the sixteenth and the middle of the eighteenth century, the voice of the masses had begun to be heard in many venues. Cromwell's grasping of power from the Crown and the American and French revolutions would have been unlikely had it not been for the invention and development of printing.

Early Attempts at Thought Control. Shortly after Cromwell's ascendancy, the Crown supported the Licensing Act of 1662, which prohibited the printing, sale, or distribution of any book in the British realm without the prior consent of the government. This notion of prior restraint did not set well with a populace that, through reading, was becoming more politically sophisticated.

John Milton in 1644 wrote his famed *Areopagitica*, in which he attacks the Licensing Act that, although it remained officially in place until 1695, became increasingly ineffective. Milton emphasized the dangers of censorship, pointing out that regardless of the integrity and wisdom of the censors, they are mere humans who will find it easier to forbid controversial material than to defend it.

John Stuart Mill, who, like Milton, wrote in defense of human rights, observes in *On Liberty* (1859): "If all mankind minus one were of one opinion, and only one person were of contrary opinion, mankind would be no more justified in silencing that one person, than he, if he had the power, would be justified in silencing mankind." Clearly, majority opinions sometimes are shallow and ill-conceived, whereas minority opinions, although they may seem heterodox to the masses, often contain insights lost on all but the deepest and most effective critical thinkers. Notions about a heliocentric universe or about evolution are typical examples of minority opinions that the majority sought to suppress.

Despite the termination of the Licensing Act, censorship affecting drama remained in force in Great Britain until 1966, the first year in which it was no longer necessary to receive approval from the Lord Chamberlain of any drama to be presented on British stages. The Lord Chamberlain himself sought to have his censorship duties discontinued.

Free Flow of Ideas Versus Control. The United States has presented a model for the practice and encouragement of free expression. Whereas political dissidents in some countries are imprisoned, exiled, or executed by those in control, the United States, through upholding the First Amendment rights that provide for freedom of speech, of the press, of peaceable assembly, and for the right to petition the government to redress grievances, has viewed dissent as healthy and freedom of information as essential to maintaining honesty and integrity in government. A free press is the requisite underpinning of such an attitude.

Many countries of western Europe have adopted policies about freedom of information similar to those espoused in the United States. Communist Bloc countries of eastern Europe, as well as the surviving communist governments in Cuba and China that outlived the Soviet Union, have regularly practiced preventive censorship through government control of newspapers, other news media, and the arts. A desirable equilibrium between personal freedom and the public good is best achieved and maintained in societies whose governments permit their members free access to the fullest possible universe of ideas. The long-term survival of any government seems dependent upon its ability to earn through its deeds the support of the citizenry it serves. No government has functioned effectively and freely in the long term without the ready exchange of ideas.

Religion and Censorship. Many attempts at censorship have been spawned by religious groups. In theocratic countries, such as Saudi Arabia or Iran, all forms of public expression are censored and, when they deviate from notions of the prevailing morality, are punished by the government. In such countries the news media are governmentally controlled. Printed material entering the country is censored to the extent that the pages of magazines may be excised, photographs blackened out, or scenes from motion pictures or television shows cut.

In 1989 the theocratic Iranian government then ruled by the Ayatollah Ruhollah Khomeini called for the assassination of author Salman Rushdie and those who, with knowledge of the book's contents, worked toward the publication of *The Satanic Verses* (1988), a novel the Khomeini regime deemed anti-Islamic and morally offensive. Other Islamic nations took the step of banning the book; still other nations denounced Khomeini's act.

In the United States religious censorship more often operates at the grassroots level, rather than at the public leadership level, given the existence of the First Amendment. Religious groups have sought to have books they considered offensive removed from public libraries or public schools.

Censorship and Education. In the United States, as well as in other countries, pressure groups on the Left and Right have sought to control what students will be exposed to in public schools, with the result that books and other media are sometimes banned by school districts. Such censorship is usually justified by their perpetrators' sometimes quite reasonable fears that a given title is not appropriate for the age group in question. Often, however, those who object do so on grounds that have to do with a narrow and provincial reaction to a book or, quite often, to part of a book. Other motivations for censorship are based upon personal religious, political, or social predilections.

The list of books that have been banned by some school districts in the United States includes such titles as Charles Dickens' *Oliver Twist* (1838), the dramas of Sophocles, many Shakespearean plays, Mark Twain's *Adventures of Huckleberry Finn* (1884), Harper Lee's *To Kill a Mockingbird* (1960), and J. D. Salinger's *The Catcher in the Rye* (1951).

Those who seek to censor often fail to understand that writing that poses searching questions may be discomfiting to those who are wedded to the status quo. Great literature is ahead of its time and great writers have ever had to answer to hostile elements in their societies. History has usually proved, however, the validity and socially desirable outcomes of good writing that searches for clues to help people understand the human condition.

Censorship and New Technologies. The invention of movable type and the printing press marked the beginning of a movement. Printing made it cheaper to disseminate ideas, and radio further increased the audience that could be served. With the invention of motion pictures, another chapter in the dissemination of ideas was opened, followed by television, which has been incredibly influential in shaping human thought and perception. Finally, the personal computer can connect people in the remotest areas with resources scattered around the world. Working from a keyboard in the remotest part of the Central American jungle or the mountain ranges of Pakistan, one can establish direct contact with people throughout the world and with libraries and other repositories of information.

Governments and other censors have sought to control this growing media revolution to some extent. In the United States, for example, the oversight of radio and television falls to the Federal Communications Commission (FCC), established in 1934 for the purpose of granting broadcasting licenses that must be renewed. The FCC, however, is prohibited from practicing censorship.

The American film industry from 1922 until 1968 abided by the judgments of the so-called Hays Office, named after a famous leading censor of the Hollywood film industry, in censoring American films. The influence of the Hays Office diminished with the increase in foreign films coming into the country and with the social upheavals of the 1960's. The film industry is now self-regulating, basing its judgments upon a system of ratings that range from X (explicit sex or heavy violence, no one under seventeen admitted) to G (approved for general audiences). Although this system is not perfect, it provides guidance for audiences.

More difficult to police is computer communication through the Internet. Minors have access to computers; pedophiles surf the Internet seeking them out. The Internet has also become a contact point for extremists seeking other extremists who will give them information about the construction of destructive weapons and other matters that threaten society. Investigations of communications of this sort are being pursued by various government agencies and censorship legislation has been enacted following the traditional motivation of the censor—to protect the public welfare.

Classified Information. Much government information, particularly during crises, is withheld from the public. A typical example would be information about the transportation of troops during wartime. Although the American public is generally willing to accept constraints during periods of national crisis, it is less willing to do so at other times. The historical pattern, however, has been that governments seek to shroud their actions in secrecy, quite often for much less noble motives than the protection of the public; the public has obtained information only with concerted effort.

Most government files are classified in categories indicating how accessible they should be to the public. Strenuous controversies arise when such materials contain sensitive information that might be damaging to those in office, as was the case with the Pentagon Papers. The papers, a long government report intended for reading only by highly placed government officials, discussed American involvement in Vietnam. The papers were more honest than official public statements about the war and the U.S. Government's aims in the war, and in some key regards contradicted what the government was saying publicly about the war. The papers were published by *The New York Times*, presenting a conflict between freedom of the press and government secrecy. The government sought to stop the papers' publication.

In 1976 the Sunshine Act made accessible to the public much material generated by federal agencies in closed meetings. When such meetings are concerned with the disposition of official matters of the agency in question, the law requires that they be open to the public.

Other Forms of Government Censorship. The United States Postal Service reserves the right to inspect all classes of mail except first class and to refuse bulk mailing rates to those who seek to use the mails to distribute lewd or lascivious materials. The postal service may also refuse to deliver unsealed materials originating in foreign countries that are deemed by the Secretary of the Treasury to contain communist propaganda. The Postal Service can prosecute those who use the mails to defraud the public.

The U.S. Customs Service engages legally in a form of censorship by refusing to permit some items to enter the country. It may seize any items it considers obscene and submit them to a federal court for final disposition. Famous examples of such actions are the seizure of copies of James Joyce's *Ulysses* (1922) and D. H. Lawrence's *Lady Chatterley's Lover* (1928), which were seized when publishers shipped these books to the United States for distribution. The court case resulting from a seizure of *Ulysses* led to a famous decision that developed the precedent that the whole of a work, rather than a part of it, had to considered in judging its obscenity.

Private Versus Governmental Censorship. Considerable censorship occurs in the public sector. If a radio or television network presents controversial programming offensive to some viewers, the viewers may, individually or as members of organized groups, refuse to view that network's offerings or, even more effectively, may boycott the sponsors of such programming. When large groups with national constituencies impose boycotts, networks are often forced to change their programming and sponsors to demand changes.

One of the most powerful censorship tools that individuals have is their refusal to view programming or patronize companies that publish or broadcast material offensive to them. In such situations, the free market system eventually creates an adjustment, quite without governmental intervention.

—R. Baird Shuman

See also Book burning; Censor; Classification of information; Comstock Act of 1873; Fear; First Amendment; Intellectual freedom; Internet; National security; Obscenity: legal definitions; Office of Censorship, U.S.; *Pentagon Papers, The*; Pornography; Prior restraint.

BIBLIOGRAPHY

Matthew Spitzer's *Seven Dirty Words and Six Other Stories: Controlling the Content of Print and Broadcast* (New Haven, Conn.: Yale University Press, 1986) is an overview of censorship in the twentieth century. In Ilan Peleg, ed., *Patterns of Censorship Around the World* (Boulder, Colo.: Westview Press, 1993), readers find a global perspective and an informative piece on censorship in the United States by J. M. Balkin. Another world perspective is offered in Kevin Boyle, ed., *Article 19: Information, Freedom, and Censorship* (New York: New York Times Books, 1988). Focusing on censorship in the 1980's is Richard O. Curry, ed., *Freedom at Risk: Secrecy, Censorship, and Repression in the 1980's* (Philadelphia: Temple University Press, 1988). Intriguing political aspects of censorship is described in Harold C. Relyea et al., *The Presidency and Information Policy* (New York: Center for the Study of the Presidency, 1981). William Noble's *Bookbanning in America: Who Bans Books?—and Why?* (Middlebury, Vt.: Paul S. Eriksson, 1990) is strong in presenting legal aspects of censorship.

Central America

DESCRIPTION: The land mass connecting North and South America, comprising the modern nations of Belize, Guatemala, Honduras, El Salvador, Nicaragua, Costa Rica, and Panama

SIGNIFICANCE: Governments in this region have historically been among the world's most ruthless suppressors of free expression

Central America, made up of the seven countries between Mexico and Colombia, has a history characterized by some of the world's worst abuses of freedom of expression. Since its colonization by Spain in the sixteenth century, Central American society has been divided, with small and powerful elites dominating social, political, and economic life, and the vast majority of people poor, weak, and frequently oppressed. Before independence, the Spanish military and administrative elite, along with the Roman Catholic church, controlled almost all information coming into the New World, through monopoly of education and the media. Since independence—which occurred in the early nineteenth century for most of the coun-

Nicaraguans await the arrival of U.S. Marines in 1912 (Library of Congress)

tries—the nations of Central America have experienced numerous civil wars and other forms of political upheaval. Censorship in Central America, as a consequence, has often taken the form of killing those speaking against the interests of particular groups—of both the Left and the Right. Numerous mechanisms have developed over the last century to control the dissemination of information in this region.

Mechanisms of Control. One of the most common forms of information control in Central America is the use of violence by state armies and private militias and security forces. These types of "unofficial" purveyors of violence have existed since the early period of Salvadoran independence, for example. The Salvadoran government has sponsored some of these forces and winked at others—such as right-wing death squads during the civil war; others have been sponsored by the government's opposition. Both the extreme right and extreme left in El Salvador have regularly used assassination to eliminate opposing voices.

During Manuel Noriega's presidency in Panama in the 1980's, more than one hundred private security agencies em-

ployed about twelve thousand thugs, who roamed the countryside, using intimidation to fix elections, and suppressing the dissemination of information that the government considered contrary to the interests of the country's elite class. Since 1978, right-wing death squads in Guatemala have murdered dozens of moderate-left leaders to prevent them from organizing opposition parties.

In addition to silencing political opposition, violence has also been frequently directed against journalists in Central America. Between 1980 and 1984, eleven Salvadoran and ten foreign reporters were murdered in El Salvador alone. In Honduras, nearly 150 journalists disappeared during this same period and many others were interrogated and their papers confiscated, by both governmental agencies and extralegal death squads.

Many Central American nations have had governmental agencies responsible for regulating the expression of opinions in society. In Panama, the Moral and Ethics Commission possessed broad and vague powers to regulate the press and entertainment industries. El Salvador's government has had the power to shut down radio or television stations at any time and for any reason. The government of Honduras can legally engage in a priori censorship on the pretext of protecting the ethical and cultural values of the nation, especially the young. Such censorship reflects the continued significant role of the Roman Catholic church, and its moral code, in Central American society.

Most Central American governments have had laws regulating specific groups that are regarded as potentially antagonistic to elite interests. Honduras, for example, has had laws against "excessive" activities by labor groups, though these groups are generally free of government controls. Journalists in Honduras must be licensed by a professional guild, which is subject to government pressure if an individual reporter discusses the wrong issues or digs too deeply in the wrong places. Frequently such reporters are dismissed by the authorities with accusations of being "Sandinista spies."

The national constitutions of Central American countries contain guarantees of free speech and press. For long periods, however, these guarantees have been suspended during official "states of siege" or declared emergencies. Freedom of expression provisions in the Salvadoran constitution, for example, were suspended from 1980 until 1987. In many countries the laws designed to protect free speech and the press are purposely vague. During the Sandinista regime in Nicaragua (1979-1990), for example, the press was free to publish information as long as it was "within the bounds of social responsibility" and not "harming the people's interests and destroying the gains achieved by the people." Such provisions have typically been used as justifications to arrest, harass, or detain journalists whose reporting political leaders have disapproved.

Treatment of Groups. One of the most frequently oppressed groups in Central American society is the press. Journalists have been subjected to harassment, both physically and professionally, throughout Central America. Opposition papers, such as *La Prensa* in Nicaragua, have been periodically suspended for excessive criticism of the government, while some have been shut down.

Since the beginning of Spanish colonization of Central America, native peoples have not been free to practice their ways of life. In Guatemala, the Indian population has scarcely been integrated into the larger society. The government has usually been swift and merciless when Indian leaders are believed to be pressing too hard for change, by seeming to threaten violence or social upheaval, for example.

The academic community is also a frequent target of censorship, often violent. Dozens of university professors and left-wing students have disappeared in Guatemala, for example. Leaders of the Roman Catholic church, to the extent that they act as opponents to elite interests, are also sometimes subjects of governmental censorship. In Guatemala, for example, Radio Catolica was shut down by the Sandinistas for a long period during the 1980's. Specific political parties, particularly communists, are often outlawed or suspended.

Late Twentieth Century Trends. After the mid-1980's, the nations of Central America began seeing some improve-

ment in the protection of expression. After the civil war in El Salvador ended in 1992, for example, news from across the political spectrum, often critical of the government, was openly discussed; however, foreign journalists were still harassed frequently. In 1990 Nicaraguan opposition parties were granted access to the media, and rules for their organization were loosened. This change enabled an opposition candidate to defeat the Sandinistas in that year's presidential election.

Despite these improvements, the expression of diverse views, particularly in the media, remained limited, largely by self-censorship, often out of fear of violent reprisals by private groups. News coverage of previously taboo topics remained relatively restrained. A continuing mechanism of news control has been the common Central American practice of putting journalists on government payrolls. Reporters' regular salaries have been so low that the danger of losing government money has kept journalists from probing into sensitive areas. Newspapers and other media are also often owned by individuals who are tied into the national elite power structure, and therefore not likely to tolerate criticism of the government in their own papers. *—Eduardo Magãlhaes III*

See also Central Intelligence Agency; Death; Exploration, Age of; Fear; Journalists, violence against; Mexico; News media censorship; Panama, U.S. invasion of; Police states; South America; Spanish Empire; Terrorism.

BIBLIOGRAPHY

Every year the journal *Current History: A World Affairs Journal* (Philadelphia, 1941) offers current descriptions of Latin American nations, which often include discussion of issues of freedom. Other excellent sources include Ralph Lee Woodward, Jr., *Central America: A Nation Divided* (2d ed. New York: Oxford University Press, 1985); Paul Boeker, *Lost Illusions: Latin America's Struggle for Democracy as Recounted by Its Leaders* (New York: Markus Wiener, 1990); James Dunkerley, *Power in the Isthmus: A Political History of Modern Central America* (London: Verso, 1988); and James Dunkerley, *The Long War: Dictatorship and Revolution in El Salvador* (London: Verso, 1982).

Central Intelligence Agency (CIA)

FOUNDED: 1947

TYPE OF ORGANIZATION: Foreign intelligence service of the United States

SIGNIFICANCE: This agency has used censorship as a means of preserving the secrecy of its personnel and activities

The CIA was created by the National Security Act of 1947, which stipulated that its director "shall be responsible for protecting intelligence sources and methods from unauthorized disclosure." This provision laid the basis for the intense secrecy that would surround all facets of the agency over the years. Its employees would be required as a condition of their employment to sign contracts preventing them from publishing any material regarding the agency, during or after their terms of employment, without agency review and approval. In the 1970's, however, in a climate of congressional investigation and media criticism, this requirement was severely challenged. A former agency official, Victor Marchetti, co-authored an exposé of the agency, *The CIA and the Cult of Intelligence*, which became the first book in American history to be subjected to prior restraint by the U.S. government. Following litigation, the book was published in 1974, with blank spaces to indicate where the agency had secured 168 deletions. Another former CIA agency employee, Philip Agee, wrote a memoir, *Inside the Company: CIA Diary*, which was published outside the United States in 1975 without the agency's review or approval. In 1977, a third former agency employee, Frank Snepp, published *Decent Interval*, about his experiences in Vietnam. Although it contained no classified information, Snepp's failure to obtain prepublication review was ruled by the U.S. Supreme Court to be a breach of his employment contract and he was forced to forfeit his royalties from the sale of the book. Hundreds of other active or former agency employees—ranging from Francis Gary Powers, the former U-2 pilot, to former directors, such as Allen Dulles and Admiral Stansfield Turner—have successfully complied with prepublication reviews of their books and articles. However, several, including Admiral Turner, have publicly complained about long delays and overcautious editing by the agency.

Beginning in the 1960's, the CIA found itself the target of increasingly aggressive investigative reporting, reaching a high point during the inquiries of the Senate Select Committee on Intelligence and the Rockefeller Commission in the mid-1970's. The agency's image was tarnished by reporting of past abuses, including mind-control experiments, foreign assassination plots, and domestic surveillance of U.S. citizens; some publications began publicly to identify agency employees working abroad under diplomatic cover. Following the 1975 assassination of Richard Welch, the agency's chief of station in Athens, Greece, steps were taken to conceal more effectively the identities of agency employees, culminating in passage by Congress in 1982 of the Intelligence Identities Protection Act, which barred the press from identifying covert agency personnel. This was followed by legislation in 1984 that partly excluded from the Freedom of Information Act the agency's operational files, which concerned sources and methods.

See also *CIA and the Cult of Intelligence, The*; Civil service; Classification of information; Espionage; Federal Bureau of Investigation; Freedom of Information Act; Intelligence Identities Protection Act; National security; Police; Prior restraint.

Cerf, Bennett

BORN: May 25, 1898, New York, New York
DIED: August 27, 1971, Mount Kisco, New York
IDENTIFICATION: American book publisher and editor
SIGNIFICANCE: Cerf led the battle to have James Joyce's controversial novel *Ulysses* published in the United States

As the publisher of the Modern Library edition and cofounder of the Random House publishing company, Cerf dedicated himself to publishing great literature in the United States. In March, 1932, he asked attorney Morris Ernst to help him defend publication of James Joyce's novel *Ulysses* (1922), which had been banned from the United States as obscene.

Bennett Cerf in 1943, sitting near many of the books for whose first U.S. publication he was responsible. (AP/Wide World Photos)

After Ernst accepted Cerf's offer—which included part of the novel's royalties if their case succeeded—Cerf met with Joyce in Paris. Promising Joyce an advance against future royalties, he signed the author to a contract with Random House.

Cerf knew that U.S. courts would refuse to consider outside literary evaluations when ruling on a work, so he and Ernst prepared a copy of *Ulysses* with laudatory reviews pasted inside its cover. After it was confiscated by customs officials, the reviews pasted in it could be admitted as evidence in court. (Cerf later donated the special copy of *Ulysses* to the Columbia University Library.) After the court declared *Ulysses* not obscene, Cerf aggressively marketed the novel, which sold spectacularly. Cerf's defense of *Ulysses* earned him praise in the publishing world. Under his direction Random House continued to publish controversial authors, including William Faulkner and Ayn Rand.

See also Book publishing; Joyce, James; *Ulysses*; Mitford, Jessica.

Chaplin, Charles

BORN: April 16, 1889, London, England
DIED: December 25, 1977, Corsier-sur-Vevey, Switzerland
IDENTIFICATION: British actor, director, and filmmaker
SIGNIFICANCE: Chaplin's political commentaries and refusal to become a U.S. citizen led to accusations of his being a communist and his exile from the United States

The son of music hall performers, Chaplin learned his entertainment craft in the halls and with a troupe under the direction of Fred Karno. After coming to the United States in 1913, he signed a one-year contract with the Keystone Company. During 1914 he worked as actor and director on thirty-five films. While making his second film, *Kid Auto Races at Venice*, he discovered the "Little Tramp" character that he kept through most of his career.

Chaplin became film's greatest star after leaving Keystone and working for Mutual, Essanay, and First National Studios. Censorship during this period came from the studios themselves; Chaplin fought for power with the studios, often losing control over the final product or creating inferior works to

Charles Chaplin in his least characteristic screen role—the murderous bigamist Monsieur Verdoux. (Museum of Modern Art/Film Stills Archive)

meet the production requirements. In 1919 he joined Mary Pickford, D. W. Griffith, and Douglas Fairbanks to form the United Artists Corporation.

Chaplin's personal life was stormy throughout his career. He married four times, had numerous affairs with younger women, and had to fight several paternity suits. In 1943 he married seventeen-year-old Oona O'Neill, the daughter of playwright Eugene O'Neill; this marriage lasted the rest of his life.

Meanwhile, Chaplin's relations with the U.S. government disintegrated. Despite making his fortune in the United States, he never applied for U.S. citizenship and he refused to fight in either world war. Instead, he concentrated his efforts on three war films: a war-bond film and the comedy *Shoulder Arms* in 1918, and *The Great Dictator* in 1941. The latter was a parody of Adolf Hitler and Benito Mussolini; a lengthy speech promoting community and harmony at its end triggered questions about Chaplin's patriotism and political beliefs. It also put him at odds with the political Right in America, since Hitler and Mussolini were not yet declared enemies of the United States.

With the onset of McCarthyism in the 1950's, Chaplin found himself the subject of scrutiny from the U.S. government, which questioned his refusal to seek citizenship and his claim that he had no country. Because of these investigations, Chaplin refused to pay taxes in the United States. In 1947 he filed a three-million dollar lawsuit against the National Broadcasting Company after broadcaster Harry Gardner called him a communist and a liar. The case dragged on inconclusively for years. The matter seemed to be on the verge of being resolved after he offered to testify before the House Committee on Un-American Activities (HUAC), but when he sailed for England in September, 1952, U.S. Attorney General James McGranery rescinded his re-entry permit and ordered the Immigration and Naturalization Service to detain Chaplin if he attempted to re-enter the country. Exiled, Chaplin and Oona stayed in Europe, and he died in Switzerland on Christmas, 1977.

See also Blacklisting; Communism; Communist Party of the U.S.A.; House Committee on Un-American Activities.

Chapultepec Declaration

DATE: 1994

PLACE: Mexico City

SIGNIFICANCE: The product of a hemispheric conference on journalistic freedom, the declaration is a vigorous manifesto in support of freedom of the press in the Americas

The Chapultepec Declaration, also known as the Hemispheric Declaration on Free Expression, is the product of a conference on free expression and freedom of the press held at the Chapultepec Castle in Mexico City in March, 1994. The Inter-American Press Association sponsored the conference, and journalists, publishers, writers, constitutional lawyers, and political philosophers drawn from North, South, and Central America attended the event. The Chapultepec Declaration enunciated principles of free expression, including the necessity of a press free from repression and from the temptation of favorable treatment according to the content of journalism. The Declaration also condemned violence against journalists and insisted that freedom of the press is a right rather than a concession from those who hold political power. In April, 1995, President Bill Clinton signed a Charter of Endorsement for the Declaration of Chapultepec on behalf of the United States, joining with the leaders of Argentina, Bolivia, Colombia, El Salvador, Guatemala, Honduras, Mexico, Nicaragua, Panama, Paraguay, and Uruguay in publicly embracing the declaration's principles.

See also Argentina; Book and Periodical Council Statement on the Freedom of Expression and the Freedom to Read; Canadian Library Association Statement on Intellectual Freedom; Central America; First Hemispheric Conference on Free Expression; Journalists, violence against; Library Bill of Rights; Mexico; News media censorship; South America.

Charlie Chan films

DESCRIPTION: Films about a fictional Chinese American detective

SIGNIFICANCE: Asian American complaints about portrayals of Chan by non-Asian actors have discouraged production of additional Charlie Chan films and contributed to the withdrawal of existing films from circulation

Earl Derr Biggers created the character of Charlie Chan, a Chinese American sleuth who is the best inspector in Honolulu's police department. Between 1925 and his death in 1933 Biggers wrote six books about Chan, beginning with *The House Without a Key*. The first Charlie Chan film, made in 1926, was based on this book. Since then Chan has appeared in approximately thirty-seven films, numerous plays, both radio and television programs, cartoons, and a newspaper comic strip. In 1974 Dennis Lynds published *Charlie Chan Returns*, an original paperback novel.

No Chinese actor has ever portrayed Chan in any film made about him. As a consequence, producers of these films have been attacked by Chinese groups who have charged that Chan's characterizations demean Asians. Defenders of the

Warner Oland (right), the best known of several white actors to portray the fictional Chinese Hawaiian detective on the screen, in Charlie Chan in Shanghai *(1935). (Museum of Modern Art/Film Stills Archive)*

films have rebutted that the consistently sympathetic characterizations of Charlie Chan reversed a tradition in the entertainment industry of portraying Chinese as agents of the "Yellow Peril." Audiences familiar with Charlie Chan films know that if any characters come off badly, they are likely to be white characters—who can do little or nothing right until Chan solves the mystery.

Actors who have played Charlie Chan most frequently were Warner Oland (during the 1930's), Sidney Toler (late 1930's and 1940's), and Roland Winters (late 1940's). In the late 1950's, J. Carroll Nash re-created Chan in the television series *The New Adventures of Charlie Chan*. During the early 1970's a Charlie Chan film made for television was never broadcast because of complaints about the casting of white actor Ross Martin as Chan. However, two spoofs of the Chan character made over the following decade raised no major objections. Peter Ustinov played Chan himself in *Charlie Chan and the Curse of the Dragon Queen* in 1980, and Peter Sellers played a similar character in *Murder by Death* (1976)

See also Asian Americans; Film adaptation; *Miss Saigon*; Race; Television.

Chase, Samuel

BORN: April 17, 1741, Somerset County, Maryland
DIED: June 19, 1811, Baltimore, Maryland
IDENTIFICATION: Justice of the U.S. Supreme Court
SIGNIFICANCE: Chase faced impeachment for violating the Sedition Act of 1798 because he denounced the Jefferson presidential Administration

An anti-British member of the Maryland Assembly before the American Revolution, Chase demonstrated with the Sons of Liberty against the Stamp Act, participated in the First Continental Congress, and signed the Declaration of Independence. He was one of eleven members of Maryland's ratifying convention members to oppose adopting the U.S. Constitution, and he proposed several amendments, including clauses to protect trial by jury and freedom of the press. After the Constitution was ratified, he represented Maryland in Congress until he changed his political affiliation to the Federalist Party in 1795. Shortly afterward President George Washington appointed him to the Supreme Court in January, 1796.

Chase supported republicanism as a means to freedom, but rejected mass democracy as a necessary component of liberty. His federalism offended Thomas Jefferson's Republican administration, which sought to limit federal judiciary powers. As a justice Chase was heavy-handed in his treatment of a treason case and a sedition case; he opposed Maryland's manhood suffrage (fearing "mobocracy"); and he fought the repeal of the Judiciary Act of 1801. After he attacked Jefferson and his administration for being weak, the president suggested he be impeached for violating the Sedition Act in May, 1803. On March 12, 1804, the House of Representatives voted 73-32 for impeachment, but the Senate acquitted Chase on March 1, 1805. After this scandal, Chase remained on the Supreme Court but contributed little.

See also Federalist Party; Jefferson, Thomas; Revolutionary War, American; Sedition Act of 1798; Stamp Act.

Chernobyl disaster

DATE: April 26, 1986
PLACE: Chernobyl station, Ukraine, Soviet Union (now part of the Ukraine)
SIGNIFICANCE: The Soviet government initially attempted to cover up history's worst nuclear accident, but surveillance from outside the country compelled its leaders to acknowledge the full scope of the disaster

On Saturday, April 26, 1986, one of the most frightening catastrophes of modern industrial history occurred at the Chernobyl nuclear plant in what was then the Soviet republic of Ukraine. Two explosions destroyed a building housing a reactor, sending flames one hundred feet high and releasing a heavily radioactive plume in the air. Over the next ten days gases streamed out of the ruins, spewing deadly radioactive material over vast areas of the Soviet Union and Western Europe. Approximately 100,000 people were evacuated from the area around the accident, including eighteen thousand who were sent to clinics for examination. The official reported loss of life was only thirty-one persons, but the total human casualties numbered in the thousands, with thousands more who suffered from various forms of radiation sickness or birth defects.

The accident resulted from improper procedures that had been carried out by an inexperienced team testing a voltage-regulating system on a turbogenerator. However, the problem went beyond mistakes of personnel. The Chernobyl reactor, known as a RBMK-1000 type, was by Western standards an inferior 1950's design with inherently dangerous features. One particularly serious safety defect was its lack of a protective containment structure.

The Soviet government's public reaction to the accident seriously undermined the credibility of Mikhail Gorbachev's administration and raised doubts about his new policy of *glasnost* (or openness). The government initially deceived not only the outside world but its own people, to the serious detriment of those living near the site of the accident. Although it was aware of what had happened within hours, the government kept its news out of the press for almost three days. Western embassies were not notified until the radiation cloud reached Sweden on the Monday after the accident. Soviet press releases contained information that was incomplete, inaccurate, and designed to downplay the magnitude of the damage. Radiation levels published by the press were 1 percent or less of what authorities knew to be their true levels.

Fearing panic and perhaps a damaging public reaction, the government reported that everything was under control. The respected Soviet physicist and political dissident Andrei Sakharov was approached by government agents pretending to be chance passer-bys. They asked him about Chernobyl, secretly videotaped his responses, and then broadcast an edited version of his interview to reassure an anxious public. Meanwhile, the lack of reliable information from the government fed rumors throughout the country that in many instances portrayed events as being even worse than they really were.

Gorbachev himself waited more than two weeks before he reported to the public on television. The thrust of his report was a bitter attack against the U.S. news media, whom he accused of spreading "lies—very shameless and malignant lies." Subsequently, the Soviet government changed its tactics and revealed details of what had happened at a special conference of the International Atomic Agency in August. The economic and political damage caused by the Chernobyl accident contributed significantly to the Soviet Union's collapse five and a half years later.

See also Communism; Gorbachev, Mikhail; Nuclear research and testing; Sakharov, Andrei; Science; Soviet Union; TASS; Three Mile Island.

Chicago Art Institute furors

DATE: May, 1988; February 17 to March 16, 1989
PLACE: Chicago, Illinois
SIGNIFICANCE: Controversies surrounding two student art exhibitions raised strong calls for censorship

The School of the Art Institute of Chicago (SAIC) was cast into the national limelight in May, 1988, when black city aldermen marched from the city council chambers to the school—an internationally recognized private art school whose sister institution is the Art Institute of Chicago—and removed a painting from a student exhibition being held in a nonpublic part of the school. The offered rationale for seizure of *Mirth and Girth* by David K. Nelson was prevention of a possible riot. The confiscation took place after a city council debate on a resolution that claimed that the artist had "demented and pathological mental capacities." Nelson's painting is a crude, full-length portrait of the first black mayor of Chicago, Harold Washington, who had died a short time before. The painting presents him as clothed only in women's underwear, with a bloated belly, clutching a pencil in his right hand. The portrait was simultaneously construed as racist, homophobic, and an insult to the macho tradition of politics in the city. In response to intense public pressure as well as a threat from the city to withhold funds not only from the school but the Art Institute as well, the SAIC issued an apology in the city's major newspapers and promised to increase its efforts in minority faculty hiring. Nelson's painting was returned to him damaged, and a lawsuit was waged on his behalf by the American Civil Liberties Union.

Following this incident was a second controversy that focused extensive national attention on the SAIC. The episode centered around an interactive work titled *What is the Proper Way to Display an American Flag?* by Dread Scott, a graduate student at the School in 1989. Scott's work consisted of the title in text on the wall and a small photographic collage featuring an American flag-burning demonstration in South Korea and coffins draped with American flags. Below the photo was a ledger on a wall shelf used to register viewers' reactions. Directly below the shelf lay a three-foot by five-foot unfolded American flag on the floor. The work was part of a minority student group exhibition and opened on February 17. Within a week, the work was provoking daily demonstrations. There was political grandstanding by defenders and detractors as well as periodic rituals of veterans picking up the flag, ceremoniously folding it, and putting it on the wall shelf. Secu-

rity guards would then unfold it and reinstate it in its intended place. Street demonstrations denouncing the exhibit had an estimated 2,500 to 7,000 participants. Some veterans tried to confiscate the flag and close the show. The city and state legislatures passed bills making it a crime to deface and defile the American flag, including laying it on the floor. The Chicago law was later repealed. Financial support was withdrawn from the SAIC and new policies were made to guarantee the right of the institute to determine when and where student work would be shown and to remove any work that the institute saw as hazardous to viewers or disruptive to the educational process.

See also American Civil Liberties Union; Art; First Amendment; Flag burning; Fourteenth Amendment; Fourth Amendment; Hypocrisy; President's Commission on Obscenity and Pornography.

Child Pornography Law (Canada)

ENACTED: 1993
PLACE: Canada (national)
SIGNIFICANCE: This amendment to Canada's criminal code and customs tariff laws defined and criminalized child pornography

In August, 1984, Canada's ministers of health and justice appointed a body known as the Badgley Committee to investigate sexual offenses against children and youths as part of a government program to regulate pornography and prostitution. The committee recommended new legislation that would punish importation of child pornography and using children to produce, manufacture, sell, or distribute pornography with prison sentences of up to ten years. The following spring another body, the Fraser Committee, called for even stronger actions against child pornography in its own report, which recommended that purveyors of child pornography be subject to the severest punishments. The Fraser Committee report advised criminalizing the inducing, inciting, or coercing of persons under eighteen years of age to participate in explicit sexual acts, as well as the possession of adult pornography with the intent to sell it.

Legislative efforts to incorporate the recommendations of the Badgley and Fraser committees into law regulating child pornography failed in 1986 and 1987. However, the Supreme Court of Canada's 1992 *Rex v. Butler* ruling, which upheld the constitutionality of the obscenity provisions in the Criminal Code, provided the momentum necessary to introduce a bill in May, 1993, that defined and criminalized child pornography. Both houses of Parliament quickly passed this bill; it received the Royal Assent on June 23, 1993, and was proclaimed in force on August 1, 1993.

Canada's 1993 Child Pornography Law defines child pornography as any photographic, film, video, or other visual depiction of persons who are—or who are depicted as being—under the age of eighteen engaged in explicit sexual activities. Included in the law's definition is any written or visual material that advocates or counsels sexual activity with persons under the age of eighteen years. Persons who make, print, publish, import, distribute, sell, or possess for purposes of publication or sale child pornography may be guilty of indictable offenses and liable to terms of imprisonment of up to ten years.

The law acknowledges some exceptions. For example, if a court determines that visual representations or written materials that have been accused of being child pornography have artistic merit or educational, scientific, or medical purposes, the accused parties can be found innocent of the offense of child pornography. The law gives judges discretionary power to determine on reasonable grounds whether materials are pornographic and to issue warrants for the seizure of alleged pornography. Materials judged to be in violation of Canada's Child Pornography law are forfeited to the state for destruction.

In December, 1993, the Toronto artist Eli Langer and Toronto's Mercer Union Gallery were charged with violating the Child Pornography Law because the gallery was displaying forty sketches and paintings by Langer containing images of young girls in sexually suggestive poses with adult men and with each other. Langer claimed that because the images came from his imagination—not from live models—they were not child pornography. The gallery's owner also argued that the pictures were not child pornography, but were art that had the power to provoke discussion of important societal issues. Pressure from arts groups concerned with freedom of expression stimulated a national debate on the question of whether charges such as those made against Langer might affect all Canadian artists and writers and stifle their creativity. In February, 1994, the Crown dropped all charges against Langer and the gallery and applied, unsuccessfully, to the courts for his work to be forfeited so that it could be destroyed.

See also *Butler v. The Queen*; Canada; Mann, Sally; Obscene Publications Acts; Obscenity: legal definitions; Pornography; Pornography, child; Pressure groups.

Child Protection Restoration and Penalties Enforcement Act

ENACTED: 1988

PLACE: United States (national)

SIGNIFICANCE: Civil liberties groups regarded the language of this law as dangerously vague because its definitions of obscenity purveyors might be interpreted to apply to legitimate publishers, book dealers, and libraries

The Child Protection Restoration and Penalty Enforcement Act was part of a larger bill introduced by conservative senator Strom Thurmond, with the support of the Moral Majority and other conservative groups. The act made production or ownership of child pornography a federal crime. It broadened the general enforcement of antiobscenity laws by defining as an illegal business any that sell or transfer at least two "obscene" items with the intent of making a profit. The law strengthened enforcement of its provisions by placing certain burdens of proof on the accused. For example, it required producers of books, films, videos, commercial art, photographs, or other media to maintain records of the ages of the models and actors they used to make their materials. Failure to keep such records was deemed an assumption of guilt that could leave a business responsible for proving its own innocence. The act has defined

distributors as any persons, organizations, or groups that sold or lent at least two obscene works.

Passage of this law alarmed American publishers, booksellers, and libraries because its language was broad enough to encompass such institutions. Various amendments have attempted to tighten the vague language in order to allow it to be successfully enforced, but none of these has clearly defined what constitutes a distributor of obscenity.

See also American Library Association; Moral Majority; Obscenity: sale and possession; Pornography, child; Thurmond, Strom.

Children's Hour, The

TYPE OF WORK: Play

FIRST PRODUCED: 1934

PLAYWRIGHT: Lillian Hellman (1905-1984)

SUBJECT MATTER: The lives of two women running a private school are ruined by a pupil's charge that they are lesbians

SIGNIFICANCE: The play's first productions were banned in Boston and Chicago because it dealt with lesbianism; in later years U.S. overseas libraries removed copies because of Hellman's leftist politics

The Children's Hour is a combative play that challenged the moral values of contemporary American society. Its story is about two women who run a private school for girls. When they are unjustly accused by a pupil of being lesbians, outraged community members withdraw their children, forcing the school to close. When one of the women realizes that she is sexually attracted to her colleague, she commits suicide.

Playwright Lillian Hellman. (Library of Congress)

Before Lillian Hellman wrote *The Children's Hour*, several Broadway plays had addressed lesbianism; however, her own play struck harder at the pieties and conventions of contemporary life. It suggested that intolerance could result in witch-hunts ruining careers and lives. As much as its implied sexual content, the play's implicit political content led to its censorship. In 1952, during the midst of McCarthyist attacks on leftists and communists, for example, Hellman's leftist political beliefs made revival of *The Children's Hour* again a *cause célèbre*. The Broadway production of the play was not censored; however, copies of the play were removed from overseas U.S. libraries, and Hellman was blacklisted in Hollywood.

Hellman adapted her play to the screen in 1936, changing its title to *These Three* and altering its plot, so that it involved a heterosexual love triangle instead of lesbianism. A more faithful adaptation was filmed in 1962, when censorship standards had been relaxed.

See also Blacklisting; Drama and theater; Film censorship; *Front, The*; Hollywood Ten; Homosexuality.

Chile

DESCRIPTION: Independent South American nation at the southern tip of the continent

SIGNIFICANCE: From its independence in the early nineteenth century until the 1970's, Chile had a good record of tolerating freedom of expression; that changed under the socialist government of Salvador Allende and its military successor

After Chile won its independence, it avoided many of the chaotic wars of the early nineteenth century that afflicted its neighbors and remained a stable republic. Employing censorship of political opponents, courts that quickly convicted enemies of the regime, and enjoying the support of the Roman Catholic church, its strongman ruler Diego Portales maintained order. By mid-century many of the most oppressive restrictions were lifted, and Chile maintained a free press that welcomed writers and political opponents of neighboring regimes. Although there were occasional brief periods when presidents abused their powers, the tradition of a vigorous press persevered through a civil war in 1891 and a 1925 coup, and Chileans prided themselves on their civil liberties.

Throughout the 1950's and 1960's Chile's politically inconsistent regimes fluctuated on reforms and social questions. This gave rise to a spirited debate in the press as conservatives, socialists, and communists vied for power in free elections. By the 1960's Chile's press represented a broad spectrum of ideas, from pro-Castro publications to those supporting a conservative's responses to calls for reform. In 1970 election of Salvador Allende, the candidate of the socialist-led Popular Unity coalition, brought dramatic changes in the relationship of government to citizens. In his attempt to establish a socialist society in Chile, Allende encountered increasing resistance from the middle class and the wealthy. Despite the increasing intensity of opposition, however, the tradition of a free press persisted. Allende had promised to uphold Chile's Statute of Democratic Guarantees, which included freedom of the press, as part of his agreement with other parties that helped him gain the presidency. Nevertheless, his government did attempt—

unsuccessfully—to take over one of two private companies that controlled production of newsprint. Such control would have given him the ability to shut down opposition newspapers. Eventually Allende gave up on trying to effect dramatic changes constitutionally, and attempted to do so outside the accepted legal framework until he was killed in a bloody coup instigated by the military in September, 1973.

The coup led by General Augusto Pinochet produced one of most brutal and repressive regimes in the history of South America; it abused human rights, censored free speech, and controlled the press and broadcast media. Under the new military government thousands of people suspected of supporting Allende's regime were detained; many were tortured, and hundreds were murdered. Political prisoners were routinely detained without warrants, and many people were arrested for minor infractions, such as painting antigovernment graffiti, protesting government torture, or demanding accountings of persons who had disappeared in police custody.

The end of the military regime in 1990 and the ascension of an elected president dramatically eased restrictions on most forms of expression and exiled Chileans returned from abroad. The last decade of the twentieth century brought a return of the freedoms to which Chileans had long been accustomed.

See also Argentina; Brazil; *CIA and the Cult of Intelligence, The*; Music; South America.

Chilling effect

DEFINITION: Indirect negative effect on protected speech resulting from certain laws or government policies

SIGNIFICANCE: Otherwise unobjectionable laws and policies are sometimes invalidated by U.S. courts because they might "chill," or discourage, speech protected by the First Amendment

The U.S. Supreme Court has often repeated that freedom of speech needs "breathing room." Laws that serve appropriate ends may nevertheless creep so close to a regulation of protected speech that they discourage people from speaking for fear of adverse legal consequences. The concern for chilling effects on speech therefore surfaces in a variety of First Amendment contexts. For example, the Court has frequently overturned vague regulations of speech which—if written more clearly—would probably have survived constitutional challenge. Vague speech regulations have an "in terrorem" effect. Because they do not distinguish crisply between permissible and impermissible speech, such regulations risk deterring or chilling speech protected by the First Amendment as well as speech that government might otherwise be free to limit. Fearful of exposing themselves to government sanction, individuals might refrain from engaging in speech that falls within the First Amendment's umbrella of protection. To preserve First Amendment values, the Court routinely overturns such chillingly vague statutes. In *Smith v. Goguen* (1974), for example, the Court held unconstitutional a statute making it a criminal offense to treat the United States flag "contemptuously." The statute, according to the Court, was impermissibly vague, since what is "contemptuous to one man may be a work of art to another."

A concern for possible chilling effects on protected speech also lies at the core of the overbreadth doctrine. An overbroad statute is one that is designed to restrict or punish speech that is not constitutionally protected. As it is drafted, however, an overbroad statute reaches not only unprotected speech but speech that is guarded by the First Amendment. The overbreadth doctrine allows individuals to complain of a statute's overreaching even if the speech of these individuals is otherwise unprotected. The doctrine essentially allows such individuals to champion the cause of unnamed speakers whose protected speech might be subject to sanction under an overly broad statute. For example, in *Houston v. Hill* (1987), the Supreme Court invalidated as substantially overbroad a Houston, Texas, ordinance making it a crime to "assault, strike or in any manner oppose, molest, abuse or interrupt any policeman in the execution of his duty." The Court acknowledged that some speech directed against police officers might be punished. However, it ruled that the statute reached too broadly, since "the First Amendment protects a significant amount of verbal criticism and challenge directed at police officers." By overreaching, therefore, the local ordinance would inevitably have the effect of stifling such protected criticism. As such, the ordinance was overturned as substantially overbroad.

See also Constitution, U.S.; Courts and censorship law; First Amendment; Free speech; Prior restraint; Unprotected speech.

China

DESCRIPTION: East Asian nation with the largest population of any country in the world

SIGNIFICANCE: Government censorship has been an important function from ancient times to modern times

The ancient period known as the Spring and Autumn and the Warring States, which lasted from the fifth to third centuries B.C.E., was perhaps the era of greatest intellectual freedom in Chinese history, even though it experienced restless wars and political disorder. During this period, the five major Chinese philosophies—Confucianism, Menciusism, Legalism, Mohism, and Taoism—were formed. This glorious cultural period ended in 221 B.C.E., when China was unified under a single centralized feudal government by Emperor Shih huang-ti.

During the early third century B.C.E. Shih huang-ti undertook such great projects as building the Great Wall to prevent attack by northern barbarians, standardizing systems of weights and measurements, standardizing the characters of written language, and burning books. Under his order, all the books of history, poetry, and philosophy except official records of himself were subject to being burned. Hundreds of scholars were executed and thousands were put into forced labor to help build the Great Wall. This cultural catastrophe left an irreparable gap in the historical records of Chinese civilization.

Han Dynasty (206 B.C.E.-220 C.E.). During the Han Dynasty, Emperor Han Wudi (141-87 B.C.E.) adopted Confucianism as the sole official philosophical theory for the foundation of the Chinese feudal system. He started a campaign of censorship that banned all schools of thought other than Confucianism. However, his censorship policy was comparatively moderate; no books were burned, and no scholars were executed.

In the late Han Dynasty, Confucian scholars developed an interesting style of public criticism, known as "pure criticism" (*Qingyi*). This took the form of discussions about current events or ruling authorities, especially when there was general misrule. As this style of public criticism became fashionable throughout China, it came to bring instant fame or disgrace to ruling officials. At first, however, as this form of public criticism arose, conflict developed among scholars and the eunuchs who served the emperors. The eunuchs' efforts to censor public criticism led to severe persecutions of scholars that were remembered as "party inquisition." These persecutions included the murder of several hundred scholars, imprisonment of more than a thousand university students, and exile or killing of scholars' relatives.

Southern Song Period (1127-1279) and Yuan Dynasty (1271-1368). In the Southern Song period, a movement of student petitions emerged when the country was in danger of the invasions from Jin (Manchus) and Mongols. In this movement, scholars and students of the imperial colleges expressed their protests to the government with joint petitions and assemblages of large numbers of people at the palace gates. In expressing public criticisms against political corruption, they demanded the dismissal and punishment of some officials, including premiers. This movement was dangerous because the premiers were the de facto rulers of the empire at a time when the emperors themselves were weak. To suppress this movement, a premier named Jia Shidao arranged murders, arrests of students, and bribes.

During the Yuan Dynasty, the Mongolian conquerors established a severe censorial system as an essential instrument of control over the bureaucracy and Chinese peoples' lives. More than a hundred censorial officials from three central offices and twenty-two locally based surveillance offices were constantly on inspection tours, examining all government documents and seeking out violations of law so as to purge wayward officials, maintain the probity of government, and prolong the life of the dynasty.

Ming Dynasty (1368-1644). The Ming rulers developed a unique system of imperial censorship. They censored not only public opinions but government officials, from the premiers down to the lowest magistrates. The imperial censors were regarded as the "eyes and ears" of the emperor. This system was established according to the earliest Chinese philosophy that an emperor's power was based on the goodwill of the people, and that when an emperor had lost that, he was doomed to collapse. However, under this censorship system, many honest scholars who dared to challenge corrupt officials risked their lives by petitioning the emperors to impeach corrupt officials.

In the late Ming Dynasty, a great movement of political criticism led by the scholars of Donglin College lasted for half a century. When the Donglin scholars clashed with the most powerful eunuch of all time, Wei Zhongxian, they were prosecuted by him on the charge of forming a political party. Most of the Donglin scholars were sentenced to death they were tortured into admitting their guilt.

Qing Dynasty (1644-1911). After the Manchu—a minority tribe that once lived in the northeastern parts of China and Siberia—conquered China, Manchu rulers were so sensitive to racial issues and the security of their reign that they would not tolerate any dissent from Han scholars. Their censorship was strict and their punishment severe. All anti-Manchu or pro-Ming literature was banned, and people involved in writing or disseminating such literature were persecuted.

During the reign of the Emperor Kangxi in the late seventeenth and early eighteenth centuries two remarkable "literary inquisitions" happened. The first case was that of a businessman who, with the help of some scholars, edited and published a critical book titled *An Abridged History of the Ming*. Almost two hundred people were punished, including those who participated in compiling the book and members of their families. Even the corpse of the businessman who died before the conviction was disinterred and put on display. Another case was publication of a book titled *Anthology of Southern Mountain*, written by Dai Mingshi, a major compiler of the Royal Bureau of Historiography. Because the late history of the Ming described in this book offended the Manchu, Dai was sentenced to a slow death by slicing; all his family members and more than three hundred other people connected with his book were sentenced to be decapitated or exiled.

In order to scour the entire country for anti-Manchu literature, Emperor Qianlong (1735-1795) ordered the compilation of a massive collection called *The Complete Works of Four Treasures*, which was to include all ancient and modern Chinese literature. Although the compilation had its significance in the collection of books into the imperial library for preservation and the development of methods of cataloging, the losses were far greater than the achievement. According to various historical records, more than two thousand works were partially or entirely destroyed.

The Twentieth Century. In 1911 the Manchu rulers were overthrown by the Chinese nationalist revolution and the first Chinese republic was established. From this time until 1927 different parts of China were ruled by local warlords, and people had comparative freedom to speak, write, and publish. During this same period communism was introduced to China. After Chiang Kaishek took control of the nation, he began to employ extreme censorship policy against communist and left-wing ideologies. Hundreds of communists and leftist writers were tortured or killed, and thousands were jailed. A complex censorship system was established. Every government branch and level had a censorship bureau. All were under the control of the Central Publicity Department of the Nationalist Party. The persecution and censorship forced the communists to turn to the underground and rural areas to organize guerrilla wars against the Nationalist Government. Finally, the communists led by Mao Zedong (Mao Tse-tung) defeated Chiang Kaishek, who retreated to Taiwan in 1949.

Since 1949 Chiang Kaishek and his successors have effectively ruled Taiwan as an independent country and the Nationalist regime has continued its censorship policies there. Any opinions favorable to communism or independence for Taiwan were banned. In 1988 Taiwan authorities finally lifted martial law and began a series of political reforms. As a result Taiwan's people have enjoyed greater free speech than any other people in China's history.

People's Republic of China. Soon after the People's Republic of China (PRC) was founded by the Communist Party in October, 1949, censorship was employed by the new government. During Mao's rule, which lasted until 1976, the government waged several campaigns to eliminate political enemies and suppress opposition opinions. Among these political campaigns, the "Anti-Rightist Movement" and the "Culture Revolution" are most significant.

Government censorship helped to keep Chinese intellectuals docile during the early 1950's. To make better use of available talent that was needed for China's development, the Communist Party began a campaign called the "Hundred Flower Blossom movement of 1956-1957." Mao invited intellectuals to express their views freely to help expose "bureaucratism, sectarianism and subjectivism." Relying on Mao's apparent liberalism, intellectuals began expressing criticisms of the government. Regardless of whether Mao's invitation to speak out was genuine, the ferocity of the criticisms expressed went beyond what he had expected. In June, 1957, he retracted his call for free expression and began to denounce "rightist" elements whom he claimed had tried to sabotage the socialist revolution. He then started the "Anti-Rightist Movement," under which hundreds of thousands of intellectuals were labeled as "rightist." Some went to prison or labor camps, and some were simply demoted within their places of work.

After Mao died in 1976, Deng Xiaoping gradually took control of China and began introducing economic and political reforms. There was a short period of a liberalized atmosphere for public opinions in the late 1970's. When Deng became a target of criticism as a dictator, he stopped easing censorship restrictions and announced the "Four Cardinal Principles": socialism, the dictatorship of the proletariate, the leadership of the Communist Party, and Marxism-Leninism-Mao Zedong Thought. Implicit in his declaration of these Four Principles was the message that the people could no longer openly criticize the government. Deng started a new round of censorship campaigns by introducing the "antispiritual pollution" and "antibourgeois liberalization" movements. However, these campaigns did not stop Chinese intellectuals' enthusiasm for pursuing democracy. The struggle between censorship and freedom of speech largely contributed to the confrontation between the government and the democratic movement led by Chinese students in 1989. Eventually, the student movement was bloodily suppressed by the government.

In Tibet government censorship has focused on suppressing pro-independence opinions and literature. Many Tibetan nuns and monks have been imprisoned, tortured, and in some cases killed for advocating independence. Buddhist temples participating in the independence movement have been shut down. The government has also censored foreign press reports from Tibet.

By the 1990's China ranked among the most repressive nations in the use of censorship and media controls. Publication of all newspapers, periodicals, books, and films, as well as the broadcast of radio and television, has not only been subject to multiple government regulatory controls, but it has also been enmeshed within the supervisory controls of the Communist Party. The constitution of the People's Republic of China has a free speech and free association clause similar to that of the U.S. Constitution; however, China has not had an independent judicial system that can enforce and protect these constitutional protections. Despite periodic moderation in the intensity of the Communist Party's control, the primary function of the Peoples' Congress and the judicial system throughout the communist era has been to foster support for Communist Party policies.

—Wei Luo

See also Buddhism; Confucius; Cultural Revolution, Chinese; Mao Zedong; Shih huang-ti; Tiananmen Square; Wall posters.

BIBLIOGRAPHY

Yutang Lin's *A History of the Press and Public Opinion in China* (Chicago: University of Chicago Press, 1936) is the best work covering the press methods and media from ancient China through the Republic of China; it also discusses some important historical censorship events. Luther Carrington Goodrich's *The Literary Inquisition of Ch'ien-Lung* (Baltimore: Waverly Press, 1935) discusses Chinese literary censorship during the late eighteenth century. The best article covering book censorship in Chinese history is Wenxian Zhang's "Fire and Blood: Censorship of Books in China," *International Library Review* 22 (1990). A fine article covering the Anti-Rightist movement is W. J. F. Jenner's "The Hundred Flowers," in *Index on Censorship* (1980). See also Alexander Ya-Li Lu's *Political Control of Literature in Communist China, 1949-1966* (Ann Arbor, Mich.: University Microfilms, 1973).

Chomsky, Noam

BORN: December 7, 1928, Philadelphia, Pennsylvania

IDENTIFICATION: American linguist and political and social activist

SIGNIFICANCE: Chomsky is a leading intellectual critic of de facto censorship in American society

The New York Times has called Chomsky "the most important intellectual alive today." He is most noted for revolutionizing the scientific study of language by introducing a theory that explains the creative and innovative nature of language. Often an outspoken critic of government policy, Chomsky has argued that as in fully censored societies the American media manipulate the population, whom he has called the "bewildered herd." By suppressing information, selectively choosing topics, distorting political discussion, by portraying the United States as an innocent and benevolent bystander in world affairs, and by misrepresenting foreign policies, the media have prevented people from fully understanding and dealing with the "real" problems. Further, he has charged that the media perpetuate the power of the rich and sanction inequalities, oppression, and violence in American society. Rather than calling this mind-control censorship, Chomsky has called it manufacturing of consent, manipulation, and diversion of the masses, and collusion between the government and the media.

Chomsky has explained his own virtual exile from, and marginal status in, American mainstream media as part of the conspiracy to deride him as anti-American, Marxist, and a conspiracy theorist. Internationally, however, he is considered one of the world's most brilliant intellectuals. Chomsky does not deny that the United States is an open society giving its citizens the freedom to criticize and challenge and free access to massive amounts of information. However, the public relies on mainstream news for information which has been constructed to practice ideological control. Chomsky claims that overt censorship might not exist in the United States but "the results remain much the same as if there were censorship."

See also Censorship; Intellectual freedom; News media censorship.

Christian Science

FOUNDED: 1879

TYPE OF ORGANIZATION: Boston-based worldwide Christian denomination that believes sickness, sin, and death can be overcome through mastery of the principles of Jesus Christ's original teachings

SIGNIFICANCE: The church has assumed the public spotlight many times as a minority of members have complained about its founder's system of governance, which forbids dissent over church management and doctrine, and forbids "unauthorized" publication of religious literature

Mary Baker Eddy founded the Church of Christ, Scientist, to propagate the biblical truths that she claimed were responsible for her life-saving healing in 1866. She published her beliefs in the book *Science and Health* in 1875. Four years later she established The Mother Church, the First Church of Christ, Scientist, in Boston, Massachusetts, and then fostered the growth of branch churches worldwide. The Christian Science Publishing Society, a variety of broadcast operations, and *The Christian Science Monitor* newspaper also became part of the denominational structure.

An intelligent and articulate woman, Eddy was frequently involved in protracted personal disputes with followers in the early years, as she fought to manage the growth of her movement's churches, religious rhetoric, and publications. Members who disagreed with her aims sometimes characterized her as a jealous and irritable tyrant. Often these members left the fold, or were expelled for their unfaithfulness. Eddy accused dissenters of carrying out mental "mesmerism" to bring evil influence against her or her church.

At the root of most complaints over the years has been *The Manual of the Mother Church*, a 138-page document written by Eddy and modified regularly until her death in 1910. The manual established rigid guidelines for church governance, election of officers, admission of members, and organization of services. It barred church-sanctioned social gatherings, established "taxation" of members, and presented guidelines for the private, personal conduct of Christian Scientists. The manual also states members may not "buy, sell, nor circulate" any religious materials not sanctioned by the official Christian Science Publishing Society. In the view of a severe critic of Eddy, Mark Twain, the manual allowed Christian Scientists "no more voice in the management of the church than has the audience in the management of a theater."

Despite the church manual's stern warnings, dissenting Christian Scientists became more outspoken in the late twentieth century, even to the extent of forming an independent society that publishes Christian Science works written by Eddy and others in direct opposition to Eddy's wishes. In 1993 pressure from some Christian Scientists, along with a conditional $50 million bequest, resulted in the Publishing Society's agreement to release *The Destiny of the Mother Church*, a hagiography that compares the church's "discoverer and founder" to Jesus Christ. Though written by a former trustee of the Mother Church, the book takes a position on Eddy's role that Eddy herself would not have approved.

During the 1990's the church was forced to defend itself against a lawsuit filed by members who claimed that the church hierarchy "recklessly and wrongfully" spent $450 million dollars in a failed bid to establish a satellite television network. Two Monitor Radio reporters were dismissed after refusing to apologize for a news story on AIDS that was judged theologically inconsistent with church teachings. Unrelated lawsuits were filed, alleging that the church was partially responsible for the deaths of gravely ill children who were under the care of Christian Science prayer treatment.

To some, the future of Christian Science has seemed to be limited by its aging membership and church prohibitions against the types of recruitment and social and charitable agendas carried out by most other Christian denominations. However, others point to growing endowments, a multimillion dollar renovation of The Mother Church, expansion of Monitor Radio news broadcasts, and new church publications as evidence that the movement has continued to address the world's spiritual needs.

See also Christianity; Mormonism; Twain, Mark.

Christianity

DEFINITION: Religions predicated on belief in the divinity of Jesus Christ

SIGNIFICANCE: From the Middle Ages into modern times, Christian organizations have often suppressed writings and other media which challenge, contradict, or ridicule their beliefs

In its earliest days, Christianity was a major target of persecution, especially by the rulers of the Roman Empire. Under Roman rule the religion itself was illegal; Christians were often put to death, and Christian writings were carefully hidden. However, the fact that some early Christian writings have survived to this day suggests that there was no great effort on the part of the empire to impose censorship.

The situation changed greatly in the year 324 C.E., when Emperor Constantine converted to Christianity himself and the faith became accepted. Almost immediately Christians began imposing censorship, often on other Christians. The major concern at the time was heresy, defined by those in power as anything which contradicted the Church's official point of view.

It is impossible to determine accurate figures relating to the early Christian population, because they had to remain secret.

The historian Edward Gibbon estimated that Christians in the city of Rome at the time of Constantine numbered about fifty thousand, accounting for only about 5 percent of the city's total population. Once the religion became legitimized, however, it grew rapidly; within a few centuries it became the dominant power in most of Europe.

The Inquisition and the Index. While various heresies were condemned and punished for many centuries, the first major challenge to the Roman Catholic church began in the sixteenth century, when Martin Luther publicly denied the authority of the pope. Protestantism of various sects began to spread rapidly, especially in northern Europe. In southern Europe, especially in Italy and Spain, the Catholic church responded with the Inquisition. The Inquisition had a number of targets, including Jews and Muslims, but the clearest threat to the primacy of Catholicism was Protestantism, because it offered liberalized rules of living without denying Christianity itself.

One of the most important tools of the Inquisition was the series of indexes of forbidden books known as the *Index Librorum Prohibitorum*. The publishing of banned books, or their importation into an affected nation, was often punishable by death. In addition, the Renaissance Church developed the Imprimatur, a "stamp of approval" that Catholic writers and publishers were required to have on their works. The last *Index* was printed in 1948. In 1966 the Vatican admitted publicly that censorship of all the world's books was no longer possible from one central authority, and local bishops were given the task of deciding what was acceptable.

Throughout the Middle Ages and the Renaissance, the Church used censorship almost exclusively as a tool to prevent unwanted religious ideas from being spread. In England Thomas More was condemned for refusing to acknowledge King Henry VIII as the religious leader of the nation. In Spain and Italy works by Jews, Muslims, and Protestants were condemned. At the same time, however, many works that later became targets of Christian censors in the United States were acceptable. For example, the works of Geoffrey Chaucer and Giovanni Boccaccio, two of the most popular writers of the Middle Ages, had a great deal of explicit sexual content. The use of what much later would be considered offensive language was also commonly used, and such use was not objected to by religious authorities.

Early American Christians. A large proportion of the early European settlers in what became the United States were European religious dissenters who had come to America to escape religious persecution. The best known of these groups were the Puritans, who dominated the population of early New England. Here, the focus of censorship shifted considerably. The U.S. Constitution (1789) guaranteed freedom of speech and of religion, so heresy could not be censored. Obscenity, however, was considered to be unprotected, because it was conceived as leading to immoral actions.

The first obscenity trial in the United States involved a novel called *The Memoirs of Fanny Hill*, written in 1747 by John Cleland, who was in debtors' prison at the time. No publisher in his home state of Massachusetts would publish the book, but it was printed in London in 1748. It did not sell well, however, and was banned in England eighteen months later, at which time Cleland returned to prison. No attempt to publish the book was made again until 1821. In that year publisher Peter Holmes finally published the book and was immediately put on trial in Boston. He was convicted of publishing an obscene work, and the work did not again become available to the general public until 1963.

By the late nineteenth century Boston had become famous as the home of the old Puritan heritage, and "banned in Boston" became a slogan used to indicate that a book was obscene. The chief censor at this time was the Boston Watch and Ward Society, a Protestant organization dedicated to banning obscene materials. In the 1920's the Protestants of Massachusetts found allies in the growing Irish Catholic population; between them they formed the Boston Booksellers Committee.

The Religious Right and Secular Humanism. In 1962 the U.S. Supreme Court ruled that prayer in schools was unconstitutional. The following year the Court determined that devotional readings of the Bible and recitation of the Lord's Prayer were also forbidden. These decisions, however, were not unanimous, and the opinions published left room for study of the Bible as literature. The first surge of Fundamentalist revival in the United States was precipitated by these Court decisions, and, to some extent, by the election of the first Catholic president, John F. Kennedy. Generally, however, the religious Right did not have a great deal of success until the 1970's. The most important event at that time, from the point of view of Fundamentalists, was the decision in *Roe v. Wade*, in which the Supreme Court determined that until a fetus was six months old, the government could not prohibit abortion.

In the 1970's and afterward, a variety of Fundamentalist groups gained power. They found that many of their views were shared by political conservatives, and an alliance between Born Again Christians and the political Right was formed. Primary aims of the new religious Right included making abortion illegal once again, fighting "godless" communists, and protecting the state of Israel. They also, however, became heavily involved in trying to determine what should be taught in public schools.

Evolution and "Creationism." During the 1920's several states had passed laws making teaching evolution illegal. In 1925 the most famous test of such a law took place, the Tennessee "Monkey Trial" of John Scopes, who was accused of teaching evolution in high school. After Scopes was convicted Tennessee's law remained on the books until 1968, when the Supreme Court decided it was unconstitutional.

After that time Christian Fundamentalist groups took a different tactic. Instead of insisting that evolution be banned from the classroom, they tried to have laws passed requiring schools to teach "creationism," the Fundamentalist term for the creation story in Genesis, along with evolution. In a few states they succeeded. The reasoning used by Fundamentalists since about 1970 has been that public schools were teaching a point of view they called secular humanism, which denied the existence of God. As such, secular humanism was itself a religion that should not be taught in public schools. Otherwise, it should be

taught as one of many alternative religions, including Christianity, Judaism, and other God-based religions. This point of view has been treated variously in different cases. The Supreme Court has carefully avoided making a definitive statement, instead rendering decisions relating only to specific cases.

The Opposing Viewpoint. A variety of groups in the United States oppose censorship, including that imposed or attempted by conservative Christian groups. Pornography, one of the major targets of Fundamentalists, has often been attacked on the basis that it can hurt children. Opponents, however, have suggested that children young enough not to be exposed to pornography are also not old enough to be interested in it.

Another major target of Fundamentalists has been supernatural literature, which is supposedly anti-Christian. The opposition suggests that because ghost stories and tales of the supernatural are popular among children, banning them in effect discourages children from reading. Closely allied to this view are Christian objections to role-playing games, such as *Dungeons and Dragons*, that assume a mythical world that is not Christian. Opponents of such censorship counter that playing such games encourages healthy development of imagination. —*Marc Goldstein*

See also Atheism; Bible; Blasphemy laws; Judaism; *Pentagon Papers, The*; Reformation, the; Roman Empire; Scopes trial; Secular humanism; Vatican.

BIBLIOGRAPHY

Joan DelFattore's *What Johnny Shouldn't Read: Textbook Censorship in America* (New Haven, Conn.: Yale University Press, 1992) discusses attempts by Fundamentalist groups to censor books in schools. Herbert N. Foerstel's *Banned in the U.S.A.: A Reference Guide to Book Censorship in Schools and Public Libraries* (Westport, Conn.: Greenwood Press, 1994) is a study of the books most frequently banned in American schools and libraries. *Censorship: For and Against*, edited by Harold H. Hart (New York: Hart Publishing, 1971), is a collection of essays representing many viewpoints. William Noble's *Bookbanning in America: Who Bans Books?—And Why* (Middlebury, Vt.: Paul S. Eriksson, 1990) traces the history of censorship in the United States, from colonial times to the late twentieth century. Robert Zwier's *Born-Again Politics: The New Christian Right in America* (Downers Grove, Ill.: InterVarsity Press, 1982) discusses Christian evangelism, particularly during the 1970's.

CIA and the Cult of Intelligence, The

TYPE OF WORK: Book
PUBLISHED: 1974
AUTHORS: Victor Marchetti (1940-   ) and John D. Marks (1945-   )
SUBJECT MATTER: Classified information on the Bay of Pigs invasion, the Vietnam War, South Africa, and the assassination of Salvador Allende in Chile
SIGNIFICANCE: Marchetti was the first writer in U.S. history to be subjected to prior restraint as a result of a secrecy agreement he had signed with the CIA as a condition of employment

Victor Marchetti, an intelligence agent who had risen to the level of special assistant to the executive director of the U.S. federal government's Central Intelligence Agency (CIA), left after becoming disillusioned with the CIA's covert actions to destabilize governments considered unfriendly to the United States. When he submitted an article to *Esquire* magazine, the CIA charged that his manuscript contained classified information and won an injunction to enjoin it from publication. Marchetti appealed, but the U.S. Court of Appeals for the Fourth Circuit held that the secrecy agreement Marchetti had signed when he was hired by the CIA should be enforced. This agreement required Marchetti—like all CIA agents—to submit his manuscripts to the CIA for approval before publishing them. In *Marchetti v. United States* (1968), the Court of Appeals thus held that the CIA had the right to prevent publication, and Marchetti became the first writer in U.S. history subjected to such a censorship order. Marchetti appealed to the U.S. Supreme Court, but it denied *certiorari*. He later tried to turn his manuscript into a novel, *The Rope Dancer*. Although the CIA tried to prevent its publication, they finally approved it after Marchetti removed all the portions to which the CIA objected.

Marchetti and a co-author John Marks, a former State Department employee who had also signed an agreement not to disclose classified information learned during his employment, wrote the book *The CIA and the Cult of Intelligence*, which they submitted to the CIA for prepublication review. The CIA required them to delete 339 passages, comprising 15 to 20 percent of the entire manuscript. Particularly heavy deletions were made in chapters on the Bay of Pigs invasion, the Vietnam War, and the CIA's attempt to prevent Salvador Allende from being elected president of Chile. With their publisher, Alfred A. Knopf, the authors sued. The government argued that they were not enjoining the press from publication, as in the Pentagon Papers case; they were merely enforcing a contract between Marchetti and the CIA. They therefore claimed that their case was not a First Amendment case; it was just a contract action to uphold the secrecy agreements Marchetti and Marks had signed. By the time of the trial, the CIA had reduced the number of deletions from 339 to 168. The U.S. District Court for the Eastern District of Virginia permitted publication of all but 26 of the 168 passages, at which point all parties appealed.

In *Alfred A. Knopf v. Colby* (1975), the U.S. Court of Appeals for the Fourth Circuit ruled that if the government could prove that each item deleted disclosed classified information, then it could require deletion of those items solely on that basis. Furthermore, the court said that Marchetti and Marks had in effect given up their First Amendment rights regarding disclosure of classified information when they signed the secrecy agreements. The appeals court remanded the case to a district court, ruling that the authors could disclose only information which they had obtained after leaving the CIA and State Department. Ultimately the CIA permitted twenty-five of the twenty-six missing passages to be printed in whole or in part, leaving unanswered the question of why the passages had been deleted in the first place.

See also Central Intelligence Agency; Courts and censorship law; Espionage; *Inside the Company: CIA Diary*; National Security Decision Directive 84; Official Secrets Act (U.K.); Prior restraint; *Snepp v. United States*; *Spycatcher*.

Cicero

BORN: January 3, 106 B.C.E., Arpinum, Latium (Italy)
DIED: December 17, 43 B.C.E., Formiae, Latium (Italy)
IDENTIFICATION: Roman writer, orator, and politician
SIGNIFICANCE: After speaking out against the destruction of the Roman Republic, Cicero was silenced by assassins

Cicero stands forth as one of the greatest writers and politicians of Rome's republican era. Born into a wealthy and prestigious Italian family, he was educated in philosophy and rhetoric at Rome, Athens, and Rhodes. After returning to Rome around 76 B.C.E. he pursued a career in the courts and in politics. He was elected to several prestigious governmental posts and soon came to be regarded as one of the most eloquent and determined defenders of the republic.

Cicero developed a long-standing opposition to Julius Caesar and actively supported Caesar's rival, Pompey. Nevertheless, he was pardoned and allowed to return to nonpolitical pursuits. However, following Caesar's assassination in 44 B.C.E., Cicero rejoiced in the news and openly stated that Marc Antony should have been killed as well. In a series of public speeches, delivered between September 44 and April 43 B.C.E., he argued unsuccessfully that the Roman Senate should declare Antony a public enemy. With the formation of the so-called Second Triumvirate, consisting of Antony, Octavian (later Emperor Augustus), and Lepidus, Cicero's days were numbered. After a half-hearted attempt at flight, he was caught by soldiers sent by Antony and the other triumvirs.

Faced with death, Cicero submitted stoically to his fate. His head and hands were cut off, later to be displayed in Rome's Forum as silent testimony to the price of republican devotion and eloquence. But whether Antony's purpose was accomplished may be judged by Plutarch's comment: "At such a sight the Roman people shuddered, for they seemed to see there not the face of Cicero, but the image of Antony's soul."

See also Death; Ovid; Roman Empire; Seneca the Younger.

Cinematograph Act

ENACTED: 1909; amended in 1952
PLACE: United Kingdom (national)
SIGNIFICANCE: Ostensibly designed to regulate safety issues associated with the showing of films, this law authorized the British government to censors films

The Cinematograph Act placed film theaters under the same safety statutes as other mass entertainment facilities, such as drama and music halls. It enabled local county councils to dictate the requirements for the licensing of film theaters on whatever terms and conditions the councils chose.

A year after it was enacted the law saw its first use as a censorship tool when the London County Council invoked it to ban showings of a film in which African American boxer Jack Johnson defeated boxer Jim Jeffries for a world championship. Also in 1910, the London council barred cinemas from showing films on Sundays, Good Friday, and Christmas Day. When one theater defied the ban, a court upheld the ban, ruling that the Cinematograph Act did indeed confer such powers upon local authorities.

By 1912 the British Board of Film Censors (BBFC), a private regulatory agency, and Britain's county councils worked together, with the BBFC issuing censorship recommendations that local authorities enforced. Film distributors agreed to submit all of their work to the board, and the board agreed to act as an impartial screening agency.

Amendments to the Cinematograph Act that were enacted in 1952 expanded the law's authority over licensing power and regulation of safety, health, and welfare issues, and added new protections of children involved in the film industry.

See also British Board of Film Censors; United Kingdom.

Citizen Kane

TYPE OF WORK: Film
RELEASED: 1941
DIRECTOR: Orson Welles (1915-1985)
SUBJECT MATTER: Pseudodocumentary life story of fictional newspaper mogul Charles Foster Kane

SIGNIFICANCE: Newspaper tycoon William Randolph Hearst regarded Welles's film as an unflattering portrayal of his own life and tried to suppress it

In collaboration with Herman Mankiewicz, Orson Welles wrote the script for *Citizen Kane*. He also directed the film and played the title role. The film opens with the death of a powerful newspaperman named Kane. The rest of the film follows a reporter's quest to understand the significance of Kane's last word, "Rosebud"—which seems to be a lament for the childhood taken from him when he inherited the fortune that made his fabulous newspaper career possible.

When William Randolph Hearst, then one of the most powerful newspapermen in the United States, learned that *Citizen Kane* closely mirrored his own life, he launched a vigorous campaign to prevent its being shown. In addition to the fact that both Kane and Hearst were both ruthless newspaper tycoons, parallels between the men are both clear and unflattering. For example, Kane's obsessive desire to see his untalented young wife become an opera singer resembles Hearst's wish for his young (but truly talented) mistress, Marion Davies, to become a film star. Likewise, Kane's excessively opulent private palace in Florida, "Xanadu," recalls Hearst's palatial estate at San Simeon, California.

John Foster Kane (Orson Welles) and his mistress (Dorothy Comingore, left) confront Mrs. Kane (Ruth Warrick) in Citizen Kane. (Museum of Modern Art/Film Stills Archive)

To prevent *Citizen Kane*'s release, Hearst ordered his many newspapers not to publish anything about the film's production company, RKO Pictures. At first, Will Hays, the head of the Motion Picture Association, expressed doubts that *Citizen Kane* could be released and RKO cancelled its scheduled opening. However, Hays's office eventually let the film be released. Nevertheless, Hearst's campaign clearly damaged the film's commercial success; it may also have contributed to Welles's receiving no Academy Awards for the film that many critics now regard as the finest American film ever made.

See also Film censorship; Hays Code; Hearst, William Randolph; Motion Picture Association of America.

Citizen Tom Paine

TYPE OF WORK: Book
PUBLISHED: 1943
AUTHOR: Howard Fast (1914-   )
SUBJECT MATTER: Fictional biography of the famed English supporter of the American Revolution
SIGNIFICANCE: Attempts to remove this book from New York libraries were unsuccessful, but they remain a prime example of the harassment of the American Left in the years following World War II

On January 18, 1949, the New York School Library Association was ordered to remove all copies of *Citizen Tom Paine* from library shelves. The apparent instigator of the censorship, Federal Bureau of Investigation director J. Edgar Hoover, also sent agents to the New York Public Library and to main libraries in other cities, ordering the destruction of the writer's other books. In his autobiography, *Being Red* (1990), Fast reported that the New York Public Library immediately invited him to speak, assured him that it did not burn books, and said it would preserve the books until they could be safely restored to the shelves. Ironically, seven years earlier Fast had been widely admired as a patriotic novelist; he had been hired to write copy for the fledgling Voice of America and had received high praise for *Citizen Tom Paine*'s pro-American themes.

The change in attitude was due to the virulent wave of anticommunism which had swept the United States after World War II. Fast had joined the Communist Party in 1944, and as his sympathies became known, the FBI subjected him to increasing pressure. The harassment did not end with *Citizen Tom Paine*; in 1951 Fast's novel *Spartacus* was rejected by half a dozen major publishers because of FBI intimidation; Fast finally published the novel himself in 1952.

See also Blacklisting; Communist Party of the U.S.A.; Federal Bureau of Investigation; Hoover, J. Edgar; Libraries; Paine, Thomas; Voice of America.

Citizens for Decent Literature (CDL)

FOUNDED: 1957 (Children's Legal Foundation since 1989)
TYPE OF ORGANIZATION: Pressure group opposed to immorality in entertainment
SIGNIFICANCE: This body grew from a local group into a nationwide organization working to eliminate pornographic and violent publications, television programs, and films

The CDL was founded in 1957 in Cincinnati by Charles H. Keating, Jr., a parent who was dismayed by displays in entertainment media of what he thought immoral. (Keating would later serve prison time for his part in the financial misdealings of a savings and loan.) He recruited local clergy and businessmen with the aim to pressure local law enforcement to close outlets for pornography. By the late 1960's the CDL had become a nationwide organization, with more than thirty local chapters. In 1968 it proved its strength as a lobby group in the public campaign against Abe Fortas' nomination to an associate justiceship on the U.S. Supreme Court.

In 1970 President Richard Nixon appointed Keating to the President's Commission on Obscenity and Pornography. Unhappy with what he regarded as the overly liberal conclusions of the commission's report, Keating and CDL members lobbied to ensure the report's rejection.

In 1973 the CDL changed its name (but not its acronym) to Citizens for Decency Through Law, and continued with its lobbying efforts. A decade and a half later, the body found that its campaigns were becoming less effective, so it again changed its name in 1989, this time to Children's Legal Foundation (CLF).

The group has worked to create an awareness in the United States of the harms associated with pornography and its distribution. The CLF assists law enforcement agencies and legislatures in enacting and enforcing ordinances and regulations that control pornography and obscenity that maybe harmful to youth. It publishes *The CLF Reporter*, a monthly newsletter distributed free to law enforcement agencies, churches, and libraries.

See also Morality; Morality in Media; National Organization for Decent Literature; Pornography; President's Commission on Obscenity and Pornography; Pressure groups.

Civil Rights movement

DATE: Mid-1950's-late 1960's
PLACE: Southern United States
SIGNIFICANCE: In a decade of militant action the Civil Rights movement reversed a century-long trend of the South's effectively censoring the African American voice by preventing them from exercising their full rights as citizens

The decade from the mid-1950's to the mid-1960's saw a new militancy in the battle for civil rights and social justice in the United States. Southern whites assured themselves that their struggle against school integration was entirely with forces and enemies external to their society: the Supreme Court, the National Association for the Advancement of Colored People (NAACP), Northern liberals, and Northern blacks. Southern whites justified much of their resistance to change as an effort to restore racial tranquillity and prevent contamination of the innocent Southern blacks from outside agitation. Belatedly Southern whites realized that Southern blacks had become the energizing source for the assault on discrimination.

In 1956 President Dwight D. Eisenhower proposed legislation to protect the right to vote that was guaranteed by the Fifteenth Amendment, but was persistently and flagrantly denied to African Americans. In 1957 he renewed his recommen-

Civil rights marchers converge on Washington, D.C. on August 28, 1963. (Library of Congress)

dation to protect voting rights, though Southern senators offered angry opposition. A compromise bill passed both chambers by overwhelming majorities. On September 9, 1957, Eisenhower signed the first civil rights act since the Grant Administration. The new bill created a Commission on Civil Rights, which had power to subpoena witnesses in its investigations of all violations of the right of citizens to vote based on color, race, religion, or national origin, and which was to report to the president. Creation of the commission was a direct blow to the censoring of African American voting activity.

In late 1955 African Americans exercised a First Amendment right and began boycotting public buses in Montgomery, Alabama. The segregated bus lines censored the races in compliance with state law and city ordinances. The boycotts challenged the direct action strategy utilized by leaders in the movement. The boycott continued throughout 1956, though white authorities attempted to censor activity by violent arrests and jail sentences. In November, 1956, the U.S. Supreme Court held the segregation laws invalid as violations of the Fourteenth Amendment, thereby rejecting the doctrine of separate but equal facilities, set forth by the Court in *Plessy v. Ferguson* in 1896.

In 1960 the NAACP launched an effective boycott of retail stores which practiced segregation at their lunch counters. Though the Ku Klux Klan, a censorship organization by design, worked vigorously to prevent the organization of African

Americans, the NAACP historically flourished under persecution and censorship. Efforts by Southern states to destroy or interfere with the NAACP were frustrated by a series of court decisions vindicating a citizen's right to expression by joining that organization.

Three significant factors contributed to equal rights and the erosion of censorship for all citizens: first, a series of Supreme Court decisions disposing of the last remnants of the separate but equal fiction, striking down the more overt forms of discrimination and giving some reality to the guarantees of equality; second, an aroused awareness of the potential power of the African American vote; and third, the decision to create interracial unity in the Civil Rights movement.

Presidential Influence. Passage of the Civil Rights Acts of 1957 and 1960 was speeded along by the bus boycott of 1955 and the sit-in demonstrations of 1960. In May, 1961, the Civil Rights movement was augmented by a freedom ride campaign initiated by the Congress of Racial Equality. As a result of this strategy, the executive branch of government was forced to take a stand. The Kennedy Administration voiced early criticism of Martin Luther King, Jr.'s campaign as it was launched in April, 1963, an indication of Kennedy's inclination to do little more than modestly improve civil rights legislation.

Once the events of the civil rights movement began to unfold and the repressive and censoring behavior of the police surfaced, President John F. Kennedy could no longer remain a neutral spectator. In the summer of 1963, approximately a quarter of a million people from various parts of the country converged on Washington, D.C., to dramatize demands for racial justice.

President Kennedy's posture on civil rights grew out of his confrontation with Governor George Wallace over a court order to admit two blacks to the University of Alabama. Kennedy delivered a dramatic attack on racial injustice, segregation, and discrimination and committed himself openly to strong and comprehensive legislation on civil rights. He later spelled out legislative proposals in a special message to Congress that gave birth to the Civil Rights Act of 1964. The president's death in late 1963 provided the final impetus for the early passage of this act in 1964.

Court Action. The U.S. Supreme Court took an increasingly active part in the defense of civil rights and liberties. By the 1960's, two thirds of its business was taken up by civil rights issues. Under Chief Justice Earl Warren the Court upheld guarantees of free speech and press against all kinds of censorship by striking down the libel charge against a newspaper and the reporting of racial injustice. The civil rights legislation strengthened the guarantees of the Fourteenth and Fifteenth amendments. The Civil Rights movement of the 1950's and 1960's contributed to the promises of equality and democracy. Millions of African Americans voted in the election of 1964 and provided an illustration of the power of African Americans in politics as well as the power of the Civil Rights movement. *—Lessie Bass Artis*

See also African Americans; King, Martin Luther, Jr.; Ku Klux Klan; National Association for the Advancement of Colored People; Newspapers, African American; Warren, Earl.

BIBLIOGRAPHY

H. J. Abraham in *Freedom and the Court* (New York: Oxford University Press, 1967) addresses the Supreme Court's role in the dismantling of segregation. Martin L. King, Jr., in *Where Do We Go from Here: Chaos or Community?* (Boston: Beacon Press, 1967) presents the quality and forces of interracial unity and community making. Benjamin B. Ringer in *"We the People" and Others: Duality and America's Treatment of Its Racial Minorities* (New York: Tavistock Publications, 1983) presents two decades of research into American race relations. Allan Nevins and Henry S. Commager in *A Pocket History of the United States* (New York: Washington Square Press, 1986) present detailed facts on the civil rights movement. Kermit L. Hall in *The Supreme Court of the United States* (Oxford University Press, 1992) presents topics on censorship in the United States and the Civil Rights movement.

Civil service

DEFINITION: Nonmilitary administrative staff responsible for implementing government programs

SIGNIFICANCE: Efforts to limit the politicization of a government's bureaucracy may limit public servants' freedom of expression

The development of bureaucracy as a form of public administration in the United States was popularized in the nineteenth century. It responded to the criticism that governmental positions were dispensed through a "spoils system" that rewarded party loyalists with government jobs. In some European countries, such jobs were literally purchased by wealthy individuals and families. This system did little, however, to ensure the objectivity, or even competence, of public servants. It also subjected the entire system to massive employee turnover whenever political leadership changed. To remedy this, the system of bureaucracy was designed to provide for the efficiency, objectivity, and accountability of public administration. (The British were among the first to successfully implement such a system on a large scale.) As defined by sociologist Max Weber and others, the bureaucracy should be a professional corps of government workers whose duty it is to implement policies and programs with a minimum of latitude.

As part of the development of bureaucracy, a system of civil service was established in various countries as a way to isolate personnel decisions from political exigencies. Hiring and promotion is accomplished through standardized tests and other criteria, and firing of employees with civil service status can only be carried out for documented reasons that meet established criteria. In all these ways, civil servants are protected from political pressures and retribution for such actions as "whistle-blowing." At the same time, however, the civil service places certain special restrictions on employees. As representatives of the government and not of particular parties or factions within it, civil servants have been barred from various forms of political expression. In addition, due to the crucial nature of governmental operations, civil servants have frequently been prevented from striking. These two sets of restrictions may constitute forms of censorship.

Restrictions. The prohibition on political activity by public employees has a long history in the United States. The 1883 Civil Service Act (Pendleton Act) created a Civil Service Commission (replaced in 1978 by the Office of Personnel Management and the Merit Systems Protection Board). Among other provisions, the Civil Service Act prohibited all employees of the U.S. government from making political contributions and endorsements. The act responded to the widespread perception, which rapidly escalated to public outrage after the Civil War, that federal employment had become a spoils system. The need to return the federal bureaucracy to its nonpoliticized ideal was assumed to outweigh restrictions upon federal employees' freedom of political action.

Further restrictions were adopted in later years. A decree by President Theodore Roosevelt in 1902 prohibited civil service employees from taking "any active part" in political campaigns. During the McCarthy era, many public employees were subject to loyalty oaths, which required that they renounce various political affiliations and beliefs. The Act to Prevent Pernicious Political Activities (passed in 1939 and amended in 1940, together known as the Hatch Act) elaborated on the provisions of Roosevelt's 1902 decree, prohibiting such activities as the raising of money for partisan causes, making campaign speeches, and distributing campaign material. It also barred federal employees from running for or holding political office themselves. The Hatch Act was inspired by revelations that federal employees were being coerced into contributing to partisan campaigns to protect their jobs. The restrictions on political activity were challenged twice in the Supreme Court, which upheld the constitutionality of the law both times. The Democrat-controlled U.S. Congress repeatedly tried to liberalize the Hatch Act in the 1970's and 1980's, but Republican presidents consistently vetoed reform measures that were passed.

A bill to reform the Hatch Act passed the Congress and was signed by Democratic president Bill Clinton in 1993. Under this legislation, federal employees were now permitted to engage in partisan political activity and to hold positions in political party organizations. Prohibitions against political activity during work hours, soliciting campaign funds, and the running for partisan political office remained, however.

Government employees also have been limited in their ability to launch "job actions." Many countries, including the United States, treat governmental employment as a public trust. This understanding places civil servants under a special set of regulations concerning hiring, firing, wages, raises, benefits, and other aspects of employment. Some of these, particularly restrictions on the ability to strike against what are perceived to be unfair working conditions, might be construed as limitations on expression. Yet many governments consider strikes to be a violation of sovereignty, in that they concede governmental authority to interest groups. There are also practical considerations about the necessity of delivering public services.

Various limitations of this type were placed upon federal employees in the United States during the twentieth century. President Theodore Roosevelt's 1902 decree prohibited employees in the U.S. executive branch from soliciting pay increases. Federal employees were granted the right to organize in 1912, but collective bargaining was still severely restricted. Federal employees are not permitted to strike, as affirmed in the Taft-Hartley Act of 1947. The act held that striking federal workers would be "discharged immediately . . . and shall forfeit [their] civil service status, if any, and shall not be eligible for employment for three years by the United States or any such agency." A strike by federal air traffic controllers in the 1980's highlighted this issue, and President Ronald Reagan's subsequent firing of the striking workers underscored the government's determination to enforce the law's provisions.

The administration of governmental programs and policies through a civil service thus draws in a number of censorship issues. If the civil service is required to be nonpolitical and nonpartisan, limitations upon political activity by civil servants clearly are necessary. The need for restrictions is underscored by the corruption that has been manifest in their absence. Further, if the provision of some governmental services is understood to be critical, then restrictions on job actions must be in place. The debate concerning such limitations upon civil servants entails, as it often does with censorship issues, the balance between individual rights and the public good.

—Steve D. Boilard

See also Classification of information; Federal Bureau of Investigation; Hatch Act; House Committee on Un-American Activities; Loyalty oaths; Military censorship; National security; Political campaigning.

BIBLIOGRAPHY

For a general overview of civil service in the United States, see Robert Maranto and David Shultz's *A Short History of the United States Civil Service* (Lanham, Md.: University Press of America, 1991). On political aspects, including limitations on political activity, see Robert P. Dwoskin, *Rights of the Public Employee* (Chicago: American Library Association, 1978); Yong S. Lee, "Free Speech and Organizational Politics," chapter 3 of his *Public Personnel Administration and Constitutional Vices* (Westport, Conn.: Quorum Books, 1992); Robert B. Denhardt, "The Political Context of Public Administration," chapter 2 of his *Public Administration: An Action Orientation* (2d ed. Belmont, Calif.: Wadsworth Publishing, 1995); and Ronald D. Sylvia, *Critical Issues in Public Personnel Policy* (Pacific Grove, Calif.: Brooks/Cole, 1989). Comparative analysis can be found in Bruce L. R. Smith, ed., *The Higher Civil Service in Europe and Canada: Lessons for the United States* (Washington, D.C.: Brookings, 1984).

Civil War, U.S.

DATE: 1861-1865

PLACE: United States

SIGNIFICANCE: The Civil War proved that public communications could provide vital information to the enemy; policies developed during the war served as precedents for future censorship policies

Technologies developed during the decades preceding the Civil War allowed news and information to be transmitted more rapidly and efficiently. The telegraph enabled reporters to send stories to their home offices almost immediately. The steam printing press increased production and lowered costs, and throughout the nation newspaper circulation rose dramatically. New transportation systems, especially railroads, permitted the speedy distribution of newspapers and mail over wide areas. These remarkable changes posed unprecedented challenges for military and civilian leaders in the North and the South at the outbreak of the Civil War in April, 1861. The easy transmission of information raised fears that military secrets could intentionally or inadvertently be made available to the enemy.

Early Censorship. Lacking clearly established precedents for censorship, the Union government's early policies were conducted in a haphazard fashion. Authorities were uncertain as to which government department was responsible for creating and implementing censorship policies. The Post Office waited for days after war had been declared before it refused to send mail into enemy territory. Although the State Department began censoring telegraph communications from Washington, D.C., in April, 1861, transmissions between the North and South continued for more than a month until Union officials seized thousands of telegrams that implicated Northerners in Southern plots.

In July, 1861, the commander of the Union Army, General Winfield Scott, issued a censorship order that banned telegraph companies from transmitting any military information without his approval. Scott changed the order a few days later, permitting reporters to send reports concerning battles in progress that did not include information about troop movements. Less than two weeks later, during the disastrous Union defeat at Bull Run, the first major battle of the war, Scott again changed his order and imposed full censorship on reporters. Unaware of the battle's true outcome, newspapers in New York and Washington reported a fantastic Union victory. The confusion that resulted in the Northern press and populace as a result of Scott's censorship orders indicated the need for a more coherent policy.

In August, 1861, several prominent Northern reporters met with Union general George B. McClellan and agreed not to report any information that would assist the enemy. In return for their voluntary self-censorship, the reporters would receive full government cooperation in obtaining and reporting all other news. McClellan could not ensure government cooperation, however, because the official censor, H. E. Thayer, was under the authority of the State Department. When Secretary of State William H. Seward ordered Thayer to ban all telegraph communications from Washington, D.C., concerning military and civil operations, the press argued that the government had violated the agreement and the voluntary censorship plan was abandoned.

Press complaints about Seward's order prompted a congressional investigation in December, 1861. Released four months later in March, 1862, the investigating committee's final report cited the numerous failures of the censorship policy, including inefficiency, favoritism toward certain reporters, and the censoring of material that violated no military secrets. The report concluded that Seward's censorship order was far too broad and that censorship should be limited to military information that would be useful to the enemy.

By the time the committee released its report important policy changes had already occurred. Congress had already clarified the issue of departmental authority in January, 1862, when it granted the president the power to regulate the use of telegraph transmissions. Secretary of War Edwin M. Stanton requested that President Abraham Lincoln transfer responsibility for controlling the telegraph lines from the State Department to the War Department, a request that Lincoln approved that same day. Stanton immediately acted to articulate and enforce a new censorship policy.

Stanton and Censorship. On February 25, 1862, Stanton issued a new censorship order that required all telegraph communications regarding military operations to receive official military approval before they were transmitted. Stanton appointed a military supervisor to manage all telegraph messages and a military superintendent to manage the telegraph lines and offices throughout the United States. Stanton also threatened to punish any newspaper that published unauthorized military news by prohibiting that paper from using the telegraph or the railroads. This threat raised such an outcry from the press that Stanton quickly modified that order to ban only the publication of military news that had occurred that same day.

Stanton hoped that his strict censorship order would eliminate sensitive military information from news reports, but the order proved difficult to enforce. Censors did a poor job,

newsman looked for alternative methods for sending stories to their editors, and officers could be convinced to release a questionable story in return for a positive mention in the press. The main achievement of Stanton's order was the establishment of a precedent of a formal censorship policy and the clarification of lines of authority for that policy.

Generals in the field proved the most effective enforcers of censorship. Many generals hated reporters, whom they believed put the military's plans and its men at risk when they wrote their stories. Weary of press criticism, General Henry W. Halleck banned all noncombatants from his army. While Halleck justified the order as a security measure aimed at Southern spies, press correspondents claimed that the general intended to silence the press. Union general William T. Sherman nursed a special contempt for the press. He had little patience for reporters, accusing them of informing the enemy and of sowing dissension in the Union ranks. In return reporters constantly attacked Sherman—a story published early in the war claimed that he was insane. Angered by a *New York Herald* story, Sherman had the reporter, Thomas Knox, arrested on charges of spying. Sherman knew that Knox was not a spy, but hoped to set an example. Knox was later acquitted of the spying charge, but he was banned from the army. By banning most reporters from the field, Halleck, Sherman, and other generals censored the press and prevented the passage of information to the enemy and to the American public.

Although military leaders often scorned newspaper reporting, attempts at total censorship of military information proved disastrous to the war effort. In late 1862 General Halleck ordered a complete news blackout on information concerning the Army of Virginia, which was responsible for protecting Washington, D.C. In the absence of any reliable news, rumors spread through the city that the army had been defeated and the Confederates were preparing to invade. Confusion and a sense of crisis seized the populace, and confidence in the government waned. The blackout ended and government leaders learned that the public required reliable news in order to support the war. Selectivity, not a complete gag on the press, was required for censorship to be effective.

Military news was not the only information subject to censorship in the North. Opposition to the war, especially from Northern Democrats known as Copperheads, resulted in harsh criticism of the government and the military. President Lincoln was a frequent target. Northern officials had to determine at what point the expression of opposition became detrimental to the conduct of the war, or perhaps even treasonous.

In April, 1863, Union general Ambrose E. Burnside issued General Orders Number Thirty-eight, which declared that anyone expressing sympathy for the enemy would be arrested and face possible execution if found guilty of violating the order. Former Ohio congressman Clement Laird Vallandigham, a vocal opponent of the war who detested Lincoln, responded to the order by giving two speeches in which he fiercely attacked the president. Burnside had Vallandigham arrested three days later. Convicted of violating the order, Vallandigham was sentenced to prison. Lincoln ordered Vallandigham transported to Confederate lines and banished from the Union. While Lincoln and his cabinet supported Burnside during the Vallandigham episode, Lincoln later decided that the government had exceeded its authority in the incident.

Press stories and criticism also brought official reaction. In May, 1864, two New York newspapers printed a forged presidential document ordering the drafting of 400,000 men. The printing of the false document could have caused bloody draft riots similar to those that racked the city in 1863. Military censors leaped at the chance to suppress the papers, both of which had been critical of the war. The papers were closed, and their editors were imprisoned for two days. In the Midwest, Wilbur F. Storey, owner and publisher of the *Chicago Times*, published a series of editorials condemning abolition and the conduct of the war. In late May, 1864, the paper printed a story that maligned General Burnside, Republican leaders, and the president, whom the article implied had become mentally unbalanced. Two days later Burnside ordered the paper closed for three days. While Lincoln sympathized with Burnside's reaction, he deemed his response as too extreme and politically imprudent. The order was rescinded. Lincoln's cautious attitude toward the Vallandigham and Storey cases reveals that the president believed that speech and press censorship were politically sensitive issues in a democracy. Requiring public support to continue the war, the president could not alienate potential allies who might be offended by a strict censorship policy. Lincoln ably balanced the needs of a nation at war with the tradition of a free press in America.

Southern Censorship. Lacking adequate resources to cover the war, several Southern publishers met in 1862 and formed a pool for sharing correspondents and information. Headed by J. S. Thrasher, the Press Association of the Confederate States of America fought military censorship of news dispatches. Thrasher met with Confederate general P. G. T. Beauregard in 1863 to protest censorship policies. He maintained that Southern newspapers held to the highest standards and would never publish sensitive information. Impressed by Thrasher's arguments, Beauregard ordered military commanders to assist reporters in transmitting their dispatches. Compliance was spotty, however, and throughout the war obstinate Confederate officers refused to aid reporters.

Although Southern military commanders often attempted to prevent the press from using telegraph lines to send messages, the most significant problems that Southern publishers faced stemmed from popular attitudes and material conditions. Always ready to criticize the government and the military for their failures, the Southern press nonetheless supported the Confederate cause. Any editor unwise enough to condemn the ultimate aims of the South faced the public's wrath and indignation. Southern publishers who might hold unpopular attitudes toward slavery or the Confederacy imposed a degree of voluntary censorship on their editorial policy out of self-interest. As the war progressed, manpower and paper shortages limited the effectiveness of the Southern press far more than any government censorship policy.

—Thomas Clarkin

See also Democracy; Mexican-American War; Military censorship; Newspapers; Sedition; War.

BIBLIOGRAPHY

J. Cutler Andrews' *The North Reports the Civil War* (Pittsburgh: University of Pittsburgh Press, 1955) presents detailed information on press censorship. Sidney Kobre's *Foundations of American Journalism* (Westport, Conn.: Greenwood Press, 1970) includes a brief discussion of Civil War censorship, while Michael Emery and Edwin Emery's *The Press and America: An Interpretive History of the Mass Media* (6th ed. Englewood Cliffs, N.J.: Prentice-Hall, 1988) offers a concise chapter on the same subject. Stephen W. Sears's article "The First News Blackout," in *American Heritage* 36, no. 4 (June-July, 1985), discusses the issues facing the press and military during the war. Frank Luther Mott's *American Journalism: A History, 1690-1960* (3d ed. New York, N.Y.: Macmillan, 1962) provides information on the problems of the Southern press.

Clan of the Cave Bear, The

TYPE OF WORK: Book
PUBLISHED: 1980
AUTHOR: Jean Auel (1936-   )
SUBJECT MATTER: Novel about a young woman living during the Ice Age
SIGNIFICANCE: This popular best-selling novel detailing prehistoric society contains naturalistic depictions of human sexuality that have prompted controversy in school districts

The Clan of the Cave Bear, the first book in Jean Auel's *Earth's Children* series, attempts to re-create an Upper Paleolithic (Ice Age) community complete with all its social components, including sexuality. In this prehistoric environment, sexual acts occur in a naturalistic manner—sometimes with violence—without recourse to religious decrees or principles. Numerous censorship conflicts resulted after the book's publication. In 1993 Tom Baldwin, a trustee of the Moorpark Unified School District in Ventura County, California, attempted to remove it and other Auel novels from the eleventh grade recommended reading list. The book, he maintained, contained "hardcore graphic sexual conduct." A seven-member committee unanimously defeated his action and Auel's novels stayed in the high school library. English teacher Peggy Blakelock argued that "the right to read what you want is basic to democratic society." Earlier, in 1985, parents at a San Antonio, Texas, high school disrupted school board meetings in an attempt to have the novel removed from library shelves.

See also Banned Books Week; Libraries; Libraries, school; Sex in the arts.

Classification of information

DEFINITION: Government use of specific secrecy categories to control access to information
SIGNIFICANCE: Originally designed to protect military secrets, document classification has also been used to restrict public knowledge of government activity and limit access to information

Governments have always tried to keep information on their military and diplomatic activities secret. The more authoritarian the system, the more information is kept from the public, whether by classification systems or deliberate censorship. In the former Soviet Union, not only military data but also information on economic, political, and cultural affairs were state secrets unless release served some national purpose. Publication of data on the size of grain harvests—information that often deviated from official propaganda—was punishable as espionage. Relentless censorship made it difficult or impossible for anyone to evaluate official claims and policies critically. Democracies have also used strict controls during wartime, but not until the onset of the Cold War in the wake of World War II did the U.S. government begin to keep massive amounts of information about its activities secret.

Formal Classification. The formal use of classification systems that specified different degrees of secrecy to be observed in protecting various information developed in the twentieth century. The American and Canadian systems copied that of Great Britain. The earliest use of such a system by the United States occurred during World War I, when the American Expeditionary Force in France adopted the terms used by the British. The use of such designations in the United States, however, was sporadic and unofficial until the onset of World War II.

The backbone of the British system was the Official Secrets Act of 1911, enacted during a diplomatic crisis with Germany, which went beyond previous laws that had dealt only with spying. This act made it a criminal offense, punishable by fines or imprisonment, to receive and retain official information as well as to disclose it. Although the act applied to all government documents, not merely those with classification marks, some documents were stamped with designations indicating the degree of care to be observed in preventing unauthorized access to them. The World War I classification categories were "Restricted," "Confidential," and "Secret" ("Most Secret" or "Top Secret" would be added by the 1940's).

The act tended to be used more to restrain the press from printing classified information than to punish civil servants who might purposely or inadvertently release information. Armed with the threat of prosecution under the act, the government could issue a so-called D-notice to the press indicating that publication of certain documents could result in criminal charges. Only those willing to sustain a costly and lengthy court battle would ignore such a notice. As originally drawn, the language of the 1911 act seemed to apply to all official information, no matter how innocuous. The 1989 revision of the Official Secrets Act reduced the number of classes of restricted information while increasing possible penalties for publishing leaks.

Canada, which follows British parliamentary traditions, has its own Official Secrets Act that criminalizes leaking classified documents. The United States has never enacted an official secrets law. Its classification system developed through presidential executive orders; violations are punishable as crimes under espionage statutes.

World War II and the Cold War. After the end of World War I, the U.S. Army and U.S. Navy continued using "Secret," "Confidential," and "Restricted" security markings for internal documents, even though the practice had no basis in law. Procedures in the State Department were even less formal. In

March, 1940, President Franklin Delano Roosevelt, worried about possible espionage and sabotage after World War II began in Europe, issued an executive order regularizing use of the armed forces' three security markings. President Harry S Truman added "Top Secret" as a fourth designation in 1950.

These executive orders defined "Top Secret" information as military, diplomatic, and intelligence data the disclosure of which could result in exceptionally grave damage to the nation; "Secret" applied to information that could cause serious damage to the nation. The "Confidential" classification covered material considered prejudicial to the national defense, while "Restricted" identified information intended for official use only and not to be given to the general public.

The Atomic Energy Act of 1946, which established federal control over all aspects of atomic energy research and development, provided that all data on nuclear materials was, in effect, "born classified." No decision was necessary to determine whether the information needed protection; its publication required an active decision that removal of secrecy was in the national interest.

As the Cold War intensified, fears of Soviet espionage and internal subversion opened the way for Senator Joseph McCarthy's accusations that the Truman Administration was riddled with spies and communist sympathizers. Truman responded in 1951 by extending use of the security classification system beyond the traditional military field. Secrecy was justified in the name of "national security," a vague and infinitely expandable category. All civilian agencies of the government were authorized to use classification marks and to withhold documents and information from the public; elaborate rules were developed for the physical protection of classified documents.

The expanded use of classification to keep information from the public and the increasing number of secret documents led to many complaints. Critics claimed that agencies used the classification system to cover up mistakes, that overclassification kept much information secret that needed no protection, and that failure to declassify older documents hindered public understanding of past official activities and policies. The complaints led to a series of efforts to reform the classification system.

Reform Efforts. Every American president from Dwight D. Eisenhower to Jimmy Carter attempted to reduce use of the classification system. Objections to the Truman system led Eisenhower to issue an executive order in November, 1953, limiting the number of agencies that could use classification markings, defining more precisely the purposes of classification, and eliminating the "Restricted" category.

Other executive orders by both Eisenhower and John F. Kennedy attempted to reduce the volume of classified material by further narrowing the number of people and agencies authorized to classify and by establishing procedures for declassifying and downgrading secret documents. Their efforts had little effect. Bureaucrats found it safer to classify than to risk being accused of revealing secrets.

The problem of overclassification intensified. Eliminating "Restricted" made "Confidential" seem a weak category, and material that might otherwise have been so classified was often designated "Secret." Over time, a number of categories above "Top Secret" developed (classifications so secret that their names themselves are classified), as agency heads tried to limit access to information even among those cleared for "Top Secret" materials. In 1968, Secretary of Defense Robert McNamara, testifying before the Senate Foreign Relations Committee, mentioned that he held some twenty-five separate clearances for access to material classified beyond "Top Secret."

Provisions in the Eisenhower and Kennedy executive orders requiring those responsible for classification to designate dates when the documents would automatically be declassified had little effect; there were too many grounds for exceptions that agency heads could exploit. Most records, once classified, remained classified. When it was politically useful, officials could always anonymously "leak" classified material to friendly reporters.

Discontent with this situation led Congress to pass the 1966 Freedom of Information Act, designed to make the right to know, rather than secrecy, the basic principle of American information policy. The act provided that if a federal agency refused a request for information, citizens could seek relief through the courts. The act provided nine general exemptions to shield defense and intelligence data, as well as information that would violate personal privacy. By creative use of these provisions, and by various obstructive tactics—denying that the information requested existed, claiming difficulty in finding documents, or demanding excessive sums for copying them—agencies could nevertheless effectively evade the intent of the act.

When the House of Representatives began hearings on complaints about classification in 1972, President Richard Nixon moved to maintain presidential control of the field and prevent legislative action. He issued an executive order reducing the number of agencies authorized to use secrecy classifications and provided for automatic declassification of documents after thirty years. The many exceptions to the order, however, meant it had little effect on government secrecy. In 1978, President Jimmy Carter reduced the automatic period to twenty years and urged that, in cases of doubt, lower or no classification be used.

Reagan and Clinton Administrations. In 1982, Ronald Reagan issued a classification order that for the first time in thirty years provided less public access to information and called for more classification. The order eliminated automatic declassification, increased the number and types of records to be kept secret, extended the power to classify to new agencies, and encouraged agencies to classify when in doubt. Reagan also empowered agencies to reclassify and recall documents previously declassified and published, making it impossible to use information in these documents in discussions of public policy. Other Reagan directives introduced a vague new category, "nonclassified but classifiable." Federal employees were instructed to keep such material secret.

Not until President Bill Clinton issued an executive order on April 17, 1995, were the Reagan Administration policies over-turned. Once again, the rule was to be, "When in doubt, do not classify." A new procedure, to be phased in over the following five years, would automatically declassify all documents more than twenty-five years old. Officials wanting to exempt a document from this procedure would have to justify the decision before a Security Classification Appeals Panel. No one knew how many documents might be affected by this process. The National Archives estimated that it held some 300 million to 400 million classified documents dating from the World War I era to 1956; possibly as many more recent records were locked in departmental files.

Critics were skeptical that Clinton's order would be any more effective than past attempts at reform, given the record of obstructiveness and creative use of the power to make exceptions that government agencies had shown in the past. Classifying information had proven too useful in facilitating official lying, and in preventing official embarrassment by hiding incompetence and illegality, for bureaucrats to surrender such a powerful protective device willingly.

Others worried about the effect of elaborate classification systems on the processes of democratic government. Revelations of the abuse of secrecy to cover up government misconduct and lying under President Nixon in the Watergate affair and during the Iran-Contra scandal of the Reagan years eroded public confidence in government. Secrecy might be needed in some military and intelligence areas or be vital in autocratic regimes, but its compatibility with democracies during peacetime remained an open question. Overclassification and delays in declassification could hide vital information about public policy, leaving Congress and the voters unable to evaluate or control the actions of the administration. The greater the degree of secrecy, the nearer the approach to authoritarian patterns. By shielding official acts from public knowledge, secrecy makes government accountability difficult.

—Milton Berman

See also Archival laws; Defense ("D") notices; Espionage; Freedom of Information Act; Iran-Contra scandal; Nixon, Richard M.; Nuclear research and testing; Official Secrets Act (Canada); Official Secrets Act (U.K.); *Pentagon Papers, The*; Police states; Reagan, Ronald; Watergate scandal.

BIBLIOGRAPHY

United States Government Information Policies: Views and Perspectives, edited by Charles R. McClure, Peter Hernon, and Harold Relyea (Norwood, N.J.: Ablex, 1989), is a collection of articles on the classification system and other aspects of government information policy. Carol M. Barker and Matthew H. Fox's *Classified Files: The Yellowing Pages; a Report on Scholars' Access to Government Documents* (New York: Twentieth Century Fund, 1972) describes the development and operation of the classification system. *Secrecy and Foreign Policy* (New York: Oxford University Press, 1974), edited by Thomas M. Frank and Edward Weisband, provides a careful examination of policy considerations, as well as comparative material on Canada and Great Britain. *Government Secrecy in Democracies* (New York: New York University Press, 1977), edited by Itzhak Galnoor, compares secrecy policies in ten democratic countries. David Wise's *The Politics of*

Lying: Government Deception, Secrecy, and Power (New York: Random House, 1973) includes a detailed description of the use of classification markings. Richard Thurlow's *The Secret State: British Internal Security in the Twentieth Century* (Oxford, England: Blackwell, 1995) is a thorough history of the British system, including consideration of the revised Official Secrets Act of 1989. Walter Laqueur's *A World of Secrets: The Uses and Limits of Intelligence* (New York: Basic Books, 1985) contrasts intelligence activities and secrecy policies of Communist and Western nations.

Clean Up Television Campaign (CUTV)

FOUNDED: 1978

TYPE OF ORGANIZATION: American group dedicated to promoting decency in television programming

SIGNIFICANCE: This group has been responsible for pressuring the sponsors of television programs they deemed objectionable

The CUTV is an American organization based on a similar British body that began in the 1960's. It is made up of religious and civil groups that felt insulted by the indecent acts represented on daily television programs, such as scenes of adultery or sexual perversion and scenes portraying immoral acts as humorous. The CUTV has initiated boycott campaigns against product sponsors of programs thought to be offensive and negative influences on young people. The CUTV achieved some success in revising television programming in the early 1980's. Its most notable achievement was helping to hasten cancellation of the popular sitcom *Soap*.

See also Action for Children's Television; Coalition for Better Television; Foundation to Improve Television; National Federation for Decency; Television.

Clear and present danger doctrine

DEFINITION: A legal test to decide whether certain kinds of speech are protected by the First Amendment of the U.S. Constitution

SIGNIFICANCE: This test permits restraint of the First Amendment freedoms of speech and press only where there is an immediate threat to what the government may legitimately protect

The need to balance the interests of society against the rights of the individual is one of the great themes of American constitutional law. The balancing process is never an easy one; however, it is particularly difficult where the security of the nation is juxtaposed against fundamental First Amendment freedoms. Supreme Court efforts to achieve a workable balance have produced several tests for determining when governments may restrain speech.

The first and most famous of these tests, the clear and present danger doctrine, was developed by Justice Oliver Wendell Holmes in a case arising under the World War I Espionage Act of 1917. Writing for the Supreme Court in *Schenck v. United States* (1919), Justice Holmes adopted a nonabsolutist interpretation of First Amendment rights. "The character of every act," he noted, "depends upon the circumstances in which it is done. The most stringent protection of free speech would not protect a man in falsely shouting 'fire' in a theater, and causing a panic. . . . The question in every case is whether the words used are used in such circumstances and are of such a nature as to create a clear and present danger that they will bring about the substantive evils that Congress has a right to prevent."

Although the clear and present danger test was used in *Schenck v. United States* to sustain wartime restrictions of speech and press, it is actually a demanding test of government's ability to restrain fundamental freedoms. First, the state must demonstrate an intent to cause the evils that governments may legitimately prevent; then it must prove that the accused's activities caused, or would have caused, those evils to occur. By contrast, most other tests fashioned by the Supreme Court in this area have been more favorably disposed toward sustaining government action. The "bad tendency" test fashioned a year after the Schenck decision, for example, essentially reduced the government's burden of proof to showing that the proscribed activities have a tendency to result in antisocial or antigovernment behavior (*Schaefer v. United States*, 1920; *Gitlow v. New York*, 1925). Likewise, in the Cold War case of *Dennis v. United States* (1951), the Supreme Court dropped the immediacy requirement of the clear and present danger in sustaining national security legislation aimed at countering the threat posed to the country by the international criminal conspiracy represented by the Communist Party of the United States. Where such conspiracies exist, the Supreme Court held, the state need only show the probability that, over time, proscribed activities might endanger the United States.

The clear and present danger rule has remained a basic judicial tool used by courts in trying to draw the ever difficult line between what the government may legitimately restrain and what the First Amendment protects. Famous cases testing the clear and present danger rule have ranged from the right of neo-Nazis to march through a predominantly Jewish neighborhood to the right of computer users to disseminate bomb-building instructions over the Internet.

See also Espionage Act of 1917; First Amendment; Holmes, Oliver Wendell, Jr.; Internet; National security; *Schenck v. United States*; Skokie, Illinois, Nazi march; World War I.

Coalition for Better Television (CBT)

FOUNDED: 1981

TYPE OF ORGANIZATION: Mississippi-based body dedicated to combatting negative images on television

SIGNIFICANCE: An organization formed to voice its objection to vulgarity and violence on television

The CBT was formed in Tupelo, Mississippi, by the Reverend Donald Wildmon. Claiming to represent more than five million families, the organization has vowed to battle the violence, profanity, sex, and obscenity that is available to everyone through commercial television. It began as a branch of the National Federation for Decency, also based in Tupelo, and has since been absorbed into that body.

See also Action for Children's Television; Clean Up Television Campaign; Foundation to Improve Television; National Federation for Decency; Television.

Coercion Acts

DATE: 1817

PLACE: United Kingdom (national)

SIGNIFICANCE: This legislation was designed to restrict basic English civil liberties during a period of civil unrest

Fueled by the liberal sentiments of the French Revolution and by post-Napoleonic War unemployment and inflation, radical disturbances swept Great Britain in 1816-1817. In the Midland region, for example, rioters known as Luddites destroyed factories and mills. In London a meeting called by John Cartwright erupted into a riot that resulted in loss of life and property destruction. Fearful that such civil unrest might provoke a revolution, Britain's Tory cabinet pushed a series of bills restricting basic civil liberties through Parliament during a single week in 1817. Collectively known as the Coercion Acts, these three bills suspended the Habeas Corpus Act of 1697, extended the provisions of the Seditious Meeting and Assembly Act of 1795, and refined the definition of treason under the Treasonable and Seditious Practice Act of 1795. The Coercion Acts restricted rights to a speedy trial, required a magistrate's permission for any type of meeting—even scholarly lectures—and classified as treason any attempt to subvert the loyalty of military personnel.

Denouncing the Coercion Acts as governmental "gagging" of civil liberties, a group of petitioners called Blanketeers (after the blankets that they carried for nighttime shelter) began a protest march from Manchester to London. They failed, however, to deliver their petition to Parliament once their leaders were arrested. They disbanded at Macclesfield.

See also Censorship; Fear; Free speech; Police states; Sedition; United Kingdom.

Colonialism

DEFINITION: European rule over African and Asian countries

SIGNIFICANCE: When the colonized peoples began striving for independence, the European colonial powers typically responded by attempting to keep revolutionary parties and literature out of their colonies although the colonizing powers themselves usually had long traditions of political and intellectual freedom

Colonialism consisted of the political, social, and economic control of large populations and geographic areas by foreign powers. Colonialism is an ancient concept, but its most extensive period of development occurred between 1880 and 1960, and concerned the major European powers and the continents of Africa and Asia. Censorship was one of the major tools the imperial countries used to diffuse the desire for independence that the populations of the colonies had in the later stages of the colonial era.

Censorship can be defined as the suppression of certain types of literature by government agencies because of its politically volatile nature. In the case of the modern colonial powers, such literature included the expression of independence movements and nationalistic rebellions. Censorship can also be defined as the suppression of certain types of political thinking, expressed by membership in nationalistic or revolutionary political parties. For example, the European powers made membership in certain political parties, especially the Communist Party, illegal in their colonies. Finally, censorship was not only the exclusion of certain types of literature or of certain types of thinking, but the propagation of "approved" literature in the hope that it will encourage politically volatile information to be ignored or discounted. An example is government-sponsored political parties, whose purpose was to lure membership away from radical, or independence-minded, parties.

Asian Colonies. Great Britain's major colony in Asia was India. The development of newspapers there was the method by which ideas such as freedom and democracy permeated the Indian middle class. The development of these newspapers was entirely due to private enterprise, and official British policy was to regard them with varying degrees of suspicion. Ironically, it was the lack of censorship that allowed *The Calcutta Press* to publish inflammatory articles against British policy in 1905. Those articles began a process that led to Indian independence in 1947. The leader of the Indian independence movement, Mohandas Gandhi, was the main target of British censorship because he became popular and his ideas were taken seriously. To silence Gandhi, the British jailed him, eventually triggering a hunger strike that produced a general protest resulting in his being released. Continuing to preach independence, Gandhi successfully resisted attempts at British censorship.

Between 1880 and 1895 the major European powers divided China into "spheres of influence," wherein the economic interests of the Europeans were paramount. In response, a secret Chinese society known as the Boxers came into being and began to agitate for the expulsion of the Europeans. Despite vigorous attempts to suppress the Boxer movement by the Europeans and the Americans, the Boxers revolted in 1899. The revolt triggered a response by American, European, and Japanese troops, who quickly put down the rebellion. The attempt by powers such as the United States, with long traditions of freedoms of the press and speech, at censorship in China was viewed by Chinese patriots as evidence of Western duplicity. It was undoubtedly one of the causes of later animosity between China and the Western world.

France's control of its Indo-Chinese colonies rested on its efforts to suppress the Vietnamese independence movement. French censorship of independence literature focused on the writings of Karl Marx and Ho Chi Minh. French efforts to censor Vietnamese thought spilled over into political life. In its attempt to censor the Communist Party, France appeared two-faced to the Vietnamese because of the long tradition of socialist involvement in French home politics. After the French were evicted from Vietnam in 1954 they were effectively replaced by the Americans. Attempts by the United States to censor Vietnamese politics made the Americans appear as duplicitous as the French had been.

In order to retain possession of the Dutch East Indies (Indonesia), The Netherlands also felt compelled to suppress nationalist literature. To do this, they required schools to teach only in the Malay and Javanese languages. This policy helped the Dutch keep the Indonesians away from revolutionary literature by slowing the penetration of European ideas of freedom and nationalism into Indonesia. Through such subtle censorship the Dutch maintained their empire well into the twentieth century.

African Colonies. In response to Kenya's so-called Mau Mau Rebellion in the 1950's, the British declared an emergency that lasted almost ten years. In order to prevent a recurrence of apparently random violence, many African leaders were jailed without benefit of trial. Jomo Kenyatta, the leading proponent of Kenyan independence, was jailed in order to silence his claim that violent revolution was the quickest route to independence.

British censorship in Africa contrasted sharply with the political freedoms exercised in Great Britain and India. Generally, Britain suppressed independence movements and those who spoke out in favor of them in Africa throughout the period in question.

France's African colonies were ruled by governor generals who possessed the right to interfere with local African politics. Although Africans were allowed to hold government positions, only those educated in France or in French schools were accepted. This policy was itself a form of censorship because it prevented native cultures and languages from achieving positions of respect in upper governmental levels. In Algeria, France's assimilation policy met stern resistance by the independence movement that gained momentum after World War II. By the 1950's the French were engaged in a policy of systematic repression of this movement and strict censorship of independence literature. Membership in the Algerian Freedom Party was made illegal, and suspected leaders of the party were either jailed or forced into exile.

Prior to World War II, Belgium attempted to control the population of the Belgian Congo by a system known as paternalism. In order to keep workers content, government-sponsored villages were constructed near where the men worked. These villages provided schools, medical care, churches, and other services to the workers and their families. Belgium's "cradle-to-grave" care can be regarded as a form of censorship because its intention was to keep the Congolese pacified and content with few political rights. With education controlled by the government, topics such as African history and political theory were omitted in order to prevent their spread. After the breakdown of paternalism, other attempts at censorship were made. In January of 1959, riots broke out over the issue of independence in the city of Leopoldville. Radio Leopoldville discounted the severity of these riots and even denied their existence. Belgian motives remain unclear, but because the denial of the disturbances ultimately resulted in their increasing violence, they may have been an attempt to discredit the methods of the Congo's independence parties.

All of the major colonial powers in Africa felt it necessary to prevent the spread of the writings of Marcus Garvey. His philosophy of black nationalism, the idea that black people throughout the world shared a common history and a common destiny, was deemed dangerous to European interests. Garvey claimed that Africa should be "redeemed" from white rule and to that end he created the Universal Negro Improvement Asso-

ciation (UNIA). The UNIA was made illegal in most African colonies.

Arguments for Censorship. The colonial powers, including the United States, approved the use of censorship in their colonies. One argument in favor of censorship was the claim that colonized peoples, being new to Western civilization, did not understand where their best interests lay. This thinking held that the older, more sophisticated European countries had the colonial people's interests at heart. In a world of dangerous ideologies, allowing colonial people to choose for themselves might result in their destruction. Because of their innocent condition, colonial people should be protected, for their own good, from the more dangerous types of political thinking. At some time in the future, the argument continued, when the colonial people were "mature," they would be allowed to choose their reading material and their politics for themselves. Censorship, in this argument, became a positive good because it would prevent dangerous philosophies and political beliefs from inflicting people who were not mature or sophisticated enough to separate good from evil. The colonial powers would provide the service of protecting the colonized people from those dangerous doctrines which could destroy them, until such time when they could safely decide for themselves.

Another argument for censorship was the idea that colonized people were vulnerable to the economic exploitation of private monied interests. As their protectors, the European powers would prevent the exposure of colonized people to the lure of profit, until such time as the colonies became economically mature.

Arguments Against Censorship. The first argument against the use of censorship in the colonies was the long tradition of freedom of the press and speech in the imperial powers' home countries. Comparing their censored environment to the freedoms enjoyed by the colonialists, the colonial subjects might develop an inferiority syndrome which could spill over into the postcolonial period and stunt the growth of democratic institutions.

The second argument threw doubt upon the commitment of the colonial powers to their colonies' better interests. Claiming that the colonialists merely wanted to remain in power, the suppression of revolutionary literature and revolutionary parties was simply the method by which that end was achieved. Colonies existed to benefit the mother countries economically; once a colony achieved independence, its mother country would lose money. Communist literature and nationalistic parties were censored to keep the colonized people from learning this lesson, and the imperialists were able to remain in power.

A final argument against censorship was the claim that it fostered hostility among the African or Asian peoples and the European powers. The argument held that in the long run censorship damaged the interests of the imperialists. After independence the hostility created by censorship would cause the newly independent nation to cut all economic ties with the Europeans. Conversely, an open and free environment during the colonial period would result in a continuing economic relationship in the post-colonial period. —*Tim Palmer*

See also Burma; Garvey, Marcus; India; Indonesia; Vietnam; Zimbabwe.

BIBLIOGRAPHY

No thorough work on censorship in European colonies in the twentieth century exists, but Stewart C. Easton provides some examples in *The Twilight of European Colonialism* (New York: Holt, Rinehart and Winston, 1960). An explanation of Western behavior in Asia and the Asian response is given in Paul H. Clyde and Burton F. Beers's *The Far East* (4th ed. Englewood Cliffs, N.J.: Prentice-Hall, 1966). Percival Griffiths offers a detailed account of the political growth of India in *The British Impact on India* (Hamden, Conn.: Archon Books, 1965). French colonial policy is discussed in Brian Harrison's *South-east Asia: A Short History* (New York: St. Martin's Press, 1966). Halford Hoskins describes European colonial policy in *European Imperialism in Africa* (New York: Holt, 1930). *Belgian Administration in the Congo* (London: Oxford University Press, 1961) by Georges Brausch helps to understand the colonial problems encountered by many European bureaucrats in Africa.

Color Purple, The

TYPE OF WORK: Book
PUBLISHED: 1982
AUTHOR: Alice Walker (1944-   )
SUBJECT MATTER: Novel about an African American woman's search for her true identity
SIGNIFICANCE: This book has been banned from some libraries, and its film adaptation was condemned by many African Americans

Actors Danny Glover and Whoopi Goldberg star in the 1985 film adaptation of Alice Walker's The Color Purple. *(Museum of Modern Art/Film Stills Archive)*

Written in the form of a series of letters, Alice Walker's novel portrays the transformation of an African American woman from a physically and psychologically abused person to what Walker has elsewhere called a "womanist"—a strong and independent person who re-creates herself out of the legacy of her maternal ancestors. Under her friend Shug's influence, Celie matures into a person courageous enough to challenge the traditional social values that have kept her down. The book has been criticized for its realistic depictions of domestic violence, incestuous and homosexual relationships, and its ostensibly irreligious themes. Many schools and libraries have banned the book.

In 1986 the book was filmed by Steven Spielberg with Walker serving as a consultant. Although the film earned eleven Academy Award nominations, it won no Oscars—possibly because of the strong criticism it had received from prominent African Americans. Several critics, including authors Ishmael Reed and Charles Johnson, complained that both the novel and the film did harm by helping to perpetuate negative stereotypes of African American men. They suggested that Walker should focus her work on intercultural rather than intracultural conflicts. Other critics also argued that the film's glossy Hollywood production values betrayed Walker's original thematic intention.

See also African Americans; Film adaptation; Film censorship; Homosexuality; *I Know Why the Caged Bird Sings*; Literature; Race; Violence.

Comic books

DEFINITION: Short books in which illustration is a key feature
SIGNIFICANCE: Comic books have been attacked as corrupters of youth

In 1886 *Yellow Kid* became the first comic strip to appear in a newspaper. The public gave it that name when the newspaper, *World*, tested its new yellow ink by printing it on the image of the Kid's clothing in the comic strip. Comic books soon developed from comic strips. The first collection of strips was published in 1897 in a magazine called *Yellow Kid Magazine*. In 1933 the first comic book, rather than a collection of newspaper strips, appeared. The boom of comic book publishing began with *New Comics, Fun Comics, Popular Comics,* and *Famous Funnies*. More than 150 titles were published in 1940 and more than 200 million copies sold.

In 1948 *Time* magazine described how several copycat crimes were committed by children who had read crime comics. Crime comics were implicated in influencing juveniles to commit burglary, a hanging, and a murder by poisoning. In the same year Dr. Frederic Wertham, a senior psychiatrist for the New York Department of Hospitals, headed a symposium, The Psychopathology of Comic Books. Wertham concluded that comic books glorified crime and violence, and he found them to be "abnormally sexually aggressive." Additionally, an ABC radio broadcast, "What's Wrong with Comics?" was one of the many factors that influenced the formation of citizen's groups for regulating and in some cases banning of certain comic books from local newsstands. Some public schools joined in and even had comic book bonfires on school grounds.

In reaction to criticism of their comic books, publishers Bill Gaines, Leverett Gleason, and others formed the Association of Comics Magazine Publishers (ACMP) in July, 1948. The ACMP formed a code of standards for decency in comic books. Any comic book that met the standards could carry the ACMP stamp of approval. This attempt at self-regulation was not successful, however, because major publishers boycotted the ACMP. Smaller publishers who relied on blood and violence to sell their books were not interested in going out of business. The media and grassroots groups continued to criticize the industry. In 1949 *Parents' Magazine* published the findings of the Cincinnati Committee on the Evaluation of Comic Books. It found that 70 percent of all comic books contained objectionable material, which included images ranging from sadistic torture to sexually suggestive and salacious actions.

In 1950 a U.S. Senate committee investigated the effects of violence in comic books in juvenile delinquency rates from 1945 to 1950. The results did not establish a clear connection between comic books and delinquency. The report reprimanded those comic books that glorified violence and that made some criminals into heroes. There were three central factors that contributed to censorship of comics. The first was Wertham, who published *Seduction of the Innocent* in 1954. This book describes the alleged negative consequences of reading comic books about crime, sex, and violence. Wertham's book is generally regarded as a classic example of research based on anecdote rather than science. His conclusion was that abnormal and delinquent children read comic books; therefore, comic books caused aberrant behavior and delinquency. Public hearings were held by a Senate subcommittee regarding the harmful effects of comic books on children. Thirty-two bills introduced in sixteen state legislatures had a negative effect on sales of comic books to children. The second factor in comics censorship was the Code of the Comic Books Association. Its objective was to eliminate all traces of violence, crime, horror, and sex in comic books. Horror and crime comics dramatically decreased in quantity, Westerns became less violent, and romance lost its sexual overtones. The third factor was mothers in America. They were inspired by Wertham and encouraged by the code. Bridge clubs changed into committees pressuring news dealers into suppressing offensive material.

New Beginning. The Comics Code Authority seal of approval was first affixed on the covers of comic books of major publishers' March, 1955, issues. The code specified that "all scenes of horror, excessive bloodshed, gore or crimes, depravity, lust, sadism, masochism shall not be permitted." The Comics Code Authority proudly proclaimed itself the most oppressive censoring body in America. In theory the code was designed to protect the book business, and it did satisfy those in the public who had been angered over the violence and lewdness allegedly found in comic books. What protected the industry generally resulted in the elimination of a number of major publishers. Artists hurriedly redrew heroines and softened violent episodes to make them conform to the required restrictions. EC Comics, headed by William Gaines, replaced his horror line with softened thrillers. Marvel comics ceased publication of its superhero division.

The code had a devastating effect on the comic book industry. In 1955 three hundred titles were being published annually, a 50-percent drop from the year before. Publishers attempted to spark interest in their publications by adding to their old titles and by trying opportunities in the mystery and suspense fields. In 1956 DC Comics launched a new superhero, Flash, the fastest man alive. It revived a dying industry. The revival also sparked an updating of the superheroes of the 1940's.

Underground Comics. Underground comics had their beginnings in the 1930's during the Depression. These were small, pocket-sized pamphlets devoted primarily to the theme of sexual intercourse. These comics were referred to by various names, including the eight pagers. The eight pagers were not concerned with redeeming social values, according to the courts, and operated between plagiarism and parody. Rather than exploring their themes in a legitimate, thought-provoking manner, they sought to exploit their sources. Eight pagers would often portray notorious criminal figures directly from headlines. Criminals defied a social structure that was in a state of distress. Armed aggression and sexual power were symbolically equated, since success with violence, according to the comic book, created success with sex.

A more significant group of underground comics have been a more public phenomenon. The first important title was *Zap*, which appeared in 1968. *Zap* number four was prosecuted for obscenity in New York City and banned in 1973. It has since been sold without prosecution, and the work of its creators has appeared in the Museum of Modern Art. Robert Crumb was the chief exponent of this new genre, not only because he contributed many of the best underground newspaper comics but also for making the underground comic book a viable form. The underground comics criticized the Vietnam War, urban chaos, materialism, capitalism, and bourgeois values.

New Comics. New comics are an outgrowth of the underground comics. They are also known as alternate comics. Cartoonists Art Spiegelman, Will Eisner, and Dave Sim have become widely recognized for publications such as: *Raw*, *American Splendor*, and *Love and Rockets*. The underground comics of the 1960's and 1970's gave way to nihilism and skepticism. The new comics prophesy doom and humorous exhilaration. Magazines such as *Weirdo*, by Robert Crumb, and *Raw*, by Art Spiegelman, deal with the postindustrial urban wastelands. Frank Miller and Alan Moore helped push the theme of superhero comics into mature levels. In 1986 Friendly Frank's, a comics store in Lansing, Illinois, was raided for selling obscene comics. Under attack were *Weirdo*, *Omaha the Cat Dancer*, *Bodeyssey*, and *Bizarre Sex*. In appellate court, the store manager was acquitted of all charges.

Television, Comic Books, and Violence. Two surveys in Australia showed that there is a positive association among teenage males between their attitude favoring the use of force and exposure to violence in the media. The first survey involved a sample of 375 teenagers before the introduction of television; the favoring of force was greater among those who read more violent comic books. The second survey involved more than ninety teenagers after the introduction of television. Comic book reading was less frequent. The amount of exposure to television and a preference for violent programs were also positively associated with the holding of such an attitude.

In 1987 another study concluded that early exposure to television violence had a consistently positive association with aggressive behavior as much as thirty years later in life. As adults, those who watched television violence early in life tended to be more punitive with their children. Aggressiveness of the children and their preference for violent entertainment, in turn, were positively correlated. The implication is that media experiences may have a crucial role in establishing behavior. —*Thomas Cappuccio*

See also American Civil Liberties Union; Books, children's; Copycat crime; Crumb, Robert; *Doonesbury*; Hypocrisy; MAD magazine; Morality; Symbolic speech; Violence.

BIBLIOGRAPHY

Mike Benton's *The Comic Book in America* (Dallas: Taylor Publishing, 1989) is an excellent illustrated history of comics. *Comix*, by Les Daniel (New York: Outerbridge and Dienstfrey, 1971), traces the evolution of comics in terms of their uses, social value, censorship, and the major publishers. Steef Davidson's *Political Comics* (New York: Penguin Books, 1982) analyzes connections between comics and the political issues of the 1960's and 1970's. In *The New Comics*, Bob Callahan (New York: Collier Books, 1991) reviews trends, ideas, and developments and the significance of various types of new comics. Mark James Estren's *Underground Comics* (Berkeley, Calif.: Ronin Publishing, 1993) surveys underground comics from the 1970's to the 1990's. *Comics, Anatomy of a Mass Medium* by Reinhold Reitberger and Wolfgang Fuchs (Boston: Little, Brown, 1970) and Richard Reynolds' *Super Heroes* (Jackson, Miss.: University Press, 1992) relate the main superheroes to their mythic origins and trace the popularity and influence of the superhero. George Comstock's *Television and the American Child* (San Diego, Calif.: Academic Press, 1991) offers evidence from social and behavioral science research regarding television viewing and children.

Commercial speech

DEFINITION: Ideas expressed in advertising

SIGNIFICANCE: Commercial speech historically has been among the least protected forms of expression

In the twentieth century the trend has changed somewhat to offer increased protection to commercial speech. Canadian courts, for example, consider commercial speech within the constitutional protection afforded all speech, and seek to balance the interest in free speech against the reasons offered for the limitation on the speech. American courts apply a more complex three-step analysis to commercial speech restrictions.

After *Central Hudson Gas and Electric Corp. v. Public Service Commission* (1980), a court must first determine whether the speech is protected by the First Amendment of the U.S. Constitution. To be protected, the speech must promote lawful activity and must not be misleading. States may ban altogether commercial speech promoting illegal activities (such as illegal drug use) and advertising that is inherently misleading. But states may not completely ban advertising that is only potentially misleading.

In the second step, a court examines whether the asserted governmental interest in regulation is substantial. This requires some important state interest, and courts have acknowledged that protection of citizens and preservation of community aesthetics are both suitable interests. In the final step of the analysis, the court examines whether the regulation directly advances the governmental interest asserted and whether it is not more extensive than is necessary to serve the asserted interest. A court will apply an intermediate standard of review, inquiring whether the "fit" between the asserted governmental interest and the regulation of speech is reasonable. A state need not employ the least restrictive means to accomplish its interests, but it must select a means narrowly tailored to achieve the desired objective without unreasonable burdens on commercial speech.

See also Advertising as the target of censorship; Courts and censorship law; *44 Liquormart, Inc. v. Rhode Island*; Smoking; Tax laws; Telephone law; Unprotected speech.

Generic industry symbols, such as the "California Raisins," have been increasingly used in television commercials and advertisements that have touched on questions of commercial free speech—such as whether individual members of related industries can be forced to help pay for generic advertising. (AP/Wide World Photos)

Committee to Defend the First Amendment (CDFA)

FOUNDED: 1979

TYPE OF ORGANIZATION: U.S. fundraising body dedicated to protecting the First Amendment

SIGNIFICANCE: This organization has provided funds for legal services and assistance to those whose First Amendment rights are in jeopardy

The CDFA is a nonprofit organization administered by a board of directors. Its members are professionals from the fields of media, education, law, and religion who are interested in protecting rights to free speech. It has provided funding for legal services in cases that involve First Amendment issues. The CDFA also provides informational material for organizations, government agencies, and the general public about limitations and violations of First Amendment rights, the place of such rights in society, and why they need to be protected.

In 1984 the CDFA changed its name to First Amendment Research Institute and began concentrating more on educating the public through research and mailings about First Amendment issues.

See also First Amendment; First Amendment Congress; Reporters Committee for Freedom of the Press.

Communications Act of 1934

ENACTED: June 19, 1934

PLACE: United States (national)

SIGNIFICANCE: This law broadened the federal government's regulatory powers beyond radio broadcasting to encompass all areas of telecommunications

Through passage of this law in 1934 the U.S. Congress replaced the seven-year-old Federal Radio Commission with the Federal Communications Commission (FCC). The new law was predicated on the belief that the broadcast spectrum was a public resource that must be owned and retained by the people. This theory held that the broadcast industry must be regulated by the federal government to ensure that a diversity of viewpoints are aired. The act broadened the government's authority beyond radio, giving it the power to regulate all telecommunications.

Regulation or Censorship? Section 326 of the Communications Act specifically prohibited censorship by stating that nothing in the law should "be understood or construed to give the commission the power of censorship" over radio broadcasting and that no regulations or conditions should be promulgated that would "interfere with the right of free speech by means of radio communication." Although the law forbade the FCC from forcing stations to air—or to stop airing—specific programs, the law simultaneously directed the commission to regulate broadcasting so that it would be "in the public interest." This directive gave the FCC the power to revoke, or not renew, broadcast licenses in cases of flagrant disregard of broadcasters' responsibility.

Under the act, the FCC could determine who should broadcast, on which wavelengths, with what power, and when. Since the FCC was authorized to grant broadcast licenses for limited numbers of years at a time, license renewal proceedings gave the FCC the power to influence station policies, ranging from their advertising techniques to the amounts of time they devoted to news and public service programming. However, the FCC rarely used this power to cancel or refuse renewal of licenses. Instead, it has typically used indirect pressure to influence the content of broadcasts.

Equal Time Rule. There has been widespread disagreement on how far the FCC should go in forcing licensees to serve the public interest. Section 315 of the Communications Act required broadcasters providing news coverage of political campaigns to cover candidates of every party seeking the same political offices equally. Some people have argued that this "equal time rule" amounts to a form of reverse censorship that violates broadcasters' First Amendment rights.

In 1959 the equal time rule was tested when members of the FCC voted 4-3 that a Chicago television station had to offer a candidate twenty-two seconds on its news program in order to balance the time it had devoted to showing Mayor Richard Daly greeting a foreign official. Both men were candidates in the Chicago mayoral election. Congress responded by amending the law to exempt noncampaign news coverage of an incumbent.

The following year Congress temporarily suspended section 315 to allow television networks to broadcast the debates between presidential candidates John F. Kennedy and Richard M. Nixon without having to include third-party candidates. In 1975 the FCC made this exception a permanent rule by declaring that stations could carry debates among pairs of major party candidates without the participation of minor party candidates.

The equal time rule required that stations offering broadcast time outside of their regular news programs to political candidates must offer equal time to the candidates' opponents. However, the rule also permitted stations to cover news events in which candidates appear without having to offer equal time to their opponents. The equal time rule does not apply to appearances of candidates on regular "bona fide" newscasts, news interviews, and news documentaries in which candidates appear incidentally. The difficulty for broadcasters has lain in deciding what constitutes "bona fide" news.

Political Advertising. Section 315 of the Communications Act has been most often applied to situations involving political advertising. The equal time rule states that if a licensee permits a legally qualified candidate for public office to use its station, it also must "afford equal opportunity to all other such candidates for that office." Broadcast stations that sell advertising time to political candidates thus cannot refuse to sell equal numbers of spots in the same time periods—and at the same prices—to candidates of other parties seeking the same offices.

The FCC has refined its rules on political advertising in order fully to implement section 315's requirements. These guarantee access to broadcast advertising for all candidates for federal office, ensure equal broadcast advertising opportunities to rival candidates for public office, require the lowest-unit rate charges for political advertising, and forbid censorship of the content of political advertisements—even if such content violates other FCC regulations, such as those pertaining to indecent language or broadcasts.

Fairness Questions. Some of the problems of adhering to the equal time principle in political news coverage disappeared after Congress' 1959 ruling. However, the root issue of ensuring "fairness" in access to the airwaves and in presenting various sides of controversial issues remained. The FCC's so-called fairness doctrine, which was enforced until 1985, was based on the argument that because the airwaves are public property the FCC should direct licensed broadcasters to operate "in the public interest, convenience, and necessity." The belief is that the public interest is best served when the airwaves are accessible to differing viewpoints.

The difficulty of attempting to legislate "fairness" led the FCC to abandon the fairness doctrine. Broadcasters had long argued that extreme efforts to include opposing viewpoints in coverage and interpretation of controversial issues led to less, rather than better, coverage of important social issues. They argued that if stations had to seek out other viewpoints to air on every issue they wished to address, they would tend to avoid covering controversial issues. Broadcasters argued that this likelihood was increased by the fear that groups or individuals dissatisfied with a station's coverage might have grounds to oppose the station's license at renewal time.

Cynics claimed that broadcasters protesting the fairness doctrine really wanted to be free from pressure from minorities, women, senior citizens, and others demanding balanced coverage. This led to an unusual alliance of advocates for minority causes and big business, who had long felt discriminated against by network coverage of national issues, particularly since the social unrest of the 1960's and the Watergate era of the early 1970's heightened mistrust of established authority. The commission sided with broadcasters, whose voices included leading journalists usually sympathetic to minority viewpoints. Walter Cronkite and Eric Severeid, for example, argued that average citizens have so many ways to obtain differing viewpoints on social issues that it was no longer necessary to require broadcasters to seek out diverse perspectives themselves.

Although the FCC concluded that the fairness doctrine did not serve the public interest, it left intact the general licensing requirement that broadcasters present issue-responsive programming. When a station's license renewal is challenged, this issue-responsive programming can become a major ingredient in a its ability to show that it has operated in the public interest. Thus the obligation that broadcasters provide balanced coverage of important public issues remained even though details on how they should do this were deregulated.

The Future. The strongest argument against continuing the regulations imposed by the Communications Act of 1934 has been the erosion of a central part of the philosophical basis for which the law was originally enacted. The argument that the airwaves belong to the public was based largely on their presumed scarcity—the notion that because the number of broadcast frequencies is finite, the federal government had to ensure that radio and television broadcasting was not dominated by those with the most money and power. Since the act was passed, however, there has been a steady growth in the number of licensed frequencies in the United States. By the mid-1990's there were more than eleven thousand radio stations and more than fifteen hundred television stations. There has also been a great expansion of cable television. These and other technological advances have mitigated against the old scarcity argument.

The 1994 election of the first Republican-controlled Congress in the telemedia age prompted many advocates of deregulation to favor a major overhaul of the Communications Act of 1934. Although many deregulatory changes were instituted through the Telecommunications Act of 1996, the rules pertaining to equal time, political advertising, and balanced news coverage of controversial issues remained.

—Gerard Donnelly

See also Communications Decency Act; Fairness doctrine; Federal Communications Commission; *New Worlds*; Radio; Television.

BIBLIOGRAPHY

Erwin G. Krasnow and Lawrence D. Longley's *The Politics of Broadcast Regulation* (New York: St. Martin's Press, 1973) is an introduction to the inherent conflict between the FCC directive to regulate "in the public interest" and the section of the Communications Act that forbids censorship. Verne E. Edwards, Jr., explores examples of "reverse censorship" resulting from the equal time provision in *Journalism in a Free Society* (Dubuque, Iowa: William C. Brown, 1970). The theory that the broadcast spectrum should be considered public property is discussed by Lawrence W. Lichty and Malachi C. Topping in *American Broadcasting: A Source Book on the History of Radio and Television* (New York: Hastings House, 1975). Mitchell Stephens stresses the importance of the equal time provision for political advertising in *Broadcast News: Radio Journalism and an Introduction to Television* (New York: Holt, Rinehart and Winston, 1980). Edwin Emery and Michael Emery trace the evolution of the equal time rule in *The Press and America: An Interpretive History of the Mass Media* (5th ed. Englewood Cliffs, N.J.: Prentice-Hall, 1984), which discusses congressional actions that have allowed exceptions to a strict interpretation in favor of the broader requirement of "fairness." The possibility of deregulation is described by Morrie Gelman in "75 Years of Pioneers: A Personalized History of the Fifth Estate from Frank Conrad to Rupert Murdoch," *Broadcasting and Cable* 125, no. 45 (November 6, 1995).

Communications Decency Act

ENACTED: February 8, 1996

PLACE: United States (national)

SIGNIFICANCE: Title V of the Telecommunications Act of 1996, this act revised earlier laws to mandate that telecommunication service providers be held criminally accountable if they fail to censor "indecent material"

In 1995 Nebraska's Democratic senator J. James Exon responded to increased public concern over the growing use of telecommunications technologies to transmit pornography and to engage children in inappropriate contacts with adults by

INTERNET DISCLAIMER

After passage of the Communications Decency Act in early 1996, online providers of sexually oriented materials went to great lengths to protect themselves from prosecution by requiring customers to sign off on disclaimers such as the following.

Terms and Conditions

Please read them before proceeding.

DO NOT ENTER UNLESS YOU ARE AT LEAST 18 YEARS OLD AND INTERESTED IN
SEEING SEXUALLY EXPLICIT MATERIAL!

By entering this site you are certifying that you are of legal adult age and are entering this website with full knowledge that it contains adult oriented material. Furthermore you are certifying that the viewing, reading, and downloading of the images in this website do not violate the community standards of your street, village, city, town, county, state, province or country. You also certify that you are wholly liable for any false disclosures and responsible for any legal ramifications that may arise from viewing, reading, or downloading of images or material contained within the website and that Adult Features, Inc. can not be held responsible for any legal ramifications that may arise as a result of fraudulent entry or use of this website and material contained herein. All models are 18 years or older depicting sexually consenting adults. If you are not interested in such material please forget this address.

Under penalties of perjury, I solemnly declare and affirm as follows:

- I am an adult of at least 18 years of age.

- I believe in the principles of the First Amendment: free adult citizens have the right to decide what they will read and view in the privacy of their own homes without government intervention or by any person or group.

- I am ordering this material for myself and for my own private interests and am not ordering it to use against Adult Features, Inc. or any person in any manner whatsoever and I waive all legal rights to do so in the future.

- I am not a law enforcement official, postal inspector, or a member of any censorship group.

- I have not asked the U.S. Postal Service to "protect me" from receiving sexually oriented or sexually explicit material. I hereby waive any requirement that an inscription such as "Sexually Oriented Ad" be made on any mail or email Adult Features, Inc. sends to me.

- I have not caused my name to be placed on any list being accumulated by the U.S. Postal Service or any other government agency which forbids my being sent sexually oriented ads through the mails or over the Internet. Further, should my posture in this regard change, I agree to notify you in writing before doing so.

- I will not sell, rent, or duplicate in any manner whatsoever any material you send me or that I purchase. I understand that such unauthorized use is a violation of U.S. Federal and International Copyright laws. All materials are for my personal use only.

- I will not exhibit any material you send me to a minor nor will I expose it to any person whose privacy or sensibilities may be offended. I believe this material meets my current community standards. Adult Features, Inc. members are personally responsible for all use of the service under your user ID (including payment for orders placed), even if you allow someone else to use your ID. Illegal, Fraudulent or abusive use of any ID or the service is grounds for termination of the Adult Features, Inc. Membership, and may be referred to law enforcement. Enrolling or using an ID on the Service under a name other than your own is Prohibited! When using our "Check Bank Draft System" you will be charged for any Returned Bank Drafts due to NSF, or any other reasons. You will be subject to a $20.00 service fee! All orders are non-refundable exchanges only. If you have become a Member you will have to renew each month as we will delete your username and password after time expires. If you agree with these terms please proceed by clicking below. If you do not agree with the terms or are under the age of 18 years do not enter this site!

introducing a bill called the Communications Decency Act. Exon complained that the Internet contained "not simply nude pictures of 'cheesecake,' but the most debased, lewd material one can imagine." There is no valid reason, he said, that "these perverts should be allowed unimpeded on the Internet." His goal was to "help make the information superhighway safer for kids and families to travel."

Exon's bill broadened the protections already existing in the Communications Act of 1934, and increased penalties for their violation. A key aspect of the law was its replacing of the term "telephone" with "telecommunications device" in order to encompass facsimile (fax) machines, computer modems, and other devices. The act made it a criminal offense to use interactive computer systems to send communications to specific persons, or to persons less than eighteen years of age, that depict or describe sexual or excretory activities or organs in manners that might be deemed patently offensive—as measured by local community standards. The law made violations punishable by prison terms and fines up to $250,000. The act specifically excluded from liability telecommunications and information service providers, system operators, and employers who do not knowingly participate in such violations themselves.

Immediately after the act's original bill was introduced to Congress, it met strong criticism from the American Civil Liberties Union (ACLU); the telecommunication, computer, and publishing industries; and such professional organizations as American Library Association; Human Rights Watch; Association of Publishers, Editors and Writers; American Booksellers Association; and American Society of Newspaper Editors.

On February 1, 1996, Exon's bill was passed overwhelmingly in both houses of Congress and became part of the Telecommunications Act of 1996, which President Bill Clinton signed into law a week later. Minutes after the president signed the act—the ACLU and nineteen other groups filed suit at a federal court in Philadelphia to block the new law by challenging its constitutionality. These groups argued that the law would criminalize forms of expression that were protected under the First Amendment.

On June 12, 1996, a federal court voted 3-0 to grant a motion for a preliminary injunction on the law's "indecency" provisions. The court also found that the act went too far in restricting the First Amendment rights of all computer users in its effort to protect children. On July 1 the Justice Department filed papers in Philadelphia asking the Supreme Court to let the law take effect, as President Clinton and a majority of senators and representatives intended. Conservative groups supporting the act promised to help Congress write new legislation if the lower court's ruling was allowed to stand.

See also American Civil Liberties Union; Communications Act of 1934; Computers; Courts and censorship law; First Amendment; Internet; Obscenity: legal definitions; Pornography, child; Prior restraint; Unprotected speech.

Communism

DEFINITION: System of government in which the state owns the means of production

SIGNIFICANCE: Communist governments and their defenders are noted for their willingness to repress independent thought

Communism is a political and economic system that grew out of the writings of Karl Marx. A variety of communist parties and movements have arisen in a number of countries. Communism, however, remains more an ideal than a reality; as an ideal, it is the shared and just distribution of wealth. In historical example, however, communism has been the rule of dictatorships.

Communism means many things to many people. As a political and economic system, it involves organizing and controlling the distribution of power in society as well as the production and distribution of goods and services. The distribution of power and goods is made according to certain basic principles. As an ideology, communism asserts that private property is the basis of capitalism, a system that allows for controlling the means of production by owners in search of profit. Marx's historical analysis argues that capitalism is ultimately the source of many social ills; communist philosophy amplifies on this. The evils of capitalism include the exploitation of workers by the moneyed class, chronic unemployment, poverty, urban squalor, and environmental destruction. Abolishing private property, nationalizing industry, and providing universal education are the typical solutions to these problems offered by communists.

Communism, in its mature form found in industrial societies, must be distinguished from primitive communism. A system of communal ownership found in traditional preliterate societies, primitive communism is common among nomadic hunters and gatherers. These small-scale societies display little social stratification—few class distinctions—and, concomitantly, little or no surplus wealth. People in these societies are extremely dependent on one another and regularly participate in cooperative or communal activities. Such societies may be called communal rather than communist, to distinguish them from those societies that are large in scale and modern in technological development.

Marxism and Communism. Marx's economic, political, and social thought provided the inspiration for modern communism. According to his view of history, the mode of production in any particular society determines the character of the social, political, and spiritual life of that society. The mode of production is the prevailing type of productive techniques used in producing goods and services. This may range from simple handwork to craft production using very basic technology to highly specialized, fully automated operations. The economic base of society is the foundation or substructure of society according to Marx. Marx, in other words, was one of the first social and historical analysts to point out that to understand how a society works, one should watch how money is made in that society and where the money goes. All other social and cultural institutions—law, art, government, literature, and religion, for example, which he called the superstructure of society—develop out of the economic foundation.

All history is the history of class conflict, according to communist ideology. The economic history of Western society involves the evolution from slavery involving masters and slaves, through the feudal society of lord and serf, to the capitalist system of bourgeoisie (owners) and proletariat (workers). In capitalist societies, class conflict between owners and workers is hostile. With increasingly complex and efficient industrial technology and with the private ownership of the land, labor, capital, and machinery used in production, owners continually profit at the expense of the workers. Wealth is increasingly concentrated in fewer hands. Workers, who do not own the means of production, have only their labor to sell in the marketplace for wages. What is in the best interest of owners—increasing productivity and profits—is seldom in the best interest of workers. What is in the best interests of workers—higher wages, better fringe benefits, and improved working conditions—is seldom in the best interest of owners. The widening gap between owners and workers is seen in differences in education, income, ideas, and lifestyles.

Communists argue that as the conditions of life for workers worsen, the working class will eventually overthrow the existing bourgeoisie control of the means of production. Society will pass through a transitional period of socialism which, according to communist doctrine, will itself wither away and be replaced by a communist society. Most societies regarded as communist refer to themselves as "socialist"; although their industry has been nationalized—taken over by the government—private property, such as household items and consumer goods, has not been eliminated. State ownership of industry, itself, must also eventually cease because government is a vehicle for class domination and communism represents the end of classes and the end of class exploitation. The communist ideal of "from each according to his abilities, to each according to his needs" will also not be realized until the emergence of a true communist society. In contrast to this ideal, in socialist societies people continue to be paid according to their work rather than their needs.

The Basis of Censorship. During this transitional socialist period, communist theory argues, communists must use whatever power, including force, is necessary to gain control of the means of production. In the process of nationalizing industry, all opposition to the revolutionary social and economic changes needed to create a socialist state must be crushed. Rather than withering away, the state must create political and economic arrangements that will concentrate authority in the hands of workers, the proletariat, as represented by the communist party. The state must grow stronger before it can wither away. This dictatorship of the proletariat remains a class rule rather than a classless rule.

Given the powerlessness and lack of organization of workers, the working class must be guided and led by a small highly motivated party of revolutionary intellectuals who better understand the laws of history leading to communism. This dedicated vanguard of communist party members must have access to and control over the masses if the transition to communism is to succeed.

The fall of communism in the former Soviet Union and throughout Eastern Europe has exposed communism to increased scrutiny. Communism continued to exist in 1996 in various forms in such diverse settings as Cuba, North Korea, and China as a political and economic system. In these countries and in the countries of the formerly communist Eastern Europe, sophisticated forms of censorship were devised and practiced, ranging from prior restraint to subtle pressures to assassination.

By assuming that the working class could not be trusted to discover and realize its own true interests, that, if left alone, workers would possibly follow the path of forming trade unions to bargain with owners over wages, fringe benefits, and working conditions, communists could assign themselves the responsibility for guiding the workers of the world. This guidance would include educating workers, using propaganda, brainwashing, and even force to convince workers that only communists understand the revolutionary struggle leading to socialism and ultimately to communism. By gaining control of not only the economy, in terms of the means of production, but having a monopoly of political power, communists had the means to bring all mass organizations, such as labor unions and religious organizations, under their control.

Class Consciousness and False Consciousness. To justify the temporary centralization of power through the dictatorship of the proletariat, communists have cited Marx's notions of class consciousness and false consciousness. Class consciousness is the awareness, especially among the working class, of their common economic, political, and social conditions. Typically, workers tend to lack a shared sense of being exploited. They often accept the status quo of being dominated by a ruling class. Class consciousness among workers, the communist argument has gone, will only emerge when workers appreciate that there is a working class, that they are part of it, and that they share not only a common way of life but common hopes, objectives, and enemies. No transition to a socialist society and, ultimately, to a communist society will be successful until a significant number of workers understand the sources of their oppression. Then and only then can workers begin to organize to change the status quo. The transformation of society requires collective commitment and collective action.

Research has indicated that among workers in the United States and many other industrial societies class consciousness is not well developed. Workers continue to aspire to middle-class and upper-middle-class membership, holding out hope for some measure of upward social mobility. The beliefs of the ruling class in democratic society concerning the importance of individual initiative and enterprise in determining an individual's success in life remain widespread, even among workers. These beliefs and attitudes are not in accord with the actual or objective situation of workers in capitalist societies. Such false consciousness accounts for the lack of commitment and action among workers to change their circumstances.

Formulating the notion of false consciousness allows communist parties to determine the interests and needs of workers, which workers themselves do not understand. This, in turn, becomes the basis for the communist parties' attempt to carefully censor the flow of information in society. Following Marx's admonition that whoever controls the "means of mental production" will eventually control the definition of reality in society, communists became increasingly adept at influencing the production and distribution of ideas. Through tightly regulating the broadcast and the print media—the content of radio, television, newspapers and magazines, and the educational system—communist rulers sought to control the flow of information. In many societies, communist parties have employed a small army of censors to review the content of broadcasts and printed materials before they are presented to ensure they are consistent with prevailing communist beliefs and ideas.

Under the dictatorship of the proletariat, as the Communist Party extends its control over people's lives, through censorship and a variety of other means, it continually centralizes its power and control over the economy and production. Centralized government planning rather than consumer preferences, as expressed through the market, determines what goods and services are produced for consumers. Government planners also determine the price of various goods and services. As the communists strengthen their hold on society, they are able to further control the flow of information in society by abolishing any competing political parties.

With minor variations, communist parties in all societies have been governed by a central executive committee. Once the party apparatus has arrived at a decision, it is expected that all in the party will carry out the decision to the best of their ability. One of the major problems in many socialist societies was that the Communist Party and the government it established became increasingly rigid in their attempt to direct every aspect of life. Art, music, literature, drama, even science—every branch of learning—became a potential threat to the grip of the party and the state. In an effort to purge any trace of independence, the expanding bureaucracy of the party, the state, the police, and the military became increasingly unresponsive to the lives and needs of the masses. For example, centralized government planning and control resulted in an economic system that usually produced consumer goods that were of poor quality and in insufficient quantities.

Not surprisingly, rather than witnessing the rise of communism out of the demise of socialism, in Russia and throughout Eastern Europe the demise of socialism was accompanied by the overthrow of the Communist Party. Although communist parties continue to function in a number of societies, serious doubt has been cast on the continued existence of communism. The image of a world communist society as the culmination of a long series of class struggles, as a lengthy process of economic and political changes has dimmed. For many, the triumph of modern communism has become more myth than reality, more likely to be the subject of a romance novel than a viable alternative for modern living. The rise of trade unions, company profit sharing plans involving workers, and the decentralization of the ownership of the means of production (in the form of millions of owners of stock in tens of thousands of companies worldwide) are all important developments. Marx and other early communists could not anticipate these developments. These and other developments have contributed to reducing the notion of a communist society where there is the free sharing of material goods to a utopian ideal.

—*Charles E. Marske*

See also Censorship; Christianity; Communist Party of the U.S.A.; Cuba; Lenin, Vladimir Ilich; Marx, Karl; Police states; Socialist Realism; Soviet Union.

BIBLIOGRAPHY

Donald Shanor's *Behind the Lines: The Private War Against Soviet Censorship* (New York: St. Martin's Press, 1985) offers an examination of mass media censorship in communist societies in the form of a case study of the former Soviet Union. A variety of documents are cited in *Censorship and Political Communication in Eastern Europe*, edited by George Schopflin (New York: St. Martin's Press, 1983), to illustrate the role of censorship in the former communist states of Eastern Europe. Issues surrounding freedom of the press in these societies are also discussed. For an overview of the various censorship techniques employed in a communist society, Carlos Ripoll's *Harnessing the Intellectuals: Censoring Writers and Artists in Today's Cuba* (Washington, D.C.: Cuban American National Foundation, 1985) is insightful. This work examines the extent to which freedom of information exists in communist Cuba and how, through censoring literature, the arts and intellectuals in general and the production and dissemination of information can be controlled. For a historical account of the censorship of twentieth century Russian literature read John and Carol Garrard's *Inside the Soviet Writers' Union* (New York: Free Press, 1990).

Communist Party of the U.S.A. (CPUSA)

FOUNDED: 1919

TYPE OF ORGANIZATION: Political party advocating establishment of a socialist dictatorship in the United States

SIGNIFICANCE: Existence of the CPUSA has tested the commitment of the U.S. government to its constitutionally guaranteed freedoms of expression and association

Throughout most of its history, the primary goal of the CPUSA has been to establish a socialist political system in the United States modeled after that which existed in the former Soviet Union. Whereas the U.S. political system has placed great value upon individual liberty, the Soviet system placed primary emphasis on equality. Throughout Soviet history, individual freedom and initiative were sacrificed for the collective goals defined and directed by the Communist Party of the Soviet Union. It was to these goals that the CPUSA became committed.

The U.S. government is based on the rule of law as established by the Constitution. Some of the most cherished constitutional liberties—liberties guaranteed to all American citizens—are freedom of speech, freedom of the press, and freedom of association. The activities of the CPUSA have periodically raised serious and volatile debates both within the U.S. government and U.S. society generally as to the extent to which the government is obligated to protect the liberties of citizens whose avowed wish is to topple the government.

Within the U.S. political system, the courts have the responsibility of interpreting and bringing clarity and definition to principles embodied in the Constitution. The U.S. Supreme Court is the highest court of law in the United States. In a number of cases involving the CPUSA, the Court has drawn the line for the U.S. government as to how far it can go in protecting itself from threats posed by CPUSA activities, while also ensuring that the constitutional rights of the CPUSA itself and its members are protected.

Sedition and Treason Cases. The federal Espionage Act of 1917 made it illegal during wartime intentionally to publish false or misleading reports about military operations, to promote the success of the enemies of the United States, or to obstruct the drafting of U.S. military personnel. Following the passage of this act, an American communist newspaper published a number of articles denouncing World War I and the participation of the United States in it. The U.S. postmaster general responded to the newspaper's actions by revoking its second-class mailing privileges. This action meant the newspaper was nonmailable and could no longer be delivered by the U.S. Post Office to its readers. The justification given by the postmaster for his action was that the Espionage Act gave him the right to stop mail if, in his view, the mail violated provisions of the act. The publisher of the CPUSA paper sued the postmaster on the grounds that its constitutional rights to free expression were being abridged. In the 1921 case of *United States ex rel. Milwaukee Social Democratic Public Publishing Company v. Burleson*, the U.S. Supreme Court found that the actions of the postmaster were permissible under the Espionage Act, and that the nonmailable matter provisions of the act were constitutional.

In 1940 a new law, the Smith Act, came into effect in the United States. The Smith Act made it a crime to advocate overthrowing the U.S. government by force or violence through the use of speech, printed materials, or instruction. The law also made it illegal to organize a group or to be a member of a group that advocated the overthrow of the U.S. government. In the 1951 case of *Dennis v. United States*, the Supreme Court upheld the conviction under the Smith Act of Eugene Dennis, a leading member of the CPUSA. Dennis had argued that the Smith Act was unconstitutional because it violated his freedoms of expression and association. The Supreme Court concluded that an individual's freedom of expression and association could be restricted by law if the person's activities posed a "clear and present danger" to the security of the United States. A similar finding was made by the Supreme Court in the case of *Scales v. United States* in 1961, when it again upheld the conviction of a member of the CPUSA, Junius Scales, under the Smith Act.

In the 1957 case of *Yates v. United States*, the Supreme Court refined its interpretation of the Smith Act by ruling that the mere teaching or advocacy of communism, in and of itself, did not pose a threat to the security of the United States, and was, therefore, protected by the U.S. Constitution. In the 1961 case of *Noto v. United States*, the Supreme Court reversed a conviction under the Smith Act because the Court was of the opinion that the intent to incite immediate action to bring about the overthrow of the U.S. government had not been proven.

Registration and Loyalty Oath Cases. In 1950 the Subversive Activities Control Act became law in the United States. The 1950 act required all communist parties or organizations in the United States to register with the U.S. government. Additionally, they were required to provide a list of their officers and all past and present members, a financial statement, and a list of all the printing presses at their disposal. In the 1961 case of the *Communist Party of the United States v. Subversive Activities Control Board*, the Supreme Court held that the registration provisions of the 1950 Act were constitutional because they were regulatory, not prohibitory, in nature. Such provisions did not outlaw or ban communist party activities, so they did not violate the U.S. Constitution.

One final Supreme Court decision affecting the CPUSA came in the case of the *Communist Party of Indiana v. Whitcomb* in 1974. This case involved the denial by the state of Indiana to allow communist candidates a place on the ballot in the 1972 general election because they refused to swear a loyalty oath pledging not to advocate the overthrow of local, state, or national government in the United States by force or violence. The Supreme Court concluded that the required loyalty oath was a violation of the First Amendment of the U.S. Constitution because it attempted to proscribe advocacy of the use of force without making a determination if such advocacy would result in imminent lawless action against the government.
—*Samuel E. Watson III*

See also American Civil Liberties Union; Assembly, right of; Clear and present danger doctrine; Communism; Espionage Act of 1917; Loyalty oaths; Nonmailable matter laws; Sedition; Smith Act; Soviet Union.

BIBLIOGRAPHY

For additional information on attempts made by the U.S. government to censor the activities of the CPUSA, consult John Diggins' *The American Left in the Twentieth Century* (New York: Harcourt Brace, 1973), James Bales's *J. Edgar Hoover Speaks Concerning Communism* (Washington, D.C.: Capitol Hill Press, 1970), Peggy Dennis' *The Autobiography of an American Communist* (Westport, Conn.: Lawrence Hill, 1977), William Foster's *A History of the Communist Party of the United States* (Westport Conn.: Greenwood Press, 1968), and Joseph Starobin's *American Communism in Crisis, 1943-1957* (Cambridge, Mass.: Harvard University Press, 1972).

Community standards

DEFINITION: Local norms of sexual decency

SIGNIFICANCE: In the United States, the concept of community standards has played a critical role in the determination of whether particular works are legally obscene and thus open to censorship

The idea of using community standards of decency in order to determine whether pornographic material is legally obscene first appeared in the decision of the U.S. Supreme Court in *Roth v. United States* (1957). The idea's later usage, however, stems from the Court's 1973 *Miller v. California* case. In that decision, the Court affirmed that while obscenity was not protected under the First Amendment, the criteria for what constitutes obscenity should be determined by the individual states. Behind the Court's endorsement of using community standards to determine obscenity stood the belief that it was unrealistic to pose a national standard for obscenity in a country as large and as diverse as the United States.

Another Supreme Court decision in 1973, *Paris Adult Theater v. Slaton*, concerned two Georgia theaters that were prevented from showing pornographic films; this case pointed up the fact that employing community standards to define obscenity could lead to situations in which a film could be judged as obscene in one state but not in another. A persistent problem with the concept of community standards has been in determining precisely what they are for any particular community. In the 1990's new legal questions arose regarding the place of "electronic community" standards in determining the obscenity of material distributed over computer networks.

See also Internet; *Miller v. California*; Obscenity: legal definitions; *Roth v. United States*.

Computers

DEFINITION: Electronic devices for managing and processing information

SIGNIFICANCE: The ease with which computers send and receive information has made them the target of censors; computers also are used to effect censorship

There are two principal kinds of censorship methods, formal and informal. Formal censorship is explicit legal control of expression. Informal censorship takes place in the absence of a specific law. Pressures subtle and unsubtle can squelch or alter an expression that a given power does not want disseminated. Computer censorship has been formal and informal.

Informal computer censorship works by the same means as informal censorship with other media. Informal censorship is generally personal, in which a more powerful person influences a less powerful one, often without explicit instructions, to present information that will not displease the more powerful one. Since such censorship depends on such human factors as organizations, institutions, and the interactions that guide them, informal computer censorship is not much different than informal censorship generally.

On-line Communication. Formal censorship in the United States recalls the First Amendment to the Constitution, which allows for freedom of speech and of the press. "Speech" has been taken to include writing and other forms of expression, including such expression as may be captured in an electronic format. The Fourth Amendment, in turn, states: "The right of the people to be secure in their persons, houses, papers, and effects, against unreasonable searches and seizures, shall not be violated; and no warrants shall issue, but upon probable cause." These two rights guarantee a significant amount of freedom for a person with a computer. Controversy has arisen, however, as to how far such rights extend. For example, there has been debate about the amount of constitutional protection that on-line communications enjoy. The U.S. government has sought to increase its power to monitor on-line communications; opponents have cited the Constitution as allowing them great freedom in on-line communications. Issues such as encryption technology, which would prevent any monitoring agency from being able to understand the communications passing between two computers, and pornography on the Internet, which minors may access, came to the fore as on-line technology became widely available. The U.S. government

argued for the placement of a chip on all computers that would allow the government to defeat encryption, and passed, on February 8, 1996, the Communications Decency Act of 1996, which mandated that telecommunication service providers be held criminally liable if they fail to censor indecent material. Civil libertarians protested both actions.

The U.S. Secret Service, in another example, confiscated microcomputer equipment of the publisher of the on-line journal *Phrack* for reportedly publishing a Bell South document outlining some of the technical details of how their 911 service worked. The agency seized the equipment of a developer of role-playing games in Austin, Texas, claiming that the person had compiled and was publishing what amounted to a how-to book of computer crime.

International Issues. Increased computer usage, on a global scale, has brought about diverse forms of expression, which have raised issues of privacy and censorship. In countries such as Iran and China, for example, computers, with their capacity for small-scale publishing and for on-line communication, have been subject to strict monitoring and censorship. Privacy International, based in Washington, D.C., is an independent organization established in 1990 to protect personal privacy and to monitor surveillance by governments, financial institutions, intelligence agencies, media, political groups, police, and other organizations. At the invitation of its members and member organizations throughout the world, Privacy International has conducted successful campaigns against computer surveillance in Asia, Europe, and North America. Many of these campaigns have raised awareness about the dangers of proposals for identity cards, national numbering systems, computer linking programs, and the like. Rather than censoring the computer, such systems exploit the computer's great power to censor. For example, it could be made law that a person had to use a national identity card for a large number of transactions, including those currently handled by a bank debit card, by library cards, voter registration cards, drivers' licenses, and similar cards. Each time the card was used, the government could record information about the user. Such systems have Orwellian implications for personal freedom, including the freedom of expression.

Internationally, information and communications technologies are generating an industrial revolution already as significant and far-reaching as that of the past. In 1993 the European Council disseminated a report in Brussels on specific measures to be taken into consideration by the Community and the member states regarding infrastructure in the sphere of electronic information. On the basis of this report, the council adopted an operational program defining precise procedures for action and the necessary means for protection or censorship of certain information.

Potentials for Abuse. All revolutions generate uncertainty, discontinuity, and opportunity. The information society has the potential to improve, as well as curtail, the quality of life for its global community. However, the main risk of an information-dependent populace lies in the creation of a two-tier society of haves and have-nots.

In the United States many people have been concerned

about actual and possible abuses of data, and the proliferation of inaccurate data. Accordingly citizens have pressed for protective legislation. Examples include the Fair Credit Reporting Act, the Freedom of Information Act, the Education Privacy Act, the Privacy Act, and the Communications Decency Act. The Fair Credit Reporting Act gives individuals the right to examine credit records maintained by private organizations. The Freedom of Information Act gives individuals and organizations the right to inspect data concerning them that are maintained by agencies of the federal government. The Education Privacy Act protects the privacy of students concerning grades and other types of evaluations maintained by schools. The Privacy Act offers protection to individuals and organizations from data-gathering abuses by the federal government.

Computers are applied in countless settings where data are processed on a regular basis. Scientists use computers to store and quickly find the results of experiments. Libraries use computer catalogs to carry information about their collections. Hospitals use computers to sustain records about their patients. Governments maintain election returns and census information on computers. Computers also enable investors to obtain information about stocks, bonds, currency exchange rates, and prevailing prices around the world. Banks also maintain a variety of records on computers. Governments keep records—public and classified—on computer. Such information is easy to copy or transmit.

The decreasing cost of computer hardware and software enables many users to have access to the enormous quantities of information attainable on the Internet. Technology has amplified the ability to censor information (and the need to keep private information private) on a worldwide level.

A computer that is part of a network resembles a room with many doors. Intruders who slip through these doors are difficult to trace. One alternative is to keep key computers physically isolated from others; this is inconvenient but is practiced when the need for security is important enough. On the positive side of the privacy issue is the fact that governments, corporations, and special interest groups alike have motivation to safeguard stored information from unauthorized access. Who should be authorized, however, and who should be allowed unmonitored expression across computer networks, has proven to be a complicated issue. —*Ritchie R. Latimore*

See also China; Classification of information; Communications Decency Act; Free speech; Intellectual freedom; Internet; Iran; Technology.

BIBLIOGRAPHY

Steven Leven's *TechnoMania: The Future Isn't What You Think* (New York: Newsweek, 1995) is a broad depiction of the impact of information technology on issues of privacy, decentralization, censorship, education, and reality of cyberspace. Walter G. Olesky's *Science and Medicine* and *Education and Learning* (New York: Facts On File, 1995) surveys the practical applications of new technology, showing how computer technology has promoted censorship. Terry O'Neill's *Censorship: Opposing Viewpoints* (St. Paul, Minn.: Green Haven, 1985) is a survey on the pros and cons of censorship. Richard Rosenberg's *Free Speech, Pornography,* *Sexual Harassment, and Electronic Networks* (Vancouver, B.C.: University of British Columbia, 1993) deals with the issue of pornography on the Internet.

Comstock, Anthony

BORN: March 7, 1844, New Canaan, Connecticut
DIED: September 21, 1915, Summit, New Jersey
IDENTIFICATION: American crusader against "vice," especially pornography
SIGNIFICANCE: The most conspicuous figure in the history of American censorship, Comstock effectively promoted the passage of the nation's strongest antiobscenity law, which he helped enforce as a postal official

Raised in a modest family of ten children, Comstock experienced the early death of his mother and a strict upbringing in fundamentalist Puritanism. After being forced to leave school at eighteen, he went to work as a clerk in a general store in Winnipauk, Connecticut. Serious and pious at that age, he killed a loose rabid dog, then smashed up the liquor store of the dog's owner. Comstock later pointed to this incident as prophetic of his career, and he often referred to his opponents as "mad dogs" who endangered the community.

Comstock's Early Career. During the Civil War, from late 1863 until the summer of 1865, Comstock served as a volunteer in the Union Army. During this period he kept a diary, which reveals a person obsessed with the notion of sin, especially in the realm of sexuality. After the war he worked in New York City as a shipping clerk and dry-goods salesman, and at the same time he became an active member of the Young Men's Christian Association (YMCA), an organization that shared his moral values. As early as 1868, after a friend was allegedly "led astray and corrupted" by pornographic books, Comstock began a crusade to promote the enforcement of the state's antiobscenity laws. These first efforts led to the conviction of three publishers, one of whom attacked and wounded Comstock with a knife. After a publicized attack on two free-thinking editors, Victoria Woodhull and Tennessee Claflin, Comstock went to work as a full-time reformer and activist for the YMCA in 1873. That same year he was the principal founder and first secretary of the New York Society for the Suppression of Vice, which he served as secretary until his death.

Immediately after the Civil War, the Congress had made it illegal to use the mails for sending any "publication of a vulgar or indecent character." In 1873 Comstock successfully lobbied a sympathetic Congress to make the postal regulations more restrictive. The resulting Federal Anti-Obscenity Act, commonly called the "Comstock Law," was signed by President Ulysses S. Grant in March. The law provided for criminal penalties of up to five years for the first offense of sending books and other materials judged to be "obscene, lewd, or lascivious," including birth control materials. The law also created special agents in the Post Office Department, giving them broad discretion to seize and prosecute suspected materials. Comstock himself was appointed an unpaid agent, a position of great power that he retained until his death forty-one years later.

The Mature Crusader. Comstock was tireless in his efforts to enforce the 1873 law. He had little interest or ability to distinguish between good art and bad; with a characteristic lack of subtlety, he was generally impatient with any art or literature that deviated from his own standards of Victorian morality. After his first year as a postal official, he could boast that he had seized 130,000 pounds of "bad books," 194,000 indecent pictures and photographs, and 60,300 "articles of rubber used for immoral purposes." By the time of his death, it was estimated that he was personally responsible for the destruction of 160 tons of "obscene" materials.

Comstock usually concentrated his efforts on keeping the grosser forms of commercialized pornography out of the mails, but his list of prohibited works included such "respectable" writers as Theodore Dreiser, Margaret Sanger, Havelock Ellis, and Sigmund Freud. He was especially opposed to works such as Marie Dennett's practical manual on sexuality, written from a liberal point of view. Comstock was normally willing to allow classical works containing eroticism, such as Boccaccio's *Decameron*, to be sent to libraries where they could be read by mature scholars, but he was determined to keep such works out of the hands of impressionable young people. Comstock's personal standards usually prevailed in courtrooms because of the "Hicklin rule," which allowed for confiscation and prosecution based on the harmful influence of isolated passages on the most susceptible person in society.

In pursuing his censorship aims Comstock was ruthless and inspired a great deal of fear. It is estimated that he was responsible for the arrest of more than thirty-six hundred men, women, and children. One of his major methods was to use agents posing as customers in order to entrap dealers of illegal materials, and then he would strike with furious and well publicized raids. Convinced of the righteousness of his cause, he never expressed any sympathy or pity for those he prosecuted. For example, when Madam Restell, a prominent abortionist and dealer in contraceptives, committed suicide after being tricked into a confession in 1878, Comstock commented, "A bloody ending to a bloody life," and boasted that Restell was the fifteenth person whom he had driven to suicide. In addition to fighting against obscenity, Comstock directed many of his efforts against dishonest advertisers and promoters of fraud and medical quackery. When he was prosecuting such abuses, even his critics admitted that he did some useful work.

Comstock's views about morality and vice are clearly expounded in his two books and several pamphlets. *Frauds Exposed* (1880) is his account of a "moral hero" (basically a self-portrait) who struggles against cowardly villains who are agents of Satan. *Traps for the Young* (1883) warned about "Satan's traps" for boys and girls, especially half-dime novels, materialistic advertisements, gambling, the practice of free-love, and the antireligious messages of "infidels and liberals."

Anthony Comstock, the most notorious censor in U.S. history. (Library of Congress)

In his pamphlet, *Morals Versus Art* (1887), Comstock insisted that he was not against serious art in museums, but he warned that lewd pictures and photographs "appeal to passions and create impure imaginations."

Comstock's Last Years. By the end of the nineteenth century, Comstock's views were increasingly outside those of the mainstream of public opinion, and he was becoming less successful in his efforts to proscribe art and literature. With his overweight body and prominent whiskers, he became a favorite subject of political cartoonists, and George Bernard Shaw coined the term "comstockery" as an epithet for moralistic censorship. Nevertheless, Comstock continued to have many prominent supporters, and he continued to seize contraband and make arrests until the last year of his life. He died shortly after President Woodrow Wilson appointed him to represent the United States at the International Purity Congress. In spite of the ridicule of libertarians, his Comstock Law remained on the books, and the courts did not significantly liberalize its enforcement until almost half a century after his death.

—Thomas T. Lewis

See also Birth control education; Comstock Act of 1873; Fear; Helms, Jesse Alexander; Hicklin case; Morality; Obscenity: legal definitions; Obscenity: sale and possession; Shakespeare, William; Society for the Suppression of Vice, New York; Sumner, John; Woodhull, Victoria.

BIBLIOGRAPHY

Heywood Broun and Margaret Leech's *Anthony Comstock: Roundsman of the Lord* (New York: A. & C. Boni, 1927) provides a critical portrait. Charles Gallaudet Trumbull's *Anthony Comstock, Fighter: Some Impressions of a Lifetime Adventure in Conflict with the Powers of Evil* (2d ed. New York: Fleming H. Revell, 1913) is excessively adulatory but useful. James Paul and Murray Schwartz's *Federal Censorship: Obscenity in the Mail* (New York: Free Press of Glencoe, 1961) and Robert Haney's *Comstockery in America: Patterns of Censorship and Control* (New York: Da Capo Press, 1974) provide informative accounts of the legal history. Paul Boyer's *Purity in Print: The Vice-Society Movement and Book Censorship in America* (New York: Scribners, 1968) also includes much interesting information.

Comstock Act of 1873

ENACTED: March 3, 1873

PLACE: United States (national)

SIGNIFICANCE: The most restrictive antiobscenity statute ever passed by the U.S. Congress, this law expanded existing federal obscenity statues and effectively outlawed the advertisement and transportation of birth control and drugs that induced abortion

Anthony Comstock—from whom the act takes its popular name—lobbied for this law with the support of the Young Men's Christian Association. Officially titled the Act for the Suppression of Trade in and Circulation of Obscene Literature and Articles of Immoral Use, the law expanded the provisions of the Federal Obscenity Statute of 1872, which defined criminal sanctions for the transportation of obscene literature through the public mails. The Comstock Act also explicitly forbade trafficking in contraception and abortion. This statute was patterned after an 1869 New York state law prohibiting pornography, the dissemination of birth control information, and the advertisement of abortion services. New York's law made it illegal to give contraception information either verbally or in writing.

The Comstock Act's definition of pornography was broad and vague; however, its prohibitions regarding use of federal mail were specific, closing many loopholes present in an antecedent statute of 1872. The act included five sections prohibiting the mailing of obscene literature, contraceptive devices, contraceptive advertisement or information, abortifacients, and abortion advertisement.

Comstock's extraordinary lobbying efforts pushed the bill through Congress at the moment that a special committee was investigating illegal government financing of the Union Pacific Railroad. This public scandal made members of Congress reluctant to oppose Comstock's moral crusade, for fear of generating a fresh public controversy. Comstock used members of the press who were covering the congressional scandal to his advantage by publicly displaying pornography, contraceptives, and abortifacients while he awaited the introduction of his bill. His bill was originally scheduled for introduction in January, but delays caused by the railroad scandal permitted Comstock and his obscenity exhibits to remain on display for six weeks. The bill eventually passed by the Senate on March 2 and was signed into law the next day.

The Comstock Act had immediate and profound ramifications, precipitating additional legislation in virtually every state. Twenty-four states adopted legislation forbidding transportation and advertisement of obscene materials, contraceptives, and abortifacients. Fourteen states added prohibitions on speech regarding these subjects. Connecticut enacted the most restrictive legislation by forbidding the use of any contraceptive technique or device.

Efforts to repeal or modify the Comstock Act began shortly after its passage. In 1878 the National Liberal League collected more than sixty thousand signatures from persons demanding that the act be repealed. As early as 1881 some states amended their own laws to allow physicians to prescribe birth control for the prevention of disease. It was not until 1936, however, that birth control became legal. A three-judge panel from the Second District Court of Appeals found that the original intent of the Comstock law was not to forbid the use of contraception but simply to protect the public from obscene and dangerous practices. Local ordinances that had been initiated by the Comstock law remained in effect until 1970 when Congress finally changed the federal law, removing the obscenity classification from contraception.

See also Abortion gag rule; Birth control education; Comstock, Anthony; *Little Review, The*; Obscenity: legal definitions; Sanger, Margaret; Sumner, John.

Confessions of Nat Turner, The

TYPE OF WORK: Book

PUBLISHED: 1967

AUTHOR: William Styron (1925-   )

SUBJECT MATTER: Fictional memoir narrated in the voice of the leader of the biggest slave insurrection in U.S. history

SIGNIFICANCE: Many African American writers objected to the presumption of a white Southerner writing a novel from a black slave's point of view

In 1835 Nat Turner led the most successful slave insurrection in American history—a Virginia uprising that lasted more than two months and killed more than fifty white people. Styron published his novel about Turner at the height of the Black Power movement during the 1960's, at a time when African American writers and activists championed black separatism over integration. Narrated by Turner himself, Styron's novel is daringly speculative about Turrner's private life, and particularly his love for one of his white victims, Margaret Whitehead.

Black novelist James Baldwin, a personal friend of Styron, praised *The Confessions of Nat Turner*, and the novel won a Pulitzer Prize. However, other novelists, historians, literary critics, and psychologists published *The Confessions of Nat Turner: Ten Black Writers Respond*, angrily attacking Styron as a white Southerner whose attempt to enter the mind of a black slave demeaned Turner. They condemned both the execution of the novel and the idea behind it. In defending his right to imagine a black slave's life, Styron was vigorously supported by Eugene Genovese, one of the leading historians of American slavery.

The controversy over the book proved so great that director Norman Jewison abandoned his plans to film the story, even though the celebrated actor James Earl Jones had agreed to play Turner.

See also African Americans; Literature; Miscegenation; Race; *Uncle Tom's Cabin*.

Confucius

BORN: 551 B.C.E., state of Lu, China
DIED: 479 B.C.E., Ch'u-fu, state of Lu, China
IDENTIFICATION: Chinese philosopher and educator
SIGNIFICANCE: Confucius' teachings became the official state philosophy of China and remained the dominant philosophy there until the mid-twentieth century

Born late in the Chou dynasty, Confucius was reared in poverty by his mother. He studied ancient texts and learned the arts of a courtier. Early in his life he held minor public posts, but is best known for his teachings during his later life. The Chou Dynasty had fallen into a state of disintegration by the time Confucius was born, and the established authority and traditional rituals were violated daily. During this time of social upheaval Confucius emerged as a teacher who valued constancy, trustworthiness, and the reestablishment of the rational feudal order of previous times. Even though he was respected as a great teacher he never held a major government post. Late in his life he became a wandering philosopher-teacher. Like Socrates of Greece, Confucius became known as a teacher primarily through the preservation of his teachings by his disciples. From 206 B.C.E. until the twentieth century the philosophy of Confucius, known as Confucianism, dominated China and many other East Asian countries.

While Confucius and his philosophy enjoyed almost complete acceptance for more than two millennia, he did attract some objections. Confucius held a minor official position in the year 500 B.C.E., based mostly on his reputation as a teacher. Although he supported ritual as a form of moral improvement, he downplayed the spiritual aspects of it. He was forced to resign from his position because his denial of the spiritual was deemed improper. Due to this event and his ideas about ritual he was never again able to obtain a government position. Two hundred and fifty years after Confucius' death the Chou Dynasty finally came to an end. The Ch'in Dynasty came to power in 211 B.C.E. and put an end to free philosophical thought. Confucianism in turn was outlawed and writings about it were burned. The Ch'in Dynasty was short lived, however. In 206 B.C.E. the new Han Dynasty instituted Confucianism as the state philosophy.

With the communist assumption of power in 1949, Confucianism again officially came to an end as the state philosophy on mainland China. Confucian belief in tradition and hierarchy are directly opposed to the Marxist beliefs that the People's Republic of China then adopted. Confucianism remained a major philosophy among East Asians outside of mainland China.

See also Asian Americans; Book burning; China; Communism; Mao Zedong; Shih huang-ti.

Twelfth century print of Confucius. (Library of Congress)

Congress, U.S.

FOUNDED: 1789

TYPE OF ORGANIZATION: U.S. national legislature, consisting of the House of Representatives and the Senate

SIGNIFICANCE: Except in times of national emergency, Congress has steered away from censorship legislation; a notable aberration was its passage of the Sedition Act of 1798

Seeking to prevent the rise of a power hungry national legislature, the Framers of the Bill of Rights included the phrase "Congress shall make no law . . . abridging the freedom of speech, or of the press" in the First Amendment. Thus, free and open discussion of governmental policies and unrestricted media debate of issues concerning the American people seem guaranteed in the Bill of Rights. Despite this extensive protection of the citizenry from congressional encroachment upon civil liberties, however, the U.S. Supreme Court has ruled, as late as 1988, that Congress may censor speech and the media, provided that such action "is necessary to serve a compelling state interest and that it is narrowly drawn to achieve that end." Therefore, idealistic guarantees are diluted by the fine print of pragmatic politics and "compelling state interest."

Alien and Sedition Acts. Historically, Congress has been cautious about encroaching upon the freedoms outlined in the First Amendment. In the summer of 1798, however, a Federalist-dominated Congress passed a series of four measures, usually called collectively the Alien and Sedition Acts, which clearly were designed to restrict the participation of the main rival political faction, Thomas Jefferson's Democratic-Republican Party. There were at the time about twenty-five thousand aliens in the United States. Many were refugees from oppressive authorities in their homelands, and they tended to align themselves with the Jeffersonians, who believed in as little government as possible. Others were propertyless and not acceptable to the Federalists, a political party of the "prosperous and well born."

One provision of the legislation was an extension of the naturalization period for immigrants from five to fourteen years. Another clause empowered President John Adams, a Federalist, to deport aliens judged by him to be subversive. Obviously, the alien provision was aimed at the newly arrived supporters of Vice President Jefferson.

The Sedition Act was an attempt to muzzle the Democratic-Republican media. The law declared that "if any person shall write, print, utter, or publish . . . any false, scandalous and malicious writing . . . against the government of the United States, or either house of the Congress . . . or the President . . . to excite against them the hatred of the good people of the United States . . . " that such a person "shall be punished by a fine not exceeding two thousand dollars, and by imprisonment not exceeding two years."

By passing the Alien and Sedition Acts, Congress undermined the basic liberties provided in the First Amendment. Uncensored speech and an unshackled press had made the nation a beacon of freedom to the rest of the world. George Washington, one year away from death, rose from his bed to warn against the threats posed by the Alien and Sedition Acts. Unfortunately, the Federalists, who dominated both houses of Congress, failed to heed Washington's warning.

Fisticuffs erupted on the floor of Congress. U.S. Republican Matthew Lyon, an Irish immigrant and follower of Jefferson, had served as a colonel in the "Green Mountain Boys" during the American Revolution. One afternoon in the House of Representatives, Roger Griswold, a Federalist supporter of the Alien and Sedition Acts, criticized Lyon's war record. Lyon spat in Griswold's eye; the next day, the two legislators fought each other with canes and fire tongs. The Federalist-controlled Congress tried to expel Lyon from the House but failed to garner the required two-thirds vote.

In an attempt to settle the score, Lyon was then charged with violating the Sedition Act. The Democratic-Republican had published a letter to an editor accusing President Adams of "ridiculous pomp, foolish adulation, and selfish adulation." Tried and convicted before a Federalist judge, Lyon became a martyr for those who championed uncensored speech and media. Reelected to Congress, Lyon led a twelve-mile-long caravan to the capital, which at that time was in Philadelphia.

As the 1800 presidential election approached, the argument became a clear one: Did the Constitution or the Alien and Sedition Acts take prior-

Contemporary newspaper caricature of congressmen Mathew Lyon and Roger Griswold fighting over the Sedition Act of 1798 on the House floor. (Library of Congress)

ity? The election became a referendum on censorship and Jefferson and his congressional supporters were swept into office. Seeking to ease fears, Jefferson calmly proclaimed, "We are all Federalists. We are all Republicans. We are all Americans." As Jefferson assumed office, the acts expired and the new president promptly pardoned all those who had been convicted under the acts and he canceled remaining trials.

These congressional measures, which struck so brutally at liberty, were the last such acts until the country entered World War I. The Espionage Act of 1917 mandated heavy fines and imprisonment for those individuals considered to be impeding the war effort. A section of this law empowered the postmaster general to censor mail such as German-language newspapers. The *American Socialist* and the Industrial Workers of the World's *Solidarity* could not be mailed. Forty-four papers lost their mailing privileges under the Espionage Act, and thirty others had to agree to remain silent on the war.

Congress passed two other laws to restrict free expression. The Trading with the Enemy Act of 1917 censored international communications. The following year Congress approved the Sedition Act, which made it a crime to write or publish "any disloyal, profane, scurrilous or abusive language about the form of government of the United States or the Constitution." Additionally, Congress forbade language that brought "into contempt, scorn, contumely or disrepute" the nation's governmental institutions. Both measures remained on the books for use in World War II by the Office of Censorship.

Congress' wartime actions were generally supported by the American people, as were similar World War II policies. Mainstream publications avoided scrutiny as the government targeted socialist and German media outlets. When the Red Scare of 1919 erupted, two thousand persons were prosecuted under the two wartime laws. Evangelist Billy Sunday summed up the widespread feeling: "If I had my way with these ornery wild-eyed Socialists and IWW's, I would stand them up before a firing squad."

Regulating the Broadcast Media. By the 1920's, the public had become mesmerized by the new medium of radio. Congress became more regulatory toward broadcast media than it had been with the fringe publications of the World War I era. Congress has used two major reasons to justify tighter federal regulation of broadcast media than of newspapers. First, space on the radio spectrum—the range of frequencies used for all electronic communications—is limited, so a limited number of channels must be allocated among broadcasters. In the mid-1920's, when radio broadcasting first became popular, stations frequently drowned out one another's signals. The Radio Corporation of America (RCA), the dominant radio manufacturer of the day, joined angry consumers in calling for government regulation of frequencies. The Radio Act of 1927 created the Federal Radio Commission to assign broadcasting licenses. In 1934 the Federal Communications Commission (FCC), an independent regulatory agency, was created. The FCC took over federal management of all kinds of electronic communications (now including telephones, AM and FM radio, over-the-air and cable television, satellites, telegraph, and citizens band radio). The FCC, now a massive

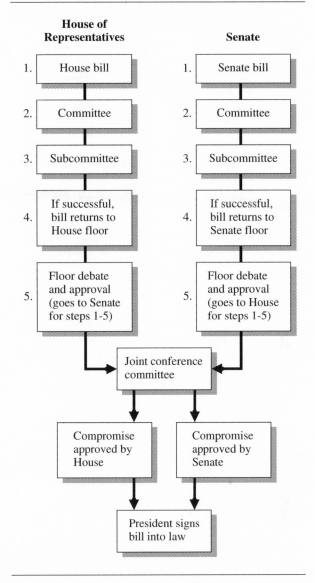

THE CONGRESSIONAL LEGISLATIVE PROCESS

Source: Adapted from Jay M. Shafritz, *The Dorsey Dictionary of American Government and Politics.* Chicago: Dorsey Press, 1988. Primary source, Auraria Library, Government Documents Section, Denver, Colo.

agency controlled by a five-member commission, is instructed by law to regulate broadcasting in "the public interest, convenience, or necessity."

The second major justification for tighter federal government regulation of the broadcast media is the public-interest argument: Broadcasters use public airwaves. Because they use public resources to serve the public, they should be regulated, as public utilities are. Secretary of the Interior Herbert Hoover was a major architect of federal radio regulation. In 1924 he argued that "radio communication is not to be considered as merely a business. . . . It is a public concern impressed with the public trust and to be considered primarily from the standpoint of public interest to the same extent and upon the same general principles as our other public utilities." Even if radio frequencies had not been scarce, Hoover and other public-interest-oriented politicians of the era would likely have called for regulation. Hoover's antibusiness sentiments ran deep; several times he expressed doubts about whether commercial advertisements should be allowed on radio.

The FCC and Congress have created policies that define technical standards, licensing procedures, and broadcasting standards. All broadcasting station licenses must be periodically renewed, and the renewal process gives the FCC a chance to deny licenses to stations that break its rules. Two of the most controversial aspects of FCC decisions have concerned content regulation and the ownership of broadcasting facilities.

One of the goals of federal regulation is to guarantee a diversity of views in the media. Diversity in the "marketplace of ideas," a popular metaphor, is prized in a democratic society because it offers citizens the freedom to make up their own minds. One-sided coverage in the print media is generally not worrisome; people with different points of view can start new newspapers or find existing papers that will print an opposing opinion. Broadcast frequencies are scarce, however, and diversity is therefore limited.

Regulation balances the free speech rights of broadcasters with the audience's "right to know." For example, during political campaigns, the equal-time provision in federal law requires that if one major candidate for office is allowed to buy commercial time, then other candidates must be similarly accommodated. The rule does not apply to news stories but only to paid time and "free time" broadcasts, such as talk shows.

Other regulatory policies have been much more controversial. The bill that created the FCC explicitly forbade censorship or interference with the right of free speech on the radio. Nevertheless, in 1949 the FCC adopted a policy known as the fairness doctrine. The fairness doctrine required broadcasters to provide "reasonable opportunities for the expression of opposing views on controversial issues of public importance." The doctrine applied to public affairs shows, entertainment, and some advertising, and critics called it censorship. The Supreme Court upheld the fairness doctrine as a reasonable policy designed to "preserve an uninhibited marketplace of ideas." The Court argued that "it is the right of the viewers and listeners, not of broadcasters, which is paramount." The Court has struck down fairness-oriented regulations on newspapers because they violate the First Amendment, but broadcasting regulations are justified by the scarcity argument.

During the Ronald Reagan era, conservative appointees to the FCC gained a majority and took many steps to deregulate broadcasting. To name only three, they discontinued FCC supervision of radio broadcast formats, eased restrictions on indecent broadcasts during some parts of the day, and removed limitations on the number of commercial messages permitted during children's television shows. By far the most notable change, however, was the abolition of the fairness doctrine.

Fearful of such a step, Congress passed a law that required the commission to administer the fairness doctrine, but on June 19, 1987, President Reagan vetoed the bill. His veto message said that content-based regulation by the federal government was "antagonistic to the freedom of expression guaranteed by the First Amendment." Reagan claimed that the scarcity argument no longer held: The rapid expansion of cable television afforded many outlets for different ideas. The fairness doctrine's supporters did not have the votes to override the veto; shortly thereafter the FCC formally abolished the doctrine. The doctrine's supporters continue to work actively for its passage through Congress.

A sizable group in Congress has continued to believe that the broadcast media should be regulated in the public interest. In 1988 Congress passed a bill to limit commercials and require educational service for children. Reagan vetoed the law, stating that "the Constitution simply does not empower the Federal Government to oversee the programming decisions of broadcasters." Support remained strong for the idea, however, leading to passage of the Children's Television Act of 1990, which requires television stations to serve the "educational and informational needs of children." The FCC promised active supervision, but was embarrassed when the Center for Media Education inspected station records and found that many stations were using commercial cartoons and situation comedies to satisfy their educational programming requirements.

On balance, Congress has restrained itself from the tendency to regulate print and electronic media. With rare exceptions, Congress has advocated the free exchange of views. When "compelling state interests" have been present—as they were during both world wars—Congress has felt compelled to proceed down the pathway to censorship. After peace has been restored, however, Congress has resumed its generally benevolent approach to press and speech freedoms.

—Joseph Edward Lee

See also Communism; Communist Party of the U.S.A.; Presidency, U.S.; Sedition; Sedition Act of 1798; World War I; World War II.

BIBLIOGRAPHY

A useful general history of Congress is Alvin M. Josephy, Jr., *On the Hill: A History of the American Congress* (New York: Simon and Schuster, 1979). An essential tool is Norman Ornstein's *Vital Statistics on Congress* (Washington: Congressional Quarterly Press, 1987). Also valuable is *Congressional Quarterly's Guide to the U.S. Congress* (4th ed. Washington: Congressional Quarterly, 1991). Primary sources may be found in the *Congressional Record* (1873-   ) and its predecessors. Louis Hartz's *The Liberal Tradition in America* (New York: Harcourt Brace, 1955) is a classic examination of the search for truth in American culture. Steven S. Smith's *The American Congress* (Boston: Houghton Mifflin, 1995) is a recent look at the dynamics of the federal legislative branch. Fred R. Harris, *Deadlock or Decision: The U.S. Senate and the Rise of National Politics* (New York: Oxford University Press, 1993), is a pessimistic treatment of the forces behind legislation. James M. Smith's *Freedom's Fetters: The Alien and Sedition Laws and American Civil Liberties* (Ithaca, N.Y.:

Cornell University Press, 1956) explains the fourteen indictments that took place under these laws. James R. Mock, *Censorship 1917* (Princeton, N.J.: Princeton University Press, 1941) examines the efforts by Congress to regulate the flow of information in wartime. Theodore F. Koop, *Weapon of Silence* (Chicago: University of Chicago Press, 1946), offers an interesting view of voluntary censorship.

Constitution, U.S.

RATIFIED: 1789

PLACE: United States (national)

SIGNIFICANCE: When the U.S. Constitution was originally ratified it contained only implicit guarantees of freedom of expression; explicit guarantees were written into its Bill of Rights, which was ratified two years later

The U.S. Constitution has long been celebrated as a model of federalism. While the system of government that it created was framed on an assumption that popular opinion unfettered by censorship would play a crucial role in forging democratic political consensus, the document itself contained no explicit guarantees of individual freedom of expression.

The Constitution written in 1787 was concerned mainly with the structure of government. Its preamble implies the nature of consensual government that Thomas Jefferson held to be crucial to his cardinal values of "life, liberty, and the pursuit of happiness." To Jefferson and many other Founders, promotion of the "general welfare" to "secure the blessings of liberty" implied the specific rights that were later defined in several amendments.

The Constitution itself outlined the structure of the legislative, executive, and judicial branches of government, and established the relationships among them. For example, the document explained how differences of opinion between the legislative and executive branches should be settled. It also defined the relationship between the federal government and the governments of the individual states—by prohibiting, for

---

BILL OF RIGHTS

First Amendment

Congress shall make no law respecting an establishment of religion, or prohibiting the free exercise thereof; or abridging the freedom of speech, or of the press, or the right of the people peaceably to assemble, and to petition the Government for a redress of grievances.

Second Amendment

A well regulated Militia, being necessary to the security of a free State, the right of the people to keep and bear Arms, shall not be infringed.

Third Amendment

No Soldier shall, in time of peace be quartered in any house, without the consent of the Owner, nor in time of war, but in a manner to be prescribed by law.

Fourth Amendment

The right of the people to be secure in their persons, houses, papers, and effects, against unreasonable searches and seizures, shall not be violated, and no Warrants shall issue, but upon probable cause, supported by Oath or affirmation, and particularly describing the place to be searched, and the persons or things to be seized.

Fifth Amendment

No person shall be held to answer for a capital, or otherwise infamous crime, unless on a presentment or indictment of a Grand Jury, except in cases arising in the land or naval forces, or in the Militia, when in actual service in time of War or public danger; nor shall any person be subject for the same offence to be twice put in jeopardy of life or limb, nor shall be compelled in any criminal case to be a witness against himself, nor be deprived of life, liberty, or property, without due process of law; nor shall private property be taken for public use without just compensation.

Sixth Amendment

In all criminal prosecutions, the accused shall enjoy the right to a speedy and public trial, by an impartial jury of the State and district wherein the crime shall have been committed; which district shall have been previously ascertained by law, and to be informed of the nature and cause of the accusation; to be confronted with the witnesses against him; to have compulsory process for obtaining witnesses in his favor, and to have the assistance of counsel for his defence.

Seventh Amendment

In Suits at common law, where the value in controversy shall exceed twenty dollars, the right of trial by jury shall be preserved, and no fact tried by a jury shall be otherwise re-examined in any Court of the United States, than according to the rules of the common law.

Eighth Amendment

Excessive bail shall not be required, nor excessive fines imposed, nor cruel and unusual punishments inflicted.

Ninth Amendment

The enumeration in the Constitution, of certain rights, shall not be construed to deny or disparage others retained by the people.

Tenth Amendment

The powers not delegated to the United States by the Constitution, nor prohibited by it to the States, are reserved to the States respectively, or to the people.

example, any state from imposing duties on goods imported from another, and by affirming that a citizen of any given state is also a citizen of all others.

The Constitution's provisions for admitting new states and for amending itself implied that debate and discussion about these matters should be open and free. In addition, the checks and balances built into the Constitution implied that government decisions should be made by the many—as opposed to the few—a view that implied a need for uncensored discussion and debate.

Several amendments to the Constitution, in addition to the first, also implied a need for uncensored exchange of information. For example, the long-standing tradition of open police and court records in the United States owes as much to the Sixth Amendment as it does to the First Amendment. The principle of uncensored public access to the mechanisms of justice has also been invoked to expose instances of "cruel and unusual punishment," which the Eighth Amendment outlawed. The Ninth and Tenth amendments reserved undelegated powers to the individual, again implying an uncensored cacophony of voices. This might also be said about the Thirteenth Amendment, which outlawed slavery; the Fifteenth Amendment, which forbade discrimination on condition of "race, color, or previous servitude"; and the Nineteenth Amendment, which extended the right to vote to women.

Despite adoption of the Bill of Rights in 1791, censorship legislation soon followed. The Constitution's first major test in this area was the Sedition Act of 1798.

See also Assembly, right of; First Amendment; Fourteenth Amendment; Fourth Amendment; Jefferson, Thomas; *New York Times Co. v. Sullivan*; Sedition Act of 1798.

Convention for the Protection of Human Rights and Fundamental Freedoms

DATE: Signed 1950; came into force 1953
PLACE: Europe
SIGNIFICANCE: This international declaration in favor of free speech has become law in many Western European nations

The European Convention for the Protection of Human Rights and Fundamental Freedoms was drafted to protect freedom of expression, thought, conscience, religion, peaceful assembly, association, and a number of other freedoms from violation by governments. The convention is law in most European countries.

A commission and a court were created to enforce the convention. The commission investigates violations and tries to get the parties involved to settle the dispute. If no settlement can be reached, the case is often referred to the court for a binding determination. Court decisions are final and have the force of law in the European signatory countries.

The court has been successful in getting various European governments to change laws which violate the freedoms supported by the convention. It has said that freedom of expression is an essential foundation of a democratic society, and a basic condition for social progress and individual development. Such freedom is based on concepts of pluralism, tolerance, and broadmindedness, and covers even speech that offends, shocks, or disturbs the government or any sector of a country's population.

The convention allows governments to limit freedom of expression if it is necessary in a democratic society. Grounds for such limitations are public safety, prevention of crime, protection of health and morals, protection of reputations, and maintenance of the authority of the judiciary.

The court has been particularly careful to extend freedom of expression to such areas as artistic expression and debate on public issues and political affairs. It struck down an order prohibiting a newspaper from printing an article about a court case, even though the article might have made the trial more difficult. Another newspaper was allowed to portray a high government official as undignified and immoral in handling a political issue. Laws regulating advertising have also been struck down as interfering with freedom of expression.

Obscenity is more likely to be subject to government regulation. Books containing material judged to be obscene can be severely regulated or even banned when directed to children and teenagers. Public displays of obscene artistic works can also be regulated or banned.

Any forms of speech that amount to slander or libel are not protected if they are false and they damage the persons attacked. Speech may be subject to greater protection if made against a high political official.

See also Defamation; First Amendment; Free speech; Obscenity: legal definitions.

"Cop Killer"

TYPE OF WORK: Rap song
RELEASED: 1991
WRITER AND PERFORMER: Ice-T (Tracey Marrow, born c. late 1950's)
SUBJECT MATTER: Social protest against police brutality
SIGNIFICANCE: The song's message explicitly advocating that victims of police brutality retaliate by killing the police evoked such strong and widespread protests that the song was pulled from release

In 1992 the heavy metal rap group Body Count led by Ice-T released a self-titled recording "Body Count" on Warner Bros. Records, a subsidiary of Time Warner. The most controversial song on the recording was "Cop Killer," whose lyrics contained the message that victims of police brutality should retaliate by killing the police. After the album debuted in 1991, it received little attention until after the verdict in the Rodney King police brutality trial. In 1992 the Texas Fraternal Order of Police threatened a boycott of all Time Warner products if the song were not pulled from release.

U.S. president George Bush denounced Time Warner as "wrong" and labeled Ice-T "sick." Former National Security Council aide Oliver North led his Freedom Alliance to form a petition to bring the executives at Time Warner to trial for "sedition and anarchy." Sixty members of Congress signed a letter of protest calling the song "vile and despicable." Police representatives and critics, including actor Charlton Heston, attended the 1992 Time Warner shareholders' meeting to denounce the company for the recording.

People protesting Ice-T's song "Cop Killer" demonstrate outside a Warners Corporation shareholder's meeting in Beverly Hills, California, in July, 1992. (AP/Wide World Photos)

During the controversy, Ice-T claimed that his fifteen-year-old daughter had been pulled from her school class and questioned about her father. He has also stated that Warner Brothers Records staff members received death threats.

On July 28, 1992, Ice-T pulled the song from the release. He contended that the choice to pull the song was his, not the record company's. The company then reissued the recording without the "Cop Killer" track. Also in 1992, Ice-T was released from his recording contract.

See also Music; Parents' Music Resource Center; Rap music; Recording industry; Sedition; Shakur, Tupac; Suicide; 2 Live Crew.

Copernicus, Nicolaus

BORN: February 19, 1473, Thorn (Torún), Prussia
DIED: May 24, 1543, Frauenburg (Frombork), Prussia
IDENTIFICATION: Polish astronomer
SIGNIFICANCE: Copernicus' theory that the sun, not the Earth, was the center of the solar system was attacked by Protestant and Catholic theologians; his treatise on the subject was placed on the Index of Forbidden Books in 1616

From the age of ten, when his father died, Copernicus was raised by an uncle who was later a Roman Catholic bishop. Following Copernicus' education in Poland, his uncle arranged for him to travel to Italy, where the young man obtained a doctor's degree in canon law and studied astronomy, mathematics, and medicine. His upbringing, religious studies, and long service in religious office made Copernicus an odd candidate to defy church teachings.

His astronomical studies and interest in the truth, however, led him on a path of conflict with established religious doctrine. At that time, religious authorities taught that the earth was at the center of the universe, and that all objects in the sky moved around it. Humankind thus occupied a "special position" at the center of all creation. This view, first formalized by the Greco-Egyptian astronomer Ptolemy in the second century, continued to dominate human belief through the sixteenth century.

However, Copernicus observed flaws in the Ptolemaic model by comparing the predicted and observed positions of the planets. Copernicus formulated a new model of the solar system, in which the earth and the other planets orbited around the sun, reviving an idea proposed more than seventeen hundred years earlier by Aristarchus of Samos. Copernicus circulated this idea among friends in a manuscript titled *Commentariolus*, but he refrained from the widespread distribution of the manuscript. Nonetheless, it came to the attention of Pope Clement VII in 1533; however, the pope took no action to suppress it.

The first serious attacks on the Copernican model came from Protestant religious leaders, with Martin Luther claiming that "this fool wants to turn the whole art of astronomy upside down!" Perhaps because of these attacks, or perhaps because of his own reticence, Copernicus did not publish a full description of his idea, entitled *De Revolutionibus Orbium Coelestium*, until 1543, when he was near death. Even then, Andreas Osiander, who supervised production of *De Revolutionibus Orbium Coelestium*, urged caution, suggesting that the introduction should state that planetary motion could be explained either by the hypothesis of Copernicus or by that of Ptolemy. Copernicus rejected this compromise, but Osiander removed the introduction Copernicus had written and substituted his own unsigned preface. Presenting the theory as a hypothesis kept Roman Catholic theologians from attacking the book for many years. *De Revolutionibus Orbium Coelestium* was not placed on the *Index Librorum Prohibitorum* until 1616.

Had Copernicus widely discussed and defended the details of his model, it might have gained acceptance during his lifetime. As it was, few people were willing to accept his revolutionary idea. However, astronomers and astrologers used his book because it was a more accurate way to predict planetary positions than the Ptolemaic method. The Copernican model only gained widespread acceptance as the true description of nature when it was revived by the work of Galileo Galilei and Johannes Kepler in the seventeenth century.

See also Astronomy; Galileo Galilei; *Index Librorum Prohibitorum*; Luther, Martin; Reformation, the; Science; Vatican.

Copycat crime

Definition: Misbehavior inspired or triggered by news reports of criminal activity

Significance: Society's need to discourage copycat crime has often been cited as a justification for censorship

One of the more frequently stated reasons why speech should be censored is the impact that certain ideas might have on weak-minded or immature individuals. In particular, the discussion or depiction of criminal behavior within the various media has frequently been alleged to lead to copycat crimes. Examples include the Tylenol tampering incidents of 1982, the assassination attempt depicted in the 1976 film *Taxi Driver*, and the availability of information, on the Internet and in book form, on how to make bombs. It has been alleged, for example, that information from the Internet was used to construct the bomb that destroyed the Oklahoma City federal building in 1995.

The idea that media descriptions and depictions have a strong impact on behavior has been referred to in the media effects literature as the "hypodermic needle" model. Like a drug injection, the ingestion of violent or antisocial conduct impacts the psyche and may lead to repeating the behavior. Typically, however, those favoring censorship of criminal depictions do not believe they are impacted in such a way,

but, nevertheless believe that some are. Children, imbeciles, the emotionally vulnerable, the undersocialized, and publicity seekers have been cited as in need of protection from portrayals of crime. Since it is impossible to predict how many might react by repeating the crimes, censorship helps to protect society from the possibility of copycat behavior.

Empirical Evidence. Until the 1980's there was little empirical research dealing exclusively with copycat crime. Empirical studies of media influence do not support the anecdotal evidence. For example, an Australian study used a three-year time frame to compare police data on bank and other armed robberies with local newspaper stories on robberies during the same period. Robberies were compared for two seven-day periods immediately before and after the date of any newspaper story reporting a successful robbery. There was no evidence of any copycat effect following newspaper stories or after possible word-of-mouth communication about the commission of high-value bank robberies. Research results did not support the idea that newspaper reports of successful bank robberies stimulate copycat robberies of banks or other targets.

Ray Surette has done extensive research on copycat crimes since the mid-1980's. He argues that copycat crime is a persistent social phenomenon, common enough to influence the total crime picture, but mainly by influencing crime techniques rather than the motivation to commit a crime or the development of criminal tendencies. A copycat criminal is likely to be a career criminal involved in property offenses rather than a first-time violent offender. The specific relationship between media coverage and the commission of copycat crime is currently unknown, and the social-context factors influencing copycat crimes have not been identified. Certainly, it cannot be proven that a media depiction might stimulate an otherwise ordinary person to commit a crime. Although research has established the media's influence on some deviant behaviors, it has not established a direct causal connection between media stimuli and specific deviant behaviors apart from other variables appearing in combination. Simply because a media depiction is followed by the reoccurrence of a similar event does not indicate a connection. In some cases, alleged copycats have stated they knew nothing of the previous publicized incident.

Surette also noted that copycat crimes revealed identifiable similarities among incidents. The copycat criminals seemed to fall into at least four groupings with some overlap. "Mode" copiers were those who already intended to commit a crime and who received a method from the media event. For example, a potential car thief copies the techniques seen on a television police drama for breaking into and hot-wiring a car. "Group" copiers were those who copied acts in groups. In 1995 a group of Tampa, Florida, teens bragged to police they stole cars and shot at robbery victims because earlier in the same week a twelve-year-old repeat robber had been granted probation rather than prison. The case had been given major media attention. The other two categories were mentally ill or mentally deficient copiers, and terrorists. Since terrorism is partially driven by media attention, it is not surprising that terrorists choose to repeat methods that have produced high media ratings in the past. This has led concerned media executives to consider carefully how much attention they focus on terrorist acts.

In spite of the fact that the evidence for copycat behavior is inconclusive, pressure groups continue to advocate voluntary and mandatory controls on media depictions of crime and violence. Hearings were held in the U.S. Congress several times in the early 1990's addressing these issues.

—Cecil E. Greek

See also *Beavis and Butt-head*; Clean Up Television Campaign; Communications Decency Act; Film censorship; First Amendment; Gangster films; Morality in Media; *Natural Born Killers*; News media censorship; Pressure groups; Shakur, Tupac; Violence.

BIBLIOGRAPHY

Justice and the Media (Springfield, Ill.: Charles C Thomas, 1984) and *The Media and Criminal Justice Policy* (Springfield, Ill.: Charles C Thomas, 1990); and *Media, Crime, and Criminal Justice* (Pacific Grove, Calif.: Brooks/Cole, 1992), edited by Ray Surette, offer considerable discussion of copycat crimes and censorship. See also "Newspaper Reports of Bank Robberies and the Copycat Phenomenon" in *Australian and New Zealand Journal of Criminology* 25, no. 1 (March, 1992), by Ronald V. Clarke and Gerry McGrath. On attempts to censor the popular culture forms perceived to be dangerous in the 1950's, see James Gilbert's *A Cycle of Outrage* (New York: Oxford University Press, 1986), which draws parallels to later campaigns, such as attempts to censor crime stories.

Copyright law

DEFINITION: National legislation and international agreements designed to protect the rights of creators of intellectual and artistic properties

SIGNIFICANCE: The first copyright laws were enacted to encourage and protect authors, while allowing the public free and easy access to information; modern trends in technology and law have put both goals in jeopardy

A copyright is the exclusive right to publish and sell the expression embodied in a literary, musical, or artistic work, or any work that involves original creative effort. Copyright protection provides creators with power to control the various modes of reproduction, public distribution, performance, display, and adaptation of their works. Ownership of copyright can be transferred. For example, authors may grant certain of their rights under copyright to publishers, recording companies, motion picture studios, or broadcasters.

The concept of intellectual property rights was intended to reward and stimulate the creation of works of authorship and their distribution for maximum public benefit. The most important idea embodied in copyright law is that ideas, systems, methods, processes, and principles cannot be copyrighted, but their "literary expression" can be. In other words, only specific strings of text—such as the words on this very page—are protected. The ideas they express, however, are available for free dissemination so that others may make use of them.

Since independence the U.S. Congress has passed two major revisions of the federal statute, in 1909 and 1976, and a third, minor revision in 1988. A purpose of the 1909 and 1976 revisions was to accommodate copyright to new technologies of expression and increase the term of protection so that authors might profit longer. The major purpose of the 1988 revision was to move toward meeting the requirements of the Berne Convention, an international treaty for the protection of copyright.

The 1976 U.S. Copyright Law. In 1976 Congress passed a new copyright law that covers "original works of authorship" that are "fixed in tangible form," whether published or unpublished. This new definition of "original works" thus extended federal copyright protection to all works from the moment of their creation. Under earlier law such protection attached only at the moment of publication or, in the case of some unpublished works, at the moment of their registration. Works of authorship include literary, musical, and dramatic works; pantomimes and choreographic works; pictorial, graphic, and sculptural works; motion pictures and other audiovisual works; sound recordings; compilations; and derivative works. For works created on or after January 1, 1978, the 1976 act measures the term of copyright (with some exceptions) by the life of the author, or authors, plus fifty years. The 1909 law had set the term at twenty-eight years from the date of first publication; copyright was renewable once for an additional twenty-eight years.

Fair Use. The 1976 law codified a concept that had arisen in previous case law known as "fair use." The law's fair use rule permits limited use of copyrighted material under specific conditions, generally for private or noncommercial uses. The fair use provision allows copying from a work for the purposes of criticism or commentary, news reporting, teaching and scholarship. Persons accused of violating someone else's copyright often raise "fair use" defenses. Whether an infringement falls under fair use depends on many factors, including the purpose of the use, the nature of the original work, the amount of the original work used in the secondary work, and the possible effect of infringement on the market for the original work.

Since 1976 teachers and professors have felt confident in their rights to make multiple copies of material for their students. Only during the early 1990's did this practice come under legal scrutiny, discouraging many teachers and administrators from taking chances on fair use defenses. In the 1991 decision *Basic Books, Inc. v. Kinko's Graphics Corporation*, for example, a federal district court ruled that a private for-profit company could not copy large amounts—in fact entire chapters—from books for redistribution as parts of "reading packets" for university students. The ruling and the penalty sent waves of fear throughout faculties, which had relied on reading packets as inexpensive ways to distribute information and multiple perspectives to students.

In 1996, however, the same federal court that had ruled against Kinko's said that coursework packets produced by a company in Ann Arbor, Michigan, did not violate the Copyright Act. The court ruled that the company had complied with the act's "fair use" provision. The difference between the cases is that Kinko's copying was done as a profit-making venture, not as an educational one. Nevertheless, the two court rulings contained ambiguous and apparently contradictory directives that offered no clear guidance on the matter of duplicating to instructors and copy services. The decision did, however, contribute to an erosion of confidence in educational fair use that made educators cautious.

Parodies. One way to comment on or criticize a work is to parody it. Courts have generally allowed free use of original works for parody, arguing that such expressions are necessary for open debate in a democratic society. However, there have been several attempts to limit protection for parodies since passage of the Copyright Act of 1976. One of the most publicized such cases involved a 1964 song, "Oh, Pretty Woman," written by Roy Orbison and William Dees. In July, 1989, the rap group 2 Live Crew released an album titled *As Clean as They Wanna Be* containing a song called "Pretty Woman." The group claimed the song parodied Orbison and Dees's original piece, which focused on the mundane concerns of middle-class white society. The U.S. Supreme Court in 1994 ruled unanimously that the controversial rap group did not break federal copyright laws by recording a raunchy parody of the hit song. In a 2-1 ruling, the Sixth U.S. Circuit Court of Appeals in Cincinnati, Ohio, had found the version violated the law because it was "blatantly commercial" and hurt the marketability of the original. However, the Supreme Court ruled the parody was protected by the fair use exemption because it commented on the original. While the creators of the parody in this case were successful, fear of being sued could deter creators from taking such chances in the future.

Enforcement Problems. New late twentieth century technologies, particularly high-quality digital reproduction of recordings and distribution of electronic media by computers and electronic networks, have threatened one of the major purposes of copyright law: protecting authors. Using inexpensive scanners, computers, and simple software, almost anyone can duplicate songs, paintings, photographs, or texts and distribute them virtually for free over the Internet, which connects millions of computer users around the world. Because the Internet is inherently diffuse and because it evades any clear sense of geographic jurisdiction, legal protection of copyrighted material distributed on it has seemed futile. As soon as a work is posted on an Internet site, literally millions of people all over the world can duplicate and save it in their homes and offices, leaving no effective way of retrieving their copies or punishing the copiers.

If authors, musicians, and artists cannot be assured of financial rewards for creating their work, they may not have sufficient incentive to create and distribute it. Such a development might create a chilling effect on the creative community by increasing the supply of their products beyond any market demand, resulting in the creation of fewer new works.

—*Siva Vaidhyanathan*

See also Biography; Book publishing; Computers; Internet; Libraries; McGuffey Readers; Photocopying; Scientology, Church of; 2 Live Crew; Video games.

BIBLIOGRAPHY

Useful introductions to broad copyright issues can be found in Mark Rose's *Authors and Owners: The Invention of Copy-*

right (Cambridge, Mass.: Harvard University Press, 1993) and L. Ray Patterson's and Stanley W. Lindberg's *The Nature of Copyright: A Law of User's Rights* (Athens: University of Georgia Press, 1991). For considerations of the new issues raised by modern electronic media, see Anthony L. Clapes, *Software, Copyright and Competition: The "Look and Feel" of the Law* (New York: Quorum Books, 1989); Paul Goldstein, *Copyright's Highway: From Gutenberg to the Celestial Jukebox* (New York: Hill and Wang, 1994); and John S. Lawrence and Bernard Timberg, eds., *Fair Use and Free Inquiry: Copyright Law and the New Media* (Norwood, N.J.: Ablex Publishing Corp., 1989). In *Copyright, Fair Use and the Challenge for Universities: Promoting the Progress of Higher Education* (Chicago: University of Chicago Press, 1993) Kenneth D. Crews examines copyright issues relating to academia.

Cormier, Robert Edmund

BORN: January 17, 1925, Leominster, Massachusetts

IDENTIFICATION: American journalist, essayist and author of young adult novels

SIGNIFICANCE: During the 1970's Cormier introduced young adult readers to a "new" realism, depicting the darker side of life in a corrupt and oppressive world

Robert Cormier has claimed that he writes about youngsters, not directly for them, yet his reading audience is composed mainly of young adults. They find his books complex, hard-hitting, almost cinematic in style, with memorable characters and unexpected plot twists. Cormier's adult detractors, however, have objected to his "vulgar" language and "ugly" sexual images; to his depressing endings, in which the good individual is often defeated; and to the subjects he has dramatized: child murder, sadism, government and religious corruption, suicide, and terrorism.

Critics have contended that Cormier's novels are often political in nature, detailing the struggle of an individual with a malevolent institution. For example, the protagonist in Cormier's most celebrated novel, *The Chocolate War* (1974), refuses to sell chocolates in a private school fund drive. He becomes an outcast, is victimized by his conforming peers and corrupt school administrators, and is nearly murdered. The sequel, *Beyond the Chocolate War* (1985), continues the same theme of cruelty and conformity. While students have raved about the realism of these ground-breaking novels, censors have banned the books from schools or had them put on restricted lists. Censors have condemned Cormier because of his sexual descriptions, curse words, and his derogatory portrayal of teachers, school officials, and religious ceremonies.

While censors immediately attacked *The Chocolate War* upon its publication, they did not challenge *I Am the Cheese* (1977) for nearly ten years. In 1986 three separate incidents of successful censorship occurred. In one episode, in Panama City, Florida, a teacher received death threats for teaching the novel, and a woman who publicly defended the book on television had her car firebombed. The censors attacked the book because of its coarse language, portrayal of government as an evil institution, and premise that parents lie to their children.

Their complaint that the novel is too complex has, perhaps, a grain of truth: The tale is told by Adam, fourteen years old, as his mind disintegrates under the pressures of a ruthless government agency that is supposed to protect his family from gangland revenge.

Cormier's later novels have also provoked controversy, largely because of his pessimistic view of human nature and the devastating endings of his novels, in which evil often destroys innocent youth. In *After the First Death* (1979), children die during a terrorist hijacking. In *The Bumblebee Flies Away* (1983), terminally ill youngsters face death in an experimental hospital. *Fade* (1988) deals with recurrent manic violence, while *We All Fall Down* (1991) chronicles high school seniors vandalizing and maiming other youngsters. For his part, Cormier has maintained that his chief worry is not outright censorship but the "quiet censorship" practiced by librarians and teachers who sometimes are afraid to order and teach the novels due to the pressures and threats which are often put upon these school officials by outraged members of the community.

See also Books, children's; Libraries, school; Morality; Offensive language; Sex in the arts; Violence.

Coughlin, Father Charles Edward

BORN: October 25, 1891, Hamilton, Ontario, Canada

DIED: October 27, 1979, Bloomfield Hills, Michigan

IDENTIFICATION: Roman Catholic priest and radio broadcaster during the 1930's

SIGNIFICANCE: Coughlin's outspoken expression of his political views and his anti-Semitic views led to his losing his radio programs on both network and independent stations

Ordained a Roman Catholic priest in 1916, Father Coughlin was assigned to Saint Theresa Parish in Royal Oaks, Michigan, in 1926. After he arrived at his new parish, the local Ku Klux Klan burnt a cross in his lawn as a hate warning. As a countermeasure, Coughlin arranged for baseball great Babe Ruth to speak at his church. Encouraged by the publicity that he received at this event, and needing to raise money for his church, Coughlin started a weekly program on radio station WJR in Detroit. By 1929 stations in Chicago and Cincinnati had added his Sunday program.

The advent of the Great Depression resulted in Coughlin's adopting stronger political perspectives on the air. Adamantly anticommunist, he believed that the best way to fight godless communism was for capitalism to provide decent standards of

The Reverend Charles E. Coughlin, who earned a national reputation with his strident radio speeches, attacks President Franklin D. Roosevelt at a meeting in July, 1936. (AP/Wide World Photos)

living for all workers. In 1930 the Columbia Broadcasting System (CBS) began broadcasting Coughlin's Sunday afternoon program, "Golden Hour of the Little Flower," across the nation. As many as thirty million Americans were estimated to listen to his program.

Coughlin supported capitalism, but believed that it needed to be regulated by government for the betterment of all. He was particularly vocal about the evils of international bankers as the cause of the Depression. In January, 1931, he planned to charge that the Treaty of Versailles would lead Europe into another war. CBS vice president Edward Klauber asked Coughlin to tone down his broadcasts, especially on his upcoming Sunday topic. Coughlin assured CBS that he would have an entirely different topic that next Sunday. On January 4, 1931, Coughlin devoted his entire hour on national radio exposing CBS's attempt to censor him. Over a million people wrote letters of protest to embarrassed CBS stations nationwide. Outraged by Coughlin's actions, CBS refused to renew his contract the following spring. Coughlin attempted to buy time on the National Broadcasting Company (NBC) but was also turned down. Despite his later attempts to get on a national network, neither NBC nor CBS would ever agree to broadcast his radio programs again.

Using money sent in by his listeners, Coughlin built his own network of forty-three independent radio stations in the late 1930's. He then became increasingly anti-Semitic, viewing the international communist movement as Jewish-financed and inspired. He flirted with fascism by saying that the Nazis were effectively stopping communism, and he began to charge that President Franklin D. Roosevelt was a communist sympathizer. Coughlin's message of hate eventually took its toll on listeners, and gradually his popularity declined. After the start of World War II, Coughlin continued to extol the theory that international Jewish bankers were the cause of the war. The Roosevelt Administration put pressure on the Catholic church to censor his broadcasts. On May 1, 1942, Archbishop Edward Mooney ordered Coughlin to terminate all nonreligious activities. Coughlin spent the remainder of his life as a parish priest in Royal Oaks, Michigan.

See also Broadcast media; Communism; Cushing, Cardinal Richard James; Moral Majority; Presidency, U.S.; Radio; Televangelists.

Courtrooms

Definition: Venues for civil and criminal trials

Significance: In the interest of protecting defendants' rights to fair trials, judges often issue gag orders, sequester juries, or restrict courtroom attendance and camera coverage

The First Amendment to the U.S. Constitution promises freedom of speech and press, and the Constitution's Sixth Amendment grants to criminal defendants the right to public trials by impartial juries. Sometimes these two rights conflict. For example, if the public attending a trial loudly proclaims its views on the proceedings, insisting that the defendant is guilty, the defendant can claim that the trial was not fair. More subtle forces may also influence a public trial. To balance the rights of the defendant and the public, judges may issue orders that restrict the rights of the public to attend a court proceeding or to view it on television. In addition, judges may restrict out-of-court statements made by attorneys and, in rare circumstances, may attempt to limit information the press reports about a case. Judges also may decide that the sensational nature of a case requires that the jury be sequestered, or isolated, for the length of the trial. Thus, a judge has considerable discretion to fashion remedies ensuring a defendant's right to a fair trial. In doing so, there is some infringement, or censorship, of the First Amendment rights of the public, the press, the jurors, attorneys, and other trial participants.

Problem and Solutions. The U.S. Supreme Court has offered guidance to judges faced with a free press-fair trial conflict. In *Sheppard v. Maxwell* (1966) the Supreme Court ruled that regardless of the press's role in sensationalizing a story it is the judge's job to control the courtroom and ensure a fair trial. Dr. Sam Sheppard was a Cleveland, Ohio, physician who was convicted of murdering his wife in 1954. There was intense media interest in the case before and during Sheppard's trial. In overturning the doctor's conviction, the Supreme Court found that the "carnival atmosphere" surrounding the proceedings had denied the defendant a fair trial. The Supreme Court rebuked the trial judge for failing to take action to safeguard Sheppard's rights. "Of course, there is nothing that proscribes the press from reporting events that transpire in the courtroom," the justices said. "But . . . courts must take such steps by rule and regulation that will protect their processes from prejudicial outside interferences." The Supreme Court said the judge could have changed the location of the trial or delayed it until publicity died down. He could have thoroughly questioned potential jurors, isolated jurors during the trial, and warned jurors not to read or view news stories about the case. The judge also could have limited the type of out-of-court statements made by attorneys, witnesses, and other trial participants. Restrictions of this sort are often referred to as gag orders. Finally, regarding the press, the Supreme Court said that any judge overseeing a highly publicized case must control the use of the courtroom by journalists.

Gag Orders and the Press. While the Supreme Court was highly critical of the press's sensational coverage of the *Sheppard* case, the court did not suggest press censorship as a remedy. Nevertheless, gag orders aimed at the press were not uncommon afterward. In 1975 a Nebraska judge issued an order that stopped the press from reporting about the murders of six members of the Kellie family. The order also prevented the press from reporting on public pretrial proceedings against the man charged with the crimes. The judge feared the defendant's right to a fair trial would be compromised by the publicity. Journalists challenged the gag order and, in *Nebraska Press Association v. Stuart* (1976), the Supreme Court established guidelines that made it difficult for judges to gag the media. The court called censorship of speech and publication "the most serious and least tolerable infringement on First Amendment rights," and said three conditions had to be met before a gag order against the press could be justified. The court said judges had to determine the nature and extent of pretrial news coverage, whether there were other solutions

Although the right to "a speedy and public trial" is guaranteed by the Sixth Amendment to the U.S. Constitution, citizens must be vigilant to ensure that that right is maintained. (Betty Lane)

available to counteract pretrial publicity, and whether a gag order aimed at the press would, in fact, be effective in preventing prejudice against a defendant.

Access to Proceedings. Another way to curb prejudicial publicity and safeguard a defendant's right to a fair trial is to prevent access to the courtroom. A judge can close the doors on a pretrial proceeding or trial, but only under strict conditions set by the Supreme Court. American courts are generally open to the press and public. And when there is privacy, it is likely to affect only part of a proceeding. In reviewing a Virginia judge's order to close his courtroom for the fourth trial of a murder defendant, the Supreme Court noted in *Richmond Newspapers v. Virginia* (1980) that the trial judge had not considered alternatives to the closure and that he should have. The High Court said that First Amendment guarantees "prohibit government from summarily closing courtroom doors which had long been open to the public at the time that amendment was adopted." Don R. Pember, author of *Mass Media Law* (1996), summarizes access to legal proceedings by noting that there is "virtually an unqualified right for any citizen, including reporters, to attend a criminal or civil trial, and there is a strong but qualified right for the press to attend most other kinds of judicial proceedings and to inspect most court documents."

Cameras in the Courtroom. Most states allow cameras in some or all of their courts, but Pember notes that judicial or other permission is required in thirty-one states before cameras can be used. In the O. J. Simpson trial, for example, the judge had the power to remove the camera from the proceedings. Two cases illustrate the Supreme Court's history with cameras in the courtroom. In *Estes v. Texas* (1965), the Court reversed the conviction of a Texas financier on grounds that television had denied him a fair trial. "The heightened public clamor resulting from radio and television coverage will inevitably result in prejudice," the Court said. "Trial by television is, therefore, foreign to our system." That 5-4 decision slowed state experimentation with cameras in the courtroom. By 1981, however, camera technology had improved—and so had the Court's view on the matter. In *Chandler v. Florida*, an appeal of the burglary convictions of two Miami Beach police officers, the Court was unanimous in its opinion that the presence of cameras in court is not inherently prejudicial to a defendant. The Court noted that, while there is always a risk of prejudice, that prejudice has to be demonstrated to the Court's satisfaction. In this case, the Court said the police officers had not proven that the presence of the cameras harmed jurors' ability to render a verdict based on the evidence. The Court said states were free to experiment with cameras in court if they chose.

—*Diane M. Pacetti*

See also Courts and censorship law; Gag order; Prior restraint.

BIBLIOGRAPHY

ABA Standards for Criminal Justice: Fair Trial and Free Press (3d ed. Washington, D.C.: American Bar Association, 1992) covers legal rules. Douglas S. Campbell's *Free Press v. Fair Trial: Supreme Court Decisions Since 1807* (Westport, Conn.: Praeger, 1994) gives a history of Court decisions regarding the relation of the First and Sixth amendments. *Censorship, Secrecy, Access, and Obscenity*, edited by Theodore R. Kupferman (Westport, Conn.: Meckler, 1990), has articles on a variety of the ramifications of the court censorship issue. Peter E. Kane's *Murder, Courts, and the Press: Issues in Free Press/Fair Trial* (Carbondale: Southern Illinois University Press, 1992) discusses the sensational murder trial, which is often the source of controversial decisions regarding court censorship. Don R. Pember's *Mass Media Law* (7th ed. Madison, Wis.: Brown & Benchmark, 1996) establishes a context for court censorship issues.

Courts and censorship law

DEFINITION: Federal and state trial and appellate courts decide numerous cases involving censorship issues

SIGNIFICANCE: In Great Britain and the United States judicial review has played a crucial role in defining censorship laws

The courts had played a complicated and often misunderstood role in deciding questions of censorship. They often decide whether particular regulations, statutes, or executive decisions constitute unconstitutional censorship or lawful exercises of governmental authority. The American court system encompasses several distinct judicial institutions. There are fifty-one separate court systems—one federal system and fifty state systems. Generally, civil and criminal cases begin in a trial court (known as a district court in the federal system);

STRUCTURE OF THE FEDERAL COURT SYSTEM

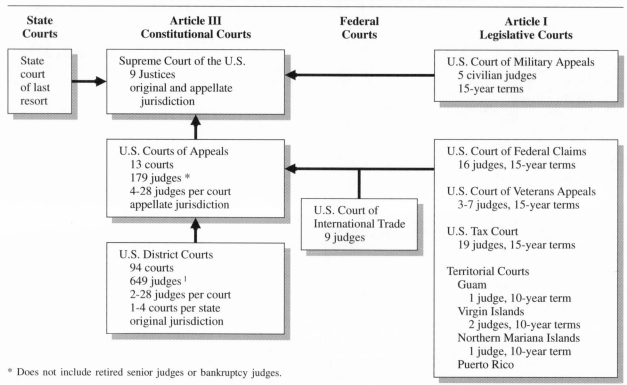

State Courts	**Article III Constitutional Courts**	**Federal Courts**	**Article I Legislative Courts**
State court of last resort	Supreme Court of the U.S. 9 Justices original and appellate jurisdiction		U.S. Court of Military Appeals 5 civilian judges 15-year terms
	U.S. Courts of Appeals 13 courts 179 judges * 4-28 judges per court appellate jurisdiction	U.S. Court of International Trade 9 judges	U.S. Court of Federal Claims 16 judges, 15-year terms
	U.S. District Courts 94 courts 649 judges [1] 2-28 judges per court 1-4 courts per state original jurisdiction		U.S. Court of Veterans Appeals 3-7 judges, 15-year terms

* Does not include retired senior judges or bankruptcy judges.

U.S. Tax Court
19 judges, 15-year terms

Territorial Courts
Guam
1 judge, 10-year term
Virgin Islands
2 judges, 10-year terms
Northern Mariana Islands
1 judge, 10-year term
Puerto Rico

---

many cases end there. If appealed, cases proceed through one and possibly two appellate courts. In the federal system, there are courts of appeal, followed by the U.S. Supreme Court. In most states, there are courts of appeal and a state supreme court, followed by review in the U.S. Supreme Court. Cumbersome at first glance, these multiple levels of appeal ensure that decisions are subject to critical review.

Judicial Review Doctrine. The courts derive their authority to judge the constitutionality of statutes from the doctrine of judicial review, which is nowhere expressly mentioned in the U.S. Constitution. It was not until John Marshall's opinion in *Marbury v. Madison* that the Court granted itself the power to strike down statutes found to conflict with the Constitution. This power, which is often misunderstood by members of the public who believe that a democracy is controlled by majority vote, has since been exercised by courts at every level. The power of judicial review has placed responsibility on all judges, from municipal courts to the U.S. Supreme Court, to entertain constitutional challenges to every manner of statute, regulation, and governmental action.

In discharging this duty courts are often accused of making law rather than interpreting it. This distinction ignores the fact that the act of interpretation involves deciding whether a statute applies. The court thus "makes" law for those found liable and "makes" exceptions for those found not liable. It is also a matter of personal interpretation when one decides whether or not a court "makes" or "interprets" law when it decides a case based on judicial review. When a court decides that a state statute prohibiting the burning of a cross on private property, if done as an act of political protest, is an unconstitutional violation of freedom of speech, for example, whether such an act is interpretation or lawmaking typically depends what an observer thinks of the result.

Critics of the judicial system accuse judges of pursuing ideological agendas, under which they work backward from finish to start, instead of applying neutral principles to the facts and finding the appropriate result. It is noteworthy that Supreme Court justices from both ends of the liberal-to-conservative spectrum, such as William H. Rehnquist and William J. Brennan, Jr., have been accused of being "result-oriented."

That judges have previously considered the contours of great constitutional questions before actual cases are presented to them for decision should come as no surprise. Indeed, at least at the appellate level, judges are chosen for the depth of their scholarship and study of the law. Nominees to the U.S. Supreme Court have been criticized (or even disbelieved) when they have testified at confirmation hearings that they had not seriously considered controversial constitutional and public policy issues. The legitimacy of judicial opinions does not turn on whether judges are result-oriented or not. It turns on whether they exhibit a principled rationale, based on well-established precedents and a fair and accurate summary of the facts.

A judge with a long history of decisions upholding (or for that matter) rejecting First Amendment challenges to governmental regulations, who decides new cases in a principled manner, is less vulnerable to criticism than a judge who disclaims any result orientation, but decides new cases by misstating the facts or relying on inapplicable precedents or ones that have been overruled.

Judicial Balancing. Proponents of censorship often call on courts to balance First Amendment rights against other competing interests. Opponents of censorship respond that the Founders did all the balancing necessary when they wrote the Bill of Rights and that inevitably "balancing" is a code word for "censorship" that undermines cherished First Amendment rights, because virtually any act of government can be justified on the basis of any number of legitimate or valuable purposes and thereby trump the First Amendment. Civil libertarians argue that the identification of a legitimate governmental interest is only the beginning, not the end, of the inquiry in First Amendment cases.

Independent Judicial Review. Deciding First Amendment issues brings into play special judicial rules given the preferred position of individual rights in the constitutional system. In conventional cases, not involving constitutional rights, courts tend to defer to the presumed expertise of government officials and agencies. Likewise, appellate courts defer to the factual findings of trial courts who have heard the evidence and observed the witnesses.

When freedom of speech or the press or other rights protected by the Constitution are at stake, however, these general rules are replaced by the doctrine of independent review. To guarantee maximum protection for constitutional rights, the courts carefully scrutinize governmental actions without giving them the benefit of the doubt. Appellate courts independently examine the court record to satisfy themselves on the facts involved in constitutional challenges, without blindly accepting whatever the trial court has found.

Another safeguard used by the courts in censorship (and other constitutional) cases, is to apply strict scrutiny in judging whether the government has demonstrated a compelling interest sufficient to justify a restriction on protected speech. Normal legislation involving economic or business regulation is judged under the lesser rational basis standard—such laws raise no constitutional problems so long as they are reasonable. Few laws will run afoul of the minimal rational basis standard. Laws that on their face or by application purport to restrict First Amendment rights, however, are strictly scrutinized to detect whether any censorial motivation was behind the legislation, in which case the legislation is vulnerable to invalidation on constitutional grounds. In many cases, the difference between a successful and unsuccessful First Amendment challenge will depend entirely on which standard of scrutiny is applied.

Prior Restraint. In censorship cases, the courts' most draconian power is prior restraint—enjoining speech even before it is uttered. Many constitutional scholars believe that prior restraint is the single most ominous threat to freedom of speech, and that prior restraint in England prompted the passage of the First Amendment. Courts rarely if ever grant a prior restraint of speech even in the face of urgent claims by the government that unless speech is banned prior to publica-

tion serious damage to the national security will result. Such cases demand that judges display keen fidelity to the letter and spirit of the Constitution and to resist the temptation to accept the dreadful predictions of government lawyers who are seeking to enjoin speech before it is published.

Few areas of the law place the courts under greater public scrutiny than censorship cases. Aside from highly visible criminal prosecutions or notorious political scandals, the public rarely takes notice of most trials or appeals, unless they involve controversial battles over free speech, free press, or the separation of church and state. Censorship cases have involved flag-burning, cross-burning, pornography, and Nazis marching in Skokie, Illinois; in such cases, the courts' decisions are not going to please everyone and many are displeased when the courts uphold First Amendment protections. Public confidence in the judicial system is severely tested when the courts are called on to protect hateful or offensive speech in the face of majority condemnation.

—*Stephen F. Rohde*

See also Brennan, William J., Jr.; Censorship; Clear and present danger doctrine; Constitution, U.S.; Courtrooms; First Amendment; Free speech; Gag order; Holmes, Oliver Wendell, Jr.

BIBLIOGRAPHY

Edward J. Cleary's *Beyond the Burning Cross* (New York: Random House, 1994) is a personal account of the landmark First Amendment decision in *R.A.V. v. St. Paul* by the lawyer who represented the controversial defendant. The book traces, in illuminating detail, the progress of a constitutional case through the courts. Richard Hixson's *Mass Media and the Constitution: An Encyclopedia of Supreme Court Decisions* (New York: Garland, 1989), is a useful collection of synopses of more than two hundred U.S. Supreme Court decisions in the areas of broadcasting, business, censorship, commercial speech, copyright, fair trial, Freedom of Information Act, free speech, libel, news gathering, obscenity, and privacy. Stephen B. Presser's *Recapturing the Constitution* (Washington, D.C.: Regnery Publishing, 1994) is a scholarly polemic that decries "result-oriented jurisprudence" in the areas of race, religion, and abortion, but ultimately reveals that the author is not as concerned with the fact that judges pursue their own political and social agendas but that they pursue political and social agendas with which the author disagrees. David G. Savage's *Turning Right: The Making of the Rehnquist Supreme Court* (New York: John Wiley & Sons, 1992) is a behind-the-scenes look at how U.S. Supreme Court justices have decided critical constitutional cases. In the First Amendment area, the book examines flag burning, election campaigns, abortion counseling, student newspapers, Christmas displays, and nude dancing. Rodney A. Smolla's *Free Speech in an Open Society* (New York: Alfred A. Knopf, 1992) is a readable and accessible discussion spanning First Amendment issues, including the rationale of constitutional protection of freedom of speech and press, flag-burning, hate speech, libel, public funding of the arts and education, money and politics, prior restraint, censorship during the Persian Gulf War, and the challenges of new technologies.

Cover art

DEFINITION: Artwork decorating the covers of books, especially paperback editions

SIGNIFICANCE: Designed for immediate visual impact, cover art often uses visceral motifs or suggestive treatments that attract the attention of both customers and censors

Cover art became an important element of book marketing with the rise of the mass market paperback in the 1940's and early 1950's. Free paperback Armed Service Editions had been distributed to soldiers in World War II; to keep these people reading books in the postwar years, publishers developed new lines of novels to sell at twenty-five cents each. These books were designed for working and middle-class males who had not bought books regularly before the war. The art used on covers of these books was comparatively free for its time in depicting sexual themes.

Typical paperback covers of that era featured paintings of nubile young women, scantily clad or in seductive poses. Props ranged from square-jawed hero, to guns and pools of blood for suspense stories. Although some novels reflected the sexual emphases promised by their covers, similar covers were also used on such sexually restrained works as Sinclair

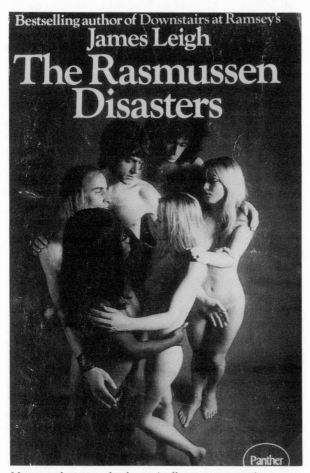

Mass-market paperbacks typically use provocative covers that may or may not have anything to do with the contents of the books. (Arkent Archive)

Lewis' *Babbitt* (1922). Sold through drugstores, bus stops, and variety stores, paperbacks were both more widely available and more visible than hardbound books.

Many censorship attempts resulted from this cover art. Challenges to lurid paperback covers were raised in varied arenas, from local boycotts and police actions to the national level. Titles were singled out either for their covers alone, or because their covers suggested objectionable content within the books themselves. Among the books most frequently challenged for their cover art were the 1948 edition of John Erskine's *The Private Life of Helen of Troy* (1925), whose cover illustration revealed a woman's nipples, and Tereska Torres' *Women's Barracks* (1950), whose cover hinted at a subtext of lesbian relationships. In 1952 a select committee of the U.S. House of Representatives chaired by Ezekiel Candler Gathings held hearings on "immoral, obscene or otherwise offensive" paperbacks. The committee interviewed only two publishing industry officials while inviting many judges, ministers, and police officials to testify against the books. These witnesses often cited lurid cover art to make their points.

The congressional hearings produced few direct results; however, they bolstered other efforts to censor cover art. For example, the U.S. Post Office banned a book by Guy de Maupassant because its cover depicted female nudity. Intimidated publishers soon stopped using provocative covers. (Ironically, these "good girl" and "bad girl" paperback covers later became collector's items.)

Evocative cover art that pushes the limits of acceptability has remained a major marketing tool for paperbacks, however. Certain shocking and sensual motifs have become standard symbols for books that fall within specific subgenres. For example, pictures of horrific creatures with dead humans indicate horror novels, and pictures of muscular men embracing women in low-cut gowns indicate historical romances—which are often termed "bodice rippers." Attacks on individual books are not unknown; however, the larger censorship impact is upon selection, as many libraries and bookstores refuse to carry books that feature gory and sexually suggestive covers.

See also Art; Caldwell, Erskine; Nudity; Postage stamps.

Crimean War

DATE: October, 1853-April, 1856

PLACE: Crimea, Russian Empire (now Ukraine)

SIGNIFICANCE: Wartime censorship prevailed in Russia, Turkey, France, and Sardinia, but new professional war correspondents for Great Britain's free press influenced the war itself, and ultimately led to British military censorship

In 1853 Tsar Nicholas I demanded greater authority over Christians in Turkey's autonomous Balkan provinces of Moldavia and Wallachia, and a Russian protectorship over Bulgaria and Serbia. With British and French encouragement, Turkey resisted, whereupon Russia invaded Moldavia and Wallachia. In October, 1853, Turkey declared war on Russia. French emperor Napoleon III sought joint action with the British, who tried to negotiate a diplomatic solution. However, a Russian naval victory in the Black Sea on November 30 was sensationalized by London newspapers as "the massacre of Sinope." Britain's coalition cabinet, indecisively headed by George Hamilton Gordon, Lord Aberdeen, was swept along by press agitation; on March 28, 1854, Britain joined France in declaring war on Russia.

Newspaper expectations of a major war were disappointed when Baltic naval operations stalled, and when the Russians, threatened by Austrian intervention, left the Balkans. The *London Times* then urged an attack on Russia's Black Sea naval base at Sebastopol, and in September, 1854, French, British, and Turkish troops invaded the western Crimea. After battles at the Alma River, Balaclava, and Inkerman, the Crimean War developed into a nearly year-long siege of Sebastopol.

Russia's war journalism during this conflict was limited to official communiques, fairly accurate and up-to-date, thanks to telegraphic connections, but firmly under the control of the tsar's already stringent censorship. Turkey's fledgling and government-subsidized press was also "official," apart from some items copied from foreign papers. The French press sent correspondents and illustrators to the Crimea, but even the opposition papers published no serious criticism of Napoleon III's management of the war. Sardinian press coverage in 1855-1856 was by regulation limited to official sources, but the regulations were not strictly enforced on Italy's reporters.

The British also issued official bulletins, but these complacent accounts were in glaring contrast to the charges of incompetent army administration published by the London press. Earlier "serving correspondents" had been under military authority, and newspapers had sometimes been harassed by "seditious libel" prosecutions, but the British press of 1854 was not subject to any army or government censorship, and had an important influence on middle-class voters and their political leaders. *The Times*, once a government supporter but since 1817 a "voice of the people," was especially significant because its circulation was about ten times that of its competitors. Also, *The Times* covered the Crimean War with several able correspondents, including the war's star reporter, William Howard Russell.

Russell was not the first war correspondent, but he became the exemplar for the profession. He supplied long eye-witness accounts, keenly observant and rich in descriptive detail, conveying the excitement of the charge of the Light Brigade, the discomforts and humor of camp life, and the human cost of casualty reports. That the British army was ill-prepared for the Crimean winter and a cholera epidemic was clear in all newspaper reports. Russell's columns, however, made the rain, mud, flies, disease, hospital filth and army bureaucracy living and present realities for his readers.

Britain's Crimean army commander, Fitzroy Somerset, Lord Raglan, naturally resented slurs on his military record by a civilian journalist. He did not ban correspondents from camp (as did the French), but by ignoring them he encouraged his staff to treat reporters with malign neglect, while he also complained to his government's cabinet that press reports were aiding the enemy. London editors and Crimean reporters were asked to be self-censors, and Russell offered to submit his dispatches to army review, but in November and December of 1854 both the army situation and the news reports steadily worsened.

Wretched hospital conditions at Scutari, as described by Thomas Chenery of *The Times*, led the paper to propose sending out, and raising financial support for, the female nursing mission headed by Florence Nightingale. This in turn led to bruising conflicts over the scope of her authority at Scutari. On December 23, *The Times* editor John Delane opened an editorial attack on Lord Aberdeen's government for mismanaging the war. The London papers were soon filled with letters from junior officers supporting the press criticism. Among several government responses, a commission on hospital care eventually exposed such army incompetence as hoarding medicine and equipment at Varna, Bulgaria, while sending sick and wounded soldiers to die of neglect at Scutari, about two hundred miles away. After Nightingale was vindicated, and given broader authority over the army's hospital program, she became, for the press and the public, the most outstanding heroic figure of the war.

Aberdeen's embattled coalition lost its parliamentary support early in 1855, and was succeeded on February 5 by a Whig administration under Henry John Temple, Lord Palmerston. Military reforms already in progress, plus Sardinia's participation, helped the allied cause. Lord Raglan's illness, retirement, and death were widely blamed on Russell's reporting. With the death of Tsar Nicholas in March, and the fall of Sebastopol in September, 1855, the conflict languished. The second winter in the Crimea was less difficult for the allied armies, but also less interesting for the correspondents and their readers. On February 25, 1856, General Sir William Codrington, as British commander-in-chief, belatedly issued regulations for censoring what little news remained. By the treaty of peace signed on March 30, 1856 in Paris, Russian demands were dropped, but most of her losses were restored. In their newspapers, both sides claimed to have won the war.

In the postwar decade, Russian censorship was slightly relaxed in 1855 and 1865, and Napoleon III liberalized French press laws in 1866. By contrast, the Ottoman Empire increased its censorship of "Young Turkey" literature in 1865 and 1869, and Sardinia's free press again became "official" during the 1859-1860 war of Italian unification. In Britain the newspapers gave themselves credit for winning the war, but the politicians took a different view. They felt that *The Times*, in particular, had helped push the country into war, insisted on invading Russia, forced changes in army organization and command, and howled down a government with such headline charges as "Army Sacrificed," "Last Chance Is Gone," "Woe and Misery," "Serbonian Bog of Despair," "Catastrophe," "Disaster," "Doom." The Whig politicians, determined to curb "the vile tyranny of *The Times*," in March, 1855, repealed the penny tax on all newspapers weighing less than four ounces. This left only *The Times* subject to the tax, and opened the way for penny press competition that reduced "the Thunderer's" relative influence. "Billy" Russell went on to other wars and an eventual knighthood. He always defended his Crimean despatches against the charge of aiding the enemy, but even he came to agree that in wartime even Britain's free press needed some intelligent censorship. —*K. Fred Gillum*

See also Civil War, U.S.; France; Italy; Military censorship; Nicholas I; Russia; Spanish-American War; Turkey; United Kingdom; War; World War I.

BIBLIOGRAPHY

For W. H. Russell, see Alan Hankinson's *Man of Wars* (London: Heinemann, 1982), Philip Knightley's *The First Casualty* (New York: Harcourt Brace Jovanovich, 1975), and Russell's own published accounts. On British journalism, *The History of the Times*, 6 vols. (New York: Macmillan, 1935-1993), edited by Stanley Morison, is defensive; Alexander Kinglake's *Invasion of the Crimea*, 8 vols. (New York: Harper & Brothers, 1863-1887), is critical; and Olive Anderson's *A Liberal State at War* (New York: St. Martin's Press, 1967) is objective. Charles A. Ruud's *Fighting Words* (Toronto: University of Toronto Press, 1982) covers Russian censorship. See also Ahmed Sureyya Emin, *The Development of Modern Turkey as Measured by Its Press* (New York: Columbia University Press, 1914).

Criminal syndicalism laws

DEFINITION: Laws against belonging to a criminal organization

SIGNIFICANCE: Criminal syndicalism laws, passed by most U.S. states around the time of World War I, were designed to facilitate the prosecution of members of radical organizations

Criminal syndicalism laws generally outlawed the advocacy of violence to bring about social and political change. The laws were drawn so broadly that simply being a member of an organization deemed to advocate such ideas, printing or distributing such a group's literature, or even renting a hall to such groups would violate the law. It was unnecessary to prove that particular individuals associated with the groups used violence or even advocated it. Criminal syndicalism laws were used legally to crush such groups as the militant labor organization the Industrial Workers of the World (IWW).

The laws were also used as a model for later sedition laws used to prosecute the Communist Party of the United States. The clear purpose and the actual use of criminal syndicalism laws was to facilitate the jailing of members of radical organizations without evidence of individual participation in the organizations' work, thus effectively suppressing target groups that were deemed subversive without the need to prove that they had actually used violence or otherwise violated the law.

The model of later criminal syndicalism laws were laws passed by four states in 1902 and 1903 in the wake of the 1901 assassination of President William McKinley by an anarchist. These so-called criminal anarchy laws, such as the 1902 New York law, banned advocating the doctrine that government should be overthrown by force, violence, or assassination, with penalties for those who personally advocated such beliefs, who helped disseminate such doctrines, or who organized, joined, or voluntarily assembled with any group advocating such beliefs. During the 1917-1920 period of American involvement in World War I and the postwar Red Scare, similar laws, more broadly drawn to outlaw advocacy or member-

ship in organizations that advocated violence as a means of bringing about economic or political change, targeted the IWW and the American Communist Party. Such laws were passed by more than twenty states. These laws were especially enforced in California and the Pacific Northwest, where the IWW was especially active; for example, between 1919 and 1924, more than five hundred people were arrested for criminal syndicalism in California alone, of whom 264 were prosecuted and 109 were convicted.

After 1924 criminal syndicalism prosecutions in California and elsewhere largely disappeared, partly because the IWW had been effectively suppressed through such prosecutions and other legal forms of repression. However, criminal syndicalism laws were one of the models for the 1940 federal Smith Act, which was used to suppress the Communist Party of the United States during the Cold War. The laws were periodically resurrected during times of high social tension, such as the Great Depression and the Black Power and antiwar movements of the 1960's. Criminal syndicalism laws were effectively interred, however, in a series of Supreme Court rulings, and especially in the 1969 Supreme Court case of *Brandenburg v. Ohio*. In this case the Court ruled in a criminal syndicalism prosecution brought against a Ku Klux Klan leader that the states could not forbid even individual advocacy of violence unless it was "directed to inciting or producing imminent lawless action and is likely to incite and produce such action," a standard which could virtually never be met and which paved the path for future rulings expanding free speech protections, such as the 1989 and 1990 decisions protecting flag burning as a form of political expression.

See also Advocacy; Communist Party of the U.S.A.; Flag burning; Ku Klux Klan; Sedition; Smith Act; *Texas v. Johnson*.

Criminal trials

DEFINITION: Legal proceedings that determine the guilt of defendants accused of crimes

SIGNIFICANCE: The tradition of public trials has often pitted the right of defendants to receive fair hearings against the right of the people to know and the principle of free press

Attempting to balance the right of freedom of speech with the defendant's right to an unbiased verdict is the source of many censorship issues, which are numerous and varied. The issues generally can be traced to attempts at reaching an appropriate balance between the rights of the defendant to a fair trial and the rights of those who are not the defendant to free speech. What is considered an acceptable balance between these rights varies from society to society and from era to era.

At one time courts were almost completely open to the public. Trials in general and especially certain criminal trials were a very popular form of entertainment. The public's right to know, to have open access to court proceedings, tended to take precedence over the defendants right to a fair trial. Too much privacy also limits the defendant's right to a fair trial; historical examples of secret trials in which the verdict was a foregone conclusion led the Founders of the United States to guarantee a public trial to the defendant. That public trials are typically in the defendant's interest can be shown by example.

For example, many juvenile courts in California in the 1990's were not open to the public, for the stated reason that the privacy protects minors. Critics argue, however, that such privacy has led to the minors' rights being undervalued in abuse cases, in which only court-appointed lawyers are the children's advocates in court. Critics have argued that public oversight of such trials could combat the bureaucratic inertia that has led, they claim, to an institutional bias for the parents.

To the extent, however, that the right of a free press translates into uncontrolled access to criminal trials, and the right to speak and write freely about those trials is uncontested, then the individual's right to a fair trial becomes increasingly difficult to achieve. In the late twentieth century, the increasing emphasis on individual rights, as seen in the Civil Rights movement and in expanded rights for defendants, has led to limitations on the press coverage of trials as well as access to court proceedings. Under these circumstances, censorship typically increases.

Contemporary Censorship Issues. Courts once were virtually open to the public. This openness has been replaced by closed doors, strict security, and judicial dress, procedures, and jargon that are often incomprehensible to the public. Such developments have made it difficult for the average person to raise rational questions concerning the courts. Of the possible censorship issues that arise in conjunction with criminal trials, the following are of particular significance: pretrial publicity, cameras in the courtroom, jury sequestration, witness protection (which defendants may argue is "coaching"), and privileged communications.

Pretrial publicity can be prejudicial, at times to the extent that jury verdicts and judicial decisions are influenced. What is reported, how it is reported, and when it is reported by the media are all crucial. Speculative, inaccurate, and sensationalized reporting of criminal trials is particularly problematic. Pretrial publicity that occurs prior to jury selection can make selecting jurors that are capable of reaching a verdict on the basis of the evidence presented in the case especially difficult. Pretrial publicity about evidence that is damaging but inadmissible can be particularly prejudicial, to the extent a guilty verdict becomes more likely. The extensiveness of the pretrial publicity surrounding a criminal trial can significantly affect the trial.

The use of television cameras in the courtroom became a matter of heightened public debate with the O. J. Simpson trial in 1995. Some states and jurisdictions allow cameras in the courtroom, others do not. Some criminal trial lawyers support allowing cameras in the courtroom, others do not. Supporters believe it is not healthy in a democratic society to keep judicial proceedings from public observation. Television cameras allow for greater public observation and scrutiny. Opponents of cameras in the courtroom contend they interfere with maintaining a dignified and fair trial. Arguments against allowing television cameras in the courtroom have weakened in light of recent technological developments that have made cameras very compact, portable, and able to operate in ordinary room light. Such cameras can be operated so unobtrusively they need not interfere with court proceedings.

Attempts to limit possible prejudicial pretrial publicity range from attempting to limit the release of information by the media to using a variety of approaches to shield jurors from publicity. In extreme cases, in response to excessive media attention courts can use their authority to hold members of the media in contempt if they persist in releasing inflammatory or prejudicial information. Fines or imprisonment can be levied against reporters and other media representatives if a court order regarding pretrial publicity is violated.

Change of venue (moving the trial to another jurisdiction in another city or county) is another strategy employed to limit the influence of pretrial publicity on jurors and on the trial generally. In addition, judges can caution jurors against being influenced by any pretrial publicity they hear or read. A judge's instructions to jurors, however, seldom can overcome the influence of extensive pretrial publicity. Yet another alternative strategy is for a judge to grant a continuance in a criminal case that is beset by extensive pretrial publicity. This tactic is based on the notion that by postponing a criminal trial the emotional, inflammatory atmosphere surrounding the case will subside. The use of *voir dire* can be a valuable tool for assessing the impact of pretrial publicity as well as a means of limiting its impact on criminal trials. *Voir dire* involves examining witnesses and potential jurors, under oath, to determine their competency.

Jury sequestration, such as occurred in the O. J. Simpson trial, involves keeping the jury in seclusion while the trial is underway as a means to shield jurors from the media coverage surrounding a publicized case. While sequestered, attempts are made to keep jurors from being exposed to radio, television, magazine, and newspaper reports of the trial. In addition, efforts are made to keep jurors from discussing the case while sequestered so no conclusions are reached before all evidence is presented.

Generally, the level of media attention given to a criminal trial parallels the level of public interest in the case. Sequestration of jurors is typically only utilized in those cases when there is such extreme media coverage surrounding a criminal trial that it would be impossible for jurors not to be significantly influenced by the extensive coverage.

Witness protection programs are designed to protect witnesses from threats to their safety and well-being. Gangs, for example, can be a serious threat to witnesses who testify against one of their members. Witnesses under protection are often uprooted, moved to new surroundings, and cut off from family and friends. Under such conditions, witnesses often complain that they feel censored, unable to communicate with anyone they know.

Privileged communications include sidebar discussions between the judge and attorneys, which are held at the bench out of hearing of the jurors and the public. Extended sidebars can take place behind closed doors in the judge's chambers. The widespread use of privileged communications has become a censorship issue.

Responses to Censorship. Unfortunately, many of the responses to the aforementioned censorship issues often create further censorship and additional problems. When continuances are granted and cases are postponed, for example, witnesses move away and disappear, some may die, and memories fade and recollections weaken. Defendants are given the right to a fair and a speedy trial. Poor defendants in criminal cases may not be able to afford bond. When continuances are granted they may remain in jail for lengthy periods of time even though they have not been found guilty of any crime.

Jury sequestration can, if not carefully supervised, provide jurors increased opportunities to share their thoughts, influence one another, and reach conclusions before all evidence and testimony has been presented. Jury sequestration, as are witness protection programs and case continuances, is expensive, requiring additional court, law enforcement, and correctional personnel and other resources. All these responses to censorship place increased burdens on jurors, witnesses, judges, and other court personnel and require careful planning and supervision.

As crime has grown in volume and as public outrage over crime has increased, and as communications have become more rapid and pervasive, the necessity of establishing procedures that meet the needs of a free press and a fair trial has become increasingly significant. The passage of sunshine laws in many states, which require court proceedings—including hearings, motions, and trials—be open, underscores the importance of developing these procedures. Sunshine laws allow for hearings and other court proceedings to be closed only when clear and compelling reasons, such as the safety of a witness, can be demonstrated. There is no perfect or complete solution to the censorship problems that arise in criminal trials. Policies and procedures are needed that attempt to balance or better accommodate the defendants' right to an unbiased verdict and the rights of a free press. A number of recommendations have been made by scholars who study censorship issues that arise in reference to criminal trials.

One recommendation is that court proceedings that are supposedly open must be made so in reality. The use of public address systems and keeping all conversations and extraneous noise to the absolute minimum in the courtroom can be a logical first step in improving public access to criminal trials. Sidebars and other private meetings and conferences involving the judge and attorneys must be limited.

Other recommendations concern a problem that contributes to the censorship of press coverage of criminal trials. Press reports are often inaccurate and superficial. Judges and the legal profession could help remedy this situation in several ways. Judges ought to experiment with ways to educate and inform journalists about the background surrounding a particular case. They could meet regularly with the press for informal discussions or for more formalized presentations to discuss legal terms, procedures, and current ideas.

Other recommendations concern uniform standards for judging when pretrial publicity is so prejudicial as to justify a change of venue or the sequestration of jurors. These standards ought to be based on the overall circumstances or atmosphere surrounding the case rather than primarily on the judge's personal viewpoint. Also, rather than banning modern technology from the courtroom, it can in certain cases be employed to protect defendants' constitutional rights. For example, closed-circuit television can help to protect children in sexual abuse cases without sacrificing the defendant's right to a fair trial—including the right to confront their accuser. Closed-circuit television with two-way audio and visual interactive capabilities is preferable to pretrial videotaping of the child's testimony. The child, testifying in a "child's room," can testify during the court proceedings and the child's testimony can be seen in a separate room by the defendant and others. Such procedures can allow the defendant or the defendant's representative to confront and question the witness without so intimidating the witness as to make the witness' testimony unreliable. Multiple cameras and multiple monitors can be used. Due to the interactive capabilities of the closed-circuit system, the defendant's right to cross-examination is also protected. To the extent the child feels more comfortable to testify freely and openly, to that extent the child's viewpoint is represented rather than censored by the emotional strain of physically confronting the defendant and a roomful of extremely serious-looking adults.

The necessity of maintaining defendants' right to a fair trial is well established. Democratic societies, however, pay a high price if censorship becomes a fundamental means of ensuring this right. It is dangerous in a democracy to close its court system to the public. The public pays for the courts, the public serves as jurors, members of the public find themselves on trial, and ultimately the public is most influenced by the quality of justice available in courts. —*Charles E. Marske*

See also Courtrooms; Courts and censorship law; Gag order; Privileged communication; Simpson, O. J., case; Witnesses, protection of.

BIBLIOGRAPHY

Access Denied: The Politics of Press Censorship (Washington, D.C.: Sage Publications, 1978), edited by Sean Kelly, provides an overview of the relationship between government and the press. In editing *Landmark Decisions of the United States Supreme Court* (Beverly Hills, Calif.: Excellent Books, 1991) Maureen Harrison and Steve Gilbert provide summaries of landmark court decisions dealing with censorship issues, including *New York Times v. the United States* (1971), a significant press censorship case.

Crop-ears

DEFINITION: Name given to persons who had their ears cut off for criticizing English political or religious leaders during the 1600's

SIGNIFICANCE: Ear-cropping was a common form of censorship in seventeenth century England and its colonies

The practice of cropping the ears of political and ecclesiastical critics reaches back at least to the tenth century and continued sporadically until the eighteenth century. It was a form of punishment, however, most widely used during the religiously tumultuous years of the seventeenth century. In the 1630's especially, when King Charles I and Archbishop William Laud sought to quell criticism of the Church of England by Puritans, ear-cropping was a mainstay of official policy.

When many Puritans fled from England to the New World to escape the wrath of Charles I, they included among their own repertoire of criminal sanctions the ear-croppings that the king had visited upon them. In 1631 Phillip Ratcliff earned an ear-cropping from the Massachusetts Bay Colony Puritans for making scandalous speeches against the colony's government and one of the colony's churches. Twenty-five years later the colony became exasperated by an influx of Quakers who, being repeatedly banished from Massachusetts, refused to stay banished. To quell this religious zeal, the Puritans revived the practice of ear-cropping, at least for males. But even this deterrent proved insufficient to dissuade the Quakers from reentering the colony, and the Puritans ultimately found it necessary to execute three Quakers on the Boston commons in 1659 and 1660.

See also Death; Leighton, Alexander; Prynne, William; Puritans; Reformation, the; Religion.

Crossman Diaries

TYPE OF WORK: Book
PUBLISHED: 1975-1977
AUTHOR: Richard Crossman (1907-1974)
SUBJECT MATTER: A detailed account of how British cabinet ministers and civil servants conducted government business
SIGNIFICANCE: By permitting publication of this controversial diary, British courts made it easier for newspapers and book companies to publish accounts of the inner workings of the British government

A cabinet minister in the Labour government of Prime Minister Harold Wilson, Richard Crossman served as minister of housing and local government (1964-1966), leader of the House of Commons and lord president of the Council (1966-1968), and secretary of state for social services (1968-1970). While he was a minister, he kept a detailed diary of the inner workings of government, particularly high-level discussions involving cabinet ministers and senior civil servants. Following his death in 1974, his literary executors wished to honor his instructions by publishing his diaries in three volumes titled *The Diaries of a Cabinet Minister*.

In June, 1975, the British government moved for an injunction to bar publication of the Crossman diaries because they had not been approved by the cabinet office. The case was heard before Lord Chief Justice Lord Widgery. Attorney-General Sam Silken decided not to invoke the Official Secrets Act. Instead, he argued that such a breach of confidentiality was not in the public interest, since it would undermine the constitutional principle of collective responsibility and inhibit cabinet ministers from speaking frankly and senior civil servants from giving controversial advice. The government contended that the common law of England had accepted over a period of time a number of "conventions" and "parameters" that limited how much information former government officials could release to the public. The defense contended that the principle of confidentiality extended only to marriage and industrial secrets, that confidentiality had been breached by a number of previously published books, and that if there was a problem, legislation would be the best answer.

On October 1, 1975, Widgery delivered his judgment. He stated that because the first volume of Crossman's diary dealt with events that had occurred a decade earlier and because there had been three general elections in the interval, no substantive case existed for preventing its publication. At the same time he effectively ruled that in the publication of future volumes of this diary, or any other diaries and memoirs, each individual case had to be decided on its own merits. Most legal observers believed this meant that future governments would have a more difficult time proving it was in the public interest to have information suppressed. The two remaining volumes of the diaries were published without incident. No other high-profile case involving an attempted suppression of memoirs occurred until the *Spycatcher* controversy of the late 1980's.

See also Book publishing; Civil service; News media censorship; Official Secrets Act (U.K.); *Spycatcher*; United Kingdom; *Valachi Papers, The*.

Crumb, Robert

BORN: August 30, 1943, Philadelphia, Pennsylvania
IDENTIFICATION: American graphic novelist
SIGNIFICANCE: Crumb's work has been attacked as pornographic and obscene

The son of a career U.S. Marine, whom his sons describe as an "overbearing tyrant," Crumb began working as an artist at the American Greeting Card Company in Ohio in 1962 and also worked as an artist for the Topps Company in New York City. He then began to do freelance portraits and cartoons in Atlantic City, New Jersey. Since then he has published under many different names: Crud, Crumarums, Brumbum, Crumski, Crum the Bum, Crunk, and others.

Crumb has more than twenty publications to his name. His comic-book art has been both praised as the work of a genius and condemned as obscene. His cartoons are typically sexually explicit and graphically violent. His *Zap Comix: No. 4* and his *Snatch* series were the subject of obscenity trials and were removed from circulation on both the East and West coasts, as well as in Britain. According to his defenders, Crumb is a hero of imaginative freedom. He attacks mainstream values, draws things so that they look cute, while using them to attack mainstream values or to tell offensive stories. His most famous creations are Fritz the Cat, Mr. Natural, and Angelfood McSpade. He also created the well-known "Keep on Truckin'" logo.

Crumb's Angelfood McSpade character is a sex symbol who represents the hidden desires of white civilization. His Whiteman represents a stereotypical uptight businessman. Mr. Natural is a capitalist guru; and Flakey Foont, Natural's bumbling disciple, is a hopelessly repressed city-dweller seeking easy solutions to the world's most complex problems who is repeatedly used and abused by Mr. Natural.

In Crumb's "Ooga Booga" strip he initially seemed to denigrate African Americans, but this was merely a satire on black stereotypes. Crumb feels that if his art displays a deep seated racism or sexism, it is because such feelings are deep seated in the white male American psyche.

The popularity of Crumb's Fritz the Cat is due to the film of the same name, directed by Ralph Bakshi. Ironically, Crumb was so displeased with the film that he waged a successful legal battle to have his name removed from its credits. Still, Crumb's work has had an impact on changing American mores. Millions of baby boomers remember his hilarious, obscene, psychedelic satires, so-called underground comic books during the late 1960's and early 1970's.

In 1994 a close friend of Crumb, Terry Zwigoff, directed a documentary film about his life that was honored by critics as the best documentary of the year. The film looks over Crumb's shoulder as he works, drawing on table napkins, bus tickets, and whatever is available. Zwigoff interviews *Time* magazine art critic Robert Hughes, who sees Crumb as a modern successor to Pieter Brueghel, Francisco José Goya, and Honoré Daumier. Two women are also interviewed: Deirdre English, a former editor of *Mother Jones*, and cartoonist Trina Robbins. They praise Crumb's talent while deploring his evident hostility toward women. Crumb's work does not intend to evoke sexual arousal or hatred, but to laugh at the expense of hypocrisy or political righteousness.

See also Art; Books and obscenity law; Censorship; Daumier, Honoré.

Cuba

DESCRIPTION: The largest island in the Caribbean and the only communist nation in the Western Hemisphere

SIGNIFICANCE: State monopolization of all means of mass communication has ensured ideological compliance since Fidel Castro took power in 1959

Censorship has taken a variety of forms throughout Cuba's complex cultural history. Until the late nineteenth century, Cuban law was mandated by Spanish colonial authorities. Cuba's war for independence from Spain was spearheaded by efforts to gain full political and civil rights for all Cubans. On October 10, 1868, Cuban rebel leaders issued a manifesto that included demands for freedom of expression. Freedom finally came after the Spanish-American War of 1898. In 1901 the newly independent Cuban Republic drafted a constitution that explicitly gave citizens the right to "express their thoughts freely" without "prior censorship." This principle served as the basis for the constitution of 1940, which reaffirmed the right of every person "to express his thoughts freely in words, writing, or any other graphic or oral means of expression."

Despite these constitutional guarantees of free speech, successive dictatorships throughout the first half of the twentieth century gradually eroded civil liberties and fueled civil discontent. Geraldo Machado's government "reforms" in 1928, for example, restricted the civil rights granted by the constitution of 1901. A military coup led by Fulgencio Batista in 1952 imposed statutes that severely limited freedom of speech. Batista's censorship practices also included manipulation—newspaper editors were bribed to curtail reports of antigovernment guerrillas. By the time that Fidel Castro's guerrilla army toppled Batista in 1959, many Cubans had grown weary of foreign intervention and domestic government corruption. Many wel-

A U.S. Coast Guard vessel picks up Cuban political refugees attempting to cross the Florida Straits in open boats in 1994. (AP/Wide World Photos)

comed Castro, who had publicly declared the revolution's "absolute and reverent respect" for the 1940 constitution.

Despite these and other emancipatory declarations, however, one of the new revolutionary government's first steps was to shut down or take over all independent newspapers and magazines. Censorship then became less a matter of legal reform than one of monopolization; the state became the sole owner of all major forms of communication—from television stations to publishing houses to film companies. Many Cuban writers and artists had supported the revolution and had looked forward to a flourishing of creative freedom; however, it soon became evident that art was to serve ideology. Castro's famous 1961 speech, "Words to the Intellectuals," set the tone for the new society: "What are the rights of the revolutionary or nonrevolutionary writers and artists? Within the Revolution, everything; against the Revolution, no right." The socialist constitution of 1976 allowed freedom of expression that was "in keeping with the objectives of socialist society." The penal code prescribed up to fifteen years in prison for anyone who incited revolts against "the socialist state by means of oral, written or any other kind of propaganda."

As a result of these laws, many Cuban artists have been harassed, fired, exiled, or imprisoned for expressing views deemed "counterrevolutionary." Some writers, such as Armando Valladares, Angel Cuadra, and Jorge Valls, managed to smuggle manuscripts out of prison while serving long sentences. Others, such as Heberto Padilla, were forced to make public retractions for writing "enemy propaganda."

The nationalization of the communications media in Cuba provided the state with its most powerful ideological tool, binding individual expression to the country's vast political machinery.

See also Bay of Pigs invasion; Central America; Colonialism; Communism; Haiti; Martí, José Julián; Police states; Radio Martí; South America; Spanish-American War; Spanish Empire.

Cultural Revolution, Chinese

DATE: 1966 to 1976
PLACE: China
SIGNIFICANCE: In an attempt to transform China into a "pure" socialist state, Mao Zedong mobilized millions of workers and students to burn books and attack anyone deemed "bourgeois," leaving him the only voice in China

Mass persecution of intellectuals is a Chinese tradition that started with Emperor Shih huang-ti in the third century B.C.E. Shih had hundreds of Confucian scholars killed, and he burned many books in order to establish an ideology favorable to his regime. After the founding of the People's Republic of China in 1949, the Communist Party, led by Mao, launched several movements to suppress dissenting intellectuals and officials, thereby sowing the seeds for the future Cultural Revolution. In 1957 Mao advocated the "Hundred Flower Blossom" movement, inviting intellectuals to criticize party leadership. However, when criticism turned on one-party dictatorship, Mao abruptly declared his critics "rightists" and sent a half million of them to labor camps. Two years later, when Defense Minister Peng Dehua criticized Mao's "Great Leap Forward" movement—an ambitious economic program that had created a nationwide depression—Mao launched a campaign to purge Peng and his friends. During the early 1960's, in the midst of the open debate and split with the Soviet Union, Mao conducted the "Socialist Education Movement" to "rectify party powerholders who take the capitalist road." Mao aimed to prevent China from becoming like the Soviet Union, which he regarded as a capitalist country in disguise. The final catalyst of the Cultural Revolution came from Wu Han, a leading nonparty intellectual and deputy mayor of Beijing, who published a historical play, *Hai Rui Dismissed from Office,* depicting an honest official in the Ming Dynasty who lost his job after pointing out the mistakes of the emperor's land program. In late 1965 radical communists in Shanghai called the play a veiled defense of ousted Peng and—by extension—an attack on Mao, sparking a nationwide debate on Wu's play and works by other intellectuals.

Cultural Revolution: First Phase. As criticism of Wu and other intellectuals spread in schools across the country in early 1966, some party officials such as Peng Zhen, the mayor of Beijing, partly succeeded in organizing the debate as an academic one, instead of one symbolizing life-and-death struggles among the proletariat and bourgeoisie and true Marxists and party reactionaries—the view Mao favored. In May, 1966, the first big-letter wall poster appeared at Beijing University, charging the administration of trying to suppress the Cultural Revolution. The poster, published nationwide by Mao's order,

rallied millions of people, who used wall posters to denounce intellectuals and government cadres as "bourgeois reactionaries." In June, Mao's political opponents, Chairman of the Republic Liu Shaoqi and Party Secretary General Deng Xiaoping, dispatched to universities and schools workteams which led counter-attacks on many students, teachers, and low-level cadres, calling them "reactionaries." The tide turned again in August when Mao criticized the workteams for suppressing "revolutionary students" and ordered their withdrawal. Mao also published his own big-letter poster—"Bombard the Headquarters," which endorsed the Red Guards (students and workers), whom he used to sweep his political enemies, Liu, Deng, and their allies out of power. In the frenzy of eradicating "bad elements," the Red Guards beat up, killed, and imprisoned millions with "bourgeois ideology" or born into a "bourgeois family." They also burned and banned books written by Westerners and ancient Chinese authors.

While attacking and seizing power from intellectuals and government officials, the Red Guards also turned on one another as different internal factions tried to prove that they alone were true Mao loyalists and others were disguised bourgeois defenders. In late 1966 and 1967, oral debates on university campuses turned into armed clashes and bloodshed in many cities, stopped only when teams of soldiers and factory workers were sent to schools to take control. Starting in late 1968, as most radical students were sent by Mao to the countryside to be re-educated, order gradually returned to schools and factories, and studying Mao's works became the focus of the revolution. In April, 1969, Lin Biao, the designated successor of Mao, declared the Cultural Revolution to be in a new phase.

Issues and Debates. Intense as they were, no debates among the people and factions of Red Guards during the Cultural Revolution were free of Mao's own political framework, which was published in party newspapers. Every debate—whether it be on Chinese traditional music, school reform, or industrial policy—was conducted with an underpinning theme: to discover the class struggle between the proletariat and the bourgeoisie. Everything was seen as a two-line struggle between Mao's proletarian ideology and Liu's bourgeois ideology. The central concern of the debates and the reforms that emerged from them was how to promote Mao's line and suppress the bourgeois line. For example, the central issue of the "revolution in education" was how to bridge the gap between intellectuals (representing the bourgeoisie) and manual laborers (representing the proletariat) through reforming or re-educating intellectuals and students so that they would acquire the proletarian ideology. The debate led to a number of reforms, such as recruiting college students only from among workers and peasants with five years of work experience, and sending millions of high school graduates to the countryside to be re-educated by peasants. Similarly, the debate on the "revolution in art" led to the abolishment of the traditional Peking Opera, which was based on stories of emperors and Confucian intellectuals. It was replaced by "Modern Peking Opera" featuring proletarian heroes.

Cultural Revolution: Second Phase. From April, 1969, to October, 1976, when the Communist Party formally declared the end of the Cultural Revolution, there were additional large-scale political campaigns and debates. However, they were no longer spontaneous; they were orchestrated by the government to promote Mao's ideology or to discredit political opponents. For example, in 1972, after Lin Biao died in a plane crash during a coup attempt, a nationwide campaign was launched and millions were instructed to criticize him and Confucius, for Lin was discovered to have admired Confucius greatly. In April, 1976, Mao's wife, Chiang Ch'in, and her allies mobilized the masses to criticize Deng as the unrepentant bourgeois capitalist. After Mao's death and the arrest of his wife and her friends in October, 1976, Deng's allies launched campaigns to discredit them, blaming them for all the sufferings caused by the Cultural Revolution.

Aftermath. The Cultural Revolution's decade-long destruction of schools and teachers, and its discredit of Confucianism, left a generation of Chinese youths with little education or sense of cultural heritage. The damage it did was still evident decades later. At the same time, however, the Cultural Revolution's many political flip-flops greatly weakened the public's faith in communist ideology. After the Cultural Revolution, intellectual freedom not seen since the founding of communist China began to flourish, even though direct criticism of the government was still forbidden. *—Fan A. Shen*

See also China; Communism; Confucius; Dine, Jim; Intellectual freedom; Mao Zedong; Shih huang-ti; Wall posters.

BIBLIOGRAPHY

Jean Daubier's *A History of the Chinese Cultural Revolution* (translated by Richard Seaver; New York: Vintage, 1974) and Julia Kwong's *Cultural Revolution in China's Schools, May 1966-April 1969* (Stanford, Calif.: Hoover Institution Press, 1988) offer useful outlines of the Cultural Revolution. *China in Ferment: Perspectives on the Cultural Revolution*, edited by Richard Baum (Englewood Cliffs, N.J.: Prentice-Hall, 1971), and *New Perspectives on the Cultural Revolution*, edited by William A. Joseph and others (Cambridge, Mass.: Harvard University Press, 1991), handy sources for background information, key documents, and interpretations of the Cultural Revolution. Nien Cheng's *Life and Death in Shanghai* (New York: Grove Press, 1987) provides a personal memoir that is indispensable to understanding the extent of oppression during the Cultural Revolution.

Culture ministries

DEFINITION: Government departments that control national arts

SIGNIFICANCE: In attempting to promote particular conceptions of arts and culture, culture ministries often practice de facto censorship of artistic and cultural expression

The governments of many countries include divisions or departments whose duty it is to promote culture. Some of these culture ministries act as patrons of the various arts within a country; others seek to preserve recognized aspects of the country's national culture. The power and activities of culture ministries vary from country to country. This variety is reflected in their official names: Greenland's Ministry of Culture, Education, and Ecclesiastical Affairs; Austria's Ministry of Science, Research, and the Arts; North Korea's Ministry of Culture and Sport; and Indonesia's Ministry of Education and Culture.

Activities. Some ministries of culture define their duties in terms of advocacy and patronage. Greece's Hellenic Ministry of Culture, for example, has instituted cultural festivals, overseen the development of museums, and sought the return of Greek antiquities taken from the country. In some provinces of Canada, ministries carry out cultural advocacy as part of a mission to promote tourism. Japan's Agency for Cultural Affairs is charged with sponsoring various cultural events in Japan and abroad and preserving and restoring Japan's "cultural properties." A major part of the work of these culture ministries is to support national music, literature, and other arts through financial grants and publicity. Such activities are similar to those carried out by the National Endowment for the Arts in the United States.

The work of culture ministries sometimes involves political measures that amount to censorship. For example, the ministries of culture in authoritarian countries often politicize culture as a tool of control and indoctrination. Nazi Germany's Reich Cultural Organization (established in 1933) enlisted and supported artists as part of its propaganda campaign, and persecuted those who did not follow its dictates. More recently, analogous control of the arts was undertaken by communist regimes during the Cold War, including the Soviet Union's Ministry of Culture (earlier known as the People's Commissariat of Enlightenment). The communist ministries of culture sought to restrict the types of art that could be produced and performed. Only works that conformed to the political and aesthetic standards of Socialist Realism were approved, and unauthorized works could earn the artist a jail sentence or worse. Even after the conclusion of the Cold War, China's Ministry of Culture continued systematically directing the arts as a propaganda tool, although its techniques became less oppressive after the Cultural Revolution.

Regimes that claim religious authority may utilize culture ministries as a tool of censorship and control. Iran's Ministry of Higher Education and Culture is one example. The Ayatollah Ruhollah Khomeini, who led the Islamic revolution in Iran at the end of the 1970's, ridiculed the shah's Ministry of Culture as a source of corruption and decadence. Khomeini reorganized a ministry to promote Islamic teachings and values. Overall, the ministries of culture in authoritarian states such as these represent the most blatant forms of censorship.

Yet some of the activities of culture ministries in democratic states can also be construed as censorship. In the mid-1990's, the French Ministry of Culture under Jacques Toubon gained notoriety for its proposed language laws. The ministry was responding to the perception that the French language was being corrupted by the introduction of foreign words and phrases (primarily English). The legislation, adopted in 1994, prohibited the use of foreign expressions where official French substitutes had been identified. Penalties were prescribed for advertisers, publishers, and others who violated the law. France's Constitutional Court subsequently restricted the scope of the law to apply only to governmental bodies. Nevertheless, the French Ministry of Culture has also pursued censorship in other forms. The ministry has required that at least 40 percent of all songs broadcast on French radio stations be of French origin. It has also limited the proportion of American-produced television programs that can be aired and American-produced films that can be shown in French cinemas.

Slovakia successfully gained its independence by dissolving the Czechoslovakian federation in 1993, spurred largely by the sense that its society and culture were dominated by the Czechs. Its newly established Ministry of Culture immediately undertook efforts to protect Slovakian language and culture. Some of these measures resulted in controversial laws, including a language law that some saw as discriminatory and tantamount to censorship.

Norway's Ministry of Cultural Affairs, along with other governmental agencies, has undertaken measures to preserve the Norwegian language and promote Norwegian literature. It has sought to encourage the publishing of Norwegian-language books, for which there is virtually no market beyond Norway's population of about four million. The government offers subsidies to augment the royalties of Norwegian authors. Special additional subsidies are provided for books of particular use in promoting Norwegian language and culture, including classic Norwegian books and illustrated children's books. The government also requires that Norwegian bookstores stock all new Norwegian books for at least three years after publication. Additionally, the government commits to purchase the first thousand copies of most fictional works. Although all of these measures can be justified on the basis of promoting Norwegian culture, they provide a significant market advantage to works that conform to the government's criteria. If this advantage is large enough, it could be construed as de facto censorship of competing works that do not meet governmental criteria.

Considering the meaning and purpose of art, there are those who object to any government involvement in the arts, even as an advocate. But this may be an idealistic philosophy, given the reliance upon patronage by many artists. The question of potential censorship by the government is actually one of degree.

It is clear that many culture ministries occasionally engage in censorship. Less clear is the extent to which such censorship is justified. The goal of promoting the arts is in itself fairly noncontroversial. Even the more partisan objective of protecting and preserving a national culture has generally been recognized to be a legitimate governmental undertaking. But some of the methods chosen for accomplishing that objective can invite criticism. Defining the particular national culture of a country can be even more politically contentious. And finally, the doctrine of multiculturalism, particularly for multinational states, has been used to challenge the concept of a single national culture. —*Steve D. Boilard*

See also Art; Book publishing; Cultural Revolution, Chinese; Degenerate Art Exhibition; Language laws; National Endowment for the Arts; Socialist Realism.

BIBLIOGRAPHY

For a detailed examination of the relationship between law and culture, see Lawrence M. Friedman, *The Republic of Choice: Law, Authority, and Culture* (Cambridge, Mass.: Harvard University Press, 1990). For a critique of the administration of the arts, see Denis Donoghue's "The Cherishing Bureaucracy," in *The Arts Without Mystery* (Boston: Little, Brown, 1983). On Japan's Agency for Cultural Affairs and related policies, see Thomas R. H. Havens, "Arts and the State," chapter 3 of *Artist and Patron in Postwar Japan: Dance, Music, Theater, and the Visual Arts, 1955-1980* (Princeton, N.J.: Princeton University Press, 1982). On Nazi Germany's treatment of literature, see Sander L. Gilman, "Literature in German, 1933-1945," chapter 11 of Charles Budick et al., eds., *Contemporary Germany: Politics and Culture* (Boulder, Colo.: Westview Press, 1984). Erika Repovz and Nikolai Jeffs report a lengthy and illuminating interview concerning cultural nationalism in "Culture, Nationalism, and the Role of Intellectuals: An Interview with Aijaz Ahmad," in the *Monthly Review* 47, no. 3 (July-August, 1995).

cummings, e. e.

BORN: October 14, 1894, Cambridge, Massachusetts
DIED: September 3, 1962, North Conway, New Hampshire
IDENTIFICATION: American poet and author
SIGNIFICANCE: Cummings' first book and many of his poems were censorsed

When cummings gave his father the manuscript of his book *The Enormous Room* (1922) to deliver to Boni and Liveright for publication, his instructions were explicit: No changes were to be made in his work. When the autobiographical narrative appeared in print, however, he found that several chapters had been omitted. Horace Liveright maintained that

e. e. cummings before his political beliefs got him into trouble. (Library of Congress)

he had removed only a few obscenities to make the book's publication possible. He suggested that cummings' father was responsible for the missing chapters, a charge strongly denied by Edward Cummings.

Prior to sending *The Enormous Room* out to reviewers, Liveright received word of an intended raid by John Sumner, head of the New York Society for the Suppression of Vice. To avoid trouble with Sumner, an office worker went through every copy of the book to ink out a word deemed offensive. Nevertheless, some reviewers still complained that the work was full of crudities and gratuitous filth. The book was eventually reprinted in an edition that included all materials from the original manuscript.

Editors also often censored cummings' poems by substituting inoffensive words, or dashes or periods, for words that they regarded as obscenities. Vehemently opposed to such alterations, cummings stated that the one way government could assist writers would be by abolishing censorship. He also satirized the feared censor John Sumner in his poem "the season 'tis, my lovely lambs."

See also Liveright, Horace; Poetry; Society for the Suppression of Vice, New York; Sumner, John.

Cushing, Cardinal Richard James

BORN: August 24, 1895, Boston, Massachusetts

DIED: November 2, 1970, Boston, Massachusetts

IDENTIFICATION: Roman Catholic cleric in Massachusetts

SIGNIFICANCE: Cushing played a leading role in promoting censorship after World War II

Cushing served as Catholic archbishop of the Boston diocese from 1944 until his death in 1970. In 1958 Pope John XXIII elevated him to the rank of cardinal. Considered one of the most influential Catholic leaders of his time in the United States, Cushing became embroiled in a post-World War II censorship movement that attacked films, television, and books. Groups such as the Legion of Decency, National Organization for Decent Literature, and the National Office of Literature served as watch guards for Catholic bishops examining the moral content of visual and written material. In 1946, for example, Cushing supported Irish Catholics who tried to ban the series *Duffy's Tavern* from television because they thought it portrayed a demeaning image of Irish Americans. He also pushed to censor the language content of the play *Life with Father*.

In the late 1940's Cushing was asked by Catholic groups to have the controversial film *Forever Amber* banned in Boston. Cushing found nothing in the film objectionable enough to justify its being banned. He did, however, take a hard stand on risqué Boston nightclubs and the selling of erotic literature. In 1951 he issued a pastoral letter in his diocese reminding clergy and lay members alike of their responsibility in helping to stem the tide of entertainment that glorified sex.

When Henry Morton Robinson's novel *The Cardinal* was filmed in 1963, Cushing was invited to view the film in order to judge whether it might be interpreted as an attack on New York's procensorship champion, Cardinal Francis J. Spellman. Cushing saw no resemblance between the film's central char-acter and Spellman; he even reviewed the film favorably in a leading Catholic paper.

See also Boston; Boston Watch and Ward Society; Coughlin, Father Charles Edward; Ireland; Legion of Decency; National Organization for Decent Literature; Spellman, Cardinal Francis Joseph; Vatican.

Customs laws, Canadian

DEFINITION: Legislation controlling the importation of foreign goods

SIGNIFICANCE: Literature and other works entering Canada are subject to customs approval and may be detained if they are deemed to contain treasonous, seditious, or obscene material, or hate propaganda

Canadian law regulates the importation of material that is of a questionable moral or political nature. Implementation of customs laws has given rise to a continuing legal and ethical discourse. A tariff code governs the prohibition of undesirable objects entering Canada and allows officials to detain material that is deemed to be obscene, hate propaganda, treasonous, or seditious.

When administrative policies relating to tariff code were updated in September, 1994, changes were made in an effort to establish revised guidelines for the classification of material that fell into any of the prohibited categories. It has been argued by violators of the law that such detention and prohibition infringe basic rights to freedom of expression and freedom of the press, and that they therefore effectively constitute censorship. Revenue Canada, the federal ministry governing Canada's customs, refutes this argument, however, claiming that the code's prohibition of certain material involves the same enforcement that applies to domestically produced works. These conflicting positions are illustrated by a case involving a bookstore in Vancouver, British Columbia The defendants claimed that review by Canada customs effectively constituted censorship and that because the books in question had to pass customs, they were scrutinized and evaluated more stringently than similar material produced in Canada would have been.

More than half of Canada's tariff code pertains to the definition of obscene representations in any form. Approximately 40 percent is concerned with the definition of hate propaganda, and less than 10 percent is concerned with treasonous and seditious matter. During the year prior to the code's 1994 revision, there were some eleven thousand detainment or prohibition cases concerning obscene material or hate propaganda. According to Revenue Canada, there has never been a detainment case concerning either seditious or treasonous material. Clearly, then, the greatest perceived threat to the national cultural fabric lies in the importation of material that is allegedly obscene or that promotes hate against identifiable groups. The definitions of such terms as "obscene," "hate," and "identifiable groups" are open to wide and contradictory interpretation, however, leading to ongoing problems in enforcement.

Definitions. The tariff code refers to the criminal code for clarity of intent, but many of the same words are used in both texts, necessitating a reversion to standard dictionary definitions. Since 1868 enforcement has been based on the British Hicklin test, which focuses on the potential "corrupting impact" of the material. Later interpretations of obscenity have rested on a judgment of "undue exploitation of sex" in works being considered. A key case in the application of this clause was the consideration of customs clearance for D. H. Lawrence's 1928 novel *Lady Chatterley's Lover* in 1962.

Other salient phrases such as "disgusting object" and "indecent show" have led to challenges of unconstitutional infringement of freedom of expression as guaranteed by a section of the Canadian Charter of Rights and Freedoms. A rigid interpretation of these phrases led customs officials, in a celebrated case, to detain and charge a Canadian returning from the United States who was wearing a button bearing the message "Fuck Iran"; all charges against him were later dismissed in court. The test applied in determining indecency is that of "the community standard of tolerance." The relevant consideration is whether a display is inappropriate or an object disgusting according to Canadian standards, given the nature of the audience and the context in which a display takes place.

In Canadian social discourse, the developing openness concerning sex and sexuality, together with a greater sensitivity to freedom of expression, have been reflected in changing judicial opinions. Community standards, as articulated by Justice Freedman in 1964, "are not set by those of lowest taste or interest. Nor are they set exclusively by those of rigid, austere, conservative, or puritan taste and habit of mind. Something approaching a general average of community thinking and feeling has to be discovered." Community standards obviously are not written in stone, and alterations in such standards are reflected in the influence of the women's movement of the 1970's, when feminist objections to various depictions of sexual activity began to have an effect on the definition of obscenity. Furthermore, the term "community standards" is itself problematic. For example, court decisions have held that the intended audience is irrelevant in determining obscenity despite the argument that certain depictions are inoffensive within the gay community.

Obscene Goods. A 1994 interpretation of the tariff code described goods—which may be in the form of books, drawings, paintings, prints, photographs, films, sound recordings, and videotapes—that are prohibited because of their obscene nature. Obscene goods are those that depict sexual acts that appear to degrade or dehumanize any of the participants, including "depictions of sex with violence, submission, coercion, ridicule, degradation, exploitation or humiliation . . . which appear to condone or otherwise endorse such behavior for the purposes of sexual stimulation or pleasure." A greater part of the act outlines prohibited depictions of sex with violence, including rape, nonconsensual sex or sex achieved by force or deception; bondage or external control in a sexual context; the association of sexual pleasure with pain, suffering, mutilation, or the lack of basic dignity for a human being; sexual gratification gained through physical pain or humiliation, including extreme roughness and spanking; mutilation or killing in the context of sexual arousal; sexual suggestive-

ness with persons actually or apparently under the age of eighteen; incest; bestiality; and necrophilia.

Hate Propaganda. Goods constituting hate propaganda under the criminal code are those advocating or promoting genocide or promoting hatred against any identifiable group that may be distinguished by color, race, religion, or ethnic origin. In particular, hate propaganda includes goods that blame an identifiable group for serious economic or social problems; that allege a certain group manipulates the media, trade, finance, government or world politics to the detriment of society; that allege that a certain group is racially inferior; or that allege a certain group seriously threatens society. While attempting to assess goods under this provision, Canada customs policy advises that freedom of expression should be recognized and that works should be assessed in their entirety in the context of their overall nature, dominant characteristics, and themes. Such was the process for Salman Rushdie's 1989 novel *The Satanic Verses*, which some countries deemed hate literature, but which received Canada customs approval for importation.

Emergent Issues. The evolution of certain technologies, such as broadcasting and the Internet, has effectively circumvented the protective intent of customs regulations, thereby raising several communication issues. These are illustrated by the sensational 1993 murder trial of Karla Homolka. In Canada, a total publication ban had been court-ordered, but the trial was widely reported in the U.S. press, over which the order had no jurisdiction. American reporting of that trial was not prohibited from entry into Canada under customs regulations. Although U.S.-purchased accounts of the trial were not stopped at the border, once inside Canada, they were illegal. Furthermore, while cable-carried trial information was restricted by the Canadian Radio-Television and Telecommunications Commission (CRTTC), the banned information was widely available to many Canadians via the Internet and over-the-air broadcasting from border stations, neither of which media falls under the purview of any Canadian regulatory agency.

—*Hilary Horan*

See also Books and obscenity law; *Butler v. The Queen*; Canada; Child Pornography Law (Canada); Community standards; Customs laws, U.S.; Denmark; Hate laws; Hicklin case; Judicial publication bans; *Lady Chatterley's Lover*; Obscenity: legal definitions; Official Secrets Act (Canada).

BIBLIOGRAPHY

Gordon Hawkins and Franklin Zimring's *Pornography in a Free Society* (New York: Cambridge University Press, 1988) reviews findings of several commissions on pornography and discusses pornography's social impact. *Martin's Annual Criminal Code 1994*, annotated by Edward L. Greenspan, (Aurora, Ontario: Canada Law Books, 1993) is an annual publication that provides the texts of every act of Canada's criminal code. Alan W. Mewett and Morris Manning's *Mewett and Manning on Criminal Law* (3d ed. Toronto: Butterworths, 1994) discusses the fundamental concepts on which Canadian criminal law is based, paying special attention to constitutionally guaranteed freedoms. James R. Robertson's *Obscenity: The Decision of the Supreme Court of Canada in R. v. Butler*

(Ottawa: Library of Parliament, 1992) provides a concise synthesis of the underlying issues and the considerations leading to the decision in the Butler case, which became the basis for determining criminal obscenity. *Freedom of Expression and The Charter* (Scarborough, Ontario: Thomson Professional Publishing Canada, 1991), edited by David Schneiderman, focuses on the implications of Canada's Charter of Rights and Freedoms.

Customs laws, U.S.

Definition: Laws regulating the importation of materials from outside of the country

Significance: The U.S. federal government has used its postal and customs powers to censor the internal movement of undesirable material and its entry from abroad

The first article of the U.S. Constitution grants to Congress the power of customs and of establishing post offices. Congress has therefore enacted customs laws, some of which have included provisions for stopping obscene material at customs and preventing it from being mailed within the country. Such federal censorship powers are controversial with respect to citizens' right of free speech as protected by the First Amendment of the U.S. Constitution.

Statutory Language. In passing the customs law of 1842, Congress made its first attempt to include a provision for censoring imported materials in the law. This statute contained a section to prohibit pictorial art from being imported if it was "indecent or obscene." From time to time the areas of customs censorship have been expanded.

The Tariff Act of 1930 was the first comprehensive customs law; it consolidated previous customs laws into one coordinated statute. Although the 1930 act has been repeatedly amended, it is still the basic customs statute. Before enactment of the act, the customs officers often exercised their power arbitrarily, excluding many acknowledged masterworks of art and literature. Section 305 of the Tariff Act is a revision of all sections of previous laws about customs censorship and became the basic source of statutory authority for customs censorship. Section 305 has been codified within Title 19 of U.S. Code, Section 1305, which concerns immoral articles, the importation of which is prohibited.

The code prohibits all persons from importing items belonging to four categories into the United States from any foreign country. The first category is any book, pamphlet, paper, writing, advertisement, circular, print, picture, or drawing containing any matter advocating or urging treason or insurrection against the United States, or forcible resistance to any law of the United States, or containing any threat to take the life of or inflict bodily harm upon any person in the United States. The second category is any obscene book, pamphlet, paper, writing, advertisement, circular, print, picture, drawing, or other representation, figure, or image on or of paper or other material, or any cast, instrument, or other article which is obscene or immoral. The third category is any drug, medicine, or any article whatever for causing unlawful abortion. The fourth category is any lottery ticket, or any printed paper that may be used as a lottery ticket, or any advertisement of any lottery

(except those printed in Canada for use in connection with a lottery conducted in the United States).

The law also authorizes customs officers to seize and forfeit the entire contents of the package in which the prohibited articles are imported, including other goods entitled to entry. It provides further that the secretary of the treasury may, at his discretion, admit classics or books of recognized and established literary or scientific merit, but may, in his discretion, admit such classics or books only when imported for noncommercial purposes.

Constitutionality of Censoring Imported Materials. After the enactment of the Tariff Act of 1930, Congress also passed a few laws related to censoring communist political propaganda materials from abroad, such as the Foreign Agents Registration Acts of 1938 and 1942, and the Communist Political Propaganda provision of Public Law 87-793 in 1962 (this provision was later repealed). In practice, it has been less controversial that these statutes empowered the Customs Bureau and the Post Office to detain communist political propaganda mail from abroad. The issue of censoring imported obscene materials derived from Section 305 of the Tariff Act has been very controversial. Many cases were brought in the federal courts to challenge the constitutionality of Section 305.

One of the main issues is whether Congress has constitutional power to enact such laws as Section 305. This power has been affirmed by the U.S. Supreme Court in many cases based on Article I, Section 8, of the Constitution, which gives Congress broad comprehensive powers to regulate commerce with foreign nations. The most controversial issue is whether Section 305 violates the right of free speech, as protected by the First Amendment of the Constitution if imported materials are for private, personal use. In *United States v. Twelve 200-Foot Reels of Super-8 Millimeter Film* (1973), a majority of the Supreme Court held that a prohibition under Section 305 of the Tariff Act against importation from any foreign country of any obscene materials, is not unconstitutional. In this case, the claimant Paladini sought to carry movie films, color slides, photographs, and other printed and graphic materials into the United States from Mexico. The materials were seized for being obscene by customs officers at a port of entry, Los Angeles Airport, and made the subject of a forfeiture action under Section 305 of the Tariff Act. The claimant contended that under the First Amendment and the Supreme Court's decision in *Stanley v. Georgia* (1969), the right to possess obscene material in the privacy of the home creates a right to acquire it or import it from another country. The District Court of Central California agreed with the claimant's argument and dismissed the government's complaint. The Supreme Court later overruled the district court's decision. The Supreme Court's holding was based on the grounds that *Roth v. United States* (1957) had established that obscene material was not protected by the First Amendment; also, the Stanley case's emphasis was on the freedom of thought and mind in the privacy of the home, but a port of entry is not a traveler's home; finally, Congress had not authorized an exception for private use of obscene materials.

Customs Censorship Abroad. Censorship provisions in customs laws and censorship practice on imported materials or foreign mails are different in democratic and authoritarian countries. Among the Western democratic countries, customs censorship laws and practice vary from country to country depending upon the public and government views on sex, race, religion, and politics.

Canada has obscenity laws that are much more strict than those in the United States. Not surprisingly, the Canadian customs has a long history of seizing obscene materials, especially materials on gay and lesbian topics.

Generally, Western European countries tolerate more sex but less violence than the United States. European censors often cut violent scenes in American films before distribution, or ban the films altogether. Sweden is considered the toughest country in censoring films for violence. For example, the Walt Disney film *Beauty and the Beast* (1991) might be considered relatively harmless, but some scenes involving violence were cut before the film was shown in Sweden.

New Zealand's customs censorship appears to be the most rigid in the Commonwealth. The New Zealand Customs Act focuses on the concept of "indecency" rather than "obscenity." Therefore, New Zealand's law makes it unlawful to import documents that are indecent. New Zealand does not have a large publishing industry, so customs control over imports, a form of precensorship, is of primary importance.   —*Wei Luo*

See also Child Pornography Law (Canada); Constitution, U.S.; Customs laws, Canadian; Disney films; Foreign Agents Registration Act of 1938; Pornography; Pornography, child; Postal regulations; *Roth v. United States*; Sweden; Vietnam War.

BIBLIOGRAPHY

Jay A. Sigler's "Customs Censorship," in *Cleveland Marshall Law Review* 15 (1966), is an overview. Edward T. Byrne's "Government Seizures of Imported Obscene Matter: Section 305 of the Tariff Act of 1930 and Recent Supreme Court Obscenity Decisions," in *Columbia Journal of Transnational Law* 13 (1974), describes the central legal issues involved in U.S. Customs censorship. Joan H. Hillenbrand's "The Customs Authority to Search Foreign Mail," in *International Law and Policy* (1973), discusses the law within the larger context of international law. Margaret A. Blanchard's "The American Urge to Censor: Freedom of Expression Versus the Desire to Sanitize Society—from Anthony Comstock to 2 Live Crew," in *William and Mary Law Review* (Spring, 1992), offers opinion on the censorship issue.

D

Dahl, Roald

BORN: September 13, 1916, Llandaff, Wales

DIED: November 23, 1990, Oxford, England

IDENTIFICATION: British screenwriter and author

SIGNIFICANCE: Dahl's children's books have been among the most frequent targets of censorship in U.S. education

Although Dahl was one of the world's most successful children's authors, parental critics have charged that his books revelled in vulgarity and cruelty. Criticism of his books has come from both the Right and the Left, as well as from other ideological factions. Feminists, for example, have denounced *The Witches* (1983) for its unflattering portrayals of women, while Christian Fundamentalists have attacked the book out of fear that it will entice impressionable children into the occult. Dahl's private opinions—especially anti-Semitism expressed in letters to friends—have also fueled arguments against exposing children to his books. Critics have also objected to unflattering racial depictions in *Charlie and the Chocolate Factory* (1964) and *The BFG* (1982).

Dahl's *Revolting Rhymes* (1982), one of the most frequently banned books in U.S. schools, parodies traditional fairy tales. Objections to it center on both its language and its violence—such as the beheading of Cinderella's stepsisters. Dahl's other banned works include *George's Marvelous Medicine* (1981), in which a boy allegedly murders his grandmother, and *James and the Giant Peach* (1961), which has been targeted for its language, sexual imagery, and abusive situations.

Some U.S. publishers have bowdlerized Dahl's books, removing allegedly offensive passages, such as *Charlie and the Chocolate Factory*'s description of a fat boy. In an essay about censorship published in 1987, Dahl contended that adults are more disturbed by his books than are children—who he claimed are more vulgar and cruel than grownups.

See also Banned Books Week; Libraries, school.

Dalí, Salvador

BORN: May 11, 1904, Figueras, Spain

DIED: January 23, 1989, Figueras, Spain

IDENTIFICATION: Spanish artist, writer, and filmmaker

SIGNIFICANCE: As one of the most eccentric and popular creative figures of the twentieth century, Dalí invited controversy with many of his well-known works

As an adolescent, Dalí experimented with various painting styles. In 1921 he was admitted to the San Fernando Academy of Fine Arts in Madrid, Spain. His rebellious nature ran counter to the more traditionalist approach of the academy, however, and he was suspended in 1923. He returned to the academy the next year, but was permanently expelled in 1926 for his disruptive behavior.

By the late 1920's he found himself drawn to the surrealist movement. He settled in Paris in the fall of 1929 and offi-

cially joined the movement. During his years of association with the surrealists, Dalí created many of his most striking and disturbing paintings, including *Portrait of Paul Eluard* (1929), *The Invisible Man* (1929), *Imperial Monument to the Child-Woman* (1929), *The Great Masturbator* (1929), and probably his most famous surrealist painting *The Persistence of Memory* (1931), with its limp watches on a barren landscape. By exploring the subconscious mind, Dalí was able to create surrealist paintings that successfully linked illusion with reality.

In 1928 Dalí collaborated with the Spanish filmmaker Luis Buñuel on the screenplay for Buñuel's surrealist short film *Un Chien andalou* (1928; *an Andalusian dog*). The film horrified its Parisian audiences and brought notoriety to both Buñuel and Dalí. They collaborated once again on the surrealist film *L'Age d'or* (1930). This film caused an even greater scandal than *Un Chien andalou*. *L'Age d'or* spoke out against repression in society by including shocking scenes of eroticism and anti-Catholicism. It had received approval from the French censors and was first shown in Paris at Studio 28 on November 28, 1930. On December 3, members of the Patriots' League and the Anti-Jewish League disrupted the showing of the film

Portrait of Salvador Dalí made by Carl van Vechten in 1939. (Library of Congress)

by throwing ink at the screen and by destroying some of the paintings by Dalí, Joan Miró, and others displayed in the foyer of the theater.

After the incident right-wing editorials called for the film to be banned. A Paris police authority called for the Municipal Council to meet. The Ministry of Public Education also became involved and, on December 6, the manager of Studio 28 was ordered to remove several scenes from the film that contained Catholic bishops. This action by the manager, however, did not satisfy all government agencies. On December 11, the Board of Appeals of the Bureau of Censorship viewed the film and concluded that it should be banned. Copies of the film were confiscated, and Viscomte de Noailles, the man who financed the making of the film, was forced to resign from the Jockey Club. The scandal surrounding *L'Age d'or* reached such a pitch that Noailles also was threatened with excommunication from the Roman Catholic church.

Although the *L'Age d'or* scandal made Dalí a household name, there were several potential buyers of his paintings who hesitated to purchase them because of the uproar. With would-be buyers shying away, Dalí turned his creative mind to several ideas he had for inventions. Over the years, he learned to be a master at self-promotion and thrived on the various scandals he instigated. Throughout his long and illustrious career, Dalí never strayed very far from the center of controversy in the art world.

See also Art; Film censorship; France; Mapplethorpe, Robert; Serrano, Andres; Whistler, James Abbott McNeill.

D'Annunzio, Gabriele

BORN: March 12, 1863, Pescara, Italy
DIED: March 1, 1938, Gardone, Italy
IDENTIFICATION: Italian novelist, poet, dramatist, and soldier
SIGNIFICANCE: D'Annunzio's works were placed on the Roman Catholic *Index Librorum Prohibitorum* because they emphasized sensual gratification and promoted non-Christian values

D'Annunzio published his first collection of poetry in 1879, and he served as a deputy in Italy's Parliament from 1884 to 1904. In politics, he gained attention because of the literary quality of his fluent rhetoric, but he behaved unpredictably, creating scandals with his many love affairs, and he was forced into bankruptcy in 1910 because of his extravagant spending. A fervent Italian nationalist, he was a daring member of the national air force during World War I, and he was outraged when Italy did not receive its territorial claims after helping to win the war. In 1919, he led three hundred soldiers who captured the port city of Fiume (now Rijeka, Yugoslavia), and held it by force for a year.

D'Annunzio was an early advocate of many fascist ideas, and his own troops introduced the black shirt which became a symbol of the Fascist Party. Always maintaining close ties with the Fascist regime that came into power in 1922, he gave every appearance of supporting Benito Mussolini's authoritarian policies—including tight regimentation of the press. In 1926, Mussolini arranged for a government-sponsored edition of D'Annunzio's complete works, even though most of them were then on the *Index*. In 1937, Mussolini appointed D'Annunzio president of the Royal Italian Academy.

A versatile writer, D'Annunzio was praised for his imaginative and melodious style, but most critics considered the content of his many novels and plays to be superficial, melodramatic, and often flowery. Novels such as his *The Child of Pleasure* (1898) and *The Triumph of Death* (1894) reveal preoccupations with reckless courage, sensual gratification, the beauty of nature, and the desire for happiness. Probably his best-known novel was *The Flame of Life* (1900), one of several works based on his turbulent affair with actress Eleanora Duse. It appears that D'Annunzio was a skillful plagiarist who often borrowed themes and ideas from Renaissance writers, as well as from Émile Zola and Friedrich Nietzsche.

Many critics disliked D'Annunzio's values, particularly his glorification of sensual gratification. In 1898, the Boston Watch and Ward Society tried, but failed, to convince a jury that D'Annunzio's *The Triumph of Death* was obscene. The Roman Catholic church was the institution that attempted most strongly to limit the availability of his works. In 1911, the Vatican placed all his love stories and most of his plays on the *Index*, and by 1948, the prohibition for faithful Catholics was extended to the totality of D'Annunzio's writings. In 1936, the bishop of Pompeii forbade Catholics to attend D'Annunzio's play, *The Martyrdom of Saint Sebastion*, and the government tourist bureau indefinitely postponed its presentation. Mussolini banned D'Annunzio's biography in 1935, but when D'Annunzio died in 1938, Mussolini and his cabinet joined thousands of Italian patriots who assembled to honor his memory, and the Vatican issued a statement denying that it had excommunicated D'Annunzio.

See also Boston Watch and Ward Society; *Index Librorum Prohibitorum*; Italy; Vatican; World War I; Zola, Émile.

Dante Alighieri

BORN: May, 1265, Florence, Italy
DIED: September 13 or 14, 1321, Ravenna, Italy
IDENTIFICATION: Medieval Italian writer
SIGNIFICANCE: Perhaps the greatest poet of his time, Dante was—for political reasons—driven into exile from his native city and his works were condemned as heretical by the Roman Catholic church

Dante was an only child in a family that belonged to Italy's lower nobility. By his own account, the most significant event of his childhood occurred when he was nine and first gazed upon a nine-year-old girl named Beatrice, his lifelong secret love who inspired much of his poetry. (The girl later became the Florentine noblewoman Beatrice Portinari). Dante spent most of his youth circulating in Florence's cosmopolitan literary community, in which he developed an interest in literature.

Dante's political troubles began in 1300, when he was elected to Florence's municipal council. In the political turmoil that plagued Italy at the time, Dante allied with the nationalist faction known as the Ghibelline against the Guelphs, who supported the papacy. During Dante's tenure on the council, he played a role in banishing Guelph leaders from the city. In 1301, while he was away from Florence, the

Guelphs engineered a coup and banished him from his beloved home. He remained in exile until his death in 1321.

Dante's insistence on writing in Italian instead of Latin was a revolt against traditional thought and expression that helped to break the monopoly that Latin had long held over literary communication. His epic masterpiece, *The Divine Comedy*—which he completed shortly before he died—describes a journey through Hell, Purgatory, and Paradise. It also reflects Dante's philosophical and political ideas. It was banned by the Roman Catholic church in the sixteenth century as part of the Inquisition, the Church's campaign to combat the spread of Protestantism.

The Divine Comedy was a poetic narrative, not a philosophical treatise. It was in *On Monarchy* (ca. 1310), the most strongly antipapal tract of the Middle Ages, that Dante provided the fullest philosophical exposition of his political thought. This work makes a case for universal monarchy. What made Dante's theory of world government revolutionary was his rejection of the traditional medieval view of authority. He totally severed the temporal authority of government from the ecclesiastical authority of the Church, arguing that both pope and universal monarch are superior in their own spheres, and both receive their authority directly from God. Therefore, Dante concluded, the Church should not be permitted to exercise any worldly power.

So offended by Dante's attack upon papal authority was the Roman Catholic church that Pope John XXII declared *On Monarchy* heretical and ordered it burned in 1329. In the sixteenth century that book joined *The Divine Comedy* on the *Index Librorum Prohibitorum*, the catalogue of condemned books considered dangerous to the faith, that Catholics were forbidden to read under threat of excommunication. Dante's books remained on the list until the nineteenth century, when they were removed as no longer dangerous.

See also Book burning; Heresy; *Index Librorum Prohibitorum*; Italy; Poetry; Vatican.

DARE program

FOUNDED: 1983

TYPE OF ORGANIZATION: Government-sponsored drug education program for children

SIGNIFICANCE: The effectiveness of this program's work has been challenged in a study whose results were suppressed by the U.S. Justice Department

In 1983 a drug education program, DARE, was implemented in schools in Los Angeles and quickly spread to become one of the most popular in the nation. After a 1994 study, the program came under scrutiny as to its effectiveness and controversy resulted when the Justice Department chose not to publish the results. Drug Abuse Resistance Education, or DARE, was a program in which fifth and sixth graders were given forty-five-minute to one-hour sessions for seventeen weeks by a local law enforcement official. The curriculum emphasized building self-esteem while teaching children the effects of drug use.

Criticism of the program evolved when the Research Triangle Institute in North Carolina completed a research project commissioned by the National Institute of Justice, a division of the Justice Department. After three years of study, the institute concluded that although the program improved social skills and general drug knowledge, it was statistically ineffective as compared to other programs designed to deter drug use. Advocates of the DARE program argued that the curriculum studied was not the improved version introduced in late 1994, that it was unfairly compared to unrelated programs, and that the test group was too small. They further stated that in the age group studied, drugs were not a significant problem yet, and little research had been done on the long-term effects. The institute chose to make the results available but refused to publish because they did not agree with the conclusions.

See also Drug education; Police.

Darwin, Charles

BORN: February 12, 1809, Shropshire, England

DIED: April 19, 1882, Downe, Kent, England

IDENTIFICATION: British naturalist and author

SIGNIFICANCE: Darwin's writings on biology established natural selection as a major mechanism in the evolution of species

In 1859 Darwin published *On the Origin of Species*, the first of a series of texts explaining the role of natural selection in the evolution of biological species. Central to his theory was a search for a mechanism of evolution; he also suggested that humans and other primates evolved from common ancestors. Darwin's ideas were formulated primarily from his travels on

Naturalist Charles Darwin, whose name has become synonymous with scientific controversy. (National Archives)

the *Beagle*, a British ship that had sailed on a five-year voyage around the world during the 1830's in order to map the globe and to collect flora and fauna. When Darwin published his account of the voyage in 1845, his ideas on evolution were already developing; however, it was another fourteen years before these ideas were formally published. Reasons for this long delay remain unclear. The most likely explanation is that Darwin's materialistic view of evolution—which attributed natural selection to random variation—was so at odds with the views of religion and society that he was afraid of committing professional suicide with its publication. It was only after evidence supporting his view became more abundant that Darwin decided to publish his work.

The first public forum for Darwin's theory came in June, 1860, at an Oxford meeting of the British Association for the Advancement of Science. As part of the public debate, Samuel Wilberforce, the bishop of Oxford, argued vehemently against any theory suggesting that humans were descended from apes. However, other scientists strongly defended Darwin's arguments. Most prominent among them were the naturalist Thomas Huxley and botanist Joseph Hooker. Although Hooker had long opposed theories of evolution, he provided Darwin's strongest defense. He accused Wilberforce of distorting Darwin's work, and explained how he had become convinced of the truth of evolution.

Belief in evolution eventually became the norm among scientists. Prior to Darwin's work, most naturalists believed that species were immutable, and that each had been created separately. Most notable among such "creationists" in the United States was Louis Agassiz, arguably the most important naturalist of nineteenth century America. However, while some scientists remained skeptical that natural selection was the driving force behind evolution, most became convinced that evolution itself was real. Thomas Huxley became known as "Darwin's bulldog" for his strong advocacy of the theory. Although Huxley was an eloquent speaker, his extreme view of the Church often forced critics to take an opposing stand. Nevertheless, Darwin's additional works on the subject of evolution, most notably *Variation of Animals and Plants Under Domestication* (1868) and *The Descent of Man* (1871), contained such strong arguments in favor of his theories that most critics were eventually quieted. By the early twentieth century, even most organized religions found little conflict with the idea of evolution or Darwin's theories to explain it.

See also Evolution; Science; Scopes trial; Vesalius, Andreas.

Daughters of the American Revolution (DAR)

FOUNDED: August 8, 1890

TYPE OF ORGANIZATION: Conservative patriotic women's group

SIGNIFICANCE: Since its founding, the DAR has used patriotism to justify censorship

In 1890 President Benjamin Harrison's wife, Caroline Harrison, founded the DAR, a national patriotic organization for female descendants of Americans who served in the Revolution. Congress chartered the organization in 1895. Since then the DAR has promoted patriotic history education, but its opposition to liberal social reform has attracted criticism. As a primarily white organization it has also often been accused of racism. In 1939 it denied use of its headquarters, Constitution Hall in Washington, D.C., to the black contralto Marian Anderson for a concert sponsored by Howard University. When black pianist Hazel Scott was barred from the hall in 1945, DAR member Bess Truman—the wife of President Harry Truman—compared DAR policies to Nazism. In the 1960's, the group denounced the National Association for the Advancement of Colored People as left-wing and anti-Christian.

The DAR opposed the New Deal, and it rejected both the League of Nations and later the United Nations as unpatriotic. While Senator Joseph McCarthy hunted communists in the late 1940's and early 1950's, the DAR accused the United Nations Education, Scientific, and Cultural Organization (UNESCO) of using formal education to indoctrinate children with socialism. DAR and John Birch Society members also attacked textbook publishers. Of 214 texts evaluated in *DAR*

After the DAR refused to let Marian Anderson sing in its hall, First Lady Eleanor Roosevelt resigned from the organization and persuaded Secretary of the Interior Harold Ickes to invite Anderson to perform at the Lincoln Memorial, where the contralto sang for more than 75,000 people on April 9, 1939. (Library of Congress)

Textbook Study 1958-1959, only forty-nine met the group's minimum standards for patriotism. "Dangerous" works included four Pulitzer Prize winners, as well as Theodore Dreiser's *An American Tragedy*, Aldous Huxley's *Brave New World*, John Hersey's *Hiroshima*, and writings by Margaret Mead and Lincoln Steffens.

See also Education; National Association for the Advancement of Colored People; Pressure groups; Textbooks.

Daumier, Honoré

BORN: February 20 or 26, 1808, Marseilles, France
DIED: February 11, 1879, Valmondois, France
IDENTIFICATION: French artist
SIGNIFICANCE: Daumier was imprisoned in 1832 for satirizing the king of France in a newspaper caricature

Daumier's reputation for political satire arose in the early 1830's, when he published prints in two newly founded French periodicals, *La Caricature* and *Le Charivari*. The reigns of Charles X and Louis Philippe provided political events that were ripe for caricature. A state ordinance to muzzle the press resulted in the censoring of several Daumier lithographs during the early 1830s.

"Gargantua," which Daumier published in *La Caricature* in December, 1831, depicted Louis-Philippe as the monstrous glutton invented by François Rabelais in his 1530's satire, *Gargantua and Pantagruel*. While graffiti on Parisian walls had depicted the king with a pear face (the French word for pear meant "dullard" in French slang), Daumier rendered him fat, pear-headed, and seated on an enema chair in the Place de la Concorde. Unlike his anonymous counterparts, Daumier had dared to attack the king in a public forum. As a result, the printers' lithographic stone was seized by the police and Daumier himself was tried, along with the printers, in February, 1832, for "hatred and contempt of the government and insulting the king's person." Each defendant was fined five hundred francs and was sentenced to six months in prison. Daumier served five months of his sentence.

Daumier later expressed his indignation toward the government in "Rue Transnonain, 15 April 1834," a graphic account of the unjustified murder of Parisian citizens by French troops. The stone and copies of the print were confiscated by the police.

See also Art; Caricature; France; *Doonesbury*.

Davis, Angela

BORN: January 26, 1944
IDENTIFICATION: Professor of philosophy and activist for radical leftist and African American causes
SIGNIFICANCE: Davis' Communist Party affiliations and her association with the Soledad Brothers made her a target of conservatives who have tried to ban her from teaching in state-supported institutions

Davis grew up in Birmingham, Alabama, where her parents were involved with the National Association of Colored People and the Southern Negro Youth Congress. She received a scholarship to attend a progressive private high school on scholarship in New York, where she first attended Communist

Though briefly imprisoned during the early 1970's for her alleged role in a courtroom shootout and subsequent escape of prisoners in California, Angela Davis was acquitted on all charges in 1972. (Library of Congress)

Party youth meetings. After graduating from Brandeis University with high honors with a degree in 1965, she did graduate work in modern philosophy at the University of Frankfurt, then returned to the United States and earned her masters degree from the University of California at San Diego.

In 1968 she joined the Communist Party of the United States (CPUSA) and worked with the Student Nonviolent Coordinating Committee and the Black Panther Party. The following year she was hired as an assistant professor at University of California at Los Angeles (UCLA), where she was completing work on her doctoral dissertation. Citing a state law that prohibited Communist Party members from teaching at state universities, California's Governor Ronald Reagan fired Davis. Davis took her case to the courts, where the law under which she was fired was declared unconstitutional. After being reinstated at UCLA, she was again fired in 1970 because of her outspoken support of Jonathan Jackson and George Jackson, the "Soledad Brothers," radical African American prisoners in California's Soledad prison. This time a university faculty committee ruled that Davis had not compromised her faculty position by her involvement.

Later that same year Davis' name made the most-wanted list of the Federal Bureau of Investigation. After Jonathan Jackson seized hostages while trying to negotiate a deal for the Soledad brothers during a trial at the Marin County courthouse, it was discovered that the guns he used had been purchased by Davis. Both Jackson and a judge were killed; Davis was seen as Jackson's accomplice and was charged with murder, kidnapping, and conspiracy. For two months Davis was a fugitive. In

1972 the case went to trial, and Davis was acquitted of all charges. Afterward she continued her teaching and political activism. She remained active in the Communist Party and was its vice-presidential candidate in the 1980 and 1984 elections.

See also Communism; Federal Bureau of Investigation; Lennon, John; Prisons; Universities.

Day They Came to Arrest the Book, The

TYPE OF WORK: Book
PUBLISHED: 1982
AUTHOR: Nat Hentoff (1925-   )
SUBJECT MATTER: In this book, which is geared toward students in junior and senior high school, a teacher assigns her history class *Adventures of Huckleberry Finn*, setting off an uproar among parents, students, teachers, and school administrators
SIGNIFICANCE: The novel deals directly with the question of the freedom of teachers to assign books that are widely considered masterpieces, in spite of the objection of parents

The character Nora Baines's assignment of Mark Twain's classic novel as required reading is challenged by a student and his father for its use of the word "nigger." They want the book removed from the school. This is not the first attempt at censorship in the school; a former librarian had resigned because of the principal's pressuring her to remove other questionable books. When the principal asks Baines not to teach *Adventures of Huckleberry Finn*, she refuses and requests that the novel be submitted to a school censorship committee. She continues to teach the novel; some students leave her class, but one black student remains, feeling that he should make up his own mind. The lively debate that ensues touches on all sides of the censorship problem and First Amendment rights.

Objections to Hentoff's novel have focused on the way it allegedly encourages students to disobey school administrators. One student, for example, after carefully thinking things over, decides that the school's principal is wrong to ban the book, and the teacher is right to assign it. In 1990 the novel was challenged in the Albermarle Middle School in Charlottesville, Virginia, for being inflammatory and encouraging students to defy legitimate authority.

See also *Adventures of Huckleberry Finn*; Freedom to Read Foundation; Libraries, school; Twain, Mark.

Dead Sea Scrolls

DATE: 1946 to 1956
PLACE: Qumran, Israel
SIGNIFICANCE: Publication of the ancient scrolls has been delayed as much as forty years, raising charges of religious or political censorship

In late 1946 or early 1947, Palestinian Bedouins discovered the first of what by 1956 proved to be hundreds of ancient scrolls in eleven caves in bluffs overlooking the Dead Sea. These scrolls can be divided into two categories: biblical and sectarian. Dated to the second and first centuries B.C.E., they may be the oldest surviving manuscripts of both types of Jewish literature.

The texts of the earliest discovered scrolls were published quickly, and the Jordanian government allowed the chief archaeologist at Qumran to form an eight-person team that would publish the remaining manuscripts. Since then, all the texts from Cave 1 and a small number from eight other caves have been published. By 1990, only a few of the many scrolls in Caves 4 and 11 had appeared, however, leaving about 55 percent of the scrolls unpublished. Many scrolls from Cave 4 crumbled in their containers and had to be reassembled like jigsaw puzzles. That task was finished by the early 1960's. Shortly thereafter a photographer made infrared pictures of the scrolls, copies of which were stored for security in California, Ohio, and England. The original scrolls were kept in the Palestine Archaeology Museum.

When the West Bank came under the control of the State of Israel after the 1967 Arab-Israeli war, the Israeli government assumed responsibility for the scrolls and promised speedy publication of the remaining texts—a promise it has not kept. Since 1967 four members of the original publication team have died, one retired, and one became a recluse. Several team members passed their scrolls to hand-picked successors, while others have used their own graduate students to speed up publication. Meanwhile access to the scrolls has been denied to some of the foremost biblical scholars in the world.

Fragments of the Dead Sea Scrolls that California's Huntington Library made available to scholars for the first time in 1991, despite protests from the Israeli government. (AP/Wide World Photos)

Publication delays have raised charges of censorship. Some critics claim that the Vatican made a deal to suppress texts that might undermine Christian teachings. Critics have implicated both the Jordanian and Israeli governments in the scheme. However, no public evidence supports such claims. Nevertheless, it is clear that the Israeli government has entrusted the scrolls to a very few scholars—some of whom have admitted to keeping the scrolls to themselves for their own professional gain. Other critics have leveled charges of deliberate tampering with texts because of apparent differences between photographs of the same texts taken at different times.

Over the years the physical condition and legibility of the scrolls—as well as some of the original photographs and negatives—have deteriorated, raising the fear that some texts will never be published. In 1989 the Israeli government's antiquities department announced a "suggested timetable" for publication of the remaining scrolls. When new delays occurred, "unofficial" publication of the scrolls began. As early as 1988 a concordance to the scrolls was published by young scholars in West Germany. Three years later the Biblical Archaeology Society published a computer-generated version of the unpublished scrolls based on that concordance, as well as a two-volume set of the photographs of the previously unpublished texts.

These publications did not resolve the dispute, however. Publication team members denounced the computer-generated texts as inaccurate and several law suits were filed. Meanwhile, the changing political climate in the region left the future of the scrolls uncertain.

See also Archaeology; Bible; Israel; Jeremiah's Book of Prophesies, burning of; Judaism; Religion; Talmud; Vatican.

Death

DEFINITION: Silencing critics by killing them

SIGNIFICANCE: Governments and other groups have often resorted to this ultimate form of censorship

Those who exercise their right to free speech may pay with their lives when governments treat criticism as equivalent to treason. State authorities may first try to silence such voices by harassment and imprisonment. Execution is a formal and official act of the state (often preceded by a trial meant to demonstrate legality); state-sponsored murder and assassination are extra-judicial. Such brutal sanctions against heroic figures often backfire, however, when the victims' words and acts are remembered more reverently in death than in life.

Assassination of Critics. The covert killing of a dissenter removes the critical voice while concealing governmental responsibility. A famous example of this practice is associated with Henry II of England. His rash words—"Who will free me from this turbulent priest?"—led to the assassination in 1170 by underlings of his former friend Thomas Becket, who had become a surprisingly independent and troublesome archbishop of Canterbury.

The kidnapping and murder of another priest, Father Jerzy Popieluszko provides a twentieth century example of this censorship technique. When the independent Polish trade union Solidarity arose in 1980 to challenge the legitimacy of the communist regime in Soviet-occupied Poland, Popieluszko praised Solidarity from the pulpit and instituted what was called a Mass for the Homeland, which became a rallying point for Solidarity activists on the last Sunday of each month. Modern technology facilitated the distribution across Poland of the popular priest's sermons through tapes and reprints. So beloved was the humble, slight Father Jerzy that silencing him become a priority for the government.

After the suspension of Solidarity in late 1981, a campaign of harassment, ranging from punctured car tires to constant surveillance and to repeated interrogations, was directed at Popieluszko. The first attempt on the priest's life came in 1982, when a bomb that failed to explode was thrown through his window. A year later, he was arrested for possessing illegal pamphlets and munitions, which it was later revealed (in his murderers' trial), had been planted in his apartment by the state authorities. The indictment included the "abuse of freedom of conscience and religion" as one of his "crimes." He rejected an offer to give up the Masses for the Homeland in exchange for dismissing the indictment (which was later dropped as part of a general amnesty).

The regime publicly warned that his activities could no longer be tolerated after his July, 1984, Mass for the Homeland drew fifteen thousand people. Father Jerzy was kidnapped on October 19, 1984, following a church service in Bydgoszcz, although his driver escaped to tell the tale. When his tortured body was found in a reservoir, he became a national martyr representing the Polish quest for independence. Lech Walesa (later the elected president of a free Poland) eulogized the priest with these words: "Solidarity lives, because you died for it." The government maintained its innocence while convicting four secret police officials of Popieluszko's murder.

Execution of Dissenters. Socrates was executed by the Athenian government in 399 B.C.E. for "corrupting" its youth by promoting skepticism and thoughtful analysis of right conduct. He was put on trial as a public offender on the charge that "he does not recognize the gods that the state recognizes." Probably his accusers were expecting Socrates to flee rather than risk conviction and the death penalty. Socrates ardently defended to the jury his commitment never to give up teaching philosophy. Moreover, he asserted that being a "gadfly" made him a precious commodity to Athens. During the weeks between his conviction of impiety and his execution, Socrates rejected opportunities to escape. His emphasis on rationally based ethics led him to conclude that he must obey state laws, including his own death sentence. Socrates sustained a philosophical discourse with his students during his imprisonment, even to his last moments after drinking hemlock. Socrates remains a dramatic champion across the ages to all advocates of critical thinking in the face of oppressive authority.

Jesus Christ, the founder of Christianity, was executed in about 33 C.E. primarily for claiming to be the son of God. Many Jews were awaiting the redeemer of Israel as a political leader, the king of Israel, who would overcome the Roman domination of Judea. The Romans wanted no uprising against their rule, be it religiously inspired or otherwise. They arranged to have Christ found guilty of blasphemy in a trial

NOTABLE PERSONS KILLED FOR EXPRESSING THEIR OPINIONS

Year	Person	Identification	Place	Method	Reason given
399 B.C.E.	Socrates	philosopher	Greece	made to take poison	misleading youth
1431	Joan of Arc	peasant	France	burned at stake	religious heresy
1535	Sir Thomas More	chancellor of England	England	beheaded	denying King Henry VIII's religious supremacy
1600	Bruno Giordano	philosopher	Italy	burned at stake	religious heresy
c. 1700?	Dai Mingshi	historian	China	dismembered	publishing book critical of the ruling dynasty
1797	François Noël Babeuf	Jacobean writer	France	beheaded	writing against the French Revolution
1830	David Walker	journalist	United States	lynched	publishing abolitionist tracts
1837	Elijah Parish Lovejoy	journalist	United States	lynched	writing against slavery
1976	Don Bolles	journalist	United States	killed by bomb	investigating crime
1984	Jerzy Popieluszko	Roman Catholic priest	Poland	murdered	supporting Solidarity movement
1994	Vladislav Listyev	journalist	Russia	murdered	investigating crime
1995	Ken Saro-Wiwa	writer	Nigeria	hanged	opposing national government

before the ruling council of Jewish authorities, who for their part feared a futile political upheaval. He was then turned over to the Roman procurator of Judea, Pontius Pilate, who reluctantly authorized Jesus' death by crucifixion. Christianity later became the world's largest religion.

Ken Saro-Wiwa was a prisoner of conscience who neither advocated nor employed violence in exercising his freedom of speech. Saro-Wiwa was executed in 1995 by the Nigerian military regime of General Sani Abacha. Saro-Wiwa was convicted in a trial (described as a "travesty" by *The New York Times*) of murder; what lead to his execution, however, was his political activism on behalf of the people of his region. As public relations officer (and later president) of the grassroots Movement for the Survival of the Ogoni People (MOSOP), he campaigned against the Abacha dictatorship on three issues. The first issue was the dictatorship's nullification of the 1993 democratic election of Chief Moshood K. O. Abiola, who was later arrested for treason for proclaiming himself president of Nigeria. The second issue lay in the dictatorship's rejection of autonomy for Ogoniland, home to the 500,000 Ogoni people of the Niger Delta River States. The third issue reflected the dictatorship's indifference to the killing of the Ogoni people. Years of collusion between the government and powerful multinational companies, especially Shell Oil Company (which corrupted numerous officials with bribes stemming from the enormous oil profits taken out of Ogoniland) left the Ogoni in abject poverty and illness amidst massive oil pollution of their farming soil and fishing water.

MOSOP escalated its demands in 1992 to $10 billion in oil royalties plus environmental compensation from Shell and the government. After sporadic destruction of Shell equipment, the government's Internal Security Forces destroyed some thirty Ogoni villages and engaged in perhaps one hundred extrajudicial murders. Saro-Wiwa was arrested on June 21, 1993, for inciting a mob, at a rally he had not attended, to murder four pro-Abacha Ogoni chiefs whom he had months earlier described as "vultures." Saro-Wiwa and eight other Ogoni leaders were hanged on November 10, 1995, despite vigorous condemnation by the United Nations, other groups, and private individuals around the world.

—Nancy N. Haanstad

See also Athens, ancient; Bolles, Donald F., Jr.; Intellectual freedom; Joan of Arc; Journalists, violence against; Obituaries; Poland; Police states; Rushdie, Salman; Saro-Wiwa, Ken; Socrates; Walker, David.

BIBLIOGRAPHY

Amnesty International makes an annual survey of human rights standards in each state, such as "Nigeria," in *Amnesty International: Report 1996* (1996). *Index on Censorship* monitors free speech, along with other such organizations, including Human Rights Watch and Article Nineteen, concerning political advocacy cases. Roger Boyes and John Moody detail Popieluszko's heroism in *The Priest and the Policeman* (New York: Summit Books, 1987). Grazyna Sikorska highlights the religious commitment of the slain Polish leader in *Jerzy Popieluszko: A Martyr for Truth* (1985). I. F. Stone's *The Trial of Socrates* (Boston: Little, Brown, 1988) is a lively presentation of the meaning and context of Socrates' fate. The Bible tells the story of Christ's murder at the hands of political authorities.

Death of a President, The

TYPE OF WORK: Book

PUBLISHED: 1967

AUTHOR: William Manchester (1922-   )

SUBJECT MATTER: Historical account of the assassination of President John F. Kennedy in 1963

SIGNIFICANCE: Efforts of the Kennedy family to censor the book's contents led to controversy and demonstrated the difficulties in writing an authorized history

After the assassination of President John F. Kennedy in November, 1963, it immediately became clear that the public had a large appetite for information about the late president. Disturbed by the prospect of books that might commercialize her husband's death, Jacqueline Kennedy asked journalist William Manchester to write an accurate account of the assassination, in February, 1964. By formal agreement Manchester gained exclusive access to the Kennedy family, he agreed that publication of his book would be contingent on the family's approval, and he granted a large part of the book's expected profits to the Kennedy presidential library that was to be built. Manchester then spent two years researching and writing a lengthy manuscript, which was reviewed by representatives of the Kennedys. Members of the family requested more than a hundred changes; they were particularly interested in having less said about Jacqueline Kennedy's private life and about the physical details of the president's death. After sixteen weeks of revision work, Manchester received what he interpreted as the family's final approval; however, his sale of the book's serialization rights to *Look* magazine for $665,000 so alarmed Jacqueline Kennedy that she sought to censor additional details about herself. When Manchester balked, she filed a lawsuit to halt his book's publication. Manchester and the Kennedys eventually reached a settlement that permitted the book's publication with the deletion of only sixteen hundred words of text. Perhaps in part because of the censorship controversy, it became a best-seller and, in so doing, generated more than $1 million for the new Kennedy library.

See also Biography; Kennedy, John F., assassination of; Presidency, U.S.

Debs, Eugene

BORN: November 5, 1855, Terre Haute, Indiana

DIED: October 20, 1926, Elmhurst, Illinois

IDENTIFICATION: American socialist politician, author, and antiwar activist

SIGNIFICANCE: Debs was an outspoken opponent of censorship who was himself a frequent casualty of censorship

A socialist politician, Debs firmly believed in the unlimited right of Americans to express their opinions. However, because of his opposition to censorship and his uncompromising

Eugene Debs addressing a labor convention at the height of his career. (Library of Congress)

anticapitalist beliefs, his work was frequently ignored and occasionally even banned. When Fred Warren was arrested for writing against the imprisonment of labor leaders, Debs argued that his fellow Socialist Party member was punished for his ideas—much as British governors had punished outspoken American colonists before the American Revolution. Eugene Debs publicly urged the American people to raise their voices and demand "free speech, a free press, and a free people!"

During his 1912 presidential campaign, which captured 6 percent of the popular vote, Debs drew impressive crowds to his speeches, only to find the mainstream press almost completely silent. This subtle censorship extended to his writings and printed copies of his speeches, which were largely refused distribution or sale outside of the Socialist Party. As the United States moved closer to entry into World War I, this conspiracy of silence increased. Debs campaigned fiercely against American involvement in the war; afterward he blamed "the ruling classes of all nations engaged in the conflict . . . [who] must be overthrown."

After the United States entered the war, hostility toward antiwar views caused thousands to be indicted under the Espionage Act of 1917. Indignant, Debs wrote to one indicted socialist, "I cannot yet believe that they will ever dare to send you to prison for exercising your constitutional rights of free speech." Meanwhile, due to the increased suppression of the socialist press, Debs found it difficult to publicize his own antiwar arguments. The only option left to him was to undertake a national lecture tour. Beyond promoting his antiwar cause, Debs used his tour to test the constitutionality of the Espionage Act. He hoped to be arrested so he could publicize his belief that such censorship violated the First Amendment. Government officials initially refused to cooperate, but Debs got his wish on June 16, 1918, in Canton, Ohio. At his trial, he not only refused to let his lawyers fight the charge on technical legal grounds, but also openly admitted to the charges against him. His only defense was an appeal in favor of free speech as guaranteed by the First Amendment. Despite bringing tears to eyes of many jurors, he was convicted and given a ten-year prison sentence.

After an international campaign for clemency in Debs's behalf, he was pardoned by President Warren G. Harding in 1921. However, Debs refused to recant his views. Despite advanced age and greatly weakened health, he returned to his life as a socialist agitator and defender of free speech. Not only did he continued to attack censorship in America, he harshly criticized restrictions on free speech in the Soviet Union, despite his warm support for the Russian Revolution.

See also Draft resistance; Espionage Act of 1917; Labor unions; Sinclair, Upton; Soviet Union; World War I.

Deep Throat

TYPE OF WORK: Film
RELEASED: 1972
DIRECTOR: Gerard Damiano
SUBJECT MATTER: After a woman who cannot experience orgasm in normal sexual intercourse learns that her clitoris is in her throat, she finds satisfaction in fellatio
SIGNIFICANCE: Banned in twenty-three states for obscenity, this X-rated film represents the only instance in which an American artist was federally prosecuted for his work

Deep Throat was directed by New York hairdresser Gerard Damiano. Harry Reems, who received a hundred dollars for a single day's work, starred as the physician who discovers that the young woman's (Linda Lovelace) clitoris was misplaced by nature. Critics and audiences agreed that the acting performances in this low-budget film were terrible. A New York City criminal court judge, for example, called it "a Sodom and Gomorrah gone wild before the fire." Nevertheless, the film played on college campuses and fashionable theaters throughout the country and grossed more the twenty-five million dollars. It soon gained such notoriety that its title became the code name of a mysterious criminal operative in Washington's Watergate scandal. Meanwhile, numerous state and local governments banned the film.

Between 1972 and 1981 *Deep Throat* was banned in twenty-three states for obscenity. In 1974 the U.S. Department of Justice decided to crack down on commerce in erotica by using federal laws concerning the interstate shipment of obscene materials. In July officers of the Federal Bureau of Investigation arrested Reems and charged him with participating in a nationwide conspiracy to transport "an obscene, lewd, lascivious, and filthy motion picture" across state lines. This arrest made Reems the first artist or performer to be prosecuted by the federal government for his work. Eventually,

Operators of this midtown New York City theater were prosecuted in 1972 on charges of promoting obscenity. (AP/Wide World Photos)

twelve different persons, five corporations, and ninety-eight unindicted co-conspirators—including theater projectionists and ticket takers—were named in the federal indictment. The defendants were convicted in April, 1976. Harvard law professor Alan Dershowitz orchestrated Reems's appeal, which was granted largely because the U.S. Supreme Court's *Miller vs. California* decision—which tightened the definition of obscenity—had been decided in 1973, after the film was made.

See also Bruce, Lenny; Film censorship; Miller, Henry; *Miller v. California*.

Defamation

DEFINITION: Publication—in print or orally—of false statements that hold persons up to public ridicule or injure their good reputations

SIGNIFICANCE: Laws governing defamation have historically allowed allegedly injured parties to discourage public debate

The civil injury known as defamation has two forms: Written defamation is called libel; spoken defamation is called slander. This distinction is primarily a matter of legal procedure. Although the effects of both varieties of defamation may be the same, libel and slander constitute different legal actions. Historically, laws governing defamation have favored plaintiffs, requiring defendants to demonstrate their own innocence—usually by offering proof of the truth of the offending statements. U.S. courts have come to recognize a number of privileges that can act as a defense in defamation actions—even those concerning false utterances. These privileges have applied to cases involving discussion of issues of public interest, ranging from art to politicians.

In 1964, in its *New York Times Co. v. Sullivan* decision, the U.S. Supreme Court employed the First Amendment to defeat a libel action brought by an Alabama public official. Afterward a more lenient standard—allowing only "reckless disregard" for the truth to take precedence over First Amendment rights—was extended to cover other "public figures." Although these changes in the law made it easier for defendants to prevail in defamation cases, the costs of such litigation have continued to have a chilling effect on free speech, thereby fostering self-censorship among the news media.

See also Anti-Defamation League; Chilling effect; Free speech; Libel; *New York Times Co. v. Sullivan*.

Defense ("D") notices

DEFINITION: A system of censorship of the British press based on an agreement between military officials and press representatives

SIGNIFICANCE: The D-Notice system was designed to clarify for the British press what information could be published without fear of prosecution under the Official Secrets Act of 1911

Following the enactment of the Official Secrets Act in 1911 and its broad sweep of restrictions, the British government was in a position of having to clarify for the British press what published information might be considered to pose a threat to national security. Thus was formed the Services, Press and Broadcasting Committee, consisting of sixteen members: five top government officials and eleven press and broadcasting representatives. This committee developed the D-Notice system, which alleviated for the press the fear of prosecution and offered assurance to the government that technical and strategic information would not be disclosed. The twelve D-Notices were distributed to newspaper editors and covered a range of spying, internal security, and military activities.

Although the protections the system offers are apparent during wartime, it is questionable whether these protections are not outweighed by the general public's mistrust of the British government that results from the secrecy surrounding the system. Compliance with the system has steadily declined since World War II.

See also Leafletting; National security; News media censorship; United Kingdom; War; World War I.

Defoe, Daniel

BORN: 1660, London, England
DIED: April 26, 1729, London, England
IDENTIFICATION: English novelist and political pamphleteer
SIGNIFICANCE: Defoe's political pamphlets were censored by English libel laws, and his novels were listed on the *Index Librorum Prohibitorum* and seized by U.S. Customs

The author of 547 publications, Defoe was a ministerial student, a merchant, an importer, and a political agent for the English monarchs William and Mary. He was representative of the English intellectual revolution that denounced traditional authority and questioned even sacrosanct subjects, making him too radical for both Whigs and Tories. In 1685 he participated in Monmouth's Rebellion against King James II, narrowly escaping Judge Jeffrey's Bloody Assizes. As part of William and Mary's triumphal procession into London (1689), Defoe wrote pamphlets advocating William's policies.

Defoe's best-known novels, *Robinson Crusoe* (1719), *A Journal of the Plague Year* (1722), and *Moll Flanders* (1722), examine contemporary social problems but avoid politics. He was censored in England for his controversial political pamphlets about religious minorities, the Jacobite threat, the Scottish Union, the standing army, the Act of Settlement, and King George's accession. When Defoe's mentor, King William, died in 1702, Tories attacked Defoe as a Whig radical.

Defoe's most famous pamphlet, *The Shortest Way with Dissenters* (1702), ridiculed church bigotry, outraging both non-Anglican "dissenters" and Anglican officials. Defoe was tried for seditious libel in early 1703, under a law that defined libel as any criticism of government that reduced "the affection of the people for the king or his ministers and thereby encouraged rebellion." The trial forced Defoe to repudiate his Whig beliefs. After he pleaded guilty, he was fined, sentenced to stand in the pillory three times, and given an indeterminate prison sentence. In order to secure Defoe as his personal propagandist, Robert Harley, speaker of the House of Commons, secured his release from Newgate Prison in June, 1703.

In 1713 both Whigs and Tories were offended by two of Defoe's pamphlets, which, ironically, celebrated the hypothetical benefits of an absolutist Jacobite king for England.

After Queen Anne died in August, 1714, the Whigs made George of Hanover king. Powerful Whigs tried and convicted Defoe for libel in July, 1715, forcing him to serve as an undercover Whig, while pretending to advocate Tory beliefs.

Even Defoe's use of "immoral" heroines in his nonpolitical novels, *Moll Flanders* and *Roxanna* (1724), aroused censorship. His novels were prohibited by the Roman Catholic *Index Librorum Prohibitorum*, a list of books forbidden to Catholics because the church considered them contrary to Catholic faith or morals. *Moll Flanders* was prohibited because its protagonist unwittingly married her own brother, thereby committing incest. *Roxanna* was forbidden because its heroine was a prostitute.

Defoe's political pamphlets, which attacked contemporary social and political topics, aroused government censorship through libel trials, but interest in censoring them waned when the controversies abated. It is ironic that Defoe's nonpolitical novels were censored as immoral as late as 1930. U.S. Customs had the power to ban obscene material in enforcing tariff restrictions. U.S. censorship laws allowed local customs officials arbitrarily to ban books, subject only to sporadic review by the U.S. Customs Court, which began to place certain items under a general ban. Thus, Defoe's novels, written in the early 1700's, were banned as immoral by U.S. Customs in 1930.

See also Books and obscenity law; Cushing, Cardinal Richard James; *Index Librorum Prohibitorum*; Literature; Prostitution; Sedition.

Degenerate Art Exhibition

DATE: July 19, 1937

PLACE: Munich, Germany

SIGNIFICANCE: Germany's National Socialist government mounted an exhibition of allegedly degenerate art to demonstrate that government censorship was necessary to ensure that art conform with Nazi ideology

In 1937 four years after Adolf Hitler gained power in Germany, about 650 paintings and sculptures—confiscated by the Propaganda Ministry from public museums and private collections—were exhibited in an attempt to vilify modern art. The exhibition brochure denounced the undesirable artists as Jews, or as artists who had failed to comply with Adolf Hitler's dictates to support the culture of the master race. Although many professors (Otto Dix, among others) had been removed earlier from their teaching positions, this attempt to censor modern art made many artists aware that adhering to international art movements—such as cubism, expressionism, constructivism, and others—would no longer be tolerated and that in the future they would be forced to create the kind of social realism advocated by Hitler. In fact, the official art organization denied them not only employment but also forbade any artistic expression.

At the opening, the audience was warned that the exhibition would "inspire horror and disgust." The catalogue printed comments on how the feigned primitivism, seen in this display, duped the general public and that artists in reality were nothing but swindlers. The banished works were arranged in nine narrow rooms according to themes. One cubicle showed how modern art violated the churches; defamatory slogans spoke of "painted hocus-pocus." German expressionist works, such as Karl Schmitt-Rottluff's *Christ*, a veristic woodcut dated 1918, and Max Beckmann's *Deposition*, an oil painting of 1917, were misrepresented as caricatures. Otto Freundlich's cubistic stone mask *The New Man* (1912, later destroyed) was discredited by being labeled "created by a Jew." Other social comments addressed the mockery of German womanhood. Presenting Karl Hofer's depiction of lesbians, the Nazis played on viewer homophobia. Dadaism was ridiculed, and abstract works by Paul Klee and Wassily Kandinsky were displayed under disparaging headings. The negative messages were directed also against the museum directors that had purchased the images (although the Nazis sold some of the best paintings exhibited at the exhibition at an auction on June 30, 1939, in Lucerne, Switzerland, for hard currency).

In the history of art censorship, Hitler's strategy to defame modern art may have been unique; the works were neither burned nor kept from public view. On the contrary, Hitler encouraged Germans to visit this carefully orchestrated propaganda traveling display to gain public approval for his actions. The officially sanctioned art was exhibited in Munich's new German Art Museum. Cultural suppression of modern art, which climaxed in 1937, continued until 1945 and had worldwide repercussions. Josef Albers, Max Beckmann, and Piet Mondrian, to name a few, left Europe and took refuge in the United States. In 1991 the Los Angeles County Art Museum revived, with anticensorship intentions, the infamous exhibition.

See also Art; Bauhaus, the; Germany; Grosz, George; National Socialism (Nazism); Nolde, Emil; Socialist Realism.

De Grazia, Edward

BORN: February 5, 1927, Chicago, Illinois

IDENTIFICATION: American attorney, law professor, and author

SIGNIFICANCE: A well-known defender of writers and artists accused of obscenity, de Grazia has written widely on censorship

After obtaining his law degree from the University of Chicago, de Grazia practiced law, specializing in cases involving the First Amendment, many of which involved censorship of materials deemed by the government as either obscene or pornographic. His most famous cases have involved such works as Aristophenes' *Lysistrata*, Henry Miller's *Tropic of Cancer*, William S. Burroughs' *Naked Lunch*, and the Swedish film *I Am Curious—Yellow*.

In addition to practicing law, de Grazia has also written on the subject of censorship, particularly censorship involving the arts. His books include *Censorship Landmarks* (1969), featuring important censorship cases of the past century; *Banned Films: Movies, Censors and the First Amendment* (1982; written with Roger K. Newman), giving information about censored motion pictures; and *Girls Lean Back Everywhere: The Law of Obscenity and the Assault on Genius* (1992), which contains information from writers and artists who have been censored. He has also written several plays, and his articles have appeared in such periodicals as *The New Republic* and *The Nation*. He has taught at Georgetown University and is among the founding faculty of the Benjamin N. Cardozo School of Law at Yeshiva University in Manhattan. He is also a member of the PEN American Center's Freedom to Write Committee.

See also Censorship; Courts and censorship law; *I Am Curious—Yellow*; Miller, Henry; *Naked Lunch*; Obscenity: legal definitions; Seldes, George; *Tropic of Cancer*.

Deliverance

TYPE OF WORK: Book
PUBLISHED: 1970
AUTHOR: James Dickey (1923-   )
SUBJECT MATTER: Novel about four city men who test their survival skills on a wild river trip, responding in different ways to the perils they encounter
SIGNIFICANCE: Censors have attacked stark, realistic fiction such as this novel as unsuitable for high school students

In this novel, four businessmen taking a weekend canoe trip down the untamed Cahulawassee River battle both nature and hill people in "kill-or-be-killed" situations. In lean prose, Dickey graphically details such incidents as a man being savagely sodomized at gunpoint, threats of castration, the sexual overtones of the death climb up a cliff, and the earthy epithets of men stalking and killing others.

The 1970 novel became popular with school-age readers after release of the highly successful 1972 film version, featuring Burt Reynolds and Jon Voight. However, in challenges occurring in Maryland and Virginia schools, the book was found "obscene." In Drake, North Dakota, in the 1970's, the book became part of a much-publicized book-burning and teacher-dismissal case.

The American Booksellers Association has cited two reasons for the frequent bannings of *Deliverance* in public schools and libraries: its inappropriate themes for the young and its objectionable language. Challengers have deemed the book inappropriate because of its relentless and unnerving violence, depicting how decent men under pressure can revert to primal behavior. Challengers have also questioned the loose morality of the book's conclusion: The survivors find deliverance back in the civilized world, unrepentant and unpunished after killing several men, disposing of their bodies, and lying repeatedly to the law.

See also Libraries, school; Morality; Offensive language; Sex in the arts; Violence.

Democracy

DEFINITION: Democracy is government by the people, with majority rule being a guiding principle
SIGNIFICANCE: Of all forms of government, democracy is arguably the most antithetical to censorship

Democracy requires the wide dissemination of politically relevant information, argument, and ideas for consideration of citizens, who as collective sovereign, cannot deliberate adequately without freedom of the means of dissemination of information. There are various types of democracy, however,

that must be considered. Democracy is possible in several forms. Liberal democracy, for example, is democracy that protects nonpolitical expression in addition to protecting political discussion. In a liberal democracy, freedom to pursue private expression and interests is protected by law. But democratic regimes may be nonliberal or antiliberal, and, while protecting political expression, they may censor or otherwise prohibit a range of nonpolitical expression. Thus, censorship of the arts is entirely consistent with nonliberal democracy, as proposed by Jean-Jacques Rousseau, who countenanced the abolition of the theater in his native Geneva to preserve its mores.

Liberal Democracy and Censorship. Only with the development of modern liberalism in the eighteenth and nineteen centuries was a private sphere recognized that, within limits, was considered beyond legitimate government interference. A perennial issue in liberal democracies, including the United States, is what those limits should be. That they should be wide has acquired broad acceptance. American jurist Benjamin Cardozo famously remarked that "freedom of thought and speech" is "the matrix, the indispensable condition of every other form of freedom."

The latitude of definition of forms of private expression has changed over time in the direction of greater liberty. In the view of some, this freedom has been taken beyond the boundary where liberty becomes license. Others back the wide latitude in personal expression championed by English philosopher John Stuart Mill in his book *On Liberty* (1859).

Censorship among Western democracies varies, although wide freedom regarding political speech is common to all. There are, however, limits on speech in Western liberal democracies. In some countries, hate speech and some forms of political advocacy that are particularly reprehensible are outlawed. Germany, a liberal democracy, does not tolerate advocacy of Nazism, for example. Western nations also differ on nonpolitical subjects, especially erotica. In the twentieth century, Great Britain, Canada, and Ireland have had significantly less liberty in this area than the majority of Continental democracies.

In most parts of the United States there is great latitude in tolerated private expression, although individual communities may prohibit certain public displays and practices or the sale of items deemed indecent or obscene. Everywhere, however, there are "time, place and manner" restrictions on expression. Expression of outlandish political speech is tolerated, for example, but not with loudspeakers in sleeping neighborhoods at midnight.

American law does tolerate some requirements of official approval for certain forms of expression. Radio and television broadcasting must be licensed, as well as parades, demonstrations, and distributing leaflets. But the courts do not allow official discretion over what is expressed.

With respect to freedom of political expression, the U.S. Supreme Court's opinion in *New York Times Co. v. Sullivan* (1964) has become the centerpiece of American law. In this landmark case, the Court allowed errors to be made with impunity in political speech. False statements must be allowed, the Court reasoned, if freedom of expression is to be protected.

Censorship prior to publication, known as prior restraint, is usually not allowed in liberal democracies, although there are exceptions. American films were once subject to prior censorship. In Britain, an official board of censors reviews all films.

National Security Issues. Issues of prior restraint have been most pronounced in cases involving national security. Secrecy has in some instances undoubtedly been necessary for preserving the state's, and, usually, citizens' safety, typically in times of war. Diplomacy, it may be argued, requires considerable secrecy, as does development of weapons for defense.

However, the degree of secrecy required for security of the governed, rather than the power and convenience of fallible governments, is hotly disputed. The burden of historical experience is that, if allowed, governments tend to aggregate powers to themselves far beyond what is necessary, using such excuses as national security to cloak questionable or reprehensible actions.

An unfettered press can hope to challenge the abuse and aggregation of the powers of modern governments before the bar of public opinion, but in certain situations the publication of state secrets may wreak catastrophe. In this regard, war has been a principal occasion of censorship in democracies. A basic norm, however, is that democracy does not cease during wartime. The ancient Romans, adhering to the motto *Salus populi suprema lex est* ("the well-being of the people is the highest law"), instituted dictatorship during wartime or national emergency, handing power to one man, who regulated society as he pleased, but only for a limited period. Modern democracies, in law at least, have never adopted this practice, preferring to retain the norm of constitutionalism (limited government) and its requirement of the rule of law. Thus, during World War II, the British Parliament was free to replace Winston Churchill as prime minister, and the American electorate was free to reject Franklin Roosevelt.

Censorship was routinely practiced during World Wars I and II. Reporters submitted stories to military censors, who deleted whatever they considered of aid to the enemy, including depressing facts that might lower civilian moral. Before the 1960's, American reporters freely cooperated with military censors.

The system of cooperation broke down during the Vietnam War, when a deep divide opened between press and government. Government restriction of information was viewed as a means to shore up morally questionable policy by ensuring public ignorance of facts about the war. Matters came to a head in *New York Times Co. v. United States* (1971), the Pentagon Papers case, in which the U.S. Supreme Court rejected the government's contention that publication of the papers should be restrained.

The Freedom of Information Act is a centerpiece of the public effort to enshrine in American law the public's right to know what government does in its name. Government secrecy must be subject to strict limits and considered an anomaly, even a pathology, of liberal democracy. Advocates of secrecy bear a heavy burden of proof in justifying each excep-

tion to liberal democracy's need for public openness and free expression.

The inability of reporters to cover freely the U.S. entry into Grenada in 1983 and Operation Desert Storm against Iraq in 1991 resulted from the adversarial relationship between government and press that was established during the Vietnam War.

Conflict Among Values. A further consideration is that free publication of some information may involve conflict among accepted democratic values. The accused's right to a fair trial may conflict with freedom of the press; government's need for secrecy in national security and other matters may conflict with a democratic public's right to know. Freedom of expression for one person may conflict with another's right to privacy or right not to be defamed. In each conflict, law must find its way to uncertain accommodation. The Internet and its international scope add new legal complexities, as views of what is permissible speech conflict across geographic areas.

—*Charles F. Bahmueller*

See also Constitution, U.S.; France; Freedom of Information Act; Germany; Military censorship; Mill, John Stuart; Milton, John; National security; *New York Times Co. v. Sullivan*; *Pentagon Papers, The*; Rousseau, Jean-Jacques; United Kingdom; United States; World War I; World War II.

BIBLIOGRAPHY

The seminal work of modern liberal thought on the subject of censorship is John Stuart Mill's *On Liberty* (1859). Kermit Hall, ed., *The Oxford Companion to the Supreme Court of the United States* (New York: Oxford University Press, 1992) has numerous articles relevant to democracy and censorship. Pat M. Holt's *Secret Intelligence and Public Policy: A Dilemma of Democracy* (Washington D.C.: CQ Press, 1994) suggests remedies for conflicts between the necessity for secrecy and requirements of an open society. Harry M. Clor's *Obscenity and Public Morality* (Chicago: Chicago University Press, 1969) presents a comprehensive discussion of the issues. Thelma Adams, ed., *Censorship and First Amendment Rights: A Primer* (Tarrytown, N.Y.: American Booksellers Foundation for Free Expression, 1992) gives arguments against censorship in liberal democracy. Jonathan Rauch's *Kindly Inquisitors: The New Attacks on Free Thought* (Chicago: University of Chicago Press, 1993) discusses late twentieth century feminist and other arguments for censorship. Nat Hentoff's *Free Speech for Me—But Not for Thee: How the American Left and Right Relentlessly Censor Each Other* (New York: HarperCollins, 1992) is a cogent essay on censorship issues in American politics.

Democratic National Convention of 1968

DATE: August 25-29, 1968

PLACE: Chicago, Illinois

SIGNIFICANCE: National Democratic Party officials and the mayor of Chicago attempted to manipulate media reporting in order to prevent unfavorable news coverage from reaching the public

Political conventions typically receive considerable media attention, and the Democratic National Convention held in Chi-

Eight hundred armed National Guard troops surrounded a Chicago hotel where 2,500 antiwar protesters had gathered to demonstrate against the Democratic National Convention in August, 1968. (AP/Wide World Photos)

cago in August, 1968, promised to be especially newsworthy. The press anticipated a divisive convention as Democrats struggled to resolve conflicts over the party's platform and the conduct of the Vietnam War. In addition, thousands of demonstrators planned to protest in the city streets during convention week.

The Democratic National Committee (DNC) was determined to prevent the convention from degenerating into a spectacle on national television. At previous conventions media representatives had been allowed considerable freedom. The resulting news reports angered party leaders, who believed that the coverage gave misleading impressions about convention activities. In order to control members of the press, the DNC limited access to the convention floor. In 1964 the DNC had issued two hundred floor passes; at Chicago, they issued only eighty. They limited the three major television networks to one mobile camera each on the floor. Reporters complained that the DNC wanted coverage to focus on the podium events, offering viewers a highly organized political presentation that distorted the truth about convention politics.

Reporters also discovered that live coverage would be limited to the convention proceedings. In order to resolve a labor dispute with striking communications workers, the mayor of Chicago, Richard Daley, had agreed that microwave relays necessary for live broadcasts would be installed inside the

convention hall but nowhere else. Coverage of demonstrations on the city streets would be limited to film or tape, which could take an hour to process before being shown on television. Media representatives charged that Daley had crafted the bargain with the striking workers in order to prevent coverage unfavorable to the Democratic Party or the city of Chicago.

In Chicago reporters encountered dozens of minor restrictions that limited their ability to cover stories. Police banned news cameras from sidewalks; fire department officials ordered the rewiring of equipment vans; filming from hotel windows was not allowed. Media members contended that city officials and the DNC were attempting to prevent coverage of the planned demonstrations; convention organizers responded that the measures were intended to ensure the safety and security of convention delegates.

As anticipated, the protests degenerated into fights between the Chicago police and demonstrators. The police often focused their hostility on members of the press. Several reporters and photographers were clubbed or maced when they tried to cover the protests. In some cases police intentionally destroyed cameras and tape recorders. Although the police were instructed to respect the rights of reporters, incidents of harassment and violence continued throughout the week.

Despite the violence and the manipulation of the press by convention officials, opinion polls revealed that most television viewers sided against the media. Viewers believed that convention coverage had been biased and distorted and blamed the media for encouraging the antics of irresponsible protestors. Criticism of the press raised new questions about the role of the media in a democracy.

See also News media censorship; Political campaigning.

Democritus

BORN: c. 460 B.C.E., Abdera, Thrace
DIED: c. 370 B.C.E., Abdera, Thrace
IDENTIFICATION: Greek philosopher
SIGNIFICANCE: Democritus developed a mechanistic and materialist philosophy whose implicit atheism provoked attempts to suppress it

Democritus traveled widely and studied mathematics in Egypt. He is reported to have written seventy-two works, only fragments of which remain. In developing the philosophy of atomism originated by Leucippus of Miletus, Democritus reduced all reality to individual particles of matter that could be "cut" no smaller. These immutable "atoms" move in an infinite void, eternally coagulating to form and re-form worlds. Democritus also developed a theory of perception based on the interaction of atoms.

As a physical philosophy Democritus' atomism can be viewed as a precursor to the law of the conservation of matter in modern chemistry and atomic physics. However, attempts to explain all reality as merely atoms in motion imply that souls—and even the "gods"—are made of atoms. All beings will thus perish with the next coagulation of atoms. Plato reportedly so disliked Democritus' ideas that he wanted to burn his writings. Aristotle criticized atomism for denying independent existence to souls.

Epicurus modified Democritus' mechanistic atomism to allow for free will. Lucretius, the Roman poet, popularized atomism and its inherent religious skepticism; however, opposition to the theory can be seen as late as 1624, when the Parliament of Paris decreed the death penalty for the teaching of atomism in opposition to Aristotle.

See also Anaxagoras; Aristophanes; Aristotle; Atheism; Plato.

Demonstrations

DEFINITION: Mass gatherings, usually in public places, for purposes of political protest
SIGNIFICANCE: A form of assembly, demonstrations are given qualified protection from censorship by the First Amendment, as long as they are peaceable

Demonstrations are a form of assembly, given protection from control or censorship by the U.S. Constitution so long as they are "peaceable." Demonstrations are always assumed to be forms of political protest; thus, a rock concert, for example, would not necessarily be well protected. "Peaceably" is the key word in the First Amendment's command that "Congress shall make no law . . . abridging . . . the right of the people peaceably to assemble." The First Amendment divides the free expression of ideas into three categories: speech, press, and peaceable assembly. The Congress (and since the 1930's state and local governments) may not exercise a prior restraint over either speech or press. The presence of the word "peaceably" in connection means assemblies can be, and routinely are, subject to censorship or prior restraint.

Forms of Free Expression Distinguished. Speech and press differ from assembly in that they are assumed to have a more passive character, allowing government to grant them greater protection. While it is possible to imagine someone making a speech before an assembly that would incite a riot, it is difficult to imagine a crowd silently reading a book, reaching a dramatic line at the same moment, and then rioting. Originally, none of the First Amendment applied to the states before the passage of the Fourteenth Amendment. Section one of that amendment requires that no state deny any person the "right to life, liberty, or property without due process of law." This language has been held to incorporate most of the important rights in the Bill of Rights and apply them to the states. This has been done on a case-by-case basis and assembly was incorporated and applied to the states at least partially in the case of *DeJonge v. Oregon* (1937), although this was more clearly stated in *Hague v. Congress of Industrial Organizations* (1939). *Hague* is the basis for the essential rule that while assemblies may be restrained in time, place, and manner, and permits may be required for those who wish to use public parks and streets for assemblies, the permits may not be denied in a discriminatory manner and must be open to all who wish to use them on an equal and evenhanded basis. There must be no censorship of the ideas that are involved. To understand how this works, one must consider demonstrations as mixed speech and assembly controversies, as with street oratory cases. Since there is no prior restraint for speech, but there can be prior restraint for assembly, one need find a balance between two rights.

Conflict with Riot Laws. The U.S. Constitution's framers never intended to prohibit censorship of assemblies or demonstrations. Many laws on all levels forbid or limit the size of assemblies, such as limits on the numbers of people who may occupy enclosed spaces, but this is not a free expression issue. Regulations may require advance permission or prohibit demonstrations during commuting hours to allow the free movement of traffic for people going to and from work. Neither kind of regulation has anything to do with the content of the ideas. If the police knew that a speaker planned to provoke a riot, such an assembly could also be restrained.

Difficulties arise when speakers address peaceful assemblies with no intention of starting riots, but express ideas so offensive to their audiences that some listeners seek to silence them with violence. When the U.S. Supreme Court first considered such a case in *Feiner v. New York* (1951), it decided that the police could arrest speakers, even though they had no intention of starting a riot, apparently putting the blame on the peaceable speaker instead of violent audience. Eighteen years later, in *Brandenburg v. Ohio* (1969), the Court reversed itself by holding that the police should protect for those who assemble peaceably, even if they express unpopular ideas, from members of the audience who might threaten them.

To see how far the court has gone to protect those who

express unpopular ideas, consider the famous case of the American Nazi Party members who planned a demonstration in Skokie, Illinois, a city with a large Jewish population. Using the swastika, flags, and paraphernalia of the German Nazi Party, these American Nazis espoused vicious anti-Semitic views. Skokie's Jewish groups threatened violence if the Nazis were allowed to demonstrate and the city government passed three separate ordinances to block the march, saying that the audience would not be peaceable, even if the Nazis were.

The American Civil Liberties Union (ACLU) joined in the suit on behalf of the Nazi Party, despite the ACLU's opposition to Nazi ideals, because the ACLU thought it vital to protect free assembly. They prevailed when a federal district court struck down the Skokie ordinances; the U.S. Supreme Court upheld the lower courts in *Collin v. Smith* (1978) and *National Socialist Party v. Village of Skokie* (1977). Despite the lack of a Supreme Court opinion in the case, the Court's decision strengthened freedom of assembly. Ironically, after the case was over, the Nazis did not actually march in Skokie, since they had already achieved their true goal of winning nationwide publicity.

Unlike assemblages of people who gather to watch nude dancers or attend concerts, demonstrations are usually regarded as a protected form of political expression, but their leaders must be peaceful. If so, the police are required to protect them from hostile onlookers. Since freedom of assembly is restricted to peaceable assembly, there are limits on demonstrations that do not exist for press, although prohibitions against censorship do apply.   —*Richard L. Wilson*

See also Assembly, right of; Censorship; Fourteenth Amendment; Free speech; Offensive language; Picketing; *Schenck v. United States*; Skokie, Illinois, Nazi march; Street oratory.

BIBLIOGRAPHY

The best way to begin studying this complex subject is to turn to Henry J. Abraham and Barbara A. Perry's *Freedom and the Court* (6th ed. New York: Oxford University Press, 1994). For the opposite view of Abraham on the Fourteenth Amendment and the incorporation doctrine, see Raoul Berger, *The Fourteenth Amendment and the Bill of Rights* (Norman: University of Oklahoma Press, 1989). For a thoughtful analysis of free expression, see Kent Greenawalt's *Speech, Crime, and the Uses of Language* (New York: Oxford University Press, 1989). More specifically, Kent Greenawalt's *Fighting Words* (Princeton, N.J.: Princeton University Press, 1996) provides an excellent comparative analysis of Canadian and U.S. conceptions of the distinctions between protected words and unprotected actions. For a section-by-section examination of the Bill of Rights, see Eugene W. Hickok, ed., *The Bill of Rights: Original Meaning and Current Understanding* (Charlottesville: University Press of Virginia, 1991). Wallace Mendelson's *The American Constitution and Civil Liberties* (Homewood, Ill.: Dorsey Press, 1981) contains useful excerpts from the most important Supreme Court cases on censorship and other free expression issues. A comprehensive symposium on the entire Bill of Rights can be found in Geoffrey R. Stone, Richard A. Epstein, and Cass R. Sunstein, eds., *The Bill of Rights in the Modern State* (Chicago: University of Chicago Press, 1992).

Denmark

DESCRIPTION: Scandinavian constitutional monarchy located in Northern Europe

SIGNIFICANCE: During the 1960's, Denmark was in the forefront of countries that repealed most of their obscenity laws

A constitutional monarchy was first instituted in Denmark in 1849 by King Frederick VII, who called for a constitution to be written. It was not until the 1953 Danish constitution, however, that legislative authority would rest with both a parliament and the monarch. Along with Frederick VII's constitution came many sweeping educational and social changes that were codified into law. One change involved the removal of censorship restrictions from the Danish press. The tradition of a free press continued into the twentieth century. Although journalists have the right to protect their sources, the law stipulates that all stories must have a named author. In addition to protecting the freedom of the press, Denmark made it clear in its 1953 constitution that individuals have the right to "publish their thoughts in printing, in writing, and in speech." The only instances in which free speech can be curtailed involve defamation of character or hate speech against a person's racial or ethnic background.

During the 1960's Denmark reexamined its antiobscenity laws. Prior to this time, it had been illegal to publish or distribute obscene material. In 1964 the Permanent Criminal Law Committee was given the task of studying the effectiveness of the current laws by the minister of justice. The committee published its findings in 1966, recommending that the obscenity laws be completely overhauled because there was no hard evidence that pornography did substantial harm to individuals or society at large. In June, 1967, the Danish legislature voted to do away with virtually all laws that regulated the publishing of obscene material. The only restrictions that would remain in the penal code involved the selling of obscene material to minors. The new law took effect in August, 1968, while laws regulating visual material would not be struck down until July, 1969.

Because of the changes in Danish obscenity laws, Denmark was viewed around the world as a country that had lost its moral bearings. Conservative forces in the United States, for example, spoke out loudly against allowing pornography laws to be abandoned as they had been in Denmark. The Danish documentary *Pornography in Denmark* (1970) was banned in Essex County, New Jersey, in 1971, and the semidocumentary film *Sexual Freedom in Denmark* (1970) was banned in New York City during the same year. Although many other countries took issue with Denmark's position on pornography, Denmark believed that it had found a rational approach to the issue. There were some excesses after the new obscenity laws took effect in regard to child pornography and live sex shows, but modifications to the laws were made and such activities became criminal offenses.

Since the 1980's Denmark has grappled with the issue of hate speech. Although it has been illegal to speak out against another person's race or ethnic background, an exception in the law takes into consideration the concept of "in the public interest." In 1989 the Danish Supreme Court decided a case concerning two television journalists who had broadcast an interview with a known racist group called the Green Jackets. A lower court had found the journalists guilty of aiding and abetting hate speech; the Supreme Court upheld the conviction, stating that there was no larger public interest that outweighed the rights of others who could be harmed by the racist thoughts of the Green Jackets.

In another controversial case, an American named Gary Rex Lauck was extradited to Germany from Denmark so that he could stand trial for smuggling pro-Nazi and racist publications into Germany. A native of Lincoln, Nebraska, and the leader of the National Socialist German Workers' Party— Foreign Organization, Lauck had become known to American authorities as the "Farm-Belt Führer." From his base in Nebraska, he published neo-Nazi and racist pamphlets in several languages and distributed them around the world to subscribers. After German authorities had confiscated some of his publications in Berlin in March, 1995, Germany requested that Danish law enforcement officers arrest Lauck while he was in Denmark. Lauck was arrested on suspicion of smuggling and held until the legal details could be worked out for his extradition. On August 24, 1995, the Danish Supreme Court ruled that Lauck could be sent to Germany. Following this decision, Lauck filed a petition asking for political asylum in Denmark. His application was denied, and he was sent to Germany to stand trial. A year later a German court found Lauck guilty of hate crimes and sentenced him to four years in prison. At the trial, Lauck refused to testify. It was his lawyer's contention that since Lauck was an American citizen that his activities were protected under American law and that a German court would have no jurisdiction.

Although it has been legal to publish and distribute neo-Nazi and white supremacist literature in the United States, laws covering such matters are different in many European countries, including Denmark and Germany, both of which have stringent laws concerning hate speech.

See also Film censorship; Germany; Hate laws; Pornography; Pornography, child.

Descartes, René

BORN: March 31, 1596, La Haye, Touraine, France

DIED: February 11, 1650, Stockholm, Sweden

IDENTIFICATION: French mathematician, scientist, and philosopher

SIGNIFICANCE: Considered a founder of modern philosophy, Descartes held philosophical views concerning the existence of God and the nature of the universe that were subjected to indirect pressure by religious authorities

Descartes was an accomplished mathematician, scientist, and philosopher whose works include the *Discourse on Method* (1637), *Meditations on the First Philosophy* (1641), *Principles of Philosophy* (1644), and *The Passions of the Soul* (1649). Often considered the father of modern philosophy, he discarded the absolutist systems of the scholastic philosophers

who had preceded him, and subjected all knowledge to universal doubt, through which he attempted to establish new foundations for knowledge of the physical world and of God. He was the victim of posthumous censorship, as various of his works were banned after his death by the Roman Catholic church and, much later, by the Soviet Union.

Descartes' relationship to censorship is primarily interesting, however, because it illustrates the ways in which policies of censorship can influence the direction of a philosopher's thought. In November, 1633, Descartes wrote to a friend that he was surprised and dismayed to learn that Galileo Galilei's *Dialogue Concerning the Two Chief World Systems* (1632) had been confiscated and destroyed, and that Galileo himself had been fined by the Catholic church in Rome for arguing that the earth orbits the sun. Descartes was surprised, he said, because he knew that Galileo was an Italian whom he believed to be in good standing with the pope. He was dismayed because Descartes himself was one of a growing number of thinkers who had followed Nicolaus Copernicus in rejecting the geocentric model of the universe. The prospect of what trouble he, a French Catholic of no special standing with the pope, might incur, was enough for Descartes to suppress publication of his own work on cosmology, *The World*, which would not published until twenty-seven years after his death. It is possible that Descartes' learning of Galileo's condemnation marked the beginning of a new emphasis in his thought. Prior to the end of 1633, Descartes had worked primarily in the natural sciences and mathematics. After the condemnation of Galileo, however, metaphysics assumed a new prominence in his thinking, a prominence that includes the attempt to found his entire philosophical and scientific worldview upon proofs for the existence and veracity of God.

While learning of Galileo's condemnation may well have influenced the direction of Descartes' research, it would be misleading to suggest that Descartes built his philosophy and science upon a theistic foundation only because he wanted to avoid the wrath of the Church. Such a view is hard to reconcile with the attention and effort that Descartes had long devoted to natural theology. It is also belied by a letter he wrote three years before Galileo's condemnation, in which he states that it was the attempt to know God that had enabled him to discover the foundations of his physics. It would likewise be misleading to suggest that the condemnation of Galileo was the sole cause of the new focus of Descartes' intellectual efforts after 1633. However, it is possible that Galileo's condemnation played a role in the dramatic shift of emphasis in Descartes' thought, which appears to have occurred near the end of 1633.

See also Copernicus, Nicolaus; Gabler, Mel, and Norma Gabler; *Index Librorum Prohibitorum*; Science; Vatican.

Devlin, Bernadette

BORN: April 23, 1947, Cookstown, Northern Ireland

IDENTIFICATION: Northern Ireland political and radical leader

SIGNIFICANCE: As an outspoken advocate of Roman Catholic civil rights in Northern Ireland, Devlin devised innovative stratagems to make her voice heard

Devlin was born into a poor Roman Catholic family in a small town in Northern Ireland. While attending Queen's University in Belfast, she helped found People's Democracy, a student movement dedicated to promoting Catholic civil rights under British rule. The student group tried protests and marches to spread their mostly socialist ideology, but encountered opposition from the police. In March of 1969 the group entered candidates for Britain's general parliamentary elections as a means of spreading their doctrines. Since the police were required by law to protect parliamentary candidates, the student candidates used their protection to pass out literature and conduct public meetings. Devlin stood for a parliamentary seat, but lost. A year later, however, she entered a special by-election and won. At age twenty-one she became the youngest woman ever to sit in Great Britain's Parliament.

In August of 1969 Devlin was present at the barricade construction in Bogstad, North Ireland, which led to the Battle of Bogstad. Because of her role in this skirmish she was sentenced to a six-month prison term shortly after she was reelected to Parliament. That same year, while touring the United States to raise support for Northern Irish relief, she received a key to New York City from the mayor and handed it over to members of the Black Panther Party.

Due in part to her contempt for regular politics, Devlin lost her parliamentary seat in 1974. Although she has not held another political office, she has remained an outspoken supporter of Irish Catholic civil rights. In 1981 she and her husband were seriously wounded in an assassination attempt by members of an extremist group from Ulster.

See also Ireland; Irish Republican Army; Northern Ireland; United Kingdom.

Diary of Anne Frank, The

TYPE OF WORK: Book
PUBLISHED: 1947 (English trans., 1952)
AUTHOR: Anne Frank (1929-1945)
SUBJECT MATTER: Journal of an adolescent Jewish girl whose family lived in a secret attic during the German occupation of the Netherlands in World War II
SIGNIFICANCE: One of the most popular published accounts about the Holocaust, this work has been periodically attacked as unsuitable reading material for schools and libraries

When Anne Frank was thirteen years old in 1942 she began keeping a diary. Written for herself alone, it described in explicit detail her thoughts and feelings during the two years that she was confined with seven other people in which she called the "Secret Annex." Eventually, they were all arrested, and Anne, her sister, and her mother perished in German concentration camps. After the war, Anne's father edited and published an abridged version of her diary which omitted comments about her growing sexual awareness, as well as her critical remarks about her mother and others who shared her hiding place. This version was also adapted to a popular play and a film.

Although Anne's diary has often been recommended on high school reading lists, parents have complained to school boards in such states as West Virginia in 1982 and in Alabama

Extract from Anne Frank's diary entry for October 10, 1942, which translates: "This is a photo as I would wish myself to look all the time. Then I would maybe have a chance to come to Hollywood." (AP/Wide World Photos)

in 1983, condemning the contents as overly sexually explicit or depressing.

An unabridged, definitive edition, retranslated and published in 1995, has restored all of Anne Frank's original entries and contains nearly 30 percent more material.

See also Abridgment; Banned Books Week; Books, young adult; Holocaust, Jewish; World War II.

Dickens, Charles

BORN: February 7, 1812, Portsmouth, Hampshire, England
DIED: June 9, 1870, Rochester, England
IDENTIFICATION: British novelist
SIGNIFICANCE: Dickens' work has been the target of censorship efforts because of its depiction of the Jewish character Fagin in *Oliver Twist*

Dickens is generally considered to be the preeminent novelist of Victorian England. His novels include *Oliver Twist* (1838), *A Christmas Carol* (1843), *Bleak House* (1852-1853), and *A Tale of Two Cities* (1859). His novel *Oliver Twist*, about an

Charles Dickens' Jewish corrupter of youth, Fagin (Ron Moody), instructs the Artful Dodger (Jack Wild) in pickpocketing in the film Oliver! *(1968), a musical adaptation of* Oliver Twist. *(Museum of Modern Art/Film Stills Archive)*

orphaned boy who runs away from a workhouse and falls under the influence of an unscupulous Jewish thief named Fagin, was the subject of a censorship effort in New York in 1949. The case of *Rosenberg v. Board of Education of the City of New York* involved a complaint made in the New York courts against the reading and study of *Oliver Twist*—as well as William Shakespeare's play, *The Merchant of Venice*—in New York City secondary schools. Charging that both works contained offensive portrayals of Jews, the complainants urged the court that the works would prompt hatred of Jews as individuals and as a race. However, the court determined that because no school officials or instructors had selected the works in order to promote anti-Semitism their censorship would be inappropriate.

See also Education; Judaism; Literature; Race; Shakespeare, William.

Dictionaries

DEFINITION: Reference books containing alphabetically arranged entries that provide information about individual words, phrases, parts of words, abbreviations, and symbols
SIGNIFICANCE: As comprehensive summaries of the meanings and usages of words in languages, dictionaries are subjected to cultural codes of social and linguistic decorum that have often amounted to tacit forms of censorship

The dictionaries with which most people are familiar list, in varying degrees of comprehensiveness, the words in a language, providing their standard and alternative spellings and definitions. There is a general perception among the public that dictionaries should be authoritative guides to language. This view holds that the spellings and usages contained in a dictionary are correct, and that those that are not are incorrect. Therefore, if a slang locution such as "ain't" is not listed in a dictionary, it should not be used.

The earliest English language dictionaries often veered toward a kind of whimsicality that reflected the backgrounds and prejudices of their compilers. Samuel Johnson's *A Dictionary of the English Language* (1755), for example, defined "oats" as "a grain that in England is generally fed to horses, but in Scotland supports the people." Variant spellings were more common and more widely tolerated before the eighteenth century than they were after it, largely because of increased public literacy and the proliferation of standardized spellings in printed material.

In addition to the general, word-definition dictionaries with which most people are familiar, specialized dictionaries exist that focus on specific vocational or other areas. Some dictionaries emphasize such aspects of language as etymology, pronunciation, dialects, or synonyms and antonyms. Others offer such encyclopedic information as that found in biographical or geographical dictionaries. Still others provide bilingual equivalencies for non-native speakers of a language, such as those found in bilingual dictionaries.

Prescriptive and Descriptive Dictionaries. Until 1961, when *Webster's Third New International Dictionary* was published, dictionaries were largely prescriptive. That is, they set standards of usage, provided rigid rules for spelling, and essentially dictated how language should be used properly. *Webster's Third New International Dictionary* was the first wholly new unabridged dictionary produced by the Merriam-Webster Company since 1934. Earlier dictionaries were typically built around the principles of a Latinate grammar that did not easily accommodate the conventions of English, which is a Germanic, rather than a Romance, language. As a result, many dictionary users found their prescriptive rules difficult to apply to the realities of English language.

During the 1940's and 1950's much was learned about language by those who had taught intensive language courses to the military during World War II. Language came to be viewed more as something alive and dynamic than as something static with a fixed set of rules whose violation represented—at least in the public mind—grammatical errors. Since that time, modern grammarians have advanced the idea that any language that communicates successfully is grammatically acceptable, regardless of whether or not it is socially acceptability.

To grammarians concerned with describing language, a phrase such as "I ain't got none" communicates the idea that its speaker intends just as well as "I do not have any" (or "I have none"). One level of society tends to use locutions such as the former, while another uses the latter. The old prevailing belief that two negatives ("ain't" and "none") necessarily make a positive may be accurate in mathematics, but it is absurd in real English usage. Even such revered writers as William Shakespeare often achieved emphasis by using double (or triple or quadruple) negatives.

The word order and sentence structure in both sentences cited above are standard. Neither is grammatically incorrect when viewed in the context of modern descriptive grammar. An utterance that is truly grammatically incorrect might be something such as "I store to the went"—a statement that no native speakers of English would ever make, regardless of their social or educational levels.

Modern lexicographers have been almost unanimously descriptive, rather than prescriptive, in their approaches to dictionary making. The public at large, however, has been slow to catch up with them. It was for this reason that after *Webster's Third International Dictionary* appeared that subsequent dictionaries such as *Webster's Seventh New Collegiate Dictionary* (1963) and *The American Heritage Dictionary* (1969) were designed to be considerably more prescriptive than *Webster's Third* had been.

The editorial board of *Webster's Third* and its chief editor, Philip B. Gove, refused to make moral judgments about many words and usages that earlier editions had dismissed as slang, colloquial, or substandard English. Because modern linguists consider spoken language more reflective of true usage than written forms of the language, citations of authority for many usages in *Webster's Third* were made to popular entertainers such as Marilyn Monroe or Elvis Presley, rather than to the hallowed literary sources used cited in dictionaries. This was a departure that disturbed many of the edition's critics.

Obscenity, Profanity, and Scatological Language. Although most modern dictionaries contain words that are at least mildly profane, they usually do not contain words that are considered obscene, despite their pervasive presence in modern literature, as well as a not inconsiderable body of English writing dating back to the Middle Ages. Description of coarse words has generally been left to more specialized reference works, such as the *Dictionary of American Slang* (first published in 1960) and the *New Dictionary of American Slang* (1986). There has, however, been a trend toward including words of every stripe in comprehensive dictionaries. The *Oxford English Dictionary* (1884-1928), for example, is a compendious multivolume dictionary that carefully traces the history of every word it defines. It has always striven for completeness, but it did not originally include many vulgar words, such as those commonly used to describe sexual acts. Modern revisions of this very inclusive dictionary, have, however, become even more inclusive.

After the *Dictionary of American Slang* was first published in 1960, it was summarily banned from the public and school libraries in several states—including California and Texas. Max Rafferty, California's state superintendent of schools in the late 1960's, publicly railed against the book, attracting such attention that the resulting furor spurred the book's sales to many people who otherwise would probably not have been aware of its existence.

Limitations of Size. The most frequently sold dictionaries are single-volume works, such as those typically purchased by students and secretaries. Unabridged dictionaries might contain as many as 600,000 entries, but editors of smaller dictionaries must exclude from their editions whole categories of terms. At times the editors make censorship decisions of sorts, typically by omitting potentially offensive terms. Otherwise, such dictionaries usually omit technical terms that can be found readily in specialized works designed for such fields as medicine, law, or engineering. Many small dictionaries eliminate whole sections, such as the biographical entries or geographical gazetteers typically found in larger dictionaries. Some dictionaries, such as *The American Heritage Dictionary*, incorporate biographical and other specialized entries into their main texts, conserving space by condensing the definitions greatly.

Most purchasers of single-volume dictionaries expect these editions to be authoritative and are generally unmoved by the explanations and justifications that grammarians and linguists make about language usage. Publishers of such volumes are thus constrained by the demands of the books' users from radically departing from prescriptive approaches.

—R. Baird Shuman

See also Abridgment; Banned Books Week; Book publishing; Censorship; Gabler, Mel, and Norma Gabler; Libraries; Libraries, school; Obscenity: legal definitions; Webster, Noah.

BIBLIOGRAPHY

A good starting point for research into dictionaries is Yakov Malkiel's *Theory and Method in Lexicography* (Ann Arbor: University of Michigan Press, 1980)—a broad discussion of how dictionaries are constructed. Herbert C. Morton's *Philip Gove's Controversial Dictionary and Its Critics* (New York: Cambridge University Press, 1994) offers a detailed account of Philip Gove's vision for *Webster's Third New International Dictionary*, and captures well the firestorm that his dictionary ignited. Another good overview of the controversy can be found in the essays collected in *Dictionaries and That Dictionary* (Chicago: Scott, Foresman, 1962), edited by James Sledd and Wilma R. Ebbitt. *Censorship: A Threat to Reading, Learning, Thinking* (Newark, Del.: International Reading Association, 1994), edited by John S. Simmons, contains twenty-one articles that provide a comprehensive view of school censorship in the modern United States. Herbert N. Foerstel's *Banned in the U.S.A.: A Reference Guide to Book Censorship in Schools and Public Libraries* (Metuchen, N.J.: Scarecrow Press, 1994) cites many instances of school and library censorship.

Diderot, Denis

BORN: October 5, 1713, Langres, France
DIED: July 31, 1784, Paris, France
IDENTIFICATION: French author and editor
SIGNIFICANCE: As editor of the *Encyclopédie* and as a creative writer, Diderot helped lead France's Enlightenment struggle for freedom of expression and became a frequent target of censorship

One of the principal leaders in the late eighteenth century Enlightenment, Diderot is best known as the editor of *L'Encyclopédie: ou dictionnaire raisonné des sciences, des arts et des métiers* (1751-1772, *Encyclopedia or Rational Dictionary of the Sciences, Arts and Crafts*), a twenty-eight-volume work designed to examine social and physical phenomena in strictly rational terms. Human experience—rather than God or the dictates of organized religion—anchored the enterprise, which became the first great modern work of reference. Diderot's efforts on behalf of the *Encyclopédie* began in 1746. Working initially with mathematician Jean Le Rond d'Alembert, he enlisted as contributors many of the most influential French thinkers of the era, including Voltaire and Jean-Jacques Rousseau. Montesquieu, too, is often associated with the *Encyclopédie*, although he wrote nothing specifically for it. The complete work comprised seventeen volumes of text and eleven of plates.

Beginning with the publication of the first volume, the *Encyclopédie*—which exposed clerical and judicial abuses—was persistently attacked by the Jesuits, Jansenists, the General Assembly of the Clergy, the Parlement of Paris, the king's council, the pope, and defenders of the old orthodoxies and the Old Regime. In 1752, its first two volumes were suppressed for their political and religious outspokenness, but two years later King Louis XV issued a personal privilege for the continuation of the project. Soon after the seventh volume appeared in 1757 d'Alembert abandoned Diderot. The next blow came in 1759, when King Louis responded to political pressure by forbidding further publication of the *Encyclopédie*. Shortly after the king's reversal, all existing volumes were listed on the *Index Librorum Prohibitorum* on the grounds that they promoted godlessness and undermined religion. Despite the great condemnation the *Encyclopédie* received, Diderot persevered, managing the formidable editorial responsibilities

and writing many of the articles himself. The final ten volumes of text were brought out in 1765 under a false imprint. Unfortunately, publisher Andre-Francois Le Breton censored the work without Diderot's knowledge. Disheartened, Diderot continued with the project until the publication of the final two volumes of plates in 1772. Although he considered it a monstrosity, the work's survival constituted an important step in the Enlightenment and the history of the modern book.

Like the *Encyclopédie*, Diderot's innovative novels, essays, and other literary efforts exude a philosophical boldness that often brought him into conflict with official morality. His book *Philosophic Thoughts* (1746) was placed on the *Index Librorum Prohibitorum* in 1766. *Letter on Blindness for the Use of Those Who See* (1749), an argument for biological determinism, landed him in prison for several months. *The Nun* (1796)—Diderot's sexually explicit novel about the abuses of monastic life—was far too scandalous for prerevolutionary France. In fact, although it was written in the 1760's, it was not published until more than a decade after Diderot died. *The Nun* has been censored for its portrayal of Catholicism, but was never relegated to the *Index Librorum Prohibitorum*. However, Diderot's other posthumously published novel, *Jack the Fatalist and His Master* (1796), appeared on the *Index Librorum Prohibitorum* in 1804. Students of censorship have also followed the fate of *The Indiscreet Jewels* (1748), an erotic satire about Louis XV and his court.

See also Atheism; France; *Index Librorum Prohibitorum*; Montesquieu; Rousseau, Jean-Jacques; Voltaire.

Dine, Jim

BORN: June 16, 1935, Cincinnati, Ohio
IDENTIFICATION: American artist
SIGNIFICANCE: Artworks that Dine exhibited in London in 1966 were confiscated as obscene

Dine's best-known work has affiliations with the "pop art" of the mid-1960's. His subject matter, which focuses on banal and everyday objects—hearts, hand tools, bathrobes—has been viewed by many as warm-hearted, honest, and emotion-laden. His semi-abstract collage works, which were exhibited in London in 1966, are characteristic of this same spirit. Construed as a visual journal of Dine's visits to London, some of the works were made in collaboration with British sculptor Eduardo Paolozzi. Included within the images were those with scatological content and phallic drawings, one of which featured a phallus wrapped in rose-strewn wrapping paper from a well-known department store of the time. Acting on a warrant under the Obscene Publications Act of 1959, London's Metropolitan Police (Scotland Yard) confiscated twenty-one works from the exhibition as well as the show's catalog—which was later annotated and justified by a Jesuit priest.

Fraser was subsequently tried under the British Vagrancy Act of 1838 and found guilty in "exposing or causing to be exposed to public viewing an indecent exhibition." He was fined twenty pounds and court costs. The art works remained impounded by the police pending appeal.

See also Art; Dalí, Salvador; Degenerate Art Exhibition; Hypocrisy; Serrano, Andres.

Disney films

DEFINITION: Family-oriented feature films released by the Disney Company since the late 1930's

SIGNIFICANCE: Although Disney films have long dominated the field of G-rated film entertainment, protests have been raised against their content and Disney itself has occasionally been accused of practicing forms of censorship in its adaptations of materials from other sources

Live-action and animated films produced by the Walt Disney Company have been generally accepted as "family fare," containing little to offend young viewers. At times when Hollywood films were threatened by external censorship, Disney provided the film industry with a safety valve of "safe" viewing.

This reputation for child-friendly film was jealously guarded by Walt Disney and his successors at the studio, even when it hampered creative efforts, as happened to Mickey Mouse, the enormously successful animated star that made Disney's first fortune. Mickey began as a somewhat amoral rascal or trickster, living by his wits; after he became one of the most recognized figures in the film world, however, his rougher edges were smoothed. Walt Disney decreed that Mickey should be a model of respectability, with no off-color humor or naughty behavior. Eventually, Mickey was so cleansed of bad habits that studio animators had difficulty finding things for him to do. A new, more aggressive and physical character, Donald Duck, had to be invented to exploit the comedic potential of animated film.

The First Animated Features. When Disney began to develop animated features, beginning with *Snow White and the Seven Dwarfs* (1937), characters and situations were similarly altered to make them more acceptable to an audience of children and, most important, their parents. *Pinocchio* (1940), for instance, is based on Carlo Collodi's 1882 novel about a wooden puppet who turns into a real boy. Collodi's Pinocchio misbehaves seriously and suffers significant punishment before he is allowed to become fully human. Disney's film tones down the character, turning Pinocchio into a good little boy who is led astray by bad companions, rather than as Collodi's amoral puppet who must learn to be good.

Disney's animated films were initially hailed as highly crafted works of cinematic art, but even at the beginning, there were some who argued that his work tampered too much with its source material, bowdlerizing it in the name of a mediocre, middle-class aesthetic. Ironically, there were also concerns that the films were often dangerously traumatic for children. The violence and terror of scenes such as Snow White's flight through the woods were thought by some observers likely to inspire nightmares among the very young. The question of whether these films should be viewed by young children was seriously debated by film critics, parents, and teachers.

Similar concerns were raised about later films, from *Bambi* (1942), which featured the violent death of the young fawn's mother, to *The Lion King* (1994), with the even more traumatizing violent on-screen death of the cub's father. *Bambi* was also perceived by outdoors enthusiasts as antihunting propaganda; many hunters refused to allow their children to watch it, and several outdoors magazines claimed that it was libelous.

"Disneyfication." The most persistent criticisms of Disney films have come from educators and librarians concerned about the films' tendency to eclipse the original materials on which they were based. Regardless of their sources, all Disney films have shared certain traits of animation style, characterization, and plot development. Film critic Richard Schickel coined the term "Disneyfication" for this process of making films conform to the studio's style. Disney's enormous success in marketing its films has contributed to these concerns, as the "Disney version" tends to replace the original story in the cultural memory. By driving out traditional versions of fairy tales and other classic children's works, Disney films effectively make them unavailable and substitute versions that eliminate sexuality and other presumably disturbing content, while substantially altering characters and plots.

Disney has been directly accused of censorship by the creator of one of the appropriated works in at least one notable case, that of Igor Stravinsky's ballet *The Rite of Spring*, which provided the musical accompaniment for a segment in Disney's animated musical feature *Fantasia* (1940). Stravinsky's composition was significantly rearranged and rescored to match the film narrative, without indicating to the audience that what they heard was anything but Stravinsky's original music. The composer objected but was unable to get Disney to accede to his wishes, since the piece was not protected under U.S. copyright law. *Fantasia* was also the occasion for one of the few instances of official censorship of Disney projects, when the Hays office decreed that the female centaurs in one segment must have their bare breasts covered.

Concern about Disney's appropriation of cultural materials ebbed somewhat following Walt Disney's death in 1966, as the quality of the studio's product declined in most critics' and viewers' estimation. Several relatively unsuccessful films over the next two decades suggested that Disney domination of the children's film market was at an end.

The Resurgence of Disney Films. Beginning with *The Little Mermaid* in 1989, Disney enjoyed a resurgence with a new string of hit animated films. The new Disney was, if anything, an even more powerful marketing engine, resurrecting concerns about its treatment of source materials and adding a new objection: misrepresentation of minority groups and cultures. Ironically, these objections arose from the studio's efforts to be more inclusive, working from materials originating outside Western culture, as in *Aladdin* (1992), or attempting to be sensitive to minority perspectives, as in *Pocahontas* (1995). Both films were attacked by the groups represented. Arab American protests caused Disney to rewrite lyrics in one of *Aladdin*'s songs, and the film was withdrawn from distribution in Indonesia because of claims that it was anti-Islamic. Several American Indian spokespersons argued that *Pocahontas*, which attempted to present an Indian perspective on the British colonization of Virginia, in fact injured Indian children because the film's colonists used the term "savage" to refer to Indians—as the Indian characters themselves did when referring to the white colonists. Such protests rarely result in direct censorship of later Disney films, but they have produced calls to boycott the films and various merchandising spin-offs.

—A. Waller Hastings

See also Abridgment; *Alice's Adventures in Wonderland*; Comic books; Film adaptation; Film censorship; Hays Code; Islam; Motion Picture Association of America; Native Americans.

BIBLIOGRAPHY

Leonard Maltin's *The Disney Films* (3d ed., Westport, Conn.: Hyperion, 1995) provides a comprehensive overview of Disney films, complete with detailed plot summaries and cast and credit lists. The essential starting point for any examination of Disney's role in popular culture is Richard Schickel's *The Disney Version: The Life, Times, Art and Commerce of Walt Disney* (rev. ed., New York: Simon and Schuster, 1985). Other useful studies include two books by Eric Smoodin: *Animating Culture: Hollywood Cartoons from the Sound Era* (New Brunswick, N.J.: Rutgers University Press, 1993) and *Disney Discourse: Producing the Magic Kingdom* (New York: Routledge/American Film Institute, 1994). Frances Clarke Sayers' "Walt Disney Accused" in *Horn Book* 41 (1965) articulates the case that many educators have made against Disney. Also useful is "The Instrumentalization of Fantasy: Fairy Tales, the Culture Industry and Mass Media" in Jack Zipes's *Breaking the Magic Spell: Radical Theories of Folk and Fairy Tales* (Austin: University of Texas Press, 1979).

Djilas, Milovan

BORN: June 12, 1911, Podbbišće, Montenegro

DIED: April 20, 1995, Belgrade, Serbia

IDENTIFICATION: Yugoslav government official and author whom Tito jailed for writing a critique of communism

SIGNIFICANCE: Djilas was the first post-World War II communist official in Eastern Europe to rebel against communist dogmatism and the corruption of power

Djilas joined Yugoslavia's Communist Party as a student and participated in its quest for power before and during World War II. He quickly rose to high government posts and became a close friend of Tito. In 1953 he publicly accused government officials and party members of corruption and betrayal of communist ideals in an article, appropriately titled "Anatomy of a Moral," and was forced to resign from his posts. He was also expelled from the party and was jailed three years later. While in jail, he wrote additional books of criticism, for which he received additional prison sentences and was not released until the end of 1966. Meanwhile, he became the most celebrated dissident in the postwar communist world.

Djilas wrote several books of fiction and on political and historical subjects. Perhaps the most important is his early work *The New Class* (1957), which mercilessly pilloried the communists for rising to power only to improve on the corruption of the bourgeois predecessors against whom they revolted. This book's title, "The New Class," entered political terminology and has since been applied almost exclusively to communists. Djilas followed that book with *Anatomy of a Moral* (1959), a collection of satirical articles in which he continued his attack on bureaucracy and corruption. *Conver-*

sations with Stalin (1962) moved his criticisms into the international sphere, drawing a devastating portrait of moral degradation of the Soviet dictator and justifying Yugoslavia's break from the Soviet Bloc in 1948.

In *Wartime* (1977) Djilas chronicled the events in Yugoslavia in World War II. It pays homage to the struggle of the partisans and reveals several secrets, such as the meeting between the partisans and the Germans in 1943—which ostensibly took place to discuss a prisoner exchange, but which in reality planned a joint resistance to a possible Allied landing in the Balkans. Djilas' uncompromising honesty and courage of conviction have made him a reliable witness to the events of World War II and the ensuing Cold War.

The changes in Djilas' thinking over the years merit emphasis. From a fervid communist he eventually became a social democrat; however, at heart he remained a communist who regretted the missed opportunities of putting Marxist theory into a successful practice.

See also Communism; Havel, Václav; Police states; Soviet Union; Stalin, Joseph; Translation; World War II.

Dole, Robert

BORN: July 22, 1923, Russell, Kansas

IDENTIFICATION: American politician

SIGNIFICANCE: As a Senate leader, Dole strongly supported the censorship activities of Republican presidents Richard Nixon, Ronald Reagan, and George Bush; in the 1990's he led calls for censorship of the media

Despite suffering wounds near the end of World War II that left him without the use of his right arm and hand, Dole completed a law degree in 1952 and entered Kansas politics. After serving eight years in the national House of Representatives, he moved to the Senate in 1968 and won re-election in 1974, 1980, 1986, and 1992.

As a Republican congressman, Dole criticized the Democratic administration of John F. Kennedy, accusing it of being soft on communism. In the Senate he fervently supported President Richard Nixon, defending all Nixon's actions so effectively that Nixon chose him in 1971 to chair the Republican National Committee during the 1972 campaign. Although Nixon asked Dole to resign in November, 1972, Dole defended Nixon during the Watergate scandal, insisting that Nixon had not committed any crimes.

Dole ran as vice-presidential candidate with Gerald Ford in their unsuccessful 1976 campaign, earning a reputation of hatchet man for his abrasive, harsh campaign style. He won national attention again in 1979 when his conduct of Senate committee hearings on religious cults was attacked as a threat to freedom of religion. After an abortive run for the Republican presidential nomination in 1980 against Ronald Reagan, Dole returned to the Senate, where he became chairman of the Finance Committee in 1981, majority leader in 1984, minority leader in 1987, and majority leader again in 1994. As administration spokesman in the Senate he faithfully supported the censorship policies of presidents Reagan and Bush.

Even when running against Bush for the presidential nomination in the hotly contested primary campaign of 1988, Dole defended Bush against accusations that he had had a major role in the Iran-Contra scandal. When Bush called for a constitutional amendment to modify the Bill of Rights after the Supreme Court ruled that flag burning was a protected form of speech in 1989, Dole led the Senate effort to secure passage of Bush's amendment. When the effort failed, Dole blamed Bush for not exerting enough pressure on doubtful senators.

As Dole prepared to try for the presidency again in 1996, he launched a series of attacks on the media which, although not calling for official censorship, exerted pressure for self-censorship on commentators, publishers, movie studios, and record companies. In 1992 he led a Senate Republican attack on federal funding for the Corporation for Public Broadcasting, arguing that its programming spread left-wing and anti-American propaganda. On May 31, 1995, he launched a withering attack on the entertainment industry for producing movies and records that he claimed undermined the social fabric and character of the nation. The Time-Warner media conglomerate shortly thereafter decided to stop producing controversial rap records.

See also Armenian genocide; Bush, George; Congress, U.S.; Fear; Flag burning; Iran-Contra scandal; National Public Radio; Nixon, Richard M.; Political campaigning; Public Broadcasting Service; Reagan, Ronald; *Texas v. Johnson*; Watergate scandal.

Doonesbury

TYPE OF WORK: Syndicated newspaper cartoon strip
FIRST PUBLISHED: 1970
ARTIST: Garry Trudeau (1948-   )
SUBJECT MATTER: Contemporary American life and politics
SIGNIFICANCE: A topical cartoon strip that has often used the names of real people, *Doonesbury* has occasionally contained such barbed satire that newspapers have hesitated to print it

A life-long New York resident, Garry Trudeau is best known for his comic strip *Doonesbury*, which has been syndicated in as many as 850 different newspapers. In 1975 he won a Pulitzer Prize for editorial cartooning, and he was nominated for an Academy Award for his animated film, *A Doonesbury Special*, in 1977. The film also won a special jury prize at the Cannes Film Festival.

Noted for the controversial nature of his editorial cartooning, Trudeau has lampooned such public figures as singer Frank Sinatra, Attorney General John Mitchell, Senator John Warner, and Philadelphia mayor Frank Rizzo. In October, 1980, he poked fun at "the mysterious world of Ronald Reagan's brain." In one strip drawn during the 1980 presidential campaign the narrator comments: "The brain of Ronald Reagan has been shrinking ever since 1931, whereas Jimmy Carter's brain has only been dying since 1944. To the trained scientist, this represents a clear choice." Whether film producers and cartoonists may legally satirize or misrepresent public persons has long been debated. Trudeau has often been accused of willful misrepresentation of public figures.

At times editors have decided not to print Trudeau's cartoons out of fear of legal problems. In November, 1993, the

San Diego Union-Tribune, Orange County Register, Los Angeles Times, and *Escondido Times-Advocate* decided not to use six *Doonesbury* cartoons that depicted a couple in Malibu, California, who panic when they think a neighbor's yard is on fire and that their own house will burn next. Later it is discovered that the fire—which is quickly extinguished—has been caused by a tipped barbecue. One newspaper editor thought that the strip was in bad taste at that moment because Southern California was recovering from several devastating fires, including one in Malibu that destroyed several hundred homes and killed three people. Although the editors removed the cartoons out of sensitivity for the feelings of the readers, readers accused them of censorship.

Another series of *Doonesbury* cartoons suggested that Vice President Dan Quayle had taken illegal drugs and that there was a federal "cover-up" of Quayle's "file" in the Drug Enforcement Administration. One character says that "the file didn't actually surface until late in the '88 campaign." Although *Doonesbury* is acknowledged to be merely a comic strip that need not be taken seriously, some critics have charged that the contents of the widely distributed strip are believed to be at least partly true by many readers.

See also Caricature; Comic books; Crumb, Robert; *Far Side, The*; Flag burning; MAD magazine; News media censorship; *Ronde, La*.

Dostoevski, Fyodor

BORN: November 11, 1821, Moscow, Russia
DIED: February 9, 1881, St. Petersburg, Russia
IDENTIFICATION: Russian author of novels, short stories, and political writings
SIGNIFICANCE: One of the great writers in world literature, Dostoevski was almost executed for rebelling against czarist absolutism during his youth

As a fledgling writer, Dostoevski was drawn to humanitarian idealism. Opposing the absolutist rule of Czar Nicholas I, he attended meetings of a revolutionary group called the Petrashevsky Circle, but more out of curiosity than from true revolutionary zeal. In 1849 he and others were arrested at a meeting; he was imprisoned for eight months, tried, and sent to Siberia. But before this sentence was announced, Dostoevski was among the members of the Petrashevsky who were tied to posts and told they were about to be executed until a pardon arrived from the czar at the last moment. This experience had a traumatic affect on Dostoevski, aggravating the epilepsy with which he was already afflicted.

In December, 1949, Dostoevski was sent to a prison in Siberia. After spending four years there, he spent another four years in the Russian army in the Far East. From these experiences later came one of his most impressive works, *Memoirs from the House of the Dead* (1861). Ironically, the experiences also brought about his conversion to conservatism and gave him respect for Russia's authoritarian system. This change was effected by Dostoevski's admiration for the simple Russian peasants he met in prison, their stoic suffering despite injustice, and their deep religious faith in God and the czar.

Dostoevski returned to St. Petersburg in 1859 with a new philosophical and political outlook. Two years later he began to express his conservative views in *Time*, a political journal that he edited with his brother. It advocated a democratic and Christian nationalism and faith in the peasants. After having trouble with censors who suppressed the publication of some issues for alleged subversive material, the Dostoevski brothers were forced to reissue their journal in 1864 as *The Epoch*. Financial difficulties and the deaths of Dostoevski's wife and brother eventually forced Dostoevski to abandon this journal. Later, however, he published *An Author's Diary* (1876-1877, 1880-1881), with a similar outlook. He was also forced to go abroad, but mostly because of his gambling debts.

In his novels, Dostoevski based his conservative views on humanism and the need to support the poor and oppressed. In *Insulted and Injured* (1862) he sided with those who were kept down by life circumstances and by the insensitivity of fellow man. In *Crime and Punishment* (1866) he showed understanding for a young woman who was forced into prostitution in order to help her family. In *The Brothers Karamazov* (1879-1880) he again spoke for an innocent Russian against the accusations and conviction brought on by the authorities. For such stances he was often criticized in some quarters and by authorities, but he persisted in championing the oppressed.

See also Gogol, Nikolai Vasilyevich; Literature; Nicholas I; Prisons; Prostitution; Russia; Tolstoy, Leo.

Douglas, William O.

BORN: October 16, 1898, Maine, Minnesota
DIED: January 19, 1980, Washington, D.C.
IDENTIFICATION: Associate justice of the U.S. Supreme Court (1939-1975)
SIGNIFICANCE: Douglas served longer on the Supreme Court than any other justice; during his tenure he championed personal freedom and opposed censorship

Although he was born in Minnesota, Douglas is most closely identified with the state of Washington, where he grew up in poverty and battled against polio in childhood by hiking and walking in the Cascade Mountains near his Yakima home. Both experiences affected him greatly in later life; the former gave him empathy for society's underdogs, while the latter provided him with a love of nature and a feeling of kinship with Franklin D. Roosevelt, the polio-afflicted president who later appointed him to the Supreme Court.

Douglas worked his way through college with various odd jobs, at one point living in a tent. After graduating with honors in economics in 1920, he taught high school in Yakima for two years. In 1922 he enrolled in Columbia Law School in New York, from which he was graduated second in his class. Discontented after two years in a Wall Street law firm, he returned to Yakima to practice law. Less than a year later, however, he returned to New York, teaching at Columbia Law School until leaving the next year. He was employed as a professor at Yale Law School from 1929 until President Roosevelt appointed him to the Securities and Exchange Commission (SEC) in 1936. In 1937 he became chair of the SEC. His tenure there

William O. Douglas, one of the strongest proponents of unfettered free speech to sit on the U.S. Supreme Court, early in his judicial career. (Library of Congress)

was a stormy one, during which he defended the interests of the average citizen and demanded reforms in the New York Stock Exchange's network of patronage.

In 1939 Douglas was appointed to the U.S. Supreme Court. During his thirty-six years on the Court, he supported free expression and condemned censorship, writing more than twelve hundred opinions. With Justice Hugo Black, he is considered one of the Court's most strident civil libertarians, persistent in his opposition to censorship. Consistent with his support for the rights of women, minorities, and the poor, Douglas was a lifelong defender of freedom of speech, both for mainstream and for fringe elements in society. For example, in *Terminiello v. Chicago* (1949), he noted that "the right to speak freely and to promote diversity of ideas and programs is . . . one of the chief distinctions that sets us apart from totalitarian regimes." In *Dennis v. United States* (1951), perhaps his best-known dissenting opinion, Douglas stated the case against censorship succinctly when he wrote, "We have deemed it more costly to liberty to suppress a despised minority than to let them vent their spleen. We have above all else feared the political censor. We have wanted a land where our people can be exposed to all the diverse creeds and cultures of the world."

See also Black, Hugo; Courts and censorship law; First Amendment; Free speech; Warren, Earl.

Douglass, Frederick

Born: February, 1817(?), Tuckahoe, Talbot County, Maryland

Died: February 20, 1895, Washington, D.C.

Identification: American abolitionist, author, newspaper publisher, and public official

Significance: By writing books and publishing his own newspapers, Douglass was able to speak free of the restraints that publishers and critics sought to impose upon him

Born a slave, Frederick Bailey escaped to freedom in 1838, changed his name to Douglass, and soon began delivering speeches throughout the North for William Lloyd Garrison's American Antislavery Society. In 1845 the society published *The Narrative of the Life of Frederick Douglass, An American Slave*. The book became a best seller and secured Douglass' position as the leading black abolitionist in the United States. The volume was also published overseas, despite the efforts of Douglass' British publisher to censor his criticism of Christian slaveholders as hypocrites.

In 1847 Douglass split with Garrison and began publishing an antislavery newspaper, *The North Star* (renamed *Frederick Douglass' Paper* in 1851). Garrison's supporters tried unsuccessfully to prevent Douglass from producing a periodical to rival *The Liberator*, the American Antislavery Society's jour-

nal. Douglass editorialized in his newspapers about slavery, prejudice, politics, and other issues. In 1855 he published *My Bondage and My Freedom*, which was more critical of slavery and slaveholders than the *Narrative* had been.

After the Civil War Douglass stood as the most influential African American of his era. He later served as marshal of the District of Columbia and U.S. minister to Haiti.

See also Abolitionist movement; African Americans; Civil War, U.S.; Newspapers, African American.

Draft-card burning

Definition: Destruction of identification cards that men eligible for the military draft were required to possess

Significance: During the Vietnam War, burning one's draft card became a common expression of political protest

Following a series of highly publicized draft-card burnings to protest the Vietnam War, the U.S. Congress outlawed such activity in August, 1965, passing a bill without hearings within nine days of its introduction. Failure to possess a draft card was already a violation of draft regulations; the law's purpose was to silence a form of dissent that had received widespread media coverage. A 1968 U.S. Supreme Court decision upheld a 1965 law forbidding draft-card burning. In *United States v. O'Brien* (1968), the law was upheld as designed to facilitate the administration of the selective service system rather than

Antiwar demonstrators burn their draft cards outside of the Northampton, Massachusetts, Selective Service office in early 1970. (AP/Wide World Photos)

as aimed at suppressing dissent. The Court also declared that such prohibitions of expression that involved conduct could only be upheld where they were "unrelated to the suppression of free expression," a guideline that the Court later used to expand protection of "symbolic speech," as in the 1989 and 1990 rulings that struck down laws that banned flag desecration. The Court ruled that there was no nonsuppressive intent behind laws against flag desecrating. Thus, outlawing draft-card burning led indirectly to greater protection for symbolic speech.

See also Flag burning; Symbolic speech; *Texas v. Johnson*; Vietnam War.

Draft resistance

DEFINITION: Refusal of individuals either to serve in combatant roles in the armed forces, or to serve in any capacity at all in the armed forces, when ordered to do so

SIGNIFICANCE: Governments that impose military conscription are often tempted to suppress the advocacy, in print or other media, of conscientious objection or draft resistance, and to censor news about draft resistance

Draft resistance may arise not merely from deep-rooted pacifist convictions, but also a manifestation of objections to specific wars or specific political situations. Draft evasion, unlike draft resistance, is furtive rather than openly defiant. In the United States the inherent tension between the government's power to raise armies and the First Amendment's guarantee of freedom of speech was eased by the shift to a volunteer army in 1973.

U.S. Civil War. In both the North and the South, Quakers, Mennonites, and members of the Church of the Brethren objected to military service on moral grounds. Northern Quakers felt torn between pacifism and hatred of slavery. Most Northern draft resisters, such as the Irish immigrant mobs who rioted in New York City in July, 1863, opposed the Union's post-1862 war aim of emancipating the slaves and they resented the draft law because it permitted purchase of exemption from service. Although Northerners suspected of disloyalty to the Union were often arrested without trial, Northern newspapers that assailed the war and the draft suffered only sporadic suppression.

World War I. The draft was revived by the U.S. Congress after war was declared against Germany in 1916. It was opposed by socialists and anarchists, as well as religious pacifists. Draft-age members of the peace churches, theoretically eligible for conscientious objector status, felt great social pressure to serve as soldiers. Socialist publications were denied access to the mails. Under wartime legislation that criminalized attempts to interfere with army recruitment, both the native-born socialist leader Eugene Debs and the foreign-born anarchist Emma Goldman served prison terms for their public speeches. In *Schenck v. the United States* (1919), the U.S. Supreme Court upheld the conviction of Socialist Party official Charles Schenck for mailing antidraft leaflets to prospective soldiers. Because of government repression and propaganda, the draft functioned smoothly until its abolition shortly after war's end.

World War II and the Early Cold War. The U.S. Congress enacted a peacetime draft in September, 1940. After Japan bombed Pearl Harbor on December 7, 1941, the war effort against Japan and Germany enjoyed near-universal popular support until victory was won in 1945. Because the American wartime consensus was so solid, and because no pacifist organization tried to obstruct the war effort, pacifist publications were tolerated. The thirteen thousand draft resisters imprisoned during the war were mostly religious pacifists, including four thousand Jehovah's Witnesses. Those granted conscientious objector status had to either accept noncombatant army service or perform unpaid labor in civilian public service camps, whose locations far from major cities minimized the objectors' influence on the rest of the population. Antiwar and antidraft demonstrations were not reported in the press or on the radio, although future Vietnam War protester David Dellinger remembers being arrested for passing out leaflets in 1943.

After 1941 objection to World War II on nonpacifist grounds was confined mainly to anti-Semitic rightists, some of whom were illegally granted conscientious objector status by their local draft boards. Perhaps convinced of the rightists' powerlessness, the Supreme Court justices frustrated some federal prosecutions of them. In 1944 they reversed the conviction of Emil Hartzel for mailing criticisms of the war to selective service registrees. In 1945 they overturned the conviction of Gerhard Wilhelm Kunze, leader of the German-American Bund, for urging Bund members to refuse to cooperate with the draft.

From 1948—when the draft, which had expired in 1947, was revived because of tension with the Soviet Union—until the early 1960's, there was little popular sympathy or judicial tolerance for pacifist advocates of draft resistance despite American involvement in the Korean War. In 1949 Larry Gara, a college history teacher, went to prison for advising someone to resist the draft. In 1956 the same fate befell a woman newspaper editor, for the same reason.

The Vietnam War. In August, 1965, as the United States was escalating its military involvement in Vietnam, Congress voted to criminalize the burning of draft cards at antiwar demonstrations. The participation of draft-exempt university students in antiwar demonstrations prompted Selective Service Director Lewis Hershey to threaten, in December, 1965, to reclassify protesters as immediately eligible for military service. In *United States v. O'Brien* (1968), the Supreme Court declared that draft-card burning was not protected by the First Amendment. However, in two other cases, it ruled the punitive reclassification of protesters unconstitutional. In *Cohen v. California* (1971) the Court reversed the conviction of a young man who had expressed opposition to the draft with a slogan on his jacket incorporating a four-letter expletive.

In October, 1967, Dr. Benjamin Spock, a sixty-four-year-old expert on baby care, signed a manifesto offering financial and moral support to those who refused to fight in Vietnam. The following January he and four other men were indicted for conspiring to aid and abet draft resisters. The verdict of guilty, issued in June, 1968, for four of the defendants, was overturned on appeal by a three-judge panel in July, 1969.

The Spock trial could not stifle antidraft sentiment. The coverage of public draft-card burnings by newspapers and television, even if initially unsympathetic, kept news of antidraft protest from being smothered by the government. In large cities, draft counseling centers, staffed by volunteers, sprang up to advise draft-eligible youth about conscientious objection and other alternatives to the military, thus counteracting the neighborhood and family pressures exerted on young men to serve in the army when called. Applicants for conscientious objector status now came from Jewish, Roman Catholic, mainstream Protestant, and secular backgrounds, as well as from peace churches.

Conscientious Objection After 1975. After the U.S. draft was replaced by a volunteer army in 1973, and the Vietnam War ended in 1975, the issue of resistance did not arise again until 1980, when Congress imposed registration for a draft (but not actual conscription). During the Persian Gulf crisis of 1990-1991, Army doctor Yolanda Huet-Vaughn and some other soldiers who unsuccessfully sought conscientious objector status received little sympathy from the mainstream media.

Other Countries. During World War I forty-four-year-old British philosopher Bertrand Russell went to prison under the censorship provisions of Great Britain's Defence of the Realm Acts, for his writings on behalf of the No Conscription Fellowship, which championed the cause of conscientious objectors. During World War II, British conscientious objectors were treated with greater tolerance than in World War I.

In Nazi Germany dictator Adolf Hitler persecuted pacifist religious sects and suppressed news about German draft resistance. For example, the story of Franz Jagerstatter, who was executed for refusing military service during World War II, was not well known until a biography by the American pacifist Gordon C. Zahn was published in 1964.

In France more than one hundred intellectuals signed a manifesto in February, 1960, urging support for young Frenchmen who refused to fight in Algeria. The government harassed both those who signed the manifesto and the newspapers that printed it. The antidraft movement had no access to French television, which was government owned. However, France passed a law in 1963 that recognized conscientious objection. In 1983 France's long-standing legal ban on propaganda in favor of conscientious objection was eliminated.

Canadian draft resistance during World War II was fiercest among French Canadians unwilling to fight for Great Britain. In 1940 the mayor of Montreal was jailed for urging noncompliance with draft registration. However, debate over conscription was never suppressed (draftees were not sent overseas until 1944); and, as in the United States of the 1960's, wartime controversy over the draft paved the way for its eventual abolition.

During the 1980's the advocacy of conscientious objection and draft resistance—which had been viewed by many Americans in the 1960's as a Trojan horse for international communism—helped undermine several communist regimes in Eastern Europe. The Swords to Plowshares movement in East Germany, for example, and the Peace and Freedom Movement

in Poland both promoted conscientious objection. In both countries communism was overthrown in 1989. In the Soviet Union—which had been fighting a war in Afghanistan since 1979—Mikhail Gorbachev relaxed censorship, allowing criticisms of the draft and news about draft evasion to be voiced publicly for the first time after he came to power in 1985. Draft resistance, inspired by secessionist nationalism, in the Soviet republics of Georgia and Lithuania contributed to the breakup of the Soviet Union in late 1991.

In 1988 the white minority government of South Africa suppressed the publications of the End Conscription Campaign. Nonetheless, this antidraft campaign, which appealed to draft-age whites reluctant to shoot at rebellious blacks, probably contributed to the eventual dismantling of white minority rule in 1994.

—*Paul D. Mageli*

See also Berrigan, Daniel, and Philip Francis Berrigan; Cable television; Civil War, U.S.; Debs, Eugene; Draft-card burning; Espionage Act of 1917; Goldman, Emma; Jehovah's Witnesses; Panama, U.S. invasion of; *Schenck v. United States*; Vietnam War; World War I.

BIBLIOGRAPHY

Despite its strong pacifist bias, Stephen M. Kohn's *Jailed for Peace: The History of American Draft Law Violators, 1658-1985* (Westport, Conn.: Greenwood Press, 1986) is useful on the years from 1948 to the Vietnam War. For more detail on the Spock case, see Benjamin Spock, "The Conspiracy to Oppose the Vietnam War," in Bud Schultz and Ruth Schultz, eds., *It Did Happen Here: Recollections of Political Repression in America* (Berkeley: University of California Press, 1989). David Dellinger's *From Yale to Jail: The Autobiography of a Moral Dissenter* (New York: Pantheon Books, 1993) offers insights on the World War II era. Charles Moskos and John Whiteclay Chambers II, eds., *The New Conscientious Objection: From Sacred to Secular Resistance* (New York: Oxford University Press, 1993), provides information on eastern Europe, France, and South Africa, as well as the United States. On French draft resistance during the Algerian war, the best source is John Talbott, *The War Without a Name: France in Algeria, 1954-1962* (New York: Alfred A. Knopf, 1980). On Nazi Germany, see Gordon Zahn, *In Solitary Witness: The Life and Death of Franz Jagerstätter* (Boston: Beacon Press, 1964). Thomas P. Socknat, *Witness Against War: Pacifism in Canada, 1900-1945* (Toronto: University of Toronto Press, 1987), covers Anglo-Canadian conscientious objectors. J. L. Granatstein and J. M. Hitsman's *Broken Promises: A History of Conscription in Canada* (Toronto: Oxford University Press, 1977) deals with French-Canadian draft resistance. On British conscientious objectors, Caroline Moore, *Troublesome People: Enemies of War: 1916-1986* (London: Hamish Hamilton, 1987), is best for the general reader.

Drama and theater

DEFINITION: Closely related terms for public performances in which actors use words or gestures to convey scripted ideas and actions

SIGNIFICANCE: Throughout world history, drama and theater have attracted close government regulation and censorship

Since its beginning, theater has faced censorship at the hands of governments, the clergy, and powerful individuals. The communal nature of theater—the fact that plays are typically performed before masses of people, who need not be literate to understand their messages—has raised special concerns about the power of theater to instill potentially dangerous ideas and incite action in its audiences. A case from the life of Great Britain's premier playwright, William Shakespeare, provides an example. In 1601, on the eve of an attempt by the Earl of Essex to depose Queen Elizabeth, those planning the insurrection, presumably to drum up support for their cause, paid Shakespeare's acting company to revive his *Richard III*, a play about the deposition and killing of a monarch. It is unclear whether this performance had any impact on the public's opinion of the queen or if it helped Essex and his coconspirators. In any case, Essex's uprising failed. However, Elizabeth's fury at the fact that the popular theater had been unleashed against her illustrates an important point. Essex's belief that the play's performance would help his cause and Elizabeth's belief that the play would harm her cause illustrate the power attributed to this art form.

Such concerns have been part of the heritage of theater since ancient times. One of the earliest advocates of stage censorship in the western world was Plato, who attacked theater in both the *Republic* and the *Laws*. The ancient Greek philosopher opposed all forms of mimesis, or imitative art, and as theater is the quintessential form of imitation, it came in for his especially harsh criticism. Plato's writings are only a small part of the history of antitheatrical bias arising from the idea that theater can be dangerous and subversive. Because of this attitude, censors have often treated drama and theater differently from other forms of literature and art. In many cases, theatrical censorship has remained strict, even in times and places where other forms of expression have enjoyed relative freedom.

North America. There has never been widespread, systematic prior restraint in the United States, where drama is treated the same as other printed matter and theatrical productions are protected by the constitutional guarantee of free speech. However, this is not to suggest that there has been no censorship of theater in America. It means, rather, that such censorship has been local rather than national in scope and has been pursued sporadically in different times and places. The earliest incidents of American theatrical suppression sprang from the puritanism of the English settlers, whose religion made them deeply suspicious of theater and acting. In the early days of the American colonies, plays of all sorts were denounced as immoral and unchristian. In the late eighteenth century, several of the original colonies—and, after independence, many states—adopted strict laws forbidding theatrical performances. However, as populations grew in size and religious diversity, demands for theatrical entertainment also grew, until it was no longer practical to outlaw dramatic performance. Slowly, the authority for regulating plays devolved to the cities in which performances occurred. After this, censorship became quite idiosyncratic, relying as it did upon the moral, political, and religious convictions of widely varying local authorities.

Owing to laws protecting freedom of expression, only a few American cities—most notably Boston and Chicago—ever attempted prior restraint of theater. For the most part, productions of plays and other entertainments were allowed to open, and, if they were found objectionable, the local police would raid the theaters and close them down, sometimes fining or even imprisoning the actors and theater managers. For much of the nineteenth century, however, American playwrights shared the conservative standards and tastes of the general public, so relatively little government censorship was deemed necessary. By the late nineteenth and early twentieth centuries, however, vaudeville and burlesque theaters were becoming infamous for their vulgar comedy and shocking—by Victorian standards—dance acts. It was upon these entertainments that local restrictions were increasingly enforced.

At the same point in history, though, the "legitimate" theater was also experiencing expansion of the subject matter and stage business it saw fit to attempt. Daring plays by such foreign authors as George Bernard Shaw and Henrik Ibsen were performed—sometimes while still banned in their home countries—and even American playwrights were beginning to tackle such sensitive issues as divorce and gender roles. This new freedom on the stage led to a new outcry against drama and theater, with clergy, newspaper editors, and members of the public demanding stricter controls by the authorities. Thus, at the very time when much of Western Europe was campaigning for a relaxation of censorship laws, many in America were asking to have such laws strengthened.

The outcry, however, did not result in any action on the national level, and censorship remained very much a local issue that flared up from time to time with greater or lesser violence. Among the most famous cases of local prosecution in the early twentieth century were Jane Mast's 1926 play *Sex* (for performing in which actress Mae West was arrested and jailed for several days), Eugene O'Neill's *Strange Interlude* (1928), and Lillian Hellman's *The Children's Hour* (1934). In midcentury, many theater workers—like their counterparts in the film industry—faced persecution that amounted to censorship at the hands of Senator Joseph McCarthy's anticommunism campaign. Playwrights Lillian Hellman and Bertolt Brecht were perhaps the most famous theater professionals called to testify before the House Committee on Un-American Activities (HUAC), where both refused to indict their fellow writers and actors. Meanwhile, throughout the twentieth century, theaters continued to push the boundaries of what could be staged, until late in the century little remained that still constituted grounds for closing a play. It was at this point, however, that many began to scrutinize, and in some cases to suppress, the quasi-theatrical form known as "performance art."

United Kingdom. Theatrical censorship in Great Britain is notable because it was for many years more severe and more regularly enforced than in the rest of Europe. In addition, until the late twentieth century, the theater was censored with far more vigor than the press and the other arts in the same country. Beginning in the Middle Ages, the burden of theatrical censorship fell to the Master of the King's Revels, a minor court official responsible for arranging royal entertainments.

EXAMPLES OF THEATER CENSORSHIP IN NINETEENTH CENTURY EUROPE

Year*	Play	Playwright	Form of censorship
1821	Marino Faliero, Doge of Venice	Lord Byron	play was so severely expurgated by its London producer that it failed
1824	King Ottokar's Rise and Fall	Franz Grillparzer	reportedly banned on a whim of a German censor
1825	Boris Godunov	Alexander Pushkin	banned in Russia until 1870 because of Pushkin's refusal to accept Czar Nicholas I's suggestions for expurgations
1825	Woe from Wit	Alexander Griboyedov	banned in Russia until expurgated by Griboyedov in 1831
1831	Marion de Lorme	Victor Hugo	banned in France for its unfavorable depiction of King Louis XIII
1834	Masquerade	Mikhail Lermontov	Lermontov was forced to revise the play because of its unacceptable criticism of costume balls
1840	Vautrin	Honoré de Balzac	shut down after one performance in France because its lead actor appeared in a wig that mimicked King Louis Philippe
1843	Arnaldo da Brescia	Giovanni Battista Niccolini	banned throughout Italy because of its appeal to Italian nationalism and reunification
1852	La Dame aux camélias	Alexander Dumas, fils	banned in England and declared offensive to public morality in France
1853	La Pierre de touche	Emile Augier	Augier was forced to remove a line of dialogue stating that society was "ill ordered"
1873	The Happy Land	W. S. Gilbert and Gilbert à Beckett	expurgated by England's Lord Chamberlain because several characters were made up to resemble cabinet ministers
1881	Ghosts	Henrik Ibsen	banned in England because its characters "appear to be morally deranged"; also banned in much of Germany
1885	The Mikado	W. S. Gilbert and Arthur Sullivan	banned in England in 1907 to avoid offending a visiting Japanese prince
1888	Miss Julie	August Strindberg	banned in Copenhagen, but permitted in Berlin
1890	A Man and His Picture	Hermann Sudermman	banned by Berlin police because "it just suits us."
1893	The Weavers	Gerhart Hauptmann	banned throughout Germany until 1890 because of its depiction of a weavers revolt
1894	Mrs. Warren's Profession	George Bernard Shaw	banned in England until 1925 because of its frank treatment of prostitution
1906	The Enemies	Maxim Gorky	banned in Russia for its portrayal of a struggle between textile workers and their employers

*Year of original publication or production

In order to ensure that nothing would offend the royal family, this official made sure that no blasphemy was uttered on stage and that no offensive remarks were made about members of the royal household. It soon became the task of this office to screen scripts intended for production in the kingdom. Various office holders took the job's responsibilities more or less seriously, but in general the post had a reputation for corruption, caused in part by the fact that fees were charged for reading scripts and licensing theaters—a practice suggesting that the office holder might not be wholly disinterested.

In the eighteenth century, however, the onus of censorship was transferred to the office of the Lord Chamberlain. Concerned with the amount of antigovernmental satire appearing on stage, particularly in works by Henry Fielding, Parliament swiftly passed the Licensing Act of 1737. This law gave the Lord Chamberlain the duty of reviewing all new plays and issuing licenses before performances were allowed. The Lord Chamberlain, with the assistance of the examiner of plays, could insist upon specific deletions and changes or deny performance outright for any reason. Not only was he not required to explain his decisions, he was responsible to no other agency and was unavailable for appeal. Those who refused to abide by his decrees were heavily fined and risked losing their theatrical licenses.

Over the years, a number of playwrights and others expressed outrage at the degree of censorship imposed on the

British theater. Fielding gave up writing plays and turned to novels (a far less regulated form) after the passage of the Licensing Act. While the law remained in effect, other authors—including Thomas Hardy and H. G. Wells—suggested that they might have written drama were it not for fear of the censor. English drama thus suffered a great deal in the eighteenth and nineteenth centuries as artists turned to genres that allowed them greater freedom of expression. Some British plays, in fact, had their foreign performances long before they were staged in their native land. Many authors, of course, still chose to write for the theater, and of them George Bernard Shaw (himself a target of the censor) was perhaps the most vocal in his campaign for a reduction in the Lord Chamberlain's powers. This chapter in the history of British censorship ended when the Theaters Act of 1968 finally abolished prior restraint, leaving the theater to be regulated in the same manner as other arts.

Western Europe. During Europe's Middle Ages, the predominant censor was the Roman Catholic church. Much drama was religious in nature, and the clergy felt it necessary to regulate the content of scripts and performances. After the Reformation, Protestant churches also became involved in theatrical suppression, attempting to delete references to catholicism. There were particularly severe restrictions on performance in Spain in the sixteenth and seventeenth centuries. This church-sponsored censorship was based in part on religious objections to the "immorality" of much stage business. But an even greater objection was to the presence of women on stage—which seemed by the standards of the day a great breach of decorum.

In France as well, the authorities were concerned with the threat to morals posed by theater. For a part of the seventeenth century, for instance, Italian comedies were banned in France as lewd and corrupting. Censorship through much of France's history was enforced by the royal government, which kept guard over the state theater monopoly until the revolution of 1789 brought increased freedom to the arts generally. Still, some restrictions on the building and ownership of theaters remained until 1864, and along with these controls came the ability to restrict performance on both moral and political grounds.

In Germany, as elsewhere in Europe, governmental permission was required to open a theater and strict censorship was the rule. In the eighteenth century, for instance, an attempt was made to elevate the tone of theatrical performance, which the authorities feared might have a corrupting influence on the populace. King Joseph II placed new, strict regulations on comedy and forbade the kinds of dramatic improvisation of which Germans were fond. Throughout Germany's early history, state control was intended to ensure morality and order and ostensibly to serve the public welfare. When the Nazis rose to power in Germany in the 1930's, however, their suppression of theater was swift and well organized. They outlawed drama and theater by such "undesirables" as Jews and communists. They also banned plays by non-Germans—with the notable exception of Shakespeare, whom they regarded as sufficiently Nordic in spirit to satisfy Adolf Hitler's government. To replace the theater that they suppressed, the Nazis simultaneously began a campaign to bring to the populace as much propagandistic German theater as possible.

Russia and Eastern Europe. There is a long history of theatrical repression in Russia and Eastern Europe. Under the rule of Russia's czars, all plays were potentially subject to restraints on political grounds. The late eighteenth century's Empress Catherine II and mid-nineteenth century's Nicholas I became notorious for restraining theater and other arts. Soviet Russia, as well, was known for strict control during the twen-

While Czech dissident Václav Havel's plays were still banned in his native country, audiences in Western countries could see them in productions such as this 1984 California staging of A Private View. *(Jay Thompson, Mark Taper Forum)*

tieth century. Mechanisms for censorship were in place, and a number of productions were, in fact, restricted in the decades before World War II, but after the war, when Joseph Stalin was at the height of his power, these restrictions increased dramatically. Socialist Realism became the only permissible form of drama, and all playwrights were expected to devote their efforts to promoting the state. Local party officials were placed in charge of each theater and saw to it that authors, actors, directors, and other theater workers conformed to the state ideals.

Among the most interesting reversals of theatrical fortune is the case of Czech playwright Vàclav Havel. His plays were banned outright by the Czechoslovakian government in 1969, and he served time in jail for his "seditious" writings. He continued to work for artistic and social freedoms, however, and became a leading voice in the revolution that toppled his country's communist regime in 1989. Afterward, he was elected president of the new Czech Republic. It has been remarked that Havel helped orchestrate the revolution as if it were a stage play and the revolutionaries actors.

When state communism collapsed in much of Eastern Europe in the late 1980's and early 1990's, state censorship vanished with it. At this time, many predicted an explosion of new drama, including bold experimentation and challenges to the old "official style" of Socialist Realism. This, however, did not occur as expected. Certainly, playwrights and performers felt less constrained, and new plays were produced. But economic hardships caused by the conversion to free-market systems intervened, making large-scale changes in culture difficult.

Latin America. As was the case elsewhere in the Roman Catholic world, Latin America for many years experienced substantial censorship from the Church. In 1739, for example, Portuguese-Brazilian playwright Antônio José da Silva was burned at the stake by the Inquisition, in part because of his stage depictions of churchmen. During the nineteenth and twentieth centuries political, rather than religious, concerns have led to the greatest restrictions on theater. The political instability in many countries of Central and South America, and the presence of both right- and left-wing dictators, has made censorship a constant part of theater in this region. In Guatemala in the early to middle decades of the twentieth century, for example, all forms of political and social satire were banned from performance. After General Augusto Pinochet gained power in Chile in 1973, his government closed watched the theaters, banning many plays before performance and closing down others after they opened. Here, as elsewhere in the region, censorship promoted a preference for light comedy and noncontroversial subjects. Despite—or perhaps because of—such restrictions, theater has remained vital in Latin America, and many practitioners consider it an ideal way to bring new ideas to the people.

Asia. This part of the world has a theatrical history as ancient and diverse as the cultures that make up the region, and censorship has long been a part of that history. In China different forms of drama were once considered suitable for the different social classes, and some were more strictly regulated

than others. A fourteenth century Mongol ruler, for example, outlawed certain classes of comedy that he deemed lewd and inappropriate. By the eighteenth and nineteenth centuries, China's government had begun to fear the large (and potentially unruly) crowds that gathered at some types of performance—which were variously restricted and even banned outright. With the outbreak of World War II, censorship in Chinese theater increased, and drama began to be used for patriotic and propagandistic purposes. Since 1949, the People's Republic of China has constantly censored the theater, more strongly during periods of political and social unrest. In Japan, a burst of new theatrical activity in the seventeenth century brought an accompanying burst of censorship. Women were banned from stage at this time, and certain subjects—including the samurai clans—were not allowed. In the nineteenth century, the Japanese emperor issued a decree that all theatrical performances must be appropriate for families and foreigners. India, too, has a history of stage censorship which, not surprisingly, is interwoven with the complex history of its religious and social upheavals. With the coming of Islam in the tenth century, the ancient tradition of Sanskrit theater was suppressed in accordance with the new religion. Later, the agencies of the British Empire used the theater to help teach British culture to their Indian subjects, and consequently they censored many native works, especially after passage of the 1879 Dramatic Performances Act.

Africa. It is difficult to generalize about a continent as large and diverse as Africa, which has more than fifty nations with more than eight hundred languages. However, some incidents of stage censorship there can be mentioned. As orthodox Islam moved into Africa from the Middle East after the seventh century, it brought with it a ban on artistic representations of human beings. This ban included actors portraying other humans on stage, so Muslim countries often restricted certain types of performance on religious grounds. More often, though, censorship has been politically motivated, and the best known case of state censorship on the continent is that of South Africa. For many years, the country's ruling white minority considered drama a way of promoting European culture, and they enforced various types of censorship as well as strict racial segregation in theaters. When the black liberation movement gained force in the 1960's and 1970's, militant theater became a tool to spread ideas and politicize the black majority. A number of playwrights, actors, and theater workers were tried and served jail time for their activities. The severity of theater censorship in this region, as in the rest of the world, might be used as an indicator of the relative stability or instability of religious, social, and political life.   —*Janet E. Gardner*

See also Examiner of plays; Federal Theatre Project; Fielding, Henry; Havel, Václav; Jonson, Ben; Licensing Act of 1737; Lord Chamberlain; Master of the Revels; Performance art; Prior restraint; Shakespeare, William; Shaw, George Bernard; Socialist Realism; Theatres Act of 1968.

BIBLIOGRAPHY

Jonas Barish's *The Antitheatrical Prejudice* (Berkeley: University of California Press, 1981) gives a thorough overview of the bias against theater, covering Western culture from Plato to the twentieth century. The history of theatrical censorship in America, from the colonial period through the mid-twentieth century, is considered in Abe Laufe's *The Wicked Stage: A History of Theater Censorship and Harassment in the United States* (New York: Frederick Ungar, 1978). Frank Fowell and Frank Palmer's *Censorship in England* (reprint, Bronx, N.Y.: Benjamin Blom, 1969), first printed in 1913, covers the history of stage censorship in Britain until the beginning of the twentieth century and includes such useful supplements as extracts from the Theaters Acts, the oath taken by the examiner of plays, and copies of play licenses. For Europe, see Robert Justin Goldstein's *Political Censorship of the Arts and the Press in Nineteenth-Century Europe* (New York: St. Martin's, 1989). A selection of American and British newspaper articles and speeches considering both pro and con positions on theatrical (and film) censorship is reprinted in Lamar Taney Beman's compilation, *Selected Articles on Censorship of the Theater and Moving Pictures* (New York: Jerome S. Ozer, 1971). Bruce Zortman's *Hitler's Theater: Ideological Drama in Nazi Germany* (El Paso, Tex.: Firestein Books, 1984) provides a clear historical account of the Nazis' suppression of theater as well as their work to promote a new theater for a national socialist Germany.

Dreiser, Theodore

BORN: August 27, 1871, Terre Haute, Indiana
DIED: December 28, 1945, Hollywood, California
IDENTIFICATION: American novelist, journalist, and essayist
SIGNIFICANCE: Because Dreiser battled censors over artistic freedom of expression during the early 1900's, later writers of realistic fiction were allowed more latitude in their subject matter

Dreiser looms as an important figure in pre-1920 American literature because his controversial novels contained powerful messages, and because he stood firmly against attempts by censors to ban his views. Dreiser broke with the literary traditions of the early 1900's, writing realistic fiction in which his characters often violate society's code of moral behavior but are not always punished for their transgressions. His battles over censorship began with *Sister Carrie* (1900), reached a crescendo with *The "Genius"* (1915), and continued sporadically throughout his life.

Sister Carrie went against the grain of the genteel tradition in which fiction always taught a moral lesson, with goodness rewarded and sin punished. Partly autobiographical, the novel chronicles the rise of an uneducated girl who discards a series of lovers, and, ultimately, becomes a celebrated actress on the stage. The book's publication resulted in a heated battle between Dreiser and his publisher, Frank Doubleday, who found the book offensive. Because Dreiser threatened litigation, Doubleday distributed only a few books, storing most copies in a basement. Censors and church groups attacked Dreiser as an immoralist who used crude, vernacular language. Although *Sister Carrie* was unsuccessful in 1900, another publisher successfully reissued the book in 1907.

The Financier (1912) and *The Titan* (1914) fomented storms of protest as well. A fictionalization of the career of

Theodore Dreiser was plagued by censors throughout his writing career. (Library of Congress)

Charles T. Yerkes, the novels traced the rise of the ruthless protagonist, Copperwood, to wealth and power. Censors attacked Dreiser for not condemning Copperwood as a dishonest, cruel, and vicious scoundrel, and for not punishing the protagonist for his sins.

Publication of *The "Genius"* (1915) generated a direct confrontation between Dreiser and his censors, with legal action following. Along with various church groups, the New York Society for the Suppression of Vice sought to suppress the book because it detailed the career of an artist driven by two motivations—a desire for a successful career, and unbridled sexual passion. The society deemed ninety-two passages of the book lewd and profane. When the publisher withdrew the book from circulation, Dreiser took him to court. Although the novelist lost, he alerted the American literary community to the dangers of censorship and eased the way for later writers of realistic fiction. Dreiser's vindication occurred later when the novel appeared uncut in 1923, and capitalized commercially on its notoriety.

By the mid-1920's, rabid censorship restrictions had eased somewhat. When Dreiser brought out the masterpiece *An American Tragedy* (1925), based on a famous murder case, there were only a few outcries about the "hero" who drowns his dowdy pregnant girlfriend so that he can court a rich girl and move into high society. The book was banned in Boston until 1935; by this time, however, a book being banned in Boston actually helped increase sales. At nearby Harvard University, meanwhile, the book was required reading.

See also Adultery; Book publishing; Faulkner, William; Hemingway, Ernest; Literature; Prostitution; Roman à clef; Society for the Suppression of Vice, New York; Steinbeck, John.

Drug education

DEFINITION: Programs designed to educate young people about the dangers of drug use

SIGNIFICANCE: Despite widespread agreement that programs to reduce drug abuse are needed, critics have charged some programs with being counterproductive because they have distorted facts

The American counterculture of the 1960's, with its psychedelic music and widespread use of mind-altering drugs helped bring what had been a marginal subculture to suburbia. Drug use had long been recognized as common among jazz musicians and other marginal groups, but few parents and educators concerned themselves with drug problems until drugs suddenly became more widely known and experienced. State and federal governments began strengthening laws relating to controlled substances, as well as increasing penalties and creating special agencies to combat drug use.

By the mid-1990's the debate over effective approaches to education to prevent drug abuse by children and adolescents had become acrimonious. While few disputed that substance abuse contributed to serious social problems, organizations ranging from the National Organization for the Reform of Marijuana Laws to the American Medical Association (AMA) expressed concern that many drug education programs engaged in censorship and distortion. Many policy analysts began to believe that the long-term effects of the government's war on drugs might be worse than the effects of the drugs themselves.

DARE. Advocates of the most popular drug education curricula in U.S. schools, the Drug Abuse Resistance Education program—known as DARE—claimed that their own educational materials significantly reduced the use of legal drugs, such as alcohol and tobacco, and illegal drugs, such as marijuana and crack cocaine. Critics of DARE, however, cited studies, including one commissioned by the U.S. Justice Department in 1993, indicating that participation in DARE had no statistically significant effect on rates of substance abuse by young people. Rather than effectively educating young people about the real dangers of various drugs, critics claimed that DARE programs distorted facts and used scare tactics, such as claiming that it was possible to overdose fatally on marijuana, that then backfired when students were exposed to conflicting information. Having learned that some so-called facts were actually fiction, students then discounted all of the DARE material. Debates such as this were nothing new, however, as the history of twentieth century drug policy was characterized by melodramatic distortions and suppression of information by government agencies and by drug advocacy groups.

Scholars in criminal justice studies have documented that much of the drug war of the late twentieth century was the product of political opportunism, racism, and media hype. Condemning drug use has always been politically safe. Many politicians have found taking harsh stands on the drug war a productive rhetorical tactic to use when campaigning for election, as no one wants elected officials who are soft on crime. Critics have noted that the pandering of politicians to public hysteria over drug abuse has contributed to ever-harsher mandatory sentencing laws; persons convicted for possession of drugs meant only for personal consumption have frequently served more time in prison than criminals arrested for violent crimes.

By the 1990's the United States enjoyed the dubious distinction of imprisoning a greater percentage of its population than any other industrialized nation. Some criminologists claimed that drug offenses accounted for as much as 80 percent of all incarcerations. Crimes that would have drawn only small fines or probation before the war on drugs were sending drug users to jail. Draconian sentencing laws often seemed irrational when examined from a historical viewpoint.

Although drug abuse has long been recognized as a social problem, government did not become involved in regulating the nonmedical use of drugs until the late nineteenth century. The first antidrug laws were passed in the late nineteenth century to control access to opium dens, which became common in cities such as San Francisco, into which thousands of Chinese workers had immigrated. Even then the initial attempts at regulation did not forbid the use of opium, but rather simply attempted to restrict who could frequent the dens. Typically, Chinese workers were permitted access to opium dens, white workers were not. Drug policy in the United States thus had racist undertones from the start. Society deplored the abuse of drugs and expressed pity for addicts, generally people who had become addicted accidentally to opiates such as laudanum (a solution of opium in alcohol once commonly prescribed for various ailments), but did not attempt to restrict access to anything. This changed in the early twentieth century with the 1906 passage of the Pure Food and Drug Act.

Pure Food and Drug Act. The federal government did not intend the Pure Food and Drug Act as a criminal law to restrict access to drugs. Its intent was to ensure that foods and drugs meant for human consumption were safe. Still, by requiring that certain substances, such as opiates, be available only through prescription, the new law greatly reduced the number of drug addicts in the United States. It also changed the demographic profile of addiction. Prior to the law's enforcement the typical opiate addict was a middle-aged woman who had become addicted accidentally through consumption of an unregulated patent medicine. After passage of the act, drug abuse and drug addiction became problems found mainly among marginalized segments of the population.

Marijuana—the drug which even during the 1990's Americans were most likely to be arrested for possessing—also fell under the Pure Food and Drug Act. Known as a mild euphoric for thousands of years, it was widely cultivated for its fibers, which were used for rope. Its seeds also were used in bird food, and its medicinal applications were also known. Beginning with Utah in 1914, states passed laws that outlawed nonmedical use of marijuana, although it continued to be sold over the counter in drugstores. Until 1930 physicians often prescribed hemp tea or hemp cigarettes to patients suffering from nervous conditions. Some historians have speculated that the drive to outlaw marijuana began in the American southwest as part of a racist reaction to its reported wide usage by Mexican migrant farmworkers; they have also speculated that the term marijuana, rather than its scientific name, *cannabis*, or the more common term, "hemp," was used to play upon racist images. Other historians have suggested that the move to ban marijuana began as part of the general prohibition movement of the early twentieth century. Having succeeded in prohibiting the sale of alcohol, the temperance movement then spread to other substances, including drugs such as narcotics and marijuana.

Tougher Federal Legislation. The federal government began cracking down on hard drugs, such as heroin, with the 1914 Harrison Act, but it initially ignored marijuana. It was not until the 1920's, following the successful prohibition of the sale of alcoholic beverages, that a national movement arose to prohibit the use of marijuana. By 1937 sufficient publicity against the drug had been generated that the federal government passed the Marijuana Tax Act. Films such as *Reefer Madness* (1936) coupled with claims by the Federal Bureau of Narcotics that use of marijuana inevitably led to insanity, violent criminal behavior, and death, convinced much of the general public that marijuana was a drug as deadly as addictive narcotics such as heroin. The Federal Bureau of Narcotics publicity campaign against marijuana was, in fact, so successful that juries found several murderers in the late 1930's to be innocent by reason of insanity after the accused criminals confessed to smoking marijuana prior to committing their crimes. One defendant testified that the drug caused him to grow fangs; another that it turned him into a giant bat. Such exaggerated portrayals of the dangers of marijuana were later recognized as ludicrous, but vestiges of them have remained in some drug education materials.

The Marijuana Tax Act of 1937 passed despite testimony from numerous scientific and medical authorities that marijuana had legitimate medical applications and posed no threat to the general public. Still, law enforcement generally treated marijuana as a less serious crime than the possession or sale of narcotics such as heroin. This tendency to treat marijuana differently continued even after the passage of the 1969 Dangerous Substances Act. That act devised a schedule for drugs that ranked them according to their potential for abuse and their medical usefulness. Schedule one drugs, such as LSD, had little medical use and a high potential for abuse, schedule two drugs had high medical use and high potential for abuse, and schedule three had high medical use and low potential for abuse. Marijuana remained classified as a schedule one drug despite recommendations from organizations such as the Americans for Compassionate Use that it be made available for wider medical use. Although a few liberal politicians were willing to listen to advocacy groups, most lawmakers continued to ignore the findings of even such traditionally conservative organizations as the AMA regarding changes in drug policy.

The DARE Program. The reluctance of politicians to modify existing policy also extends to drug abuse education efforts, particularly where programs such as DARE are concerned. In the early 1980's Los Angeles chief of police Daryl Gates created the first Drug Abuse Resistance Education program in Southern California. Gates—who once drew criticism for claiming that casual drug users should be shot—enjoyed wide success in arresting dealers who sold drugs to high school students, but realized that society needed to discourage young people from buying drugs in the first place. He designed a program aimed primarily at children in the fifth and sixth grades, although some school districts use DARE from kindergarten through the twelfth grade. DARE sends police officers into classrooms to become friends to the children. In addition to emphasizing the dangers of substance abuse, DARE strives to increase children's self-esteem to help them resist peer pressures. DARE supporters have noted that the curriculum includes much more than simply talking about drugs. DARE is also meant to help children feel comfortable coming forward to tell trusted adults—their parents, their teachers, or the local police—about issues such as child abuse and sexual molestation.

The DARE program quickly became popular with educators and lawmakers. Presidents Ronald Reagan and George Bush both supported DARE, and Congress voted millions of dollars in federal funds to help school districts and local law enforcement agencies implement the program around the country. At the same time, criticisms of DARE emerged across a wide spectrum of political beliefs. While DARE has been attacked for a variety of reasons, the main point all critics make is that DARE does not work. Numerous studies, including one by the Canadian government and another by the U.S. Department of Justice, have concluded that there is no statistically significant difference in the rates of drug abuse by young people who have gone through the DARE program and those who have not. Critics have argued that in a time of scarce resources, DARE has been diverting funds from other programs that have demonstrated success rates. Just as the information conveyed in drug education programs has often been colored more by political interests than by scientific fact, so, too, have the interpretations of the success or failure of those drug education programs. DARE, however, which has been popular among the police and conservative politicians, seemed likely to remain the dominant model for drug education for years to come. —*Nancy Farm Mannikko*

See also Birth control education; DARE program; Health epidemic news; Medical research; Sex education; Temperance movements.

BIBLIOGRAPHY

Images of Issues: Typifying Contemporary Social Problems (Hawthorne, N.Y.: Walter de Gruyter, 1995), edited by Joel Best, contains several articles showing how various political interest groups manipulated statistics or used the media to create the appearance of a drug war or an addiction crisis where none actually existed. In *America's Longest War: Rethinking Our Tragic Crusade Against Drugs* (New York: G. P. Putnam, 1993) Stephen B. Duke and Albert C. Gross present an intriguing thesis that the war on drugs actually does more harm to American society than the drug use itself, while a collection of essays edited by Rod L. Evans and Irwin M. Berent, *Drug Legalization: For and Against* (LaSalle, Ill.: Open Court Publishing, 1992), includes economic, historical, and psychological arguments from a wide range of experts on all sides of the issue. Readers interested in a broad overview of the drug use issue will appreciate H. Wayne Morgan's *Drugs in America: A Social History, 1800-1980* (Syracuse: Syracuse University Press, 1981). In *Hallucinogens: Cross-Cultural Perspectives* (Albuquerque: University of New Mexico Press, 1984) Marlene Dobkin de Rios examines the roles drugs have played in non-European cultures, including Plains Indians and Siberian tribes.

Dumas, Alexandre, père

BORN: July 24, 1802, Villers-Cotterêts, Aisne, France
DIED: December 5, 1870, Puys, France
IDENTIFICATION: French novelist and dramatist
SIGNIFICANCE: An exceptionally prolific writer, Dumas saw his works banned in 1863 and placed on the *Index Librorum Prohibitorum*

Alexandre Dumas scandalized Paris in the late 1860's by openly carrying on an affair with the younger actress Adah Isaacs Menken, who worked to publicize pictures such as this. (Library of Congress)

Dumas is best known for such romances as *The Count of Monte Cristo* (1844), *The Three Musketeers* (1844), and *The Man in the Iron Mask* (1848-1550). He claimed to have written more than twelve hundred pieces of work, but that figure is an exaggeration. Dumas dealt with many issues pertaining to the history of France in his novels and plays, and he produced his best work during his middle years, from 1835 until 1860. In 1863, Dumas along with his son—who is known as Alexandre Dumas *fils*—received a Decree of Condemnation which placed all of his writings on the *Index Librorum Prohibitorum* by the Roman Catholic church because of their emphasis on "impure love." He was branded one of the church's eleven "Condemned Novelists" and all his future novels were to be automatically listed, unless they could be shown to be acceptable. This condemnation did not extend to Dumas' dramatic works, however.

Later, some of Dumas' works were given qualified church approval by Abbe Louis Bethleem, who made a detailed study of the French authors, particularly those whose works were placed under the ban of "all love stories." Several of Dumas' minor works and his major works, including *The Count of Monte Cristo* and *The Three Musketeers*, were banned entirely. *The Corsican Brothers* (1844), a story about the intimate sympathy between twin brothers, even when separated, and *The Twin Lieutenants* (1858), a story about the career of Napoleon, along with fifteen other works were designated as suitable only for adults to read. Seventeen minor works by Alexandre Dumas are considered works which may be read by all. These include *The Chronicles of Charlemagne* (1836), a portion of Dumas' series *The Chronicles of France*. Several travel books by Dumas are listed as books that may be read only with serious precautions, including *Ten Days on Mount Sinai* (1839), a narrative of a scientific journey to Egypt and Sinai, and *A Year in Florence* (1841), a travelogue of Dumas' journey through the south of Europe. (Abbe Bethleem did not recommend lifting the prohibition on any of Alexandre Dumas, *fils* novels.)

After the church's Decree of Commendation, Dumas continued to write sparingly until his death, concentrating on dramas and serialized romances. Several of his later works dealt with the turbulent times in French history and are listed under the completely banned works of the author.

See also Balzac, Honoré de; Baudelaire, Charles; Drama and theater; Flaubert, Gustave; France; Gautier, Théophile; Hugo, Victor; *Index Librorum Prohibitorum*; Index on Censorship; Literature; Opera; Sand, George; Stendhal.

Dworkin, Andrea

BORN: September 26, 1946, Camden, New Jersey
IDENTIFICATION: Radical feminist author and philosopher
SIGNIFICANCE: A strong advocate of women's causes, Dworkin is best known for her view that pornography should be prohibited on the grounds it violates women's civil rights

In 1981 Dworkin published a book called *Pornography: Men Hating Women*. This book, more than any others that she later published, brought her to the attention of the general public. In it Dworkin firmly rejects the view that pornography is a form of expression and argues that it is an issue that should even be debated as worthy of the protections given to freedom of speech by the First Amendment to the U.S. Constitution.

To consider pornography a free-speech issue would be, in her opinion, to gloss over the horror of what pornography really is. Liberals who oppose censorship and defend access to pornography on the grounds of freedom of speech do not understand, she contends, what pornography is all about: the violent hatred of men against women, behavior comparable to terrorism. In its turn, the terrorism of pornography leads to further harmful acts by particular men against particular women, including rape and spousal abuse. Just as important, Dworkin takes pornography to be a means for men in general to harm women in general, by confining them to a "sexual underclass" within society.

Together with law professor Catherine MacKinnon, Dworkin has actively tried to influence public policy concerning pornography. In the early 1980's, they proposed antipornography ordinances for the cities of Minneapolis and Indianapolis that would have enabled women to bring civil lawsuits against those involved in the pornography industry. Defining pornography as "the graphic, sexually explicit subordination of women," these ordinances classified pornography more as a type of discriminatory behavior against women than as a form of expression. Although such measures would not have banned pornographic movies and magazines, they would have provided women the opportunity to bring charges against pornographers on the grounds their activities were a violation of women's civil rights.

Although many women supported Dworkin in her efforts to win approval for these ordinances, others, including those belonging to the Feminist Anti-Censorship Task Force, criticized her efforts. They claimed that antipornography regulations might ultimately have harmful consequences for women by playing into the hands of antifeminist groups interested in suppressing feminist sexual imagery and speech.

Both of Dworkin's and MacKinnon's attempts to bring about antipornography measures were unsuccessful. The Minneapolis ordinance was not enacted. The Indianapolis ordinance was locally approved; however, in 1986 it was found by a federal court to be unconstitutional. In its decision concerning *American Booksellers Association, Inc. v. Hudnut*, a court ruled that the ordinance did not clearly demonstrate that pornography was a form of behavior, rather than a form of speech deserving free-speech protection.

In 1988 Dworkin published a collection of lectures and essays under the title *Letters from a War Zone*. This volume documents her struggle to gain access to mainstream media such as *The New York Times* and the *Washington Post* in order to defend her antipornographic views. Because these papers and others would not publish her, she became, in her view, a victim of censorship at the hands of public guardians of the freedom of speech.

See also *American Booksellers Association, Inc. v. Hudnut*; *Butler v. The Queen*; Feminism; MacKinnon, Catharine A.; *New York Times, The*; Pornography; Women, violence against; Women Against Pornography.

E

Eagle Forum

FOUNDED: 1972

TYPE OF ORGANIZATION: Profamily, private enterprise association

SIGNIFICANCE: This conservative-action group has been important because of the visibility and impact of its founder's political activities

Phyllis Schlafly founded the Eagle Forum in reaction to the feminist movement of the early 1970's. Under her leadership the organization developed into a politically active body describing itself as "leading the profamily movement since 1972." Its goal was to encourage its members to participate in public-policy making at all levels in order to help perpetuate what it believes has made America great: "family values," private enterprise, liberty, and a strong national military. It also has encouraged parents to question the role of public school education in their children's lives.

The Eagle Forum has opposed feminism and what it calls the "hidden agenda" of the Equal Rights Amendment movement. It had also opposed centralized federal government, excessive taxes, and government subsidizing of art. It has argued that a strong national defense is important for protecting America and that allowing homosexuals and women in the military conflicts with that belief. The organization's monthly newsletter, *The Phyllis Schlafly Report*, discusses new politically relevant topics every month. The group also publishes the *Education Reporter*, a monthly newspaper addressing important educational issues.

See also National Federation for Decency; Parents' Alliance to Protect Our Children; Pressure groups.

Ecstasy

TYPE OF WORK: Film

RELEASED: 1933

DIRECTOR: Gustav Machaty (1901-1963)

SUBJECT MATTER: After a young woman finds sexual gratification in an adulterous affair, her impotent, older husband commits suicide

SIGNIFICANCE: Long considered an erotic classic because of its scene in which actress Hedy Lamarr swims nude, this Czechoslovakian film was banned in the United States because of its closeup shots of Lamarr's ecstatic face during a love scene

In the original version of *Ecstasy* the young wife played by Lamarr has her clothes carried off by her horse while she swims nude; she then runs through a rainstorm to the cabin of

Hedy Lamarr's nude swimming scene in Ecstasy *caused the film to be banned in the United States but it did not damage her acting career.* (AP/Wide World Photos)

a young engineer, with whom she makes love. At the moment the woman achieves sexual climax, the camera closes in on her face, revealing the ecstasy that she is experiencing.

In 1935 U.S. Customs seized the film as it was being imported into the country. A federal district court jury then ruled that the film's closeups of Lamarr's face during the love scene made it "obscene and immoral." The film's distributor appealed this decision, but a federal marshal meanwhile burned the seized print, and the distributor's appeal was dismissed for lack of evidence.

In 1937 a revised version of the film was imported into the United States. In this version the woman does not make love with the engineer until after her impotent husband dies and she has married the younger man. This version passed through U.S. customs; however, despite its crucial change, it was banned by the New York state censorship board. As the federal jury had done earlier, the New York board objected to the film's closeups of the woman's face during the love scene because it "unduly emphasized the carnal side of the sex relationship."

Taking his cue from a recent U.S. Supreme Court decision regarding the obscenity of James Joyce's novel *Ulysses*, the distributor of *Ecstasy* argued that the only proper question to ask was whether the film as a whole was obscene. New York's state supreme court rejected this argument, however, ruling that the state could refuse to license a film even if only part of it was objectionable. Afterward, new prints of the film from which the criticized closeups and nude scenes were removed were shown throughout the United States, but even this version did not get a Hays Code seal of approval. In 1940, a second revised version of the film was finally licensed for exhibition in New York.

See also Adultery; *Amants, Les*; Customs laws, U.S.; Film censorship; Hays Code; Motion Picture Association of America; Obscenity: legal definitions; Sex in the arts; *Ulysses*; Warhol, Andy.

Education

DEFINITION: Formal training in academic institutions

SIGNIFICANCE: Because of their central role in training youth and fostering cultural and moral values, educational systems have faced heavy censorship pressures from a variety of critics

Some have suggested that intellectual development has been replaced, at the institutions that should promote such development, by indoctrination. Nat Hentoff, for example, has charged that efforts to restrict free expression of ideas in America have been nowhere more pronounced than in the schools.

Schooling has the potential to influence how and what future adults think, as well as the way they act. For example, the teaching of the German language in U.S. public schools was restricted after the defeat of Germany in World War I. During the Red Scare of the 1950's members of allegedly subversive groups were not allowed to teach and many faculty members were required to sign loyalty oaths. Educational censorship did not go away during the 1990's. People for the American Way, a national anticensorship organization based in Washing-

ton, D.C., estimated that there were more acts of school censorship (a total of 375) during the 1993-1994 school year than at any time since it began tracking attempts in 1982.

The amount and types of censorship that have taken place in America may seem trivial compared to that in places with authoritarian regimes such as Cuba or Iran, but such regimes are not regarded as proper sources for comparison. Rather, freedom of expression as guaranteed in the U.S. Constitution is regarded as the source for comparison. It is the comparison of reality to the First Amendment that is probably most appropriate in assessing the extent and applicability of censorship in American education. Various studies indicate that approximately a third of all attempts to censor materials in American schools are successful.

Classroom Subjects and Conservatives. There are many topics of discussion and formal exploration in school that persons of one political persuasion or another think should be restricted in some way. For example, conservatives tend to believe that if any sex education must be taught in classrooms, it should consist of reproductive facts only, while reinforcing "traditional values." The conservative approach to drug education also tends to promote the idea that any exploration of the patterns of, reasons for, and history of drug use might spur adolescent experimentation. Many attempts to ban books from classrooms have been accurately attributed to the political and religious Right. William Shakespeare's *Macbeth* (1606) has been criticized because it has witches in it. *The Catcher in the Rye* (1951) has been censored because it contains—rather than advocates the use of—a word most adolescents know. The works of authors such as Arthur Miller and Kurt Vonnegut have been attacked for various reasons, although their criticism of the cultural, social, and religious mores of the United States is perhaps the central target.

The People's Republic of China overcame traditional restrictive attitudes to begin formal sex education for the first time during the 1980's in order to support government population-growth policies. On the other hand, a more developed Asian country, Japan, has quite constrained sex education, partly as a result of lobbying by the Unification Church.

In addition to sex education, conservatives have censored the teaching of evolution. Believing Charles Darwin's theory of evolution to be contrary to Christian "creationism," they have attempted to prohibit its teaching. Religious conservatives have attempted to force schools to teach "scientific creationism" as a competing perspective to evolution. Another science subject that conservatives have often censored is environmentalism. Classroom instruction in this is often seen as anticapitalist and thus, by questionable extension, un-American. Scientific findings regarding the environment have been dismissed or challenged.

During the 1990's social scientific examinations of ethnic studies, multiculturalism, and feminism have provided battlegrounds on which American liberals and conservatives have debated how these ideas should be addressed, if at all. Revisionist historians have met stiff resistance in their attempts to change curricula to reflect these perspectives. In an ironic twist, attempts have been made by religious groups to designate an ideology that they call "secular humanism" as a religion in order to get it banned from public schools under the constitutional provisions separating church and state.

Classroom Texts. There are two basic methods by which censors can influence messages conveyed in the books used in school classrooms. One is to censor existing books. This method tends to draw greater attention, bringing about controversies which in turn may bring communities to agree—though often to agree not to censor. A second method is prior restraint, which is more insidious, because it is more complicated, private, and procedural. Book publishers are in the business of seeking profits. Those that sell books to schools must have their books approved by committees. The committees, in turn, evaluate books based on criteria established by other committees. To get a schoolbook approved—or adopted as the process is called in textbook publishing—publishers examine the established criteria and produce books to meet them. Publishers generally avoid controversy because it means fewer textbook sales. Those who influence the criteria for textbook selection therefore influence the content of textbooks. Conservatives and liberals alike have pressured educational administrators to write criteria for textbook selection that favor various viewpoints.

Textbooks and Liberals. Liberals have been effective in quietly pressuring textbook publishers to make their products inoffensive to their own views. Consequently, most books published for classroom use offer positive examples of gender equality, racial and ethnic minorities in professional positions, and other images characteristic of the liberal agenda. Stories in literature textbooks have been cut for reasons as diverse as being offensive to women to endorsing junk food. Conservatives have also had success at influencing the publishing process. The result has been a widely lamented trend in textbook publishing in which engaging, detailed, and opinionated books are forced out of classrooms in favor of bland, general, and inoffensive books. For example, liberals have censored such engaging books as *Adventures of Huckleberry Finn* (1884) for alleged racial insensitivity.

Electronic Media. Most American educational institutions have computers and other technological tools. This is the newest area of interest in educational censorship. The potential censorship of cyberspace is an avenue explored by conservatives and liberals. The Internet and the world wide web have innumerable opportunities for students doing research for school assignments. Students may also encounter sexually explicit materials or hate speech on the Internet. Censors from the Left and the Right have proposed restrictions. Given the lack of hierarchy in the Internet, however, the method by which censorship could be implemented has remained unclear.

Another form of censorship applicable to computers is comparable to the censorship of textbooks. Most computer manufacturers sell their products with a variety of software products already installed. The Apple Computer company was threatened with a boycott if it did not remove something someone considered offensive from a preloaded bundle included with machines it was selling to schools.

During the 1990's some U.S. schools began using educational cable television developed specifically for schools but supported by private sponsors. Many critics from liberal and conservative camps agreed that advertising has no place in the curricula and should be censored.

Teaching and Evaluation Techniques. Certain methods by which ideas may be imparted and assessed have been challenged in America during the 1980's and 1990's. Role-playing, because it may encourage sympathy for those with "deviant" lifestyles, for example, came under attack on occasion. Values-clarification exercises, which encourage students to consider critically their beliefs, has been challenged as contributing to a rejection of parental and other authority. Techniques focusing on development of student self-esteem have been criticized as attempts to avoid the realities of teaching difficult subjects—such as math and English—in which students may, in fact, fail. Other teaching techniques that have consistently come under fire include sensitivity training, behavior modification, and situational ethics.

A 1990's trend in U.S. classroom grading and graduation standards, outcome-based education, came under attack in various areas. Critics have asserted that its emphasis on acquiring politically correct values may override the traditional values favored by most parents. They have also sought to restrict its application, arguing that outcome-based education interferes with the achievement of basic academic skills.

Libraries. Virtually all levels of formal education make repositories of books and periodicals available to students. School libraries have been subject to certain forms of censorship. The most notable form of censorship of library materials occurs when pressure groups lobby to have certain books or magazines removed. This technique is also the least likely to succeed. U.S. Courts have ruled repeatedly that the Constitution protects the free access to information. Some libraries may voluntarily remove books that are deemed offensive enough by certain groups that these groups voice strong and persistent opposition to the presence of the materials. Libraries are least likely to be susceptible to political pressure when they follow a set of written criteria for the acquisition of materials that has been developed by an omnibus committee. More insidious is the self-censorship that goes on in libraries; however, it is difficult to document.

Extracurricular Activities. Various nonclassroom opportunities intended for education have come under the criticism of certain pressure groups. Among these have been school newspapers, school plays, and support groups for certain types of students. The most serious blow against the freedom to express ideas in America came in the Supreme Court's *Hazelwood School District v. Kuhlmeier* (1988) decision. The Court ruled that school administrators do have the right to prior approval of anything to be published in school newspapers. This precedent seems to have set the stage for more arbitrary restrictions by school administrators, as well as more challenges to school materials and activities by various pressure groups.

During the 1990's in the United States, any school play carrying even the slightest supernatural theme—whether traditionally Christian or otherwise—was likely to be challenged by pressure groups of either the Left or the Right. Similarly, any theater presentation that depicts "deviant" lifestyles or other unpopular perspectives is likely to draw the ire of either liberal or conservative censors.

The Catholic Defense League launched an attack against St. Paul, Minnesota, public schools that permitted support groups for gay and lesbian students. In Los Angeles, a similar support group has sustained attacks from various censors. Misinterpretation of the constitutional guarantees separating church and state has led to denying many students in public schools the opportunity to use school facilities for their religious activities.

Objections about the celebration, or even acknowledgment, of Christian holidays in public classrooms have long been raised by the Left. Consequently, many rituals and customs associated with Christmas and Easter have been restricted from even casual classroom use. Halloween has also been attacked. Conservatives have been concerned that classroom observances of Halloween generate an interest in the occult and other anti-Christian activities. Liberals have been concerned that many of the costumed characters glorify violence, sexism, and other undesirable attributes.

The Censors. Those most desiring censorship of certain educational issues in America have been parents and pressure groups, usually working hand in hand. Parents may object to something happening in the schools and seek the assistance of existing pressure groups in order to facilitate their intended action. Pressure groups may seek the support of parents in local communities to facilitate their agenda in that locale. Parents and pressure groups, however, typically call for censorship; others actually censor.

Those who most commonly have the power to censor are school boards and school administrators. Usually, they censor at the behest—or the expectation of the behest—of vocal parents and organized pressure groups. Since school boards are composed of elected members of the community in which the schools they regulate are found, they are often responsive to community pressure. Since school administrators are often subject to dismissal if they fail to please their school boards, they are usually responsive to boards. If school boards are unresponsive to the desires of parents and pressure groups, those uncooperative members are often replaced in the next election by members who are pledged to support the agenda of offended parents and pressure groups.

Teachers and librarians are likely to be the final implementors of censorship upon orders by school administrators. Teachers also may decide on their own to censor, or they may become self-censors, wishing to avoid trouble with potential censors of either political persuasion. As is the case with textbooks, the desire not to arouse the ire of people with opposing views has led to the tepid presentation of ideas and facts in the classroom.   —*Scott Magnuson-Martinson*

See also Drug education; Environmental education; Ethnic studies; Evolution; Libraries, school; Multiculturalism; Newspapers, student; Sex education; Textbooks.

BIBLIOGRAPHY

Nat Hentoff's *Free Speech for Me—But Not For Thee: How*

the Left and the Right Relentlessly Censor Each Other (New York: HarperCollins, 1992) describes the history of attempts by various groups to restrict free expression in America. Probably nowhere else has this been more pronounced than in the schools. For a legalistic perspective on education and censorship, see Anthony Whitson's *Constitution and Curriculum: Hermeneutical Semiotics of Cases and Controversies in Education, Law and Social Science* (London: Falmer Press, 1991). Ilan Peleg, ed., presents the international picture, including educational restrictions, in *Patterns of Censorship Around the World* (Boulder, Colo.: Westview Press, 1993). Herbert N. Foerstel's *Banned in the U.S.A.: A Reference Guide to Book Censorship in Schools and Public Libraries* (Westport, Conn.: Greenwood Press, 1994) gives a thorough analysis of several major incidents in schools from 1976 to 1992, as well as a summary of the challenges to the most banned books of the 1990's. The Office of Intellectual Freedom's *Intellectual Freedom Manual* (4th ed. Chicago: American Library Association, 1992) provides ideas and approaches to circumvent censorship. Another resource for ways to deal effectively with attempted censorship is Henry F. Reichman's *Censorship and Selection: Issues and Answers for Schools* (rev. ed. Chicago: American Library Association, 1993). *CQ Researcher* 3, no. 7 (February 19, 1993) has several articles addressing aspects of school censorship. Stephen Bates's "The Textbook Wars: When Does a 'Censor' Become a 'Positive Pressure Group'? Ask Holt Rinehart," in *National Review* 45, no. 18 (September 20, 1993), looks at this issue from a different perspective. Barbara Dority explores "Public Education Under Siege" in *The Humanist* 54, no. 4 (July-August, 1994). Local polluter pressure on school discussion is addressed in Richard Wolf's "Seldom Is Heard a Discouraging Word" in *Environmental Action Magazine* 26, no. 1 (Spring, 1994). Teachers' fears of losing their jobs are explored by Elizabeth Noll in "The Ripple Effect of Censorship: Silencing in the Classroom" in *English Journal* 83, no. 8 (December, 1994).

Ellis, Henry Havelock

BORN: February 2, 1859, Croydon, Surrey, England

DIED: July 8, 1939, Hintlesham, Suffolk, England

IDENTIFICATION: English critic and sexologist

SIGNIFICANCE: Ellis' pioneering studies of human sexuality helped break down the barriers of silence and guilt that had long prevented people from understanding the sexual elements in their natures

Havelock Ellis—as he was commonly known—was born in a London suburb to a family of seafarers. However, apart from a trip around the world with his father at age seven, he grew up in the city and was educated in rather poor private schools. As he notes in his autobiography, *My Life* (1939), his real education came from extensive personal reading. At sixteen he again went voyaging with his father, but this time he remained in Australia, where he taught school for four years. During this period he began to develop a concept of values that combined the scientific and aesthetic. He also moved away from traditional religion.

Ellis returned to England and entered medical school in

1881. He was an indifferent student, sometimes just skipping exams, and failed to get licensed by the Colleges of Physicians and Surgeons, settling for credentials from the Society of Apothecaries. Fortunately, he rarely practiced. His years in school did provide opportunities. His literary bent was given expression in his work as editor of the Mermaid play reprint series, which provided the first popularly priced unexpurgated editions of many classical dramas. When he gave up that job in 1888, his skill at editing and publishing had produced a significant contribution to English culture. He was also active in scientific publishing; as editor of the Contemporary Science Series, he got many excellent contributors to produce what became standard texts.

A controversial life-style also took shape. He developed an intimate relationship with the author Olive Schreiner, writing numerous love letters to her—a practice he continued after she left for South Africa in 1889. In 1891 he married Edith Mary Oldham Lees, with whom he had a relationship that allowed both partners unusual freedom. Schreiner and Edith Ellis knew of their common connection to Ellis and when Edith died in 1916 Schreiner attended the funeral.

Although Ellis first intended to write about religion, he soon shifted his attention to human sexuality. The first volume of his magisterial *Studies in the Psychology of Sex* appeared in 1897; he published five more volumes by 1910 and a seventh in 1928. The first volume, *Sexual Inversion*, was quickly challenged. In 1898 a bookseller was indicted for selling it, and although a defense fund was organized, he pled guilty. Ellis, equally liable to prosecution under British law, left the country for a time, and avoided legal problems by publishing later volumes in the United States.

By approaching his subject openly and from a biological rather than clinical perspective, Ellis opened the subject to social science. Sigmund Freud credited Ellis with anticipating his own conclusions. Ellis' work *The Criminal* (1899) was the first English effort to deal with the psychological causes and treatment of crime. His autobiography, *My Life*, which portrays his unusual marriage, is his best-known work; *Man and Woman* (1894) is perhaps his best single volume.

See also Kinsey Report; Obscene Publications Acts; Sex education; Sex manuals; Society for the Suppression of Vice, U.K.; *Well of Loneliness, The.*

Elmer Gantry

Type of work: Book
Published: 1927
Author: Sinclair Lewis (1885-1951)
Subject matter: Novel about a handsome young man who becomes a successful Fundamentalist preacher despite his intellectual and moral shortcomings
Significance: This satirical work questioning the sincerity and sanctity of religious institutions was attacked from pulpits as well as in print, spurring sales and ensuring its author's place in literary history

It was certain that this novel would generate attempts at censorship, for its author was no stranger to controversy and its publisher, Harcourt Brace and Company, was eager to pro-

mote it as a sensational exposé rather than as the fierce satire it really was. Lewis' best-selling earlier satires, *Main Street* (1920) and *Babbitt* (1922), had lampooned the values of midwestern small town life, and he had created a firestorm in literary circles by refusing to accept a Pulitzer Prize for the novel *Arrowsmith* (1925).

Burt Lancaster won an Academy Award for his commanding portrayal of the charlatan preacher Elmer Gantry in the 1960 film adaptation. (AP/Wide World Photos)

Some objected to the spicy scenes of physical passion in *Elmer Gantry*, but most of the clergy who opposed the book were more outraged by the shallowness and hypocrisy of its main character. Much of Lewis' background research took place in Kansas City, Missouri, and ministers there were particularly angered and vociferous. However, a local Unitarian clergyman, L. M. Birkhead, defended the novel as a warning against self-righteousness. In the decades that followed, the book would become widely available.

In 1960, a film version of *Elmer Gantry* was made, with Burt Lancaster, in the title role, winning an Oscar for best actor.

See also Christianity; Lewis, Sinclair; Literature; Religion.

Ely, Richard Theodore

Born: April 13, 1854, Ripley, New York
Died: October 4, 1943, Old Lyme, Connecticut
Identification: American university educator

SIGNIFICANCE: Ely's trial by his university on charges of advocating socialism led to a celebrated affirmation of academic freedom

Ely was the son of a self-taught civil engineer and a gifted art and music teacher. After graduating first in his class at Columbia University in 1876, he earned a doctorate in economics in Europe. On returning to the United States in 1881, he joined the faculty at The Johns Hopkins University. Eleven years later he was invited to head the School of Economics, Political Science and History at the University of Wisconsin in Madison.

A prolific writer on economics, Ely early expressed sympathy for working men and women. His concern for labor led to his being accused of promoting socialism to his university students by Wisconsin's recently elected state superintendent of education, Oliver E. Wells, in 1894. Published in *The Nation*—then a bastion of conservatism—these charges received national publicity. Wells accused Ely of actively supporting efforts to unionize printers at a printing company that had a state contract. A committee appointed by the university to investigate the charges concluded that Wells had based his accusations on isolated comments taken out of context, and that Ely had no connection whatever with efforts to unionize employees.

The committee's report contained an affirmation of academic freedom afterward put on a bronze plaque affixed to the university's main administration building:

> Whatever may be the limitations which trammel inquiry elsewhere we believe the great state University of Wisconsin should ever encourage that fearless sifting and winnowing by which alone the truth can be found.

During his distinguished career in economics, Ely helped to found the school of institutional economics, which drew general principles from conditions actually observed in the economy—what Ely called the "look and see" method. He also was a founder and early president of the American Economic Association. His college textbook, *Outlines of Economics*, was widely used.

See also Intellectual freedom; Labor unions; Universities.

Emerson, Ralph Waldo

BORN: May 25, 1803, Boston, Massachusetts
DIED: April 27, 1882, Concord, Massachusetts
IDENTIFICATION: American poet, essayist, and lecturer
SIGNIFICANCE: Emerson's most famous work, an essay asserting the need for independent thought and nonconformity in the face of social conventions and dogmas, has long been a powerful argument against censorship

The son of a Unitarian minister, Emerson embarked on a clerical career of his own until a crisis of faith drove him to a different vocation. After he graduated from Harvard College in 1821, he was ordained a Unitarian minister at a Boston church in 1829, but he resigned from the ministry in 1832. In his subsequent career as a poet, essayist, and lecturer, he became the most influential spokesman of New England Transcendentalism—a school of philosophy kindred in content to Continental Romanticism.

Perhaps the best-known of Emerson's writings is his essay "Self Reliance," which celebrates individuals who remain undaunted by attempts of societies, institutions, and the masses to muzzle them. "Society everywhere," Emerson wrote, "is in conspiracy against the manhood of every one of its members." Nonconformity, he believed, was the unchanging price of manhood; dissent, its natural garb; and self-confidence, its true habitat. "It is only as a man puts off all foreign support, and stands alone, that I see him to be strong and to prevail. He is weaker by every recruit to his banner. Is not a man better than a town?"

See also Literature; Orwell, George; Poetry; Religion; Thoreau, Henry David.

English Commonwealth

DATE: 1649-1660
PLACE: England
SIGNIFICANCE: Under Oliver Cromwell's Puritan-dominated government, which briefly replaced England's monarchy, censorship controls over publishing were increased and many aspects of traditional English life were subjected to tight government regulation

In May, 1649, four months after the execution of King Charles I for treason, England was declared to be a "Commonwealth and Free State." The leader of the new government was a Puritan, Oliver Cromwell. Charles I also had been an enemy of free speech. In 1637 a Star Chamber decree established serious punishment for the printing, reprinting, or importing of any book without first obtaining a royal license. Censorship had caused John Milton to defend free speech in his *Areopagitica* (1644) on the grounds that truth will always prevail over error. While Cromwell's Commonwealth permitted a large number of Protestant writers to publish, he strictly regulated publication and imposed levels of censorship not dreamed possible by Charles I. One of Cromwell's first acts was drowning out the final words of Charles I with a roar of drums shortly before the unfortunate king's execution.

During Cromwell's rule as Lord Protector, England was divided into districts, each supervised by a major general who possessed full administrative jurisdiction. The new Puritan rulers were, by the standards of many, religious prudes. Strict morality laws were passed. Swearing and even flirting were prohibited. Field sports, musical concerts, theater, and church festivals came to an abrupt end. Dress was strictly regulated, as was personal conduct on the sabbath. The greatest attack on British culture, however, was the closing of ale houses. The banning of overt celebration of Christmas and Easter ranked as a close second. Feasting on Easter or Christmas could mean confiscation of the roast by eager soldiers. Too enthusiastic preaching on these holidays resulted in numerous ministers being taken into custody. May Day celebrations, with dancing around the Maypole, was another practice to be stamped out in an effort to turn England into a land of saints.

Cromwell's regime did tolerate a large number of diverse Protestant sects. Even Quakers, who believed in direct communion with the Spirit and hated formal worship, were tolerated to a point. This point, however, was transgressed by

James Nagler, a Quaker leader, who was tried and convicted of blasphemy. Parliament deliberated several hours over which parts of him should be cut off. The Levellers and the Diggers, who advocated a more social and political equality, found themselves purged from army ranks and silenced. The famous Barebones Parliament, which allied itself squarely behind Cromwell's religious policies, was nevertheless dissolved by Cromwell for criticizing the expense of maintaining a large standing army in times of peace.

The passing of the Commonwealth after the death of the Lord Protector in 1658, and the restoration of the Stuart Dynasty in 1660, ended the obnoxious attempts to censor a wide section of society. Merry England returned, but strict laws on literary censorship continued. The Licensing Act of 1662 forbade the printing of books or pamphlets that did not conform to the Church of England, and required all publications to be licensed and registered with the Stationers Company, a book publishing guild. The Licensing Act was ultimately allowed to lapse in 1694, when strict libel laws were substituted in its place.

See also *Areopagitica*; Licensing Act of 1662; Milton, John; Puritans; Reformation, the; United Kingdom.

Environmental education

DEFINITION: Education about the relationship between human beings and their natural and artificial surroundings

SIGNIFICANCE: Many environmental education programs are accused of fostering censorship

Environmental education has been taught in the United States since 1970. Because the Tenth Amendment, by implication, reserves education to the states, it is up to each state to decide if its students should have environmental education. In 1995 thirty states had laws mandating some type of instruction on environmental issues and concepts.

The proponents of environmental education have claimed that it has helped the nation, states, and localities make tremendous progress in protecting human health and the natural environment. Opponents of environmental education claim that it is dominated by a doomsday approach to environmental issues. Such an approach, opponents argue, uses scare tactics and guilt to induce political actions by the students. Still others claim that environmental education caters to big business and politics, thereby censoring environmentalist ideas.

Environmental Education Laws. Because each state legislature has complete choice regarding environmental education, there are many differences among state programs. Many of the state laws require that environmental education be taught in most subject matter classes and at all grade levels. Students typically learn about environmental issues in a variety of classes, including science, math, history, health, and English. All states that do choose to have environmental education construct their curriculum programs through the state legislature. Florida, Wisconsin, and Arizona have all been cited as being the leading states in teaching environmental education programs. Each state government can also go to the federal government for environmental education funding.

In 1990 the National Environmental Education Act was passed by Congress. This legislation charged the Environmental Protection Agency with the responsibility of coordinating national efforts to increase public understanding of environmental issues, and to advance and support environmental training and education throughout all fifty states. As environmental education has gained in public awareness, critics have claimed that it censors important information, such as the economic principles that, they argue, govern human resource and energy use.

Economics. Some critics of environmental education charge that it censors basic economic principles, such as the price mechanism, consumer behavior, and innovation; and as a result, environmental education misguides more than it teaches. When textbooks of environmental education use selective data to urge students to conserve natural resources, they often attempt to induce guilt among students for not caring for the earth. Rather than learning how economic realities adjust for scarcity and consumer behavior, critics contended that students are only taught that resources are finite and that students should conserve and preserve these resources to save the planet from doom. It is believed that without the teaching of economic principles, students will not learn how competition and the price mechanism stimulate technological innovation and creative solutions to environmental problems. Thus, efforts to save the planet will be inconsistent with larger economic goals that humans pursue, such as long-term economic growth and a rising per capita income. In conclusion, critics argue that by censoring or incompletely explaining economical principles within environmental education programs, textbooks and teachers are seriously miseducating students about energy and natural resource issues.

Cooption by Industry. A completely different criticism of censorship in environmental education comes from environmentalists who believe that environmental education has been diluted by extractive industries such as mining, chemical, ranching, farming, and logging who maintain powerful influences throughout state legislatures. As mentioned earlier, state legislatures have a choice of whether or not they want environmental education and also what it should and should not include. As environmental education has increased in popularity among the states, it is charged that the politicians concerned about representing economics often attempt to change the curriculum to please big business groups. For example, in 1994 the Arizona state legislature erased the state-wide mandate to teach environmental legislation and revised the curriculum language to include more diversity in political and scientific views on the environment and less advocacy. The Arizona legislature also restricted the flow of grant money to schools and transferred many environmental education funds to ranchers, farmers, and miners who were allotted the money so that they could host field trips for students to show how their businesses operate with the environment.

Different Needs and Concerns. Another element of censorship in environmental education is the problem of different needs and concerns among youth across America. Big-city students may worry more about guns and violence than rain forests. Poor rural students may be concerned about their health more in terms of farming pesticides and herbicides than city smog.

In 1995 the National Environmental Education and Training Foundation did a national survey of fourth-through twelfth-grade students on their concerns, education, and action related to the environment. The results illustrate a great disparity of needs and interests between the children of middle class school districts and students from poor school districts. Findings include: Among disadvantaged students, the environment ranks eighth among a list of ten societal issues that students from disadvantaged areas want to make better; students from disadvantaged areas are more concerned about present and immediate environmental problems than students from non-disadvantaged areas, who were more concerned about the future; all students agreed that human health was the number one reason for protecting the environment, but the margin was higher among students in disadvantaged areas; girls are more likely than boys to worry about the environment.

The survey results seem to indicate that because of the differences in needs and concerns between school districts and students, environmental education should not be implemented universally across income levels, cultures, and geographical areas. When programs are implemented without the knowledge of local living realities, it is contended that environmental education overlooks different interests between students and geographical areas and thus censors important information.

As is the case with many other education programs and subjects, environmental education has had to confront the charge of censoring certain topics and ideas. Environmental education has been the subject of criticism from all sides in the debate over environmental issues and politics. Because different parts of the United States are dominated by different political attitudes and needs, the charges of censorship vary considerably.   —*Matthew J. Lindstrom*

See also Pesticide industry; Political correctness; Saro-Wiwa, Ken; Science; Textbooks; Toxic waste news.

BIBLIOGRAPHY

Merryl Hammond and Rob Collins, *One World, One Earth: Educating Children for Social Responsibility* (Gabriola Island, B.C.: New Society, 1993), develops the thesis that students should be taught how to be political activists and act in an environmentally "responsible" fashion. Steve Jackstadt and Michael Sanera, "Environmental Education: Turning Kids into Political Activists," *The Freeman: Ideas on Liberty* (October, 1995), critiques the dominant form of environmental education, which constructs the curriculum in such a way so as to mold students around the environmentalist political agenda. In her essay "Enviro Education: Is It Science, Civics—or Propaganda?" *Garbage* (April/May, 1993), Patricia Poore claims that much of "enviro-education" is not grounded in sound science or civics, but is muddled with scare tactics to convince children to follow the course of the big environmental groups. The entire Spring, 1995, issue of *EPA Journal* is devoted to environmental education and how the EPA contributes to such education across the country.

Equal Access Act

ENACTED: August 11, 1984

PLACE: United States (national)

SIGNIFICANCE: This federal law requires public secondary schools receiving federal financial assistance that create limited open forums not to deny students opportunities to conduct meetings on their premises solely on the basis of the content of the speech at such meetings

In a 1981 case entitled *Widmar v. Vincent*, the U.S. Supreme Court ruled that a student religious group at the University of Missouri should be allowed to use campus facilities for its meetings. The state-supported public institution had previously allowed only nonreligious student groups access to its facilities. When it was approached by members of a student religious group, the university denied the group use of its facilities in order not to violate the establishment clause of the First Amendment to the U.S. Constitution. In deciding in favor of these students, the Court ruled that allowing only nonreligious groups to use the same facilities violated the religious groups' rights to freedom of speech.

Congressional Response. Following the *Widmar* decision Congress passed the Equal Access Act in 1984. This act effectively extended the Supreme Court's Widmar decision to include all pubic secondary schools that receive federal funds. The act required all such secondary schools that create limited open forums for noncurriculum-related student groups to meet during noninstructional times not to deny similar access to other student groups solely on the basis of the religious, political, philosophical, or other content of their meetings. Thus, any public secondary school that allowed at least one voluntary student-initiated and nonschool-sponsored club or group unrelated to specific classes to meet on school premises outside of normal classroom instructional settings, must allow any other student groups to conduct their meetings at school in a similar fashion.

Although broadly worded, the legislation limited the scope of access in certain situations. For example, school administrators were permitted to deny access to any student group whose meetings had the potential to interfere with the orderly conduct of educational activities within the school. Otherwise eligible student groups were also restricted in certain other ways; for example, nonschool persons could not direct, control, or regularly attend group activities. Also, if a student group were to embrace a religious orientation, school personnel could be present at its meetings only in a nonparticipatory capacity. Along these same lines, student groups would lose their eligibility under the act if they were sponsored by the school, its agents, or its employees. However, the act also provided that schools and their employees had the authority to maintain order and discipline, to protect the well-being of students and faculty, and to ensure that student involvement in group activities would be strictly voluntary.

The law gave public secondary schools the option of avoiding its requirements by simply declining to create limited open forums. Schools could accomplish this by denying the use of their facilities to all noncurriculum-related student groups, while restricting access only to groups directly connected to existing school curricula. For example, the existence of a student-initiated Spanish club in a high school that provides Spanish-language instruction would not fall under the act's jurisdiction. By contrast, groups such as a scuba club or student service club closely related to nonschool organizations probably would trigger the act, thereby opening the door for other noncurriculum-related groups to request access to school facilities. It should also be noted that any school district that would normally be subject to the Equal Access Act that forgoes federal funding is not affected by the act.

Subsequent Litigation. In 1990 the U.S. Supreme Court was asked to consider the constitutionality of the Equal Access Act and whether the establishment clause of the First Amendment prohibited a secondary school with a limited open forum from denying access to a student religious group. In *Board of Education of the Westside Community Schools v. Mergens* (1990) the Court ruled that the act was constitutional. The Court concluded that Congress had not implied an endorsement of religion when it acknowledged the presumed maturity of secondary school students in schools with limited open forums voluntarily to form religious or other types of clubs.

In reaching this decision, the Court confronted Congress' failure to define several key terms and concepts within its act. For example, since "noncurriculum related student group" was not defined, the Court had to develop its own interpretation of what Congress meant by the term. The Court held that any student club involving subject matter comparable to that in a class that was being taught—or that would soon be taught—in a regularly scheduled course would not trigger the act. Similarly, the act would not be triggered if the group's subject matter concerned a body of courses taken as a whole (such as student government), or in cases in which group participation is either required or results in the awarding of academic credit (such as school band or choir).

After the *Mergens* case was decided in 1990 at least one court ruled on the question of the durational length of a secondary school limited open forum. In *Pope by Pope v. East Brunswick Board of Education* (1993), the U.S. Third Circuit Court of Appeals held that although a school district had created a limited open forum at a high school when it recognized a noncurriculum-related student group, the district retained authority to eliminate all its noncurriculum-related student groups and totally close its forum.

Conclusion. As the Equal Access Act has been interpreted by the Supreme Court, public secondary schools that create limited open forums by allowing noncurriculum-related student clubs to meet on their premises during noninstructional hours may not arbitrarily discriminate against other student groups solely on the basis of their religious, philosophical, or political content or orientations. As the act's title implies, Congress supports the notion that all students wishing to meet for legal and nondisruptive purposes must have the same access to public facilities that is afforded to other noncurricular student clubs or groups. Whenever the act has been triggered, it has generally prevented public school authorities from unilaterally abridging the rights of secondary school students to gather and discuss topics and issues of common interest on school grounds during noninstructional time.

—*Fred Hartmeister*

See also Education; First Amendment; Religion; Religious education; School prayer.

BIBLIOGRAPHY

Arval A. Morris' "The Equal Access Act After Mergens" in *West's Education Law Reporter* (vol. 61, no. 4, 1990) provides an expanded and scholarly analysis of the relationship between the Equal Access Act and the *Mergens* decision. For a comparable examination of the same relationship, see Lawrence F. Rossow and Mark G. Rice's "The Constitutionality of the Equal Access Act: *Board of Education of Westside Community School District v. Mergens*" in *West's Education Law Reporter* (vol. 64, no. 3, 1991). A more concise overview of the act's impact on students and student groups is developed in Martha M. McCarthy and Nelda H. Cambron-McCabe's *Public School Law* (3d ed. Boseon, Mass.: Allyn and Bacon, 1992). Fred Hartmeister's *Surviving as a Teacher: The Legal Dimension* (Chicago: Precept Press, 1995) provides a similar overview from the teacher's perspective.

Erasmus, Desiderius

BORN: October 27, 1466?, Rotterdam or Gouda, The Netherlands

DIED: July 12, 1536, Basel, Switzerland

IDENTIFICATION: Dutch theologian and humanist

SIGNIFICANCE: Widely published during his time, Erasmus endured severe criticism from both sides of the Reformation and his works were placed on the *Index Librorum Prohibitorum* posthumously

The illegitimate son of a priest and a druggist's daughter, young Erasmus studied with the Brethren of Common Life where he became familiar with Humanism and learned that sound living took precedence over doctrinal quibbles. He entered the Augustinian Order but, after ordination to the priesthood, worked outside of the cloister and eventually received a dispensation from his vows. His work as a humanist scholar took him all over Europe scouring libraries for manuscripts and, along the way, he became a friend of many—and tutor of several—of the most important figures of the day, secular and religious.

Erasmus' scathing, satirical essays poked fun at ecclesiastical, educational, military, political, and linguistic foibles of his contemporaries, arousing enmity as well as admiration. During his lifetime more than 750,000 copies of his works—excluding his critical edition of the New Testament, which became a standard text in theological centers everywhere—were sold, making him, by far, the most widely read figure of his day. The works were historical, linguistic, pedagogical, theological, and ethical in subject material

It was especially Erasmus' *Colloquies* (1516) and collections of *Adages* (1500) that roused the ire of his contemporaries. The *Colloquies* criticized especially the superstitious character of many of the practices that had entered into Roman Catholic piety and religious life. This particularly upset many ecclesiastical figures because the booklets were designed to help students learn Latin and, hence, had a wide currency. One of the *Colloquies*, his *Iulius Exclusus*, satirized the recently deceased pope as one of the most unworthy figures ever to hold the See of Rome. The *Adages* were a linguistic tour de force, again widely used in the study of Latin, giving etymologies and Erasmus' own ideas about a wide array of topics.

Like many others, Erasmus found Martin Luther's opposition to much of Roman Catholic practice justified criticism, but he felt that Luther had gone too far in breaking up the Christian church. As a result, he penned a strong essay criticizing Luther's opposition to free will. Thus he found himself in the unenviable position of having strong opponents among both Reformers and Catholics, as well as strong supporters in both camps. For example, a commission of cardinals established to reform the Roman Catholic church proposed that his essays be banned from all Catholic institutions. And when Johannes Oecolampadius took over church reform in Basel, Erasmus fled into exile to Friburg, returning to Basel only to die. While his work was included in the curriculum of all Jesuit institutions, the *Index Librorum Prohibitorum* banned those same writings in 1559, under Pope Paul IV, for whom Erasmus had served as a tutor.

See also Luther, Martin; Reformation, the.

Ernst, Morris Leopold

BORN: August 23, 1888, Uniontown, Alabama
DIED: May 21, 1976, New York, New York
IDENTIFICATION: American lawyer and author
SIGNIFICANCE: One of the most important civil liberties lawyers of the twentieth century, Ernst specialized in censorship law and cases involving literary and reproductive freedom

When Ernst was two years old, his father moved the family from Alabama to New York City, where he became active in real estate. Ernst attended the New York City public schools and earned a B.A. from Williams College in 1909. While working as a bookkeeper and salesman for shirt manufacturers and furniture stores he attended law school at night, earning a LL.B degree in 1912. He was admitted to the bar the following year, and in 1915 cofounded the firm of Greenbaum, Wolff and Ernst, where he was active until his death.

In 1927, after Ernst lost a book censorship case involving the U.S. Customs Service, he determined to master this field. He eventually wrote more than two dozen books, nearly half with collaborators, and hundreds of articles for general and professional publications. His writings earned him a reputation as an expert on the laws of libel, obscenity, and especially censorship. In 1928 he published *To the Pure: A Study in Obscenity and the Censor*, coauthored with William Seagle, in which he argued that it was impossible to define obscenity and that all attempts at censorship were irrational. *Censored: The Private Life of the Movies* (1930), written with Pare Lorentz, criticized the development of movie censorship. *The Censor Marches On: Recent Milestones in the Obscenity Laws in the United States* (1940), with Alexander Lindley, surveyed important censorship cases. His 1964 *Censorship: The Search for the Obscene*, coauthored with Allan Schwarz, described court decisions on the topic from 1821 to 1963.

Ernst's books brought him a succession of notable censorship cases, all of which he won. His best-known case involved the effort to reverse the customs ban that prohibited import of James Joyce's *Ulysses* into the United States. Ernst's argument that the book should be considered in its entirety as a work of literature convinced federal district judge John M. Woolsey, whose eloquent opinion permitting import and publication of the book became a classic statement of American censorship law. Other significant victories won the right of general sale for Margaret Sanger's *Birth Control*, Dr. Marie Stopes's *Married Love*, and Radclyffe Hall's *The Well of Loneliness*.

Ernst fought government censorship of all types. As co-general counsel of the American Civil Liberties Union from 1929 to 1954 he vigorously attacked literary censorship. He argued that because no generally acceptable definition of obscenity was possible, all prosecutions were arbitrary, and speech about sex deserved full constitutional protection. As general counsel for the Planned Parenthood Federation from 1929 to 1960 he attacked laws restricting distribution of birth control information or devices. More than any other lawyer of his generation, Ernst led the fight for literary, artistic, and reproductive freedom.

See also American Civil Liberties Union; Birth control education; Books and obscenity law; Cerf, Bennett; Customs laws, U.S.; Obscenity: legal definitions; Sanger, Margaret; Sex education; Stopes, Marie; *Ulysses*.

Erznoznik v. Jacksonville

COURT: U.S. Supreme Court
DECIDED: June 23, 1975
SIGNIFICANCE: This decision, holding unconstitutional an ordinance prohibiting drive-in theaters with screens visible from public areas from showing films containing nudity, denied that government could shield citizens from all exposure to nudity in film

This case involved a challenge to the constitutionality of a Jacksonville, Florida, ordinance prohibiting drive-in theaters with screens visible from public streets or other places from exhibiting films containing nudity. After a state trial court upheld the ordinance against a First Amendment challenge, a state appeals court affirmed its ruling. When Florida's supreme court declined to overturn these lower court decisions, the U.S. Supreme Court accepted the case for review. It ultimately held, in a 6-3 decision, that Jacksonville's ordinance violated freedom of speech.

In an opinion written by Justice Lewis Powell, a majority of the Court found that the ordinance discriminated against films solely on the basis of their content—that is, whether or not they contained nudity. He noted that content-based discriminations are generally disfavored under the First Amendment.

During the course of these legal proceedings, the city conceded that not all films containing nudity are obscene and that its ordinance therefore restricted some speech which was not obscene and therefore protected by the First Amendment. However, the city urged that it was entitled to suppress nudity visible from a public place as a nuisance because of the offense some citizens might experience upon exposure to nude film images, to protect children from exposure to such images, and to enhance traffic safety by eliminating possible distractions to passing motorists.

The Supreme Court found each of these asserted justifications insufficient to warrant the city's restriction of protected speech. Citizens, the Court observed, must sometimes endure offense as the price of freedom, especially citizens who—offended by nudity glimpsed on a drive-in theater's screen—can readily avert their eyes. Furthermore, the Court continued, the ordinance could not be justified as protecting children from what might be obscene to their eyes, since not all nudity could be characterized as obscene, even to children. Finally, the Court declined to uphold the ordinance as a means of securing traffic safety, since the city had excluded only nudity in films, not other kinds of images which might also be distracting to passing motorists.

Chief Justice Warren Burger, together with justices William H. Rehnquist and Byron White, dissented. The chief justice, joined by Rehnquist, chided the Court's majority for suggesting that bystanders could simply avert their eyes from a huge projection screen. In addition, he and the other dissenters pointed out that the city certainly had authority to protect the public from actual physical nudity in public places. Consequently, these justices argued, the city should be able to pre-serve the public from unsolicited glimpses of nudity on a drive-in theater's screen just as they could protect citizens from physical displays of nudity in a public park.

See also Film censorship; *Miller v. California*; Nudity; Obscenity: legal definitions.

Espionage

DEFINITION: Spying or using spies to obtain secret information

SIGNIFICANCE: Keeping secrets from real or imagined spies often involves restraints on free expression and punishments for those who make secrets public

Censorship is the attempt, by a government or other authority, to control access to information. Espionage is the attempt to gain access to controlled information. Censorship and espionage, then, are closely connected to one another.

Those who defend the practice of censorship most often argue that it is necessary for at least one of two reasons: to protect public morality or to protect state secrets. The second reason takes on greatest weight when people feel that state secrets need to be hidden from spying enemies. In order to keep information from enemies, real or imagined, governments must also keep information from their own populations. Therefore, censorship designed to deny information to spies necessarily also denies it to citizens, and it punishes citizens for publications or statements that could be useful to foes. Perhaps the most far-reaching act of censorship in American history was the Espionage Act of 1917, which made it illegal to utter or publish "disloyal" sentiments, as well as illegal to make public military secrets.

Fears of espionage during the Cold War led the United States to develop a large body of "classified" information, government secrets that could not be made public. Publishing classified information came to be recognized as a form of espionage. For this reason, in 1985 an employee of the U.S. Naval Intelligence Support Center, Samuel Loring Morison, was prosecuted as a spy when he provided classified material to the periodical *Jane's Defense Weekly*.

Many Americans did not even recognize this classification system as a form of censorship, even though it has served as one of the most effective means of prior restraint of expression in the country's history. When Congress passed the Freedom of Information Act in 1966 to enable U.S. citizens to obtain information from the federal government, it excepted records that were classified as secret in the interest of national defense or of foreign policy. Even members of Congress themselves were sometimes

After the Soviet Union downed an American U-2 spy plane in May, 1960, President Dwight D. Eisenhower revealed the news to the public in a televised address from the White House. (National Archives)

unable to obtain these kinds of records. In 1973, the U.S. Supreme Court ruled that a report prepared for the president about the environmental impact of nuclear testing could be denied to a group of concerned congressmen, since this information had been classified as secret, and was therefore exempt from the Freedom of Information Act.

The federal agencies most directly concerned with espionage, the Federal Bureau of Investigation (FBI) and the Central Intelligence Agency (CIA), have been heavily involved in censorship through classification. The FBI is in charge of investigating espionage and sabotage within the United States and many of the bureau's activities have been classified as secret. The CIA, the chief American agency in charge of spying on other countries, has had such great control over the release of information that the agency has at times even withheld secrets from U.S. presidents.

See also Central Intelligence Agency; *CIA and the Cult of Intelligence, The*; Federal Bureau of Investigation; *Inside the Company: CIA Diary*; Intelligence Identities Protection Act; National security; Sedition.

Espionage Act of 1917

ENACTED: June 15, 1917

PLACE: United States (national)

SIGNIFICANCE: Enforcement of this act led to the suppression of free speech and the press during World War I and to the prosecution and incarceration of political dissenters

In June, 1917, two months after the United States declared war against Imperial Germany and a month after the Selective Service Act went into effect, the U.S. Congress passed the Espionage Act. Concerned about the German American and Irish American opposition to the U.S. support of Great Britain and its allies, as well as about potential interference with conscription, Congress defined three new criminal offenses. The act penalized "false statements or reports with intent to interfere with the operation" of military forces, causing "insubordination" in the military, and obstructing enlistment services.

Passage of the Espionage Act did not end Congress' efforts to suppress dissent. The attorney general of the United States, Thomas Gregory, recommended several relatively minor adjustments in the act's wording, but Congress enacted a series of amendments in 1918 that collectively became known as the Sedition Act. Among other offenses, it became a crime to "utter . . . print . . . write [or] publish" any disloyal "language intended to cause contempt" for "the form of government of the United States or the Constitution, or the flag or the uniform of the Army or Navy." Conviction could bring fines of twenty-thousand dollars, prison terms of up to twenty years, or both.

Sedition Sections of the Act. The act was used during World War I to suppress any speech or act alleged to be disloyal to the United States or disparaging of the national war effort. No one, poor or rich, prominent or unknown, was immune from prosecution. For example, a California fortune teller who told a customer that liberty bonds were worthless and that her husband had been wounded in France was sentenced to two years in prison. A German American saloon keeper in Ohio who cursed President Woodrow Wilson and the United States was given a twenty-year sentence. A would-be poet in Pennsylvania who wrote doggerel in a disrespectful letter about the Liberty Bell was sentenced to five years in prison. Rose Pastor Stokes, the wife of an aristocratic and wealthy New Yorker, was convicted under the Espionage Act for saying that she was "for the people and the government is for the profiteers." (Her conviction was later reversed by an appeals court.) An Alabama man angry at the United States for entering the war was sentenced to prison for fifteen months. In all, approximately two thousand persons—including many German Americans and Socialist Party members—were convicted under the law.

Constitutionality of the Espionage Act. The constitutionality of convictions under the Espionage Act was not decided by the U.S. Supreme Court until after the end of the war when the Court considered six cases. These concerned a Socialist Party handbill sent to military inductees, a speech by Eugene Victor Debs, two newspapers that printed objectional material, a protest against U.S. intervention in the Russian Revolution, and a pamphlet opposing the U.S. war effort. The first case, *Schenck v. United States*, was perhaps the most important in the doctrinal history of the First Amendment. Justice Oliver Wendell Holmes, Jr., wrote the unanimous opinion for the Supreme Court, enunciating the "clear and present danger" test for construing the boundaries of permissible speech. In the third case, Holmes affirmed the conviction of Debs, the three-time Socialist candidate for president who ran again from his prison cell in 1920. Debs was pardoned by President Warren G. Harding the following year.

Frohwerk v. United States. Jacob Frohwerk and Carl Glesser, the editor and the publisher of a small German-language newspaper in Kansas City, had been indicted for conspiracy to violate the Espionage Act. They had written and published twelve articles between late 1917 that were pro-German and anti-British. One article argued that it was an error in policy to send American soldiers to the trenches in France and praised the "undiminished strength of the German nation." Another referred to the Oklahoma draft riots and to the suffering of men drafted into the armed forces. Still another exhorted the American public to wake up to the fact "that we are led and ruled by England and that our sons, our taxes and our sacrifices are only in the interest of England." Glesser had pleaded guilty and had been sentenced to five years; Frohwerk had gone to trial and been convicted, fined, and given a ten-year sentence.

The *Frohwerk* case was decided by the U.S. Supreme Court in March, 1919, with, once again, Justice Holmes writing the Court's unanimous opinion. As the record in the *Frohwerk* case came to the high tribunal no evidence was present about who read the newspaper or what the attitudes and feelings of Kansas City's German community were. Only the articles themselves were presented as evidence. In affirming their convictions, Holmes wrote that the court could act only on the basis of the record as it existed, and that on that record it was "impossible to say that it might not have been found that the circulation of the paper was in quarters where a little breath

Virulently anti-German films, such as The Kaiser: The Beast of Berlin, *encouraged the American public to accept the need for the federal Espionage Act of 1917.* (National Archives)

would be enough to kindle a fire and that the fact was known and relied upon by those who sent the paper out."

Frohwerk's sentence was later commuted to one year, and Justice Holmes, after the *Debs* case, broke with his colleagues on the Court and authored dissenting opinions in *Abrams v. United States* (the handbill case protesting U.S. intervention in the Russian Revolution) and in *Pierce v. United States* (the pamphlet case criticizing the American war effort). During the war, however, the Espionage Act was a potent weapon in government suppression of civil liberties and the prosecution and persecution of political dissenters.   —*David L. Sterling*

See also Debs, Eugene; Dole, Robert; First Amendment; Holmes, Oliver Wendell, Jr.; Loyalty oaths; *Schenck v. United States*; Sedition Act of 1798; World War I.

BIBLIOGRAPHY

Zechariah Chafee, Jr., *Free Speech in the United States* (Cambridge, Mass.: Harvard University Press, 1946), is a classic study of the Espionage Act cases and later Supreme Court decisions on First Amendment cases by a civil liberties champion during and after the World War I. Donald O. Johnson, *The Challenge to American Freedoms: World War I and the Rise of the American Civil Liberties Union* (Lexington: For the Mississippi Valley Historical Association, University of Kentucky Press, 1963), examines the origins of the premier civil liberties organization in the United States. Joan M. Jensen, *The Price of Vigilance* (Chicago: Rand McNally, 1969), is a useful analysis of the record of the American Protective League, a World War I patriotic organization that helped to enforce the Espionage Act and suppress dissent. Frederick Luebke, *Bonds of Loyalty, German-Americans and World War I* (DeKalb: Northern Illinois University Press, 1974), examines the attitudes and

actions of the German American community prior to and during the participation of the United States in World War I. The best biography of the Socialist Party's standard-bearer is Nick Salvatore, *Eugene V. Debs: Citizen and Socialist* (Urbana: University of Illinois Press, 1982).

Ethnic studies

DEFINITION: Examination of the cultures, lifestyles, and literary and artistic achievements of ethnic groups

SIGNIFICANCE: Advocacy of ethnic studies has challenged traditional educational curricula, often bringing charges of censorship

The concept of ethnic studies in the United States has typically been distinguished from multicultural studies in focusing on the cultures of European immigrants, such as the Greeks, Irish, Italians, Jews, Poles, and Slavs. Special attention has been given to the continuing development of these cultures in America, especially to the reciprocal effects of Old World and New World lifestyles. Distinctions are not always sharp, but what have been called multicultural studies have typically concentrated on the cultures of Africa, Asia, and Hispanic America, as well as on historically disadvantaged groups such as African Americans, Asian Americans, Hispanic Americans, and Native Americans. Gay and feminist studies are also often included under multiculturalism.

Background. Ethnic groups are relationally located in social arenas and defined internally by specific understandings. Such groups often emerge most strikingly when group interests seem to be at stake. Ethnicity is therefore best viewed as a relational aspect of personality that overlaps with a host of other aspects of personal identity: nationality, socioeconomic class, religion, and gender. Instead of being a fixed category, ethnicity is a social construction that often represents a search for identity and meaning in response to external political and economic circumstances. People can amplify, downplay, or ignore their ethnicity in response to changing social situations.

The rise of ethnic consciousness among the descendants of immigrants to America was correlated to several political events of the 1960's: the African American and Native American civil rights struggles in the United States, emerging feminist movements in the Western world, and rebellion against participation in the Vietnam War. Moreover, ethnic consciousness may be a reaction to the alienation many feel as technology expands, centralized government solidifies, and the hold of traditional values loosens. Individuals may seek solace in immediate social bonds as a way to lessen the estrangement they experience when confronting the mechanisms of the modern state. A robust ethnicity offers a measure of security and stability in a fragmented nation that is too large and too varied to form a community.

Ethnic Studies Models. The U.S. government formally recognized ethnic studies in 1972, when Congress enacted the American Ethnic Heritage Bill. Congress appropriated $2.5 million to implement the law, which stipulated that ethnic heritage education include studies of a student's own heritage as well as that of other Americans. The money facilitated curriculum development, the training of elementary and secondary teachers, and research and teaching in colleges and universities.

Ethnic studies have developed in at least three different ways. In the independence model, ethnic courses are offered separately from standard curriculum. Such courses enjoy the benefits of autonomy and flexibility, but often suffer from their isolation from traditional departments: inferior standards of scholarship and second-class status may result. In the departmental model, traditional humanities and social science departments develop specific courses in ethnic studies that are taught as part of the standard curricula. Such courses enjoy first-class academic status, but still send the message that ethnic studies are specialty courses necessary for only a segment of students. In the full-integration model, ethnic studies

ally not been viewed as disadvantaged; they have a less persuasive case than multiculturalists that their voices have been silenced by the dominant culture. Further, European ethnics have typically intermarried in large numbers, thereby diminishing their claims to ethnic distinctiveness. Finally, ethnics have generally been less well organized politically than multiculturalists. Accordingly, ethnic studies have been mainly voluntary additions to curricula reflecting the special interests of faculty and students at particular universities. At elementary and secondary levels, however, minor doses of ethnic studies are often mandated.

Critical Attack. Critics have argued that ethnic studies embody inherent philosophical defects that generate negative practical effects. From their inception, ethnic studies have

Students occupy Columbia University's library in April, 1996, during their campaign to force the university to create an ethnic studies major. (AP/Wide World Photos)

are included in established courses. Thus a survey course in American history would include generous attention to immigration movements and the ongoing contributions of and distinctions among ethnic groups. Under this model, ethnic studies are viewed as necessary for all students, but the amount of time spent on ethnicity in any single course decreases.

Calls for mandatory inclusion of ethnic studies in the curriculum have been less frequent than demands for the inclusion of multicultural material. This difference results from several factors. Descendants of European ethnics have gener-

advanced educational ideals that are inconsistent with cosmopolitanism, universal culture, and traditional liberal-humanistic instruction. Ethnic scholars have often served as propagandists for explicitly political movements. Accordingly, ethnic studies programs have jeopardized standards of academic excellence in universities by substituting indoctrination of ethnic agendas for dispassionate searches for truth.

Critics have argued that the flawed foundations of ethnic studies have encouraged a host of societal defects: parochialism, ethnocentrism, and, in extreme cases, separatism. As such, it has been argued that ethnic studies tend to polarize groups and increase the fragmentation of society. Moreover, ethnic studies may reinforce the zeal for political correctness and campus speech codes, both of which threaten the censorship of speech historically viewed as protected by the First Amendment.

Justification. Advocates of ethnic studies have rejoined that critics have taken the worst examples of ethnic studies and assumed that they define the entire field. Although it is possible that a particular ethnic studies program could be so academically bankrupt and politically corrupt as to embody the critics' worst fears, it is not necessary that this be the case. They have further argued that people are constituted by their distinctive cultural and genetic legacies, as well as by their time, place, and circumstances. To act as if all people are all exemplars of a universal human ideal is to ignore the durability of ethnicity and to devalue the ongoing contributions various ethnic groups make to the common culture. There is no inherent contradiction between supporting the soundness of a common culture and nourishing the efforts of ethnic groups to preserve and sustain their own integrity.

Successful ethnic studies programs have examined a range of views and thinkers that have been wrongly muted in the past, exploring distinctive human behaviors in a variety of social contexts, while expanding knowledge of social possibilities. Ethnic studies must be accompanied by a vision of the public good that goes beyond a fragmented society of competing interests. Moreover, they must emphasize comparative understandings of the interrelationships of particular groups. In sum, advocates claim that ethnic studies help Americans to acquire more accurate self-knowledge, to appreciate diverse languages, arts, histories, and cultures, and to develop more effective social policies. As such, advocates argue that ethnic studies pose no threat to free speech.   —*Raymond A. Belliotti*

See also Campus speech codes; Multiculturalism; Political correctness; Universities.

BIBLIOGRAPHY

E. D. Hirsch's *Cultural Literacy* (Boston: Houghton Mifflin, 1987) and Allan Bloom's *The Closing of the American Mind* (New York: Simon & Schuster, 1987) argue that the forced introduction of new discourses, such as ethnic studies, has politicized the curriculum and eroded standards of excellence in universities. In *Seeking Identity: Individualism Versus Community in an Ethnic Context* (Lawrence: University Press of Kansas, 1995), Raymond A. Belliotti explores the relationship between personal identity and ethnicity. Charles Taylor argues in *Multiculturalism: Examining the Politics of Recognition* (Princeton, N.J.: Princeton University Press, 1994) that ethnic studies and multiculturalism are justified by the liberal political values of human respect and dignity.

Euphemism

DEFINITION: The substitution of inoffensive expressions for words that may offend or suggest something unpleasant

SIGNIFICANCE: Neutral or inoffensive words can blunt emotional reaction to what the words describe

George Orwell, the author of *Nineteen Eighty-Four* (1949)

EXAMPLES OF EUPHEMISMS FROM THE PAST AND PRESENT

Activity	Euphemisms
assassination	liquidation
defecation	going to the bathroom number two
dead person	the departed loved one
death	passing on
garbage collector	sanitary engineer
insanity	mental disorder
masturbation	playing with oneself self-abuse
military attack	preemptive strike
pregnant	in the family way in an interesting condition
public toilet	rest room comfort station lavatory
sexual intercourse	sleeping together carnal knowledge
underwear	unmentionables
urination	relieving oneself
used car	preowned vehicle

and *Animal Farm* (1945), masterpieces of political analysis, wrote an essay, "Politics and the English Language," that points out that political speech and writing "are largely the defense of the indefensible." Examples abound: bombarding defenseless villages is called "pacification," killing prisoners is called "elimination of unreliable elements." "Such phraseology is needed if one wants to name things without calling up mental pictures of them," Orwell concludes in the essay.

In 1974 the National Council of Teachers of English established, under the direction of Rutgers University English department member William Lutz, the *Quarterly Review of Doublespeak*. The review annually awards the Doublespeak Award to those who have "perpetrated language that is grossly unfactual, deceptive, evasive, euphemistic, confusing, or self-contradictory." The term "doublespeak" is a reference to *Nineteen Eighty-Four*, which uses the term to describe the deliberate use of euphemistic or contradictory language in order to make the barbarous sound civilized. Examples from the journal include calling bombing "coercive diplomacy"; referring to a fatal space shuttle accident as an "anomaly" and the astronauts' coffins as "crew transfer containers"; labeling a bullet wound a "ballistically induced aperture in the subcutaneous environment"; and calling killing the enemy "servicing the target." New taxes can be called "revenue enhancement"; layoffs, "workforce adjustments" or "headcount reduction" or "negative employee retention" or "downsizing." A corporate raider becomes an "unaffiliated corporate restructurer" and an abortion, a "pregnancy interruption." Poor people are termed "economically disadvantaged," and poor countries can be called "developing nations." Official lies become "press guidance"; to embezzle is to "wrongfully enrich" oneself; a recession is "negative economic growth." A man's beating his wife becomes "domestic abuse." Such censorship is not unique to the United States. Orwell borrowed terms for his novel from the language of totalitarian governments of Europe. In Britain, "mixed gender relationship" has been used in place of "love affair"; in South Africa, "cultural group concept" has been used for "apartheid"; in Canada, "secure facility" has been used for "jail"; and in North Korea, a dissident suffers from "mental illness."

See also Censorship; Hypocrisy; Intellectual freedom; Military censorship; Orwell, George; Police states; Political campaigning; Political correctness; Propaganda; Symbolic speech.

Evolution

DEFINITION: Evolution is the scientific theory that explains the creation and mutability of life forms

SIGNIFICANCE: Accepted by scientists as consistent with fact, the theory of evolution has been attacked in legal and political arenas by "creationists," who argue that the creation of the world, people, and animals happened literally as described in the Bible

The battle over whether to allow American schoolchildren to be taught the theory of evolution is almost as old as the theory itself. Many states enacted laws forbidding the teaching of evolution in the early years of the twentieth century, but the last of these laws was overturned during the 1960's. With the introduction of evolution into the curriculum, creationists began lobbying for, and achieving, balanced-treatment laws, which require that creation science be presented as an alternative to evolutionary science. Scientists, science teachers, and the American Civil Liberties Union have successfully argued in courts of law that creation science is religion flimsily disguised as science, so most of these laws have been overturned on constitutional grounds. Creationists have been more successful in watering down or eliminating entirely any mention of evolution in high school biology texts by pressuring publishers to change textbooks to suit the dictates of large markets in conservative regions. In 1984 People for the American Way, an organization that fights censorship, could find no mention of the theory of evolution in 17 percent of the biology texts adopted by American school boards. Creationists have been fighting to convince local school boards to incorporate creationist doctrines, as a viable scientific alternative to evolution, into biology classes.

The Nature of Scientific Theory. The underlying assumption of science is that all observed phenomena are governed by natural laws, which researchers attempt to discover, succinctly express, explain, and use to make predictions about nature. In science, experimental observations are facts. A generalization relating or explaining the facts is termed a scientific law. A scientific law typically describes some aspect of nature but provides no explanation. For example, Isaac Newton's laws of motion describe the motion of a planet or a tennis ball; they do not explain why the planet or tennis ball has such motion. The

explanation for the "whys" of natural phenomena is supplied by a scientific theory. Theories are grand conceptual schemes that usually incorporate many laws and that explain a variety of behaviors in a diversity of circumstances. In the popular usage of the word, "theory" implies a tentative or incomplete explanation based on little or no evidence; the meaning in science is quite different, almost the opposite. Usually considerable effort and many years of painstaking effort are required to formulate a valid theory; that is, a theory that explains and unifies many diverse phenomena into a coherent whole. A valid theory makes the prediction of new phenomena possible. Theories are formulated, evolve, and are discarded when better, more inclusive explanations appear. In science, theories must be modified or discarded if they cannot account for the observed facts. Finally, scientific theories deal only with what can be observed in nature. Anything outside the realm of the human senses, or extensions of human senses, is considered to be outside the realm of science, and therefore not assessable to the scientific method. For example, information gathered from observing Jupiter through a telescope is scientifically acceptable. Other people can look through telescopes and see for themselves and confirm or cast doubt upon what the first observer reports.

The Theory of Evolution. The theory of evolution, first presented in detail in Charles Darwin's 1859 book *The Origin of Species by Means of Natural Selection*, may be summarized as follows: Plants and animals produce more offspring than can possibly survive. Because of this overproduction of offspring, a large number of every species compete for a limited food supply. Genetic variations occur in all living organisms and are passed on to the offspring. Some genetic variations are favorable, others unfavorable for a given species. Since favorable traits give an advantage in the struggle for food and mates, they are naturally selected to be passed on to the next generation. Thus, species may evolve over time; they may die out; and new species may arise, as the conditions for life change.

Creation Science. The central assumptions of mainline creationism follow. First, a supernatural force, God, created the universe, energy, and life from nothing over a span of six days. Second, only micro-evolutionary fine-tuning of originally created plants and animals has occurred since then, since God created the world in a state of perfection. Third, the earth and universe are only six to twelve thousand years old. Fourth, the earth's present geography is the result of a series of catastrophes, including a worldwide flood. These events as described in the Bible are true in the most literal sense.

Historical Context. In 1831 Darwin furthered his scientific ambitions by accepting the position of naturalist on a British survey ship exploring the coastal regions of South America. It was during the course of this five-year expedition that Darwin laid the groundwork for his theory. Returning to England, he used his treasure-trove of notes, sketches, and specimens, assembled in South America, to write several specialized monographs, but not a word appeared concerning the origin of species. In the secrecy of his study, however, he slowly and painstakingly developed his evolutionary theory of natural selection, so that by 1842 a detailed outline, meticulously detailing the mechanisms of evolution, was extant. It was not, however, a politically auspicious time for introducing a scientific theory that removed God from creation, replaced a divine design with random variation, and relegated survival to the best adapted in the competition for limited resources. Darwin, in short, was aware of the religious implications of his theory, and he was aware that his theory would cause great controversy. Furthermore, the issue of the ape ancestry of human beings would likely be viewed as a degradation of the human species, and Darwin was apprehensive about the effect of this news on public morals. Although Darwin continued to gather supporting evidence for his theory for fifteen years, the theory itself remained a carefully guarded secret. Darwin may have kept his secret until after retirement, or he may have died with it, were it not that he received a letter from another biologist who, knowing nothing of Darwin's work, had arrived at the same theory, but without benefit of Darwin's vast assortment of evidence. This forced Darwin's hand; he immediately began writing a short outline of his theory of evolution. By almost imperceptible degrees it evolved into the five-hundred-page tome published in 1859.

Although Darwin had scrupulously avoided mentioning human evolution in his book, the Church of England (also known as the Anglican church) realized the implications and became the theory's bitter enemy. In an effort to discredit the theory, a debate was staged in 1860 between biologist Thomas Henry Huxley, known as Darwin's bulldog, and Anglican bishop Samuel Wilberforce, a skilled debater whose slippery argumentation had earned him the nickname "Soapy Sam." During the course of the ensuing pyrotechnics the bishop, without considering scientific aspects, used rhetorical tricks to discredit the theory, and he was demolished by Huxley's clear logic and scientific acumen. Although the day was won for Darwinism, and although the Anglican church soon conceded, the battle has continued unabated among other scientists and other churches.

Evolving Issues of Censorship in America. By 1900 Darwin's theory had proven to be so extraordinarily successful in explaining many seemingly unrelated facts that virtually all biologists accepted it and praised its brilliance. Emotional disputation, however, concerning the teaching of this theory in public schools prevailed during the early decades of the twentieth century. Biologists wished to include this important new theory, but conservative religious organizations vehemently opposed the idea. The World's Christian Fundamental Association, founded in 1919, was the first group formed for the sole purpose of keeping Darwin's theory out of the public schools. To accomplish this goal, the group lobbied state legislatures to pass laws banning evolution from the curricula, making the teaching of evolution a crime, and proscribing textbooks that referred to evolution. The group achieved a considerable measure of success: Antievolution bills were introduced in more than twenty state legislatures. By the 1920's, for example, Tennessee, Mississippi, and Arkansas had outlawed the teaching of evolution, and Texas and Florida had imposed nonbinding resolutions opposing the teaching of Darwin's theory.

The issue of censorship as related to evolution first became a legal question in the Scopes trial of 1925. John Scopes, a high school biology teacher, was being tried for violating a Tennessee statute that made it unlawful for any teacher in any public school or university "to teach any theory that denies the story of the Divine Creation of man as taught in the Bible, and to teach instead that man has descended from a lower order of animals." The battery of lawyers defending Scopes never denied the charge that he had broken the law, and Scopes was convicted and fined for this offense. The real motive behind the defense was to appeal the conviction in order to have the law reviewed by the U.S. Supreme Court. The defense lawyers' argument was to be that the law prohibiting the teaching of evolution violated the First Amendment, which prohibits the mixing of church and state. Their action was stymied because the Tennessee Su-

In early 1996, more than seventy years after the Scopes trial, Nashville high school biology teacher Wesley Roberts stood ready to challenge another proposed Tennessee law that would ban teaching evolution as a scientific fact. (AP/Wide World Photos)

preme Court rejected the conviction on a technicality. As a result, for the next thirty-five years science texts devoted little space to the concepts of evolution, and virtually none mentioned Darwin's name.

Reviewed Emphasis on Evolution. When the Soviets launched the world's first artificial satellite in 1957, Americans began to reassess the quality of their science education. The resulting extensive effort to upgrade the science curriculum included putting the theory of evolution back into the biology curriculum, thus setting the stage for the battles that followed. Several states began to enforce the antievolutionary statutes that had lain dormant for decades. The constitutional issue was finally settled in 1968, when prohibitions against teaching evolution in public schools were struck down by the Supreme Court. Susan Epperson, a high school biology teacher, successfully challenged a 1929 Arkansas law forbidding the teaching of "the theory or doctrine that mankind ascended or descended from a lower order of animals." The Supreme Court ruled that this law was an attempt to establish religion in the classroom because it sought "to blot out a particular theory because of its supposed conflict with the Biblical account."

Although the Epperson case was thought to have settled the debate by flatly declaring that laws censoring the theory of evolution are unconstitutional, the losers began fighting back on new constitutional territory. Rather than expunging evolution from the curriculum, they fought to have creationism taught as a viable scientific alternative. In the early 1970's, two institutes were formed to abet this cause, the Creation Science Research Center and the Institute for Creation Research (ICR). In addition to promoting creationism as a legitimate scientific theory, these institutes have been leading challenges to the Epperson case on the grounds that the decision is hostile to the First Amendment by not respecting neutrality toward religion. The ICR claims that evolution promotes a hostile attitude toward religion. Since the state must remain neutral on religious issues, any statute supporting the teaching of the theory of evolution as the only explanation of creation cannot, the creationists argue, be legal. The ICR proposed "scientific creationism" as a legitimate alternative to evolution and fought to have this hypothesis included in public school science curricula.

"Balanced-Treatment" Laws. Consequently, during the early 1980's, when in the political arena the fear of God was regaining ground lost to fear of the Soviets, several states enacted balanced-treatment laws prohibiting the teaching of evolution in public schools without granting creation science equal time. The law enacted in Arkansas, although manifesting a surface plausibility, floundered in attempting to define creation science by enumerating its basic precepts. Brought to court in December, 1981, creationist lawyers were not able to convince the judge that biblical beliefs, such as Noah's flood and the relatively recent creation of the universe, could be defended as legitimate science rather than religion disguised as science. The Arkansas balanced-treatment law was declared unconstitutional; the judge ruled that "Creation science is not science because it depends upon supernatural intervention." The only real effect of the law seemed to be to advance

religion by forcing biology teachers to purvey religious beliefs in science classrooms.

The balanced-treatment law enacted in Louisiana seemed to rest on firmer ground because the law required only the teaching of facts which attested a supernatural creation; the law was deliberately phrased to avoid any mention of religion. Nevertheless, the federal court and the court of appeals voted against the constitutionality of the law, noting that its intended effect was to "discredit evolution by counterbalancing its teaching at every turn with the teaching of creationism, a religious belief." The state of Louisiana, represented by the ICR's Creation Science Legal Defense Fund, put before the Supreme Court the question of whether the state statute violated the First Amendment. The court concluded that the act was indeed a violation of the First Amendment because that act lacked a clear secular purpose and was designed not to protect academic freedom but to discredit evolution.

The teaching of evolution in science classes won a clear victory in the courts, but the impact of the victories was, arguably, diminished. The consequences of consistent antievolution grassroots pressure upon textbook publishers, who respond to market forces, and upon school boards were considerably greater. For example, Texas chooses textbooks for the entire state every six years. Creationists succeeded in having the state-issued guidelines to publishers request that evolution be presented as "only a theory" (playing upon the difference between the popular and the scientific meanings of the word) and that creation science be presented as a valid alternative. In an effort to be admitted to the Texas market, publishers reduced, watered down, or even completely eliminated evolution from their biology textbooks. California's book-adoption board, however, began to fight this trend in 1986, when it circulated new guidelines for its biology textbooks. California educators suggested that biology texts should include a discussion of evolution, and stated that discussions of creation should be placed in religious books.

Fundamentalist religious groups have applied pressure to school boards, administrators, and teachers to use the "dual model" approach. Highly educated, erudite, and well-prepared spokespersons for the creationist cause have been traveling to local PTA meetings to lobby, make presentations on creation science, and "explain" the flaws of evolutionary theory. Science educators have become cautious in designing their curricula and selecting their texts. Many are fearful of treading on controversial ground because legal proceedings may be instigated or because a negative community reaction may jeopardize their jobs.

Conclusion. To the vast majority of scientists, creation science is a sectarian religious belief disguised as science. Careful examination of the assumptions and the evidence behind creation science reveal only outmoded, incorrect, and occasionally directly dishonest distortions of true science. Most creationists however, claim that there are two competing and equally valid scientific theories to explain the origin and diversity of life: evolution and creationism. Creationists argue that the acceptance of the theory of evolution implies atheism since in evolution there is no room for God. Scientists argue, in turn, that acceptance of the theory of evolution implies nothing about God; one can believe in God, if one wishes, and accept the validity of the theory of evolution. The theory of evolution and the biblical account of the creation of the world, however, are in contradiction, but only if one takes the biblical account literally. The issue as now defined by creationists is that the creationist theory is being censored by the educational and legal system. Most scientists concur that science, not censorship, is the issue. Creation science, by definition, cannot be science because the acts of a supernatural being are excluded from the realm of science. Scientists have supported litigation against equal-time bills, not as an act of censorship but because they are convinced that creation science is a wolf in sheep's clothing. It appears to be a highly sectarian religious belief system masquerading as science. Creationists counter by claiming that equal-time laws broaden the range of material presented to students and that a student's right to know is abridged if instruction concerning the creation model is censored. On the other hand, if the creationist model is indeed religion it cannot, in good conscience, be presented as a viable scientific alternative to the theory of evolution. Scientists argue that they have no interest in forbidding the teaching of creationism, which may be taught in religion classes or Sunday school; rather, they seek to avoid being compelled to teach an invalid theory that is not scientific but religious.

Creationists counter by arguing that it is an infringement of a student's rights to practice religion freely if a student is taught only evolution in the classroom. Science, however, does not teach any theory as if it were the final truth. Students are not taught to believe in evolution, they are only taught what scientists think is true of the natural universe and why.

In the final analysis, the controversy between evolution and creationism is not a battle about science. The scientific debate is settled: Evolution is a theory, creationism is not. The controversy centers on public opinion. —*George R. Plitnik*

See also Darwin, Charles; Science; Scopes trial.

BIBLIOGRAPHY

Philip Kitcher's *Abusing Science: The Case Against Creationism* (Cambridge, Mass.: MIT Press, 1982) is a broad frontal attack on creationism, refuting its tenets point by point. Christopher McGowan's *In the Beginning: A Scientist Shows Why the Creationists Are Wrong* (Buffalo, N.Y.: Prometheus Books, 1984) is geared to a general audience and covers the entire controversy. Editor Ashley Montagu's *Science and Creationism* (New York: Oxford University Press, 1984) presents critiques of creationism by various scientists. Editor Henry Morris' *Scientific Creationism* (El Cajon, Calif.: Master Books, 1974) is the source book of scientific creationism.

Examiner of plays

DEFINITION: British government office responsible for reviewing publicly performed plays

SIGNIFICANCE: Holders of this office censored the content of dramatic productions from the early eighteenth century through the mid-twentieth century

In Great Britain the examiner of plays was a functionary in the office of the Lord Chamberlain to whom, by statute, he was responsible. From the early eighteenth century, when the office was created, until its abolition in 1968, the examiner was specifically charged with reviewing and censoring public theatrical productions. Holders of the office were generally narrow-minded and conservative, wielding an authority that proved unduly repressive to artistic expression in British drama, particularly in the nineteenth century. George Colman was perhaps the most arrogant and notorious of the nineteenth century examiners, purging plays of all references to religion, identifiable prominent personalities, politics, and sexual suggestiveness. Colman's excesses were prominent among the concerns that prompted the House of Commons to appoint a select committee to review current laws on licensing and censorship in the theater in 1823. Although the committee, chaired by novelist Edward Bulwer-Lytton, recommended the abolition of censorship and the office of the examiner, Parliament rejected its conclusions. The Theatre Regulation Act of 1843 reaffirmed the Lord Chamberlain's authority and officially established the censorship responsibilities of the examiner of plays.

Some playwrights, notably George Bernard Shaw, partly circumvented and called attention to theatrical censorship excesses by printing their plays for publication. Shaw prefaced his published version of *Mrs. Warren's Profession* (1893) with an extended essay on the censorship issue.

A new committee established by Parliament in 1966 resulted in the Theatre Act of 1968. It repealed the Theatre Regulation Act of 1843 and abolished the offices of both the Lord Chamberlain and the examiner of plays.

See also Drama and theater; Lord Chamberlain; Master of the Revels; Shaw, George Bernard; Theatres Act of 1968.

Exorcist, The

TYPE OF WORK: Film
RELEASED: 1973
DIRECTOR: William Friedkin (1939-   )
SUBJECT MATTER: A teenage girl is possessed by a demon
SIGNIFICANCE: This film established new boundaries for permissible content in mainstream films, including graphic horror, sexual violence, blasphemy, and obscenity; its R rating was criticized, and it has been legally restricted or prohibited in Washington, D.C., and Great Britain

It is difficult to overstate the impact on the American public of this film adaptation of William Peter Blatty's 1971 novel about demonic possession. When it premiered in 1973, reported reactions from audience members ranged from vomiting and fainting to fears of psychological trauma. These reactions, coupled with raw language and shocking visuals unprecedented in mainstream films, made *The Exorcist* one of the most widely discussed and debated movies of the 1970's.

The Motion Picture Association of America's ratings board gave the film an R rating, which was widely criticized as too lenient in view of such scenes as the possessed girl violating herself with a bloody crucifix. Yet the U.S. Catholic Conference film board did not condemn the film, instead rating it "A-IV, morally unobjectionable for adults, with reservation." However, in Washington, D.C., the film was legally prohibited

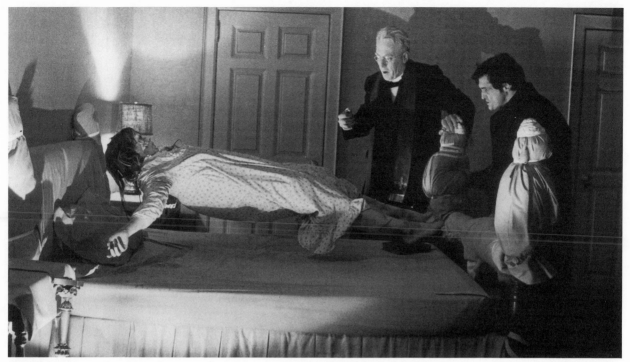

Shocking scenes in The Exorcist *compelled many filmgoers to leave their seats and rush out of the theaters.* (Museum of Modern Art/Film Stills Archive)

to persons under seventeen, and as late as 1995 the British Board of Film Censors refused to certify the film for distribution on video, though it could be shown in theaters.

See also British Board of Film Censors; Film censorship; Legion of Decency; Motion Picture Association of America; Subliminal messages; Violence.

Exploration, Age of

DEFINITION: Period of worldwide discovery and colonial expansion by European powers

SIGNIFICANCE: Each European power attempted to suppress dissemination of the knowledge gained by its own explorers, but in every case such efforts failed

The European nations involved in exploration had an interest in controlling the information they acquired. Exploration was not pursued to gain mere knowledge. Each voyage was undertaken in the hope of acquiring wealth and power, most often by locating new trade routes to the Orient or by exploiting the resources of the new lands discovered by the Europeans. Thus, new information benefited the owner most if it was unavailable to the other countries. As a result, various forms of censorship were imposed.

Spanish and Portuguese Censorship. The monarchy of Spain enacted the most comprehensive and effective censorship of its explorers' knowledge, but these policies ultimately failed. Information did reach rival powers. The continued Spanish censoring of cartographic information also was used to counter Spanish claims to territory in the Gulf of Mexico.

Spain began its explorations with little regard for secrecy. In the early voyages, Spain quite often employed experienced seamen from foreign countries. Christopher Columbus was a Genoese and his first voyage in 1492 was primarily funded by fellow Genoese. Ferdinand Magellan was Portuguese and his crew included Portuguese, Italians, and Frenchmen. Once the Spanish monarchy realized the true wealth of the New World, especially after the conquests of the Aztecs and Incas, censorship efforts were enacted. The Spanish monarchy banned all foreign ships and men from the wealthy West Indies trade area. Although this ban was partially reduced in the 1550's, stringent requirements and Spanish suspicions of all foreigners remained crucial aspects of Spanish colonial policy. Throughout this period, illegal trespassers were subject to imprisonment or execution. The monarchy also created centralized departments to oversee the new empire. In 1508 a hydrographic office was established. In addition to training navigators and collecting the new information, the office also oversaw the control of the maps being created. Although general, large-scale maps were published, important coastal charts and detailed maps were restricted. Spanish navigators were held responsible for the charts and maps they carried on their voyages. If disaster struck they were to save these materials if possible, but they were to destroy them before they let them fall into foreign hands. Despite this, pirates and foreign warships often managed to capture these valuable documents.

In the early seventeenth century, Spain expanded its censorship to include almost all information about the New World. Thus, few Spanish maps were published, and those that were published were conspicuously bare. These efforts to suppress the dissemination of information generally failed. Information leaked out through spies, disgruntled Spaniards, captured documents, and because other European powers were increasingly encroaching into Spanish territories. In fact, the lack of published Spanish maps undermined Spain's claim to the Gulf of Mexico. When France published detailed maps of the northern Gulf and claimed it as a French possession, the Spanish had no credible published maps to refute France's claims.

After Spain, Portugal employed the most successful censorship of its explorations. The Portuguese monarchy oversaw the commercial interests that typically funded the explorations and the monarchy actively controlled the trading empire established in the Indian Ocean. Like the Spanish, the Portuguese created governmental offices to coordinate their explorations, trade activities, and the defense of their new empire—which included censoring maps. From the first voyages down the western coast of Africa, the monarchy tried to control access to coastal maps and navigational information. Published maps were rare. Foreign seamen were employed less by the Portuguese than was the practice in other countries. Extensive policies restricted foreign vessels from traveling in Portuguese waters and overwhelming hostility to intruders kept most interlopers out during the sixteenth century. The Portuguese reputation for protecting their territory was so effective that for most of the sixteenth century, Portugal controlled almost all of the Indian Ocean spice trade. However, this success did not include their efforts to suppress knowledge of Portuguese territories. Both Spain and France repeatedly enticed Portuguese pilots into their service, and when they left Portugal they often brought Portuguese charts and maps with them. By the seventeenth century Portugal had become basically a conquered province of Spain and the bulk of the Portuguese empire began to fall into the hands of the Dutch, French, and British.

Northern European Empire Builders. In the early seventeenth century, the Dutch became the first of the northern Atlantic powers to break the Spanish and Portuguese monopoly on the world empires. The Dutch quickly acquired most of the Portuguese empire and established colonies in the Americas that were useful in launching piracy against the Spanish and in controlling the contraband slave trade. The Dutch parliament government and the relatively open merchant society of the United Provinces of the Netherlands made extensive censorship impractical. The Dutch did attempt to suppress initial information of their explorations—mainly because they were intruding into Spanish and Portuguese areas and they needed time to consolidate bases of operation. This censorship was at best temporary. The Dutch never effectively censored publications of maps, and they relied on seamen from various countries, which made the Dutch especially vulnerable to spies.

Of the North Atlantic powers, France had the greatest potential to suppress their explorers' discoveries. Although France had a parliament, the monarchy gained absolute authority. Censorship boards were established, and by mid-seventeenth century, all French publications required royal approval. Early French explorations were censored. Voyage logs and maps were restricted, but the details still became widely known. The explorations of Giovanni da Verrazano in 1524 and Jacques Cartier during 1534 to 1535 employed seamen from several countries. Furthermore, early French censorship was haphazard at best. By the late sixteenth century, France had adopted a strategy of suppression and propaganda. Especially in North America, the French attempted to restrict access for intruders of competing nations. France also enacted extensive secrecy in the planning and establishment of the Fort Caroline garrison in 1564 and the Robert LaSalle expedition in 1684. France, not following the policy of Spain, quickly published numerous maps of French explorations in order to further the legitimacy of its claims.

Great Britain attempted to suppress information about its early explorations, but these efforts were generally futile. The fifteenth century British voyages to Greenland and Newfoundland were likely done in secret for the dual goals of establishing trade and seeking a northwest passage to the Orient. The Portuguese at least were soon aware of the details of the voyages. Later efforts to find a northwest or northeast passage to the Orient were also quickly compromised. The British use of foreign seamen, coupled with Britain's relatively weak monarchy and the British people's antipathy for legislated censorship made suppression of knowledge nearly impossible.

—*Fred Hoover*

See also Astronomy; Central America; France; Historiography; National security; Propaganda; Raleigh, Sir Walter; South America; Spanish Empire.

BIBLIOGRAPHY

Leo Bagrow's *History of Cartography* (Chicago: Precedent Publishing, 1985) gives a thorough overview of the processes and policies involved in the creation and publishing of maps. William H. Goetzmann's *The Atlas of North American Exploration from the Norse Voyages to the Race to the Pole* (New York: Swanson, 1992) details the purpose and results of explorations in North America. In *Spain and Portugal in the New World, 1492-1700* (Minneapolis: University of Minnesota Press, 1984), Lyle N. McAlister describes the Iberian countries' policies and efforts to suppress foreign involvement in their empires. Robert Weddle, *The French Thorn* (College Station: Texas A&M Press, 1991), discusses the conflict between the French and the Spanish and their use of maps. John Wilford's *The Mapmakers* (New York: Alfred A. Knopf, 1981) provides accounts of numerous explorations and their findings.

F

Fahrenheit 451

TYPE OF WORK: Book

PUBLISHED: 1953

AUTHOR: Ray Bradbury (1920-   )

SUBJECT MATTER: In an authoritarian future society a man whose job is to burn books changes his point of view and becomes a reader

SIGNIFICANCE: To many readers, this novel is a thought-provoking depiction of a plausible future in which censorship of reading is absolute

The first science fiction novel by Ray Bradbury, *Fahrenheit 451* is an early example of a dystopian tale about a future world that is nightmarish rather than hopeful. In its imaginary world, police state "firemen" burn homes containing books, as all books are forbidden by law. The protagonist, Guy Montag, is a fireman who becomes drawn into the world of clandestine book-readers by a woman he meets. Eventually, he joins a group of outcasts trying to preserve literature by committing entire books to memory. While printed matter can be burned, memories cannot be erased.

The novel's point of view is clearly against censorship. It depicts the general population as living in darkness, with huge television screens dominating their homes and radios constantly blaring in their ears. The authoritarian government has decreed that all writing is subversive, as it is inevitably contradictory and it allows people to become aware of unpleasant aspects of society. Montag's conversion to reading is significant in that he suddenly finds himself in light rather than

In the dystopian world of Fahrenheit 451 *"firemen" do not extinguish fires, but start them—in order to burn books.* (Museum of Modern Art/Film Stills Archive)

darkness. The book's none-too-subtle message is that reading makes people aware of ideas that may be dangerous to a totalitarian state, but are absolutely necessary for clear thinking.

Although *Fahrenheit 451* is intended as a warning, not a prophecy, its anticensorship message has often been cited by opponents of book bannings in the United States.

See also Book burning; *Day They Came to Arrest the Book, The*; Intellectual freedom; Literature; *Playboy*; Police states.

FAIR (Fairness & Accuracy in Reporting)
FOUNDED: 1986
TYPE OF ORGANIZATION: Anticensorship organization based in New York
SIGNIFICANCE: FAIR seeks to redress bias, especially regarding progressive viewpoints, in the news media

FAIR has aggressively challenged the often-stated opinion that the news media have a liberal bias. Through analyses of news coverage, FAIR has concluded that the media tend to present important news stories from center-right viewpoints, muting or rejecting more liberal or progressive voices. A root of this problem, as FAIR has seen it, is that ownership of the media in the United States is too heavily concentrated among a few powerful and wealthy individuals and corporations. This control, FAIR believes, works to stifle the viewpoints of more marginalized groups, such as organized labor, grassroots environmental or public interest organizations, women, minority groups, and others who may pose challenges to the interests of those in the economic and political establishment. This censorship is further strengthened by the power and influence major advertisers are able to exert over the news media.

FAIR publishes a bimonthly magazine titled *Extra!* Since 1992 it has produced a weekly radio program that has been aired by several dozen stations in the United States and Canada.

See also Advertisers as advocates of censorship; News media censorship; Project Censored.

Fairness doctrine
ENFORCED: June, 1949-January, 1987
PLACE: United States (national)
SIGNIFICANCE: This Federal Communications Commission (FCC) policy requiring broadcasters to provide balanced and impartial news coverage of controversial community issues was designed to ensure that the public receive diverse information on important issues

A principle underlying freedom of expression in the United States is the belief that if truth and falsehood meet in an open marketplace of ideas, truth will win out. So long as sufficiently diverse opinions are expressed, the democratic process will function at its best. To ensure that such diversity exists, government must not place any prior restraints on the press. Government regulation of expression is permissible only when there are excesses that government has a right to punish.

This principle has long governed the print media, but its application to broadcast media has posed special problems. Whereas a potentially unlimited number of newspaper outlets can exist in any given geographic region, the same was not always true of broadcast outlets—which historically depended on the limited breadth of the electromagnetic spectrum to transmit their signals. Unrestricted use of the airwaves can result in signals interfering with each other so that no voices at all are heard. For this reason, the Radio Acts of 1912 and 1927 and the federal Communications Act of 1934 required broadcast station operators to be federally licensed and to broadcast in the public interest.

The fairness doctrine that arose in the late 1940's was based on the scarcity of the broadcast spectrum theory. The principle of public ownership of all the airwaves, and the concomitant belief that broadcasters must represent public interests, were invoked to justify greater government restrictions on expression in broadcasting than in the print media. The doctrine itself grew out of a practice begun in the 1920's of revoking the licenses of radio stations that broadcast one-sided propaganda messages.

In a document released in June, 1949, *In the Matter of Editorializing by Broadcast Licensees*, the FCC ruled that the Mayflower Doctrine of 1941, which prohibited editorializing, was no longer valid. In place of that doctrine's ban on editorializing, the FCC instituted a new "fairness doctrine," which held that broadcasters must provide adequate time on their station to discuss important and controversial issues, and that broadcasters must ensure that all significant viewpoints on such issues be covered. In 1969 the U.S. Supreme Court upheld the constitutionality of this doctrine in *Red Lion Broadcasting v. Federal Communications Commission*, a case arising from a Pennsylvania radio station's refusal to comply with an FCC order to grant time to the author of a critical book on Senator Barry Goldwater to rebut accusations that evangelist Billy James Hargis had leveled against him on the air.

The fairness doctrine did not require stations to provide a variety of viewpoints within individual programs, and the doctrine applied only to news and public affairs programs, not to entertainment shows. The doctrine's enforcement required monitoring news broadcasts and documentary programming over extended periods of time—a task almost impossible to execute fully. The only station to lose its license for violating the fairness doctrine was the conservative, fundamentalist radio station WUXR in Media, Pennsylvania. In 1970 the FCC refused to renew the station's license because of local complaints about its one-sided broadcasts and its attack on persons whom it denied permission to reply. Two years later a federal circuit court upheld the FCC's action in the case of *Brandywine Main Line v. Federal Communications Commission*.

Equal time. Both broadcasters and the public often confuse the fairness doctrine with section 315 of the federal Communications Act of 1934. That law required any station broadcasting a promotion for a legally qualified candidate for public office to allow all other legally qualified candidates for the same office equal opportunities to use its broadcasting facilities. Such broadcast time did not necessarily have to be free, but its cost could not exceed that charged to the first candidate. Regular newscasts and appearances by candidates in news spots, news interviews, and news documentaries were exempted, as are certain national political debates. Under fairness doctrine provisions, equal time was not required for opposing views, and stations were not required to give equal time to particular viewpoints.

Personal Attacks and Political Editorializing. Two rules that were originally part of the fairness doctrine that have remained in force involve criticisms of individuals or groups and endorsements of political candidates. If a station attacked the honesty, character, or integrity of any person or group, the fairness doctrine required the station to notify targets of its attacks within a week; it also had to provide them with summaries of the attacks, and offer them reasonable opportunities to respond on the air. Attacks on public figures and foreign individuals were allowed, however, as well as general criticisms of individuals attacking their ability or knowledge. Such attacks had to be made during discussions of controversial issues for the rule to apply.

Whenever a station endorsed a candidate for office, all other candidates for the same office had to be notified and given reasonable opportunities to respond. However, if a station opposed only one candidate for office, then only that candidate had to be notified and given an opportunity to respond. A consequence of these rules was that stations rarely editorialized about political candidates and they were more likely to express their opposition to certain candidates than their support for others.

Rise and Fall of the Doctrine. The fairness doctrine was successfully applied to cigarette advertising in 1967 but its extension to advertising generally soon became unwieldy and was dropped. In the 1980's new broadcast technologies increased the number of broadcasting voices available to any given geographical region; as a result scarcity was no longer considered a paramount problem. The old argument that a single station had to present the viewpoints of all factions in its community seemed no longer to be valid. By the late 1980's there were nearly ten thousand radio stations and twelve hundred television stations throughout the United States, compared to 1,750 daily newspapers. During the 1990's the number of broadcast stations continued to increase steadily, while the number of newspapers declined. In these changing conditions, a new rationale of broadcast deregulation, based on demands of the marketplace, came into being with the support of Republican members of Congress and Republican presidents. In 1987 the FCC ruled that the fairness doctrine was ineffective and that fairness in broadcasting could best be served by the marketplace.

A Democrat-controlled Congress tried to re-establish the doctrine rule in 1987, but President Ronald Reagan vetoed the measure. His successor, George Bush, announced that he would veto any attempts to pass such a bill. Later attempts to reenact such a doctrine also failed. Abandonment of the rule led to a rapid proliferation of politically biased talk shows, such as that of Rush Limbaugh.   —*Roger D. Haney*

See also Accuracy in Media; Advocacy; Communications Act of 1934; Federal Communications Commission; Limbaugh, Rush; Political campaigning; Right of reply; Talk shows.

BIBLIOGRAPHY

The fairness doctrine and other relevant FCC documents, such as the Blue Book, the Mayflower Doctrine, and *Red Lion* case, are collected in Frank J. Kahn's *Documents of American Broadcasting* (3d ed. Englewood Cliffs, N. J.: Prentice-Hall, 1978). Donald M. Gillmor et al., *Mass Communication Law: Cases and Comment* (5th ed. St. Paul: West Publishing, 1990), and Don R. Pember, *Mass Media Law* (7th ed. Madison, Wis.: Brown & Benchmark, 1996), cover the legal histories of the doctrine and other restrictions on media expression. Steven J. Simmons examines the doctrine's conceptual history, its implications for advertising, and the difficulty of defining issues in *The Fairness Doctrine and the Media* (Berkeley: University of California Press, 1978). Hugh Carter Donahue's *The Battle to Control Broadcast News: Who Owns the First Amendment?* (Cambridge, Mass.: MIT Press, 1989) gives a complete history of the doctrine through its demise, attempts by Congress to legislate the doctrine, and President Ronald Reagan's veto.

Fairy tales

DEFINITION: Fictional tales that typically involve elements of the supernatural, stereotypically resolved in a traditional happy ending

SIGNIFICANCE: Though long considered merely children's entertainment, fairy tales are important tools in the socialization of young people and an important literary genre with a long history of censorship

The fairy tale, or a tale that features some prominent supernatural element, is a common narrative form throughout the world. Though each country's tradition of tale-telling bears recognizable differences, enough similarity in structure exists for scholars to create categories and patterns that cross cultural boundaries. Of these, the creation of types of subgenres of tales is the most common. The term fairy tale has been interpreted to include all types of tales, from fables to miraculous legends, to anecdotes. The most-censored varieties of fairy tales fall into two categories: the literary fairy tale and the children's fairy tale. Of these, the children's tales are much better known and more popular, but each has a long history of censorship, almost as long as their existence in print.

Literary Fairy Tales. Literary fairy tales are as old as the print medium. That they have a close relationship to censorship is not surprising: Scholars have theorized that the genre developed partly as a response to censorship. Writers have long recognized the possibilities of safely changing the human objects of their criticism into ogres, animals, and other nonrealistic and fantastic forms.

Literary fairy tales also allow their authors to tap into the stories of popular culture, which are often political or utopian in nature. The most popular narratives of the Middle Ages were often compendia of folk stories placed in the framework of larger narrative structures, such as Giovanni Boccaccio's *The Decameron* and Marguerite de Navarre's *The Heptameron*.

The single most-popular work of the late Middle Ages, *Gargantua and Pantagruel*, written by a former monk and medical doctor, François Rabelais, is the tale of a family of giants who experience a series of outlandish and often obscene adventures while traveling throughout Europe. Based on popular French folk stories, the book went through numerous

Wilhelm Grimm (left) and Jacob Grimm—brothers whose names have become synonymous with fairy tales. (Library of Congress)

editions and sequels. The text begins as a parody of medieval miracle stories, with the birth of the hero Gargantua through the ear of his mother, the giantess Gargamelle. Rabelais notes that such a thing is in fact possible in reality, arguing that the Bible does not strictly eliminate such an occurrence from happening. This logic did not amuse the hierarchy of the medieval Christian church, so the book was banned in many places in Europe. Although Rabelais published the book pseudonymously, using the pen name "Alcofribas Nasier," an anagram of his own name, he was identified as the author, and found his own life in peril. He was able to find personal safety only because of the protection of his patron, Queen Marguerite de Navarre, author of *The Heptameron.*

The nation most indebted to the tradition of literary fairy tales is Germany, which is also the nation most closely identified with the fairy tale genre. Almost every German writer in the past three centuries has written literary fairy tales. Many of those tales were banned during the Nazi regime in the 1930's and 1940's; the Nazis preferred to create their own filmic fantasies, based on their close imitation of Hollywood films.

A final example of the literary fairy tale is George Orwell's transparently satirical twentieth century novel, *Animal Farm* (1945). A critique of the centralizing tendencies of twentieth century governments, the novel is an allegorical story of a farm gone bad, the institution having been taken over by the animals. At least one contemporaneous ruler, Joseph Stalin, found the characterization of the pig Napoleon too familiar for comfort, so he had the book banned in the Soviet Union.

Children's Fairy Tales. The idea of a separate literature written by adults and directed specifically toward an audience made up entirely of children is a relatively modern idea. Much of the credit for the invention of children's literature can be given to European literature, and the ideology that sprang up around Enlightenment- and Romantic-era ideas concerning culture and children. Children, the argument ran, are essentially different from adults, and therefore must be treated differently—either educated, according to Enlightenment ideas, or protected, according to Romantic ideas. The result of both practices can be seen in the anthologies of children's stories written and collected in Germany beginning in the early nineteenth century.

The first important anthology of folk writings collected in nineteenth century Germany was Clemens Brentano's *Des Knaben Wunderhorn* (1805-1808), or *The Boy's Magic Horn*, a cycle of folk songs. Brentano was the acquaintance of two brothers, Jacob Grimm and Wilhelm Grimm, whom he encouraged to compile a similar volume of stories. The result was the famous first volume of the *Nursery and Household Tales* in 1812. The text was soon banned in Vienna under the pretext that it was a work of superstition, but more likely because of its celebration of German nationalistic folk culture.

Though the work of the Brothers Grimm was in fact banned in Vienna, recent scholars have been more concerned with the collection methods of the brothers and the editing of the stories from the original volume to the much more widely distributed later editions. From the beginning the Grimms viewed their collection as an *Erziehungsbuch*, or instructional book, and not as a volume of tales amusing to children. Beginning in 1815, when Wilhelm Grimm took over the majority of the brothers' editing duties, numerous stories were abridged, edited, and expanded. In one of many examples, the little girl in "The Frog Prince" was changed from an ordinary German girl into a princess of a kingdom. In that manner, the Grimms altered the stories to make them conform to their own notions of class and nationhood, with the aim of instilling similar values in children.

In Germany, in the 1920's, fairy tales once again became a political topic, as the education and socialization of children became an overt object of all the major political parties. Writers associated with the left wing of German politics voiced disapproval of the conservative social values exhibited in the stories of the Brothers Grimm and in those of later writers such as Hans Christian Andersen. Instead of arguing for censorship, however, a group of writers led by Hans Dominick and Sophie Rheinheimer constructed an alternative set of tales, poems, and plays, which they considered to be both more progressive and more liberating. This movement came to an abrupt halt, however, with the collapse of the Weimar Republic and the advent of Nazi rule. The Nazis banned all such writing as communist propaganda and substituted their own nationalistic canon of tales. The argument was finally settled during the

Allied occupation of Germany after World War II, when all fairy tales were banned briefly because the Allies feared the nationalistic implications of the tales and their effects on the German citizenry.   —*Jeff Cupp*

See also *Arabian Nights, The*; Boccaccio, Giovanni; Books, children's; Books, young adult; Dahl, Roald; Disney films; *Little Black Sambo*; National Socialism (Nazism); Orwell, George; Stalin, Joseph.

BIBLIOGRAPHY

Bruno Bettelheim's *The Uses of Enchantment: The Meaning and Importance of Fairy Tales* (New York: Alfred A. Knopf, 1976) is the standard work on the psychology of fairy tales. John Ellis' *One Fairy Story Too Many: The Brothers Grimm and Their Tales* (Chicago: University of Chicago Press, 1983) takes a different sociological approach. Ellis is highly critical of the methods of Brothers Grimm in the collecting and marketing of their famous tales. Allen Dundes' *Cinderella: A Folklore Casebook* (New York: Garland, 1982) presents a far-ranging examination of this one well-known story. Two works by Jack Zipes focus on the often troubled history of fairy tales. His *Fairy Tales and the Art of Subversion* (New York: Wildman Press, 1983) is probably the best work on the political history of the fairy tale. Likewise, his *The Brothers Grimm* (New York: Routledge, 1988) presents much little-known material on both the Brothers Grimm and the reception given to their tales.

Falkland Islands War

DATE: April 2, 1982-June 14, 1982
PLACE: Falkland Islands, South Atlantic Ocean
SIGNIFICANCE: During this war between Argentina and Great Britain, Argentina's military junta heavily censored the press and gave it false information; the British government provided limited opportunities for press coverage

When Argentina became independent in 1816, it assumed Spain's claim to the Falkland (Malvina) Islands about three hundred miles off the coast of southern Argentina in the South Atlantic. It occupied the islands in 1829, fifty-four years after the British had voluntarily withdrawn from them. In 1833 Great Britain reoccupied the islands. Argentina continued to claim the islands but made no attempt to enforce the claim until after World War II. In 1947 Argentina began political and military initiatives to regain the islands. World opinion forced Great Britain in 1966 to begin negotiations with Argentina. Argentina claimed sovereignty and wanted the islands returned. Great Britain was not anxious to retain them but hesitated to withdraw because the inhabitants, called Kelpers, wanted to remain British. Consistently citing the principle of self-determination in the negotiations, Great Britain insisted on safeguards for the Kelpers. Negotiations continued until the war broke out.

By 1980 the military junta in Argentina had become unpopular because of the brutal suppression of any opposition, the large number of disappeared, and the disastrous economic policies that increased inflation and decreased purchasing power for the masses and the middle class.

To divert public attention from the political and economic problems, the junta decided to seize the Falklands. The junta was convinced that Great Britain would not fight for the islands, that the United States would support Argentina, that world public opinion would favor Argentina, and that Argentines would rally behind the government in a burst of patriotic fervor. The junta was wrong in the first three points and only partially correct on the fourth. Most Argentines did rally behind the government at first but turned against the government before the war was over.

Press censorship already existed; so the junta was able to censor news coverage of negotiations with England, secret preparations for war, and the war. The junta released false information to the press to hide the reverses that demonstrated the total incompetence of the military and the ineptness or cowardice of the military leadership. When the war was lost and the truth could no longer be hidden, Argentines reacted so violently that the military government was forced out. Civilians assumed control in July, 1982.

In England press coverage of peace negotiations was restricted, and war news was limited because of the isolated location of the Falkland Islands and poor communications with the islands. One of the greatest problems for the British navy was the very poor and limited communications on the islands and between the islands and England. Few correspondents were included in the British task force, and those present had little means of communicating with England while aboard the ships or on the islands. Even the war cabinet in England, which was directing the war, had little current information on the conduct of the war. It did, however, release more information to the press than the naval commanders in charge of the military effort wanted known. When Great Britain won the war, the British public quickly forgot about any inadequacies in the press coverage.

See also Argentina; Grenada, U.S. invasion of; South America; United Kingdom; War.

Family

DEFINITION: Families maintain their religious and social standing through internalized sanctions and prohibitions
SIGNIFICANCE: The nature, degree, and manner of imposition of family censorship varies widely, but it is generally present

Any system of child-rearing and family relations practices two categories of prohibitions. The first includes prohibitions common to nearly all families for maintaining health and safety, especially that of children and young adults (for example, family rules against the children's smoking). The second is intended to maintain family status in the community (for example, family rules against foul language, especially when a minister is visiting). These two categories may overlap, but family censorship involves the second category.

Sources of Family Censorship. Whatever its social and political environment, the family can never escape social and cultural influences. At one extreme, nearly all the roles and functions of the family are defined in terms of government goals and principles. At the other extreme, family lineage and clan attachment prevail over social, legal, or economic norms.

In either case, the norms are there to be followed or to be resisted.

The modern Western world's multifaceted conception of family makes defining family roles harder. For example, the phenomenon of same-gender parents introduces new social and legal questions regarding freedom, censorship, and sexuality. As the realities of the nuclear family change, the conception of the family as a training ground for children also changes. Families with sometimes radically opposing conceptions of a proper and good life use censorship to define their position in the society and to distinguish themselves from others. In one family, denigrating jokes about homosexuals or some other minority group may be de rigueur; in another, such jokes might be frowned upon.

Religious Sources of Family Censorship. Sometimes it is difficult to distinguish social, political, or cultural influences from religious ones. In most societies, including Western society, religion plays a powerful role in moral conceptions. Censorship of sexual thoughts, beliefs, and behavior usually stem from religious beliefs. The most severe moral restrictions in many Jewish, Christian, and Islamic families concern sex.

For example, the Ayatollah Ruhollah Khomeini's revolution in Iran was also a revolution against "corruption" of youth, primarily through Western sexual ideas and practices. He imposed severe censorship of Western news and entertainment; the influence of such censorship spread, as was intended, to families. Seeing women in bathing suits was bad; but during the Iran-Iraq war, hundreds of thousands of boys as young as eleven gave, with government encouragement that families felt obliged to reinforce, their lives for Islam. Khomeini attributed their willingness to accept martyrdom to his program of cleaning their minds of Western "filth."

Young people in response to biological changes exhibit sexual curiosity. Christian, Jewish, and Muslim parents expend enormous energy controlling their children's sexual behavior. In some societies, such as Islamic ones, dating in a Western manner is forbidden. Even engaged couples are not allowed to spend time together. Many marriages take place without dating. In the West, experienced teachers know that many parents who otherwise show no interest in their children's schooling will become furiously involved if sexual, religious, or racial issues are addressed directly in the classroom. Thus as society influences the family, so the family influences society; what children are told is unspeakable remains unspeakable, in many cases, when those children become adults.

According to noted thinker Sigmund Freud, severe sexual restriction and censorship in the family results in unhealthy psychological side effects. Freud believed children have sexual desires, including desires for the parent of the opposite sex. Freud argued that society invented the taboo against certain sexual practices such as incest to censure not only the act but also the thought. Although others have disagreed with his concept of the child's desire for incest, many have agreed with the point of his insight, which is that repression, including censorship, is an integral part of society, including the basic unit of society—the family.

Family Censorship and Marriage. Family censorship in the form of taboos and moral codes and practices of sexuality determines the range of acceptable conduct, especially regarding marriage. In many societies, the woman's sexual and economic subjugation to her husband through various intricate systems of censorship is accepted practice and even sometimes religiously praiseworthy. In a Hindu family the laws of marriage and courtship go back at least four thousand years; the wife is specifically accorded a lesser place to that of her husband.

In many cultures the woman loses her legal identity through marriage. To offset this, some Muslim women, for example, create considerable control over their wealth through legal ownership of their dowry. Sometimes size of dowry determines success or failure of a proposed marriage. "Bride services" are another form of dowry given in the form of service to the family of the bride by the potential husband to ensure his control and censorship over the bride in the future.

In most societies the husband or father sets the normative censorship in the family, with the exception of a few cultures, such as the Kuna Indians of Panama and the Nayar people in India. Kuna women through marriage become heads of their families and imparters of culture and morality. They control the economic and political power of the family and devise guidelines for their husbands' behavior. Nayar women go further. They do not allow the official husband to claim economic, parental, or moral responsibility. In Nayar culture there is also a form of sexual matriarchy at work. The wedding of a couple is to legitimize the woman's ability to have sexual intercourse with any man of distinction for the purpose of procreation. This kind of polyandry is a reversal of most accepted censorship and sexual practices in the world.

Censorship in courting and marriage is also used by families for purely pragmatic reasons. Parents who want to maintain wealth, power, or aristocratic culture, for example, set standards for their children's marriages. Some lower-class parents may push their children to marry persons of higher classes in hopes of social and financial advancement.

Different cultures exert different degrees of sexual censorship on choice of mate. Variations include parents' prohibition and censorship of sexual activities prior to marriage and control over choice of spouse—sometimes prescribing marriage between specific individuals and assigning mates to children before they are even born; instructing children to seek mates with specific qualifications; isolation of children from unacceptable potential mates; close or total supervision and censorship during courtship; freedom in sexual exploration, with informal control exerted by parents, relatives, and friends.

Family censorship differs from other forms of censorship in that the effect on children, who are impressionable and who are inclined to accept parental influence much more than that of an outsider, is deeper and longer lasting.   —*Chogollah Maroufi*

See also Christianity; *Garden of Eden, The*; Islam; Morality; Religious education; Sex education; Television, children's.

BIBLIOGRAPHY

For a clear philosophical discussion of morality and family, see Albert Cafegna, Richard Peterson, and Craig Staudenfaur,

Philosophy, Children, and Family (New York: Plenum Press, 1982). Harry Chlor's *Obscenity and Public Morality* (Chicago: University of Chicago Press, 1985) is a balanced account of obscenity in the media and the role of family in the debate. *The Front Lines of Sexuality Education: A Guide to Building and Maintaining Community Support* (New York: Network Publication, 1984) by Peter Scales and *Banned! Censorship in the Schools* (New York: Messner, 1988) by Donald Rogers are good sources about pros and cons of sex education in schools and placing controversial materials in school libraries, including parental involvement in the process. The first volume of Michel Foucault's *The History of Sexuality* (New York: Vintage Books, 1978) is a thorough historical account of the evolution of sexual morality and censorship in Western cultures.

Fanny Hill, The Memoirs of

TYPE OF WORK: Book
PUBLISHED: 1749
AUTHOR: John Cleland (1709-1789)

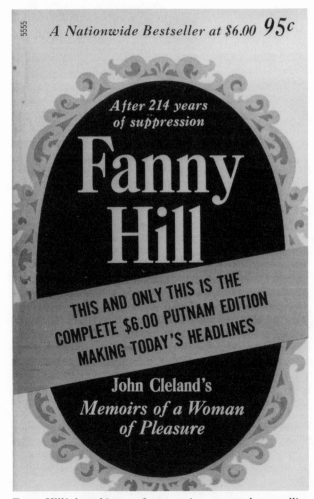

Fanny Hill's long history of suppression was used as a selling point when the book entered the world of mass-marketing in the 1960's. (Arkent Archive)

SUBJECT MATTER: A satiric erotic novel whose central character goes through a sexual awakening
SIGNIFICANCE: In 1821 this book was the first in the United States to be charged with being obscene

Fanny Hill: Memoirs of a Woman of Pleasure details the sexual adventures of a teenage girl in London. Orphaned at fifteen, Frances Hill, with little skill and education, must find a way to survive. She leaves her village for London and finds employment at Mrs. Brown's brothel. Fanny believes her new job to be legitimate, but her curiosity and sensuality are aroused when the prostitute with whom she shares a room introduces her to sex. Mrs. Brown then tricks Fanny into "servicing" a client, and the girl is nearly raped. She escapes from the bordello and falls in love with a man named Charles, who is sent to sea by his father before he can provide for Fanny. Once more destitute and alone, Fanny finds work at an upper-class brothel, where she experiences a multitude of sexual acts and discovers that sex for money is not as satisfying as sex for love. Fanny is removed from the bordello by an elderly gentleman, who cares for her, instructs her in the arts and sciences, and, after eight months, dies, leaving her his fortune. Soon after her benefactor's death, Fanny is reunited with Charles, and the two live happily ever after.

In 1821 the Commonwealth of Massachusetts tried to ban *Fanny Hill*, claiming that it was obscene. Previously ruled obscene in England in 1761, the book did not receive broad acceptance or distribution in the newly formed United States. However, since it was somewhat popular in "underground" circles, a publisher named Peter Holmes saw an opportunity to profit from printing and selling it. During the trial, the prosecutor based his arguments solely on the book's sexual content, arguing that, under common law, it should not be printed or possessed. The trial court judge agreed and found Holmes guilty of obscene libel.

Presenting his appeal before the Massachusetts Supreme Court, Holmes's lawyer seemed to accept the decision that the book was obscene, arguing for his client not on First Amendment grounds but on technical grounds, since Holmes had not published and delivered the book to a particular individual, as he had been charged, but had rather published the book "generally." In its decision the higher court stated that Holmes was a "scandalous and evil disposed person" who was contriving to corrupt the morals of the "good citizens of said commonwealth . . . and to raise and create in their minds inordinate and lustful desire." This decision would be the sole legal ruling in the United States regarding obscenity in published material until 1890.

See also Banned Books Week; *Lady Chatterley's Lover*; Literature; *Miller v. California*; Obscenity: legal definitions; Obscenity: sale and possession.

Far Side, The

TYPE OF WORK: Comic strip
PUBLISHED: 1979 to 1995
AUTHOR: Gary Larson (1950-   )
SUBJECT MATTER: Unconventional visual humor, such as reversals of animal and human behavior

SIGNIFICANCE: One of the most popular comic strips of the 1980's and early 1990's *The Far Side* was also one of the most frequently censored

Cartoonist Gary Larson's daily single-panel comic strip *The Far Side*, which first appeared in 1979, was often accused of bad taste. One popular cartoon, for example, showed two angry parents yelling at a witch, with the caption, "We hired you to babysit the kids, and you cooked and ate them BOTH?" Despite its controversial content, *The Far Side* eventually appeared in more than nine hundred newspapers. Although some publications dropped it owing to its frequent depictions of implied violence, most brought it back when loyal readers protested.

Many newspapers carried *The Far Side* but refused to print selected cartoons. *The Los Angeles Times*, for example, turned down a panel showing a peg-legged elephant speaking into a telephone, captioned, "What? They turned it into a *waste-basket*?" Other cartoons were rejected entirely by Larson's editor, such as a panel showing a surgeon offering a begging dog a morsel from a human patient's body. Larson also often drew cartoons that he never offered to his editor, knowing that they would not be published. Many of his controversial, censored, and unpublished cartoons can be found in the collection *The PreHistory of the Far Side: A 10th Anniversary Exhibit* (1989). Larson stopped drawing *The Far Side* in 1995.

See also Comic books; *Doonesbury*; MAD magazine; Newspapers; Violence.

Farewell to Arms, A

TYPE OF WORK: Book
PUBLISHED: 1929
AUTHOR: Ernest Hemingway (1899-1961)
SUBJECT MATTER: During World War I an American ambulance driver serving Italy becomes disillusioned but finds love with an English nurse
SIGNIFICANCE: Older realistic fiction, such as *A Farewell to Arms*, continues to be attacked by censors, especially when taught in public schools

Before publishing *A Farewell to Arms*, Ernest Hemingway complained bitterly about his editor's acting as censor, removing unsavory words that conveyed important truths about war and love. Despite his editor's efforts, reviews of the novel often asked if it were art or "dirt." Several cities in the United States banned the book briefly because of its language. Italy's Fascist government banned the book because it depicted the cowardice and atrocities of Italian soldiers during the retreat at

Adolphe Menjou watches Gary Cooper explore a woman's foot in the 1932 film adaptation of Ernest Hemingway's A Farewell to Arms. *(Museum of Modern Art/Film Stills Archive)*

Caporetto during World War I. The government also forced cuts in a 1932 film adaptation.

Over the years, the book continued to draw fire, especially when taught in U.S. public schools. During the 1980's, the American Library Association listed the novel as perennially challenged for three primary reasons: sex and debauchery; violent deaths and senseless brutality; and belief in a universe indifferent to people's suffering. Despite critical acclaim for the book—its honest description of war, unique writing style, and timeless story of tragic lovers—it continues to be challenged as "pacifist propaganda" and "un-American."

See also American Library Association; Hemingway, Ernest; Italy; Libraries, school; Literature; Morality; War; World War I.

Farrakhan, Louis Abdoul

BORN: May 11, 1933, New York, New York

IDENTIFICATION: Leader of the Nation of Islam

SIGNIFICANCE: Farrakhan has frequently been a center of national controversy because of his outspokenness

Farrakhan first achieved national recognition in 1984. When Jesse Jackson announced his intention to seek the Democratic Party's nomination for president of the United States, Farrakhan publicly endorsed him. He also encouraged his followers to register and vote, and had members of his special security force, the Fruit of Islam, provide protection for Jackson. During the ensuing political campaign the news media attributed several anti-Semitic statements to Farrakhan, including a remark that seemed to praise Adolf Hitler, another that described Judaism as a "gutter religion," and one implying that the media were Jewish controlled.

Since that time public appearances and speeches by Farrakhan and his associates have frequently resulted in controversy. His appearances at Syracuse University and the University of Pennsylvania, for example, were picketed by students. In New York City the Nation of Islam sued the operators of the Jacob Javits Convention Center, claiming that they had reneged on an oral agreement to rent them space for a meeting. Farrakhan eventually spoke at the center before an audience of twenty-five thousand. In Los Angeles, Jewish leaders opposed Farrakhan's 1985 appearance at the Forum, where he attracted an audience of fifteen thousand, although local leaders had characterized him as an anti-Semitic demagogue.

In early 1986 Farrakhan was invited by Great Britain's Black People's Association to speak in London, but British home secretary Douglas Hurd barred him from entering the country because of his alleged anti-Semitic remarks. In December that same year more than a third of the members of the New York Philharmonic Orchestra refused to play at a free concert at Harlem's Abyssinian Baptist Church because its minister would not denounce Farrakhan for calling Judaism a "gutter religion." During the criminal trial of Washington, D.C., mayor Marion Barry, Jr., in 1990, the judge tried to bar Farrakhan from the courtroom saying his presence might be disruptive and intimidating to jurors. Following his appeal to a federal court, Farrakhan was admitted to the courtroom.

Attempts by Farrakhan to work with more mainstream African American leaders have also generated controversy. In 1993, for example, Congressman Kweisi Mfume was criticized for inviting Farrakhan to a congressional Black Caucus meeting. The following year National Association for the Advancement of Colored People leader Benjamin Chavis was criticized for inviting Farrakhan to a conference of black leaders in Baltimore. Farrakhan's attempt to become more acceptable to mainstream leaders suffered a further setback in 1994 when his aide Khallid Abdul Muhammad gave a highly publicized racist and anti-Semitic speech at Kean College in New Jersey. Afterward Farrakhan demoted Muhammad, while defending the truths he claimed that Muhammad had expressed.

Farrakhan has consistently accused the news media of distorting his statements. In a 1984 speech in Columbus, Ohio, for example, he claimed that "as long as Jewish people control the media, Arabs, Blacks, Muslims will never have a balanced

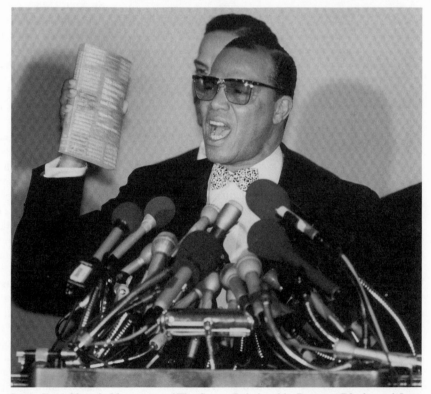

Louis Farrakhan holds a copy of The Secret Relationship Between Blacks and Jews *at a Washington, D.C., news conference in February, 1994, after dismissing an aide for publicly making anti-Semitic remarks.* (AP/Wide World Photos)

view." He also attacked the "Jewish controlled media" for its handling of Jesse Jackson's 1984 presidential campaign. After leading the "Million Man March" in Washington, D.C., in 1995, Farrakhan again criticized the media, claiming that their commentaries on the event were part of a racist plot.

See also African Americans; Anti-Defamation League, the; Islam; Judaism; Political campaigning; Race.

Faulk, John Henry

BORN: August 21, 1913, Austin, Texas
DIED: April 9, 1990, Austin, Texas
IDENTIFICATION: Television personality and author
SIGNIFICANCE: Faulk was blacklisted during the 1950's and won a major libel suit against the organization that accused him of communist sympathies

John Henry Faulk awaits the verdict in his 1962 libel suit against the investigative company whose claims that he had communist links cost him his broadcasting job. (AP/Wide World Photos)

Faulk was born to liberal-minded parents and received a master's degree in American folklore from the University of Texas. He served in the Red Cross and the Army during World War II, then started a career in radio in 1946. Faulk was a supporter of Henry Wallace's 1948 presidential campaign and other liberal causes. In 1949 he hosted a daily radio show on WPAT in Paterson, New Jersey, moving in 1951 to WCBS, where for six years he hosted the *The John Henry Faulk Show*. He also appeared on many early television talk programs.

Faulk became active in the New York local of the American Federation of Television and Radio Artists (AFTRA) in 1955. AFTRA was a union that represented television and radio artists. In December, 1955, Faulk won election as vice president of AFTRA's New York local. In February, 1956, an or-

ganization called AWARE, Inc., issued a bulletin claiming that Faulk was sympathetic to communism. AWARE was a private company that investigated and "cleared" members of the entertainment industry of suspected communist ties. Faulk filed suit against the company in June, 1956, retaining the famed attorney Louis Nizer as his lawyer. However, Faulk soon lost his job at Columbia Broadcasting System (CBS) radio and was unable to find work in the entertainment industry for several years. The suit dragged through the courts for years, but on June 28, 1962, Faulk was awarded $3.5 million by a New York jury. His suit established that blacklisting occurred throughout the entertainment industry.

Soon after the trial, Faulk returned to radio and television appearances. In 1964 he wrote *Fear on Trial*, a memoir of his legal battles. A television movie based on the book was aired on CBS in 1975. From 1975 to 1980, Faulk was a regular member of the television show *Hee Haw*. Known for his folksy wit and storytelling, he later lectured on the First Amendment to college audiences and performed in a one-man show entitled *Pear Orchard*.

See also Blacklisting; Communism; Radio; Television; Television networks.

Faulkner, William

BORN: September 25, 1897, New Albany, Mississippi
DIED: July 6, 1962, Byhalia, Mississippi
IDENTIFICATION: American novelist
SIGNIFICANCE: Although Faulkner won both the Pulitzer Prize and the Nobel Prize in Literature, his works are among those most frequently banned by public libraries and school boards

Faulkner's novels deal explicitly with such controversial topics as rape, incest, masturbation, castration, adultery, impotence, and racism. Despite the fact that such topics are always peripheral to his primary concerns, his novels have been attacked continuously as being shocking and immoral. None of his works was ever subject to direct governmental censorship, but they have often been subjected to cultural censorship.

Boni and Liveright, publishers of Faulkner's second novel, *Mosquitos* (1927), insisted on deleting passages that they felt verged on perversion. When Faulkner submitted the manuscript for *Sanctuary* (1931), which in part deals with the brutal rape of a young college student and her subsequent descent into sexual and moral depravity, to his new publishers, Cape and Smith, in June of 1929, Hal Smith wrote back saying "I can't publish this. We'd both be in jail." However, Smith eventually decided to take a chance on the book, so *Sanctuary*, Faulkner's fifth novel, was published in 1931. Reviews of the book expressed both horror at its subject matter and admiration for its power. In the public mind Faulkner became associated with sadism, violence, and decadence. His own father was outraged by *Sanctuary* and sought to have it suppressed and withdrawn from the market. Ironically, *Sanctuary* was a great financial and popular success, made Faulkner a more widely respected artist, and lead to a reexamination of his previous novels, which included *The Sound and the Fury* (1929) and *As I Lay Dying* (1930).

None of Faulkner's other novels was ever as controversial as *Sanctuary*; in fact, with the publication of *Light in August* in 1932 and *Absalom, Absalom!* in 1936, he was widely recognized as one of America's greatest novelists. His artistic achievement was acknowledged by the literary world when he received the Nobel Prize in Literature in 1950. In spite of the fact that his novels frequently dealt with sensational topics, his primary concerns were, in the words of his Nobel Prize acceptance speech: "the problems of the human heart in conflict with itself. . . . the old verities and truths of the heart, the old universal truths lacking which any story is ephemeral and doomed—love and honor and pity and pride and compassion and sacrifice." Faulkner had no sympathy for writers who wrote about sex or violence or degradation just for their own sake. He believed that sex, greed, and violence were powerful forces in human life, and, consequently, that any writer interested in dealing truthfully with mankind and the human heart must do justice to their roles in human life. He said that a writer "shouldn't be inhibited by any fear of censorship. If he knows it to be true and worth telling, then he should tell it."

Although Faulkner undertook goodwill tours for the U.S. State Department in the late 1950's and spoke out against the McCarthy hearings and racial segregation, he was essentially an apolitical man and writer. He was, in fact, passionate about the sanctity of his private life and resented intrusions of the press into his personal affairs. He felt that every citizen who was neither a criminal nor a politician had an absolute right to privacy and that the press, the government, and moral watchdog groups were destroying the last vestiges of individual privacy under the guise of freedom of the press or national security or morality. He did not advocate censorship of the press; rather he called upon his fellow citizens and the press to take the meanings of liberty, individuality, and personal freedom more seriously.

See also Literature; Morality; Prostitution; Sex in the arts; Violence.

Fear

DEFINITION: Anxious reaction to perceived danger

SIGNIFICANCE: Fear plays an important role in censorship, which is motivated by fear of words, images, or ideas that are viewed as dangerous, and which is reinforced by fear of punishment

The Psychology of Censorship. Sigmund Freud, the founder of psychoanalysis, maintained that human beings engage in a form of self-censorship that he termed repression. People have desires, including sexual desires and the desire for power. The early sexual feelings of children, Freud believed, are directed toward those closest to them, their parents. As children learn that some forms of sexuality, especially sexuality with parents, are forbidden, they repress or censor the dangerous feelings from their conscious minds, but they continue to hold their desires unconsciously. Most people can deal with this act of repression with little difficulty, but for some there is a constant, anxiety-producing struggle to push the unacceptable urges out of awareness. The fear of one's own impulses, especially sexual impulses, can lead to an intense need to stifle the thoughts and expressions related to these impulses.

This Freudian psychological perspective can help to explain why the suppression of sexual expression is such a prominent part of censorship. Sexually explicit materials seem threatening to many people because the materials provoke their own self-forbidden desires. Anthony Comstock, who founded the New York Society for the Suppression of Vice in 1871 and who became America's most famous antipornography crusader, seems to have been a case study in this type of psychology of censorship. Comstock saw indecency everywhere: in nude statues, in dime novels, and in the poetry of Walt Whitman. He attributed an enormous, evil power to sexuality in art and literature, claiming that Satan used "evil reading" to destroy families and nations.

Comstock displayed an obsessive fascination with the vices he sought to suppress, and he was known to read pornographic materials before destroying them. In June, 1878, he made headlines when he attended a sex show involving three women and sat through the entire show before arresting the women. Most psychologists would maintain that Comstock crusaded against such activities precisely because he was drawn to them, and his fear of pornography was actually a fear of his own sexuality.

Insecurity and the Fear of Freedom. Theories of fear of sexuality can provide insight into why some individuals advocate censorship, but they are not a complete explanation. Sexual expression is not the only target of censorship. Moreover, tolerance for freedom of expression varies at different times and in different places.

The psychologist Erich Fromm argued that authoritarianism, intolerance for freedom, can be produced by insecurity and that times of insecurity tend to produce calls for political control. According to Fromm, individualism is the key characteristic of modern civilization. This means that individuals have the liberty to realize their own natures and their differences from one another. It also means, though, that people may have a sense of isolation from others and of being small and powerless. Liberty therefore poses a threat to people's identities, since social groups provide human beings with their identities.

When a society undergoes economic and social hardships, people feel especially threatened, in Fromm's view, and the loneliness of freedom becomes particularly hard to bear. People come to fear freedom, and they feel the need to escape from it and to lose their isolated selves in some greater authority. By providing rules for what can and cannot be said, or even thought, authoritarian governments provide psychological stability based on a strong sense of identification with a group. Those who have escaped from freedom by submerging themselves in a group often see outsiders or people who violate the rules as demons who threaten the foundations of social life.

This group psychology perspective may help to explain why Comstock's personal obsessions became so influential in post-Civil War America. At the time that Comstock was active (1871-1915), the United States was rapidly changing from a rural, agricultural society to an urban, industrial one. Immigration was greater than at any other time in American history, and large numbers of new immigrants were arriving from southern and eastern Europe, bringing with them languages and cultures that were strange to earlier settlers. It was in New York, which had become a huge industrial metropolis in the course of a single generation and which was the port of arrival for the greatest number of immigrants, that Comstock founded his society. Support for his crusade against pornographers and

The first attempt at legal censorship in the United States, the Alien and Sedition Act of 1798, occurred when many in the new country were anxious about the nation's chances for survival. The United States was caught between warring England and post-revolutionary France. There were Americans who sympathized with each side. France's revolution had turned extremely violent, and some feared that America might fall into a similar violent upheaval. Many in the Federalist

For more than four years Senator Joseph McCarthy waged a communist witch-hunt that helped keep Americans afraid to speak their minds until the hollowness and hypocrisy of his crusade was exposed to the nation in hearings broadcast on national television in 1954. (AP/Wide World Photos)

morally impure people came from those living in an increasingly complex and unfamiliar environment who wanted to define and safeguard a pure community.

Confidence and Free Speech. Censorship can be seen as a product of fear produced by lack of political self-confidence, as well as a product of psychological insecurities. The principle of free speech is based on the idea that if all individuals express themselves without legal restraint, the community of citizens will be able to weigh all ideas, and to accept the good ones and reject the bad ones. When a nation's self-confidence is shaken, people may question whether it is safe to let citizens hear, see, and decide for themselves.

Party of President John Adams believed that the Democratic-Republican Party of Thomas Jefferson contained pro-French subversives. Democratic-Republican criticisms of the Federalist government were seen as weakening the nation to prepare it for a French invasion.

A somewhat similar faltering of national self-confidence stimulated efforts at political censorship during the 1950's. Americans became concerned over the apparent spread of communism and feared that their own national survival was in danger. As in 1798, many believed that the external threat from alien political and social doctrines was also an internal threat from subversives. Fear of communism and a lack of confidence in American institutions led to the blacklisting of suspected radicals in the movie and television industries. The Smith Act of 1940, which made it a crime to advocate the violent overthrow of the U.S. government, began to be enforced against members of the Communist Party, reflecting a fear that Americans might actually be persuaded by advocates of revolutionary violence. —*Carl L. Bankston III*

See also Communism; Intellectual freedom; Maya books, destruction of; Sedition.

BIBLIOGRAPHY

Eli M. Oboler's *The Fear of the Word: Censorship and Sex* (Metuchen, N.J.: Scarecrow Press, 1974) provides a study of the relationship between sexual taboos and censorship. Erich Fromm's *Escape from Freedom* (New York: Holt, Rinehart and Winston, 1941) is not specifically about censorship, but it is a classic psychological description of how fear of freedom can lead to political intolerance. Patrick M. Garry's *An American Paradox: Censorship in a Nation of Free Speech* (Westport, Conn.: Praeger, 1993) looks at the role of censorship in the American search for national identity. Garry argues that calls for censorship tend to arise when Americans feel anxious and insecure.

Federal Bureau of Investigation (FBI)

FOUNDED: July 1, 1908

TYPE OF ORGANIZATION: The principal investigative arm of the U.S. Department of Justice

SIGNIFICANCE: With the broadest mandate of any federal law enforcement agency, the FBI has been accused of many censorship activities

From its creation the FBI has acted to censor the behavior of some and encroached upon the civil liberties of many. In 1907 U.S. attorney general Charles J. Bonaparte approached Congress with the idea of establishing a permanent detective force within the department of justice (DOJ). On July 1 of the following year, Congress authorized the creation of the agency but did not provide the DOJ with its own investigators. Rather, the Justice Department was to borrow agents from the Secret Service, which operated under the authority of the Treasury Department. Bonaparte pointed out that such an arrangement presented numerous problems, not the least of which was the need for prior Treasury approval for the loan of agents. Bonaparte argued that this arrangement left little chance that any investigation could be kept confidential. In 1909 a Special Agent force was then created within the DOJ and named the Bureau of Investigation by the new attorney general, George W. Wickersham. In August, 1921, J. Edgar Hoover was appointed to the position of assistant chief of the bureau, a position Hoover had lobbied Attorney General Harry M. Daugherty to attain. In December, 1924, Hoover was appointed director of the agency that he would lead for the next forty-eight years. The agency received the name of Federal Bureau of Investigation in 1935.

Initially, agents of the FBI investigated violations of the relatively few federal criminal statutes that existed, such as those concerning bankruptcy frauds, antitrust crimes, and neutrality violations. The White Slave Traffic Act of 1910 offered an opportunity for government intrusion into private matters. Better known as the Mann Act, the law was passed to curb prostitution by prohibiting the interstate transport of a woman for "immoral purposes." The act was used by the bureau to develop dossiers on criminals who frequented brothels, on elected officials who received bribes, on wealthy socialites who profited as the landlords of the hotels, and on rooming houses used by prostitutes and their customers. The FBI's cozy relationship with madams allowed it to put an end to John Dillinger's criminal career in 1934.

During World War I the Bureau was given responsibility for espionage, sabotage, sedition, and draft violations. It was during this period that the bureau exercised further censorship and violated more civil liberties. With the war, anything German became anathema. Teaching the language was banned from many schools as was the performance of music by German composers. The perceived threat of spies led in quick succession to the passage of the Espionage Act (1917), the Sedition Act (1918), and the Alien Deportation Act (1919). The fact that many brewers were German aided the growth of the temperance movement and assisted passage of the Eighteenth Amendment in 1920, which initiated Prohibition.

Hoover had won Daugherty's support because of Hoover's role as leader of the earlier General Intelligence Division (GID) of the DOJ. As chief of the GID, Hoover was not only familiar with the dossiers on prominent people collected in response to investigations concerning violations of the Mann Act, but made it clear that such information would be made public if it suited him. Hoover had investigated striking labor unions and pointed out to Daugherty "the menace of Communism," the threat of the growing labor movement, and, moreover, the role of foreign-born "agitators." Under Hoover, the GID, which was organized in 1919, began infiltrating labor unions, collecting information on activists and others believed to be a threat to the status quo. Government raids on meetings of the Industrial Workers of the World (IWW) led to the deportation of some labor activists and the imprisonment of others. The FBI's activities had a stifling effect on the growth of unions.

The Selective Service Act of 1917, which required that all males between the ages of twenty-one and thirty register for the draft, inspired the DOJ to seek draft dodgers. Experimental, illegal roundups of men from street corners, pool halls, theaters, hotel lobbies and barber shops took place in major U.S. cities. Thousands had their constitutional rights violated because warrants had not been issued. Such roundups netted only a few draft dodgers, and although the American Civil Liberties Union objected, by 1921 a list of nearly a half million names of "agitators" was compiled and cross-referenced by location. The list permitted the quick identification of activists, picketing laborers, strikers, and others in the event of social unrest. Such measures had an intended chilling effect on dissent.

The Middle Years. The passage of Prohibition in 1920 prompted an increase in the number of gangsters and the growth of what became known as organized crime. Furthermore, the collapse of the stock market in 1929 put much of the nation out of work, heightened awareness of criminal activity, and prompted a need for further law enforcement. Kidnapping, bank robbery, and other acts became federal crimes in 1932 and 1934, enlarging the FBI's beat. The new statutes of the early 1930's gave Special Agents the authority to make arrests and to carry firearms and prompted the further creation of government files on citizens. While Hoover was always concerned about communists, a group he despised his entire career, by means of various presidential directives in 1936 the FBI was given authority to investigate Nazis as well. The FBI targeted union leaders of the automobile, coal, steel, and garment industries as well as those at educational institutions. Laws and presidential mandates in response to the social change prompted the FBI to intrude further into the lives of citizens by using wiretaps and other surveillance techniques. President Franklin D. Roosevelt's 1940 authorization for the attorney general to use wiretaps to eavesdrop on conversations of people suspected of being subversive was used by the FBI to justify telephone tapping U.S. citizens. Immediately following the 1941 attack on Pearl Harbor, Hoover assumed personal responsibility for acting as the government's censor of information concerning the attack.

The FBI's size and jurisdiction grew during World War II to include intelligence matters in Central and South America. At the end of the war and the beginning of the Cold War, the FBI conducted further politically motivated investigations and created additional government files. During the 1945 organizational meetings of the United Nations in San Francisco, the FBI issued scores of credentials with fictitious names to agents in the hope of collecting potentially valuable intelligence information. Additionally, background security investigations for the White House and other government agencies became the province of the FBI following the war. The FBI participated in blacklisting suspected and former communists; blacklisting not only prevented those accused from working but also effectively censored their freedoms of speech, inquiry, and creativity.

Across university campuses students and faculty became the center of inquiries concerning communists, former communists, or suspected communists. Foreign language institutes and research centers directed at understanding the Soviet Union and other nations attracted FBI interest and prompted accusations of conspiracy. Academic discourse thus was censored. A Library Awareness Program was initiated by the FBI to obtain the borrowing records of library patrons suspected of being a security risk. This program sought to bring university librarians into the fold of investigators and to mark those with foreign names as spies or political agitators. Librarians have denounced such practices. In addition to investigations of counterterrorism, white-collar crime, drugs, and organized crime, periods of social unrest—such as that during the Civil Rights and peace movements—permitted the FBI to add to the number of intelligence files on U.S. citizens. Leaders of the National Association for the Advancement of Colored People (NAACP) were targeted for their views, as were those promoting peace.

The FBI's Image. The FBI's image has been shaped by its censorship activities. In 1935 Hoover negotiated his total control of *G-Men*, a radio series that became very popular for addressing the agency's famous cases. The publication of Donald Whitehead's book *The FBI Story* in 1956, which later became a popular film, provided Hoover and the FBI further propaganda opportunities. The image of the FBI that Hoover wished to extol was made popular in the television series *The FBI* The series starred Efrem Zimbalist, Jr., and ran on television from 1965 to 1974. Each of the program's scripts required Hoover's personal approval. In addition, FBI agents monitored the film production of each story.

The FBI's 1992 role at Ruby Ridge, Idaho, against the Weaver family, as well as its involvement in actions taken against the Branch Davidians at Waco, Texas, in 1993, which resulted in the death of more than eighty people, have prompted concerns and questions of FBI censorship and cover-up.

—Turhon A. Murad

See also American Civil Liberties Union; Blacklisting; Central Intelligence Agency; Communist Party of the U.S.A.; Draft resistance; Espionage Act of 1917; Hoover, J. Edgar; Picketing; Sedition; Temperance movements.

BIBLIOGRAPHY

Sigmund Diamond recalls the cooperation various university faculty and administrators provided to the FBI in *Compromised Campus: The Collaboration of Universities with the Intelligence Community, 1945-1955* (New York: Oxford University Press, 1992). Curt Gentry's *J. Edgar Hoover: The Man and His Secrets* (New York: W. W. Norton, 1991) is a dark biography of the long-term director of the FBI. A similar dark biography of Hoover is offered by Anthony Summers in *Official and Confidential: The Secret Life of J. Edgar Hoover* (New York: G. P. Putnam's Sons, 1993) in which Hoover is scandalously described as a cross-dresser and homosexual who blackmailed various federal officials, including sitting and former presidents, because of their sexual indiscretions. *Surveillance in the Stacks: The FBI's Library Awareness Program* (Westport, Conn.: Greenwood Press, 1991), by Herbert N. Foerstel, addresses one of the FBI's counterintelligence activities that least accords with the Bill of Rights. *Hoover's FBI: The Inside Story by Hoover's Trusted Lieutenant* (Washington, D.C.: Regnery, 1995) is authored by a former FBI insider, Cartha DeLoach, who was a deputy director of the FBI. This book paints a flattering picture of the agency and its surveillance activities.

Federal Communications Commission (FCC)

FOUNDED: 1934

TYPE OF ORGANIZATION: U.S. government agency that regulates broadcasting communications

SIGNIFICANCE: The FCC has exercised various forms of control over public and private communications systems

Invention of the radio and the spread of radio broadcasting after 1920 gave rise to a need in the United States for overall regulation to ensure that individual radio stations would be assigned broadcasting frequencies that did not interfere with those of other stations. Control of some sort was required to keep order among the increasingly crowded radio frequencies. The task of assigning frequencies and regulating radio stations first fell to the U.S. Department of Commerce. Soon, however, this work became so complicated that Secretary of Commerce Herbert Hoover found that he was devoting too much of his time and effort to it. Meanwhile, despite early federal efforts to control the airwaves, some broadcasters disregarded government mandates and used whatever frequencies they wished.

National Association of Broadcasters. The chaos that characterized early broadcasting in the United States led radio station owners and managers to urge government regulation of the airwaves. Broadcasters needed to protect their own frequencies from the interference of maverick broadcasters. In 1922 a group of radio station executives formed the National Association of Broadcasters, the parent of the Federal Radio Commission (FRC), and the grandparent of the FCC. Members of Congress and other government officials were hounded by angry radio listeners who, after purchasing expensive sets, discovered that they could not listen to their favorite programs without interference from stations unwilling to respect assigned frequencies.

Initially, Secretary of Commerce Hoover wanted the FRC to function as a division of the Department of Commerce. Some skeptics suspected his motives, realizing the potential radio had as a political tool for swaying people and opinions. To counter the danger that radio might be controlled by members of the executive branch of government, California's Senator Clarence Dill drafted a bill calling for the formation of the FRC, to consist of five members, no three from the same political party, appointed by the president and approved by Congress for set terms. This bill was passed in February, 1927.

Under the Radio Act of 1927, the FRC's chief duty was to assign frequencies and to regulate broadcasting according to the "public interest, convenience, or necessity." Despite this mandate, the commissioners were denied the power to censor content, which, throughout the history of the FRC and the FCC, has been protected by First Amendment guarantees. Founded seven years after radio broadcasting began in the United States, the FRC served a necessary, limited function. It was responsible only for radio communications, with the regulation of telephone and telegraph communications falling to the Interstate Commerce Commission (ICC).

Shortly after Franklin D. Roosevelt became president in 1933, the Communications Act of 1934 established the FCC, providing for the appointment by the president of seven commissioners (during the Reagan Administration in the 1980's this number was reduced to five), whose appointments to seven-year terms required congressional approval. The president was also empowered to designate one FCC member as chair. Roosevelt recommended to Congress that the FCC be made responsible for regulating communication, both domestic and international, by wire as well as by radio, thereby expanding the functions of the commission and shifting responsibility for telephone and telegraph communications from the ICC to the FCC.

Since the 1930's the FCC has been charged with three major tasks. It must direct the orderly development of broadcasting, cable, and communications services in the United States in keeping with the limitations of technology and economics. It must also obtain and maintain efficient and dependable telephone, telegraph, and common carrier services. Finally, it must provide for the safety of life and property and for the nation's defense through communication facilities.

FCC Commissioners. FCC commissioner appointments are political. Appointees generally have little background in communications. Their responsibilities have increased significantly as communications have grown in complexity and variety. Proliferation of personal computers and communications systems, such as the Internet, has added a new dimension to the commission's work. One of the FCC's major tasks has always been to issue licenses to radio and television stations, whose numbers are huge, and to renew those licenses at regular intervals—currently every seven years for radio and every five for television stations. The commission must satisfy the agency's most important criterion in issuing and renewing licenses: the commission must be convinced that the station is serving the public interest.

In addition to the regulation of radio, television, telephones, and telegraphs, it falls to the FCC and its commissioners to regulate all other forms of radio communication, including private amateur broadcasting, police, fire, and other emergency use of the airwaves, and cellular telephones. Added to this is responsibility for overseeing such other forms of electronic communication as cable television, satellites, and even electronic garage door and gate openers.

Beyond Technical Matters. In assigning frequencies and otherwise directing radio traffic, the early FCC, like the FRC before it, was essentially concerned with technical matters. Some licenses were withdrawn for cause, although such withdrawals were infrequent, largely because the FCC was forbidden to assume the role of censor. During the 1930's, the FCC was not one of the Roosevelt Administration's most illustrious commissions. In 1939, however, with the appointment of James Lawrence Fly, a former attorney for the Tennessee Valley Authority, as FCC chair, the agency's mission expanded.

Fly thought that FCC concerns should reach beyond technical matters. For example, he believed that the public would best be served if the commission prevented any network from having more than one station in any single community. At that time the two major networks were the Columbia Broadcasting System (CBS) and the National Broadcasting Company (NBC). NBC operated the red and the blue networks, which gave it two networks in many communities. The FCC's *Report on Chain Broadcasting* (1941) outlawed this practice and, by 1943, NBC had been forced to sell its blue network, which became the American Broadcasting Company. Fly reasoned that with additional competition, the networks would improve programming and better serve the public interest. After he left the FCC in 1944, the commission entered a period of relatively routine operation.

Controversial Actions of the FCC. For most of its existence, the FCC enforced the fairness doctrine, under which air time was given for opposing views in controversial matters. This policy became cumbersome during political campaigns, however, when two or three serious candidates seeking an office had to share air time with many other candidates for the same office who had no realistic hope of success. In 1986 the fairness doctrine was abolished. Congress introduced legislation to make the doctrine law, but President Ronald Reagan vetoed the bill. When Congress could not override his veto, the FCC was free to eliminate the regulation from its official policies. Later efforts to revive the fairness doctrine failed.

In 1988 the House of Representatives voted to enact legislation that would restrict the amount of advertising permitted on children's programming. The legislation called for the FCC to take into account stations' compliance to this law when renewing licenses. President Reagan, citing constitutional violations relating to freedom of expression, vetoed the bill immediately before Congress adjourned, therefore denying it the opportunity to override his veto. The FCC repealed its regulations regarding this matter in 1984, thereby supporting Reagan's action.

Perhaps the most controversial matter with which the FCC has dealt is indecency. The question of how indecency, obscenity, or profanity are defined has perplexed the commission and the courts for years. First Amendment guarantees have generally prevailed, after several essential tests are applied to questionable material. First, does the dominant theme of the material appeal to a prurient interest in sex? Second, is material offensive because it violates contemporary community standards regarding the description or representation of sexual matters? Finally, does the material, taken as a whole, lack serious literary, artistic, political, or scientific value?

The test, as intended, cannot be applied merely to part of a work. Any work deemed offensive must be viewed as a whole. The question also arises of whether radio and television programming should be held to higher standards than some of the other arts, inasmuch as they are more easily accessible to young children and to others who might stumble upon offensive programs rather than seeking them out. The FCC, nevertheless, is forced by the mandates under which it operates carefully to observe the thin line between obscenity and art.

As the FCC involved itself in a number of obscenity cases, most were resolved by the stations in question paying token fines rather than engaging in costly litigation. In 1973 comedian George Carlin broadcast a nightclub act in which he uttered the seven obscene words that were not allowed on American radio and television stations. Carlin's use of these words was defended partly on the basis of his being a well-recognized satirist and partly because it was clear that these words themselves did not lead members of his audience to engage in prurient sexual behavior. The counterargument was that Carlin's offending dialogue was broadcast at a time when children might be listening to the radio. The FCC, however, penalized neither Carlin nor the Pacifica Foundation station that broadcast his performance. Rather it served notice indirectly that it might invoke the indecency clause in the future.

FCC Bureaus. The FCC has four bureaus. The mass media bureau assigns stations space within the available broadcast frequencies. It reviews applications for licenses and renewal requests. With the continued increase in radio and television stations and with the growth of cable television, this bureau's responsibilities have increased dramatically. The common carrier bureau determines the interstate rates and services of telephone and telegraph companies, as well as radio and satellite companies. This is a considerably smaller bureau than the mass media bureau. The private radio bureau regulates all nonpublic electronic communication, such as ham radio, radio frequencies of police and fire departments, remote control devices that use radio frequencies, and personal radio communications facilities. The field operation bureau inspects nationwide the facilities of radio and television stations and monitors their operations. This bureau works through a coordinated network of field offices and operates a substantial fleet of mobile units. Each bureau is answerable to members of the FCC and their chair, who are overseen by the Congress. The bureaus have been cognizant of the nonpolitical nature of the commission and must guard against acting as censors.

—*R. Baird Shuman*

See also Blue Book of 1946; Broadcast media; Call-in programs; Canadian Radio-Television and Telecommunications Commission; Carlin, George; *Citizen Tom Paine*; Communications Act of 1934; Communications Decency Act; Fairness doctrine; *Miller v. California*; National Association of Broadcasters; Pacifica Foundation; Radio.

BIBLIOGRAPHY

James R. Bennett's *Control of Information in the United States: An Annotated Bibliography* (Westport, Conn.: Meckler, 1987) will lead readers to many additional sources. William B. Ray's *FCC: The Ups and Downs of Radio-TV Regulation* (Ames: Iowa State University Press, 1990) provides an insider's view of the commission by an expert on broadcast law. A valuable adjunct to Ray's book is James L. Baughman's *Television's Guardians: The FCC and the Politics of Programming 1958-1967* (Knoxville: University of Tennessee Press, 1985), which, although covering a limited period, provides a useful overview of an important period of the FCC. Henry Geller's *The Fairness Doctrine in Broadcasting* (Santa Monica, Calif.: Rand, 1973) discusses a crucial concept in depth. More recent is Sydney W. Head and Christopher H. Sterling, *Broadcasting in America* (Boston: Houghton Mifflin, 1987).

Federal Theatre Project (FTP)

DATE: October 1, 1935-July 1, 1939

PLACE: United States

SIGNIFICANCE: A federal relief agency for the unemployed during the Great Depression, this government project gave work to thousands of performers and technicians, but simultaneously interfered with their freedom of expression

Establishment of the FTP in 1935 under the U.S. federal government's Works Progress Administration (WPA) afforded many unemployed performers an opportunity to work during the Depression. Relief Administrator Harry Hopkins declared that the FTP would uphold a standard of "free, adult, uncensored" theater. Hopkins appointed Hallie Flanagan national director; her goal was to unite community theaters into a federation operating under the federal government.

The promise of uncensored theater was soon challenged by preparations for production of *Ethiopia*, playwright Elmer Rice's play on Italy's recent invasion of the old African kingdom of Ethiopia. After obtaining a tape of President Franklin D. Roosevelt's radio broadcast on the Italo-Ethiopian War, the FTP producers were warned that they could not "impersonate any foreign dignitaries" while staging their plays. After much debate, it was decided that the words of the dignitaries could be used, but their voices could not be impersonated. Wary about compromise and future government censorship, Rice resigned from the project. As a result, *Ethiopia* was never produced.

The WPA remained neutral for a short time to deter skeptics who claimed government would interfere using propaganda and censorship. Flanagan continued staging productions that depicted the social and economic realities of the 1930's. While she advocated and presented many such plays, the government preferred plays that did not have controversial material. A series called the "Living Newspaper" documentaries especially created controversy; they illustrated the hardships of farmers in *Triple A-Plowed Under* (1936); the difficulties of labor organizing in *Injunction Granted* (1936); and issues of slum housing in *One-Third of a Nation* (1939). The opening of Sinclair Lewis and John C. Moffit's play *It Can't Happen Here* (1935) played to good reviews and indicted both fascism and communism. Nevertheless, critics variously charged that the play revealed that the FTP was communist, that it was pro-New Deal, that it was subconsciously fascist, or that it was propaganda for Roosevelt.

The scheduled June, 1937, opening of a prounion version of a steel strike became a target for censors. The play *The Cradle Will Rock*, written by Marc Blitzstein and to be produced by Orson Welles and John Houseman, was delayed until the end of the fiscal year—allegedly due to expected cuts in WPA funding. This move was seen as suppression and censorship because the government did not wish to incite violence in midwestern industrial cities.

The expected cuts devastated the FTP and Flanagan faced more harassment in productions. In 1938 the FTP was plagued when Martin Die's new House Committee on Un-American Activities (HUAC) attacked Flanagan and other employees as being communists. Flanagan testified and defended the project but was not allowed to make a concluding statement. None of her defending testimony was printed in the hearing reports. The FTP was cited as having embarked on a venture into entertainment and having forgotten its purpose of work relief. Congress used HUAC's claim that the FTP had been infiltrated with communists when it ended the program in 1939.

See also Communism; Drama and theater; House Committee on Un-American Activities; Lewis, Sinclair.

Federalist Party

FOUNDED: 1787

TYPE OF ORGANIZATION: U.S. political party

SIGNIFICANCE: Arguably the first political party in the United States, the Federalist Party tried to legislate away First Amendment protections of free speech

In U.S. history, the term Federalist was first used to define those supporting the ratification of the U.S. Constitution. Between 1789 and 1796 the term narrowed to define those supporting the policies of John Adams and Alexander Hamilton against those of Thomas Jefferson and James Madison. During Adams' presidency (1797-1801), the Federalists became an organized political party that supported peace with Great Britain, a strong national government, and conservative fiscal and social policies. Political partisanship became intense, and the Federalists used their majorities in Congress to intimidate opponents and stifle debate.

The Federalists enacted a series of repressive laws to try to contain the growing political strength of Jefferson and his allies. To them the crisis atmosphere of the period justified such repressive legislation as the Act Concerning Aliens, the Act Respecting Alien Enemies, the Naturalization Act, and the Act for the Punishment of Certain Crimes—popularly known as the Sedition Act—all passed during June and July, 1798.

Confronted by the possibility of the new nation's having to wage naval war against Great Britain or France or both, the Adams Administration moved to censor popular criticism of the president out of fear that the survival of the nation was at stake. To censor the expression of negative popular opinion on political issues, Federalist animosity against their opponents caused them to engage in censorship activities similar to those of the 1950's, when Senator Joseph R. McCarthy used fear of the communist threat to justify harsh censorship measures.

Republican editors convicted under the Sedition Act included James Callendar, Thomas Cooper, and William Duane. Benjamin Bache of the Philadelphia newspaper *Aurora* died before he could be convicted. Congressman Matthew Lyon of Vermont, convicted of libel based on an article in the *Vermont Journal*, cast the decisive vote for the election of Jefferson in 1801.

Opposition to the Sedition Act of 1798 was intense. The most important statements of the Republican position against the Sedition Act were the Virginia and Kentucky resolutions of 1798 and 1799. Popular anger against the Sedition Act, which failed to make criticism of Vice President Jefferson (with whom Adams was in disagreement) a crime, helped elect Jefferson president in 1800. The Federalists never regained national political power.

Modern opinion has tended to cast the Republicans as heroic supporters of the First Amendment; however, the Federalist position can be seen as defensible in the context of the 1790's. The U.S. Constitution and the First Amendment were untested when the Federalists attempted to censor the expression of opposition viewpoints by citizens, printers, and publishers. The Federalist position on libel was similar to that taken by the eighteenth century English jurist William Blackstone. The Federalists were tolerant in that they allowed truth to be a defense against libel charges. Even Jeffersonians supported harsh libel prosecutions as long as they were carried out by the states.

See also Blackstone, William; Coughlin, Father Charles Edward; Fear; First Amendment; Jefferson, Thomas; Sedition Act of 1798; United States.

Feminism

DEFINITION: Feminism is the advocacy of women's rights

SIGNIFICANCE: Some feminists have sought to censor pornography, at times with ironic results

At the beginning of the twentieth century, the feminist Margaret Sanger was the target of Anthony Comstock and the New York Society for the Suppression of Vice, which actively censored the "twin evils" of birth control and obscene literature. For decades, feminists universally decried censorship, the historical example of which, from their point of view, was a means of maintaining the lower status of women. Even Women Against Pornography, formed in New York in 1979 to protest against degrading sexual depictions of women, took pains to state that it was not intent on carving out "any new exceptions to the First Amendment."

The Appeal of Censorship. By the 1980's, however, a feminist faction focused on pornography as a primary cause of discrimination and sexual violence against women. In 1983 writer Andrea Dworkin and law professor Catharine MacKinnon drafted a model ordinance that declared pornography ("a graphic sexually explicit subordination of women through pictures and/or words") to be a "practice of sex discrimination" and that authorized civil lawsuits for damages and injunctive relief for "trafficking," "coercion into" or "forcing" of pornography, or "assault or physical attack due to pornography." The ordinance passed the Minneapolis City Council, but was vetoed by the mayor, an advocate of women's rights, on the ground that it violated the First Amendment.

In 1984 the Dworkin-MacKinnon ordinance was enacted into law in Indianapolis, with each Democratic member of the City Council voting against and each Republican member in favor. The law was supported by conservative Phyllis Schlafly, famous for her activism against the Equal Rights Amendment, and was opposed by the local chapter of the National Organization for Women.

Model Ordinance Found Unconstitutional. The Indianapolis law was struck down in *American Booksellers Association v. Hudnut* (1984, 1986), in a case filed by a coalition of booksellers, publishers, and others involved in producing and distributing material potentially punishable under the ordinance. The suit was supported by the American Civil Liberties Union and Feminist Anti-Censorship Task Force. MacKinnon criticized the Hudnut decision as "the *Dred Scott* of the women's movement," while law professor Nadine Strossen, president of the ACLU and author of *Defending Pornography* (1995), applauded it as "the *Brown v. Board of Education* of the women's movement." In 1988 a version of the Dworkin-MacKinnon law that had been adopted by voter referendum in Bellingham, Washington, was also struck down by a federal court.

In 1992 the Senate Judiciary Committee reported favorably on the Pornography Victims' Compensation Act, sponsored by Republican senator Strom Thurmond and supported by Dworkin and MacKinnon. The bill, which died when the full Senate failed to take it up before recessing, would have created a federal civil cause of action authorizing the payment of damages to the victim of a sexual assault by the publisher or producer of any sexually explicit (but not necessarily obscene) book, magazine, motion picture or video which a jury found to be a "substantial cause" of the assailant's crime. Opponents criticized the bill as a grave threat to free speech. Joyce Meskis, president of the American Booksellers Association, testifying against the legislation, argued that with 700,000 books in print and 50,000 new titles each year, nearly all of which could conceivably be accused of being the cause of a criminal's actions, the act would "produce the most pervasive censorship the U.S. has ever experienced" and would leave bookstores with no real option but to notify publishers that they will no longer stock any work with any sexual content.

Pornography as Unprotected Speech. According to antipornography feminists, the "law of equality and the law of freedom of speech are on a collision course in this country." Antipornography feminists argue that because the purpose and effect of pornography are to subordinate, degrade, and dehumanize women, sexually explicit books and movies constitute violence against women and represent discrimination on the basis of sex. Antipornography feminists define pornography as what presents women as dehumanized sex objects who enjoy humiliation or pain and who experience sexual pleasure in rape, incest, or other sexual assault. In pornography, women are tied up, mutilated, bruised, or physically hurt and are presented in postures or positions of sexual submission, servility, or display. Women's body parts, including their vaginas, breasts, and buttocks, are exhibited in such a way that women are reduced to those parts. In pornography, women are presented as being penetrated by objects or animals and are portrayed in scenarios of degradation, humiliation, injury, or torture.

The standard of obscenity under *Miller v. California* (1973) provides constitutional protection for material that has "serious literary, artistic, political or scientific value," but the definition of pornography used by MacKinnon and Dworkin recognizes no such limitation.

When Is Censorship Not Censorship? MacKinnon and Dworkin staunchly reject the charge that the legal efforts of antipornography feminists constitute censorship. Dworkin has argued that in legal terms censorship has always meant prior restraint, and the legislation that she has proposed judges a work after, not before publication. Opponents, such as Strossen, counter that aside from the fact that the model ordinance drafted by MacKinnon and Dworkin would authorize injunctions that would in fact operate as a prior restraint of speech, the First Amendment has been interpreted to prohibit *any* use of unwarranted government power that punishes protected speech before or after it is uttered. Strossen argues that the U.S. Supreme Court has recognized that censorship in civilian garb is still censorship and has held that the fear of damage awards in civil liability cases may be markedly more inhibiting upon free expression than the fear of prosecution under a criminal statute.

In her most comprehensive critique of First Amendment protection for pornography, *Only Words* (1993), Catharine MacKinnon ridicules the notion that pornography is worthy of constitutional protection. Instead, she argues that pornography is an act and as such may be regulated or punished like any other act, particularly any act of sex discrimination or sexual assault.

The First Amendment Is Not Absolute. Pivotal to the feminist antipornography argument is the recognition that the First Amendment is not absolute and admits of several exceptions, including defamation, plagiarism, mail fraud, false advertising, perjury, contempt of court, and criminal solicitation. Each of these exceptions reflects a societal judgment developed over time and ultimately adopted by the Supreme Court that, on balance, the need to punish the harm inflicted by certain speech on particular individuals, groups, or society as a whole is sufficient to outweigh First Amendment protection for free speech. Once the First Amendment is seen as the

women. (Unlike the model ordinance proposed by MacKinnon and Dworkin, however, the Court retained its existing rules that a work must be considered as a whole and that no material will be deemed obscene if it has an artistic purpose or is part of the serious treatment of a sexual theme). MacKinnon coauthored one of the briefs in the case and hailed the decision as a stunning victory for women. Other feminists disagreed. Liz Czach, a member of the Ontario Coalition Against Film and Video Censorship, stated that the law did not protect women but rather it silenced women.

Within a year of the *Butler* decision, Canada experienced what *Nation* magazine called an "epidemic of censorship." *Feminists Bookstore News*, a Canadian publication, reported

Many feminists have argued that pornography—such as advertised in this 1972 New York City street scene—degrades women and therefore violates their civil rights. (AP/Wide World Photos)

repository of societal balancing, rather than an absolute bar to government restriction on speech, antipornography feminists argue that the real psychological, emotional, and physical harms caused by pornography more than justify another exception to the First Amendment.

The Canadian Precedent. Antipornography feminists achieved their greatest judicial success in Canada. In 1992 the Canadian Supreme Court, in *Butler v. The Queen* (1992) interpreted the Canadian obscenity laws to embody the MacKinnon-Dworkin concept of pornography and outlawed sexually explicit materials that are "degrading" or "dehumanizing" to

that the *Butler* case had been used only to seize lesbian, gay, and feminist material. Within the first two-and-a-half years after the decision, more than half of all Canadian feminist bookstores had had materials confiscated or detained by customs. Two books written by Andrea Dworkin herself were seized at the border, because the works were judged to eroticize pain and bondage. By the fall of 1993, Karen Busby, a Canadian lawyer who worked on a brief filed in the *Butler* case by the Women's Legal Education and Action Fund (cofounded by MacKinnon) conceded that the *Butler* decision had been used by the Toronto police to confiscate *Bad Attitude*, a lesbian erotic magazine, which was "hardly a threat to women's equality."

The Rise of Anticensorship Feminism. In the United States, the efforts of antipornography feminists have triggered the creation of anticensorship feminist organizations, including Feminists for Free Expression and the National Coalition Against Censorship's Working Group on Women. Various feminist writers, lawyers, and activists have expressed opposition to censorship, including Judy Blume, Barbara Ehrenreich, Nora Ephron, Nancy Friday, Betty Friedan, Susan Isaacs, Molly Ivins, Erica Jong, Wendy Kaminer, Kate Millett, Marcia Pally, Katha Pollitt, Anne Rice, Wendy Wasserstein, and Faye Wattleton. —*Stephen F. Rohde*

See also Birth control education; *Bradlaugh v. The Queen*; Comstock Act of 1873; Dworkin, Andrea; Eagle Forum; MacKinnon, Catharine A.; Pornography; Society for the Suppression of Vice, New York; Women, violence against; Women Against Pornography.

BIBLIOGRAPHY

Andrea Dworkin's *Pornography: Men Possessing Women* (New York: G. P. Putnam's Sons, 1989) is an indictment of the perceived harm caused to women by sexually explicit material. Dworkin's "Against the Male Flood: Censorship, Pornography, and Equality," in *Harvard Women's Law Journal* 8 (Spring, 1985) is a review of the conflicts over the values society places on freedom of expression versus the attainment of equality. Editors Laura Lederer and Richard Delgado's *The Price We Pay: The Case Against Racist Speech, Hate Propaganda and Pornography* (New York: Hill and Wang, 1995) is a comprehensive series of essays advancing the theory that the First Amendment allows—or should allow—government regulation of hate speech, racist speech, and pornography. Catharine MacKinnon's "Pornography, Civil Rights, and Free Speech," in *Harvard Civil Rights-Civil Liberties Law Review* 20 (1985) is an analytical review of the legal and constitutional issues surrounding the regulation of pornography as a civil rights issue. MacKinnon's *Only Words* (Cambridge, Mass.: Harvard University Press, 1993) is an extended essay addressing the need to make the law more receptive to protecting women from violence and discrimination and less protective of pornography. Wendy McElroy's *XXX: A Woman's Right to Pornography* (New York: St. Martin's Press, 1995) is an unashamed and buoyant defense of pornography, including interviews with performers and a forthright attack on antipornography feminists. Nadine Strossen's *Defending Pornography: Free Speech, Sex, and the Fight for Women's Rights* (New York: Charles Scribner's Sons, 1995) is a complete historical account and legal analysis of the critical issues involved in First Amendment protection of pornography.

Ferlinghetti, Lawrence

BORN: March 24, 1919 (?), Yonkers, New York

IDENTIFICATION: American poet and publisher

SIGNIFICANCE: Ferlinghetti was tried on obscenity charges after his publishing company, City Lights Books, published a volume by Allen Ginsberg

In 1955 Ferlinghetti, the spiritual leader of San Francisco's Beat poets and owner of City Lights Bookshop, a hangout for aspiring writers, founded City Lights Books, a publishing company that would print inexpensive paperback editions of the works of emerging poets. That same year, he heard Allen Ginsberg, a Beat poet from New York, give a reading of "Howl," a rambling poem that chronicles the depressed state of young Americans who felt alienated from the prevailing materialistic culture and escaped through alcohol, drugs, and sex. Ferlinghetti agreed to publish "Howl," which included language and described sexual acts that tested the mores of the 1950's.

The first printing of *Howl and Other Poems* occurred in October, 1956. On March 25, 1957, the second edition, which was printed in England, was seized by U.S. Customs officials on the grounds that it was obscene. Charges were dropped several weeks later, and the books were released. In early June, however, San Francisco police entered Ferlinghetti's bookstore and arrested him and an employee for selling obscene books.

Ferlinghetti's ensuing trial lasted through the summer and into the fall of 1957. The American Civil Liberties Union, which defended Ferlinghetti without fees, called local critics, reviewers, and professors to testify on the literary merits of Ginsberg's poems. On October 3, Judge Clayton Horn ruled in favor of Ferlinghetti, calling "Howl" an "indictment of those elements of modern society destructive to the best qualities of human nature" that ends with "a plea for holy living."

See also American Civil Liberties Union; Book publishing; Customs laws, U.S.; *NYPD Blue*; Obscenity: legal definitions; Poetry.

Fielding, Henry

BORN: April 22, 1707, Sharpham Park, Somersetshire, England

DIED: October 8, 1754, Lisbon, Portugal

IDENTIFICATION: English novelist and playwright

SIGNIFICANCE: Fielding wrote and produced several plays satirizing Britain's prime minister that helped lead to enactment of Britain's Licensing Act of 1737

In the early years of his writing career, Fielding—who was later best known for such novels as *Tom Jones* (1749)—enjoyed considerable success as a dramatist. Between 1728 and 1737, he wrote twenty-seven plays that were staged at Drury Lane, the Little Haymarket, and other theaters. His first plays were traditional five-act comedies, but he soon discovered a talent for mocking English society and government, particularly the royal court and the government of Prime Minister Robert Walpole. Such works as *Tom Thumb* (1730) and *The Welsh Opera* (1731) revealed a savagely satiric tone that would surface later.

During the early 1730's Fielding wrote plays that were primarily entertainments, but even these works—like his earlier plays—differed from the farces of his contemporaries in offering social satire along with burlesque elements. After a three-year stint of writing more traditional burlesque, Fielding return to satire with *Pasquin* (1736), a nonpartisan, highly political, and extremely funny portrayal of corruption in English politics and society. This play's success led Fielding to

Now best known as a novelist, Henry Fielding was notorious in his own time for challenging censorship of the theater. (Library of Congress)

produce *The Historical Register for the Year 1736* (1737), a satirical piece whose name and structure both derived from the annual survey so titled. In a series of loosely related scenes, this play satirized a wide range of public figures and institutions. It targeted both Walpole and his opposition; however, when Fielding added an afterpiece to the play specifically depicting Walpole as a scoundrel, the government began to examine his dramas more closely.

During the 1730's British political satire was widely popular; in early 1737 alone, for example, more than one hundred plays satirized Walpole's government. As a result, Walpole and his allies introduced a bill in the House of Commons to censor theatrical activity. The Licensing Act became law on June 21, 1737. Fielding's theatrical career was ended by the law's provision subjecting all material for the stage to scrutiny by the Lord Chamberlain, who would have the power to approve it for public performance. Denied a venue for the production of his political burlesques, Fielding was forced to abandon his lucrative career as a playwright and impresario. He turned his attention to the law and to a new career as a novelist.

See also Drama and theater; Licensing Act of 1737; Literature; Lord Chamberlain; United Kingdom.

Fighting words

DEFINITION: Language that may cause injury or incite immediate violence

SIGNIFICANCE: The U.S. Supreme Court has ruled that fighting words are not protected as free speech

The U.S. Supreme Court once ruled that certain kinds of speech receive no protection under the First Amendment. Among these kinds of speech were fighting words, which, as the Court describes them in *Chaplinsky v. New Hampshire* (1942), "by their very utterance inflict injury or tend to incite an immediate breach of the peace."

The Supreme Court has in recent years found that the First Amendment affords at least some protection to categories of speech formerly viewed as altogether unprotected. Although the Court has not explicitly repudiated the fighting words doctrine, it has not upheld a punishment of speech as fighting words since its decision in the *Chaplinsky* case. Consequently, many observers have questioned whether the doctrine is still valid. Nevertheless, although the fighting words doctrine may have been abandoned by the Court, lawmakers and other public officials have sometimes relied on the doctrine to prohibit racial and sexist insults, commonly referred to as hate speech. The Court cast these kinds of speech regulations in doubt, however, by holding in *R.A.V. v. City of St. Paul* (1992) that even if fighting words in general may be prohibited, government cannot single out particular fighting words—such as racial or sexual epitaphs—for censorship.

See also Constitution, U.S.; First Amendment; Flag burning; Free speech; Hate laws; Offensive language; Unprotected speech.

Film adaptation

DEFINITION: The changing of a literary or other artistic work into the film medium

SIGNIFICANCE: Many have decried how literary works, when adapted to film, are censored

Many films are based on literary works, but literary works and films employ two different media, each with its own characteristics. Books contain thousands of words and feature-length films typically run approximately ninety minutes; it is impossible, for example, to read a typical book's narration aloud in voice over, with actors speaking each line of dialogue, in anything approaching ninety minutes. Therefore, it is necessary to adapt the book to film; this typically involves rewriting dialogue and presenting themes in visual images and in action rather than in narration. Based on dialogue, the play resembles film more closely than a novel, but plays, if simply filmed as they are performed, are likely to appear wooden on film. Film is obliged to use strengths—such as motion of the camera, use of close-up and distance shots, a soundtrack, and so on—that a play does not have, and to make use of such strengths, adaptation of plays also typically becomes necessary. Why and how an adaptation is performed, rather than the necessity of such adaptation, is the frequent subject of dispute.

The Nature of Film. Literary works tend to be solitary efforts that cost little to produce; films tend to be collaborative efforts costing large sums of money. The director has an idea—if all is going well—of how the film should be adapted. The many hands involved, however, in making a film virtually guarantee that it will not turn out exactly the way any one person wishes it.

Censorship occurs when powerful persons or other forces

Stanley Kowalski (Marlon Brando) grabs his sister-in-law, Blanche Dubois (Vivien Leigh), in the 1951 film adaptation of Tennessee Williams' play A Streetcar Named Desire. *(Museum of Modern Art/Film Stills Archive)*

(such as economics) effect the omission or alteration of key elements of the original work for such nonartistic reasons as avoidance of controversy, a desire to please a major talent, or to comply with prior restraint rules on what can be depicted on film.

Marketability is another factor. For example, critics generally agreed that the erotic scenes in *The Scarlet Letter* (1996), starring Demi Moore, in no sense advance the themes of the original novel. Such scenes, the speculation ran, made the film's commercial success more likely. Two endings were made for the film. Test marketing results showed that audiences preferred the happier ending over the original ending of the novel, and the film was released with the happier ending. Critics made jokes about Nathaniel Hawthorne, author of the original novel, spinning in his grave, and Hawthorne, were he alive, might claim that his novel's ideas about sin and guilt had been censored.

On the other hand, critics lauded actress and screenwriter Emma Thompson's 1995 adaptation of Jane Austen's 1811 novel *Sense and Sensibility*. In writing the screenplay, she made substantial changes to the novel, but each change seems justified as a means of bringing the novel to film. The film was also popular with audiences.

Censorship Boards. In the early 1930's, the film industry made itself subject to regulation by the Production Code Administration (PCA). Run by the major film companies and distributors, the PCA put restraints on the production and content of films. The industry decided to set up the PCA in the face of federal and state government pressures. In addition, religious groups were also putting pressure on the industry, and succeeded in establishing several criteria for censorship.

For example, Charlotte Brontë's *Jane Eyre: An Autobiography* (1847) was released as a film, *Jane Eyre*, in 1944. References could not be made to the character Mr. Brocklehurst's ministerial status because they would reflect badly on the ministry, so this omission caused a change in the film. Changes were also made to bring more attention to the male star, Orson Welles, at his request.

A Farewell to Arms (1932), starring Helen Hayes and Gary Cooper, was reedited in order to meet the demands of the PCA, toning down some of the incidents of love and war (sex and violence). The film also angered Italian officials, since it depicts the Italian military unfavorably. The author of the novel from which the film was adapted, Ernest Hemingway, expressed his disgust with the film's changed ending, in which Hayes's character rallies on her sickbed, implying that she may live and that she and Cooper's character may live happily ever after. In the novel, the character very definitely dies, crushing her lover's hopes.

Studios, eyeing the bottom line, have made many novels' endings happier; for censorship boards, obscenity, violence, sexuality, and sexual immorality are the areas of concern. Concern over content of films has risen and fallen. By the end of the 1950's the PCA had lost most of its power in the industry. Success of films that were released without the PCA seal ended its effectiveness. Films released without the PCA seal include *The Pawnbroker* (1965), adapted from a novel, in which a woman bares her breasts; *Who's Afraid of Virginia Woolf?* (1966), adapted from a play, which makes liberal use of profane language; and *Alfie* (1966), adapted from a play, which treats the topics of sexual promiscuity and abortion.

During the 1950's, several of Tennessee Williams' literary works were made into films. Williams' literary works contain sexual references, violence, and references to homosexuality. One film, *A Streetcar Named Desire* (1951), made the career of the screen legend Marlon Brando. The film, in which Brando's character rapes his sister-in-law, was censored in adaptation. For example, when one character takes too long in the bathroom, another character in the apartment asks, in the stage version, whether she fell in; in the film, this reference to a toilet was altered; the character asks if she fell asleep.

In 1968 the voluntary film rating system was established for the general welfare of children and, again, to stave off governmental censorship. The ratings were originally G, PG, R, and X. Later, the rating PG-13 was added. A film with a G rating contains minimal to no obscenity, sexual content, nudity, or violence, and is therefore deemed suitable for children of all ages. The G stands for "general audiences." The PG rating means "parental guidance"; the film contains some of the items listed above, but may still be suitable for children. The PG-13 rating means that the film may not be suitable for children less than thirteen years old. The R rating means that children younger than seventeen years old cannot view the film unless they are accompanied by a parent or guardian. The X rating means that the film is pornographic or extremely violent; no one younger than eighteen is allowed to view the film. Occasionally, sexually explicit films that have artistic merit are released without obtaining a rating, since an X rating connotes that the film is of no artistic interest, and most theaters will not exhibit a film with an X rating. Adapted films have often been censored to obtain a lower rating (for example, to change an X to an R). This has resulted in considerable arguing, during the editing process, between the filmmakers and the ratings board about how many seconds, for example, of a bare posterior must be edited out, or how many obscene words may be left in.

In 1956 a film version of George Orwell's famous novel *Nineteen Eighty-Four* (1949) was released. The filmmakers changed the novel considerably and added, for American audiences, a less depressing ending. The novel's sexual content was played down as well. In 1984 another film adaptation of the novel was released. The director, Michael Radford, and others involved in the film were determined to make it faithful to the novel, and they were successful. The film renders the novel's depressing atmosphere and imaginatively conveys a sense of what, in the late 1940's, appeared futuristic. The novel's sexual content is also brought to the film, with nude scenes that earned the film a more-difficult-to-market R rating. The book's sad ending is rendered faithfully. The production process, in turn, had a bitter ending. The film's producer, worried about the film's commercial prospects, overruled the director and obtained a soundtrack that he hoped would attract young audiences. The director was angered enough to make his dissatisfaction public. Critics and the public, however, were generally of the opinion that the soundtrack was acceptable, even good. The film was successful critically and financially. —*Sharon Mikkelson*

See also Art; Censor; Censorship; Film censorship; Hays Code; Legion of Decency; Literature; *Man with the Golden Arm, The*; Motion Picture Association of America; Performance art.

BIBLIOGRAPHY

For information on film adaptation and screenwriting refer to Linda Seger's *The Art of Adaptation: Turning Fact and Fiction into Film* (New York: Holt, 1992). Tino Balio's *The American Film Industry* (Madison: University of Wisconsin Press, 1985) is a history that includes a discussion on censorship. Stories about William Faulkner's film adaptations can be read in Gene Phillips' *Fiction, Film, and Faulkner: The Art of Adaptation* (Knoxville: University of Tennessee Press, 1988). Another excellent source on the nature of the media and adaptations is *Novels into Film* (Berkeley: University of California Press, 1957) by George Bluestone. A source on Tennessee Williams is John McCann's *The Critical Reputation of Tennessee Williams* (Boston: G. K. Hall, 1983).

Film Advisory Board (FAB)

FOUNDED: 1968

TYPE OF ORGANIZATION: American film industry monitoring group

SIGNIFICANCE: Created to review and rate films and collateral materials, the FAB has played a role in self-censorship of films

In 1968 the Hollywood film industry created a new rating system to replace the old Hays Code. The new code has been monitored by the National Association of Theater Owners (NATO), International Film Importers & Distributors of America, and the Motion Picture Association of America (MPAA) through the new FAB, whose membership comprises parents and other persons associated with members of the MPAA. The mission of the new rating system was to provide parents with information about films so they could make informed decisions about the films their children view.

For each submitted film, the FAB makes judgments concerning the film's handling of theme, violence, language, nudity, sensuality, drug abuse, and other areas of parental interest. All advertising for submitted films must be tagged with an "all audience" viewing rating. Therefore, all film tags, print, television, radio, and print advertising matter connected with the film must be inspected. Decisions concerning the criteria for rating films have often brought disagreements. Producers may appeal ratings, but filmmakers have usually been willing to change the content of their films to earn commercially desirable ratings.

Approximately 85 percent of all NATO theater owners use the system. National yearly surveys have indicated that 74 percent of all parents find the system useful to them. Nevertheless, some films are never submitted for review.

See also Advertising as the target of censorship; British Board of Film Censors; Censorship; Film adaptation; Film censorship; Hays Code; Motion Picture Association of America.

Film censorship

DEFINITION: Suppression of film content through industry self-regulation or through legislation

SIGNIFICANCE: As film developed into the dominant mass medium of the early twentieth century, it became a principal battleground between forces advocating censorship and those demanding freedom of expression

In 1894 an Atlantic City peep show production of *Dolorita in the Passion Dance* aroused the first U.S. protest against film immorality. In 1897 *Orange Blossoms* was banned in New York as offensive to public morals. In the socially and politically turbulent decades following the Civil War, government, religious, and civic spokespersons for conventional standards feared the spread of socially, sexually, and politically subversive ideas among the increasingly literate masses, who included freed slaves and their descendants, women agitating for rights, and unprecedented numbers of immigrants. Silent films posed even more of a threat than did printed materials, since literacy, or literacy in English, was not necessary for understanding silent films. A similar controversy stirred in Great Britain, then experiencing agitation from Irish nationalists and suffrage fighters, as well as marked class division. The British Board of Film Censors was created in 1912.

The United States. Local attempts to censor films spread rapidly. Chicago set up a municipal censorship board in 1907; the city's police chief was empowered to withhold a permit from any film he deemed offensive or obscene. In the first court censorship case, *Block v. City of Chicago* (1909), the court upheld the Chicago ordinance. That case involved two films perceived as glamorizing crime. In 1908 New York City's mayor closed all motion picture theaters; exhibitors obtained court injunctions and reopened, but could not admit children under sixteen unaccompanied by adults. In 1911 Pennsylvania passed the first state censorship law, followed in 1913 by Ohio and Kansas and, in 1916, by Maryland. In 1915 deciding the case of *Mutual Film Corporation v. Industrial Commission of Ohio*, the U.S. Supreme Court upheld the validity of the state censorship laws by ruling that First Amendment freedom of expression did not protect motion pictures, which were a business, not an organ of the press or public opinion.

Industry Self-regulation. Since New York was then the center of film production, as well as entertainment, New York exhibitors and filmmakers created a self-censorship body in 1909—the New York Board of Censorship of Programs of Motion Picture, renamed the National Board of Censorship later that year. In 1915 they created the National Board of Review of Motion Pictures, in the hope that self-regulation would eliminate local censorship and efforts, beginning in 1914, to create a federal system of censorship. In 1916 film producers and directors formed the National Association of the Motion Picture Industry (NAMPI), again to forestall censorship efforts.

Reasons for Censorship. Early film censorship was unpredictable. In 1912 Congress used interstate commerce laws to prohibit films showing boxing; this law was passed after African American heavyweight champion Jack Johnson beat the white former champion Jim Jeffries. Fear of race riots was the stated reason for the legislation. Educational birth control and venereal disease films, including reformer Margaret Sanger's film, were banned in New York in 1917. Sanger's film was banned not only because of its topic, according to New York City license commissioner George H. Bell, but also because it promoted contempt for existing law and emphasized the contrast between the lives of the rich and the poor. Most famous of the pre-World War I attempts at censorship involved D. W. Griffith's *Birth of a Nation* (1915), which, because of its racist depictions of African Americans, was challenged more than one hundred times between 1915 and 1980 and was banned or cut in about sixty cases. In Great Britain early restrictions against representing nudity and the figure of Jesus Christ were, by the outbreak of World War I, augmented by restrictions limiting, for example, the kind of dancing portrayed, the disparagement of public institutions and characters, and native customs, if offensive by British standards. No successful interracial marriages could be shown.

World War I and Communism. Censorship efforts became more vigorous with the outbreak of the war in 1914 and, by the end of the war, the fear that the successful Russian Revolution of 1917 would spread communism worldwide. European production cutbacks during the war, among other factors, made Hollywood the leader in film production, but Hollywood was strongly influenced by postwar fears of social change. Russian revolutionist Vladimir Ilich Lenin believed that film was the art form most important to revolutionary success; Russian cinema turned to the celebration of communist ideology. This reinforced fears in Western nations that film would become a vehicle for communist propaganda. In 1918 David Niles, chief of the film section of the U.S. Department of Labor, threatened federal censorship for studios that failed to consult him about representations of socialism or labor

---

FILM CENSORSHIP TIME LINE
COMPILED BY BETTY RICHARDSON

1893 Inventor Thomas A. Edison prepared peepshow films for the Chicago World's Fair. *Fatima's Belly Dance*, a film of exotic dancer Fatima, caused complaints. Edison prepared another version, etching crosshatchings to conceal the dancer's body. In Washington, D.C., a senator objected to another Edison film, *The Serpentine Dance*, in which the dancer reveals her underwear.

1894 *Dolorita in the Passion Dance* or *Dolorita's Passion Dance*, shown at an Atlantic City, New Jersey, boardwalk peepshow, was banned after an outraged local minister protested to authorities. The film was probably the first to be banned in the United States.

1896 Although *The Kiss* or *The May Irwin-John C. Rice Kiss* played for less than a minute, this forty-two foot film aroused public demand for police interference. It was filmed at the Edison studio.

1897 New York police banned *Orange Blossoms*, which showed a bride changing into a nightgown on her wedding night. They arrested the exhibitor.

1907 Chicago became first major U.S. city to authorize police to deny permits for showing films judged obscene or immoral. Chicago censors banned *The James Boys in Missouri* and *The Night Riders* as encouraging crime. This led to the first court test of censorship, which was upheld in 1909.

1908 New York City Mayor George B. McClellan ordered all theaters closed; after theater owners won injunction against him, he insisted that only educational programs could be shown on Sunday.

1909 Newly created National Board of Censorship, supported by the film industry, banned *Every Lass a Queen*, a story of a sailor with many girlfriends.

1910 The film of African American boxer Jack Johnson's defeat of white boxer Jim Jeffries was banned in Canada and South Africa and led to a U.S. federal law (July 31, 1912) prohibiting the importation and interstate transportation of films depicting boxing, a law not repealed until 1940.

1913 William F. "Buffalo Bill" Cody's reconstruction of the Battle of Wounded Knee, sympathetic to a Native American point of view, was filmed with U.S. government cooperation, but was then suppressed by the government. The government withheld the film from general release. *The Crimson Cross* and *Why Men Leave Home* were among the first twenty-two films refused approval as the newly created British Board of Film Censors (BBFC) began certifying films for English viewing. Detroit banned films showing police corruption or ways of committing crimes.

1914 *The Jungle*, the first film of Upton Sinclair's novel attacking conditions in the meatpacking industry, was banned in Chicago, a meatpacking center. *The Strike at Coaldale*, a dramatization of a railroad strike, was banned in the industrial states of Pennsylvania and Ohio as too prolabor.

1915 Director Lois Weber's *The Hypocrites*, an attack on politics, big business, and the church, was banned in Boston until Weber clothed the figure of Truth, originally portrayed as a naked woman. Sessue Hayakawa's portrayal of a wealthy Japanese art dealer in *The Cheat* provoked protests from Japanese Americans; when the film was rereleased in 1918, the villain was described as Burmese, not Japanese. *The Birth of a Nation*, originally titled *The Clansman*, D. W. Griffith's Civil War epic, aroused protests from African Americans and became the most frequently banned film in U.S. history.

1916 The French Ministry of the Interior initiated national film censorship on grounds that films were responsible for increased crime; by 1917, 198 films were banned or cut. Director Lois Weber's *Where Are My Children?*, a dramatization of

(continued)

unrest. In 1919 Secretary of the Interior Franklin Lane met with producers and distributors to discuss ways of controlling radicalism, Bolshevism, and discontent with American values. In 1926 the International Motion Picture Congress, affiliated with the League of Nations, ruled that the government and conditions of life of Soviet Russia were to be ignored.

1922 to 1941. Hollywood scandals further intensified fear that films would subvert traditional values. Although viewers demanded sensational pictures, conservative forces reacted against them and against Hollywood lifestyles, as suggested by the sensational trial of Roscoe "Fatty" Arbuckle for manslaughter in 1921 and the murder of William Desmond Taylor the following year. During 1921, almost one hundred censorship acts were introduced into the legislatures of thirty-seven states. In response, the industry organized the Motion Picture Producers and Distributors Association of America (MPPDA) to replace NAMPI, and requested Will H. Hays, postmaster general of the United States, to be president. Hays

was effective in defeating local and state legislation; despite repeated efforts, no state passed censorship legislation after 1922.

The Hays Code. In 1924 Hays presented MPPDA with a formula by which the Hays office would judge the suitability of each work considered for filming. In 1926 he created a Studio Relations Department to draw up a code of subjects unsuitable for filming. This permissive system changed in 1929 (by which time the silent film had been superseded by sound) with the writing of the Motion Picture Production Code by two Roman Catholic spokespersons, Martin Quigley and the Rev. Daniel A. Lord, foreshadowing the increasingly potent Catholic Legion of Decency (1934), which threatened organized Catholic film boycotts. At a 1934 rally in Cleveland, fifty thousand persons applauded Bishop Joseph Schrembs's vow to purify or destroy Hollywood; some priests and Catholic periodicals declared that going to the theater was a venial sin and that attendance at a film condemned by the church a

---

FILM CENSORSHIP TIME LINE—CONTINUED

abortion and birth control issues, was denied approval by the BBFC and banned in Pennsylvania. *Patria*, a William Randolph Hearst-financed serial, was probably the first U.S. film to be edited as a result of international pressure; depictions of Japanese and Mexicans brought protests from authorities in both countries.

1917 With U.S. entry into World War I, the U.S. government issued a decree prohibiting U.S. civilian cameramen from following American armed forces; the decree was reaffirmed with the establishment of the Committee on Public Information in 1917. *The Spirit of '76*, a reenactment of the American Revolution, portrayed British soldiers much as current World War I propaganda portrayed Germans. It was banned in Los Angeles, and producer Robert Goldstein was convicted under the 1917 Espionage Act for encouraging subversion and disloyalty and undermining war efforts. In Russia, director Feodor Protazanov's adaptation of Leo Tolstoy's *Father Sergius* was suppressed by the czarist government for portrayals of decadent aristocratic life.

Margaret Sanger, a pioneering advocate of birth control education, coauthored and acted in *Birth Control*, which was banned in New York. Besides objecting to the subject matter, License Commissioner George H. Bell opposed the film because it emphasized contrasts between the lives of rich and poor. Director Lois Weber's *The Hand That Rocks the Cradle*, based on Sanger's imprisonment for illegally spreading birth control information, was also banned in New York.

1919 *Damaged Goods* (British, 1919), the second film version of a much-censored French play on venereal disease by Eugène Brieux, was banned by the BBFC, which also banned two other films on the subject, *Open Your Eyes* (1919) and *Fit to Fight, Fit to Win* (1919). The latter, produced with U.S. government approval, was banned in New York.

1920 Prolabor newsreels were banned in Ohio and Pennsylvania during coal strikes.

1921 New York passed a law forcing producers to submit newsreels to censors prior to showing. About two thousand people participated in an American Legion-led march on Miller's Theater in Los Angeles to protest the opening of *The Cabinet of Dr. Caligari* (1919), in part a protest at paying dollars to German filmmakers. In *Fate*, Clara Harmon, acquitted murderess, portrayed herself, over the objections of the American Society of Cinematographers, which prohibited members from working on the film and expelled one member, André Barlatier, who did.

1922 After three highly publicized trials for the rape and murder of Virginia Rappe led to two hung juries and an acquittal, comedian Roscoe "Fatty" Arbuckle became the first film star to be blacklisted. His films were withdrawn from circulation or not released, and he was denied further work as an actor. Despite the film's antinarcotic message, *Cocaine* was rejected by the BBFC. It was allowed by some regional English censors and attracted large audiences.

1923 *Married Love*, a British film, was produced as a vehicle for the ideas of sex and birth control educator Marie Stopes, author of a best-selling book by the same title. Her film was passed by the BBFC only on condition that its title was changed to *Maisie's Marriage* and that all references to Stopes and to birth control were removed. When conditions were not fully met, the British Home Office intervened in an unprecedented step, advising local authorities that only the censored version should be shown. After Hollywood star Wallace Reid's death from drug addiction, his widow Dorothy Davenport sponsored *Human Wreckage*, an antidrug film. It was denied approval by the BBFC.

1924 *The Eternal City*, Hall Caine's 1900 novel, told of the establishment of a state based on the Christian Socialism of Giuseppe Mazzini. When Samuel Goldwyn tried to film the novel in Rome, Italian fascist leader Benito Mussolini threatened to stop the filming unless Goldwyn changed the subject to a celebration of fascist power. In Belgium, Jacques Feyder's *Crainquebille*, a retelling of an Anatole France story, was banned because it showed lack of respect for authority. The first nondocumentary film to be made in Bolivia was banned upon release because it was based on an actual scandal.

mortal sin. The twenty-two-million-member Federal Council of Churches of Christ in America threatened to seek federal censorship.

Production Code Administration. Hays welcomed the production code. In 1930 he hired publicity agent Joseph I. Breen from Quigley. In 1934 the Studio Relations Committee of MPPDA became the Production Code Administration (PCA) under Breen's leadership; apart from a brief period of employment with RKO studio, Breen remained PCA censor until 1954. PCA enforced the code through its seal of approval, without which films could not be released, exhibited, or distributed. Existing films had to be submitted for approval. Breen blocked, for example, reissue of Mae West's 1933 *She Done Him Wrong* in 1935 and 1949. He barred Edward G. Robinson's *Little Caesar* (1931) and James Cagney's *Public Enemy* (1931) until 1953. Other films were to be cut or remade.

The 1934 code was modified several times, with codes on crime (1938), costume (1939), profanity (1939), and cruelty to animals (1940) added or modified. Its basis remained three principles: No film should lower the moral standards of the audience, only correct standards of life should be shown, and no natural or human law should be ridiculed, nor should sympathy be created for law's violators. Specifically banned were portrayals of the drug traffic, sex perversion; white slavery, miscegenation, childbirth, and sexual diseases. Films about crime could not teach criminal methods, justify criminals, or inspire imitation.

Political Issues in the 1930's. By the mid-1930's, political changes created new censorship issues in the United States and abroad. After protests from the Nazi German government, for example, Breen tried to get MGM to cancel production of Erich Maria Remarque's *Three Comrades* (1937), since Remarque was among the authors banned in Nazi Germany. If the production continued, Breen urged that the story's action be changed to pre-Nazi times. He urged removal of references to anti-Semitism and book burning and asked that Nazi agita-

FILM CENSORSHIP TIME LINE—CONTINUED

1925 *Ben-Hur* was banned in China as Christian propaganda and in Italy because Romans are defeated in the film. In a decision not reversed until 1954, the BBFC refused approval to Sergei Eisenstein's *Potemkin* (also known as *Battleship Potemkin*).

1926 Because its plot was based on adultery, Nathaniel Hawthorne's *The Scarlet Letter* was considered unfilmable, but star Lillian Gish bombarded censorship and Congressional groups with letters until Frances Marion's scenario was filmed.

1927 *The Callahans and the Murphys*, a comedy of working-class Irish life featuring Marie Dressler and Polly Moran, led to complaints from Irish and Roman Catholics and theater disturbances. New York censors rescinded approval, and MGM permanently withdrew the film from circulation.

1928 In *Dawn*, Sybil Thorndike portrayed Nurse Edith Cavell, shot by the Germans as a spy during World War I. The film was censored in Germany and Australia and banned in Holland as offensive to Germans. Los Angeles film studio MGM defied Motion Picture Producers and Distributors of America (MPPDA, later MPAA) censor Will Hays, producing films based on W. Somerset Maugham's "Rain" (which portrays a prostitute sympathetically and a clergyman unsympathetically) and Michael Arlen's *The Green Hat* (1924, which portrays young people of fashion doing fashionable things), two works of which Hays had forbidden film adaptation. The first appeared as *Miss Sadie Thompson*, the second as *A Woman of Affairs*.

1929 Fascist leader Benito Mussolini banned foreign-language films from Italy. *Blackmail*, the first English talking film to reach Australia, was banned there for portrayal of crime.

1930 *L'Age d'or* a French film with the English title *The Golden Age*, was filmed by painter Salvador Dalí and Luis Buñuel, satirist and founder of surrealistic cinema. Their targets were bourgeois culture, the Catholic church, and fascism. The movie closed immediately after opening because of right-wing riots and was not shown again until 1980 in New York and 1982 in Paris. Marlene Dietrich's *The Blue Angel* was cut in Pasadena, California. New York censors cut more than 2,200 crime scenes from films between 1930 and 1934.

1931 *Little Caesar* (1930), a gangster film starring Edward G. Robinson, was banned in Australia and parts of Canada. *The Public Enemy*, a gangster film with James Cagney, was denied approval by the BBFC. The scene in which Cagney squashed a half grapefruit into Mae Clarke's face was cut in Maryland because both characters wore pajamas. In New York, censors cut shots of gangsters with guns from this and other gangster films. The horror film *Dracula* was banned in Singapore, British Malaya, and British Columbia. Massachusetts censors demanded that two scenes be deleted for Sunday showings: a skeleton in a coffin and an insect emerging from a small coffin. Boris Karloff's *Frankenstein* was banned in Belfast, South Australia, Czechoslovakia, and Sweden. Frederic March's *Dr. Jekyll and Mr. Hyde* was banned in Finland, the Netherlands, Rhodesia, and Czechoslovakia.

1932 The film studio Paramount defied the censor Hays, who had refused to allow Mae West's controversial Broadway play, *Diamond Lil* (1928) to be filmed. Paramount's film version of the play, starring West, was released as *She Done Him Wrong* in 1933. The film reveled in the heroine's success as she sought wealth, pleasure, and the unprofessional attentions of a handsome young vice squad officer. After state censors repeatedly cut the middle verses from the heroine's song "A Guy What Takes His Time," MGM cut the lines from all prints. The film was banned in Finland, Austria, Australia, and Atlanta, Georgia. Tod Browning's *Freaks* showed life and romance among the profoundly handicapped. Condemned by critics, theater owners, and parents, it became one of the most frequently banned films in movie history. New York state censors approved it only after about thirty minutes of film were cut. Australia rejected it as repulsive; the BBFC's refusal to approve it was not reversed until the 1960's.

(continued)

tors be changed to communists. In 1941 a Senate committee accused Hollywood of offending Germany with anti-Nazi films. Pro-Soviet films were locally banned, as were films, such as Walter Wanger's *Blockade* (1938), sympathetic to antifascist forces in the Spanish Civil War. The Knights of Columbus and the Legion of Decency opposed *Blockade*, after which the Legion proposed screening films for false political, religious, and moral doctrine.

1930's Politics and Film. These issues mirrored international developments. *Blockade* was banned in eleven countries. Many countries banned American gangster films, and in the 1930's political issues gained significance. In 1938 for example, France banned films apt to shock foreign sensibilities and provoke diplomatic incidents, while demanding advance approval of films relating to national defense, public institutions, and French or foreign officials. In Italy, ruled by Fascist powers under Benito Mussolini after 1922, the privately owned L'Unione Cinematrografia Educativa (LUCE)

was taken into state control and directed to make and distribute patriotic films designed to correct public taste. Screening of LUCE films became compulsory in Italian movie houses. In Germany, governed by the Nazis under Adolf Hitler after 1933, state control was comprehensive. After 1936, the film industry was purged of Jews, film criticism was abolished, and the industry was nationalized. American films were banned in 1939. In England, at the outbreak of war in 1939, a Censorship Division of the Ministry of Information imposed security censorship.

The 1940's. With U.S. entry into World War II in 1941, a law enacted during World War I went into effect again. The law dictated that all foreign films be screened and granted permits before entering the country. No national censorship law for U.S. films existed, although one was briefly proposed under the 1933 National Industrial Recovery Act, but, in June, 1942, President Franklin D. Roosevelt established the Office of War Information (OWI). While OWI claimed to oppose

---

FILM CENSORSHIP TIME LINE — CONTINUED

Island of Lost Souls, adapted from H. G. Wells's novel *The Island of Dr. Moreau* (1896) and starring Charles Laughton, was banned in England, Latvia, the Netherlands, India, South Africa, Germany, New Zealand, and Singapore. The MPPDA censors allowed rerelease in 1941 only after significant cuts, and cuts were demanded before 1958 release in England. *Scarface*, a gangster film recalling the career of famed hoodlum Al Capone, was banned in Australia. New York demanded cuts, and all references to Capone were removed. To satisfy the Hays office, a subtitle, *The Shame of the Nation*, and additional scenes were added, but censors rejected the film in New York, Ohio, Virginia, Maryland, and Kansas. City censorship boards rejected *Scarface* in Detroit, Seattle, Portland, Boston, and Chicago.

1933 Within a few months of taking power, German fascist leader Adolf Hitler formed the Ministry of Popular Enlightenment and Propaganda to control the film industry. Jews were banned from the industry; film censorship was established in 1934, film criticism was banned in 1935.

With its nude shots of star Hedy Kiesler (later Hedy Lamarr), Czechoslovakia's *Ekstase* (*Ecstasy*) was denied entry to the United States in 1935 and was destroyed. A censored version was admitted later that year but was denied MPPDA approval. The film was banned in Austria. *Red-Headed Woman*, starring Jean Harlow as a working girl who sabotages her boss's engagement so she can marry him, was cut by Massachusetts, Pennsylvania, and Ohio censors and was rejected by the BBFC. Hitler's government canceled the premiere of director Fritz Lang's *Das Testament des Dr. Mabuse* (*The Testament of Dr. Mabuse*) on grounds that criminals voiced Nazi slogans; Lang immediately fled Germany. The first full-length film made in Yiddish, *Sabra*, made in Palestine, was banned by the BBFC for leftist and anti-Arab slant. Warner Bros.' *Convention City*, a comedy of a drunken, rowdy sales convention, and Paramount's *The Story of Temple Drake*, a retelling of William Faulkner's *Sanctuary* (1931), which describes Temple Drake's brutal rape, brought demands for more rigorous self-censorship. The two films were made despite Hays's ban on use of the *Sanctuary* story and later insistence on extensive cuts.

1934 After receiving the MPPDA Production Code Administration (PCA) seal of approval, Irving Thalberg's lush production of *The Merry Widow*, a popular operetta, was called back for thirteen cuts, under threat of Catholic Legion of Decency action. Hays notified MPPDA members that criminal John Dillinger's life and crimes were not to be filmed. MPPDA censor Joseph Breen demanded that films on the Catholic Legion of Decency condemned list be removed from circulation.

1935 PCA censor Breen removed from circulation many films made before strengthened censorship of 1934. Some (for example *She Done Him Wrong*) were banned permanently, others (including another Mae West film) were permitted to finish their current runs, and some (Boris Karloff's 1931 *Frankenstein*) were permitted to be reedited to meet new PCA standards. Among censored films was director Dorothy Arzner's *Christopher Strong* (1933), starring Katharine Hepburn. Portraying a famous pilot, Hepburn's character falls in love with a married man, becomes pregnant, and commits suicide after achieving a world flying record. The film was banned from reissue because of the topics of pregnancy and suicide. To refilm Leo Tolstoy's *Anna Karenina*, first filmed in 1927, producer David O. Selznick had to cut any suggestion that passion or love justified Anna's adultery. Selznick also had to ensure an unhappy ending for both Anna and her lover. *Bride of Frankenstein* was cut to meet objections of Hollywood, Japanese, and Swedish censors, among others, but was rejected by Trinidad, Palestine, and Hungary. *Lives of a Bengal Lancer* was banned in Turkey because it dealt with imperialism.

1936 Mae West's *Klondike Annie* was banned in Australia as offensive to religion. *Green Pastures*, an African American

censorship, its Bureau of Motion Pictures attempted to prevent release of films deemed harmful to war policy or to relationships with U.S. allies. Studios were asked to submit all scripts for review. When OWI asked for review of synopses and cuts of films immediately before prints were made, the studios rebelled. OWI backed down. Nevertheless, in 1942 OWI banned exportation of films that predicted a long war, portrayals of labor or class conflict since World War I, and scenes of ungoverned lawlessness.

In 1945, at the war's end, Hays resigned as MPPDA president and was replaced by Eric Johnston, president of the U.S. Chamber of Commerce, who changed MPPDA's name to the Motion Picture Association of America (MPAA). It was based in Washington, D.C. The PCA office in Hollywood was known as the "Breen Office." While Breen upheld prewar principles of censorship in demanding changes and banning sexually explicit advertising in such films as Howard Hughes's *The Outlaw* (completed in 1941; released in 1946), new forms of

self-censorship emerged as a result of the House Committee on Un-American Activities (HUAC).

House Committee on Un-American Activities. Committee hearings on communist involvement in Hollywood began in 1947 under J. Parnell Thomas and were revived in 1951 under Senator Joseph McCarthy. Best known among those condemned by the committee, also known as the House Un-American Activities Committee or HUAC, were the Hollywood Ten—seven writers, two directors, and one producer who were blacklisted. Hundreds more suffered directly as a result of HUAC activities and of a related "gray" list of suspected communists established by the American Legion. At a November 24, 1947, meeting of the Association of Motion Picture Producers, studio heads committed themselves to refusing employment to communists or other suspected subversives. Denied work, those accused of communist activities left the country, left the profession, or found work under pseudonyms or friends' names. Although the postwar public showed

---

FILM CENSORSHIP TIME LINE—CONTINUED

religious drama, was banned in Austria, the Dutch East Indies, British Malaya, China, Latvia, Palestine, Finland, Australia, Hungary, and Ireland. *Fury*, the story of an attempted lynching, was banned in Venezuela, Peru, British Malaya, and India because of its sympathetic portrayal of violence during industrial strikes. Playwright and screenwriter Lillian Hellman, to film her successful stage play *The Children's Hour*, had to omit the play's central lesbian theme, change its title, and promise not to refer to the original play before the film could be released as *These Three*. Polish censors cut lines from Paul Robeson's song "Ole Man River" in *Show Boat* because of references to class and labor struggle.

1937   Burlesque star Gypsy Rose Lee was forbidden by Hays office censors to star in Twentieth Century-Fox's *You Can't Have Everything* until the studio agreed that she would act under her real name, Louise Hovick, to avoid exploiting her celebrity as stripper. French censorship, aimed at controlling war and crime films, tightened to ban films that ridiculed military or that might offend foreign nationals. Queen Victoria had died in 1901, but the British ban on film representations of her was not lifted until 1937, with the filming of *Victoria the Great*. The BBFC ended production or importation of horror films; the ban was not lifted until the end of World War II. *They Won't Forget*, based on a 1915 lynching of a Jew by Georgians, was opposed by censors because of its suggestion that American justice was corruptible. The film was banned in Georgia. Japanese censors banned *Mutiny on the Bounty* (1935), among other films, and cut kissing scenes from many U.S. films.

1938   *The Birth of a Baby*, a documentary about pregnancy from the first awareness of pregnancy to birth, was compiled by the American Committee for Maternal Welfare and backed by major medical organizations, including the U.S. Public Health Service, the American Medical Association, and the American Association of Obstetricians and Gynecologists. The PCA code banned the subject matter; New York state censors denied it a permit, and an appeal to the state commissioner was turned down on the grounds that the film would corrupt morals. The film was banned in Cincinnati, Omaha, and other cities and was denied approval by the BBFC. *Cupid Takes a Holiday*, banned in British Columbia, Canada, was among the first films banned as offensive to the handicapped.

Italian leader Benito Mussolini banned Mickey Mouse cartoons because they lacked the imperialistic firmness of spirit expected of Italian youth. *Professor Mamlock*, a Soviet film showing the struggle of anti-Nazis, especially communists, against Nazi tyranny, was banned in England, China, Chicago, Ohio, Massachusetts, and Providence, Rhode Island. RKO's *The Mad Miss Manton* was not approved by BBFC, which insisted that the married caretaker and his wife not be shown in the same bed. The BBFC ban on couples' being in the same bed lasted until 1948, when the BBFC censored Columbia Picture's *Her Husband's Affairs*. Playwright George Bernard Shaw's *Pygmalion* was rejected for filming by the MPPDA unless mention of Eliza's illegitimacy and her father's willingness to sell her for five pounds were deleted. The Marx Brothers' *A Day at the Races* was among films banned in Latvia as worthless.

1939   *Blondie Meets the Boss*, a film in a popular series about the cartoon husband and wife, was banned in Belgium for setting a bad example by showing children's disrespect for parents. In England, *Dark Eyes of London*, a Bela Lugosi horror film, became the first British film to receive new H certificate from BBFC, which was attempting to restrict horror films to adult viewers. The Hays office banned *Gone with the Wind*'s scenes that depicted brothels, the pain of childbirth, and Scarlett O'Hara's pleasure after rape by Rhett Butler. After considerable negotiation, producer Selznick was allowed to retain the word "damn" at the film's end.

Twentieth Century-Fox's *Hold That Co-Ed* was banned in Egypt because student rebellion against police set a bad

(continued)

interest in mature social themes, under HUAC pressure, social-problem themes in film decreased precipitously from 1947 to 1953.

Postwar International Films. As Hollywood themes narrowed, international films developed, many displaying the social realism and sexual openness prohibited in the United States. In Japan, U.S. occupation forces from 1945 to 1952 encouraged the development of Japanese productions for an international market. Japan's film industry, before the war, had been second in size to that of the United States but Japanese films were rarely seen outside Japan and Japanese-dominated territories. Although U.S. occupation forces censored films, some Japanese producers found such censorship less burdensome than prewar Japanese censorship. Postwar Italy, between 1945 and a new set of censorship restrictions in 1949, offered neorealist films, which took up the serious social issues demanded by postwar audiences. One of the most important to U.S. censorship issues was Vittorio de Sica's *The Bicycle Thief*

(1948), condemned by Breen because it portrays a child urinating and a bordello. Film distributor Joseph Burstyn defied Breen, releasing the film without a seal of approval; the film won the 1950 Academy Award for best foreign film. Major theaters showed the film, although it lacked a seal, the first major defiance since 1934.

The End of U.S. Censorship. The collapse of the studio system helped limit censorship. In 1948 the U.S. Supreme Court, in *United States v. Paramount Pictures*, ruled that studio control of production, distribution, and exhibition violated antitrust laws. As studios divested themselves of theater holdings, theater owners had greater freedom in selecting films. In 1942, as the Department of Justice pursued antitrust charges, Will Hays, on advice of attorneys, stipulated that theater owners could no longer be fined under the code; only producers and distributors could be penalized. This opened the way to the showing of films such as *The Bicycle Thief* and Roberto Rossellini's *The Miracle* (1951), in which parallels between

---

FILM CENSORSHIP TIME LINE — CONTINUED

example. *The Mystery of the White Room* was banned in Dutch East Indies for questioning the integrity of the medical profession. Under threat of boycott by the Legion of Decency, censors forced thirteen hundred feet of cuts in *Yes My Darling Daughter*, which was based on a Broadway show. The film showed a defiant girl running off for a sexless trial weekend with her boyfriend. Warner Bros. removed *Devil's Island*, a story about the French penal colony, from circulation after the French government threatened a two-month ban on all Warner features. The BBFC approved *The Wizard of Oz* for adults only because of frightening scenes. Irish censors cut a hula dance by Eleanor Powell and a native Hawaiian from the musical *Honolulu*. The scene of white Eleanor Powell dancing in front of Hawaiians was cut in South Africa. In Japan, Eleanor Powell's *Rosalie* was banned as offensive to royalty.

1940 Police in Lima, Peru, banned the showing of Alexander Korda's *The Lion Has Wings*, a British film, after riots, assumed to be instigated by German sympathizers. Similar riots occurred in Chile, where the U.S. film *Confessions of a Nazi Spy* was banned by the provincial governor of Santiago for fear of pro-Nazi agitation.

1941 *Two-Faced Woman*, Greta Garbo's last film, showed her as a wife who disguised herself as a sexier twin sister to win back her husband. New York's Archbishop Francis Spellman condemned the film in a pastoral letter to be read at masses in his diocese. The film was banned in Boston and banned and cut in other cities until MGM withdrew it and cut the suggestion that the husband believed that he was committing adultery with his wife's supposed twin. Nazi-occupied France enacted laws that banned Jews from the film industry.

1942 British Information Minister Brendan Bracken denounced the PCA in the House of Commons for insisting that profanity be cut from Noël Coward's *In Which We Serve*, the story of the destruction of a British destroyer.

1943 Howard Hughes's *The Outlaw*, a story of Billy the Kid and a Mexican woman named Rio, was given a seal of approval when first filmed in 1941. Sexually provocative advertisements later led to revocation of the seal and an antitrust suit against censors by Hughes.
      British authorities tried to suppress *The Life and Death of Colonel Blimp*, a satiric portrait of a military man. In Memphis, Tennessee, a censor banned *Brewster's Millions* because the African American servant played by Eddie "Rochester" Anderson was disrespectful.

1946 *Let There Be Light*, John Huston's documentary showing treatment of shell-shocked war veterans, was suppressed by the U.S. War Department, which had commissioned it, on grounds that showing it would violate the privacy of patients. Selznick's *Duel in the Sun* was cut to accede to Breen's demand that a religious hypocrite not be shown as a minister and that the heroine should demand that her rapist marry her.

1947 House Committee on Un-American Activities investigations led to the blacklisting of anyone associated with allegedly communist organizations. Except for those who publicly recanted, blacklisting lasted until 1960, when Otto Preminger gave Dalton Trumbo, who was blacklisted, screen credit for *Exodus*. *Crossfire*, directed by suspected communist Edward Dmytryk, began as the story of a man who murders a homosexual who is attracted to him. Censorship prohibited this theme, and the film became an attack on anti-Semitism, with victim changed from a homosexual to a Jew. An Italian law intended to strengthen national film industry imposed government censorship of scripts and allowed withholding of export licenses for films giving a negative image of Italy. Charlie Chaplin's *Monsieur Verdoux* (1947), the story of a wife killer who, when tried, compared his crimes to those of World War II, was denounced by the American Legion as un-American. Chaplin later withdrew the film from circulation. Although *Forever Amber*, the story of a Restoration sexual adventuress, received a PCA seal of approval, it was condemned by the Legion of Decency until much of the

the heroine and Mary, mother of Christ, provoked attack by the Legion of Decency, picket lines, and bomb threats. The film was banned in New York. Distributor Burstyn appealed to the U.S. Supreme Court (*Burstyn v. Wilson*), which reversed the *Mutual Film* decision of 1915. In 1952 the Supreme Court ruled that films were protected by the First Amendment.

Further Challenges. In 1953 the code was again challenged when Breen opposed release of *The Moon Is Blue* (1953) because of specific words, including "virgin" and "pregnant," and the suggestion that someone can be both immoral and likable—an impossibility under the code. Producer Otto Preminger released the film. Its banning in Kansas led to a 1955 Supreme Court case (*Holmby Productions, Inc. v. Vaughan*) that overturned the Kansas censorship and invalidated the state's censorship law. The six existing state censorship boards also were called into question when New York banned Walt Disney's *The Vanishing Prairie* (1954) because it depicted a buffalo giving birth. Other challenges to censorship

followed, both because of the increasing audience for foreign films and because Hollywood was beset by labor problems and by competition from television as well as from film imports. Studios, and increasingly important independent producers, needed to compete with European sexual openness and social realism.

Breen retired in 1954. Geoffrey Shurlock, Breen's chief assistant since 1934, became PCA director. During his fourteen-year term, he allowed expansion of what was permissible. The success of Otto Preminger's *The Man with the Golden Arm* (1955) pointed to the need for code revision; while approved by the Legion of Decency, the film, which deals with drug addiction, could not be passed under the code. The 1956 code revisions dropped the prohibition of miscegenation, drug addiction, abortion, prostitution, and kidnapping.

The 1960's. In 1966 Jack Valenti succeeded Eric Johnston as MPAA president. When *Who's Afraid of Virginia Woolf?* was denied a seal that year, Valenti recommended that the film

---

FILM CENSORSHIP TIME LINE — CONTINUED

heroine's life of luxury and her sexual pleasure were cut.

1949 *Curley* was banned in Memphis, Tennessee, because it showed African American and white children at the same school.

1950 The Italian film *The Bicycle Thief* was denied the PCA seal of approval. The film, widely lauded for its excellence, was shown in major U.S. theater chains without the seal, the first such defiance since 1934. The French film *La Ronde* (*The Round Dance*), based on Arthur Schnitzler's comedy *Riegen* (1897), was banned in New York because of its focus on sexual promiscuity. Director Ida Lupino's *Outrage*, intended to be the first extended, realistic U.S. film treatment of rape, was forced to accept PCA demands that the rapist be an acquaintance, not a stranger, and that the word "rape" never be used. Additionally, the victim could not be shown attempting to fight off her assailant.

1951 *A Streetcar Named Desire*, Elia Kazan's already censored film version of Tennessee Williams' hit play, was cut further by Warner Bros. without Kazan's consent to meet CPA and Legion of Decency complaints. Kazan's complete film was not released until 1993. The banning of Roberto Rossellini's *The Miracle* in New York led to the U.S. Supreme Court decision that, for the first time, ruled films a medium of expression protected by the U.S. Constitution. *M*, a remake of a 1932 German film about a psychopathic murderer who killed young girls and stole their shoes, was banned in Ohio.

1952 *Pinky*, starring Jeanne Crain as a light-skinned African American who passed for white, was banned in Marshall, Texas.

1953 Otto Preminger's light comedy *The Moon Is Blue* was released without a PCA seal of approval and against Legion of Decency opposition. The film's light attitude to sex was the cause of the uproar. British film giant Charlie Chaplin, while in Europe, was denied a reentry permit to United States on grounds of communist sympathies, although he had none. Some theaters canceled showings of his *Limelight* (1952). Pierre Chenal's film of Richard Wright's *Native Son* (1951) was banned in Ohio as contributing to immorality and crime.

1954 *The Wild One* was denied approval in Britain; Marlon Brando and Lee Marvin's portrayal of motorcycle gang leaders who terrorized a small town was viewed as a danger to public morals. The ban was not lifted until 1968. Walt Disney's *The Vanishing Prairie*, an Academy Award-winning documentary, was banned in New York because it showed a buffalo giving birth; an American Civil Liberties Union complaint led to a reversal of the ban.

1955 The subject of narcotics was banned by PCA, so *The Man with the Golden Arm*, a film about a heroin addict, was automatically denied PCA approval. Otto Preminger's decision to release it without a seal led to changes in the code. The film was banned in Maryland but the decision was overturned by a Maryland appeals court.

1956 The Indian government banned two British and six American films, including *The African Queen*, as unfavorably portraying African life. Elia Kazan's *Baby Doll*, the story of a thumb-sucking bride whose husband spied on her, hoping to consummate their marriage, opened, although condemned by the Legion of Decency and the Roman Catholic church. The film was banned in Aurora, Illinois. *The Brave One*, written by "Robert Rich," won an Academy Award for Best Screenplay; nobody stepped forward for the award. In 1959 Dalton Trumbo, who had been blacklisted, revealed he was the actual writer. The MPAA ban on Oscars to persons accused of communist affiliations was lifted that year. The film version of French writer Colette's *Le Blé en herbe* (1923; English film title, *The Game of Love*) was banned in Chicago because of the film's preoccupation with sexuality. Egypt banned Marilyn Monroe's films upon her marriage to the Jewish playwright Arthur Miller.

1957 *Garden of Eden*, a story of a foul-tempered man changed into a decent human being by going to a nudist camp, caused the BBFC to lift the total ban on nudity after 180 local authorities allowed viewing of the film. It was banned in New York

(continued)

be released as appropriate for mature audiences only. This opened the way to the classification system formally adopted November 1, 1968. The original ratings were G for general audience, M for mature audience, R for restricted, with no admission to young people under sixteen unless accompanied by an adult, and X, which barred persons under sixteen from admission. A Code and Ratings Administration replaced the PCA.

State and local censorship efforts continued in the United States, with court cases focusing on obscenity as in the censorship of *Deep Throat* (1972), banned in twenty-three states and *The Devil in Miss Jones* (1973), banned in eleven. Strong censorship continued to exist in other nations, especially in the Middle East. Censorship efforts, however, were increasingly frustrated by the internationalism of filmmaking in the 1980's and 1990's, as well as by technological advances, including the easy reproduction and transportation, legal or illegal, of films.   —*Betty Richardson*

See also *Birth of a Nation, The*; Blacklisting; British Board of Film Censors; Disney films; Film adaptation; Hays Code; Legion of Decency; Motion Picture Association of America; Pressure groups; Prior restraint; Raleigh, Sir Walter; *Times Film Corp. v. City of Chicago*.

BIBLIOGRAPHY

Edward de Grazia and Roger K. Newman's *Banned Films: Movies, Censors and the First Amendment* (New York: R. R. Bowker, 1982) includes a history of censorship from the 1890's to 1980 with descriptions of 122 films involved in court cases. Kevin Brownlow's *Behind the Mask of Innocence* (New York: Random House, 1990) contains considerable information on censorship during the silent film era. Murray Schumach's *The Face on the Cutting Room Floor: The Story of Movie and Television Censorship* (New York: William Morrow, 1964) and Frank Miller's *Censored Hollywood: Sex, Sin, and Violence on Screen* (Atlanta, Ga.: Turner, 1994) cover American film censorship. Gregory D. Black's *Hollywood*

FILM CENSORSHIP TIME LINE—CONTINUED

but the ban was overturned by an appellate court. A film distributor took a Pennsylvania censorship board to court after *Wild Weed* (1949) was rejected twice by the censorship board. The distributor won; the Philadelphia Court of Common Pleas struck down Pennsylvania's state censorship law, the nation's oldest. *L'Amant de Lady Chatterley*, based on the much-censored D. H. Lawrence novel *Lady Chatterley's Lover*, was banned in New York. The Supreme Court overturned the censorship ruling. The Maryland censorship board demanded deletion of all scenes showing bodies naked above the waist in a Brazilian semi-documentary, *Naked Amazon*. Philadelphia banned *And God Created Woman*, starring Brigitte Bardot. *Silk Stockings*, a Fred Astaire-Cyd Charisse musical, was banned in Uruguay as procommunist.

1958   Walt Disney's *Song of the South* (1946) was withdrawn from circulation after protests by African Americans. *Les Amants* (*The Lovers*) was banned or cut in Cleveland, Dayton, and Cuyahoga County, Ohio; Boston; Providence, Rhode Island; Portland, Oregon; Memphis, Tennessee, and the states of Maryland, New York, and Virginia. The film portrayed an unhappy wife who left her husband for a lover. In 1964 the Supreme Court ruled that the film was constitutionally protected and not obscene.

1959   Egypt banned Elizabeth Taylor's films because of her support of Israel; also, she had recently married a Jew and converted to Judaism. Chicago banned *The Anatomy of a Murder*, based on the Robert Traver novel, because of language, deemed obscene by censors, used in a court scene involving rape. The ruling was overturned in the district court. Chicago banned *Don Juan* (1956), a film adaptation of Wolfgang Amadeus Mozart's opera, because the film distributor refused to submit the print to a censor prior to showing.

1960   A musical number, "Hialeah," was cut from the musical *Bells Are Ringing in South Africa* to avoid showing African American and white singers singing together.

1963   The film *A Stranger Knocks* was banned in New York and Maryland (1964) because of explicit sex scenes; the bans were overturned upon legal appeal.

1964   A Swedish film, *491*, was banned from entry into the United States. The film concerned an idealistic social worker whose efforts were thwarted by the delinquents he asked into his home. The film was seized by U.S. Customs Service, and the decision was overturned by a federal appeals court.

1966   Berkeley, California, banned the only film of French author Jean Genet, *Un Chant d'amour*, which reflected his prison experiences and showed explicit homosexual behavior.

1967   *Titicut Follies*, a documentary about conditions in a Massachusetts state hospital for the criminally insane, was forbidden general release in 1968 on grounds that viewing the film would violate the privacy of the persons shown in the film. General release was approved two decades later. The Swedish film *I Am Curious—Yellow* was seized by U.S. Customs agents and forbidden U.S. entry as obscene because of its explicit sex scenes; when an appeals court overturned the Customs Service decision, the film was banned in Alabama, Arizona, California, Colorado, Georgia, Kansas, Maryland, Massachusetts, Michigan, New Jersey, New Mexico, Ohio, Pennsylvania, Virginia, and Washington between 1968 and 1971.

1968   *Rosemary's Baby* received a "condemned" rating from the National Catholic Office for Motion Pictures, formerly the Legion of Decency, for nudity and mockery of religious persons and practices. Violence in Sam Peckinpah's *The Wild Bunch* caused a few minutes of cuts to escape an X rating and thirty-five minutes of cuts after a disgusted preview audience left a Kansas City screening.

1970   Jean-Luc Godard's *Alphaville*, following the adventures of a private eye in a future totalitarian world, was banned in

Censored: Morality Codes, Catholics, and the Movies (New York: Cambridge University Press, 1994) shows how censorship promoted social and political conservatism. British censorship is covered by Annette Kuhn in *Cinema, Censorship and Sexuality, 1909-1925* (New York: Routledge, 1988), by James C. Robertson in *The British Board of Film Censors, 1895-1950* (London: Croom Helm, 1985).

First Amendment

RATIFIED: December 15, 1791

PLACE: United States (national)

SIGNIFICANCE: As part of the U.S. Constitution's Bill of Rights, the First Amendment embodies the chief constitutional protections against government censorship

The First Amendment of the U. S. Constitution is the central constitutional bulwark against government-imposed tyranny of the mind. Its wording is brief, simple, and direct:

Congress shall make no law respecting an establishment of religion, or prohibiting the free exercise thereof; or abridging the freedom of speech, or of the press, or the right of the people peaceably to assemble, and to petition the Government for a redress of grievances.

Proposed by the first Congress and ratified by the requisite number of states in 1791, the First Amendment has provisions guaranteeing freedom of religion, speech, press, assembly, and the right to petition government for a redress of grievances. Of these, the guarantees protecting freedom of religion and speech have become the central pillars of the Bill of Rights.

Application to States. By its terms, the First Amendment explicitly prevents Congress from dong anything to abridge the freedoms of religion and speech. As originally contemplated, the amendment restrained the federal government, but not the governments of the individual states. When the Bill of Rights was being debated, James Madison proposed an

---

FILM CENSORSHIP TIME LINE—CONTINUED

Pakistan. In Rutherford County, North Carolina, a sheriff tried to force local theaters to show only G-rated films; he lost a legal decision after an arrest of an exhibitor showing *Where Eagles Dare* (1969), an adventure story about the freeing of an American general from Nazi captivity.

1971 *Carnal Knowledge*, Mike Nichols' study of male sexual hypocrisy, was banned in Albany, Georgia, in 1972. Local police seized the film and arrested the theater manager for circulating obscene material; the manager, convicted, appealed to the Supreme Court and won.

1972 *Deep Throat*, film with explicit sex, was banned in California, Colorado, Florida, Georgia, Illinois, Iowa, Kentucky, Louisiana, Maryland, Massachusetts, Michigan, Mississippi, Missouri, Nebraska, New Hampshire, New Jersey, New York, North Dakota, Ohio, Pennsylvania, South Dakota, Tennessee, and Texas between 1972 and 1981. Federal authorities filed conspiracy charges against five corporations and twelve persons associated with the film. The convictions were overturned on appeal. *Last Tango in Paris*, a Marlon Brando film about a fatal affair between an older American expatriate and a young Frenchwoman, led to police orders forbidding its showing in Montgomery, Alabama, and to the arrest and confiscation of the film by police in Shreveport, Louisiana. In director Bernardo Bertolucci's native Italy, the film was banned from 1976 to 1978; authorities lost court cases on obscenity charges against the director, producer, and some cast members.

1973 *The Exorcist*, the story of a girl possessed by the devil, was banned in Hattiesburg, Mississippi; the state's supreme court overturned the conviction of the theater owner for exhibiting an obscene picture. *The Devil in Miss Jones*, dealing with the reprieval of a woman from hell so that she can enjoy sex, was banned in California, Florida, Georgia, Kansas, Massachusetts, Michigan, Missouri, New York, South Dakota, Texas, and Virginia from 1973 to 1975.

1975 The American Legion requested a boycott of the Vietnam documentary, *Introduction to the Enemy*, directed by Haskell Wexler, Tom Hayden, and Jane Fonda.

1976 Andrzej Wajda's Polish film *Man of Marble*, an attack on power, especially communist power, was released abroad but generally suppressed in Poland.

1977 In South Africa, *How Long* was banned, and its director Gibson Kente and some film crew members were arrested. This musical was the first film produced and directed by black South Africans.

1978 A Turkish film, *Enemy*, a study of the dispossessed underclass, was suppressed in Turkey but was allowed to be exported to show that Turkey allowed freedom of speech.

1979 The Soviet Union, with other communist nations, withdrew from a West Berlin film festival in protest against Oscar-winning Vietnam War film *The Deer Hunter* (1978); in the movie, there are cruel communist prison guards.

1990 *Henry and June*, a film about Henry Miller and Anaïs Nin, two writers of erotica, was the first film to receive an NC-17 rating and was shown in only 307 U.S. theaters. Lesbian scenes and a shot of an erotic Japanese postcard were cut to avoid an X rating before the new NC-17 classification for films was adopted.

1992 Threatened with an NC-17 rating that would limit theater showings, forty-two seconds from three scenes were cut to ensure an R rating for *Basic Instinct*. The scenes were reinserted for European release and for a director's cut for home viewing. Gay activists, upset at the negative portrayal of the film's central bisexual character, sought to disrupt the film's San Francisco shoots, also threatening demonstrations and disturbances inside theaters.

amendment that would have required states to respect "the equal rights of conscience, the freedom of speech or of the press, and the right of trial by jury in criminal cases," but his proposal failed to win support in the first Congress and was never enacted.

More than a century after the Bill of Rights was ratified, the U.S. Supreme Court was called upon to consider the effect of the Fourteenth Amendment, ratified in 1868, on the First Amendment's original scope. The Fourteenth Amendment's due process clause declares that states may not "deprive any person of life, liberty, or property, without due process of law." A key issue that the language of this clause posed is identifying which "liberties" are protected against unlawful deprivation. In a series of cases decided in the first half of the twentieth century, the Supreme Court ultimately determined that the word "liberty" in this clause included most of the liberties protected by the Bill of Rights. The Court accordingly held that the Fourteenth Amendment's due process clause made most of the provisions in the Bill of Rights—including those of the First Amendment—applicable to the states. Thus, whereas the First Amendment had originally restricted only federal encroachments on freedom of religion and speech, the Fourteenth Amendment effectively extended this restriction to state and local governments.

Original Intent. Although the Framers of the First Amendment prohibited abridgments of "freedom of speech," historians have never fully agreed on what types of government restrictions on speech the Framers intended to prevent. At the time of the amendment's enactment, two types of assault on freedom of speech were most common: prior restraints and the common law crime of seditious libel. Prior restraint is any government action designed to prevent certain types of speech from occurring at all, rather than simply punishing offenders after the fact. A prior restraint law is one that requires material that is to be published or publicly spoken to be submitted to a government official with power to grant or deny permission to utter or publish the speech based upon its contents. In the eighteenth century, the most common forms of prior restraint were licensing laws requiring government approval of books, newspapers, and other writings by a government official prior to their publication. Seditious libel, on the other hand, was a legal doctrine that allowed governments to punish persons who criticized public officials, laws, or government policies.

The First Amendment clearly was intended to prohibit prior restraints of speech, such as government licensing schemes. Less certain is the question of whether the Framers intended to abolish the crime of seditious libel as well. Less than a decade after the amendment's ratification, Federalists passed the Sedition Act of 1798, which codified aspects of the common law crime of seditious libel by making it illegal to conspire against the federal government and by providing for the punishment of writers who criticized government operations. This act was denounced by Jeffersonian Republicans; after they assumed control of the federal government, prosecutions under the law ceased before the constitutionality of the law itself was tested in court. The unusual circumstances of these events have left historians unclear as to the Framers' intent with respect to the application of the free speech clause to seditious libel.

Modern Interpretations. However limited the framers' original vision of the First Amendment may have been, the Supreme Court has read the language of the amendment expansively to protect most forms of belief, opinion, and expression during the twentieth century. The Court has read the free exercise clause to ban all deliberate attempts to suppress particular religious ideas and the practices that flow from them. Moreover, it has interpreted the establishment clause as prohibiting almost all attempts by government to censure unpopular religious beliefs, even indirectly by lending its weight to other religious beliefs, or by supporting religion generally over nonreligion.

Although the First Amendment's free exercise and establishment clauses provide some protection against government censorship, its most important limitations on censorship are its free speech and press clauses. The Supreme Court's late twentieth century interpretation of these clauses cannot be reduced to a simple formula, but it has generally provided expansive protection for most forms of speech. The Court has interpreted the free speech and press clauses to prohibit almost all attempts to censor particular messages on account of the viewpoints they express or the content they contain, unless there is a "clear and present danger" of speech producing a social harm that the government is entitled to prevent. In keeping with the intent of the Framers, the Court has treated all forms of prior restraint—such as licensing schemes and injunctions against certain speech—with special suspicion. Moreover, the Court has frequently overturned laws containing vague regulations of speech because of the likelihood such laws might deter or "chill" speech protected by the First Amendment.

The Court has not, however, treated all forms of speech the same. Obscenity, for example, receives no constitutional protection and may be restricted by federal, state, or local governments. Furthermore, certain forms of speech, while receiving some protection under the First Amendment, may nevertheless be subjected to narrower restrictions than accorded other protected speech. For example, government may regulate advertisements, pornography, certain offensive language, and defamation more readily than other protected forms of speech. Moreover, in contrast with government attempts to regulate the content of speech, government officials may more freely regulate the time, place, and manner of speech so long as they do not discriminate among various viewpoints, and so long as the regulation serves some important purpose.

—Timothy L. Hall

See also Assembly, right of; Clear and present danger doctrine; Constitution, U.S.; First Amendment Congress; Fourteenth Amendment; Free speech; Intellectual freedom; Libel; Prior restraint; Sedition Act of 1798; *West Virginia State Board of Education v. Barnette.*

BIBLIOGRAPHY

The historical background of the First Amendment is surveyed in Leonard Levy, *Emergence of a Free Press* (New York: Oxford University Press, 1985), and Thomas J. Curry, *The First Freedoms: Church and State in America to the*

First Amendment Controversies

Issue	Reasons to Limit	Reasons Not to Limit
Does the First Amendment protect the right of members of the Native American Church to smoke peyote as part of their religious rituals?	Peyote is a controlled substance. To permit its use might endanger the lives of the user and others.	The free exercise of religion by the Native American Church requires the use of peyote. Freedom of religion should not be infringed.
Does the First Amendment protect the right of art galleries to display publicly artworks that may be considered obscene or offensive?	The First Amendment does not protect pornography or obscenity. If a work is considered offensive by people in the community, it should not be displayed.	Freedom of speech and freedom of the press imply free expression. Art is in the eye of the beholder.
Does the First Amendment protect those who burn the American flag in violation of state laws?	The flag is the country's most important symbol. State governments ought to be allowed to protect it.	Burning the flag is as legitimate an act of protest as speaking out against a government policy. Preventing flag-burning would be banning a form of political expression.
Should schools and public libraries ban books that contain racially offensive terms?	Use of some racial terms is offensive and may lower the self-esteem of minority students.	Censorship restricts the flow of ideas. Students would be prevented from reading literature that was written in a time when such terms were considered more acceptable.
Should the press be allowed to print any government documents?	The press's freedom should be restricted to ensure national security.	Government decisions should be exposed to the will of the people.
Should newspapers and the media be allowed access to participants in a trial before a verdict has been delivered?	Unlimited discussion of trial-related matters in a public forum may infringe upon Fifth Amendment rights to due process.	Matters of public concern should be open for discussion.

Passage of the First Amendment (New York: Oxford University Press, 1986). Chapters 16 and 17 of John E. Nowak and Ronald D. Rotunda's *Constitutional Law* (5th ed. St. Paul, Minn.: West Publishing, 1995) discuss the modern state of First Amendment law. The relationship between the amendment and democratic values is explored in Walter Berns, *The First Amendment and the Future of American Democracy* (New York: Basic Books, 1976). Anthony Lewis' *Make No Law: The Sullivan Case and the First Amendment* (New York: Random House, 1991) and Rodney Smolla's *Jerry Falwell v. Larry Flynt: The First Amendment on Trial* (New York: St. Martin's Press, 1988) thoroughly examine two important First Amendment cases.

First Amendment Congress

Founded: 1979

Type of organization: Group sponsored by print and broadcast news reporters to promote First Amendment values

Significance: The First Amendment Congress is active in sponsoring opportunities for discussion of First Amendment issues and in developing curricular materials concerning freedom of expression

The First Amendment Congress was founded under the leadership of Jean Otto by a number of major print and broadcast news associations. The news media sensed that it was under

fire from the public and consequently sought to foster a dialogue between the public and the media to further freedom of expression. By 1995 the organization's voting members included twenty national associations, including the Associated Press, United Press International, and the Reporters Committee for Freedom of the Press. The organization operates at the University of Colorado at Denver's Graduate School of Public Affairs. Although the First Amendment Congress focused originally on issues relating to the public response to news media, it gradually expanded its concerns to include a broad spectrum of First Amendment issues. The Congress sponsors a variety of meetings for the public discussion of these issues. It has also prepared and distributed a set of lesson plans for grades K through twelve called *Education for Freedom*. The plans promote awareness among students of the First Amendment and seek to relate freedom of expression to everyday events from students' lives.

See also Associated Press; News media censorship; Reporters Committee for Freedom of the Press; United Press International.

First Hemispheric Conference on Free Expression

Date: March 9-11, 1994

Place: Mexico City, Mexico

Significance: This conference produced a proclamation of free speech principles, including a rejection of censorship, that was approved by a broad range of international representatives

In March, 1994, a group of about seventy publishers, editors, reporters, government officials, and others from North and South America met in Mexico City for a hemispheric conference promoting free expression. The conference was sponsored by the Inter American Press Association (IAPA) and was organized by publisher James McClatchy and thus tended to focus upon the censorship of newspapers. Former secretary general of the United Nations Javier Perez de Cuellar presided over the meeting as general chairman.

The conference delegates developed and approved a ten-point declaration of principles concerning freedom of expression. The declaration's preamble stated, in part, that "a free press is the foundation of liberty," and that "there must be no law abridging freedom of speech or of the press." The enumerated principles declared freedom of speech and of the press to be "inalienable" rights; called upon governments to allow their citizens access to all information; declared censorship and other "obstacles to free information flow" to be "in direct opposition to freedom of the press"; and otherwise supported free expression. The IAPA planned to obtain additional signatures from other international leaders and organizations, and to disseminate the declaration worldwide.

See also Book and Periodical Council Statement on the Freedom of Expression and the Freedom to Read; Canadian Library Association Statement on Intellectual Freedom; Chapultepec Declaration; Convention for the Protection of Human Rights and Fundamental Freedoms; Library Bill of Rights; News media censorship; Expression and the Freedom to Read; Freedom; Fundamental Freedoms.

Flag burning

DEFINITION: The willful burning or desecration of a national flag or similar symbol

SIGNIFICANCE: A controversial form of political expression in the United States, flag burning has been protected under the First Amendment; it is a highly emotional issue that illustrates differences among the courts and other branches of government in interpreting censorship

Throughout U.S. history there have been numerous attempts to make flag burning illegal. Local and state officials have advocated and, in some cases, passed legislation making desecration of the national flag illegal. Nebraska outlawed flag desecration in 1903 and Texas did so in 1986. At the federal level, laws punishing flag desecration have been advocated at various times by members of the executive branch and have been introduced in both the House and Senate.

Some federal officials, including President George Bush in 1990, have gone as far as advocating amending the Constitution to outlaw flag burning. Such an amendment was, however, voted down by both houses of Congress during Bush's administration. In 1995 the House of Representatives overwhelmingly passed a flag-burning amendment, but this time it was President Bill Clinton who opposed it. At various times, as many as forty-nine of the fifty state legislatures—the bodies

that ultimately ratify constitutional amendments—have indicated their willingness to support a flag-burning amendment. In some cases, police concerned about the legality of such laws have chosen to arrest flag burners on other charges, such as arson, disturbing the peace, or inciting to riot.

Debate over flag burning has occupied far more time and energy in America than have actual instances of flag burning. Opponents of censorship have noted that within a typical year, only five or six instances of flag burning are reported throughout the United States. These opponents have suggested that the issue has usually been raised more for political purposes during election periods than as a critical component in the debate over free speech.

Flag Burning Throughout the World. As a form of political protest, flag burning has occurred more frequently in countries outside of the United States. For example, demonstrations in the Philippines following a murder conviction in 1995 included numerous acts of desecration of the flag of the United Arab Emirates. Philippine president Fidel Ramos labeled the actions "unreasonable displays of emotion" and urged that flag burning "should be condemned by all of us, even if these are manifestations of legitimate protests." Flag burning has also been frequently used as a symbolic gesture in the Republic of South Africa, where rival ethnic factions have often desecrated the flags of rival groups.

The practice has also been common in Middle Eastern countries, where the complex relationships among political, social, and religious institutions have added extra symbolic dimensions. Indeed, in many parts of the world, flag burning is interpreted as not only an attack on the state, but an attack on religion and culture.

Judicial History. As American legislatures have debated laws to suppress flag burning, the judicial system has consistently ruled such laws unconstitutional. The U.S. Supreme Court has repeatedly ruled against flag-burning legislation; however, its members have not been unanimous in their rulings. Several of its rulings on this issue were decided by 5-4 votes. In *Street v. New York* (1969), for example, the Court upheld bus driver Sidney Street's right to burn an American flag. In 1974 the Court overturned judgments against two other protesters who had been convicted under state flag-desecration laws. One of these had sewn an American flag to the seat of his pants; the second had attached peace signs to a U.S. flag that he displayed outside his window. In some cases, however, the Court has upheld state regulations on flag mutilation in such cases as *Halter v. Nebraska* (1907) and *Kime v. United States* (1981).

Flag burning was most firmly established as a legal form of expression in the Supreme Court's 1989 decision in *Texas v. Johnson*. In 1984 a man named Gregory Johnson was arrested for burning a U.S. flag outside the Republican National Convention in Dallas, Texas. He was convicted of violating the Texas law against flag desecration. His appeal reached the U.S. Supreme Court, which ruled—in another 5-4 decision—that his act was a legitimate form of expression protected by the First Amendment. In writing the Court's majority opinion, Justice William J. Brennan stated that "if there is a bedrock principle underlying the First Amendment, it is that the Government may not prohibit the expression of an idea simply because society finds the idea itself offensive or disagreeable." Chief Justice William H. Rehnquist, in his dissenting opinion, labeled flag burning "evil" and said that it "is most likely to be indulged in not to express any particular idea, but to antagonize others."

Rehnquist's case against flag burning reflected the view that

by refusing to hear the lower court cases related to flag burning. Sharp divisions in the courts, as well as intense feelings expressed by presidents, members of Congress, and the general public over this issue demonstrated that it would not soon be resolved.

—Edward J. Lordan

See also Demonstrations; *Doonesbury*; Draft-card burning; Fighting words; First Amendment; Symbolic speech; *Texas v. Johnson*.

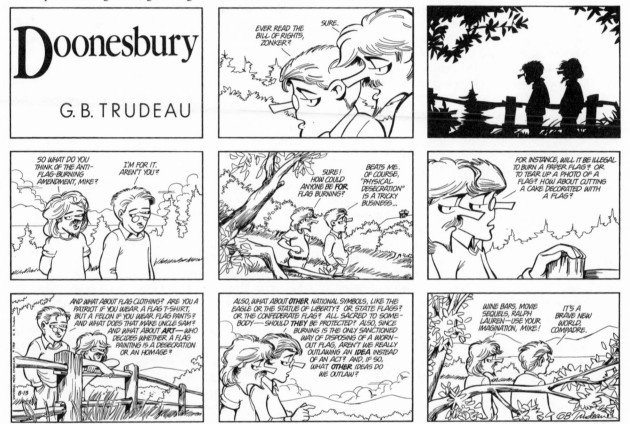

Garry Trudeau published this poignant Doonesbury *strip during the height of a national debate on flag burning in August, 1989.* (Doonesbury © 1989 G. B. Trudeau. Reprinted with permission of UNIVERSAL PRESS SYNDICATE. All rights reserved.)

such acts represent a form of "fighting words"—a concept formulated in the Court's 1942 *Chaplinsky v. New Hampshire* ruling. In that decision the Court reasoned that words likely to provoke an average person to fight or commit a breach of the peace were not protected by the First Amendment.

The Court's *Texas v. Johnson* decision rendered flag-burning laws in forty-eight states unconstitutional. However, because flag desecration is such an emotionally charged issue, state and federal officials persisted in trying to outlaw it. Congress passed the Flag Protection Act of 1989 in response to the Court's *Texas v. Johnson* ruling, but the Supreme Court immediately declared the law illegal. A year later, the Court reaffirmed its earlier ruling in *United States v. Eichman* and *United States v. Haggerty*.

In 1990 Associate Justice John Paul Stevens stated that the Court could have saved "a lot of ink" and "a lot of headache"

BIBLIOGRAPHY

Robert J. Goldstein has written three seminal books on flag desecration: *Saving "Old Glory": The History of the American Flag Desecration Controversy* (Boulder, Colo.: Westview Press, 1995), *Burning the Flag: The Great 1989-1990 American Flag Desecration Controversy* (Kent, Ohio: Kent State University Press, 1996), and *Desecrating the American Flag: Key Documents from the Civil War to 1995* (Syracuse, N.Y.: Syracuse University Press, 1996). For a broad discussion of flag burning as a symbolic act, see Haig A. Bosmajian's *Dissent: Symbolic Behavior and Rhetorical Strategies* (Boston: Allyn and Bacon, 1972) and Franklyn S. Haiman's article "Nonverbal Communication and the First Amendment: The Rhetoric of the Streets Revisited" in *Quarterly Journal of Speech* 53 (April, 1967). A practical guide to the legal ramifications of symbolic protest can be found in *The Right to*

Protest: The Basic ACLU Guide to Free Expression by Joel M. Gora, David Goldberger, and Gary M. Stern (Carbondale: Southern Illinois University Press, 1991).

Flaubert, Gustave

BORN: December 12, 1821, Rouen, France
DIED: May 8, 1880, Croisset, France
IDENTIFICATION: French novelist
SIGNIFICANCE: Attempts to censor Flaubert's writings helped win for him recognition as one of the great realist writers of his time

In 1848 a revolution toppled the last French monarchy and replaced it with a republic. The French literary world had hoped that a new government would also mean the restoration of civil liberties, but they were disappointed. Louis Napoleon, the new president, wanted power, not constitutional restraints. After two further coups, he had himself declared president for life, then Emperor Napoleon III. Political purges and press censorship followed. Twenty-seven-thousand persons were arrested; dozens of newspapers and literary magazines were closed down.

Among the victims was Victor Hugo, France's most famous writer, who went into exile, to the dismay of Flaubert, who had begun writing his great realist novel *Madame Bovary*. Flaubert detested the hypocrisy of the new industrial middle class and laid it bare in his novel. The French middle class, in turn, felt that he treated subjects that should not be discussed in refined society, such as sexuality, adultery, and suicide. Flaubert's novel might never have been published had it not been for the urging of friends who recognized its merits. It first appeared in a literary magazine in installments, beginning in October, 1856. Although Flaubert had been warned that the imperial police wanted to destroy both him and the magazine, he insisted that nothing in his novel be deleted. He then prepared for a trial.

Fortunate in having both money and powerful family connections, Flaubert was able to hire one of the best attorneys to plead his case. The hearing opened on June 31, 1857. The charge brought against him was offending public morality and religion. Flaubert's attorney pointed to passages in the classics of French literature that might be judged more offensive than those of his client. The court finally judged that the book should be censored, while acknowledging its literary merits. Flaubert himself was acquitted, to the dismay of the Roman Catholic press, which found the book to be both immoral and irreligious—fit to be listed on the church's *Index Librorum Prohibitorum*.

Charges of immorality continued to be leveled against Flaubert, who increasingly was identified only with *Madame Bovary*. American critics were especially harsh, maintaining that his subjects were sunk in vice and degradation. As late as 1935 the New York Society for the Suppression of Vice tried to have *November*, a minor and recently-translated work of Flaubert's youth, suppressed because it violated the state's law against objectionable literature. However, the magistrate ruled in the book's favor. Meanwhile, the 1857 obscenity charge and attempts at censorship haunted Flaubert the rest of his life. He thought of his trial as a whirlpool of lies and infamies and considered censorship to be a monstrosity, worse than homicide—treason against the soul.

See also Adultery; France; Hugo, Victor; Hypocrisy; *Index Librorum Prohibitorum*; Maupassant, Guy de; Morality; Obscenity: legal definitions; Society for the Suppression of Vice, New York; Suicide.

Folk music

DEFINITION: Music, often of anonymous creation, that is transmitted by oral tradition, and modern music created to follow the traditions of earlier folk music
SIGNIFICANCE: The process of oral transmission has historically been a subtle form of censorship, and modern folk music has often been censored because of its content

Strictly speaking, "folk music" is that music which is orally transmitted within particular communities or cultures. Most such music has culture significance that goes beyond its immediate entertainment value, and it has often been incorporated into secular communication, as well as sacred rituals. Modern folk music also has a popular, if less precise, definition: songs written by musicians who are inspired by authentic oral traditions, or who have displayed an empathy for the working class.

The modern definition of folk music became commonplace during the New York folk revival of the 1940's and 1950's, which featured writer-performers such as Woody Guthrie, Pete Seeger, and Huddie Ledbetter (also known as Leadbelly), who often combined original lyrics with authentic folk melodies. By the late 1950's the revival established itself commercially as an alternative to teenybopper pop music and the amplified sounds of rock 'n' roll. The Kingston Trio scored a 1958 hit with their arrangement of the traditional murder ballad "Tom Dooley." The song unquestionably belonged to Appalachian oral tradition, but the Kingston Trio's rendition, which included three-part harmonies, owed more to the college theatrical than to authentic regional performance styles.

Oral Tradition. Within oral tradition censorship most often takes the form of taboo. For instance, many Australian aboriginal cultures traditionally allowed only adult males to sound the bullroarer; women and uninitiated males were prohibited from even seeing the sacred instrument. Similarly, many college fraternities have taught their pledges songs that they may not repeat outside closed meetings. Gender taboos have played an important part in the development of folk song tradition, which has divided songs, usually by subject, into those suitable for men and those for women. For example, "bad-man" ballads generally became the province of men; romantic ballads, the province of women.

Racial divisions have also fostered musical censorship. Ragtime, blues, and jazz—all of which originated in African American folk music—were initially barred from white stages on charges of barbarism and fears of racial mixing. The advent of commercial sound recordings in the 1920's served only to increase the segregation of black and white music. A handful of record companies such as Brunswick, Vocalion, and Okeh dealt in "race records"—a term for folk music recordings produced and distributed almost exclusively to African Americans. When the Allen Brothers, a pair of whites from Chattanooga, Tennessee, learned that their blues recordings were being distributed as "race records," they insisted, successfully, that their company withdraw the product. While a few black artists, such as Bessie Smith, managed to break the color barrier, the segregation of folk music remained in place until the New York folk revival introduced black folksingers to white audiences.

Folk songs have often exhibited another form of censorship by relying upon codewords to refer to sexual activity. Blues songs, in particular, have a long tradition of employing euphemisms for sexual terms. For example, the female partner becomes the "easy rider," and her genitalia a "jelly roll," while the male becomes a "rooster" or "crawling kingsnake." Codewords have allowed blues singers to broach ordinarily taboo subjects: Homosexuals are "chicken-meat" and "bull-dykers"; "back-door man" refers not only to an illicit lover but also to anal sex.

Protest Songs. Traditional folk music has also served the social function of providing outlets for protest. American slave protest had to be concealed in nonsense phrases or codewords. A seemingly innocent song such as "Jimmie Crack Corn," for example, contained the concealed wish for the master's death: "Old massa's gone away." Even the religious traditions of white slave owners were subverted: For slaves the hymn "I'll Fly Away" expressed their desire to reach the North as much as heaven. Overt protest songs were largely performed beyond the scrutiny of whites. Frederick Douglass recorded one example with lines such as: "We bake the bread/ they give us the husk."

Communists, socialists, feminists, unionists, civil rights workers, and other groups committed to social reform have all had their repertoire of protest songs. However, these largely European American traditions have differed from those of African Americans in that they originated from more literate cultures. Authorities have generally had an easier time prohibiting such popular protest songs than authentic folk songs. Prior to the advent of sound recordings, a subversive popular song could be censored by preventing the publication or distribution of sheet music or songbooks. During the Civil War, the Confederate states prohibited not only the public performance but also the sale of sheet music of "Battle Hymn of the Republic"—a little-known hymn until after Julia Ward Howe rewrote it as an antislavery anthem.

In 1948 the government of Quebec halted importation of a songbook on the grounds that "Joe Hill" and other songs that it contained were tools of communist subversion. During the same period the Parks Authority of New York City passed ordinances, later rescinded, that banned folksinging in Washington Square Park. When song bans have not succeeded, authorities have acted against the folksingers. Labor organizer and folksinger Aunt Molly Jackson was judicially exiled from her native Kentucky in 1931 for her work on behalf of miners. On November 15, 1919, the state of Utah executed Joe Hill, a folksinger associated with the International Workers of the World, on slender evidence of his alleged participation in a murder and robbery.

Radio and television helped popularize neoprotest songs, but at the same time the commercialization of folk music ultimately served censors. For example, *The Ed Sullivan Show*, which censored popular rock music acts such as Elvis Presley and the Doors on grounds of indecency, prohibited a young Bob Dylan from performing his political satire "Talking John Birch Society Blues." Radical politics also aborted Pete Seeger's television career. The anticommunist blacklist kept Seeger off the American Broadcasting Company's television folk music program *Hootenanny*, which first aired in 1963. He finally broke the blacklist on September 10, 1967, by appearing on the Columbia Broadcasting System's television program *The Smothers Brothers Comedy Hour*. However, Seeger's performance of an anti-Vietnam War song, "Waist Deep in the Big Muddy," was deleted from the broadcast. The network did, however, allow him to sing the song on a February, 1968, appearance, but its Detroit affiliate refused to broadcast that segment and soon afterward the Smothers' show itself was canceled.

Folk song miscellanies, both academic and popular, have often distorted tradition by suppressing ribald material. Famed folk song collectors, such as Cecil Sharp and John Lomax, have bowdlerized lyrics in order to publish their discoveries. At the same time there is a kind of censorship that, during the process of oral transmission, deletes objectionable lines or even whole stanzas from popular folk songs. Songbooks have commonly omitted the following stanza from Woody Guthrie's "This Land Is Your Land":

> As I was walking, I saw a sign there,
> And on that sign it said "No Trespassing."
> But on the other side it didn't say nothing,
> that sign was made for you and me.

While some publishers, particularly during the McCarthy era, may have deleted the stanza for fear of its communist sympathies, others more recently have done so simply because this is the way the song has been transmitted.   —*Luke A. Powers*

See also African Americans; Guthrie, Woody; Music; Protest music; Recording industry; Rock 'n' roll music; Seeger, Pete; *Smothers Brothers Comedy Hour, The*; Weavers, the.

BIBLIOGRAPHY

Lawrence Levine's *Black Culture and Black Consciousness: Afro-American Folk Thought from Slavery to Freedom* (New York: Oxford University Press, 1977) explores African American protest music and illustrates examples of censorship. William Barlow focuses on the transgressive nature of blues in *Looking Up at Down: The Emergence of Blues Culture* (Philadelphia: Temple University Press, 1989). John Greenway's *American Folksongs of Protest* (Philadelphia: University of Pennsylvania Press, 1953) surveys radical folk song within the abolition and labor movements. David Dunaway's well-researched *How Can I Keep from Singing: Pete Seeger* (New York: McGraw-Hill, 1981) and Oscar Brand's witty *The Ballad Mongers: Rise of the Modern Folk Song* (New York: Funk & Wagnalls, 1962) explore censorship of the folk music revival.

Foreign Agents Registration Act of 1938

ENACTED: June 8, 1938

PLACE: United States (national)

SIGNIFICANCE: This federal law authorized the U.S. government to restrict importation of any foreign films and publications that it classified as "propaganda"

The 1938 Foreign Agents Registration Act (FARA) was designed to restrict distribution of foreign films and publications in the United States. It required that any film produced in a foreign country that could be considered political propaganda had to be so labeled. During the 1980's the law was given an expansive interpretation under the Reagan Administration. In 1982 the Department of Justice sought to require three films produced by the National Film Board of Canada to be labeled as propaganda.

Two of the Canadian films were about acid rain—a sensitive subject in U.S.-Canadian relations; the third, *If You Love This Planet* won an Academy Award. The Justice Department summarized the message of this film as: "Unless we shake off our indifference and work to prevent nuclear war, we stand a slim chance of surviving the twentieth century." The Justice Department ordered the Film Board of Canada to include a message with the films that the U.S. government did not necessarily approve of its content and that the films contained "political propaganda." Under U.S. law, the Film Board of Canada was also required to provide the Justice Department with the names of the persons and organizations in the United States who ordered the films.

The following year, in Washington, D.C., and California respectively, the American Civil Liberties Union (ACLU) and California state senator Barry Keene—who had planned to sponsor showings of these Canadian films to support his own views—filed separate suits against the Justice Department, claiming that FARA was unconstitutional. The ACLU argued that labeling the Canadian films as propaganda might prejudice potential viewers and might even deter people from viewing the films at all, because the label "denigrates the films' messages." Furthermore, the ACLU argued that requiring a listing of the names of the exhibitors might injure exhibitors' reputations because they would be stigmatized as exhibitors of "un-American" or "unpatriotic materials." In 1984, in *Block v. Smith*, the U.S. District Court for the District of Columbia dismissed the ACLU suit, ruling that the term "political propaganda" did not in itself necessarily have negative connotations. An appeals court reversed part of this decision by holding that Block, the distributor of the Canadian films, had proven "concrete harm"; however, it simultaneously affirmed the lower court's ruling that the "propaganda" label was acceptable, and that Block must still report the names of the persons who ordered his films.

Meanwhile, California's Senator Keene, objecting to being labeled a disseminator of political propaganda, advanced similar arguments. The U.S. District Court in San Bernardino, California, enjoined application of FARA to the three Canadian films; this was affirmed at the appellate level.

In 1987 the U.S. Supreme Court, in *Meese v. Keene*, held that the label of "political propaganda," when used in a "neutral and even-handed manner," is not intended as censorship, and "has no pejorative connotation." Writing for a 5-3 majority, Justice John Paul Stevens conceded there was "a risk that a partially informed audience might believe that a film that must be registered with the Department of Justice is suspect. But there is no evidence that this suspicion . . . has had the effect of government censorship." The Supreme Court thus upheld the decision to label the three Canadian films as "propaganda" under FARA.

See also Canada; Customs laws, U.S.; Film censorship; Propaganda.

44 Liquormart, Inc. v. Rhode Island

COURT: U.S. Supreme Court

DECIDED: May 13, 1996

SIGNIFICANCE: Rhode Island's efforts to ban all liquor-price advertising was held to be an unconstitutional abridgment of commercial speech

In 1956 the state of Rhode Island enacted legislation that generally prohibited liquor stores licensed in the state and out-of-state manufacturers from advertising the prices of any alcoholic products that they sold within Rhode Island. The legislation also prohibited Rhode Island media from publishing or broadcasting any advertisements mentioning prices of any alcoholic beverages. In addition, a regulation of the Rhode Island liquor control administrator provided that no placard or sign visible from the exterior of a package store could make any reference to the price of any alcoholic beverage.

On May 13, 1996, the U.S. Supreme Court, in a seminal decision broadening constitutional protections of commercial speech, struck down the statutes and regulations. Although unable to agree on an opinion as to the proper standard for determining the validity of the liquor-price advertising ban, the members of the Court unanimously agreed that the statutes and the implementing regulations abridged speech in ways that violated the First Amendment.

Six justices held that the Twenty-first Amendment did not qualify the First Amendment's prohibition against laws abridging freedom of speech. Five justices held that Rhode Island had failed to carry the heavy burden of justifying, for First Amendment purposes, the complete ban on liquor-price advertising. Four justices expressed the view that regulations that entirely suppress commercial speech in order to pursue a policy not related to consumer protection must be reviewed with "special care," and that such blanket bans should not be approved unless the speech itself is deceptive or related to unlawful activity.

The justices also said that where a state entirely prohibits the dissemination of truthful, nonmisleading commercial messages for reasons related to the preservation of fair bargaining process, there is little reason to depart from the rigorous review that the First Amendment generally demands. Moreover, Rhode Island's advertising ban could not survive the applicable "special care" review standard, as it did not directly advance the state's substantial interest in promoting temperance, and it was more extensive than necessary to serve that interest.

Finally, the Court ruled that various arguments in support of Rhode Island's claim that it had merely exercised appropriate "legislative judgment" in determining that a price advertising ban would best promote temperance would have to be rejected.

See also Advertising as the target of censorship; Alcoholic beverages; Commercial speech.

Foster, Stephen Collins

BORN: July 4, 1826, Lawrenceville, Pennsylvania
DIED: January 13, 1864, New York, New York
IDENTIFICATION: American composer
SIGNIFICANCE: Criticized for perpetuating racial stereotypes, Foster's songs about African American slaves have been targets of censorship

An American poet and composer who lived primarily in the North, Foster became famous for his numerous songs about Southern slaves before the Civil War. He wrote most of these songs for performance by black-face minstrels, who were popular in the United States in his day. Although many of his songs have been continuously popular since his time, their lyrics have come to be perceived as racist by organizations sensitive to African American interests. Many of the songs imply that slaves were happy and fulfilled with their work on plantations; the songs also use terms such as "darkeys," "massa," and "boys." Some critics have argued that the songs should either not be performed or be performed only after the removal of offensive terms.

In response to these criticisms, the lyrics of Foster's "My Old Kentucky Home" and "Old Folks at Home" were changed to serve as the official state songs of Kentucky and Florida. Public performances of Foster's songs, particularly on television and radio, have been similarly purged of potentially offensive terms. At least one of the three major television networks in the 1950's used a code specifying which words could not be broadcast. Some have viewed such alterations as "salvaging," or "updating," Foster's work for a more enlightened age. Others consider it to be revisionism and censorship.

See also African Americans; Folk music; Music; Political correctness; Race.

Foundation to Improve Television

FOUNDED: 1969
TYPE OF ORGANIZATION: Television research group
SIGNIFICANCE: The foundation's educational purpose has been to inform the public of television's influence

Founded and based in Boston, the Foundation to Improve Television has promoted the appropriate uses of television, especially concerning children. It has sponsored research on the effects of television on its viewers and maintained a library of legal briefs and related source materials. It has also carried out legal and administrative actions to encourage more positive television programming.

See also Action for Children's Television; Clean Up Television Campaign; Coalition for Better Television; National Federation for Decency; Television; Television, children's.

Fourteenth Amendment

RATIFIED: July 9, 1868
PLACE: United States (national)
SIGNIFICANCE: This constitutional amendment extends application of most of the provisions of the Bill of Rights—including protection of freedom of speech—to state and local governments

Ratified in the post-Civil War Reconstruction era, the Fourteenth Amendment of the U.S. Constitution contains two elements of crucial modern importance: the equal protection and the process clauses. The amendment made both clauses apply to state and local governments, and their ratification by the Civil War's defeated Confederate states was made a condition for the states' readmission to the Union.

The amendment's immediate purpose was to respond to attempts by Southern states to deprive newly freed slaves of basic civil rights. Southern states had limited the ability of African Americans to vote, own property, testify against whites in court, make contracts, travel, speak or assemble, or bear arms. In defining as citizens any and all persons born within the United States, the amendment clearly established that former slaves were American citizens, and it spelled out several principles designed to protect their rights. The amendment's equal protection clause, for example, guaranteed to each citizen equal protection of the law throughout the entire country. Since then the U.S. Supreme Court has interpreted this clause chiefly to prohibit certain forms of government discrimination, especially racial discrimination.

The amendment's due process clause mandated that individuals not be deprived of "life, liberty, or property" by state governments without being accorded due process of law. This clause is important principally because the Supreme Court has interpreted its language to mean that most of the provisions of the Bill of Rights are applicable to state and local governments. Although both the equal protection and due process clauses were designed primarily to safeguard African Americans from various forms of political and civil oppression, the Supreme Court later interpreted these clauses to apply in many

---

THE FOURTEENTH AMENDMENT

The first of the amendment's four sections contains what have become known as the privileges and immunities, due process, and equal protection clauses.

Section 1. All persons born or naturalized in the United States and subject to the jurisdiction thereof, are citizens of the United States and of the State wherein they reside. No State shall make or enforce any law which shall abridge the privileges or immunities of citizens of the United States; nor shall any State deprive any person of life, liberty, or property, without due process of law; nor deny to any person within its jurisdiction the equal protection of the laws.

circumstances having nothing to do with matters of racial discrimination.

The First Amendment provides that Congress cannot abridge the freedoms of speech and press; the amendment thus limits the ability of the federal government to censor speech. As originally interpreted, this amendment did not restrict the ability of state and local governments to censor speech. This view of the First Amendment changed in the twentieth century as the Supreme Court began using the Fourteenth Amendment to extend Bill of Rights protections to the states through a process known as incorporation. The Fourteenth Amendment's due process clause protects certain "liberties" from deprivation without due process of law. In the early decades of the twentieth century, the Supreme Court considered the identities of these "liberties" protected against lawless deprivation by the Fourteenth Amendment. Ultimately, it determined that most of the provisions of the Bill of Rights constituted "liberties" protected under the due process clause. In particular, the Court held, in *Gitlow v. New York* (1925), that the freedoms of speech and press were incorporated by reference in the due process clause's use of the word "liberty." The Court subsequently understood this incorporation to mean that the Fourteenth Amendment's due process clause makes the same prohibition against federal abridgments of speech and press applicable to state and local governments.

See also Constitution, U.S.; Courts and censorship law; First Amendment; Free speech.

Fourth Amendment

Enacted: December 15, 1791
Place: United States (national)
Significance: As part of the U.S. Constitution's Bill of Rights, this amendment's protection against unreasonable searches and seizures has figured prominently in matters relating to evidence in several censorship cases

Although the Fourth Amendment is not usually regarded as applying to censorship, the U.S. Supreme Court has used it to help define the limits of certain forms of permissible censorship in obscenity cases. The amendment arose out of American resentment against living under British colonial rule, which did not extend to Americans the same protections from unreasonable search and seizure that people living in Great Britain then enjoyed. The amendment guarantees the right of people "to be secure in their persons, houses, papers, and effects, against unreasonable searches and seizures." It has been interpreted to allow police to take initiatives in undertaking searches. However, in order to do so they usually must first obtain court approval—which is not necessarily granted. Evidence seized by police through unauthorized or unreasonable searches is usually regarded as inadmissible in both federal and state courts.

In a famous obscenity case, *Mapp v. Ohio* (1961), police searched the home of a woman named Dolly Mapp for drugs. Finding none, they instead arrested her for possessing obscene pictures they found which were not included in their search warrant. When Mapp's case reached the U.S. Supreme Court, the Court applied the Fourth Amendment to the states under the Fourteenth Amendment's incorporation doctrine and overturned Mapp's conviction because it had rested on an improper seizure. In a later decision, *Stanley v. Georgia* (1969), the Court carried the concept further by declaring that government could not generally interfere with adults using obscene materials in the privacy of their own homes.

In 1978 the Supreme Court passed down a contrary decision when it upheld the use of evidence seized in a college newspaper office. In *Zurcher v. The Stanford Daily*, it approved police inspection of a college newspaper's confidential files, even though these were irrelevant to the search that had been authorized by a court warrant. In response to demands from the outraged press for protection of their confidential sources, Congress enacted the Privacy Protection Act of 1980. That act restricted the use of search warrants in newsrooms to instances in which there was probable cause to believe that a news organization itself or members of its staff were guilty of criminal offenses.

See also Constitution, U.S.; Courts and censorship law; Fourteenth Amendment; Police; Privacy, right to; Privacy Protection Act of 1980.

France

Description: Western European republic
Significance: Although France has one of Europe's oldest republican traditions, its governments have frequently curbed free expression because of the pressures of national security and changing public notions of decency

Modern France's ideas about freedom of expression go back to the French Revolution of the late eighteenth century. Freedom of speech and freedom of the press were formally incorporated in the Revolution's Declaration of the Rights of Man in 1789. However, as the Revolution progressed and its leaders came to the conclusion that its survival depended on internal unity and universal loyalty, various revolutionary regimes began implementing exceptions to the principles embodied in the Declaration. In August, 1791, for example, journalists who preached disobedience to the law or defiance of public authorities were subject to prosecution for libel. Later, after the execution of King Louis XVI, revolutionary authorities imposed the death penalty for advocating the reestablishment of the monarchy in either speech or print. During the tenure of Maximilien Robespierre and the Committee of Public Safety (1793-1794), the death penalty was implemented for other expressions of political opinion, such as threatening the Republic's unity and integrity, proposing the dissolution of the National Convention, or advocating peace on terms disadvantageous to France.

After the downfall of Robespierre in July, 1794, the Directory reaffirmed total freedom of the press and speech. But it also quickly backed away from this position as the realities of governing France in a revolutionary environment became apparent. In 1796, for example, it reimposed the death penalty for anyone advocating dissolution of the government, reestablishment of the monarchy, reestablishment of the constitutions of 1791 or 1793, or attacks on private property. Indeed, the notion that freedom of expression must be curbed in order to

PORTRAIT AUTHENTIQUE DE ROCAMBOLE
PAR GILL
D'après deux photographies et un grand nombre de documents fournis par **M. le vicomte PONSON DU TERRAIL**, son illustre ami

After caricaturist André Gill's depiction of Emperor Napoleon III as the bandit "Rocambole" slipped by French censors in 1867, the magazine in which it appeared was suppressed by the government. (Robert J. Goldstein)

ensure the survival of the government that guaranteed it was born during the French Revolution, injecting a paradox into French democracy that would endure.

The Napoleonic Era. Napoleon Bonaparte, who took control of France in December, 1799, had little use for freedom of expression. He always argued that his coup d'état of 1799 had been necessary to restore order and stability and that in order to maintain stability, silence must be imposed on all political factions and potential troublemakers. He silenced parliamentary debate, thereby reducing opportunities for expressing political differences, and he implemented a system of national referendums that inhibited the development of public opinion. To restrict freedom of the press, which he considered a threat to the security of the state, he reduced the number of newspapers in Paris to four and prohibited those that did exist from covering political topics. Later, in 1809, he created a board of censors to oversee each newspaper and had his police confiscate those that violated his strict guidelines.

Restoration of the Monarchy. Restrictions on freedom of expression were relaxed after Napoleon's final downfall in 1815 and the restoration of the Bourbon dynasty under King Louis XVIII. However, when Louis' brother Charles X ascended the throne in 1824, the government launched new assaults on freedom of expression in the name of restoring the institutions of the Old Regime. Charles implemented, for example, a law against sacrilege that made certain sacrilegious acts in churches punishable by long terms in prison and even execution. Charles also enacted a severe press law that severely hampered newspaper publishers and the distributors of pamphlets and circulars. Neither measure was enforced effectively but they nevertheless suggested a serious intolerance to ideas considered incompatible with the conservative agenda of Charles X's regime.

The attempt by Charles X to restore the Old Regime eventually provoked an opposition from other sectors of the French elite—especially those who had benefited from the innovations introduced by the Revolution—and led to his overthrow in July, 1830. Many men who played important roles in this event had contributed to newspapers that fought for freedom of the press during the Bourbon Restoration. As a result, the early years of the July Monarchy—as the regime of newly installed King Louis Philippe was called—witnessed a dramatic reduction in the restrictions placed on freedom of expression. This change did not last, however. Under the pressure of several popular insurrections and mounting criticism of the regime, the July Monarchy passed the "September Laws" of 1835 that severely reduced freedom of the press. Any newspaper that incited revolution, fomented hatred of the king, demanded a change of dynasty, praised the fallen Bourbon dynasty, called for a republic, attacked property rights, or questioned any law might be suspended from publication. "Caution money"—fees that newspapers had to deposit with the authorities to receive publishing licenses—was also dramatically increased. The purpose of this law was seemingly to eliminate all newspapers that opposed the July Monarchy; many of them were forced to cease publication as a result.

Other segments of the opposition press learned to sidestep the new law by such techniques as substituting implication and innuendo for direct attacks on the regime. Ultimately, the September Laws probably did more harm than good to the July Monarchy by alienating many former liberal supporters of the regime.

The Revolution of 1848. This alienation peaked in February, 1848, with the outbreak of a new revolution, which overthrew the July Monarchy and established the Second Republic. As had been the case in 1830, this revolutionary change in regime temporarily eased restrictions that had been placed on the press over the previous fifteen years. But the Revolution of 1848 also set the stage for the rise of a truly popular political movement that threatened upper-middle-class conceptions of private property and responsible government by provoking a conservative counterattack that not only resulted in renewed restrictions on freedom of the press and other forms of political expression, but led to Louis Napoleon's rise to power. Elected president of the Second Republic in December, 1848, Napoleon used this office to seize personal and exclusive control of the government in December, 1851. His new regime, the Second Empire, resurrected many of the repressive and manipulative measures first invented by Napoleon I: plebiscites, a powerless legislature, legal persecution of political dissidents, and censorship of the press and other forms of literary expression. It was during the Second Empire, for example, that author Victor Hugo was forced into exile for his political views and saw several of his writings that were critical of Louis Napoleon banned in France.

Nonpolitical authors were persecuted on moral grounds as well during this period. Gustave Flaubert's famous novel, *Madame Bovary*, first appeared in serial form in the literary journal the *Revue de Paris* in 1856. Although the editors of the journal tried to edit the piece to appease the censors, Flaubert was still prosecuted for "offenses against morality and religion" by the government in 1857. His sensational trial captured the attention of the nation due to the angry and eloquent exchanges between the lawyers from both sides. In the end, Flaubert was acquitted and his novel appeared shortly thereafter in book form to both critical praise and popular acclaim. Charles Baudelaire was also unsuccessfully prosecuted for violating public morality for his 1857 collection of poems *Flowers of Evil* (*Les Fleurs du mal*).

The Third Republic. Although Napoleon III reduced many of his restrictions against free expression of political ideas after 1868, popular dissatisfaction with his regime combined with the disastrous French performance in the Franco-Prussian War to lead to his overthrow in September, 1870. After a brief period of chaos, his regime was ultimately replaced by the Third Republic, a parliamentary government that would control the country until 1940. Many restrictions that had formerly hamstrung the press were removed and there resulted a lively and colorful atmosphere of free political expression. In 1898 the author Émile Zola was forced into exile to avoid prosecution for writing "J'Accuse," an article in which he charged that the 1894 espionage trial of Captain Alfred Dreyfus had been a travesty of justice. The notoriety of this episode, however, came from the fact that prosecutions of this type had become rare by the late nineteenth century. Although occasionally lapsing into irresponsibility and libel, political discussion—and artistic expression—during the Third Republic was normally unrestrained by the government.

World War II and its Aftermath. France's fall to Germany in June, 1940, ended this situation. Throughout the Nazi-occupied northern part of the country, the press was absolutely controlled and public expression of ideas was severely restricted. In the southern zone, the collaborationist Vichy regime placed similar restrictions on the press and public opinion. Moreover, the Vichy regime attempted to censor mass culture in an effort to halt what it regarded as the "moral decline" of the country. Examples of such attempts at censorship included an attack on "swing" music as a negative influence on the morals of youth and prohibiting the novelist André Gide from lecturing in 1941 on the grounds that he was a "prophet of hedonism."

The war years proved to be only a temporary break in France's development of free speech under the Third Republic. After the war ended, a multitude of political parties of diverse ideological persuasions in the Fourth and Fifth republics guaranteed that political expression, both in speech and in the press, would flourish virtually without restriction. Moral censorship also became lax in modern France. Female nudity, for example, has been frequently employed in advertising. Erotic movies have also appeared regularly on television without editing.

During the 1980's French authorities expressed some concern about the spread of pornography and implemented several indirect measures, such as the creation of the "X" rating for pornographic films judged inappropriate for individuals under the age of eighteen, to restrict their proliferation. Some serious filmmakers worried that this rating system might be used against erotic films of artistic worth but such did not prove to be the case. In general, modern France seems to have come to terms with the paradox introduced during the French Revolution and came to serve as a model for Western democracies in terms of government tolerance of dissenting political opinions and free artistic and intellectual expression.

—Christopher E. Guthrie

See also Babeuf, François Noël; Balzac, Honoré de; Baudelaire, Charles; Beaumarchais, Pierre-Augustin Caron de; Daumier, Honoré; Diderot, Denis; Dumas, Alexandre, *père*; Flaubert, Gustave; France, Anatole; Gide, André; Hugo, Victor; Montesquieu; Proudhon, Pierre-Joseph; Rousseau, Jean-Jacques; Voltaire; World War I; World War II; Zola, Émile.

BIBLIOGRAPHY

No comprehensive history of censorship in France has been published in English. A general history of France that discusses censorship during the nineteenth and twentieth centuries is Gordon Wright's *France in Modern Times* (5th ed. New York: W. W. Norton, 1995). Aspects of censorship in specific historical periods are covered in Louis Bergeron's *France Under Napoleon* (Princeton: Princeton University Press, 1981), Guillaume de Bertier de Sauvigny's *The Bourbon Restoration* (Philadelphia: University of Pennsylvania Press,

1967), David Pinkney's *Decisive Years in France: 1840-1847* (Princeton: Princeton University Press, 1986), John Merriman's *The Agony of the Republic* (New Haven: Yale University Press, 1978), Stuart Campbell's *The Second Empire Revisited: A Study in French Historiography* (New Brunswick, N.J.: Rutgers University Press, 1978), R. D. Anderson's *France, 1870-1914: Politics and Society* (London: Routledge & Kegan Paul, 1977), Robert Paxton's *Vichy France: Old Guard and New Order, 1940-1944* (New York: Alfred A. Knopf, 1972), and John Ardagh's *France in the 1980s* (New York: Penguin, 1983).

France, Anatole

BORN: April 16, 1844, Paris, France
DIED: October 12, 1924, La Béchellerie, near Tours, France
IDENTIFICATION: French novelist and poet
SIGNIFICANCE: Despite France's fame as an author, his works were banned by the Roman Catholic church

Anatole France's first novel, *The Crime of Sylvestre Bonnard*, appeared in 1881. This first success was followed by many others, including *At the Sign of the Reine Pédauque* (1893); *The Red Lily* (1894); *L'Histoire contemporaine* (1897-1901); *L'Histoire comique* (1903); *Penguin Island* (1908); and *The Gods Are Athirst* (1912). He achieved great fame during his lifetime and was elected to the French Academy in 1896 and earning the Nobel Prize in Literature 1921.

France's fame did not, however, protect him from attacks from various quarters. Once he converted to socialism in the 1890's, many of his books centered on such themes as the separation of church and state, minority rights, and social reform. These themes brought the animosity of the French right wing down upon him but they were not in a position at the time to censor his works. On the other hand, his continuous attacks on the Roman Catholic church in his later works resulted in all his writings being placed on the *Index Librorum Prohibitorum* (1922). In 1953 the government of Ireland also banned his *The Mummer's Tale* on the grounds that it offended religious morality.

See also France; Gide, André; *Index Librorum Prohibitorum*; Ireland; Literature; Zola, Émile.

Frankfurter, Felix

BORN: November 15, 1882, Vienna, Austria
DIED: February 22, 1965, Washington, D.C.
IDENTIFICATION: Legal scholar and associate justice of the U.S. Supreme Court (1939-1962)
SIGNIFICANCE: Frankfurter developed a judicial philosophy claiming that freedom of expression must be tempered by consideration of other public interests

Frankfurter's opinions on the Supreme Court reflected his view that freedom of expression is not an absolute right, but one that must be defined in the circumstances and context of each case. Appointed to the Supreme Court by President Franklin D. Roosevelt, Frankfurter had earned a reputation for a brilliant legal mind during his years as a professor at Harvard Law School. He enjoyed a strong personal relationship with Roosevelt and, prior to his appointment, had served the president as a political advisor on the New Deal. Frankfurter's judicial philosophy included two basic principles: a belief that the courts must defer to the decisions of "the people" expressed through their legislatures and a sense that the exercise of the freedoms included in the Bill of Rights must be balanced by concern for other public interests. Unlike colleagues who subscribed to the notion that First Amendment rights, including freedom of expression, enjoyed a "preferred position" under the Constitution, Frankfurter brought the same sense of judicial deference to laws dealing with freedom of speech and the press as he did to laws dealing with economic regulations.

Frankfurter's opinions in three cases, *Minersville School District v. Gobitis* (1940), in which he wrote the majority opinion; *West Virginia State Board of Education v. Barnette* (1943), in which he wrote a dissent; and *Dennis v. United States* (1951), in which Frankfurter concurred, illustrate his positions with respect to the constitutional protection of freedom of expression.

In *Gobitis* the Court was asked to decide whether children reared as Jehovah's Witnesses who refused on religious grounds to salute the flag should be expelled from school. Frankfurter held that the state's interest in promoting national unity took precedence over the students' freedom of conscience.

Three years later, when the Court reversed *Gobitis* in *West Virginia v. Barnette*, Frankfurter's view was in the minority. He wrote that justices may not decide cases based on their personal sympathies with persecuted minorities but must ask only whether the state acted "reasonably" to support a legitimate purpose. If West Virginia had acted reasonably, the Supreme Court must uphold its restriction on the freedom of the Jehovah's Witnesses. He disagreed profoundly with the Court's decision that the freedoms in the Bill of Rights were beyond the reach of political majorities and must not be submitted to popular vote. His belief that the courts should bow to the will of the legislatures permitted significant restrictions on individual rights.

Dennis v. United States concerned eleven members of the Communist Party who were charged with conspiring to advocate the overthrow of the U.S. government. The Court found that the defendants' speech constituted a sufficient threat to the country to justify limiting their civil liberties. Frankfurter's concurring opinion reflected his conviction that the protection of speech depended on circumstances. In this case, national self-preservation from the "communist menace" must be balanced against free expression. He concluded that there was "no substantial public interest" in permitting certain types of speech, including "the lewd and obscene, the profane, the libelous, and insulting or 'fighting' words."

Frankfurter's commitment to free expression was always tempered by his belief that the courts must defer to the wisdom of legislative bodies and that individual rights must be balanced against the community's interest in sustaining common values.

See also Courts and censorship law; First Amendment; Jehovah's Witnesses; Pledge of Allegiance.

Franklin, Benjamin

Born: January 17, 1706, Boston, Massachusetts

Died: April 17, 1790, Philadelphia, Pennsylvania

Identification: American diplomat and author

Significance: Despite Franklin's stature as a statesman, scientist, and writer, his autobiography and other works have been frequently banned and expurgated

Colonial printer, Enlightenment philosopher, scientist, and national Founder, Franklin wrote what may be the most popular autobiography ever published. This narrative—which he began in 1771 and left unfinished at the time of his death—chronicles the fortunes of a diligent and ingenious printer's apprentice who rises from poverty and obscurity to eminence in world affairs and who helps found a new nation. Because Franklin did not live to supervise the publication of his autobiography, many incomplete and inaccurate versions have been published since the first edition—a pirated version published in French—appeared in 1791. Franklin's grandson, William Franklin Temple, published the first significant English-language version in 1817-1818, but in approximately twelve hundred instances he revised his grandfather's diction to suit his nineteenth century sensibilities. For example, Temple changed "[he] had got a naughty Girl with Child" to "had an intrigue with a girl of bad character." It was not until 1868, when Franklin's original manuscript was discovered in France, that Franklin's own language was restored.

Franklin's autobiography, which is known for its frank discussion of eighteenth century colonial life, has been both a popular school text and a frequent target of expurgation since the mid-nineteenth century. An example of such bowdlerization concerns the episode in which Franklin shared London lodgings with his American friend James Ralph. Ralph, who left his wife in Philadelphia, became intimate with a milliner living in the building, and took her as his mistress. Franklin, who was also attracted to the same woman, recorded that he "attempted Familiarities" with her; however, his efforts were "repuls'd with a proper Resentment." When Ralph learned of this incident, a "Breach" resulted between the two men. Some American editors such as D. H. Montgomery, who produced a version of the autobiography for the publishing firm Ginn in 1888, simply omitted the entire episode. In other versions, the affair between Ralph and the French woman is reported in its entirety, but Franklin's own indiscretion is either omitted or is obscured by purposely vague language. In Houghton Mifflin's 1886 edition, for example, Franklin comments, "In the mean time [other circumstances] made a breach." In an 1892 edition, Julian Abernethy has Franklin obscurely declare, "In the mean time [another matter which gave him offense] made a breach." Censorship of Franklin's masterpiece continued through the twentieth century. As late as 1987, public schools in Florida banned the autobiography.

Other writings by Franklin have also experienced censorship. His ribald "Letter to the Royal Academy at Brussels," "The Speech of Polly Baker," and "Letter of Advice to Young Men on the Proper Choosing of a Mistress," which were considered acceptably salacious in Franklin's age and were appreciated in the highest circles, were forced underground in the nineteenth century. Although they have resurfaced in recent years, they are often expurgated. By the twentieth century, Franklin became one of the most frequently expurgated writers in American history.

See also Abridgment; Adultery; Biography; Book publishing; Comstock, Anthony; Jefferson, Thomas; Paine, Thomas.

Freaks

Type of work: Film
Released: 1932
Director: Tod Browning (1882-1962)
Subject matter: Deformed carnival performers exact revenge on two able-bodied performers who try to swindle one of the unfortunate "freaks"

Significance: A horror film accused of exploiting performers with disabilities, *Freaks* ran afoul of censorship boards across America and was banned in Great Britain for more than thirty years

With horror movies suddenly in vogue during the early 1930's, Metro-Goldwyn Mayer (MGM) production executive Irving Thalberg turned to director Tod Browning and allegedly told him, "I want something that out-horrors *Frankenstein*." The resulting film, *Freaks*, succeeded mainly in driving audiences from theaters after they learned that the carnival performers depicted in the film—Siamese twins, a limbless man, a man with no torso from the waist down, and others—were not the products of special-effects wizardry but were truly disabled.

Freaks, which Browning and screenwriters Willis Goldbeck

Beautiful trapeze artist Cleopatra (Olga Baclanova) is the victim of one of the most horrifying retributions in film history after she betrays her diminutive husband, Hans (Harry Earles), and his circus friends in Freaks. *(Museum of Modern Art/Film Stills Archive)*

and Leon Gordon based on Tod Robbins' short story "Spurs," elicited a wide array of censorship activities during its initial run in 1932. A women's organization called the Better Films Council of Rhode Island tried unsuccessfully to get the film toned down, for example, while the film censor in Birmingham, Alabama, restricted it to adults over the age of eighteen; the Atlanta Board of Review, meanwhile, convinced a judge to shut it down. *Freaks* also fared poorly with the New York State Censorship Board, which demanded the excision of almost thirty minutes of material (such as a close-up of a woman pouring poison into a champagne bottle, for fear it would inspire copycat crimes). In addition, *Freaks* was banned in several countries, most notably Great Britain, where it stayed out of public view for three decades.

Freaks received decidedly mixed reviews and bombed at the box office, tarnishing MGM's image as a purveyor of wholesome, quality entertainment. Following Thalberg's unsuccessful attempt to repackage the film in 1933, MGM whisked *Freaks* out of circulation until the late 1940's, when it allowed an exploitation-film specialist to exhibit the film under such titles as *Nature's Mistakes*, *The Monster Show*, and *Forbidden Love*. The film's British ban was finally rescinded in August, 1963, a year after *Freaks* received some acclaim at the Venice Film Festival. The film enjoyed some counterculture popularity during the Vietnam War era, and in 1994 the Library of Congress added *Freaks* to the National Film Registry of significant American films.

See also British Board of Film Censors; Film censorship; *King Kong*; *Titicut Follies*.

Free speech

DEFINITION: Speaking freely is one of the fundamental freedoms guaranteed in the U.S. Bill of Rights

SIGNIFICANCE: Freedom of speech includes public speech, symbolic speech, and expressive conduct

Controversies regarding freedom of expression, as reflected in seditious speech laws, trace their origins to thirteenth century England. The reign of Edward I began in 1272 with judicial reforms and a series of acts dealing with the position of the church, landowners, regulation of trade, and enforcement of the public order. Those acts included England's first seditious speech law, punishing anyone who spoke in a disparaging manner about the king and his advisors. By the time of the Peasant's Revolt of 1381, seditious speech law had been liberalized. Outlawed was false news about "great men in the realm." If the originator of the slanderous report was not identified, the disseminators were to be punished in his stead. By the 1530's seditious speech involved impugning royal advisors or the ruling class, misinterpreting government policies, or criticizing the king's sexual practices.

During the reigns of Edward VI and Mary I, officials could no longer prosecute spoken treason, but a 1555 law set the penalty for speaking about the king or queen in a slanderous or seditious manner at the loss of both ears or a fine and short confinement. Repeat offenders received life imprisonment. A 1558 law under Elizabeth I made it a misdemeanor to speak or write with malicious intent false or slanderous words about the queen. By 1580 such written words were felonies. The felony statutes against seditious speech expired with the death of Elizabeth.

James I, Elizabeth's successor, established the Star Chamber and the basic structure of English seditious speech law in 1606. After its demise in 1641, the common law courts handled seditious speech cases, prosecuting with frequency and severity throughout the century, which was marked by religious controversy.

Colonial America. The colonists brought to the New World their understanding of seditious speech: insulting or impugning government officials, criticizing the government generally, and spreading false news. Military regulations treated seditious words as mutiny and authorized harsh punishment, but statutes designed to control nonmilitary seditious speech were less severe, often establishing payment of fines as punishment.

Regulated Speech. Seditious speech regulations have tended to change in response to changing circumstances, such as criticism of new leaders. Times of danger also brought increased levels of prosecution as well as stricter laws. This trend was also visible in twentieth century free speech law. If speech advocates imminent unlawful action, which presents a clear and present danger, the speech loses its constitutional protection. In other words, not all speech is free. One may be prosecuted for what one says, if one's speech meets specific criteria, including that of clear and present danger. The Supreme Court has viewed freedom of speech as a personal right of the individual, but whether speech is permitted depends on whether it threatens public safety. In the famous words of Justice Oliver Wendell Holmes in *Schenck v. United States* (1919): "The most stringent protection of free speech would not protect a man in falsely shouting 'fire' in a theater and causing a panic. . . . The question in every case is whether the words are used in such circumstances and are of such a nature as to create a clear and present danger that they will bring about the substantive evils that Congress has a right to prevent. It is a question of proximity and degree." Therefore, throughout twentieth century American case law, the Supreme Court has indicated that even advocacy of use of violence is constitutionally protected unless it immediately incites lawless action. If the risk of violence is high enough, however, speech may be suppressed.

Protected Speech. The First Amendment forbids Congress to pass any laws abridging the freedom of speech. The Supreme Court has added limitations, attempting to distinguish between protected and unprotected speech. Although Americans' right to free speech is vigorously protected, speakers are not given free rein to speak whenever, wherever, and however they choose. The right to free speech is ambiguous and its contours unclear. Certain categories of expression can be regulated; others are not protected at all.

"Pure" speech, which does not create any substantial danger to the public, is protected as part of the democratic process. Pure speech involves oral or written communication of a philosophy, ideology, or body of knowledge that advances public understanding. Other activities containing elements of both expression and conduct (demonstrating, marching with signs or placards, and picketing, for example), are sometimes termed "speech plus," "symbolic speech," or "expressive conduct." When speech and nonspeech elements are combined, the court will allow the regulation of the nonspeech element if a sufficiently important government interest exists. In an effort to resolve controversial issues, the Supreme Court has formulated a balancing approach in which a number of factors are assessed.

One recurring theme is that American reaction to efforts to express political, social, economic, religious, and sexual views is based on how acceptable the idea espoused is to the prevailing definition of what is acceptable in society. Fear of new ideas and challenges to the existing social order depends on the ebb and flow of social mores. What is acceptable depends on the operative definition at the time.

The judiciary has prohibited certain kinds of expression, oral or written, because of the effect they may have on society. Denial of free speech on the basis of content remains a matter of heated debate. Content-based regulation of speech may amount to discrimination or censorship depending on whether the government agrees with the speaker's point of view. Even private speech or personal expression can be limited so long as the regulation is reasonable and subject to due process of law. Laws must not be so vague that people must guess at their meaning and are in fear of exercising protected freedoms. Laws must give adequate notice of the type of speech or conduct that is permitted or disallowed. Additionally, laws may not be so overly broad as to prohibit protected as well as unprotected activities. Legislation must be constructed with narrow specificity to avoid this problem. The protected freedoms need "breathing space," according to the Supreme Court, and government regulation in the area is closely examined.

The First Amendment protects the right to engage in forms of expression intended to test the limits of tolerance, invite dispute, and challenge majority beliefs. Even those who would destroy free society if they were to prevail may express their views so long as they do not incite an imminent breach of the peace. When government regulates the content of speech, there is a risk that the restriction stems from an effort to impose a viewpoint, to stop people from being offended by certain topics or perspectives, or to prevent people from being persuaded by what others have to say. Regulating speech closes off channels of public discussion and debate, thus preventing a free exchange of ideas and totally precluding the presentation of other views. Such regulation is held to be antithetical to a democratic society.

Other limitations on speech include limitations of time, place, and manner. Often compelling reasons exist to justify imposing these limitations: for example, disturbing the peace through use of loudspeakers or speechmaking, solicitations, or demonstrating in front of a courthouse concerning pending cases. Assuming neutral content (that is, that speech on one side of an issue is as disallowed as speech on another side), these regulations are justifiable because they do not regulate the content of speech, but only its external elements. The speech may continue at another time or place or in another manner. Even these regulations are subject to strict or exacting scrutiny by the court, however, to assure that they limit dissemination of information or opinion no more than necessary to protect important government interests.

Unprotected Speech. Fighting words, which by their utterance inflict injury or tend to incite an immediate breach of the peace, are unprotected because they do not constitute an essential part of any exposition of ideas and are of insignificant social value. Obscenity is also unprotected speech because it is feared that obscene material may debase society's ethics, morals, and culture. Those who want society to take steps to protect itself from immorality, violence, and sexually explicit expression have favored censorship and the suppression of these materials. Censorship and suppression are contrary to the philosophy of free speech, however, so legal challenges have been mounted against suppression of inflammatory and obscene expression. Anticensorship victories in such cases have led to new definitions, for example, of what is obscene.

The U.S. Supreme Court has especially disfavored prior restraint: licensing schemes that require permission before dissemination of speech, motion picture, newspaper, or other communication, or restrictions before publication. Prior restraint may be justified only when publication threatens national security, incites overthrow of the government, is obscene, or substantially interferes with others' private rights. Libel and slander are also unprotected forms of expression because the injury that such forms of expression cause others outweighs the right to free speech.

Symbolic Speech. Use of actions as a substitute for words is generally protected. The type of offensive speech termed "hate speech" has also been protected as being "content neutral," and includes racial slurs, hateful religious propaganda, and cross burning. Flag burning was also upheld as a controversial but valid expression of political views deserving protection in a society promoting the free exchange of ideas. Case law has demonstrated that censorship of symbolic speech solely because it is offensive and runs counter to personal predilections cannot be tolerated. —*Marcia J. Weiss*

See also Clear and present danger doctrine; Colonialism; English Commonwealth; Fighting words; First Amendment; Prior restraint; Symbolic speech; Unprotected speech.

BIBLIOGRAPHY

Historical underpinnings of English and colonial seditious speech laws are discussed in detail in Larry D. Eldridge, *A Distant Heritage: The Growth of Free Speech in Early America* (New York: New York University Press, 1994). Margaret A. Blanchard, *Revolutionary Sparks: Freedom of Expression in Modern America* (New York: Oxford University Press, 1992), is a carefully documented and readable work emphasizing historical developments of speech law dating from the Civil War throughout the twentieth century. Peter G. Renstrom, *Constitutional Law and Young Adults* (Santa Barbara, Calif.: ABC-Clio, 1992), is a guide to the Constitution, the court system, and key provisions of the Bill of Rights, with case references. The work is comprehensive in scope and comprehensible to the general reader. Edward Samuel Corwin and J. W. Peltason, *Corwin and Peltason's Understanding the*

Constitution (11th ed. New York: Holt, Rinehart and Winston, 1988), is a general overview and a valuable reference. Nat Hentoff, *Free Speech for Me—But Not for Thee: How the American Left and Right Relentlessly Censor Each Other* (New York: HarperCollins, 1992), contains anecdotal episodes dealing with free speech and censorship. John C. Domino, *Civil Rights and Liberties: Toward the Twenty-First Century* (New York: HarperCollins, 1994), is a useful resource for those with some political science background. David P. Currie, *The Constitution of the United States: A Primer for the People* (Chicago: University of Chicago Press, 1988), is a readable resource for the general reader. Cass R. Sunstein, *Democracy and the Problem of Free Speech* (New York: Free Press, 1993), contains an assessment of the role of the First Amendment in light of new controversies and technologies.

Free Speech Movement

DATE: Fall, 1964-spring, 1965
PLACE: University of California, Berkeley
SIGNIFICANCE: The Free Speech Movement involved student demands for rights of free expression and political activity relating to off-campus issues; the movement set the stage for the late 1960's antiestablishment revolts throughout the United States

In the fall of 1964 the Free Speech Movement (FSM) began at the University of California's Berkeley campus when a small group of students resisted university attempts to prohibit their efforts to distribute civil rights protest materials and to recruit civil rights workers at the campus' busy south entrance. Although the university had a long-standing policy against political activity on the campus, that policy had not been enforced at the south entrance over the previous three years. Moreover, the disputed area was not clearly delineated as campus property distinct from the immediately adjoining city sidewalk. The students therefore claimed that any university restrictions on this site violated their constitutional right to free expression.

Some of these students had tasted political activism as civil rights workers in the South during the previous summer. Other protesters, who included many former students and nonstudents, had been part of a growing band of political activists during the early 1960's in the San Francisco Bay Area. They held rallies and demonstrations for African American civil rights and against nuclear weapons and U.S. military policy in Southeast Asia.

In May, 1960, San Francisco police used fire hoses to break up mass demonstrations against House Committee on Un-American Activities (HUAC) hearings, and they arrested sixty-four demonstrators, half of whom were University of California students. It was apparently fear of a repetition of such political activism that caused powerful conservatives—such as former U.S. senator William Knowland, publisher of the *Oakland Tribune*—to pressure the university's regents and administration to enforce the campus' dormant restrictions on campus political activity.

The administration's crackdown on political activity initially took the form of a letter from the dean of students that such activity would no longer be permitted on a designated strip of ground at the south entrance. On the following day, September 17, 1964, a "United Front" of student groups ranging from socialists to Young Republicans formed to protest the new policy through vigils, pickets, rallies, and—for all but its most conservative elements—civil disobedience. This unprecedented student reaction caused the administration to concede that campaign literature advocating specific positions on electoral propositions and candidates being contested in the coming November election could, after all, be distributed at the south entrance and eight other campus locations. Two radical student groups not tied to specific electoral politics set up solicitation tables in defiance of the partial ban that still existed. The arrests and suspensions that followed prompted escalating confrontations that climaxed in an occupation of the main university administration building, Sproul Hall, by more than eight hundred predominantly student demonstrators. They were supported by thousands more demonstrators outside the building.

By this time the central issue in the controversy had become the university's right to ban from the campus types of political activity that were constitutionally guaranteed outside the campus. After weeks of rallies, sit-in demonstrations in administrative offices, mass arrests of demonstrators, and general disruption, the faculty senate persuaded the university administration to grant the students far more liberal rules for political organizing on campus—so long as the political neutrality of the university itself was not compromised or its name invoked in partisan causes.

Many supporters of the Free Speech Movement scoffed at the university's claims of political neutrality because the university itself offered research help to vested corporate and governmental interests. They claimed that the university actually prevented students from enlisting support for persons who were oppressed by the very system that the university was helping. By the end of 1964 the issues again broadened to focus on the nature of the university as a major social institution. While the Vietnam War was then escalating, many students criticized the university's increasingly direct ties to the emerging economy based on knowledge and an ever more technologically dependent military in Vietnam. Led by the FSM's leader, Mario Savio (1943-1996), many critics—both on and off campus—particularly attacked the ideas of university president Clark Kerr, who had been consistently hostile to the student movement. Kerr had coined the phrase "multiversity" in his widely read book, *The Uses of the University*, which defined a university's purpose as turning out students to provide the brainpower to fuel the emerging knowledge-based economy. Continued student unrest in early 1965 over issues ranging from civil rights and Vietnam to obscenity eventually prompted the resignation of Kerr and most of his administration.

"Filthy Speech Movement." The issue of obscenity became associated in the public mind with the Free Speech Movement in early 1965, after the university administration banned the showing of French director Jean Genet's film *Un Chant d'amour* in a campus film festival, charging that it was obscene. The response of some student protesters, who publicly displayed signs with four-letter words, led to more arrests in March, 1965. Conservative critics and much of the media quickly adopted Clark Kerr's characterization of the activity as the "Filthy Speech Movement." In fact, most of the original movement's leaders opposed shifting from narrow political objectives to a battle against all restrictions on obscenity. In May two students, John Thompson and Art Goldberg, were convicted in a municipal court on charges of displaying obscene signs and of speaking obscene words at public rallies.

opposition to the war in Vietnam. The FSM symbolized a countercultural emphasis on music, drugs, and the sexual revolution. As the FSM enlarged the scope of free speech to include what had formerly been deemed obscene, divisions within the movement and among different left-wing elements outside the university came to symbolize the New versus Old Left.

Widespread public disgust with the disorder on the Berkeley campus, and particularly the Filthy Speech Movement,

Free Speech Movement leader Mario Savio signals "victory" in front of Sproul Hall after learning that the university's faculty have voted to support student demands to lift bans on political activity on campus. (AP/Wide World Photos)

Because U.S. Supreme Court decisions on obscenity were then becoming more liberal, these students became the last people in the United States between 1965 and the 1990's to serve prison time for obscenity convictions. Having achieved most of its original objectives and weakened by serious divisions over the issue of public obscenity, the Free Speech Movement formally dissolved itself on April 28, 1965, two days after Mario Savio resigned as leader.

Impact of the Movement. This unprecedented student movement represented far more than its originally narrow objectives. It voided the traditional university doctrine regarding students of *en loco parentis*, a policy which was virtually eliminated at most major American universities by the early 1970's. The FSM was the first major university uprising in an era of movements that included civil rights advocacy and

helped Ronald Reagan get elected governor of California—by then the most populous state—in 1966. After Reagan was elected president in 1980, he appointed as his attorney general Edwin Meese, who had taken a hard-line toward student demonstrators when he had been assistant district attorney of Alameda County at the time of the Free Speech Movement.

—*Anthony D. Branch*

See also Attorney General's Commission on Pornography; Campus speech codes; Education; Free speech; Genet, Jean; Offensive language; Reagan, Ronald; Universities.

BIBLIOGRAPHY

Max Heirich was a graduate student at Berkeley who interviewed contemporaries and transcribed tape recordings of events during the fall of 1964 which he presents thoroughly in *The Beginning: Berkeley, 1964.* (New York: Columbia University Press, 1968). Another former Berkeley student, David Lance Goines, looks back on the FSM in the broader context of the turbulent 1960's in *The Free Speech Movement: Coming of Age in the 1960's* (Berkeley: Ten Speed Press, 1993). This stout volume includes both personal commentary and detailed lists of actors and events. Clark Kerr's *The Uses of the University* (Cambridge, Mass: Harvard University Press, 1964) provides insights into the growing interrelationship between the university and the "system" that so many students protested. The differing perspectives of contemporary Berkeley faculty members, many highly critical of both the administration and student protesters, are well represented in *The Berkeley Student Revolt: Facts and Interpretations* (Garden City, N.Y.: Anchor Books, 1965), a collection edited by Seymour Martin Lipset and Sheldon Wolin. *Sixties People* by Jane and Michael Stern (New York: Alfred A. Knopf, 1990) is a fascinating account of the leading figures of the era, including several FSM leaders. Edward de Grazia and Roger K. Newman's *Banned Films* (New York: R. R. Bowker, 1982) explains how the banning from campus of a Jean Genet film on homosexuality in prison caused the obscenity issue to become a major component of later FSM activity.

Freedman v. Maryland

COURT: U.S. Supreme Court
DATE: March 1, 1965
SIGNIFICANCE: This Supreme Court decision established procedural safeguards that government must observe before it can bar exhibitions of films that it deems to be obscene

In an effort to combat obscenity, the state of Maryland enacted legislation in the 1950's providing that no film could be publicly exhibited unless the State Board of Censors gave its approval. A film exhibitor named Ronald Freedman refused to submit his film *Revenge at Daybreak* to the board prior to exhibition—even though the film was not obscene—because of his objections to the censorship process. After being convicted of violating the Maryland statute, Freedman appealed his conviction on the ground that the statute requiring prior approval by the state before showing a film constituted a form of prior restraint that violated the First Amendment to the U.S. Constitution.

Four years earlier the U.S. Supreme Court had upheld, in a 5-4 decision, a Chicago municipal code provision requiring the submission of motion pictures to a censorship board in advance of exhibition in *Times Film Corporation v. Chicago* (1961). The petitioner in that case had argued that *any* prior restraint on the exhibition of a film was unconstitutional. The Court rejected that argument but did not address the issue of whether such a censorship system must comply with certain safeguards in order to pass constitutional muster.

In his own appeal to the Supreme Court, Freedman addressed the issue left unresolved in the *Times Film Corp.* case. He argued that Maryland's statute did not afford sufficient procedural safeguards to film exhibitors whose films were rejected by the board of censors. The Court unanimously agreed, holding that a state could require its board of censors to approve films prior to their exhibition only if the process

observed certain procedural safeguards. The Court specified that a board of censors could not bar a film's exhibition without first securing a judicial order emanating from an adversary proceeding at which the board has borne the burden of establishing that the film is obscene. Because Maryland's law did not satisfy this criterion, the Court struck it down as an invalid prior restraint.

In several decisions following the Freedman case, the Supreme Court imposed procedural safeguards on censorship of other forms of communications. The Court has, for example, imposed procedural requirements in cases involving censorship of mail, parades, and distribution of flyers and leaflets. The Freedman decision led to the demise of municipal and state censor boards. In its place, the film industry adopted a rating system designating sexually explicit films X so that minors are not admitted to view them.

See also Courts and censorship law; Film censorship; Obscenity: legal definitions; Prior restraint; *Times Film Corp. v. City of Chicago*.

Freedom of Information Act (FOIA)

ENACTED: July 4, 1966
PLACE: United States (national)
SIGNIFICANCE: This federal law reversed long-standing government policies and practices regarding public access to information by establishing the right of access to government information and agency records as essential to a free and open society

The Freedom of Information Act (FOIA) grew out of many years of reform effort. Its original passage in 1966 was the result of a ten-year congressional campaign, in which media representatives played a leading role. It was drafted as a revision of the public information section of the Administrative Procedures Act (1946), which contained such expansive exceptions that most agencies could effectively avoid disclosing to the public almost anything they wished. Until FOIA went into effect in 1967, public access to federal government records and documents was governed by a "need to know" policy. Persons requesting information had to demonstrate why it should be made available.

Before 1966 the old Administrative Procedures Act (APA) permitted individual government agencies not to disclose any functions that the agencies themselves claimed either should be kept secret in the public interest, or were matters relating solely to their internal management. The APA mandated that all agency records be made available to persons who were properly and directly concerned, except information censored for good cause found. Once an agency censored information, citizens had no right of appeal.

Impact of FOIA. FOIA was enacted to give the public increased access to federal government records. On the day that U.S. president Lyndon B. Johnson signed it into law, he declared that the principle upon which the legislation was based was that "a democracy works best when people have all the information that the security of the Nation permits." FOIA's purpose was to establish a general philosophy of full agency disclosure—except in clearly delineated cases—and to provide legal procedures by which citizens and the press could obtain information wrongfully withheld. It was believed that full public disclosure would further democracy by enabling better informed citizens to scrutinize government actions and thereby discourage corruption and waste.

FOIA's original wording granted the public access only to government paper "files." In 1974 the law was amended to apply to "records"—a term that the courts have interpreted to apply to a much broader range of material, making it more difficult for agencies to censor entire files. "Records" include not only the papers constituting files, but also films—including X rays—and computer media. Other physical objects, however, such as the rifle believed to have been used to kill President John F. Kennedy, are not considered records, principally because they are not reproducible.

Federal Agencies Subject to FOIA. Government entities are considered to be "agencies" when they have authority to perform specific government functions. FOIA itself defines as agencies all government bodies other than those directly connected to the U.S. Congress, federal courts, the governments of U.S. territories and possessions, and the District of Columbia. The law specifically includes all federal executive and military departments, federal government corporations, government-controlled corporations, and other establishments in the executive branch of the federal government, including the Executive Office of the President, and independent regulatory agencies. (State and municipal government bodies are not subject to FOIA.)

Exemptions to FOIA. The law lists nine categories of government records that federal agencies need not disclose to the public. These exemptions recognize the fact that censorship of some types of information may be necessary to safeguard certain legitimate government and private interests. However, agencies claiming any of these exemptions bear the burden of showing that the information should be protected under the law.

The first exemption covers information relating to national defense and foreign policy. An executive order must be issued to classify and protect this information pursuant to established standards and procedures, including submission of affidavits showing how the release of such information might damage national security. However, the language of this exemption does not provide any substantive standard for withholding information. A specific executive order must be reviewed to give the exemption meaning. Executive Order 12356, as amended, lists ten categories of information to be considered for classification. These include information on military plans, weapons, or operations; the capabilities and vulnerabilities of systems, installations, projects, or plans relating to the national security; information on foreign governments; intelligence-gathering activities; foreign relations; scientific, technological, or economic matters relating to national security; federal programs for safeguarding nuclear materials and facilities; cryptology; confidential sources; and any information relating to national security that the president or other officials determine should be protected from unauthorized disclosure.

Some national security information, even when it falls within one or more of these categories, may nevertheless not be classified. The key question is whether disclosure—by itself or in the context of other information—can reasonably be expected to damage national security. Information cannot be classified simply for the purpose of concealing violations of the law, inefficiency, or administrative errors; to prevent embarrassment to a person, organization, or agency; to restrain competition; or to delay release of information not requiring protection in the interest of national security. Further, basic scientific research not clearly related to national security is not classifiable.

Executive Order 12356 provides that information should be declassified or downgraded as soon as national security considerations permit. Further, if the director of the Information Security Oversight Office determines that any information is classified in violation of this executive order, the director may mandate declassification. The director's decisions are appealable to the National Security Council, with the information remaining classified pending appeal.

Other Exemptions. The second exemption concerns records relating solely to the internal personnel rules and practices of an agency. Its purpose is to relieve government agencies of the burden of assembling and maintaining for public review records in which the public is unlikely to be interested. It also covers internal agency procedures, such as instructions to investigators, inspectors, and auditors, disclosure of which could damage agency operations.

The third exemption incorporates by reference various federal information nondisclosure statutes and precludes disclosure of certain information protected by other statutes. Nondisclosure is authorized when other statutes either prohibit disclosure outright, or confer to an agency discretionary power to withhold material, while providing guidelines for exercising such discretion or specifying the types of material to which discretion applies. Citizens wishing to examine agency documents that are withheld under the terms of this exemption can legally appeal to have them released under the terms of the Federal Rules of Civil Procedure.

The fourth exemption protects confidential business information. Its purpose is to protect the interests of persons, corporations, and other entities who disclose trade secrets and other confidential information to government agencies and to protect the government. Two tests have been defined to determine whether information can be classified as confidential business information. The so-called "competitive advantage test" asks whether release of the information in question is likely to cause substantial competitive injury to the entity that provided it. The "chilling effect test" questions how much the agency needs the information, and whether voluntary cooperation is required for the agency to obtain the information and whether its disclosure will impair the government's ability to collect similar information in the future. Any information that qualifies under any of these tests is exempted.

The fifth exemption encompasses the executive branch's interagency or intra-agency memoranda or letters, if they are deliberative, consultative, or within the attorney-client or attorney work product privileges. This exemption from public disclosure allows for full, frank, and uninhibited written exchange of ideas and opinions among government policy makers and advisors. Such writings may be censored if their disclosure would discourage intra-agency discussion and thereby impede the ability of an agency to perform its functions.

The sixth exemption prevents disclosure of information that would constitute a clearly unwarranted invasion of personal privacy. Examples of such information might include personal medical records. However, this exemption does not apply in cases in which it is judged that public need for release of the information outweighs any possible injury to a person's privacy.

The seventh exemption protects certain investigatory records compiled for law enforcement purposes. To qualify for this exemption it must be shown that release of such records might interfere with enforcement proceedings; deprive someone of his or her right to a fair trial or impartial adjudication; constitute an unwarranted invasion of personal privacy; disclose the identities of confidential sources, including state, local, or foreign agencies or authorities, or private institutions that have furnished information confidentially; disclose techniques, procedures, or guidelines for law enforcement investigations or prosecutions, and thereby possibly assist someone to circumvent the law; or endanger someone's life or physical safety.

The eighth exemption protects from disclosure reports prepared by or for agencies that regulate or supervise financial institutions. Its purpose is to enhance the security and integrity of financial institutions. Government reports on financial institutions often contain frank evaluations of institutions such as banks; indiscriminate disclosure of such information might, for example, lead to a harmful rush on a bank.

The final exemption allows nondisclosure of ecological and geophysical information and data concerning wells, including maps. Geological explorations by private oil companies were not previously protected by the trade secrets provisions of disclosure laws. It was believed that disclosure of seismic reports and other exploratory findings generated by oil companies could provide speculators unfair advantage over those companies which incurred the exploration costs.

FOIA's enumerated exemptions are not mandatory bars to disclosure. An agency may, at its own discretion, voluntarily disclose exempt information as it deems fit. However, when an agency elects to release exempt materials, it may limit access to such information to certain individuals.

Release of Partially Exempt Information. FOIA also addresses requests for information some parts of which are exempt and other parts are not. In such instances the agencies must release "segregable portions" that remain after the material that is exempt from release has been deleted. An agency must release any remaining material that is at all intelligible after deletions have been made. If there are any doubts about the intelligibility or responsiveness of the remaining nonexempt material, those doubts are to be resolved in favor of release.

How the Public Receives Documents. FOIA requests must typically be in writing; agencies often provide prepared forms

for this purpose. Submission of written requests trigger the running of set time limits for agencies to respond. Agencies are only required to act on requests that "reasonably describe" identifiable nonexempt records. Although one test is whether requested records can be located with reasonable efforts, the size of a request alone cannot be the measure of whether it reasonably describes an identifiable record. In contrast, a request for "all" information pertaining to a certain type of record would not be sufficiently descriptive to meet the requirement.

The government cannot consider the interests of parties requesting information before determining whether to release or censor it. Courts have consistently held that a requester's needs, purposes, or motivation do not affect the requester's right to inspect agency records.

Recourse for Agency Noncompliance. Any agency denial of a request—for any reason—for information can be appealed under FOIA. The most common reason for appeals has been the failure of agencies to respond to requests within the law's statutory time limits. Agencies commonly deny requests by citing backlogs of requests, and inadequate staffing to perform record searches. Public requests can be frustrated by long delays and expense incurred while denials are appealed. Furthermore, even if an appeal is granted and a court directs an agency to comply with the request, the agency can assert—for the first time—that the requested records are exempt. This will start the appeal process all over again.

Effect of FOIA. As drafted, FOIA has been generally regarded as a substantial improvement over the APA. In practice, however, FOIA has often proved to be an inadequate means by which to obtain government information. The law's enumerated exemptions afford government agencies many ways in which to censor documents, in whole or in part. Many cases have been reported wherein citizens have filed FOIA requests and not received their denial letters until five years after the original filing. Many court battles have been fought to determine whether certain government entities are even subject to FOIA. Each time that a court has ruled a government entity to be an agency subject to FOIA, the agency has been ordered to draft guidelines for preserving and releasing its records. Through such court battles, citizens have been granted additional rights to obtain government documents pursuant to FOIA. Furthermore, FOIA has allowed certain plaintiffs in civil court cases against the United States government, or its agencies, to obtain documents implicating the U.S. government or its agencies, which has lead to judgments or settlements against the U.S. government which could not have been obtained before the enactment of FOIA. —*David R. Sobel*

See also Classification of information; Official Secrets Act (U.K.); UFO evidence.

BIBLIOGRAPHY

American Jurisprudence: A Modern Comprehensive Text Statement of Law, State and Federal (2d ed. Rochester, N.Y.: Lawyers Co-operative, 1994) is a thorough analysis of technical aspects of FOIA. A historical perspective on the law can be found in the special spring, 1983, issue of the *Detroit College of Law Review*, which also analyzes the law's strengths and weaknesses. Christine M. Marwick's *Your Right to Government Information* (New York: Bantam, 1985) is a practical guide to obtaining information from the federal government.

Freedom to Read Foundation

FOUNDED: 1969

TYPE OF ORGANIZATION: Nonprofit foundation promoting freedom of speech and of the press, particularly regarding libraries and librarians

SIGNIFICANCE: An adjunct to the American Library Association, the Freedom to Read Foundation defends the First Amendment rights of libraries, librarians, and library patrons

In 1969 the American Library Association (ALA) formed the Freedom to Read Foundation in order to promote and protect freedom of speech and freedom of the press, protect the public's right of access to information and materials stored in the nation's libraries, to safeguard libraries' right to disseminate all materials contained in their collections, and to support libraries and librarians in their defense of First Amendment rights by furnishing legal counsel or furnishing the means to obtain it.

The foundation has assisted persons in litigation by securing legal counsel, providing funding, participating directly, or by filing briefs as a friend of the court in critical First Amendment cases. In addition, it has provided informal legal advice to libraries that have been challenged by political officials or various interest groups to remove objectionable books. Among the important and controversial works that the foundation has defended are some the greatest and most widely read works of literature by authors ranging from Aristophanes and Geoffrey Chaucer to Kurt Vonnegut and Bernard Malamud.

Among the issues that the foundation has addressed are obscenity, child pornography, creationism, satanism, abortion counseling, national security, political propaganda, religious expression, student press freedom, depictions of violence, surveillance of libraries by the Federal Bureau of Investigation, prior restraint, privacy of library records, and restrictions on cyberspeech. The foundation is "devoted to the principle that the solution to offensive speech is more speech, and that suppression of speech on the grounds that it gives offense to some infringes on the rights of all to a free, open and robust marketplace of ideas."

See also *American Booksellers Association, Inc. v. Hudnut*; American Library Association; Books and obscenity law; Child Protection Restoration and Penalties Enforcement Act; Communications Decency Act; Impressions reading series; Libraries; Libraries, school; Library Bill of Rights; Textbooks.

Freedom to Read Week

DEFINITION: Annual consciousness-raising event begun by Canada's Book and Periodical Council in 1985

SIGNIFICANCE: This promotion of intellectual freedom is one of the few national efforts of its kind in Canada

Canada's Book and Periodical Council (BPC) began sponsoring Freedom to Read Week in 1985. The purpose of the event is to focus attention on intellectual freedom. The BPC, which is made up of members of associations representing publishers, university presses, booksellers, libraries, editors, writers, and others, produces an impressive resource kit in support of the event. The kit includes strategies for involving municipal councils and provincial governments; full texts of intellectual freedom statements; annotated lists and descriptions of challenged books; detailed plans for events such as debates, discussions, public readings, displays, and press conferences for public libraries, booksellers, and educators; a reading list; and a poster and press release. The kit is useful as a tool for the promotion of intellectual freedom and as study guide for censorship issues. Freedom to Read Week is generally held during the last week of February. It is one of the few national initiatives undertaken regarding intellectual freedom in Canada.

See also Banned Books Week; Canada; Canadian Library Association Statement on Intellectual Freedom; Intellectual freedom; Libraries, Canadian; Freedom.

Front, The

TYPE OF WORK: Film

RELEASED: 1976

DIRECTOR: Martin Ritt (1914-1990)

SUBJECT MATTER: *The Front* dramatizes the plight of blacklisted writers and actors in the New York television industry in the early 1950's

SIGNIFICANCE: The film was an important Hollywood treatment of the blacklist in the entertainment industry

Michael Murphy (left) plays a blacklisted television writer who persuades his friend (Woody Allen) to front for him so that he can keep selling scripts in Martin Ritt's film The Front. *(Museum of Modern Art/Film Stills Archive)*

Produced and directed by Martin Ritt and written by Walter Bernstein, both blacklist victims, *The Front* may be seen as an act of retrospective self-justification as well as satiric social criticism. Its story begins as blacklisted television writer Alfred Miller (Michael Murphy) tells his unpolitical but streetwise buddy Howard Prince (Woody Allen) that he has been shut out of work because of his communist sympathies. He asks Prince to be his "front," to present his scripts to the network as Prince's own; after taking 10 percent of the payment for himself, Prince would pass the rest on to the writer. Prince agrees and soon is fronting for other blacklisted writers as well, becoming rich and famous, while attracting the attention of political watchdogs.

Before the film ends with the belatedly enlightened Prince's denunciation of the House Committee on Un-American Activities' (HUAC) repression of constitutional freedoms, *The Front* recalls the chilling effect on the entertainment community of HUAC investigations and the dubious activities of private "patriotic" investigative businesses, such as AWARE, Inc. and American Business Consultants, that profited from the witch-hunt hysteria.

Although *The Front* received a mixed critical reception in 1976, the nomination of Bernstein's script for an Academy Award may be read as an apology by the Hollywood establishment for the punitive excesses of the Cold War era.

See also Blacklisting; Film censorship; Hollywood Ten; House Committee on Un-American Activities; Television; Trumbo, Dalton.

CENSORSHIP

List of Entries by Category

Subject headings used in list

AFRICAN AMERICANS

ART

BOOKS: CHILDREN'S AND YOUNG ADULT

BOOKS: FICTION

BOOKS: NONFICTION

FILMS

Amants, Les
And God Created Woman
Basic Instinct
Birth of a Nation, The
Blue Velvet
Caligula
Carnal Knowledge
Citizen Kane
Deep Throat
Ecstasy
Exorcist, The
Freaks
Front, The
Garden of Eden, The
I Am Curious—Yellow
King Kong
Kiss, The
Last Tango in Paris
Life and Death of Colonel Blimp, The
M
Man with the Golden Arm, The
Miracle, The
Mohammed, Messenger of God
Moon Is Blue, The
Naked Amazon
Natural Born Killers
Outlaw, The
Pinky
Pulp Fiction
Ronde, La
Titicut Follies
Who's Afraid of Virginia Woolf?
Wild Bunch, The

FORMS OF EXPRESSION

Advocacy
Armbands and buttons
Assembly, right of
Biography
Book publishing
Bumper stickers
Defamation
Draft-card burning
Draft resistance
Euphemism
Fighting words
Flag burning
Free speech
Hoaxes
Intellectual freedom
Leafletting
Libel
License plates, customized
Literature
Loyalty oaths
Marching and parading
Obscenity: legal definitions
Offensive language
Picketing
Pledge of Allegiance
Poetry
Political campaigning
Pressure groups
Privileged communication
Propaganda
Roman à clef
Slander
Street oratory
Symbolic speech
Translation
Unprotected speech
Wall posters

GOVERNMENT AND POLITICS

Abortion gag rule
Advocacy
Assembly, right of
Attorney General's Commission on Pornography
Books and obscenity law
Central Intelligence Agency
Chapultepec Declaration
Chilling effect
Civil service
Classification of information
Clear and present danger doctrine
Communism
Community standards
Congress, U.S.
Courtrooms
Courts and censorship law
Criminal syndicalism laws
Criminal trials
Culture ministries
Defamation
Democracy
Demonstrations
Draft-card burning
Draft resistance
Espionage
Examiner of plays
Federal Bureau of Investigation
Fighting words
Free speech
Gag order
House Committee on Un-American Activities
Judicial publication bans (Canadian)
Libel
Lord Chamberlain
Loyalty oaths
Marching and parading
Master of the Revels
National Endowment for the Arts
National Endowment for the Humanities
National security
Obscenity: legal definitions
Office of Censorship, U.S.
Pledge of Allegiance
Police
Police states
Political campaigning
Presidency, U.S.
President's Commission on Obscenity and Pornography
President's Task Force on Communications Policy
Pressure groups
Prior restraint
Prisons
Privileged communication
Propaganda
Right of reply
Sedition
Symbolic speech
Terrorism
United States Information Agency
Unprotected speech
Witnesses, protection of

HISTORICAL EVENTS AND ERAS

Abolitionist movement
Alexandria library
Armenian genocide
Athens, ancient
Basque separatism
Bay of Pigs invasion
Bhopal disaster
Chernobyl disaster
Chicago Art Institute furors
Civil Rights movement
Civil War, U.S.
Colonialism
Crimean War
Crop-ears
Cultural Revolution, Chinese
Dead Sea Scrolls
Defense ("D") notices
Degenerate Art Exhibition
Democratic National Convention of 1968
English Commonwealth
Falkland Islands War
First Hemispheric Conference on Free Expression
Free Speech Movement
Greek junta
Grenada, U.S. invasion of
"H-Bomb Secret, The"
Holocaust, Jewish
Iran-Contra scandal
Jeremiah's Book of Prophesies, burning of
Kanawha County book-banning controversy
Kennedy, John F., assassination of
Kent State shootings
Korean War
Lateran Council, Fourth
Maya books, destruction of
Mexican-American War
Military censorship
Mutual Broadcasting System scandal
My Lai massacre
National Socialism (Nazism)
Panama, U.S. invasion of
Paris, Council of
Persian Gulf War
Press-radio war
Publick Occurrences
Reformation, the
Revolutionary War, American
Roman Empire
Scopes trial
Simpson, O. J., case
Skokie, Illinois, Nazi march
Soviet secret cities
Spanish-American War
Spanish Empire
Spanish Inquisition
Temperance movements
Three Mile Island
Tiananmen Square
Tonkin Gulf incident
UFO evidence
Vietnam War
War
War of 1812
Watergate scandal
World War I
World War II
Worms, Edict of
Yaqzan, Matan, affair

PEOPLE: JUSTICES AND LEGAL FIGURES

Black, Hugo
Blackstone, William
Brennan, William J., Jr.
Chase, Samuel
De Grazia, Edward

Douglas, William O.
Ernst, Morris Leopold
Frankfurter, Felix
Holmes, Oliver Wendell, Jr.
Warren, Earl

PEOPLE: MORAL CRUSADERS

Comstock, Anthony
Coughlin, Father Charles Edward
Cushing, Cardinal Richard James
Gabler, Mel, and Norma Gabler

Spellman, Cardinal Francis
 Joseph
Sumner, John
Torquemada, Tomás de

PEOPLE: MUSICIANS AND COMPOSERS

Baez, Joan
Beach Boys, the
Beatles, the
Bryant, Anita
Foster, Stephen Collins
Guthrie, Woody
Jackson, Michael
Khachaturian, Aram
Lennon, John
Lewis, Jerry Lee
Madonna
Mendelssohn, Felix

Morissette, Alanis
O'Connor, Sinead
Presley, Elvis
Prokofiev, Sergei
Robeson, Paul
Rolling Stones, the
Seeger, Pete
Shakur, Tupac
Shostakovich, Dmitri
2 Live Crew
Wagner, Richard
Weavers, the

PEOPLE: PHILOSOPHERS AND SCIENTISTS

Anaxagoras
Aristotle
Bentham, Jeremy
Confucius
Copernicus, Nicolaus
Darwin, Charles
Democritus
Descartes, René
Ellis, Henry Havelock
Erasmus, Desiderius
Galileo Galilei
Hume, David
Kant, Immanuel
Kropotkin, Peter

Leary, Timothy
Locke, John
Marcuse, Herbert
Marx, Karl
Mead, Margaret
Mercator, Gerardus
Plato
Rousseau, Jean-Jacques
Sakharov, Andrei
Sanger, Margaret
Seneca the Younger
Socrates
Swedenborg, Emanuel
Vesalius, Andreas

PEOPLE: POLITICAL FIGURES

Agnew, Spiro T.
Barnett, Ross Robert
Bush, George
Cicero
Devlin, Bernadette
Dole, Robert
Franklin, Benjamin
Giddings, Joshua Reed
Gorbachev, Mikhail
Helms, Jesse Alexander
Henry VIII

Hoover, J. Edgar
James I
Jefferson, Thomas
Lenin, Vladimir Ilich
Lyon, Matthew
Madison, James
Mandela, Nelson
Mao Zedong
Meese, Edwin III
Morison, Samuel Loring
Nicholas I

Nixon, Richard M.
Reagan, Ronald
Royal family, British
Seneca the Younger
Shih huang-ti
Stalin, Joseph

Stubbs, John
Talmadge, Eugene
Thurmond, Strom
Trotsky, Leon
Zhdanov, Andrei

PEOPLE: RELIGIOUS FIGURES

Abelard, Peter
Bacon, Roger
Biddle, John
Calvin, John
Coughlin, Father Charles Edward
Cushing, Cardinal Richard James
Farrakhan, Louis Abdoul
Ghazzali, al-
Hus, Jan
Hutchinson, Anne
Joan of Arc
King, Martin Luther, Jr.
Knox, John
Latimer, Hugh
Leighton, Alexander

Luther, Martin
Malcolm X
Mani
Muhammad
O'Hair, Madalyn Murray
Paul IV, Pope
Richelieu, Cardinal
Rutherford, Joseph Franklin
Savonarola, Girolamo
Smith, Joseph
Spellman, Cardinal Francis
 Joseph
Thomas à Kempis
Torquemada, Tomás de
Williams, Roger

PEOPLE: SOCIAL AND POLITICAL ACTIVISTS

Bakunin, Mikhail Aleksandrovich
Berrigan, Daniel, and Philip
 Francis Berrigan
Debs, Eugene
Devlin, Bernadette
Douglass, Frederick
Garvey, Marcus
Goldman, Emma
Gouzenko, Igor Sergeievich
King, Martin Luther, Jr.
Malcolm X

Mandela, Nelson
Martí, José Julián
Metzger, Tom
Mindszenty, József
Nader, Ralph
O'Hair, Madalyn Murray
Pankhurst, Emmeline
Sanger, Margaret
Sumner, John
Thomas, Norman
Woodhull, Victoria

PEOPLE: WRITERS, AMERICAN

Andrews, V. C.
Baldwin, James
Blume, Judy
Cabell, James Branch
Caldwell, Erskine
Chomsky, Noam
Cummings, e. e.
Dahl, Roald
Dreiser, Theodore
Dworkin, Andrea
Emerson, Ralph Waldo
Faulkner, William
Ferlinghetti, Lawrence
Franklin, Benjamin
Ginsberg, Allen
Helper, Hinton
Hemingway, Ernest
Hinton, S. E.
King, Stephen

Lewis, Sinclair
London, Jack
MacKinnon, Catharine A.
Mencken, H. L.
Miller, Henry
O'Hara, John
O'Neill, Eugene
Paine, Thomas
Parker, Dorothy
Paterson, Katherine
Sendak, Maurice
Silverstein, Shel
Sinclair, Upton
Southern, Terry
Steinbeck, John
Thoreau, Henry David
Twain, Mark
Vonnegut, Kurt
Webster, Noah

SCIENCE

WARS

WOMEN